Ref S ⬧ O9-BHJ-824
American presidents

$80.00

3rd ed.   ocm63125836

American Presidents

Third Edition

American Presidents

Third Edition

Volume 2
Warren G. Harding—George W. Bush
Index

Editor, First Edition
Frank N. Magill

Editors, Third Edition
Robert P. Watson
Florida Atlantic University

Richard Yon
University of Florida

SALEM PRESS, INC.
Pasadena, California   Hackensack, New Jersey

Editor in Chief: Dawn P. Dawson   *Production Editor:* Joyce I. Buchea
Editorial Director: Christina J. Moose   *Acquisitions Editor:* Mark Rehn
Project Editor: Tracy Irons-Georges   *Research Supervisor:* Jeffry Jensen
Copy Editor: Sarah M. Hilbert   *Graphics and Design:* James Hutson
Photo Editor: Cynthia Breslin Beres   *Layout:* Eddie Murillo

Cover Photo: Olivier Hoslet/EPA/Landov

Library of Congress Cataloging-in-Publication Data
American presidents / editors, Robert P. Watson, Richard Yon.— 3rd ed.
    p. cm.
Includes bibliographical references and index.
ISBN-10: 1-58765-270-6 (set : alk. paper)
ISBN-13: 978-1-58765-270-7 (set : alk. paper)
ISBN-10: 1-58765-307-9 (v. 2 : alk. paper)
ISBN-13: 978-1-58765-307-0 (v. 2 : alk. paper)
1. Presidents—United States—History. 2. Presidents—United States—Biography.
3. United States—Politics and government. I. Watson, Robert P., 1962- II. Yon, Richard.
E176.1.A6563 2006
973.09'9—dc22

2006001180

First Printing

Contents

Alphabetical List xxix

Warren G. Harding 497
Calvin Coolidge 506
Herbert Hoover 519
Franklin D. Roosevelt 537
Harry S. Truman 579
Dwight D. Eisenhower 609
John F. Kennedy 636
Lyndon B. Johnson 657
Richard M. Nixon 689
Gerald R. Ford 721
Jimmy Carter 736
Ronald Reagan 754
George H. W. Bush 776
Bill Clinton 797
George W. Bush 818

U.S. Constitution 841
Law of Presidential Succession 855
Time Line 856
Presidential Election Returns, 1789-2004 889
Vice Presidents 895
Cabinet Members by Administration 897
Executive Departments and Offices 914
First Ladies 919
Presidential Libraries 921
Museums, Historic Sites, and Web Sites 925
Glossary 933
Bibliography 943

Index 967

Alphabetical List

Adams, John **1**: 50
Adams, John Quincy **1**: 134
Arthur, Chester A.. . . . . **1**: 379

Buchanan, James. **1**: 262
Bush, George H. W. **2**: 776
Bush, George W. **2**: 818

Carter, Jimmy **2**: 736
Cleveland, Grover **1**: 386
Clinton, Bill **2**: 797
Coolidge, Calvin. **2**: 506

Eisenhower, Dwight D.. . . . . . **2**: 609

Fillmore, Millard **1**: 245
Ford, Gerald R. **2**: 721

Garfield, James A. **1**: 373
Grant, Ulysses S. **1**: 332

Harding, Warren G. **2**: 497
Harrison, Benjamin **1**: 402
Harrison, William Henry **1**: 197
Hayes, Rutherford B.. . . . . . . **1**: 356
Hoover, Herbert **2**: 519

Jackson, Andrew **1**: 150
Jefferson, Thomas. **1**: 67

Johnson, Andrew **1**: 315
Johnson, Lyndon B. **2**: 657

Kennedy, John F. **2**: 636

Lincoln, Abraham **1**: 275

McKinley, William **1**: 411
Madison, James. **1**: 94
Monroe, James **1**: 116

Nixon, Richard M.. . . . . **2**: 689

Pierce, Franklin **1**: 252
Polk, James K.. . . . . **1**: 212

Reagan, Ronald **2**: 754
Roosevelt, Franklin D. **2**: 537
Roosevelt, Theodore **1**: 428

Taft, William Howard **1**: 454
Taylor, Zachary **1**: 237
Truman, Harry S. **2**: 579
Tyler, John **1**: 204

Van Buren, Martin **1**: 180

Washington, George **1**: 19
Wilson, Woodrow **1**: 469

American Presidents

Third Edition

Warren G. Harding

29th President, 1921-1923

Born: November 2, 1865
    Caledonia, Ohio
Died: August 2, 1923
    San Francisco, California

Political Party: Republican
Vice President: Calvin Coolidge

Cabinet Members
Secretary of State: Charles Evans Hughes
Secretary of the Treasury: Andrew W. Mellon
Secretary of War: John W. Weeks
Secretary of the Navy: Edwin Denby
Attorney General: Harry M. Daugherty
Postmaster General: Will H. Hays, Hubert
    Work, Harry S. New
Secretary of the Interior: Albert B. Fall, Hubert
    Work
Secretary of Agriculture: Henry C. Wallace
Secretary of Commerce: Herbert Hoover
Secretary of Labor: James J. Davis

Warren Gamaliel Harding was the twenty-ninth president of the United States. Born November 2, 1865, in Blooming Grove, Ohio, he grew up around Caledonia, Ohio. Harding was graduated in 1882 from a two-year college, Ohio Central, where he edited the school newspaper. After teaching school for a term, he settled in Marion, Ohio, selling insurance. In 1884, he and two partners bought the ailing *Marion Daily Star*. Harding soon gained full control of the newspaper, which he eventually made into a paying enterprise. His editorial policy was to boom Marion, the United States, and business development. In 1891, he married Florence Kling De Wolfe, an outspoken and formi-

Harding's official portrait. *(White House Historical Society)*

dable woman commonly referred to by her husband and friends as the "Duchess." Her determination and ambition reinforced his drive for success.

Harding became active in politics in the 1890's out of a growing conviction that Ohio Republicanism needed a younger generation of leadership. His admiration of wealth and power eventually led him to reach accommodation with his party's aging bosses, and his budding ability as an orator gained for him recognition among Republicans. In 1899, Harding was elected to the state senate; reelected in 1901, he became the senate Republican floor leader. Eager to become governor, he found that his ambition exceeded his influence. In 1903, therefore, he had to settle for the lieutenant governorship, in which he served only one term. Not until 1910 did he receive the Republican gubernatorial nomination. Running as the candidate of a badly divided party, Harding failed to win election. He remained in demand after his defeat, however, because of his oratorical talent, although that talent ran largely to uttering hollow if resounding platitudes. At the 1912 Republican National Convention, he was chosen to nominate President William Howard Taft, his fellow Ohioan, for reelection.

Despite Taft's overwhelming defeat in 1912, things went Harding's way. In 1914, he was elected United States senator. As a senator, Harding sponsored little legislation and had a poor attendance record. He did grow in status among Republicans, however, because of the roles he assumed as an able spokesperson for his party and an apostle of Republican harmony. This attitude led to Harding's selection as the keynote speaker and permanent chair of the 1916 Republican National Convention. Later, as he became a popular critic of the Wilson administration, he was mentioned as a possible contender for the 1920 Republican presidential nomination.

Harding's attractiveness to Republicans also lay in his stands on issues. Under the credo

of "Prosper America First," he called for merchant marine subsidies, protective tariffs, immigration restriction, and territorial expansion. He was generally probusiness and antiunion, although he endorsed an eight-hour day for workers. He accepted woman suffrage and Prohibition, and he warned against bolshevism and "creeping socialism." He favored ratification of the Treaty of Versailles but with reservations designed to protect American sovereignty.

A Perfect Nominee: The Election of 1920

By 1920, Harding had become Ohio's favorite son for the Republican presidential nomination. His ability to balance issues and to ingratiate himself with a variety of Republicans made it easy for his aides to secure many second-choice commitments from among delegates to the 1920 national convention. Harding did not rank among the front-runners for the nomination, comprising General Leonard Wood, Illinois governor Frank O. Lowden, and California senator Hiram Johnson. None of them, however, had enough votes to gain nomination. Consequently, when the convention delegates tired of the deadlock among the three leading candidates, Harding was able to attract enough votes to win nomination.

Harding turned out to be an almost perfect presidential nominee. His campaign was well pitched to appeal to those Republicans, independents, and even Democrats who were vexed by rising prices, labor problems, fears of depression, and the divisive issue of the League of Nations. He also shifted to championing positive action to cope with the nation's problems instead of indulging in carping criticism of the Wilson administration and Ohio governor James M. Cox, the Democratic presidential nominee. Harding's promise to return America to "normalcy" projected an image of an agreeable, conciliatory leader who was concerned with doing the right thing as a majority of voters saw it. As a result, he was elected on his fifty-

THE FIRST LADY
FLORENCE HARDING

Florence Kling Harding was the wife of America's twenty-ninth president, Warren G. Harding. Florence was born in Marion, Ohio, in 1860. Her father, Amos Kling, was Marion's wealthiest citizen and a hard-driving, domineering man. Wishing for a son, Amos assuaged his disappointment by raising Florence to be strong, well educated, aggressive, and business-minded. In likely rebellion against her tyrannical father, Florence eloped with neighbor Henry De Wolfe and became pregnant with her only child, Marshall. Her husband soon left, and Florence supported their son by giving piano lessons.

Warren G. Harding was an extraordinarily handsome man who owned a Marion newspaper. Impressed by Florence's family name and strength of character, Harding married Florence in 1891 in spite of Kling's opposition. Plagued by nervous ill health, Warren was often away from the newspaper, and it was Florence who managed the business in his absence. Her strong business acumen soon transformed Harding's fledgling, sluggish operation into a highly profitable enterprise.

A political natural because of his good looks and easy charm, Warren Harding rose through Ohio politics, eventually becoming a United States senator and candidate for president. Florence was a key adviser to his campaign. Harding was sworn in as president in March, 1921.

During her tenure as First Lady, Florence Harding reopened the White House mansion and grounds after a long closure during President Woodrow Wilson's illnesses. Florence was a modern woman who flew in airplanes, declared herself a feminist, and supported women's suffrage. Though very popular, Florence was forced to deal with her husband's political and sexual scandals and was pained to know that scandal would be the most enduring legacy of the Harding administration.

Florence Kling Harding suffered from chronic kidney disease and died in Marion on November 21, 1924.

Twyla R. Wells

fifth birthday in November, 1920, by the largest percentage of votes ever cast for a Republican presidential nominee.

The new president looked right for his job. Over 6 feet tall, Harding weighed 210 pounds, had gray eyes, a prominent forehead, silver hair, and a strong jaw. He was always well dressed. Moreover, in public he projected affability, moderation, or seriousness, but never meanness or pettiness. He was by nature easygoing. Nominally a Baptist, he was less devoted to religion than to playing poker or golf. He used tobacco and drank, though not to excess. Also, he had had affairs with women, ascribable to Florence Harding's frostiness on sexual matters, although the presidential couple otherwise got along well. Harding was

not a disciplined thinker, tending to develop his opinions intuitively along lines suggested by copybook maxims. Intensely loyal to his friends, he was not often discreet enough in choosing or using them. The president worked hard in considering and acting on official business, although he often seemed frustrated by differences of opinion among his advisers.

Harding's cabinet was generally conservative, though well balanced in the personal and geographical background of the appointees. Several members of the cabinet, especially Secretary of State Charles Evans Hughes and Secretary of Commerce Herbert Hoover, were eminent and able men. Others, such as Attorney General Harry M. Daugherty and Secretary of the Interior Albert B. Fall, were men of dubious

Harding issued a controversial pardon to Socialist Party leader Eugene V. Debs, who was jailed as a political prisoner during World War I. *(Library of Congress)*

merit. Nevertheless, Senator Fall's appointment was so popular on Capitol Hill that the Senate confirmed him without going through the usual committee hearing.

Legislative Action: Domestic Policy

The president approached Congress soon after his inauguration in March, 1921. Calling a special session for April, he presented a long legislative agendum. He asked for higher tariffs, lower taxes, a national budget system, and action to ease the economic plight of farmers. Harding also called for strengthening the merchant marine, a national highway system, encouragement of civil and military aviation, regulation of radio, establishment of a veterans bureau and a department of public welfare, government reorganization, expansion of hospital facilities, and maternity and antilynching legislation. On foreign affairs, the president requested formal action to end World War I, promotion of international cooperation out-

side the League of Nations to prevent war in the future, and aid for European economic recovery.

Harding enjoyed considerable legislative success in 1921 and 1922. The new high-tariff and low-tax legislation helped to combat America's postwar recession and to pave the way for later prosperity. The Budget and Accounting Act established the Bureau of the Budget and the General Accounting Office to make for better control and accountability in the appropriation and expenditure of federal funds. Moreover, these tools were crucial to the administration's outstanding success in fostering economy in government. The president scored well on foreign policy legislation and on measures to develop highways, hospital facilities, and aviation, and Congress substantially reduced immigration quotas, which he had long favored. Congress also enacted significant legislation to regulate agricultural markets, stimulate the growth of farm organizations, and reduce railway freight rates. These measures did not solve the nation's agricultural problems, but as a consequence of the legislation farmers' incomes lagged behind that of others in the economy less than it would have without such legislation.

There were also defeats. Harding lost on merchant marine subsidies, and the Senate killed his antilynching proposal. Although the president failed to secure authorization for a department of public welfare, Congress passed the Sheppard-Towner Act in 1922 to promote the health of mothers and children. The credit that he received for the establishment of the Veterans Bureau was offset by the development of scandal in that agency.

The administration displayed more than legislative concerns. Harding showed his mettle in pardoning Eugene V. Debs, the socialist leader, and most other wartime political prisoners. The president also worked, especially with Commerce Secretary Herbert Hoover, to institute an eight-hour workday in the steel industry, encourage self-regulation of radio stations, and use federal action to counter the effects of the 1921-1922 recession. Harding was business-oriented, yet he promoted more enlightened operation of business to benefit the whole nation and sponsored some programs of interest to farmers and welfare advocates. He was less the instrument of business (or of the Senate) than it had been predicted that he would be.

If Harding was captive to anything, in fact, it was to his high-level appointees, although their advice so often was conflicting that he was not always their creature. He needed their help, though, in taking action. Sometimes he chose

THE VICE PRESIDENT
CALVIN COOLIDGE

Calvin Coolidge was born on Independence Day of 1872 in the small hamlet of Plymouth, Vermont. Educated in tiny schoolhouses near his birthplace and a private academy in Vermont, Coolidge graduated cum laude in 1895 from Amherst College in Massachusetts. He then studied law in the firm of John C. Hammond and Henry P. Field in Northampton, Massachusetts, and was admitted to the bar in 1897.

Coolidge became interested in politics early in his career and established a law practice in Northampton. In 1899, Coolidge served on the Northampton city council and then as city solicitor from 1900 to 1901. He was appointed clerk of courts in 1903, then elected to a full term. On October 4, 1905, he married Grace Goodhue, and the couple had two children. In 1906, Coolidge was elected to the Massachusetts House of Representatives and reelected to another term. In 1912, he was elected to the upper house in Massachusetts, becoming the Senate's president from 1914 to 1915. He was elected lieutenant governor in 1915 and then governor in 1918, taking office in January, 1919.

In 1920, Coolidge was nominated as Warren G. Harding's vice president, serving in that capacity until the president's death on August 2, 1923. Coolidge was in his childhood home in rural Vermont when the news came, and he took the oath of office in the middle of the night from his father at the family home. Coolidge completed Harding's term and was elected in 1924 to a full term as president.

After his presidency, Coolidge worked on his memoirs for a magazine and wrote a syndicated newspaper column. He also served as a trustee for Amherst College, as president of the Antiquarian Society, and as chair of the Railroad Commission. Coolidge died at his home in Northampton on January 5, 1933.

Robert P. Watson and Richard Yon

Harding's secretary of state, Charles Evans Hughes (third from right), attends the Washington Conference on disarmament. *(Library of Congress)*

wrongly, as when he supported Attorney General Daugherty's punitive injunction to end the railway shopmen's strike in 1922. This action earned for the president the enmity of many labor unions.

Foreign Policy: Soothing Troubled Relations

In foreign policy Harding generally followed the advice of Secretary of State Hughes. In 1921, his administration convinced Congress to terminate formally World War I hostilities and to ratify peace treaties with America's former enemies. Harding's and Hughes's boldest success was the Washington Conference of 1921-1922. This meeting of representatives of nine nations with interests in the Far East produced agreement on and ratification of treaties that substantially limited naval armaments and reduced tensions in the Pacific and the Far East. The Harding administration also enjoyed success in soothing the troubles it had inherited in Latin America. Negotiations were initiated to restore diplomatic relations with Mexico;

American intervention in Central America and the Caribbean was reduced; and Colombia's grievances against the United States stemming from the Panamanian Revolution of 1903 were settled. What Harding and Hughes set in motion with Latin America would be continued by Presidents Calvin Coolidge and Herbert Hoover and lead to the Good Neighbor era of Franklin D. Roosevelt. In dealing with European concerns Harding felt less confident, saying, "I don't know anything about this European stuff." Nevertheless, his administration edged its way into some cooperation with the League of Nations, set easier terms for European nations to pay their war debts to America, and negotiated some favorable commercial agreements. Harding also, contrary to Hughes's advice, sought to explore with the Soviet Union the restoration of diplomatic relations.

Harding's program was not among the most weighty offered by an American president. His legislative efforts, however, were respectable. Many of his administration's operations ranked well in efficiency, effectiveness, and especially economy. Yet Harding was beset by problems. There were the usual problems of patronage and congressional relations. In addition, agriculture was not satisfied with the administration's efforts on its behalf, organized labor was angered by Harding's favoritism toward business, and business wanted additional favors. The recession of 1921-1922 aggravated the situation. The administration's enforcement of Prohibition vexed wets, yet it was not active enough to satisfy many drys. Moreover, Harding's veto of a veterans bonus sorely irritated many World War I soldiers and sailors. The 1922 elections reflected the resulting reactions of all these groups and interests when Republicans retained only a bare majority in the two houses of Congress. Consequently, Harding would have far less legislative success during the rest of his presidency.

Failing Reputation, Failing Health

Harding liked the office of president, but he found that he had to work extremely hard. "I never find myself with all my work completed," he commented. He also worried about the decisions facing him and the criticisms directed at his administration. Harding had no illusions about his presidential performance. "I cannot hope to be one of the great presidents," he said, "but perhaps I may be remembered as one of the best loved." He did not achieve this wish. Instead, he would go down as one of America's worst presidents.

After the disappointing 1922 election, Harding called a special session of Congress to pursue the remainder of his legislative program. Unfortunately, he chose to begin with the wrong legislation, a bill creating federal ship subsidies to make the United States self-sufficient on the high seas. Congress did not agree on the need for such a measure, and as a result, much time and goodwill were lost before the Senate finally killed the bill in February, 1923. The administration's only noteworthy successes in 1923 would be the Agricultural Credits Act to make more farm loans available and the Government Reclassification Act to improve the civil service.

By 1923, Harding was being overwhelmed by his job. Illness and worry increasingly plagued him, but the scandals associated with his administration were probably what broke him. Almost from the beginning of his administration, rumors of malfeasance had circulated. Nothing of significance occurred until fall,

The front page of *The Evening Star* for August 3, 1923, announces the death of Harding. *(D.C. Public Library)*

1922, when there was an unsuccessful attempt by the House of Representatives to impeach Attorney General Daugherty, specifying some fourteen improper and illegal actions. This was, however, only a straw in the wind.

Scandal soon became a serious concern to Harding. After corruption was uncovered at the highest levels in the Veterans Bureau, the president required the resignation of its director, Charles Forbes, in February, 1923. The next month, the bureau's general counsel, Charles F. Cramer, committed suicide because of his involvement in the wrongdoing. In May, a close and shady associate of Daugherty, Jesse M. Smith, also committed suicide. All of this contributed to Harding's unease. As he said, it was his friends, not his enemies, who "keep me walking the floor nights."

On June 20, Harding left Washington on a cross-country tour intended to solicit public support and to improve his own morale. He encountered favorable reactions, but the strain of the long tour cost him his life. He died in San Francisco on August 2, 1923, probably of problems associated with high blood pressure. Harding may have died a well-loved president, but in 1924, additional evidence of corruption within his administration surfaced. Some of it related to Attorney General Daugherty, whom President Coolidge forced to resign. There was also evidence that led to Charles Forbes's conviction; proof of corruption by Alien Property Custodian Thomas Miller, who was imprisoned; and especially scandals over private oil leases at the government's Teapot Dome and Elk Hill reserves, which led to the conviction of former Secretary of the Interior Albert Fall, who had profited personally from the arrangement. The new scandals further besmirched Harding's reputation. Soon forgotten were his accomplishments.

Warren Harding was not an outstanding president. The Washington Conference and the budgetary actions were noteworthy but hardly earthshaking events in American his-

tory. Nor was he innovative; including the vice president in cabinet meetings cannot be deemed significant. The Harding administration did run very economically, and in 1921 and 1922 it enjoyed a considerable measure of legislative success. All of this is a record of some accomplishment but not of greatness. It appears substantially less when set against the disastrous scandals connected with Harding's presidency.

Donald R. McCoy

Suggested Readings

Anthony, Carl S. *Florence Harding: The First Lady, the Jazz Age, and the Death of America's Most Scandalous President*. New York: W. Morrow, 1998. Details the life and the important role of Mrs. Harding in the president's career.

Dean, John W. *Warren G. Harding*. New York: Henry Holt, 2004. A biography that seeks to find successes within the Harding administration, which was rife with scandal.

Downes, Randolph C. *The Rise of Warren Gamaliel Harding, 1865-1920*. Columbus: Ohio State University Press, 1970. A comprehensive and scholarly biography.

Ferrell, Robert H. *The Strange Death of President Harding*. Columbia: University of Missouri Press, 1996. A detailed examination of Harding's sudden death in 1923.

Frederick, Richard G. *Warren G. Harding: A Bibliography*. Westport, Conn.: Greenwood Press, 1992. Gives a comprehensive listing of resources on Harding's personal life and public career.

Giglio, James M. *H. M. Daugherty and the Politics of Expediency*. Kent, Ohio: Kent State University Press, 1978. A narrative that ably deals with a key figure in Harding's political career.

Grieb, Joseph. *Latin American Policy of Warren G. Harding*. Fort Worth: Texas Christian University Press, 1976. Explores one facet of Harding's foreign policy.

Joseph, Paul. *Warren G. Harding*. Minneapolis: ABDO, 1999. A biography of Taft for young adults.

Mee, Charles M. *Ohio Gang: The World of Warren G. Harding*. New York: M. Evans, 1981. A biography focusing on the world of political corruption that influenced the Harding administration.

Moran, Philip R., ed. *Warren G. Harding, 1865-1923: Chronology, Documents, Bibliographical Aids*. Dobbs Ferry, N.Y.: Oceana, 1970. A good source for primary and secondary documents.

Morello, John A. *Selling the President, 1920: Albert D. Lasker, Advertising, and the Election of Warren G. Harding*. Westport, Conn.: Praeger, 2001. An interesting read about the growing importance of marketing political figures during the 1920's and the attempts to craft the public image of Harding.

Murray, Robert K. *Harding Era: Warren G. Harding and His Administration*. Minneapolis: University of Minnesota Press, 1969. A thorough biography with good historical context.

Romero, Francine Sanders. *Presidents from Theodore Roosevelt Through Coolidge, 1901-1929: Debating the Issues in Pro and Con Primary Documents*. Westport, Conn.: Greenwood Press, 2002. A collection of primary documents and commentary is used to debate issues that were pertinent during the tenure of presidents serving between 1901-1929.

Russell, Francis. *The Shadow of Blooming Grove: Warren G. Harding in His Times*. New York: McGraw-Hill, 1968. A solid biography.

Trani, Eugene P., and David L. Wilson. *The Presidency of Warren G. Harding*. Lawrence: University Press of Kansas, 1977. Gives a good overview of the Harding administration.

Calvin Coolidge

30th President, 1923-1929

Born: July 4, 1872
    Plymouth, Vermont
Died: January 5, 1933
    Northampton, Massachusetts

Political Party: Republican
Vice President: Charles G. Dawes

Cabinet Members

Secretary of State: Charles Evans Hughes, Frank B. Kellogg
Secretary of the Treasury: Andrew Mellon
Secretary of War: John W. Weeks, Dwight F. Davis
Secretary of the Navy: Edwin Denby, Curtis D. Wilbur
Attorney General: Harry Daugherty, Harlan F. Stone, John G. Sargent
Postmaster General: Harry S. New
Secretary of the Interior: Hubert Work, Roy O. West
Secretary of Agriculture: Henry C. Wallace, Howard M. Gore, William Jardine
Secretary of Commerce: Herbert Hoover, William F. Whiting
Secretary of Labor: James J. Davis

Calvin Coolidge was an extraordinarily popular president. His popularity hardly waned whatever problems beset the nation, whatever the administration's ineptitude, whatever the impact of presidential actions or inaction.

Coolidge's popularity is hard to explain. A slightly built man, 5 feet, 9 inches tall, weighing only 150 pounds, with deli-

cate features, he was neither physically imposing nor handsome. Alice Roosevelt Longworth quipped that he had the facial expression of one who had been weaned on a pickle. He never

Coolidge's official portrait. *(White House Historical Society)*

dominated a gathering with his mere presence. He lacked charisma. He had cultivated no particular interests. He did not enjoy spectator sports. He unenthusiastically attended the theater and concerts. Until late in his presidency, when he took up fishing, his only regular recreation was riding a mechanical horse that he kept in the White House. Much like his father, he was not a stimulating conversationalist. Although he could become garrulous, especially when discussing politics, he said little to visitors unless he knew them well. Coolidge, then, was not the typical outgoing, facile politician. His only traditional asset was his wife. Grace Coolidge exuded those qualities so lacking in her husband—charm, gregariousness, enthusiasm, and warmth.

Nor did Coolidge bring to the White House a renowned reputation, unless it was one for winning political office. Born on July 4, 1872, Coolidge grew up in the bleak and parochial rural world of Plymouth Notch, Vermont. (Named John Calvin for his father, he dropped the John when he became a young man.) Leaving Vermont in 1891, he attended Amherst College, where he was graduated in 1895. After college, he studied law in the office of a firm in Northampton, Massachusetts. In 1898, he opened his own law practice there, which he maintained for twenty-one years.

Beginning with membership on the Northampton City Council in 1898, Coolidge rose rapidly in politics, becoming a member of the state legislature in 1906, lieutenant governor in 1915, governor in 1918, and Warren G. Harding's vice president in 1921. As a state legislator and governor, Coolidge was industrious, competent, and loyal to the Republican Party. He won national attention during the Boston police strike of 1919, when, to restore order in the city, he called out the National Guard and backed the police commissioner in his decision not to rehire any of the strikers, declaring, "There is no right to strike against the public safety, by anybody, anywhere, anytime."

As vice president, Coolidge had virtually nothing to do. He presided over the Senate, read a good deal, took his regular afternoon naps, and saved his money. Lonely, without power after years of exercising it in Massachusetts, he found the vice presidency a mockery. Rather than commanding respect pointing to a bright political future, in 1923 the idiosyncratic Coolidge had become in the eyes of many a capital "character" or "joke." Informed political observers even expected him to be dropped as Harding's running mate in 1924.

The tragic death of Harding was just the latest of many lucky breaks that accompanied Coolidge's political rise. Harding's death occurred when Coolidge was visiting his father in Vermont. There on August 2, 1923, his father awakened him with the news that he was president and, as a notary public in Plymouth Notch, Vermont, administered the oath of office to his son by candlelight in the house in which the new president had been born.

Extraordinary luck accounts in part for Coolidge's meteoric political rise, but it does not explain his continuing popularity. In the 1920's, Americans responded to a man who guilelessly argued that the national government should be as passive as possible, leaving people to pursue their economic interests largely free of government interference. The chief business of the American people, he declared in 1925, was business,

> buying, selling, investing, and prospering in the world. I am strongly of the opinion that the majority of people will always find these are the moving impulses of our life. . . . In all experience, the accumulation of wealth means the multiplication of schools, the encouragement of science, the increase of knowledge, the dissemination of intelligence, the broadening of outlook, the expansion of liberties, the widening of culture.

For the individual and society to thrive, Coolidge believed, the federal government ought to be reduced in size and function, adminis-

THE FIRST LADY
GRACE COOLIDGE

Grace Coolidge was the vivacious wife of the thirtieth U.S. president, Calvin Coolidge. She worked tirelessly for the welfare of others.

Grace Anna Goodhue was born on January 3, 1879, in Burlington, Vermont. She earned a degree from the University of Vermont in 1902 and became a teacher at the Clarke School for the Deaf in Northampton, Massachusetts. During the three years that she worked at the school, she met Coolidge, a young lawyer whose quiet personality balanced Grace's exuberance.

Grace and Calvin were married on October 4, 1905. They had two sons: John, born in 1906, and Calvin, Jr., born in 1908. The family followed a strict budget, living within their means and remaining in the same home in order to save money even when Calvin became governor in 1918.

Grace compensated for her husband's shy manner with friendliness. Her warm, open personality captivated those she met in Washington, D.C. Though frugal, Calvin did encourage his wife to buy fashionable clothing in harmony with her personality.

Grace took her obligations as First Lady seriously. When their youngest son died of blood poisoning in 1924, Grace continued with her duties, including forming an advisory committee to remodel the White House and setting an example for other women by voting and taking long walks to stay fit.

She used her influence as First Lady to support the Red Cross, Easter Seals, and the Association for the Aid of Crippled Children. Her efforts resulted in a gold medal from the National Institute of Social Sciences. In 1931, she was named one of the United States's twelve greatest living women. Later, she served as trustee for the Clarke School.

When Calvin died in 1933, Grace sold their estate, the Beeches. She built another home in Northampton, where she lived until her death on July 8, 1957.

Lisa A. Wroble

tered with greater economy, and kept ever alert to raids on the Treasury by groups whose proposals, if enacted, would restrict individual initiative. Government should be in no hurry to legislate.

The 1920's were generally prosperous, and in Coolidge the people had a president who articulated and symbolized traditional values, economic and moral. He came from a family of moderate means, from a poor state where work, thrift, and frugality were extolled and the hardship of privation endured. Certainly, his personality and lifestyle contrasted favorably with the profligate types in the Harding administration, and Americans apparently welcomed the safe, secure, and predictable following the twin traumas of war and corruption.

Coolidge and His Image: The First Master of the Media

The Coolidge image, however, was shaped largely by a very skillful manipulation of the public relations media, one orchestrated by the president himself. Discerning the crucial role of public opinion in a democratic government, Coolidge used the mass media to sell himself and the Republican program to the people and in the process developed techniques that his successors emulated or refined.

In doing so, Coolidge shrewdly exploited four available media—the press, radio, movie newsreels, and official government releases. Coolidge enjoyed a favorable press throughout his presidency, at a time when a president's primary link to the people was the newspaper. He consciously promoted amicable relations with the publishers of metropolitan dailies. Although the press conference was inaugurated by William Howard Taft, Coolidge was responsible for institutionalizing it. He held press conferences twice a week, using a format that allowed the president to control news dissemination. Questions were submitted in writing before the conference, only minimal dialogue between reporters and the president was allowed, and the president could not be quoted or identified as having been the source of the information.

In addition to the press, Coolidge used radio, then in its infancy, to communicate with the people. His initial State of the Union message, read in person to Congress in December, 1923, was the first such address to be broadcast to a near national audience. Other selected and campaign speeches were sent simultaneously over the airwaves, and on occasion Coolidge spoke from the White House only to a radio audience, an innovation that Franklin D. Roosevelt refined into his fireside chats. The newsreel also brought the president regularly before Americans, who had become avid moviegoers in the 1920's. Coolidge was keenly aware of the medium's public relations potential and used it with skill. Finally, the White House issued a large number of official releases. Coolidge sent birthday greetings and letters to prominent Americans, addressed messages to organizations holding conventions or celebrating anniversaries, and delivered patriotic statements on special days. There was, thus, no official "Silent Cal." However taciturn he may have been in private, the public Coolidge was loquacious, much in the news, the very symbol of a national leader.

Coolidge's Program: Domestic Policies and Legislative Achievements

Upon taking office, Coolidge kept the same cabinet that had served Harding, but he forced Attorney General Harry Daugherty to resign when it became clear that he had been involved in the scandals of the Harding administration.

Although the cabinet met with him as a group twice weekly, Coolidge expected each secretary to administer his own department and make decisions.

The dominant figure in the cabinet, and for that matter in Washington, D.C., during the decade, was Herbert Hoover, secretary of commerce. This ambitious subordinate not only expanded the budget, personnel, and functions of his own department but also had an influential voice in the formulation of many administration policies. James J. Davis, secretary of labor, Hubert Work, secretary of the interior, and William Jardine, after 1925 secretary of agriculture, deferred to his ambition. Coolidge relied much on Hoover's judgment, but their personalities, their work habits, and even their philosophies of government differed too greatly for the two ever to be close. Coolidge was not intimate with anyone, least of all a "shaker and mover" such as Hoover.

Secretary of the Treasury Andrew Mellon, the other major figure in the cabinet, commanded Coolidge's utmost respect, if not awe. The president warmly embraced the Mellon tax program, the secretary's prescription for an expanding and increasingly prosperous economy. He saw a correlation between government fiscal policy and the nation's economic health. Eventually, Congress enacted most of the Mellon Plan, and the public, encouraged by Coolidge and other Republican politicians, came to believe that the secretary was orchestrating the decade's prosperity.

Coolidge deferred in foreign affairs to his secretaries of state, Charles Evans Hughes and Frank B. Kellogg, and to special emissaries Dwight Morrow (Mexico) and Henry L. Stimson (Nicaragua). He probably reposed greater confidence in Hughes, but he also approved most of Kellogg's recommendations.

Soon after taking office, Coolidge began to prepare for the 1924 election. Having control of the party machinery, he won nomination easily and chose as his running mate Charles G. Dawes, former director of the budget and author of the Dawes Plan for the settlement of the German World War I reparations problem. The badly divided Democrats finally nominated John W. Davis, a conservative Wall Street lawyer from West Virginia, on the 103d ballot. The Progressive Party nominated Robert M. La Follette for president. Coolidge won a decisive victory, receiving 382 electoral votes compared with 136 for Davis and 13 for La Follette.

The program that Coolidge presented to Congress was minimal, essentially that inherited from Harding, and his success in guiding it through Congress was mixed. Revenue laws providing for reduction in the surtax on individual incomes constitute Coolidge's most popular legacy. Secretary Mellon proposed these reductions to spur high-risk investment by wealthy investors who otherwise would find tax-free securities the most attractive outlet for their capital. If they did concentrate their buying on government securities, economic growth necessary for the creation of jobs would be stunted, and the national Treasury would be denied the revenue that lower taxes would bring to it. Congress passed the key tax measure in 1926 when it lowered the maximum surtax (on incomes above $100,000) and the estate tax to 20 percent and abolished the gift tax entirely. Since the exemption for married taxpayers was $3,500, however, most Americans paid no federal income tax at all.

Other noteworthy laws were passed during the Coolidge presidency, laws that had Coolidge's approval if not the enthusiastic support accorded the administration's fiscal legislation. The Air Commerce Act of 1926 brought federal regulation to a chaotic industry that required order for development. Largely the idea of Hoover, the measure furnished aid to private enterprise through regulation of aircraft and pilots and the provision of weather information, auxiliary airfields, and subsidies for mail delivery; but it still envisaged that the investment should be private, not public as in Europe. Even the post office subsidies for air mail were only tem-porary. Once private airlines could carry the mail, in compliance with the Kelly Act of 1925 the government retreated from the scene. The Radio Act of 1927, also advocated by Hoover, created a radio commission to regulate that industry. The Railway Labor Act, an impressive achievement of the Coolidge administration, replaced the justly maligned Railroad Labor Board with a Board of Mediation for the resolution of disputes and guaranteed to railway workers the right of collective bargaining.

The Boulder Canyon Project Act authorized the construction of a huge dam on the Colorado River between Arizona and Nevada. Since the development included production of vast amounts of electrical energy, which could be sold by the government to pay for flood control, irrigation, and water storage projects, Coolidge signed the measure without enthusiasm, his thinking paralleling that of private power companies, which opposed the project. Although accepting the Boulder Canyon bill, Coolidge pocket vetoed the Muscle Shoals bill, which provided for a similar public power development on the Tennessee River in Muscle Shoals, Alabama. Under Franklin D. Roosevelt, this project was carried out by the Tennessee Valley Authority.

Legislation passed in 1926 expanded American military aviation, both army and navy, although not enough to satisfy Colonel Billy Mitchell, outspoken advocate of military air power. Coolidge was no more disposed to spend government funds unnecessarily on the military than on any domestic scheme. For most of his presidency, he publicly discounted the pleas of both branches of the service that they were underfunded and that the country's security was being placed in jeopardy. The president's Aircraft Board, established by Coolidge in September, 1925, and chaired by Dwight Morrow, vindicated his judgment that the nation was not in immediate danger from an attack by air and, taking issue with Mitchell and his congressional supporters, opposed the creation of both a separate air force and a unified department of defense. The Morrow board did recommend action that when authorized by Congress in 1926 created new assistant secretaries for air in the War, Navy, and Commerce departments. Only after the abortive Geneva Disarmament Conference in 1927 did the president seek large sums from Congress for the construction of fifteen new heavy cruisers and one additional aircraft carrier. Previously, he had opposed the appropriations necessary to build the three cruisers authorized by Congress in 1924. Even then, Congress in 1929 brushed aside presidential wishes when it stipulated a time limit in building those sixteen new vessels.

Farm relief legislation precipitated the most intense struggle between Congress and the executive branch of the period. The decade of the 1920's brought depression to American agriculture, as farm prices in the aggregate fell while costs stabilized or increased. Farmers wanted the government to assure them of parity—the same prices for their commodities relative to their costs as they had enjoyed before the war. In response to this demand, Congress twice passed McNary-Haugen bills, which would have authorized the government, in an effort to support domestic prices, to buy the surplus of certain staple commodities, dispose of them at a loss on the world market, and make good the loss and administrative costs through an equalization fee to be paid by the farmers. Coolidge vetoed the legislation, the second time using uncharacteristically passionate and vitriolic language. A McNary-Haugen Act would have meant unprecedented peacetime intervention in the farm economy by govern-

Crowded housing in a company-owned coal town. *(Library of Congress)*

ment, necessitated an initial federal subsidy to carry the export program until the equalization fee made it self-sustaining, and included a price-fixing feature. Coolidge objected to the bill on philosophical and practical grounds. Such government involvement with agriculture, he held, "was dangerously socialistic in character" and contravened the American tradition of laissez-faire. Besides, the plan would not work, since it had no provision for production control. In fact, it would encourage greater production, more dumping of farm produce abroad, and foreign retaliation. Since Congress could not override the vetoes, stalemate ensued. Cooperative marketing, the administration's long-term answer to the problem, failed to satisfy farmers, their organizations' leaders, and their farm spokespeople in Congress.

Congress regularly failed to act on some of Coolidge's recommendations, as with his railroad consolidation legislation; it modified some of his proposals, as when it made the appropriation in the Flood Control Act of 1928 much greater than the president thought necessary; and it overrode some of his vetoes, of which there were fifty.

Coolidge's difficulties with Congress included not only legislation but also Senate confirmation of his appointments. The Senate re-fused to confirm as circuit court judge Wallace McCammant, the man who in 1920 had nominated him for the vice presidency. It also turned down two Interstate Commerce Commission nominees. The ultimate embarrassment, however, was its rejection in 1925 of Charles B. Warren as attorney general. Not since the presidency of Andrew Johnson had the Senate rejected a president's choice for a cabinet position. The administration argument that the president had the right to choose his subordi-

---

THE VICE PRESIDENT
CHARLES G. DAWES

Charles Gates Dawes was born on August 27, 1865, in Marietta, Ohio. His father, Rufus Dawes, was a member of Congress. The younger Dawes was educated at Marietta Academy and went on to graduate from Marietta College in 1884. Dawes studied at the Cincinnati Law School, from which he was graduated, and he was admitted to the bar in 1886. After his studies, Dawes went to work for a railway company, becoming chief engineer, but he tired of this work and moved to Lincoln, Nebraska. In Lincoln, he established the law firm of Dawes, Coffroth, and Cunningham and went on to run numerous businesses, serving as vice president of the Lincoln Packaging Company, director of the American Exchange National Bank, president of Northwestern Gas Light, and president of the La Cross Gas Light Company.

On January 24, 1889, Dawes married Carol Blymer, and the couple had two children. He published a book on the U.S. banking system in 1892 and became a member of the Republican National Executive Committee. President William McKinley named Dawes as U.S. comptroller, a post in which he served from 1897 to 1901, receiving credit for a number of banking reforms. In 1902, Dawes ran unsuccessfully for the U.S. Senate. He published a collection of his speeches in 1915, served as a major in the Army Engineer Corps in World War I—after his duty in France he was promoted several times, reaching the rank of brigadier general—and served on the Military Board of Allied Supply. Dawes was highly decorated for his service during the war and received the Nobel Peace Prize for chairing the effort that organized postwar Germany.

However, Dawes was unsuccessful in his bid for the presidency in 1920. President Warren G. Harding named Dawes to direct the Bureau of the Budget from 1921 to 1922. Dawes then headed the Central Trust Company of Chicago. During this time, he published a book on the Great War and another on the U.S. budget. In 1924, Dawes was nominated as vice president, serving in the second Coolidge administration. In 1928, Dawes attempted a second campaign for the presidency. President Herbert Hoover, the winner in 1928, appointed Dawes ambassador to Great Britain, where he served from 1929 to 1932. In 1932, Dawes was asked to help alleviate the suffering of the Great Depression when he chaired the National Economic League and was president of the Reconstruction Finance Corporation.

After retiring from politics, Dawes remained active in the banking business and continued to write. He died on April 23, 1951.

Robert P. Watson and Richard Yon

nates conflicted with the belief of some senators that their advice and consent were legitimate constitutional prerogatives. The major concern of Senate progressives, both Democratic and Republican, was Warren's former ties to the sugar trust; they worried that his department might have to prosecute the corporation he at one time headed, which was under indictment. Such a conflict of interest never bothered the president, but it did certain progressive Republicans, who were smarting as well from the recent treatment accorded four of their progressive colleagues by the party regulars. Those senators had been stripped of their committee chairmanships and seniority because they had supported the third-party effort of Robert La Follette in 1924.

In fairness to Coolidge, it should not be inferred that had he been more forceful, Congress would have done his bidding on the Warren appointment or his legislative agenda. The most activist president would have had trouble with the politically independent Congresses of the 1920's. Party affiliation meant little, and both Republicans and Democrats were divided among themselves. After 1925 the division on key issues often was a fluid coalition of progressives and moderates against conservatives. A greater effort by Coolidge would most likely not have produced much success. Nevertheless, he did try to influence the legislation. He met regularly with Republican leaders in Congress, kept abreast of issues and canvasses, and pressed congressmen to support the administration.

Coolidge had his greatest influence on the federal government by altering the ideological complexion of the courts and government agencies to conform to his economic philosophy. His only Supreme Court appointment, Harlan F. Stone, was superlative. He was less circumspect in his nominations to lower federal courts. Ignoring the views of Chief Justice William Howard Taft, even though he was a strong Coolidge supporter, the president nominated only persons of strong conservative leanings.

Coolidge effectively politicized the regulatory commissions and the tariff commission. He killed any chance that the tariff commission might help set rates to reflect the difference in the cost of producing an item in the United States and abroad. He simply replaced the moderates on the tariff commission with high protectionists regardless of party and exercised his power almost exclusively to raise, not lower, rates. He reduced duties on only five items recommended by the commission while raising those on thirty-eight. Twice he rejected its advice to lower schedules on sugar and linseed oil. Moreover, Coolidge never accepted the commission's quasi-judicial pretensions. To him it was only a fact-finding agency whose recommendations he was free to accept or reject as he pleased. In 1926, at the instigation of George W. Norris, the Senate investigated Coolidge's emasculation of the tariff commission, but nothing came of it. The commission remained a bastion of protectionism.

As for the regulatory commissions, Coolidge appointed railroad people to the Interstate Commerce Commission and enemies of business regulation to the Federal Trade Commission. In 1925 he named to the latter William E. Humphrey, a former Washington congressman who had for years vehemently attacked the FTC. Under his leadership the commission was transformed into a friendly adviser to business. The frustrated Norris saw no reason for the continued existence of the FTC since it had become an agent of those interests supposedly being regulated. Overall, then, the Coolidge administration preferred not to harass business enterprise, not to interfere with trade associations, and not to initiate antitrust suits unless there were compelling reasons to do so, but rather to use government mechanisms to promote, to refine, and to humanize business.

Support in 1925 for rent controls in the District of Columbia excepted, indications of a

The Kellogg-Briand Pact

The President of the German Reich; The President of the United States; His Majesty the King of the Belgians; The President of the French Republic; His Majesty the King of Great Britain, Ireland, and the British Dominions Beyond the Seas; Emperor of India; His Majesty the King of Italy; His Majesty the Emperor of Japan; The President of the Republic of Poland; The President of the Czechoslovak Republic, Deeply sensible of their solemn duty to promote the welfare of mankind;

Persuaded that the time has come when a frank renunciation of war as an instrument of national policy should be made to the end that the peaceful and friendly relations now existing between their peoples may be perpetuated;

Convinced that all changes in their relations with one another should be sought only by pacific means and be the result of a peaceful and orderly process, and that any signatory Power which shall hereafter seek to promote its national interests by resort to war a should be denied the benefits furnished by this Treaty;

Hopeful that, encouraged by their example, all the other nations of the world will join in this humane endeavor and by adhering to the present Treaty as soon as it comes into force bring their peoples within the scope of its beneficent provisions, thus uniting the civilized nations of the world in a common renunciation of war as an instrument of their national policy;

Have decided to conclude a Treaty and for that purpose have appointed as their respective Plenipotentiaries, . . . who, having communicated to one another their full powers found in good and due form have agreed upon the following articles:

ARTICLE I: The High Contracting Parties solemnly declare in the names of their respective peoples that they condemn recourse to war for the solution of international controversies, and renounce it, as an instrument of national policy in their relations with one another.

ARTICLE II: The High Contracting Parties agree that the settlement or solution of all disputes or conflicts of whatever nature or of whatever origin they may be, which may arise among them, shall never be sought except by pacific means.

ARTICLE III: The present Treaty shall be ratified by the High Contracting Parties named in the Preamble in accordance with their respective constitutional requirements, and shall take effect as between them as soon as all their several instruments of ratification shall have been deposited at Washington.

Coolidge sensitivity to society's less fortunate citizens are hard to find. Although in 1924 Hoover brought together United Mine Workers and management representatives who negotiated the Jacksonville agreement, which was designed to bring peace and improved living conditions to the coal-mining area of the central United States, the administration turned away from the industry when that agreement broke down in 1927 and workers went out on what proved to be a disastrous strike. A Senate investigation revealed shocking conditions in the company towns in Pennsylvania, West Virginia, and Ohio, where inhabitants were denied essential civil liberties and a feeling of hopelessness characterized those seemingly forgotten people. Washington had no more power to act here, Coolidge believed, than it did to regulate the stock exchange. The problem was for local and state authorities to correct. Similarly, he refused to address or to acknowledge signals of mounting industrial unemployment in American cities. The administration discounted the severity of the problem and denounced as partisan election rantings the efforts of Democratic Senator Robert Wagner of New York to have the government at least gather statistics to ascertain its magnitude.

Coolidge's greatest insensitivity was reserved for African Americans. He was not unusual in failing to see any moral or political urgency in the improvement of race relations. In 1924, James Weldon Johnson, the leading official in the National Association for the Advancement of Colored People (NAACP), paid a visit to Coolidge, after which he reported that the president seemed ill at ease and had little to say, not even raising issues of concern to African Americans. Coolidge's response to grievances that they most wanted redressed, segregation in federal employment and lynching, left African Americans frustrated. The NAACP informed Coolidge in detail of every lynching of an African American during the period and urged him to make an antilynching bill a legislative priority. The president was content simply to reprove the crime in his annual messages. He condemned the Ku Klux Klan in October, 1925, when its power had already begun to wane.

Foreign Policy: Involvement Without Commitment

Coolidge came to the White House with experience in local and state government, but he was quite ignorant of international politics. From the first, he deferred to professional policy makers in this area. In December, 1923, Coolidge expressed thoughts that excited the possibility of Washington's diplomatic recognition of the Soviet Union. Secretary of State Hughes quickly dashed the hopes of those Americans who favored that course, and Coolidge acquiesced. He, moreover, allowed the State Department to exploit the communist issue in its Central American endeavors. Robert Olds, undersecretary in 1926, and Kellogg tried to link Mexico and Nicaragua to a Kremlin threat to the Panama Canal, but Americans, however hateful they were of the Soviet experiment,

failed to respond. Rather they welcomed the peaceful settlement of the dispute with Mexico over property rights of foreigners, particularly those of American petroleum companies, and an election in Nicaragua under the supervision of American military personnel after the conclusion of that country's civil war.

Unfortunately, American marines, whom Coolidge had returned to Nicaragua in 1926 after a brief withdrawal, soon found themselves warring against the forces of Augusto Sandino, a revolutionary committed to the complete withdrawal of American military forces from his country. The continued skirmishes precipitated a lively debate that saw George Norris in 1928 sponsor amendments to a naval appropriations bill that called for the partial or complete withdrawal of the marines and an accounting to the Senate if the president kept them in Nicaragua past the designated date. These antecedents of the War Powers Act, however, were voted down. Yet, under Coolidge, the United States retreated from its imperialistic past, anticipating the "Good Neighbor" orientation of Herbert Hoover and Franklin D. Roosevelt. Hughes's impromptu defense of intervention at the Sixth Inter-American Conference at Havana in 1928 constitutes the final assertion of that dubious American right.

The foreign policies associated with the Coolidge administration, then, were reasonably enlightened, if not always successful. Domestic imperatives limited the foreign policy initiatives the administration contemplated. For example, however wise World War I Allied debt cancellation or drastic reduction of intergovernmental obligations might have been, such action was in direct conflict with the fiscal commitment of the president. Even so, the United States pursued a lenient war debt policy, basing the agreement negotiated during the Coolidge presidency on the capacity-to-pay principle, in effect reducing the total debt through sharp curtailment of interest. The State Department did, however, threaten to disapprove private

Coolidge signs the Kellogg-Briand Pact. *(Library of Congress)*

fines of domestic restraints and the desire to maintain future freedom of action, the Coolidge years witnessed an American effort to stabilize Europe. A prosperous Europe would be a peaceful Europe. A prosperous and peaceful Europe would be a lucrative market for exports of American goods and capital.

The Kellogg-Briand Pact, or the Peace of Paris, was the most memorable foreign policy legacy of the Coolidge presidency. Not wanting to become part of a French security system that might involve the United States in a future European conflict, Kellogg rejected the overture of Aristide Briand, the French foreign minister, for a Franco-American pact renouncing war as an instrument of national policy. Because peace groups embraced the idea, the secretary of state countered by proposing a multilateral treaty. All signatories (ultimately sixty-two), not only France and the United States, would renounce war. The treaty, however, provided for no enforcement machinery, no commitment of a signatory to any concrete action in the future. Washington concurrently ratified this pact and launched its naval arms program.

loans to citizens, corporations, or local governments of those nations that refused to negotiate debt-funding agreements.

The formulators of the Coolidge administration foreign policy discerned the importance to American interests of European political and economic stability and the contributions the United States, through business and banking experts, should make to that stability. The Dawes Plan, involving loans by American banks to Germany to make possible reparations payments by that nation, expansion of American commercial markets abroad, and encouragement of private investments in Europe (although the State Department denied loans for certain purposes and to selected countries) were initiatives that carried with them no political commitments or obligations. The United States abstained from membership in the League of Nations and even refused to affiliate with the World Court. When the signatories raised questions about a reservation the Senate attached to American adherence to the court protocol, Coolidge adopted a take it or leave it attitude. Republican foreign policy managers developed a course best described as involvement without commitment. Within the con-

The most praiseworthy American initiatives during the Coolidge years were in East Asia. China was the scene of continual civil turmoil as various northern warlords vied for control of the central government in Peking, while rolling northward from Canton in the south was a coalition composed of Chinese Communists and a reorganized Kuomintang under Chiang Kai-shek. Victorious in 1927, with the northern armies in retreat, and with China nearly unified, the coalition collapsed when the Kuomintang turned on the Communists, launching another civil war that finally led in 1949 to the ouster of the Kuomintang from the mainland. Against this backdrop of conflict, facing the forces of revolution and nationalism, the Coolidge administration established ties with the new China, agreeing to discuss tariff autonomy, negotiating such an arrangement—thus recognizing the new regime in Nanjing—and refusing to employ force to suppress emerging Chinese nationalism.

As Coolidge left office, the prized goal he failed to attain was a naval arms pact with Great Britain extending the Washington tonnage reduction formula to auxiliary ships. In early 1929, Anglo-American relations reached their lowest point in many years, with the United States embarked on an extensive naval construction program and many Britishers in agreement with Winston Churchill, who argued against renewed Anglo-American negotiations with a president who recently had expressed "the view-point of a New England backwoodsman."

Coolidge declined to run for reelection in 1928. *(Library of Congress)*

An Unwarranted Complacence

Historians still debate the meaning of Coolidge's cryptic press conference release in 1927 that he chose not to run for president in 1928. Would he neither seek nor accept the nomination of his party, or was he angling for a draft? The more cogent judgment is that he intended to retire from the presidency and expressed that intention in the idiom of New England. According to Hoover, Coolidge worked for his nomination and he, Hoover, never questioned the statement's meaning. Several factors weighed heavily in Coolidge's decision. The death of Calvin, Jr., in 1924 at age sixteen—from blood poisoning contracted while playing tennis—was a blow from which neither he nor his wife ever completely recovered. Coolidge was also concerned about his health. In 1926, he

may have suffered a heart attack. Grace Coolidge also suffered physically in Washington, D.C. Renomination and then reelection would have required a greater effort than the president wanted to expend. He did not step down because he sensed impending economic disaster. He had, in his opinion, served his country well and it was time for a new administration. Coolidge bequeathed prosperity, peace, and public tranquility to his successor, who was committed to continuing the policies believed responsible for that state of the nation.

Richard N. Kottman

Suggested Readings

Booraem, Hendrik. *The Provincial: Calvin Coolidge and His World, 1885-1895.* Lewisburg, Pa.: Bucknell University Press, 1994. An examination of Coolidge's formative years.

Calvin Coolidge Memorial Foundation. http://www.calvin-coolidge.org/. The Web site of the organization that seeks to make accessible Coolidge's speeches and writings, as well as others' research on him.

Cornwell, Elmer E., Jr. *Presidential Leadership of Public Opinion*. 1965. Reprint. Westport, Conn.: Greenwood Press, 1979. Includes an outstanding chapter on Coolidge and public relations.

Ellis, L. Ethan. *Republican Foreign Policy, 1921-1933*. New Brunswick, N.J.: Rutgers University Press, 1968. Details the approaches to foreign policy during Coolidge's era.

Ferrell, Robert H. *The Presidency of Calvin Coolidge*. Lawrence: University Press of Kansas, 1998. An extensive analysis of the Coolidge presidency.

Ferrell, Robert H., and Howard Quint, eds. *The Talkative President: The Off-the-Record Press Conferences of Calvin Coolidge*. Amherst: University of Massachusetts Press, 1964. Contains selections from Coolidge's press conferences.

Fuess, Claude M. *Calvin Coolidge: The Man from Vermont*. Boston: Little, Brown, 1940. An older but worthy biography that is strong on Coolidge's early life and career but treats the presidential years perhaps too favorably.

Gilbert, Robert E. *The Tormented President: Calvin Coolidge, Death, and Clinical Depression*. Westport, Conn.: Praeger, 2003. Argues that after the death of his son in 1924, Coolidge suffered from clinical depression, which had significant impact on the remainder of his presidency.

Greene, J. R. *Calvin Coolidge's Plymouth, Vermont*. Dover, N.H.: Arcadia, 1997. A pictorial profile of Coolidge's birthplace.

Hawley, Ellis W. *The Great War and the Search for a Modern Order: A History of the American People and Their Institutions*. 1979. 2d ed. New York: St. Martin's Press, 1992. Gives an overview of the period, which throws significant light on Hoover and associationalism.

Haynes, John Earl, ed. *Calvin Coolidge and the Coolidge Era: Essays on the History of the 1920's*. Hanover, N.H.: University of New England Press, 1998. Originally presented in a Library of Congress symposium, the twelve essays reassess the decade and Coolidge's presidency.

Leffler, Melvyn P. *The Elusive Quest: America's Pursuit of European Stability and French Security, 1919-1933*. Chapel Hill: University of North Carolina Press, 1979. A provocative exploration of foreign policy and an accurate analysis of Republican diplomatic efforts.

McCoy, Donald R. *Calvin Coolidge: The Quiet President*. 1967. Reprint. Lawrence: University of Kansas Press, 1988. Arguably one of the most balanced biographies of Coolidge, reflecting research in numerous manuscript collections.

Sobel, Robert. *Coolidge: An American Enigma*. Washington, D.C.: Regnery, 1998. A balanced biography that contradicts the popular image of Coolidge as an ineffectual leader.

Herbert Hoover

31st President, 1929-1933

Born: August 10, 1874
    West Branch, Iowa
Died: October 20, 1964
    New York, New York

Political Party: Republican
Vice President: Charles Curtis

Cabinet Members

Secretary of State: Henry L. Stimson
Secretary of the Treasury: Andrew Mellon,
    Ogden L. Mills
Secretary of War: James W. Good, Patrick J.
    Hurley
Secretary of the Navy: Charles Francis Adams
Attorney General: William D. Mitchell
Postmaster General: Walter Brown
Secretary of the Interior: Ray Lyman Wilbur
Secretary of Agriculture: Arthur M. Hyde
Secretary of Commerce: Robert Lamont, Roy D.
    Chapin
Secretary of Labor: James J. Davis, William N.
    Doak

Herbert Clark Hoover, thirty-first president of the United States, assumed office on March 4, 1929, and relinquished it four years later after being defeated in the election of 1932. His name was long associated with the suffering and misery of the Great Depression, and in popular mythology and political rhetoric it still conjures up visions of a hard-hearted, stiff-collared reactionary mouthing individualist dogma to justify stingy relief expenditures and showing solicitude for the greedy rather than the needy. Recent scholarship on his presidency, however, has tended to por-

tray him in a more positive light. It has moved toward vindicating those who have argued that he was both "the last of the old presidents and the first of the new." Increasingly, it has associated him with a variant form of political

Hoover's official portrait. *(White House Historical Society)*

progressivism seeking to develop new managerial capacities and social safety nets but insisting that this had to be done through government-encouraged private mechanisms and public-private partnerships rather than through expansion of the public sector.

Indeed, the experience of Hoover's presidency can be read as testimony both to the strength of this strain of progressivism in American political culture and to its inadequacy when subjected to severe tests. This progressivism underlay his designs for recovery, relief, and reform as well as his resistance to competing designs; and although it contributed to the failures that made him a one-term president, it also helped to put him in the office. Its appeal made his earlier career seem ideal preparation for serving national needs.

Prepresidential Career

Hoover was born on August 10, 1874, in the Quaker village of West Branch, Iowa, the son of

---

THE FIRST LADY
LOU HOOVER

Born on March 29, 1874, in Waterloo, Iowa, Lou Henry moved to Southern California with her family when she was ten years old. There she camped with her father in the hills, learned to ride a horse with expertise, and discovered a keen interest in rocks, minerals, and mining. She obtained a teaching certificate before entering Stanford University in 1894, where she studied geology—she was the first woman in Stanford's geology department—and met Herbert Clark Hoover, whom she married in 1899. His career as a mining engineer took the young couple around the globe. The Hoovers eventually had two sons.

In World War I and the postwar period from 1918 to 1923, she helped her husband establish four war relief agencies. These activities brought her to the attention of Girl Scouts founder Juliette Gordon Low, who asked her to join the Girl Scouts' executive board. By Low's untimely death in 1927, Lou had served several terms as president and vice president and had emerged as Low's successor. She had also proven to be an especially effective fund-raiser.

At the time of Herbert Hoover's inauguration in March, 1929, she was in the midst of another campaign for the Girl Scouts. The campaign's financial success assured the organization's future, enabling an expanded training program for leaders that appealed to parents—and several popular new programs that appealed to their daughters. Membership exploded from 167,000 in 1927 to more than one million by the time of Lou's death in 1944.

Like many First Ladies, Lou Hoover had a deep commitment to public service and a strong aversion to dishonest politicians who manipulated "the thing called politics" for their own ends. Lou's dislike for politics later led to assertions that she was ill-informed and did not understand the issues during her husband's administration. However, letters to her sons indicate that she discussed the issues with her husband, offered suggestions, and was keenly aware of the impact of various proposals. In the spring of 1930, she established the first large-scale relief agency to be run by a First Lady—this one addressing the impact of the Great Depression. Using her own money, she hired additional aides to coordinate assistance for thousands between 1930 and 1933. Most never realized that the assistance they had received had come from an exceptionally modest First Lady. It was not until after Lou's death in 1944 that Herbert Hoover learned of Lou's generous charity work and noted that as a First Lady, she was "a symbol of everything wholesome in American life."

Dale C. Mayer

blacksmith and farm implement dealer Jesse Hoover and his wife, Hulda. Reared as a Quaker, he would retain much of the austere demeanor and duty-bound industriousness associated with that faith. Even more important in shaping his personality, however, were the deaths of his father in 1880 and mother in 1884, his move to Oregon to live with relatives, and the insecurities, defensiveness, and determination to succeed thus instilled. By the time he entered Stanford University's "pioneer" class in 1891, he had become what one historian has called an "aggressive introvert," seeking ways to exert influence while staying in the background. While working toward a degree in geology, he became noted among close associates for his entrepreneurial, organizational, and manipulative talents.

Following graduation from Stanford in 1895, Hoover initially had difficulty in finding suitable employment, but in 1896 he entered the employ of San Francisco mining engineer Louis Janin, and this proved to be the starting point in a meteoric rise to fame and fortune. In 1897 he was hired by the British company of Bewick, Moreing, serving first as an evaluator and manager of mining properties in Western Australia and then, from 1899 to 1901, as the Bewick, Moreing man in the Chinese Engineering and Mining Company. On his way to China, he married Lou Henry, also a Stanford graduate, and in Tientsin, at the outbreak of the Boxer Rebellion, he directed construction of barricades to protect the foreign colony. In 1901 he became a partner in Bewick, Moreing and subsequently played a key role in modernizing the company and establishing its reputation for financial probity and business progressiveness. In 1908 he left to pursue business interests of his own, particularly in Burmese tin and international oil exploration. Although calling himself a "mining engineer," he earned large fees and profits as a specialist in mining finance and the reorganization of failing enterprises. By 1914, he was both wealthy and internationally recognized.

In this rise to international prominence, one can also note three other behavioral patterns significant for Hoover's later career. One was an early and persistent interest in institutional reform and social betterment, manifested particularly in his managerial innovations, professional writings, and philanthropic projects, and leading him toward visions of a new capitalism ordered and kept productive and progressive through professionalized organizations accountable to informed public opinion. A second was his continued penchant for indirection and behind-the-scenes wire-pulling, evident not only in business dealings and "hidden-hand" philanthropies but also in public relations promotions such as that undertaken for the Panama-Pacific Exposition in 1913. A third was his considerable capacity for self-delusion when ventures and projects with which he was associated turned out badly. In such cases he tended to minimize his own role, find others to blame, and credit himself with a foresight and detachment not borne out by the record.

With the outbreak of World War I in 1914, Hoover quickly became involved in relief work, initially to rescue stranded Americans in Europe and then as organizer and director of the Commission for Relief in Belgium. In the public mind he became the "great humanitarian" as well as the "great engineer." When the United States entered the war in 1917, he became wartime food administrator, and he proceeded to develop a complex of public-private partnerships, community units, and governmental purchasing and publicity agencies through which production stimulants and distributive controls were administered. Some of the resulting arrangements would become models for the kind of societal and governmental machinery that he would advocate in the postwar period, and in operation they made him the best known and most widely acclaimed of Woodrow Wilson's war managers. To "Hooverize," meaning to economize for noble purposes, became a new addition to the American vocabulary.

Following the armistice in 1918, Hoover became director of American relief efforts in Europe, not only helping to feed millions and reconstruct wartorn economies but also engaging in heated controversies over policy toward Germany, Allied economic controls, and the use of food for political purposes. In September, 1919, he returned to the United States and in the months that followed became involved in a number of domestic developments and issues. He helped to organize the Federated American Engineering Societies, became its first president, and led it to take on projects for reducing waste and reforming managerial practice. He was vice chair of President Wilson's Second Industrial Conference, which offered schemes for solving the labor problem. He supported American membership in the League of Nations. Then, in 1920, he was an unsuccessful contender for the Republican presidential nomination. At that time he seemed to many liberals the best hope for revitalizing and advancing progressive causes.

During this same period, particularly in his engineering and political addresses and testimony at congressional hearings, Hoover was also working his way toward the variant of progressivism with which his future political career would become so firmly associated. It was a progressivism that accepted much of the era's managerial thinking. It saw, in other words, an emerging organizational society threatened by market and community failures and in need of new managerial capacities and ordering mechanisms if it were to remain progressive. Yet, at the same time, it rejected prescriptions that would meet these needs through a new managerial state or through schemes to suppress self-interestedness, accepting much of the era's antistatist and anticollectivist thought. The answer, this kind of progressivism claimed, lay in building the needed mechanisms into the social order itself, thus equipping organized social groups for responsible self-government, responsible use of their new social power, and responsible participation in the management of national progress. In this building process, envisioned as both corporate and professional, there was room for governmental work of a progressive sort.

In 1921, Hoover entered Warren G. Harding's cabinet as secretary of commerce, and over the next seven years under both Harding and Calvin Coolidge he transformed that department into a beehive of the kind of activity he had defined as progressive. It became the center of an ongoing whirl of conferences, campaigns, and committee meetings, from which emerged new structures and networks that spanned the public and private sectors and purported to give the nation new managerial capacities. The department devised new machinery for employment and business cycle stabilization, for improving the performance of problem industries, for promoting trade, efficiency, conservation, and ethical business behavior, for reducing industrial conflict and providing relief during natural disasters, and for implementing a variety of other social betterment projects. Never before, noted one commentator, had any cabinet officer engaged in "such wide diversity of activities or covered quite so much ground." Given the economic boom that developed after 1922, Hoover could claim that such activity was helping to solve long-standing national problems and speed national progress. Those who saw it as a cover for business domination, social injustice, or growing economic unsoundness were by 1928 very much in the minority.

Indeed, once Coolidge had decided against seeking reelection, there were many who wanted to make Hoover president. Both he and his progressivism were highly attractive in the context of 1928, particularly as presented by the public relations network now at his command.

Once set in motion, the Hoover campaign machinery proved strikingly successful. Easily nominated at the Republican convention, Hoover crushed Democratic opponent Alfred E. Smith by carrying forty states and polling 58 percent of the popular vote.

Before the Crash

In the early months of his administration, Hoover continued to have a strongly favorable image. He was, many believed, precisely the kind of president that the nation needed, an expert, an engineer, a businessman, a "nonpolitician," a humanitarian, and a self-made success all rolled into one. He was also physically impressive, somewhat forbidding but large and athletically built, with an "outdoors" complexion, a square chin and firm facial features, and a general aura of efficiency, mastery, energy, and seriousness. His family life, as evidenced by an enduring marriage, a talented wife, and two promising sons, seemed exemplary. So did his capacity for administration, especially his proven knacks for choosing able and dedicated lieutenants and turning lethargic or failing organizations into thriving and dynamic ones. If his protective reserve, strong sense of privacy, and lack of skill in the oratorical and political arts made the political side of his job more difficult, many in 1929 still regarded these as virtues rather than defects.

In staffing the new administration, Hoover weighed and acted on two major kinds of considerations. First, there were political powers to be recognized and political debts to be paid, which meant that Andrew Mellon remained at the Treasury and that the War, Agriculture, and Post Office departments went, respectively, to James W. Good, Arthur M. Hyde, and Walter Brown, all of whom had played important roles

Black Tuesday, 1929, at the New York Stock Exchange. *(Library of Congress)*

during the campaign. Second, there was the need for men who shared Hoover's vision of the future and could help in building the kind of organizations through which it was to be realized. Two cabinet appointments of this sort were Ray Lyman Wilbur as secretary of the interior and Robert Lamont as secretary of commerce; and below the cabinet level were numerous other "Hoover men" anxious to participate in new "Hooverization" projects. In completing his cabinet, Hoover also chose Henry L. Stimson as secretary of state, William D. Mitchell as attorney general, James J. Davis as secretary of labor, and Charles Francis Adams as secretary of the navy.

During the campaign in 1928, Hoover had talked of a "new day," to be ushered in by the kind of organizational and fact-finding endeavors with which his name had become associated; and in the early days of the administration he initiated a variety of such projects. In existence within a few months were such agencies as the President's Research Committee on Social Trends, the Commission on the Conservation and Administration of the Public Domain, and the National Commission on Law Observance and Enforcement. Also under way were efforts to improve the performance of problem agencies, particularly the Indian, Veterans, Prisons, and Prohibition bureaus. In the planning stages were projects that envisioned a public-private economic council, a new series of economic studies and conferences, and a Hoover-type organizational complex engaged in rationalizing and coordinating the nation's welfare and social service activities.

An auspicious beginning was also made in efforts to develop better organization for an agricultural sector that had been depressed throughout the 1920's. The answer here, Hoover had long argued, was a properly developed set of marketing cooperatives that would make agriculture more businesslike while preserving the virtues inherent in rural individualism. In a special session of Congress convened in April,

1929, he was able to fend off other farm relief schemes and secure passage of an Agricultural Marketing Act based on his prescriptions. Under it a new Federal Farm Board, organized to represent the various interests in agriculture, was to become the agency for building and financing a new set of marketing associations. It could provide technical and promotional assistance, make loans to facilitate orderly marketing, and form emergency stabilization corporations to deal with demoralized markets; and in operation it was soon busily engaged in such organization building.

Even as such projects got under way, however, involvement in other issues provided a foretaste of future political difficulties. Tariff revision, originally intended to facilitate agricultural adjustment, bogged down in the special session and had to be postponed. A national oil conference, intended to produce cooperative machinery for rationalizing oil production, produced little but criticism. Efforts to strengthen Prohibition enforcement, as demanded by dry supporters, brought worrisome clashes with urban politicians and civil libertarians. A "Southern policy," seeking to consolidate Republican gains in the South, was successful only in alienating Northern groups. In these political arenas, where problem solving called for political artistry more than organization building, the administration was already gaining a reputation for ineptitude.

Battling the Depression

The Great Depression, which would become the central preoccupation of the Hoover administration, is generally regarded as having its roots in the economic imbalances, excessive speculation, and shaky financial structures of the 1920's. The event, however, that separated the prosperous 1920's from the Depression decade was the stock market crash of late 1929. In trouble from September on, the great bull market finally collapsed in an orgy

A Chicago breadline—opened by mobster Al Capone—during the Great Depression. *(NARA)*

of panic selling on October 29, a date that would be remembered as Black Tuesday. Although business and political leaders kept saying that the underlying economy was still fundamentally sound, the crash not only unmasked much unsoundness but also created an atmosphere of gloom that dampened both investment and consumer spending. There would be brief upturns, but the general drift of economic indicators during Hoover's remaining forty months was radically downward. From 1929 to 1933, the gross national product fell by 29 percent, while unemployment rose from 3 to 25 percent.

Through behind-the-scenes actions, Hoover had tried to generate warnings and secure more responsible business behavior. These efforts, however, had failed to have much ef-

fect. Following the crash, he joined those who viewed the underlying economy as fundamentally sound and moved to establish counter-cyclical organizations believed capable of curbing deflationary forces and getting expansion started again. By early 1930, three of these were in operation. A National Business Survey Conference, created as an adjunct of the Chamber of Commerce and making use of the administrative machinery of some 170 trade associations, was seeking to dispel gloom and obtain compliance with pledges of wage maintenance and new investment. A National Building Survey Conference, similarly organized, was attempting to implement pledges of new or expanded construction. A Division of Public Construction was working to speed up federal building projects and obtain compliance with state and

> *Herbert Hoover's telegram to state governors regarding the Great Depression, November 23, 1929:*
>
> With view to giving strength to the present economic situation and providing for the absorption of any unemployment which might result from the present disturbed conditions, I have asked for collective action of industry in the expansion of construction activities and in stabilization of wages. As I have publicly stated, one of the largest factors that can be brought to bear is that of the energetic yet prudent pursuit of public works by the Federal Government and state municipal and county authorities.
>
> The Federal Government will exert itself to the utmost within its own province and I should like to feel that I have the cooperation of yourself and the municipal county and other local officials in the same direction. It would be helpful if road, street, public building, and other construction of this type could be speeded up and adjusted in such fashion as to further employment.
>
> I would also appreciate it if your officials would canvass the state, municipal, and county programs and give me such information as you can as to the volume of expenditure that can be prudently arranged for the next twelve months and for the next six months and inform me thereof.
>
> I am asking Secretary Lamont of the Department of Commerce to take in hand the detailed measures of cooperation with you which may arise in this matter.
>
> *Herbert Hoover*

municipal pledges to increase public works expenditures.

In addition, Hoover was able to secure a temporary tax cut, a $400 million increase in federal public works appropriations, a "labor peace" pledge from union leaders, monetary expansion measures from the Federal Reserve Board, and special antideflation lending by the Federal Farm Board. Such measures were supposed to facilitate the work of the recovery organizations, and initially much optimism was expressed about their effectiveness. A "great economic experiment," Hoover declared in May, 1930, had "succeeded to a remarkable degree." As of June, however, it was becoming clear that many economic decision makers did not share this official optimism, and as summer gave way to fall, the economy reeled under the impact of new layoffs, shrinking investment outlays, worsening farm distress, mounting bank failures, and an intensifying international trade war aggravated by passage of the protectionist Smoot-Hawley Tariff. Recovery, it seemed, could not be organized in the way attempted. Refusing to concede this, Hoover

tended to blame the deteriorating situation on foreign dumping, congressional politics, and irresponsible criticism.

Consequently, the administration's response to the developments of late 1930 was the creation of new Hoover-type organizations while resisting calls for governmental controls, federal relief, and legalized cartel agreements. In August, the administration formed the National Drought Committee to mobilize community relief machinery in distressed farm areas hit by the twin blows of depression and drought. From midsummer on, it mounted organized campaigns to reduce the acreage being planted to wheat. In October came the President's Emergency Committee for Employment (PECE), which was to serve as mobilizer, coordinator, and informational exchange for community-centered programs of relief and job creation. Modeled on the temporary relief organization that Hoover had helped to create in 1921, it was supposed to relieve suffering while preserving local and individual responsibility and saving the unemployed from the character-destroying effects of a dole.

In early 1931, as economic indicators turned slightly upward, Hoover again declared that "mobilized voluntary action" had "proved its strength." Again he spoke too soon. In May and June came the financial crash in Europe, making the Depression worldwide and having strongly adverse repercussions in the United States. Although Hoover took the lead in securing a one-year suspension of international debt payments, an arrangement known as the Hoover Moratorium, this failed to check a contraction that further discredited his policies, forced abandonment of further efforts to maintain wage rates and farm prices, and led him to replace PECE with a more business-oriented President's Organization on Unemployment Relief. Again, the contraction brought the monetary and banking system into jeopardy, leading Hoover to organize the National Credit Association through which stronger banks were supposed to aid the weaker ones. The relief thus provided proved minimal and short-lived.

Still, Hoover resisted the calls for government planning, welfare statism, and legalized creation of cartels, offering instead a program that would couple more emergency organization with supportive governmental credits and deficit-reducing fiscal action. This was the program presented to Congress and the public in late 1931, and by the summer of 1932 most of it had been implemented. A Reconstruction Finance Corporation, modeled on the War Finance Corporation of 1918, was established and authorized to make loans to needy banks and railroads and subsequently, under congressional pressure, to local relief and public works agencies. New economy and tax measures were passed. Lesser laws and actions expanded the lending powers of the Farm Loan and Federal Reserve systems, added a new system of home loan banks, tried to mobilize social pressures against hoarding, and created another network of banking and industrial committees to promote credit expansion and new invest-

ment outlays. Recovery, Hoover now held, awaited only the revival of credit and confidence.

Again, too, Hoover took the brief upturn in August and September of 1932 as evidence that his program was working. The worsening crisis of his last six months, he would argue then and later, was the result of business fears created by election uncertainties and Democratic flirtations with unsound monetary and fiscal proposals. In the eyes of most Americans, however, his recovery prescriptions and programs had now become thoroughly discredited. They were, it was being argued, based on highly fallacious assumptions about what could be done through associational action and public-private cooperation, and in operation they had only delayed recovery and prolonged suffering by blocking more effective forms of recovery action. Recovery had remained elusive despite Hoover's energetic search for it. The resulting experience had left him crippled politically and unable to prevent the forms of governmental intervention that he still held to be incompatible with a progressive national future.

A Frustrated Reformism

Meanwhile, the deepening of the Depression had also become a major factor in making Hoover's reformist and educational efforts a story of increasing frustration, lowered goals, and growing criticism. In the "new day" visions of 1928 and 1929, the presidency was to become an instrument working to fill the informational and organizational gaps threatening further progress. As noted previously, the period before the crash had witnessed the launching of several such projects. After the crash, however, these projects were forced by recovery considerations to take a backseat; and although they were never totally abandoned, they accomplished relatively little and became, in the eyes of many, prime examples of gross inadequacy, unrealistic reasoning, and political ineptitude.

In the area of economic reform, for example, the early designs for filling organizational gaps were soon subordinated to the search for emergency recovery and relief mechanisms. In agriculture, the Federal Farm Board became involved in futile efforts to stabilize farm prices, lost the support of both farm and business groups, and left relatively little imprint on agricultural organization. In business, the administration's prescriptions for problem industries came under attack from antitrusters on one side and business protectionists on the other. They produced new kinds of associational machinery for the oil, lumber, coal, railroad, aviation, and cotton textile industries, but the machinery would prove fragile and little of it survived. In labor, the major reform, the 1932 Norris-LaGuardia Act outlawing "yellow dog contracts" and other antiunion weapons, emerged from Congress rather than from the administration. Hoover signed it somewhat reluctantly. In the shaping of overarching institutions, the administration's designs for a national economic council, continuing economic surveys, and new balancing mechanisms were never realized. The only agency that seemed a step toward their realization was a Federal Employment Stabilization Board established in 1931, and contemporaries saw this as part of Senator Robert Wagner's program rather than the administration's.

The outcome of conservation reform, another area in which Hoover had long been interested, was also frustrating. Here the administration was able to get the Hoover Dam project under way, expand the national park system, and conduct some valuable experiments in improved forestry and oil reserve management, but its hopes for a national waterway plan, improved developmental practices in the natural resource industries, and new partnership arrangements in administering the public lands were never fulfilled. It was also unsuccessful in bringing the kind of development it envisioned to the St. Lawrence and Tennessee River Valleys. Its treaty with Canada for St. Lawrence development was never ratified, and the stalemate it had inherited on Tennessee River development persisted. Hoover vetoed the Norris bill for development by a federal corporation, and its proponents blocked serious consideration of his scheme for a developmental agency composed of private sector and local government representatives.

Frustrating, too, were the efforts to fill organizational and informational gaps in the nation's social service system. Here the Research Committee on Social Trends became an industrious amasser of social data, but its apolitical standing was in constant jeopardy, and the accompanying scheme for creating national coordinating and promotional agencies in the fields of housing, child welfare, recreation, education, and public health was in large measure abandoned. Only two of the projected national conferences, those on child welfare and housing, were ever held, and neither the follow-up machinery produced by these nor the promotional machinery of study groups examining the educational and medical systems ever accomplished what was originally intended. By 1932, moreover, a social service community once strongly supportive of Hoover had become highly critical. In its eyes the great problem had become one of shrinking funds, not inadequate information or organization. Increasingly, its solutions called for expanding the public sector in ways that Hoover still strongly opposed.

A similar pattern was also apparent in efforts aimed at improving the lot of racial minorities. A new leadership for the Bureau of Indian Affairs made a start toward modernizing its administrative structure and improving its services. Some concern also was shown for the need to improve black education, housing, and business opportunities and to develop a better basis for racial progress in the South. The Depression, however, kept programs that cost money to a minimum, and the administration's distaste for such militant groups as the Indian

Hoover Dam. *(NARA)*

Defense Association and the National Association for the Advancement of Colored People (NAACP) heightened these groups' disenchantment with the administration's policies. They criticized it not only for stinginess but also for having assimilationist attitudes toward American Indian cultures, discriminating against African American soldiers and Gold Star mothers, embracing "lily-whiteism" in its Southern policy, and doing essentially nothing about lynching atrocities in the South. Unknown at the time was Hoover's consideration of a plan for making federal troops available to assist local authorities, a plan finally shelved after administration lawyers questioned its constitutionality.

Two other reform projects were also disappointing in the results achieved. One was the effort to reorganize the executive branch in the interests of greater efficiency and rationality. This finally culminated in a series of reorganization plans proposed under a 1932 economy bill, all of which were rejected by Congress. The other sought to reduce lawlessness and improve the nation's law enforcement and judicial system. It led to altered appointment procedures and bureau reorganizations, limited reform of the prison system, new exercises in federal-local cooperation, and much fact-gathering by a National Commission on Law Observance and Enforcement. Political resistance blocked much that was attempted, however, and the tendency of the lawlessness issue to become intertwined with the Prohibition debate exacerbated the political difficulties and made for an increasingly negative press.

In all the areas noted, Hoover's can be regarded as a reform presidency, unsatisfied with things as they were, but the elitist, quasi-privatist, antistatist style of reform that he had identified as "truly progressive" was not well suited to the changing economic and political context of the early 1930's. The result was a frustrated reformism having unintended consequences, one achieving few of its objectives but having some significance as a conduit for reform-minded professionals on their way to the New Deal and as a negative experience strongly indicating that effective reform would have to be sought along other paths.

Foreign Policies

The story of the Hoover administration's foreign policies is also largely one of frustrated hopes. It began with visions of completing the "American system" of the 1920's, a system that would use new fact-gathering, business, and legal mechanisms to achieve the ordered world prosperity that had not and could not be achieved through international politics, military interventions, or utopian peace movements. In particular, Hoover hoped to build on earlier progress toward curbing irrational arms races, developing international adjudication agencies, and bringing American-style business organization to the international economy. The Depression and the impact that it had on politics at home and abroad, however, would create a context increasingly hostile to such initiatives and turn most of them into exercises in futility and frustration.

One area in which Hoover hoped to build on the achievements of the 1920's was that of naval limitations. Here he did have some initial success. He offered a new "yardstick principle," which would "measure" navies by taking into account their ages, armaments, and other fighting capacities as well as their tonnage. This allowed the British to accept parity with the United States without giving up the larger cruiser tonnage on which they had long been insisting. The eventual result was the London Naval Treaty of 1930, extending the limitations agreed to at Washington in 1921 and adding a new set of limitations in the previously unrestricted categories of cruisers, destroyers, and submarines. The latter, however, was accepted only by Britain, the United States, and Japan. Efforts to bring France and Italy into the system were unsuccessful. In operation, the structure not only would prove shortlived but also would later be seen as a shortsighted legitimation of Japanese dominance in the western Pacific.

A second area to which Hoover devoted considerable energy was relations with the countries of Latin America. Before his inaugural he made a goodwill tour of the region, and early in his administration came actions upgrading the diplomatic service there, encouraging more inter-American economic cooperation and cultural exchange, and creating a special commission to arrange military withdrawal from Haiti. The Monroe Doctrine, moreover, was no longer to serve as justification for police actions in the area, and despite pressure from American investors Hoover rejected collection of debts by force and allowed the wave of debt repudiations and political disturbances accompanying economic contraction to run its course without American intervention. Some have interpreted his policies as an important shift from Gunboat Diplomacy to Good Neighborism. Others have noted a harder side, particularly his unsympathetic attitude toward debt relief and economic assistance proposals. By 1931, conditions in Latin America were making a mockery of the visions of growth and stability set forth earlier.

In Europe, too, initial appearances of diplomatic success soon gave way to conditions markedly at variance with what the Hoover administration had hoped to achieve. An international business committee headed by American industrialist Owen D. Young devised a new reparations settlement, and through the work of Elihu Root a formula emerged for American membership in the World Court. The resulting court treaty, however, was not ratified, and the Young settlement had no chance of survival after the Depression became worldwide. The need, so various analysts argued in 1931 and 1932, was for debt cancellation, emergency credits, tariff revision, and joint monetary actions, but the Hoover administration rejected such proposals and rebuffed Allied efforts to tie reparations reductions to reductions in the war debts owed the United States. Its willingness to provide relief was limited to the Hoover Moratorium of 1931 and a supplementary "standstill agreement" on repayment of private loans to Germany. These measures did not, as was hoped, allow the European nations to get their finances in order and their people and resources back to work.

In 1932, the Hoover administration urged arms reductions as a means of providing financial relief. Under the Hoover Plan, as proposed to the Geneva Disarmament Conference, all military forces would be reduced by one-third. This came to nothing—a victim, Hoover thought, of French attitudes and intransigence.

Similarly unfruitful were the slowly developing plans for a world economic conference and Hoover's calls in late 1932 for a new debt commission to reconsider capacities to pay. All the debtor nations except Finland would repudiate their war debts, and the economic crisis would bring to power a German regime bent on scrapping the Versailles Treaty and the system it had established.

Even as the Versailles system crumbled in Europe, moreover, developments in the Far East shattered hopes that the Washington treaty system of 1921-1922 could provide a framework for stability and peaceful development there. In Japan the economic crisis and growing resistance to Japanese economic designs in China undermined the prestige of Western-oriented liberals. In September, 1931, the Japanese began a conquest of Chinese Manchuria followed by open defiance of Western efforts to invoke moral sanctions under the League of Nations, the Washington treaties, and the 1928 Paris Peace Pact outlawing aggressive war. The major American response was a doctrine of "nonrecognition" of "immoral" and "illegal" Japanese conquests, enunciated in early 1932 and generally known as the Stimson Doctrine. Stimson himself wanted to threaten economic sanctions, but Hoover feared that such a move would only strengthen the Japanese militarists, and he decided instead to offer assurances that no such sanctions would be used.

Viewed in terms of the goals set forth in 1929, Hoover's foreign policies must be regarded as failures. The visions associated with the American system were not realized, and nothing effective was done to curb or control the economic and political forces eventually responsible for another world war. Study of the period's diplomacy, however, has shown it to be less isolationist and more sophisticated than once thought; some historians have argued that in its perceptions of the limits of American power and its skepticism about political entanglements and military solutions, it showed more wisdom than the diplomacy that followed.

Changing Political Configurations

Meanwhile, the years of persisting depression, a frustrated reformism, and shattered diplomatic hopes had also become years of mounting political discontent, heated political controversy, and changing political allegiances and alignments. Ironically, a president who prided himself on being a nonpolitician, who tended to equate good government with decisions made outside or above politics, and whose projects for improving national life would in general diminish the roles played by professional politicians now found himself in an increasingly politicized environment. In this environment he did not fare well. His once-favorable image became increasingly negative, particularly among the newly politicized; his hopes for using his reputation to build an administration bloc in Congress were soon shattered; and his association with the Republican Party became a political liability for the party, helping to convert it from majority to minority status.

One aspect of the changing political situation was a growing reservoir of anti-Hooverism from which political opponents could draw. In part this reflected the need for a Depression scapegoat. In part it was systematically sown and nurtured by the Democratic Party's publicity apparatus. Also involved were the overselling done earlier, a breakdown of relations with the press, a growing gap between Hooverian values and those of a populace battered by Depression forces, a negative fallout from Hoover's deficiencies as a political leader, and a personality and temperament ill suited to coping with such adversities. By 1932, the president's image had become almost the reverse of that in 1929. He was perceived now as stony-hearted, incompetent, irritable, dogmatic, out of touch, and insensitive to human needs, a man concerned only with the "big fellows" and more

THE VICE PRESIDENT
CHARLES CURTIS

Charles Curtis was born on January 25, 1860, in Topeka, Kansas. Educated at public schools, he studied law in Topeka and was admitted to the bar in 1881. Curtis established a legal practice in his hometown and married Anna Baird on November 27, 1884. The couple had three children.

Curtis began his career in politics by becoming prosecuting attorney for his county, serving from 1885 to 1889. In 1892, he was elected to the U.S. House of Representatives, where he served from 1893 to 1907. Curtis continued his service in Congress, gaining a seat in the U.S. Senate. During his Senate years, which spanned 1907 to 1913, he rose to the position of president pro tempore. In spite of his years of service, Curtis was defeated for reelection in 1912. However, he regained the office in 1914 and served until 1929, a time that saw him also serve as Republican whip and leader. Curtis also attended both state and national Republican conventions as a delegate.

Curtis was nominated as Herbert Hoover's vice president in 1928 and served the entire term. After the ticket's defeat in 1932, Curtis returned to the legal profession, establishing a practice in the nation's capital. He died on February 8, 1936, in Washington, D.C.

Robert P. Watson and Richard Yon

with saving mules and cattle than with saving human beings.

Association with the president was clearly not an asset in the midterm elections of 1930 and the special elections of 1931. Identifiable Hoover men did badly, and the Republican Party lost control of the House of Representatives and became dependent on party irregulars for control of the Senate. The results reflected the strong tendency of newly politicized ethnic and labor groups to vote Democratic, the collapse of efforts to make Republicanism respectable in the South, and the growth of protest politics in the rural Midwest, all developments helping to transform the party system under which Hoover was elected and to usher in an era of Democratic Party dominance.

The rise of antiadministration forces in the electorate was also accompanied by a parallel development in Congress. Initially, an administration bloc had formed there, led by Hoover men such as Senators Henry J. Allen and Arthur Vandenberg and occupying a middle position between the Republican Old Guard and Western Republican insurgents, neither of

whom had been happy about Hoover's rise to the presidency. Hopes of expanding the bloc's influence were soon shattered, however; and in the 1930 battle over Hoover's nomination of Judge John J. Parker to fill a vacancy on the Supreme Court, an antiadministration coalition formed and dealt administration forces a major defeat. Although an able jurist, Parker proved vulnerable to charges of racial and antilabor bias and could not be confirmed. His critics succeeded in putting together a winning senatorial alliance of Democrats and liberal Republicans.

In the lame duck session that followed the elections of 1930, this antiadministration coalition reappeared, particularly in the heated battles over drought relief and employment service legislation and in overriding the president's veto of a bonus bill authorizing federal loans to holders of World War bonus insurance certificates. After the Seventy-first Congress gave way to the Seventy-second, congressional rebellions became a regular feature of the political landscape. On most of its recovery program in 1932, the administration was able to secure the cooperation of the Democratic congressional leadership, but antiadministration rebellions forced significant modifications in the farm and relief programs, gave the administration much difficulty on the bonus issue, and turned back efforts to raise new revenue through a federal sales tax. The sales tax rebellion has been viewed as particularly significant, since it foreshadowed congressional alignments that would be characteristic of much of the subsequent New Deal period.

Most of these legislative battles contributed to further growth of Hoover's negative image. Following congressional adjournment in 1932, a "bonus riot" incident did more damage. Involved here were the remnants of the "bonus army" of World War I veterans who had gathered in Washington, D.C., to lobby for immediate maturity-value redemption of their bonus insurance certificates. Although the lobbying failed, some had stayed on; and when efforts were made to remove a group of them from federal properties along Pennsylvania Avenue, the result was violence in which two veterans were killed. Hoover then decided to use federal troops, and on July 28 a special riot force under General Douglas MacArthur proceeded to clear the riot area. Violating Hoover's orders, MacArthur also cleared and destroyed the veterans' camp at Anacostia Flats, an action that Hoover subsequently defended as necessary to deal with a dangerous group increasingly controlled by communists and criminals. The defense, however, was not persuasive, and the outcome tended to strengthen perceptions of Hoover as insensitive and paranoiac. Added to the image of hard-heartedness and dogmatism was that of a man who had turned the nation's arms against the very people who had saved the nation in 1918.

Defeat, Interregnum, and Postpresidency
At the Republican convention in 1932, Hoover encountered much pessimism but no serious challenges from other contenders. He and Vice President Charles Curtis were easily renom-

inated. In the campaign that followed, he occasionally seemed convinced that economic upturns, concessions to the antiprohibitionists, proper education about his administration's achievements, and better appreciation of how he had saved the country from "chaos and degeneration" would somehow turn his political fortunes around. He also believed that in nominating Franklin Delano Roosevelt, the Democrats had provided him with the weakest of several possible opponents; and he tended to discount much of the Democrats' criticism as irresponsible political propaganda that would be ineffective with sensible portions of the citizenry.

Hoover's hopes for reelection, however, rested mostly on misperceptions. Roosevelt proved to be a confident and effective campaigner, able to unite his party, take advantage of the anti-Hooverism pervading the political scene, and associate himself with the Depression-bred values of compassion and economic morality. Hoover remained on the defensive, punctuating his speeches with warnings that a Democratic victory would delay sound recovery and imperil future progress, and employing an increasingly conservative rhetoric to mobilize groups fearful of where current political and social agitation could lead. Rhetorically at least, he was moving to the right, whereas much of the United States was moving in the opposite direction. The result was to diminish even further his political appeal. On election day he carried only six states for an electoral count of 59 to Roosevelt's 472; in the popular column he lost by a count of 27,821,857 to 15,761,841.

Hoover's last four months in office, a period generally known as the interregnum, saw the Depression reach its lowest point. Unemployment climbed to 25 percent, and a new banking crisis produced near paralysis of the nation's financial machinery. Many states were forced to declare bank holidays, closing the banks or severely restricting their functions. Since the lame duck president and the president-elect could not agree on the causes of or cures for the situation, no remedial program was forthcoming. For Hoover, confidence remained the key. In a series of exchanges with Roosevelt, he tried to commit the incoming administration to the program he believed necessary to restore confidence in the system and its future, a program consisting essentially of budget balancing, gold standard maintenance, war debt renegotiation, and banking law revision. These exchanges, however, came to nothing. As Roosevelt saw it, Hoover was not only out to trick him and tie his hands in making needed reforms but also trying to shift the blame for the crisis to those who had defeated him at the polls.

Accordingly, the change of administrations on March 4, 1933, came at one of the nation's darkest economic hours; and partly because of the burst of activity and change of mood that followed, the Hoover administration entered public memory as a time of do-nothingness, despair, and defeatism. Largely forgotten were the activism and hopes with which it began, the optimistic innovativeness with which it attempted to short-circuit the business cycle, and the numerous reform projects that remained a part of its agenda. Also badly distorted because these things were forgotten was the political philosophy that shaped its attitudes concerning proper and improper forms of governmental intervention and led to policies that in the eyes of some meant unnecessary misery and suffering.

After leaving the presidency, Hoover continued to play active roles in Republican Party politics and public policy debate and from 1933 through 1938 became an outspoken critic of the New Deal, especially in *The Challenge to Liberty* (1934) and in a series of "addresses upon the American road." He also gave much attention to Stanford University, particularly to its Hoover Institution, and as World War II approached, he worked to keep the United States at peace and tried unsuccessfully to establish a food relief program for populations in German-occupied countries. After the war, as both he and attitudes toward him mellowed, he assumed the role of elder statesman, was asked to head several special agencies, and served successively as coordinator of the European Food Program in 1947, chairman of the Commission for Reorganization of the Executive Branch from 1947 to 1949, and chairman of a second Commission on Reorganization from 1953

Hoover visits children in Poland in 1946 as part of his humanitarian efforts following World War II. *(Library of Congress)* to 1955. In addition, he published his memoirs, wrote and published histories of Woodrow Wilson's "ordeal" and America's post-World War I relief operations in Europe, and worked on but failed to publish a history of communist influences on the West. He died on October 20, 1964, and is buried on a hillside in West Branch near his birthplace and the presidential library that houses his papers. Ninety years old at the time of his death, he lived longer than any president since John Adams.

General Assessment

Among historians of the Hoover administration, its nature and place in American history have been subjects of continuing controversy. Initially, the controversy was between those who contrasted it negatively with Roosevelt's New Deal and those who contrasted it positively, both seeing Hoover as an anti-Rooseveltian but the former deploring Hoover's stance against needed forms of government intervention and the latter deploring the nation's movement away from his wisdom. Yet from the beginning a few questioned the terms in which this debate was framed. The similarities and linkages between the Hoover and Roosevelt administrations, they argued, were as great as or greater than the differences and disjunctures. Both had been reformist-oriented, and both had rejected classical economic formulas for dealing with business crises and had attempted to develop new political and social machinery for that purpose. In this larger sense they had formed a continuum, with the dividing line between the old and the new coming in 1929 rather than in 1933.

As serious research on the period got under way, moreover, particularly in the 1960's, it tended to provide more support for those questioning the framework of the initial debate than for those engaged in it. Much of the research amounted to the rediscovery and documentation of the reformist, activist, interventionist side of the Hoover administration, the thinking that underlay this, and the heritages that it had bequeathed across the rhetorical divide of 1933. It found in the records a story at odds with the images of rugged individualism decried by pro-New Deal interpreters and idealized by their conservative rivals. As research and re-thinking proceeded, the new scholarship began to alter the whole framework of the interpretive debate, undercutting the premises of established positions and bringing new questions to the fore.

Increasingly, although somewhat grudgingly, participants in the older debate have had to concede that Hoover's was a reform presidency, that it had attributes foreshadowing a new managerial role for the American presidency, and that its policies seem best explained by the Hooverian variant of progressivism that guided their formulation. Most interpreters, however, would still make fairly sharp distinctions between the Hooverian and New Deal orientations, both in the role of the state and the degrees of responsiveness to insurgent political groups and antiestablishment critics. Also continuing to generate debate were the suggestions of some reinterpreters that Hoover's progressivism had been wiser and potentially more capable of realizing liberal ideals than had the New Deal variety. This view had its supporters, particularly among certain critics of the New Deal state and its failures. Most studies of Hoover's system in action, however, have concluded that the mechanisms envisioned or created were inadequate to deal with the problems they were seeking to solve and that in some cases these mechanisms tended to evolve quickly toward the use of illiberal and undemocratic methods. Scholarship would seem to support the view that although the Hoover presidency was reformist, activist, principled, and intellectually sophisticated, it was also a failed presidency, economically, politically, and in its prescriptions for social distress.

Ellis W. Hawley

535

Suggested Readings

Burner, David. *Herbert Hoover: A Public Life.* New York: Knopf, 1979. A thorough biography.

Burns, Richard D. *Herbert Hoover: A Bibliography of His Times and Presidency.* Wilmington, Del.: Scholarly Resources, 1991. A comprehensive listing of resources on Hoover's personal life and public career.

Fausold, Martin. *The Presidency of Herbert C. Hoover.* Lawrence: University Press of Kansas, 1985. An informed and authoritative analysis of Hoover's policies, especially his response to the Depression.

Ferrell, Robert H. *American Diplomacy in the Great Depression.* New Haven, Conn.: Yale University Press, 1957. Examines foreign policy decisions and how they were tempered by the Depression.

Herbert Hoover Presidential Library. http://www.hooverassociation.org/dedication address.htm. The Web site of the official library and museum of Hoover.

Hoff-Wilson, Joan. *Herbert Hoover: Forgotten Progressive.* 1975. Reprint. Prospect Heights, Ill.: Waveland Press, 1992. One of the best biographical works on Hoover.

Hoover, Herbert. *Memoirs.* 3 vols. New York: Macmillan, 1951-1952. Hoover's autobiography.

_____. *The Ordeal of Woodrow Wilson.* 1958. Reprint. Baltimore: Johns Hopkins University Press, 1992. Covers the successes and challenges of foreign policy and the presidency as a whole.

Huthmacher, J. J., and Warren Sussman, eds. *Herbert Hoover and the Crisis of American Capitalism.* Cambridge, Mass.: Schenkman, 1973. Explores the roots of the Depression and Hoover's response to it.

Joseph, Paul. *Herbert Hoover.* Minneapolis: ABDO Press, 2000. A very accessible biography intended for young adults.

Liebovich, Louis W. *Bylines in Despair: Herbert Hoover, the Great Depression, and the U.S. News Media.* Westport, Conn.: Praeger, 1994. An analysis of the treatment of Hoover by the press during the Depression.

Nash, George. *Life of Herbert Hoover: The Humanitarian.* New York: Norton, 1983. Examines the entry of Hoover into public life as he administered the Commission for Relief in Belgium during World War I.

O'Brien, Patrick. *Herbert Hoover: A Bibliography.* Westport, Conn.: Greenwood Press, 1992. Gives a comprehensive listing of resources on Harding's personal life and public career.

Robinson, Edgar E., and Vaughn Davis Bornet. *Herbert Hoover: President of the United States.* Stanford, Calif.: Stanford University Press, 1975. A solid biography and examination of the Hoover administration.

Romasco, Albert. *The Poverty of Abundance: Hoover, the Nation, the Depression.* New York: Oxford University Press, 1965. Examines the myriad responses of the Hoover administration as the Depression took force.

Schlesinger, Arthur M., Jr. *The Crisis of the Old Order.* Boston: Houghton Mifflin, 1957. A work that engages in the interpretive debates about the administration.

Walch, Timothy, ed. *Uncommon Americans: The Lives and Legacies of Herbert and Lou Henry Hoover.* Westport, Conn.: Praeger, 2003. A joint biography of the president and the first lady in essays written by several scholars.

Walch, Timothy, and Dwight M. Miller, eds. *Herbert Hoover and Franklin D. Roosevelt.* Westport, Conn.: Greenwood Press, 1998. Analyzes Hoover's relationship with Franklin D. Roosevelt, both before and after Hoover's presidency.

Warren, Harris. *Herbert Hoover and the Great Depression.* New York: Oxford University Press, 1959. Examines Hoover's policies relating to the Depression.

Franklin D. Roosevelt

32d President, 1933-1945

Born: January 30, 1882
    Hyde Park, New York
Died: April 12, 1945
    Warm Springs, Georgia

Political Party: Democratic
Vice Presidents: John Nance Garner,
    Henry A. Wallace, Harry S. Truman

Cabinet Members

Secretary of State: Cordell Hull, E. R.
    Stettinius, Jr.
Secretary of the Treasury: William H. Woodin,
    Henry Morgenthau
Secretary of War: George H. Dern, Harry H.
    Woodring, Henry L. Stimson
Secretary of the Navy: Claude A. Swanson,
    Charles Edison, Frank Knox, James V.
    Forrestal
Attorney General: H. S. Cummings, Frank
    Murphy, Robert Jackson, Francis Biddle
Postmaster General: James A. Farley,
    Frank C. Walker
Secretary of the Interior: Harold Ickes
Secretary of Agriculture: Henry A.
    Wallace, Claude R. Wickard
Secretary of Commerce: Daniel C. Roper,
    Harry L. Hopkins, Jesse Jones,
    Henry A. Wallace
Secretary of Labor: Frances Perkins

Franklin Delano Roosevelt was not born in a log cabin, and unlike many nineteenth century aspirants to the presidency, he never pretended that he had been. His birth took place instead in a modest mansion commanding a magnificent view of the Hudson River as it flows below Hyde

Park, New York. The ten-pound baby to whom Sara Delano Roosevelt gave birth on January 30, 1882, entered a family of considerable means. Born in an era noted for its self-made men, Franklin Roosevelt never had an opportunity

Roosevelt's official portrait. *(White House Historical Society)*

to "make" himself, at least not in an economic sense. He was financially secure from birth. His childhood was anything but disadvantaged, and for one who chose to enter American politics, just such a privileged upbringing was potentially a distinct disadvantage.

In fact, however, Franklin Roosevelt's nurturance in an affluent society was one of the most important contributors to the character he would display as one of America's most important presidents. His father, James Roosevelt, was a man of impeccable lineage and sub-

THE FIRST LADY
ELEANOR ROOSEVELT

Eleanor Roosevelt was one of the most beloved First Ladies ever to occupy the White House. She also served the longest in that capacity. During the more than twelve years of Franklin Delano Roosevelt's term of office, she was highly visible and outspoken on issues that touched her heart. In the years following his death in office, she became renowned as a humanitarian.

She was born Anna Eleanor Roosevelt on October 11, 1884, in New York City. Her mother was Anna Rebecca Hall Roosevelt (1863-1892), and her father was Elliott Roosevelt (1860-1894), a brother of President Theodore Roosevelt. As a child she was rather plain-looking and had low self-esteem.

When she was fifteen, Eleanor was sent to Allenwood, a finishing school outside London. During her three years there, she overcame her lack of self-confidence. After returning home in 1900, she taught at the Rivington Street Settlement House.

On March 17, 1905, at the age of twenty, Eleanor married Franklin Delano Roosevelt, her fifth cousin. The Roosevelts had six children: Anna Eleanor (1906-1975), James (1907-1991), Franklin (born and died in 1909), Elliott (1910-1990), Franklin Delano, Jr. (1914-1988), and John Aspinwall (1916-1981).

During their early married life, Franklin and Eleanor lived in New York City and on the family estate at Hyde Park, New York. With the help of her husband's adviser, Louis Howe, Eleanor began to create her own identity. However, her career plans were put on hold in 1921 when Franklin was stricken with polio. Eleanor helped nurse him through this difficult time. When Franklin was running for governor of New York and later for president in 1932, Eleanor campaigned for him.

As First Lady, Eleanor voiced her opinion on the most pressing issues of the day and was a trusted adviser to her husband. She spoke out for the rights of African Americans, even resigning from Daughters of the American Revolution when that organization refused to let African American singer Marian Anderson perform at a segregated concert hall. She also spoke out for the poor living in the rural areas of Appalachia and identified with the plight of working women and migrant workers during the Great Depression.

Following the attack on Pearl Harbor, she traveled all over the free world advancing the cause of democracy and freedom. She also helped entertain visiting Allied leaders and had a radio program while continuing to give inspirational speeches.

After leaving the White House upon the death of her husband in April, 1945, Eleanor became active in the National Association for the Advancement of Colored People (NAACP) and the League of Women Voters. She was appointed to the board of the newly founded United Nations, where she helped to frame the Declaration of Human Rights. During the last years of her life, she was revered and honored for her advocacy of humanitarian causes.

Eleanor Roosevelt died in New York on November 7, 1962, at the age of seventy-eight.

Dean M. Shapiro

stantial property. His income from coal and transportation holdings provided solid financial security for his family, but James Roosevelt never achieved acceptance into the select millionaires. He left an estate of $300,000, in itself enough to make his family secure, but his marriage to Sara Delano improved the family's financial position substantially. Her father, Warren Delano, had made a fortune in the China trade and established himself on the other side of the Hudson from Hyde Park. The Delanos were also across the political river from the Democrat Roosevelts. "I will not say that all Democrats are horse thieves," Franklin's maternal grandfather often proclaimed, "but it would seem that all horse thieves are Democrats." The one million dollars he left his daughter helped to prepare a nonthieving Democrat—his grandson—for the nation's highest office.

The security that social station and wealth gave to the Roosevelts was a central fact in young Franklin's upbringing. His mother was twenty-six years younger than his father, who was fifty-four when Franklin was born. The child immediately became the center of attention in the family. He remained Sara's only child, and so never had his serenity upset by the intrusion of a new rival for the affection of his parents. A full platoon of servants supplemented the parents' attention. It would be difficult to disagree with his mother's assessment that Franklin "had many advantages that other boys did not have."

From the Hudson to Harvard

The "River families" of the Hudson were the closest parallel in post-Civil War America to the British or European country gentry. They taught their children not only the benefits to be enjoyed by their wealth and position but also the responsibilities that their position entailed. Franklin was reared, as his mother put it, to "grow up to be like his father, straight and honorable, just and kind, an upstanding Ameri-

Eleanor Roosevelt in 1898. *(FDR Library)*

can." If this was a rather vague aspiration, the future president showed in his undergraduate thesis, written in 1901, what he understood his heritage to mean. He ascribed the "virility" of the Roosevelts to their "democratic spirit": "They have never felt that because they were born in a good position they could put their hands in their pockets and succeed," he wrote. "They have felt, rather, that being born in a good position, there was no excuse for them if they did not do their duty by the community, and it is because this idea was instilled into them from their birth that they have in nearly every case proved good citizens."

Franklin Roosevelt's aristocratic upbringing and status as an only child gave him an extraordinary degree of self-confidence, optimism, and sense of noblesse oblige. The last quality was reinforced by at least one of the private tutors who guided his early education. It was further developed under the tutelage of

Rector Endicott Peabody at Groton School, where Roosevelt enrolled at the age of fourteen. Peabody had founded the school a little more than a decade before as an American version of an exclusive English public school, one that would educate the children of the elite, giving them moral and physical training as well as any academic instruction for which they could find time. Roosevelt acquitted himself well enough in this new environment, but at no point in his schooling did he ever distinguish himself intellectually or show any particular interest in scholarship. The Groton experience with the rector's stern moralism and his father's annual holiday season readings of Charles Dickens's *A Christmas Carol* added to the sense of stewardship and social responsibility that Roosevelt had acquired on the banks of the Hudson.

In 1900, young Roosevelt moved on from Groton to Harvard and quickly settled into the Boston social scene. He clearly wanted to excel at something, but it was still not education that held his interest. He did his best at sports but was too slight to succeed at varsity athletics. Harvard society was ranked by the social clubs that students were invited to join. Despite his lineage and habit of quite literally sticking his nose in the air (by throwing his head back), Roosevelt was not asked to join Porcellian, the most prestigious of the clubs. This rejection was a bitter experience for a young man accustomed to having his way at all times. Some biographers see the episode as significant in adding to the future president's sympathy for less fortunate people, but this is probably placing too much importance on it.

Roosevelt found his opportunity for success on the college newspaper, winning the editorship at the end of his third year in Cambridge. Although still a casual student, Roosevelt could have graduated in three years but chose to stay a fourth in order to edit the *Crimson*. His concerns were nothing out of the ordinary for a college editor: school spirit, a winning football team, and more fire extinguishers in student residences. In his classwork, Roosevelt took several courses in history but absorbed little of the subject's import and managed to escape the burden of economic theories that would lose their credibility after 1929. All in all, though, his Hudson gentry heritage had a far greater impact on the future president than did his formal education.

Politics and Paralysis

By the time he left Harvard, Franklin Roosevelt had chosen both a career and a bride. For both he looked no farther than his own family. He entered Columbia Law School, but not out of any desire to make a career in the law or to do as his mother wished and follow the path of his father, who had died while Franklin was a freshman at Harvard. Rather, young Roosevelt had decided to emulate his fifth cousin, Theodore Roosevelt, who was then president of the United States. The ambition was a lofty one, but Roosevelt was lacking in neither ambition nor self-confidence, and in his still boyish fantasizing he developed a career plan that had already been tested: Harvard, Columbia Law School, the New York state legislature, assistant secretary of the navy, governor of New York, and president of the United States. If a Republican Roosevelt could do it, why not a Democratic one? Roosevelt outlined these ambitions to friends at least as early as 1907. What was remarkable, however, was not that he should have such dreams but that, with only a few changes along the way, he was to follow the script all the way to its climax in the White House.

Franklin Roosevelt's admiration for members of the Oyster Bay branch of his family soon encompassed Theodore Roosevelt's niece as well as the president himself. Anna Eleanor Roosevelt, the daughter of Theodore Roosevelt's younger brother Elliott, suffered from a childhood as unhappy and insecure as Franklin's was happy and secure. Her mother, Anna

Hall Roosevelt, made little attempt to hide her distaste for a daughter who had not inherited her beauty. Eleanor worshiped her father, but he slipped into alcoholism and followed his wife into an early grave, leaving Eleanor an orphan at the age of ten. Although parentless children of the Roosevelts' social position were spared the rigors of life in an orphanage, Eleanor Roosevelt did not fare well. The grandmother who took charge of her had no more liking for the girl than had her mother. The childhood rejections suffered by Eleanor Roosevelt helped awaken in her a lifelong feeling of compassion for those facing hardship.

As fifth cousins once removed, Franklin and Eleanor Roosevelt had played together at a few family gatherings in their early years. It was not until the latter part of his college career, however, that Franklin became reacquainted with the suddenly grown-up distant relative and quickly fell in love with her and determined to marry her. The cousins were married at an early 1905 ceremony in which the president stood in for his deceased brother and gave away the bride.

"Well, Franklin," Cousin Ted said to the groom after the ceremony, "there's nothing like keeping the name in the family"—nor, from Franklin's perspective, was there anything like joining more closely the family of his idol. As it turned out, though, Eleanor Roosevelt was to be a far greater asset in her own right than as a link to the presidential family. Her compassion and sense of social justice helped give direction to her husband's political ambitions and amorphous sense of stewardship. The first decade of marriage, however, found Eleanor Roosevelt assisting her mate in the more traditional manner. Without inordinate complaint she bore six children and endured the domineering practices of her mother-in-law.

Franklin Roosevelt spent these years going through the early phases of the political career he had planned for himself. After being admitted to the New York bar, he left Columbia without completing his law degree. He took a position in a Wall Street law firm and could easily have slipped into a comfortable, conservative, respectable, but largely meaningless, upper-class life—but such was never his intention. He was awaiting his chance to get into politics. It came in 1910, when New York Democrats asked him to run for the Dutchess County seat in the state assembly. Roosevelt was enthusiastic but soon disappointed when the Democratic incumbent changed his mind and decided to seek reelection. Now if Roosevelt wanted to run, it would have to be for the state senate, in a larger, more Republican district. His supreme confidence leading him on, Roosevelt agreed to the greater challenge. Benefiting from a national split in the Republican ranks and his own flair for innovate campaigning—especially getting around to voters in a red Maxwell touring car—Roosevelt became only the second Democrat since before the Civil War to win in this senate district. His campaign was of the traditional upper-class sort: frequent calls for "clean government" but little in the way of the genuine social progressivism then sweeping the country.

In Albany, the twenty-eight-year-old freshman legislator rapidly made a name for himself by assuming leadership of a group of insurgent Democrats who opposed Boss Charles F. Murphy of Tammany Hall when he sought to name "Blue-eyed Billy" Sheehan as the new United States senator from New York (the state was one of those in which the legislature still picked the senators). Although eventually obliged to accept another Murphy-backed candidate, Roosevelt received nationwide publicity in the struggle against Tammany. Only later did he come to understand that the machine was not entirely evil and that some degree of accommodation was essential to successful political practice.

In 1912, Roosevelt backed the successful presidential candidacy of Woodrow Wilson. His reward was the post he most coveted at this

The Vice President
JOHN NANCE GARNER

John Nance Garner served as vice president in the first two administrations of Franklin D. Roosevelt. Garner was born in Red River County, Texas, on November 22, 1868. His father was a former officer in the Confederate Army. After attending local public schools, Garner took courses at Vanderbilt but did not graduate. He did, however, continue his education by studying law with the Sims and Wright law firm in Clarksville, Texas, and was admitted to the bar in 1890.

A new attorney, Garner opened a law practice in Uvalde, Texas, where he also edited the town's newspaper. Garner's entry into politics came when he was elected judge, serving from 1893 to 1896. On November 25, 1895, he married Ettie Rheiner, and the couple had one child. After his term as a judge, Garner was elected to the Texas House of Representatives, serving from 1898 to 1902. The following year, he took his seat in the U.S. House of Representatives, serving until 1933. During his political career, Garner was a delegate to the Democratic National Convention in 1900, 1916, and 1924, and he rose in Congress to the position of minority leader and Speaker of the House.

Garner was selected as Roosevelt's vice president during the 1932 campaign and served from 1933 to 1941. Although Roosevelt ran for a third term in 1940, Garner was not on the ticket. The decision was mutual between the two men, because the conservative southerner opposed parts of the president's New Deal program and the decision to seek a third term. After his vice presidency, Garner returned to Texas and enjoyed success in the real estate, banking, and ranching businesses. Garner gave some of his vast wealth to Southwest Texas Junior College. He died on November 7, 1967, in Uvalde.

Robert P. Watson and Richard Yon

point in his career: assistant secretary of the navy. Roosevelt loved ships almost as much as he loved following the trail of Cousin Ted. He proved to be a capable administrator and an advocate of a bold foreign policy and a big navy. His service in the Navy Department ran four times longer than had Theodore Roosevelt's, although this was not for the lack of trying to move on at the same pace as had his famous kinsman. Franklin made a disastrous attempt to win his party's U.S. Senate nomination in 1914. His heavy loss convinced him that he must learn to work with the better elements in the Tammany machine.

Ever since the days of Andrew Jackson—or, for that matter, George Washington—fighting in a war and gaining a reputation as a hero has been a most helpful step toward the presidency. When the United States entered World War I in 1917, Franklin Roosevelt tried once

more to do as Theodore Roosevelt had done, this time by leaving Washington, D.C., in search of battle. President Wilson, however, insisted that Roosevelt was needed more in the Navy Department. Finally, toward the end of the war, Roosevelt persuaded his superiors to send him on an inspection tour to Europe, and he briefly came under fire before contracting double pneumonia during the terrible influenza epidemic of 1918.

When Roosevelt returned home in a weakened condition, his wife unpacked his luggage and discovered in it a group of love letters he had received from Eleanor's social secretary, Lucy Mercer. In fact, Roosevelt and Mercer had been carrying on an affair for more than a year. Eleanor suggested divorce, and Franklin might have accepted had it not been for the realization that such a step would end his political career. Instead, Franklin and Eleanor agreed that she would remain his wife in public, but not in private, and that he would not see Lucy again. This contract was kept by only one partner. Franklin met Lucy Mercer Rutherfurd secretly from time to time throughout the remainder of his life.

Roosevelt's next political opportunity came in 1920, when he was the surprising choice of Democratic presidential candidate James M. Cox to be his running mate. It turned out, however, that Americans were tired of liberalism and Wilsonian internationalism, and they voted overwhelmingly for Warren G. Harding's promise of a return to "normalcy." Roosevelt chalked up the defeat to experience and settled down to wait for the political pendulum to swing back from conservatism.

While he waited, Roosevelt suffered a setback much worse than he had received at the polls. In the summer of 1921, while vacationing at the family's retreat at Campobello, Roosevelt was stricken with polio—then commonly called infantile paralysis. He was in excruciating pain for several weeks, and after the crisis, his legs remained paralyzed. Had he been the "mama's boy" that many claimed he was, Roosevelt would at this point have retired quietly to the life of a wealthy invalid. Instead, his lifelong experience of having his own way gave him the optimism to struggle on. With the help of his wife and political adviser Louis Howe, he worked through the 1920's to preserve his political career as he worked simultaneously to strengthen his legs.

Roosevelt's bout with polio ranks behind only his aristocratic upbringing, the influence of his wife, and the impact of the Great Depression in shaping his character as president. He was thirty-nine years old when he contracted polio; his basic character had long since been formed, but his previously vague sense of noblesse oblige now blossomed into a genuine understanding of suffering. Without his disability, a man with Roosevelt's background might never have had a true feeling for the hardships his countrymen underwent during the Depression, nor would Depression victims have been likely to have responded as warmly to Roosevelt's optimism had he not faced and overcome a terrible burden of his own.

From Albany to Washington

During the remainder of the 1920's, Roosevelt became a bit more liberal, in defiance of the popular movement toward conservatism, and waited for circumstances to push opinion in his direction. It is most ironic, though, that for all his planning Roosevelt took his decisive final step toward the White House with great reluctance. When New York governor Alfred E. Smith won the Democratic presidential nomination in 1928, he and state party leaders insisted that Roosevelt run for governor to help the ticket in upstate New York. Knowing that "Republican prosperity" was at high tide, Roosevelt feared that he would lose and that, should he win, he would be propelled toward the 1932 presidential nomination. Calculating that the conservative trend would not yet have waned by that time, Roosevelt thought it better to aim for 1936, but he could not risk the appearance of unwillingness to help the party, and he did not say that he would refuse to run if drafted. When he learned of his nomination, Roosevelt said, "Well, if I've got to run for governor, there's no use in all of us getting sick about it!" In November, 1928, Roosevelt won the governorship by a very narrow margin while Al Smith was losing his home state along with the nation as a whole.

As governor when the Depression hit in 1929, Roosevelt established a solid record as one of the leading liberals in America. His conservation programs carried forward the family tradition begun by Theodore Roosevelt, and his establishment of a state relief program, wholly inadequate though it was in the face of the immense needs created by the Depression, served as a model for other states and for federal relief efforts after Roosevelt reached the

White House. Yet one fact was brought home repeatedly as Governor Roosevelt sought to counter the effects of the Depression in New York: The economic disaster was a national problem, and no individual state could do much to solve it. Even so, the progressive measures supported by Roosevelt led him to a decisive reelection victory in 1930. His winning margin of 725,000 votes was more than twenty-eight times larger than his margin two years before, and Roosevelt showed great strength in the rural upstate counties where Democrats usually did poorly. He automatically became the favorite for his party's 1932 presidential nomination.

Although Roosevelt's perceptions of the early Depression were not unlike those of the Republican president, Herbert Hoover, the New York governor differed with the man in the White House in a fundamental way. Hoover was an idealist, but Roosevelt was by this time decidedly pragmatic in his approach to social problems. Although Hoover did not steadfastly reject government intervention in all areas, he was a firm believer in voluntarism. Roosevelt quickly came to see government as a necessary tool in dealing with the economic crisis. As governor, he demonstrated one more critical difference from Hoover: Roosevelt was able to put forth the image of a dynamic, caring leader who knew what needed to be done, or at least was willing to experiment. Hoover, in contrast, appeared to the public to be incapable and uncaring.

Before he could get into the ring with the opponent in the White House in the 1932 election campaign, Roosevelt would have to knock out his Democratic rivals. The problem here was that the party still required a nominee to win the backing of two-thirds of the delegates in the nominating convention. Roosevelt had no trouble getting a simple majority, but several other candidates held key delegations that kept Roosevelt short of two-thirds. One of those other candidates was Al Smith, who turned

against Roosevelt as the latter began to overshadow him.

To win the nomination, Roosevelt became more daring in his rhetoric. Realizing that the American people had grown tired of the ineffective economic practices of the past and increasingly bitter toward big businessmen, bankers, and the rich in general, Roosevelt emphasized the traditional Democratic alternative to the Republican "trickle-down" approach to prosperity for all. In an April, 1932, radio address, the candidate called for plans "that build from the bottom up and not from the top down, that put their faith once more in the forgotten man at the bottom of the economic pyramid." Such rhetoric enraged Smith, but it seems to have pleased a large portion of the electorate.

The opposition to Roosevelt held firm on the first two ballots at the 1932 Democratic convention and came very close to turning the tide against him on the third, before the Roosevelt forces reached agreements with House Speaker John Nance Garner and influential publisher William Randolph Hearst and won the nomination for Roosevelt on the fourth ballot.

Roosevelt's flair for the dramatic was immediately displayed when he violated the tradition of waiting for weeks to be notified officially of his selection as his party's nominee and instead flew from Albany to Chicago to deliver an acceptance speech directly to the convention. He told the delegates that he intended his action to be symbolic of his willingness to break with "foolish traditions." The nominee denounced the "Tory" idea of helping the rich in hopes that "some of their prosperity will leak through, sift through, to labor, to the farmer, to the small businessman." Roosevelt pledged himself "to a new deal for the American people."

Certainly, that is what most Americans desperately wanted in 1932. The only thing they wanted more than a "new deal" was to put Her-

FDR delivering the second fireside chat of 1934. *(FDR Library)*

cific about how he would eliminate the causes of poverty, saying that it was not proper to talk politics on Sunday. "You cannot quarrel with a single one of his generalities . . . ," reporter Elmer Davis wrote, "But what they mean (if anything) is known only to Franklin D. Roosevelt and his God."

None of this mattered. Hoover complained with some justification that his opponent was "a chameleon on plaid," but the American people wanted a change, and in a two-party system Roosevelt was their only other real choice. His overwhelming victory, with nearly 23 million votes to fewer than 16 million for Hoover and the electoral votes of forty-two states to the Republican's six, was more a repudiation of the incumbent than an endorsement of the vague "new deal" promised by the challenger.

bert Hoover out of office. Franklin Roosevelt was the means to achieve both of these objectives, and he needed to do almost nothing in order to be elected over Hoover. Still, Roosevelt chose to undertake a strenuous campaign, demonstrating to the voters that he was physically capable of handling the duties of the presidency.

In his campaign speeches, Roosevelt hedged on most controversial questions. He shocked adviser Raymond Moley by looking at two drafts of a tariff speech, one favoring free trade and the other strong protectionism, and telling Moley to "weave the two together." Only in an address at San Francisco's Commonwealth Club did Roosevelt give a clear indication of the direction he would take as president. In other speeches the Democrat lashed at Hoover as a spendthrift and one who wanted "to center control of everything in Washington as rapidly as possible." Mostly, Roosevelt declined to take any forthright stand during the general election campaign. In one speech he refused to be spe-

Bold, Persistent Experimentation

Not since Abraham Lincoln had an American president taken office in the midst of a great national crisis such as that which prevailed when Franklin D. Roosevelt—or FDR, as he came to be known—repeated the oath on March 4, 1933. The Depression had grown steadily worse in the months since the election. One-fourth of the nation's workforce was unemployed; private charity and state and local relief funds were woefully inadequate; hunger was widespread; and the nation's banking system was in nearly complete collapse.

Although such conditions were horrible, Roosevelt could not have asked for a better scene in which to make his entrance. He immediately found himself in a position to accom-

Excerpt from Franklin D. Roosevelt's first inaugural address, March 4, 1933:

This is preeminently the time to speak the truth, the whole truth, frankly and boldly. Nor need we shrink from honestly facing conditions in our country today. This great Nation will endure, as it has endured, will revive and will prosper.

So, first of all, let me assert my firm belief that the only thing we have to fear is fear itself—nameless, unreasoning, unjustified terror which paralyzes needed efforts to convert retreat into advance. In every dark hour of our national life, a leadership of frankness and of vigor has met with that understanding and support of the people themselves which is essential to victory. And I am convinced that you will again give that support to leadership in these critical days.

plish more than any other peacetime president. His inaugural address began the process of restoring confidence to the shattered national psyche. This is just what Hoover had been saying was needed for three years, but he had been singularly unable to induce confidence in the people. Yet when Roosevelt intoned the words, "So, first of all, let me assert my firm belief that the only thing we have to fear, is fear itself—nameless, unreasoning, unjustified terror which paralyzes needed efforts to convert retreat into advance," the spirits of a downcast nation began to revive. Sensing the popular mood, Roosevelt took a few verbal swipes at the "money changers" and said, "This Nation asks for action, and action now."

He gave it action by calling the Congress into special session and closing all the nation's banks. Roosevelt could have obtained almost any banking legislation he wanted when the new, heavily Democratic Congress convened five days after his inauguration. It is therefore a measure of FDR's moderate approach that he endorsed an emergency banking bill that had been drawn up by Hoover appointees and bankers. The new president signed the measure into law eight hours after its introduction into Congress. Then Roosevelt demonstrated his abilities as the first media president by giving a "fireside chat" over radio to explain the banking crisis. He spoke in fatherly, soothing terms that his listeners—and, Will Rogers said, even bankers—could understand. As a result of

FDR's assurances that those banks that were allowed to reopen were safe, people stopped their withdrawals and began again to make deposits. Raymond Moley exaggerated only slightly when he said, "Capitalism was saved in eight days." Part of Roosevelt's motive in remaining conservative on banking was his penchant for catching opponents off guard. By pushing the conservative banking measure and an even more conservative economy bill that would cut federal spending, Roosevelt pleased businessmen and paved the way for the most intense period of reform in American history.

The quick actions of Roosevelt's first week in office lacked substance, but they excited the public. The new president realized, though, that people would soon look for results. He was in the fortunate position of having goals that largely coincided with the public desires of the Depression years. Both the American people and Franklin D. Roosevelt had a vague desire for an economy based more on fairness, justice, and humanitarianism than had been the case in the past. This coincidence of goals was one of the reasons that Roosevelt was able to become such a successful leader. It is always easier to lead people in the direction they are already headed. FDR usually did this, although he sometimes had to move rapidly to catch up to his followers.

Roosevelt decided to continue the special session of Congress he had called to deal with the banking crisis so that he could accomplish as much as possible while his own popularity was at its highest. Next to the banking question, the farm problem was most pressing. American agriculture had been in depression while much of the rest of the country was prospering in the 1920's. Roosevelt had argued during his campaign that the fundamental imbalance in the economy was attributable to the failure of farm income to rise sufficiently to enable farmers to buy the products of industry. Whatever the merits of this view as an explanation of the Depression, Roosevelt was determined to take steps to raise farm prices.

There was no lack of proposals for solving the agricultural problem. Roosevelt's goals were to satisfy as many different farm groups as possible and at the same time to produce a law that would give him maximum freedom to try different policies as he saw fit. Accordingly, he insisted that the leaders of the various farm groups agree among themselves to a bill before he would endorse it. The result was the omnibus Agricultural Adjustment Act (AAA), an amalgam of contradictory farm panaceas. Like many of Roosevelt's measures, it was politically sound—but economically somewhat incoherent. The basic goal was to raise prices through induced scarcity. The president and the leaders of the newly created Agricultural Adjustment Administration could choose among a variety of means to achieve this end, but mainly they used government payments, financed by a tax on food processing, to farmers who reduced their acreage under cultivation.

THE VICE PRESIDENT
HENRY A. WALLACE

Henry A. Wallace served as vice president in the third term of Franklin D. Roosevelt's presidency. Born on October 7, 1888, on a farm in Adair County, Iowa, Wallace's father was a well-regarded politician who would go on to serve as the secretary of agriculture in the administrations of Warren G. Harding and Calvin Coolidge. The younger Wallace attended public schools in Iowa and then Iowa State College. On May 20, 1914, he married Ilo Bowne, and they had three children.

Wallace edited a farming newspaper that was founded by his father and gained a reputation during the 1920's for developing experimental agricultural techniques and corn hybrids. In addition to publishing books on these topics, he chaired the Agricultural Round Table at the International Institute of Politics in Massachusetts and served as a delegate to the International Conference on Agricultural Economics in England.

In his capacity as secretary of agriculture from 1933 to 1940, Wallace emerged as one of the most influential advisers to Roosevelt on farm policy and a key architect of the agricultural component of the New Deal. Wallace played a major role in farm relief, soil conservation, and the Agricultural Adjustment Administration. He was selected as Roosevelt's running mate in the 1940 election and went on to serve as vice president from 1941 to 1945. Opposition to Wallace remaining on the ticket for the 1944 reelection campaign emerged, and he was replaced by Harry Truman and served as Truman's secretary of commerce. However, Wallace's public criticism of Truman's policies led to his dismissal by the president in 1946.

Henry Wallace remained active in politics after his vice presidency. In the 1940's, he served for a short time as editor of *The New Republic* and published two noted books—*Democracy Reborn* (1944) and *The Century of the Common Man* (1943). He ran unsuccessfully in 1948 on the Progressive ticket for the presidency. He died on November 18, 1965, in Danbury, Connecticut.

Robert P. Watson and Richard Yon

Just what planned scarcity meant was soon apparent. Since controversies over portions of the agriculture bill kept it from becoming law until mid-May, the growing season was well under way and crops already planted had to be plowed under. Many people could not see the point of destroying food while millions were hungry. The economic system had failed to bring the food to those who needed it but could not pay for it. Roosevelt's hope was to stimulate recovery by putting more money in the pockets of farmers.

The plan did not work as hoped. Many farmers took their worst land out of production and worked their best acres more intensively. In many cases the end result was greater production than before the AAA went into effect. Thanks more to the massive drought that made a dust bowl of the Great Plains than to the AAA, farm prices rose by 50 percent during FDR's first term. This proved too little to have much of an effect on reviving the economy, and the farm problem continued to plague the administration into Roosevelt's second term.

While Congress considered the farm bill, the president continued to send other proposals to Capitol Hill. Among his firmest beliefs were the need for conservation and the desirability of giving urban youths the advantages of the rugged life of the outdoors. In both respects, he was a worthy successor to Cousin Ted. Here, too, was an appropriate concern for one brought up in the tradition of the country gentleman. The lord of the manor had a responsibility to care for the land as well as the people. FDR embodied these objectives in a bill he sent to Congress in the second week of the special session. Ten days later, Congress, on a voice vote, created the Civilian Conservation Corps (CCC). The agency took unemployed young men and put them to work at reforestation and other conservation tasks, sending most of their meager paychecks home to help their families. The CCC was one of the New Deal's most popular and successful programs, and Roosevelt's personal role in its founding was a source of great pride to him.

Roosevelt's personal popularity was enormous during the first Hundred Days of the New Deal. He took advantage of this circumstance to push through some of his favorite ideas. Along with conservation, FDR was committed to planned use of the land and to public electric power projects. He combined all three when he asked Congress in April, 1933, to create the Tennessee Valley Authority (TVA). The TVA was in part a proposed solution to the battle that had raged for more than a decade between progressives and conservatives in Congress over the disposition of the Wilson Dam on the Tennessee River in northern Alabama. Conservatives wanted the government-built facility at Muscle Shoals to be sold to private power interests, whereas progressives led by Senator George Norris of Nebraska insisted that it be operated by the government. Roosevelt had long been aligned with the public power advocates, but he now went far beyond the Wilson Dam controversy and called for a development program for "national planning for a complete river workshed."

The Tennessee Valley was one of the most depressed and underdeveloped areas in the United States. The TVA, which was created by large congressional majorities within five weeks of Roosevelt's proposal, was designed to invigorate the local economy by providing cheap hydroelectric power, to stop soil erosion and provide flood control, to uplift the people through education and recreation programs, and to provide a yardstick by which to measure the fairness of electricity rates charged by private companies. In almost all respects, the TVA was a great success—so much so that frightened private power interests loudly denounced it as a form of socialism in order to block Roosevelt's intention to create several similar regional development programs. Success, not failure, prevented the duplication of the TVA elsewhere.

FDR visits the Norris Dam construction site in 1934 with Eleanor Roosevelt and TVA director A. E. Morgan. *(TVA)*

Although Roosevelt was sincere in his desire for government economy and a balanced budget—he even called for slashing payments given each month to war veterans totally disabled in civilian life from $40 to $20—he did not suffer from Hoover's single-mindedness. Roosevelt explained the contradiction of pressing for vast relief and recovery expenditures while calling for government economy by saying, "You cannot let people starve." This simple humanitarian pragmatism gave FDR the support of millions of people who had rejected Hoover's more consistent but less practical approach.

Like Hoover, Roosevelt always feared that a federal dole might destroy the self-reliance of recipients and make them dependent. Still, he also recognized that people had to be provided the basic necessities of life. On the same day that he sent the CCC bill to Congress, therefore,

he asked for authorization to name a federal relief administrator and to provide federal grants to the states for direct relief payments to the jobless. Both houses responded quickly with heavy majorities in favor of this step into federal relief.

Roosevelt appointed Harry Hopkins, who had headed his relief program in New York, to oversee the Federal Emergency Relief Administration (FERA). Hopkins thought much as Roosevelt did—that direct relief was not desirable but was necessary. Hopkins said that a dole took from people "their sense of independence and their sense of individual dignity"— yet no short-term alternative existed. The relief administrator responded to the argument that one proposal would "work out in the long run" by noting that "people don't eat in the long run—they eat every day." Setting up a desk in a hallway, Hopkins spent five million dollars in his first two hours on the job. Both Roosevelt and Hopkins saw the FERA as what its name implied—an emergency agency, not a long-term solution to poverty. Accordingly, Hopkins concentrated on distributing as much money to as many needy people as quickly as he possibly could. Some critics complained that such an approach wasted public funds, but there was surprisingly little waste or corruption in the FERA programs.

Another massive problem area emerging from the Depression led to an innovative proposal from the Roosevelt administration during the Hundred Days when the president asked in April for legislation to assist home owners threatened with foreclosure. Foreclosures had reached the frightening rate of a thousand per day. The most basic part of the American Dream—home ownership—was being undermined. The Home Owner's Loan Corporation (HOLC) refinanced mortgages at lower interest rates and saved many home owners from foreclosure. Its greatest beneficiaries, though, were the bankers and other lenders, repayment of whose loans was now guaranteed by the federal government. Eventually, 20 percent of American homes came under the protection of the HOLC.

The special session of Congress was nearing its end, and Roosevelt had proposed no legislation to deal with what most people saw as the nation's most basic need: industrial recovery. The new president had sincerely believed that recovery in agriculture, combined with increased relief spending, would stimulate the economy sufficiently to reinvigorate industry. Many in Congress and the general public were less sanguine. Senator Hugo L. Black of Alabama introduced a bill, supported by the American Federation of Labor, that would limit the hours of all workers connected with interstate commerce to thirty per week. The Senate passed this work-spreading bill, and the House appeared likely to go along. Roosevelt was unhappy with Black's proposal, since it would not give the president the flexibility that other early New Deal measures provided.

It was the need to sidetrack the Black bill that led FDR to propose his own recovery legislation. The result was the National Industrial Recovery Act (NIRA), requested by Roosevelt on May 17 and enacted a month later. The goal, the president said in his message asking for passage of the bill, was "a great cooperative movement throughout all industry in order to obtain wide reemployment, to shorten the working week, to pay a decent wage for the shorter week and to prevent unfair competition and disastrous overproduction." This was a tall order, even for a New Deal law. The basic means by which the NIRA sought to achieve its multiple objectives were the establishment of codes that would establish minimum wages, maximum hours, and standards of working conditions in each industry. The underlying idea, though, was *self*-regulation, that is, action by the businesses themselves. The largest companies in each field dominated the creation of the codes for these industries.

Title II of the NIRA created a huge program of public construction projects, the Public Works Administration (PWA). To head the program, Roosevelt named his interior secretary, Harold Ickes. Ickes was nominally a Republican and fervently a progressive. He was absolutely committed to the efficient use of the public funds. As a result, the PWA had a remarkable record of useful construction without any significant corruption. In contrast to Harry Hopkins, Ickes believed in going slowly and carefully when the public purse strings were opened. Consequently, the PWA never provided the rapid stimulus for economic recovery that Roosevelt had intended when it was paired with the National Recovery Administration (NRA).

The NRA was supposed to introduce a modicum of rationality and planning into the American free market economy. This was in no sense an antibusiness move. On the contrary, the law that Roosevelt called "the most important and far-reaching legislation ever enacted by the American Congress" created "a partnership in planning" between business and government. The NRA codes, in effect, put the federal government behind cooperative arrangements among separate businesses in each industry. This flouting of the antitrust laws was excused with the argument that such planning was necessary to bring about recovery and that concessions were also being given to labor. The latter were contained in Section 7(a) of the NIRA, which provided for collective bargaining, but this section was soon watered down by decisions of the National Labor Relations Board.

In fact, the NRA under the leadership of General Hugh Johnson became little more than an effort at cheerleading. The old Hoover idea of restoring confidence was pushed by parades, songs, advertisements, and the omnipresent NRA symbol, the Blue Eagle. It was all quite exhilarating, but it produced little in the way of lasting recovery.

A Liberal Conservative

The first hundred days of Roosevelt's presidency were marked by the "bold, persistent experimentation" that he had said the American people demanded. The actions were dramatic but lacking in consistency. Franklin D. Roosevelt was a politician, not an economist or a philosopher. As a political practitioner, he sought to please as many voters as possible. He was uninterested in general concepts; he preferred concrete problems and direct attempts to deal with them. He chose advisers and associates on the basis of personality and character, not ideology. The consequence was a wide variety of voices reaching the presidential ear in the first years of FDR's administration.

Yet presidents sometimes inspire more than they intend. Much as John F. Kennedy did three decades later, FDR launched a more liberal movement than he would initially have endorsed. The excitement engendered by the newly active government and the charismatic leader brought thousands of idealistic young men and women to Washington, D.C., to join the multiplying "alphabet agencies" of the New Deal. These tireless young New Dealers came firmly to believe in active government as a tool of the community's will. They gave the Roosevelt administration an increasingly liberal aura, even before the president himself made a decisive move to the left in 1935. They were so committed to active government that most of them would not tolerate a hint of corruption, and there was very little of it in the early years throughout the wide array of government agencies.

If the New Dealers were decidedly liberal, the same cannot so easily be said of the man whose shuffling of the cards inspired them—at least not during his first two years in the White House. In many respects, FDR's policies during the early New Deal resembled the classic conservatism of the eighteenth century British political philosopher Edmund Burke. This conservatism, to be sure, was a far cry from the ideas of those who had misappropriated the conservative label by the 1920's and 1930's. These people, principally wealthy businessmen, became the most bitter opponents of the New Deal. To them, conservatism meant a philosophy of egoism, the suppression of change, and concern only for immediate self-interest, with little thought of interests of others in the present or of future generations.

If this is what one understands as conservatism—and it is what the word came to mean in the minds of most twentieth century Americans—plainly Franklin D. Roosevelt was no conservative; but if one looks to the classic conception of conservatism, the early New Deal nearly fits. In the first two years of his presidency, FDR sought—through such programs as the NRA—to achieve a consensus above the clamoring of interest groups. He attempted to promote cooperation among government, business, labor, farmers, and other groups. He

In a 1934 cartoon, FDR tries several "New Deal remedies" to treat an ailing Uncle Sam. *(Library of Congress)*

did identify himself with those at the bottom of the economic pyramid, but not yet by opposing those at the top. President Roosevelt tried valiantly in these years to convince businessmen that change was necessary if the system from which they had so much benefited were to be saved. "Reform if you would preserve," he told them in the words of classic conservatism.

Despite the harsh rhetoric of his right-wing critics, Roosevelt was not moving in those early years in anything approaching a socialistic direction. With the sole exception of the TVA, Roosevelt resisted all suggestions of government ownership, remaining a firm believer in an economic system based on private ownership. What he sought was a wider distribution of property, not its elimination. Moreover, like classic conservatives, Roosevelt believed that each generation is entrusted with the society built by the past and is obligated to preserve and improve that society for those who will inherit it in the future.

Although Roosevelt possessed many of the characteristics and beliefs of the classic Burkean conservative, views that saved the capitalistic system and helped produce conditions that enabled business profits to rise rapidly, the right wing organized into a bitter, unflinching opposition to the president and his programs. This opposition centered in the Liberty League, an organization launched in mid-1934 by some of the leading corporate executives in the nation joining forces with Al Smith and other anti-New Deal Democrats. Roosevelt could not understand the bitterness of these people. He summed up the situation with a parable: "In the summer of 1933, a nice old gentleman wearing a silk hat fell off the end of a pier. He was unable to swim. A friend ran down the pier, dived overboard and pulled him out; but the silk hat had floated off with the tide. After the old gentleman had been revived, he was effusive with thanks. He praised his friend for saving his life. Today, three years later, the old gentleman is berating his friend because the silk hat was lost." Roosevelt approvingly quoted a friend as saying that organizers of the Liberty League believed in two things: "Love God and then forget your neighbor."

This statement of what he opposed demonstrated the heart of Roosevelt's beliefs. Never a systematic thinker, he cannot accurately be placed in any philosophical category but perhaps can be best described as a pragmatic humanitarian. He placed the need for concern about the fate of one's neighbors above any philosophical consistency. He would try many different—apparently contradictory—approaches to improve the general well-being of the community. Both the classic conservatism of 1933-1934 and the modern liberalism of 1935 and later years were grounded in FDR's upbringing as a responsible country gentleman. His sense of stewardship was close to the essence of classic conservatism and became the main feature of the twentieth century liberalism that had started with Theodore Roosevelt and Woodrow Wilson and was crystallizing in the New Deal. The new liberalism that issued from Franklin D. Roosevelt's presidency combined the best elements of Burkean conservatism—elements that had been abandoned by most of those who took up the conservative banner in the twentieth century—and Jeffersonian liberalism. Following the path of Cousin Ted, Franklin D. Roosevelt came to see government in a democracy as a tool of the people, not as their enemy. He therefore was able to employ Hamiltonian means of big government to try to achieve Jeffersonian ends of the common good and wider distribution of private property.

Which Side Are You On?

Most presidents enjoy a "honeymoon" with the American people and the Congress in their early months in the White House, but never was a honeymoon more romantic and exciting—or as long-lasting—as that of Franklin D. Roosevelt. His brimming confidence, particularly in contrast to Hoover's sourness, combined with the terrible crisis to make Roosevelt a leader most people were prepared to follow almost without question. One congressman called FDR a Moses leading the nation out of the wilderness. Many, perhaps most, Americans had much the same impression. When he spoke, a Kansas man wrote of the president, "it seems as though some Moses had come to alleviate . . . our sufferings." A letter written in March, 1933, by several Brooklyn residents to Senator Robert F. Wagner summarized Roosevelt's effect on a dispirited citizenry: "It makes one raise the head and square the shoulders, feeling that now indeed we can place confidence in those chosen to lead the destiny of our Country. We now feel that in truth

Washington is the throbbing heart of U.S.A. Fear has gone."

Roosevelt's popularity in 1933-1934 was in all likelihood among the greatest ever enjoyed by an American president. FERA investigator Martha Gellhorn filed a report from the Carolinas in 1934 reflecting the common view of FDR:

Every house I visited—mill worker or unemployed—had a picture of the President. These ranged from newspaper clippings (in destitute homes) to large coloured prints, framed in gilt cardboard. The portrait holds a place of honor over the mantle; I can only compare this to the Italian peasant's Madonna. And the feeling of these people for the President is one of the most remarkable emotional phenomena I have ever met. He is at once God and their intimate friend; he knows them all by name, knows their little town and mill, their little lives and problems. And, though everything fails, he is there, and will not let them down.

Letters from ordinary Americans poured into the Roosevelt White House at a rate four times greater than they had during any other presidency. The great majority of these communications from the public were laudatory. Many put their perception of the Roosevelts' benevolence into concrete terms. "I do think you and the President is the Mother and Father of this Great USA," a Toledo resident wrote in a typical 1936 letter to Eleanor Roosevelt.

Franklin D. Roosevelt occupied a position that is the dream of every politician. A majority of the voters praised him for everything they liked in the New Deal and blamed others for what they disliked. Those writing to the Roosevelts often complained about economic conditions, relief policies, or other problems, but they usually went on to absolve the president, like the Californian who wrote, "You are wonderful. But surely this treatment is unknown to you." Roosevelt was such a masterful politician that many people who had a strong distaste for politicians excused his calling. "Your husband is *great*. He seems lovable even tho' he's a 'politician,'" a Denver woman wrote to Eleanor Roosevelt. "I wish him all the success in the world." Any endeavor is lifted to the level of an art when it can be made to seem effortless and natural. In these qualities, Roosevelt was the American politician who most deserves to be called an artist.

FDR's political artistry notwithstanding, his hopes to please everyone and achieve consensus government could not be realized for any lasting period. Terrible crisis may lead various groups and individuals to give up their separate interests for the duration of their extreme apprehension, but as soon as the crisis gives any sign of easing, the resuscitated businessman will begin to look for his silk hat, and his counterparts in other constituent groups will begin again to seek their own interests. Roosevelt's very success in lifting the hopes—and, to a lesser extent, the economy—of the United States meant that his consensus would be short-lived. Eventually, he would be obliged to heed the words of the union song that came out of the bitter labor conflict of Harlan County, Kentucky, in the early 1930's: "Which side are you on?"

That choice became imperative as Roosevelt's great popularity began to decline in late 1934 and early 1935. It was not that very many Americans outside the Liberty League were recoiling from the New Deal. The Democrats won an unprecedented victory in the congressional elections of 1934, reducing Republican representation to 25 in the Senate and 103 in the House—the first instance in modern American history in which the president's party gained congressional seats in a nonpresidential election year. Surely, these results were heartening to FDR, but there were also portents of trouble for him in the politics of 1934. When the choice before voters was a New Deal Democrat versus an Old Guard Republican, the Democrat almost invariably won. Signs appeared in

1934, however, indicating that the people were moving farther to the left than their president. A minimum of thirty-five candidates who preached the need to go beyond the New Deal were elected to Congress that November.

In Minnesota, the Farmer-Labor Party, led by Governor Floyd Olson, swept the state. Olson had declared that he was not a liberal but a radical, and implied that many businessmen were "burglars and thieves and pirates." In neighboring Wisconsin, the sons of Progressive hero Robert M. La Follette also took the third-party route to a point somewhat to the left of the New Deal and won. In California, veteran socialist novelist Upton Sinclair infiltrated the Democratic Party, proposed a radical program to "end poverty in California" by setting up a production-for-use economic system, and won the Democratic nomination for governor with a record number of votes. Although Sinclair finally lost in an extremely dirty campaign, the popularity of his essentially socialist proposals provided another indication of the leftward drift of American public opinion.

Numerous other signs of the same phenomenon surfaced. The year 1934 saw one of the largest waves of strikes in American history—eighteen hundred strikes involving almost one and a half million people were called in that turbulent year. In Toledo, Minneapolis, and San Francisco, huge strikes precipitated violent clashes that bordered on class warfare. Wealthy residents of both Minneapolis and San Francisco, seeing strikers taking over their cities, fled out of fear that the revolution had finally come. There was little danger that it would go that far, but Roosevelt's bold economic actions seemed to have touched off a new spirit among American workers, a spirit that went beyond anything the president had intended. Workers, like voters in many parts of the nation, were restless in 1934 and demanding a more rapid move toward economic justice.

The same demand was picked up in one way or another by three nationwide move-

Huey P. Long. *(Library of Congress)*

ments led by charismatic figures. In the late 1920's, Father Charles Coughlin of Royal Oak, Michigan, had begun giving sermons over the radio to counteract the anti-Catholic activities of the Ku Klux Klan. By 1930, he had broadened his subject matter to include economic questions and had secured a network radio contract. Initially, Coughlin fixed his oratorical wrath on such immobile targets as communists, bankers, and Herbert Hoover. As the Radio Priest demanded "social justice," his audience grew rapidly until he had an estimated thirty million listeners in 1934 and 1935. For a time Coughlin wavered in his treatment of Roosevelt, but then more and more often he attacked the president. Although Coughlin later made his anti-Semitism and pro-Hitler views plain, at the peak of his popularity in the mid-1930's he seemed to be challenging the New Deal from the Left, not the Right.

In the fall of 1933, Francis Townsend, a retired physician living in California, launched a plan to end the Depression by paying two hun-dred dollars a month to every American above the age of sixty. Support for the Townsend Plan spread like wildfire, particularly among those older citizens who would be its greatest beneficiaries. Townsend proposed to finance his plan through what would have amounted to a massive sales tax. Although Townsend's lavish scheme was wholly unworkable, this fact deterred the movement not at all, and between 1934 and 1936 more than twenty million people signed petitions calling for the Townsend Plan. Pressure was mounting on politicians to endorse the plan or face the wrath of a very large group of voters.

As threatening as the Coughlin and Townsend movements were, the loudest claps of the mid-1930's thunder on the Left emanated from the hills and bayous of Louisiana. By preaching redistribution of wealth and attacking the Standard Oil Company, "Kingfish" Huey P. Long had become governor of the state in 1928. After securing virtual dictatorial powers there, Long moved on to the United States Senate in 1932. That year he helped Roosevelt win the Democratic presidential nomination, but Long's ambitions were too great for him to remain in the shadow of another politician. Early in 1934 he created the Share Our Wealth Society and demanded that the fortunes of the rich (whom he described as "pigs swilling in the trough of luxury") be divided among all Americans. This was an idea with great appeal in the Depression years, and tens of thousands of enthusiastic letters came into Long's Senate office each week.

Whatever the ultimate aspirations of such figures as Olson, Sinclair, Coughlin, and Townsend, no doubt whatsoever existed about where the Louisiana Kingfish had set his sights. The pond Huey Long sought to dominate was already occupied by Franklin D. Roosevelt, but by 1935, the Southern demagogue was picking up enough support around the country to make his goal seem realizable. There was no chance that Long could take the 1936 Democratic nomination from FDR or that he could win the presidency that year at the head of a third-party ticket. What worried Roosevelt and his aides was that Long might siphon off enough votes from the president's left flank to give a Republican victory in 1936. A secret poll commissioned by the Democratic National Committee in 1935 indicated that a Long candidacy might win between three and four million votes. Roosevelt was not anxious to find out whether he would have that many to spare.

The president would have to choose sides if he wanted to avert a possible large defection of voters anxious for more rapid change toward egalitarianism than the New Deal had so far produced.

Tacking to Port

Several forces combined to push Franklin D. Roosevelt to the left in 1935. One was the now-bitter attacks on him by businessmen who charged that he was a "traitor to his class." The president deeply resented these fusillades, and he wondered why such wealthy individuals could not understand that he was saving their necks—or at the very least the bulk of their stock portfolios. "One of my principal tasks," he said in 1934, "is to prevent bankers and businessmen from committing suicide." As the vicious and frequently personal abuse continued from the right, however, Roosevelt's patience wore thin.

The Supreme Court gave FDR another shove toward the left when it invalidated several of the early New Deal programs. In the most noted of these decisions, the Supreme Court declared the NRA unconstitutional. Roosevelt protested loudly, charging that the Court had returned the Constitution to the "horse and buggy days," but the "nine old men" may have done him a favor by executing the terminally ill Blue Eagle.

In any case, the original New Deal concept of cooperation among government, business, and labor seemed no longer viable: Many busi-

nessmen would not cooperate, labor was restive, the NRA had not brought about sufficient recovery, and now the Supreme Court said the NRA violated the Constitution. Yet, by the time the Court issued its rebuke to the NRA, Roosevelt had already begun his decisive move to the left. His principal motive was to solidify his support among lower- and middle-class voters who wanted more change. In the spring of 1935, the president told adviser Raymond Moley that something must be done "to steal Long's thunder." That something clearly had to involve a turn to the left.

Such a shift materialized in the "second New Deal" of 1935. In the late spring and early summer of that year, FDR called for, and the heavily Democratic Congress enacted, a series of laws that rank the period with the Hundred Days of 1933 and Lyndon Johnson's Great Society programs of 1964-1965 as the three most significant spurts of reform legislation in twentieth century American history.

In April, Congress agreed to Roosevelt's request for an unprecedentedly large appropriation for relief. The Emergency Relief Appropriation Act of 1935 provided $4.88 billion, a figure representing 10 percent of the national income for the previous year. After Congress appropriated the funds, Roosevelt used a large portion of the money to launch a new work relief program, the Works Progress Administration (WPA), which he placed under the direction of Harry Hopkins. Both Roosevelt and Hopkins had long been unhappy with direct relief payments to the jobless, a feeling they shared with most of the public and with most relief recipients. Everyone realized that working for relief payments helped to maintain a person's self-respect. The only drawback was the cost of work relief, but now that a new stimulus to the economy seemed advisable before the 1936 election year, the president agreed to try work relief.

Although the WPA was the target of much conservative criticism, it was a remarkably successful program. Under it, thousands of schools, hospitals, playgrounds, and other public facilities were constructed, and at the same time work, a degree of self-respect, and a subsistence wage were given to millions of Americans. Among the most daring of Hopkins's experiments was the use of a small part of the WPA funds to create programs that for the first time made the American government a patron of the arts. WPA projects for theater, art, music, and writing brought plays and live music performances to areas of the country that rarely saw them; put visual artworks in public buildings across the nation; preserved life-history narratives of workers, farmers, and former slaves; and wrote guidebooks to the states. The federal arts projects also fostered the careers of dozens of the most important figures in twentieth century American arts and letters.

Part of Roosevelt's shift to the left in 1935 meant stiffening his stand against the greedy. He was careful to point out that he was not condemning businessmen in general but only that minority who misused their positions for completely selfish ends. (Contrary to popular impression, many businessmen, especially in newer industries such as motion pictures and business machines, strongly supported Roosevelt.) Two of the developments of the second New Deal helped to draw the line Roosevelt sought to place between himself and such wealthy magnates. One was the Wheeler-Rayburn Act, which outlawed some public utility holding companies, although its final version failed to abolish them entirely. The other was a tax message that FDR sent to Congress in June. In it the president went a great distance toward stealing Huey Long's "soak the rich" thunder. Denouncing the "unjust concentration of wealth and economic power" in the United States, Roosevelt called on Congress to enact a series of new taxes aimed at the wealthy. The legislation that resulted was of little consequence, but Roosevelt had dramatically placed himself in opposition to the very wealthy.

The other two major laws of the second New Deal reemphasized FDR's stand as champion of the needy. The Wagner (National Labor Relations) Act and the Social Security Act were probably the two most important domestic accomplishments of FDR's presidency.

Roosevelt had never before been especially identified with the cause of organized labor. He had, nevertheless, been partly responsible for inspiring the hopes among workers that produced the upheaval from below in the mid-1930's. Others were more attuned to the sounds of this new force, and Roosevelt endorsed New York Senator Robert F. Wagner's bill to protect the rights of workers to form and join unions of their own choosing when it became clear that Congress would pass the legislation anyway. By making it possible for the new Congress of Industrial Organizations (CIO) to unionize most mass production workers, the Wagner Act helped to lift a large segment of American laborers into the middle class.

Of no less lasting importance was the creation of the Social Security system. Spurred by the Townsend movement, Roosevelt recommended an old-age pension plan in January, 1935. His August, 1935, signing of the Social Security Act, which made the United States the last major industrial nation in the world to establish a social insurance program giving protection against poverty among the aged and against unemployment among all ages, was the capstone of the second New Deal.

In mending his fences on the left, Roosevelt had prepared the way for his 1936 campaign for reelection. The basis of that campaign was to recognize the sharp class division that the Depression had created and to identify the president with the lower and middle classes. Early in the election year, Roosevelt linked himself with the image of Andrew Jackson and lashed rhetorically at "the forces of privilege and greed."

THE VICE PRESIDENT
HARRY S. TRUMAN

Harry S. Truman served as vice president for Franklin D. Roosevelt's brief fourth administration. Truman was born on May 8, 1884, in rural Lamar, Missouri. When he was a child, his family moved a few times around Missouri, and he was educated at public schools. Lacking the financial means to attend college, Truman worked in a number of jobs, including timekeeper with a railroad, in the mailroom of the *Kansas City Star* newspaper, and in banks in Kansas City.

In 1905, Truman joined the National Guard and worked from 1906 to 1917 on his family's farm. Because of his father's declining health, Truman returned home to work on the family farm from 1906 to 1917. On his father's death, Harry Truman assumed his father's position as overseer of roads for the county in 1914. In 1915, he was named postmaster of the town of Grandview. With U.S. involvement in World War I, Truman was a first lieutenant in charge of a field artillery battery in 1917 and was shipped off to France the following year. In Europe, Truman commanded Battery D of the 129th Field Artillery and was promoted to captain, returning to the United States a hero in 1919.

Although Truman found happiness in marrying the longtime object of his affection, Elizabeth Wallace, on June 28, 1919, he did not find success economically. Truman's haberdashery went out of business in 1922, but he was elected to the position of county judge that year and in 1926 presiding judge of Jackson County, where he served for several years. In 1934, Truman was elected to the U.S. Senate; he was reelected in 1940. In the Senate he gained notoriety for chairing the Senate Special Committee to Investigate the National Defense Program, and his work saved the country untold amounts of money through his investigations. After being selected as vice president in 1944, Truman served only a few weeks until Roosevelt's death on April 12, 1945, thrust him into the White House. He was elected in his own right in 1948.

After his presidency ended in 1953, Truman returned to Independence, Missouri, where he penned his memoirs, helped establish the Truman Presidential Library, and remained keenly interested in politics. Considered one of the greatest presidents, Truman died on December 26, 1972.

Robert P. Watson and Richard Yon

The rest of the Roosevelt strategy for 1936 was simply to emphasize the president and the difference between the dark days of 1932 and the hopeful and relatively better days of 1936. On both counts, Roosevelt stood to fare extremely well. His opponent, Governor Alfred M. Landon of Kansas, was a moderate Republican who vacillated between endorsing parts of the New Deal and heeding the demands of Hoover and the Old Guard Republicans to attack the Roosevelt program savagely. The danger to the president from the left had subsided with Huey Long's assassination in September, 1935. Although the remnants of the Long, Coughlin, and Townsend movements joined to form the Union Party, they were unable to mount an effective campaign for their candidate, Representative William Lemke of North Dakota.

By the end of the campaign Roosevelt had turned his class rhetoric up to full blast. "Never before in all our history," he told a New York audience, "have these forces [of organized money] been so united against one candidate as they stand today. They are unanimous in their hate for me and I welcome their hatred."

The side with which Roosevelt had cast his lot—the victims of the Depression and those who believed in active government to improve social conditions—turned out massively on Election Day, giving him an electoral vote victory of 523 to 8, the largest in a contested election in American history.

A Second-Rate Second Term

With an immense mandate from the people and huge Democratic majorities in both houses of Congress, Franklin D. Roosevelt seemed to be in a perfect position to move on to new triumphs that would assist the "one-third of a nation" that, as he pointed out in his second inaugural address, remained "ill-housed, ill-clad, ill-nourished." As it happened, though, Roosevelt's second term proved to be far less significant than either his first or third term.

Huge election victories have often led presidents into mistakes based at least in part on the notion that the voters will support anything they propose. The 1936 victory seemed an expression by a large majority of Americans of personal faith in Roosevelt. It also represented a clear endorsement of the New Deal. One major obstacle, however, blocked the path of the president's reforms. The Supreme Court had invalidated a series of New Deal measures in 1935 and 1936, and with its personnel unchanged there seemed little reason to believe the Court would not continue to strike down social legislation. Roosevelt had served an entire term without the occurrence of a single vacancy on the high bench. He had for some time been considering taking some action to reform the Court. Now with his great mandate from the people, he decided the time for bold action had arrived.

In February, 1937, FDR startled both Congress and the public by presenting a proposal to permit the president to appoint a new justice for every member of the Court who failed to retire within six months of his seventieth birthday. Although no one doubted that his purpose was to create a court more favorable to the New Deal, Roosevelt did not admit this. Instead, he insisted that the reform was needed because the nine aging justices were overworked.

A storm of criticism broke almost immediately. Many people feared that the proposal would upset the balanced government created by the Constitution. Even those who had complete confidence in Roosevelt were concerned about what some future president might do with such power. In the age of Adolf Hitler, Benito Mussolini, and Joseph Stalin, Americans were particularly protective of their democratic system and especially aroused at anything that hinted of dictatorship. Roosevelt's proposal was a long way from dictatorship, but a fear existed that it might be a step in that direction.

Roosevelt's frustration with the Court was understandable, but his poorly handled reform proposal proved to be one of his worst mistakes. It gave members of Congress who were anxious to show their independence but fearful of the president's popularity a legitimate issue on which to oppose him. The result was the reemergence of a conservative coalition of Republicans and Southern Democrats, a coalition that harassed New Dealers' attempts at further social reform during the remainder of FDR's presidency. What made the error of Court "packing" even more galling was that it was unnecessary. In the weeks following Roosevelt's proposal, the Court announced several decisions upholding New Deal legislation. Shortly after, one of the conservative judges retired, giving Roosevelt a chance to make a normal appointment. Still, the damage to Roosevelt's reputation was done, and he henceforth had to deal with a more recalcitrant Congress. Presidential hubris had done in lesser men than Franklin D. Roosevelt. The Supreme Court episode did not by any means finish him off, but it left him chastened.

Other problems followed in a year that had seemed to promise great success for Roosevelt. The president had never accepted the new economic doctrine propounded by John Maynard Keynes, calling for the purposeful creation of large budget deficits to stimulate a depressed economy. Roosevelt tolerated deficits as a necessary evil, the only way to avert mass deprivation, but his goal was to balance the budget as quickly as possible. With some improvement in the economy by 1937 (although unemployment still stood at 14 percent), FDR decided the time had come to cut back spending sharply. Drastic cutbacks were made in the WPA and PWA. In August, 1937, the economy took a new nosedive. For months this recession left Roosevelt bewildered. He began issuing statements on the fundamental strength of the economy. Such talk was distressingly reminiscent of the words of Herbert Hoover in the early 1930's.

The continuing decline left Roosevelt no choice. In the spring of 1938, he asked Congress for a massive new relief appropriation. This provided the stimulus that was needed to turn the economy around, but the improvements were still not sufficient to bring the nation out of the Depression. At no time before the military buildup for World War II was Roosevelt willing to prescribe a sufficiently large dose of deficit spending to cure the nation's economic illness. Instead, he kept injecting maintenance doses that kept the patient alive but allowed the sickness to continue.

Only one major reform of lasting impact was enacted in Roosevelt's second term. The president sought legislation that would define the minimum permissible wages and the maximum hours of labor per week. Opposition was intense, especially from Southern states with notoriously low wage rates. To get the bill passed, Roosevelt and its sponsors had to agree, as they had done in the case of Social Security three years before, to exclude from the bill farm and domestic labor, two major black occupations in the South. Thus made more palatable for some members of the Congress, the Fair Labor Standards Act of 1938 became law. In those occupations that fell under the law's coverage, wages of at least twenty-five cents per hour had to be paid, and workers' hours were limited to forty per week.

A political cartoon in the *San Francisco Chronicle* for March 24, 1937, criticizes FDR's Supreme Court proposal. *(FDR Library)*

By this time, the majority coalition Roosevelt had constructed out of urban Democratic machines, the Solid South, farmers, African Americans, immigrants, organized labor, and intellectuals was showing cracks. The CIO unions had found a powerful weapon in the sit-down strike, in which workers occupied the factories rather than form picket lines outside. Although successful in bringing such corporate giants as General Motors to recognize the demands of their workers, the sit-down strike seemed to many Americans to be an assault on the rights of private property. Caught in a difficult position in such industrial disputes, Roosevelt tried to take a middle ground, and in the midst of a bitter steel strike in 1937 the president said of labor and management, "A plague on both your houses." This served only to add to the strength of his opponents on both sides.

The Court fight, the labor unrest, and the recession left Roosevelt in a mood to strike back at those who had opposed him. He was especially angry at big businessmen, with whom he believed the blame for the recession rested, and conservative Democrats who had deserted him on the Court issue and other important congressional votes. The president struck a blow at the first group in April, 1938, when he called on Congress to enact measures that would tighten laws against monopolies. Congress responded in typical fashion by appointing a committee to investigate concentration in the economy. Roosevelt's antimonopoly campaign soon fizzled out when heightened military production took precedence over concerns about business concentration.

When it came to punishing opponents within the party, Roosevelt made a much bolder move. During the first years of his presidency, FDR had tried to rule by consensus. In 1935, he had identified himself with the lower and middle classes and maintained that stance through his landslide reelection the following year. He had moved during the first term from bipartisanship to partisanship. In 1938, he tried to go beyond partisanship and realign the parties. There should be some meaning to party labels, he reasoned, and those Democrats who consistently opposed their president's programs had no place in the party. At the beginning of the summer, Roosevelt announced that he would support in primary elections the opponents of certain conservative Democrats.

Roosevelt's attempted purge (the word had especially sinister connotations at the time of Stalin's horrible purges in the Soviet Union) failed. The reasons were several: The president had started too late; his personal popularity was not easily transferable; and those he opposed made an issue of state pride in not allowing an "outsider" to "dictate" to them. The failed purge was followed by substantial Republican gains in the general election of 1938. The GOP, reduced after 1936 to a minuscule 88 seats in the House, rose to 170 seats and picked up 8 in the Senate. Although the Democrats still held large majorities in both houses, Roosevelt could hardly expect to achieve new social reforms from the incoming Congress when the previous, overwhelmingly Democratic one had not been cooperative. The innovative period of the New Deal was over.

The Depression was not. In 1939, unemployment still hovered around 17 percent. It is clear that the New Deal had not solved the nation's economic woes. Roosevelt's policies had, however, brought great relief to many of those suffering the ravages of the Depression, and they had produced substantial reforms that changed the United States in lasting ways. Where the New Deal had not succeeded was in the other *R*, recovery. This failure was, it can be argued, not one of policy so much as it was of courage. The sorts of programs Roosevelt pushed could have brought about recovery, but neither the president nor the Congress had the courage to push them far enough to end the Depression.

Roosevelt's constant fear of deficit spending was, according to this view, the greatest impediment to recovery. Had he—and Congress—been willing to spend on domestic social programs the way the government did for military purposes after the outbreak of World War II, it is very likely that recovery from the Depression would have been achieved at a much earlier date. As it was, World War II ended the Depression.

Toward War and Reelection

As the New Deal was sputtering to a standstill in Roosevelt's second term, the president was giving increasing attention to foreign affairs. The rise of Hitler to power a few weeks before FDR took office in 1933 was a cause for worry from the outset of Roosevelt's presidency. In the early years of his administration, though, Roosevelt had to concentrate heavily on domestic economic matters. As Nazi Germany, Mussolini's Italy, and Japan started military adventures in the second half of the decade, Roosevelt became alarmed at the drift toward another world war. Not only were foreign problems becoming more pressing but also domestic ones had become so intractable that a turn to events abroad was a welcome change for the president.

The barriers to serious diplomatic action were formidable. Isolationism, rooted both in American tradition and in the conviction that bankers and munitions manufacturers—"merchants of death"—had led the nation into World War I, was a powerful force in the nation at large and even more so in the Senate. In 1935, as Italy invaded Ethiopia, FDR agreed to a Neutrality Act that embargoed arms shipments to all belligerents. Early in 1936, Nazi troops moved into the Rhineland, violating the treaties of Versailles and Locarno. A few months later, Fascists under General Francisco Franco began a civil war to overthrow the Spanish republic. The American response was to extend the provisions of the Neutrality Act to cover civil wars, thus preventing aid to the beleaguered republic. In mid-1937, the Japanese began a full-scale war in China.

In October, 1937, Roosevelt decided to test American sentiment on aggression. In a speech in Chicago. the president suggested that aggressor nations ought to be "quarantined" as were patients with contagious diseases. The quarantine speech amounted to running a bolder foreign policy up the flagpole to see how many would salute. Few did. "It's a terrible thing," FDR lamented, "to look over your shoulder when you are trying to lead—and to find no one there."

With the public adamant about not getting involved in overseas problems, Roosevelt could do little but watch as the dictators moved the world toward war. In March, 1938, Hitler seized Austria. Later in the year, he demanded that Czechoslovakia give him a large part of its territory. Hitler was of a mind to take the territory by force but was persuaded by Mussolini to invite the heads of the British and French governments to a conference at Munich, where the Western leaders would approve the German aggrandizement. Roosevelt's role in these maneuvers was minimal. When British prime minister Neville Chamberlain accepted Hitler's invitation to Munich, FDR wired, "Good man." The American president, however, had no illusions about Hitler. Seeing him for the madman that he was, Roosevelt was only waiting for American public opinion to catch up with him before taking a larger part in the world crisis.

Meanwhile, Hitler was tightening the noose around the Jewish people of Germany. Here was an area in which the American government could have taken humanitarian action of great consequence by allowing Jewish refugees to immigrate into the United States, but given the continued high unemployment rate, American public opinion ran strongly against easing the immigration quotas. When the Nazis went on a particularly terrible binge of destruction and assault against Jews in November of 1938, Roosevelt said, "I myself could scarcely believe that such things could occur in a twentieth-century civilization"—but 83 percent of the public opposed letting in more immigrants, and Roosevelt did not push to arouse the nation's conscience. It was not his finest hour.

In March of 1939, Hitler broke the pledge he had made at Munich five months earlier and seized the rest of Czechoslovakia. The next month Roosevelt sent cables to Hitler and Mussolini directly asking them whether they would promise not to attack thirty-one nations that the president listed. Hitler's response was delivered in a speech in which he sneeringly read the thirty-one names and indicated that the United

States was a greater threat to peace than was Germany.

This occurred only four months before the Nazis signed a nonaggression pact with the Soviet Union, carving up Poland in the process and precipitating World War II. The sympathies of Roosevelt, like those of most Americans, were clearly on the side of the British and the French, but still the overwhelming majority of Americans wanted their country to stay out of the war.

As the European crisis deepened, an American election year approached. No president (except, under unusual circumstances, an earlier Roosevelt) had ever broken the precedent established by George Washington of not seeking a third term. FDR, however, had remained noncommittal about such a possibility. This was good politics, since it lessened the problems created by being a lame duck from which second-term presidents usually suffer. With the war in Europe, the possibility grew that Roosevelt might run again.

If Roosevelt was to break the anti-third-term tradition, he would have to do so by answering the draft of his party and the people. In this way it could be said that he was not seeking a third term but was accepting a call to duty during a time of great crisis. Such a draft by the Democratic convention was inevitable with the president not having said he would refuse the nomination. God would provide a candidate, Roosevelt told his aides.

By the time Roosevelt was renominated in July, events in Europe had turned ominous. Hitler's Blitzkrieg had swept over Denmark, Norway, the Low Countries, and—shockingly—France. As the crisis worsened, Roosevelt took two defense-related steps that also were helpful to the cause of his reelection. In May, he

Adolf Hitler addresses a crowd on April 14, 1938. *(Library of Congress)*

asked Congress for funds to build "at least 50,000 planes a year." This appropriation provided a sharp stimulus to the lagging economy and marked the beginning of the end of the Depression. By the first Tuesday after the first Monday in November, the economic improvement would be obvious. Late in June, just before the Republican Convention, Roosevelt appointed Henry L. Stimson, who had been Hoover's secretary of state, as secretary of war, and Frank Knox, the 1936 Republican vice presidential candidate, as secretary of the Navy. The concept of bipartisan government in the face of international danger helped to blunt the third-term issue.

The Republicans nominated the previously little known Wendell L. Willkie, and for a time in the fall, his chances of unseating Roosevelt looked promising. The British, with their backs to the wall, were pleading for American assistance. In September, Roosevelt announced an exchange of fifty overage American destroyers for long-term leases on bases in British possessions in the Western Hemisphere. It was a noble and courageous act on Roosevelt's part, for the political risks were great. Willkie approved of

563

the idea, but he denounced Roosevelt for acting on his own, without congressional approval. The GOP nominee began charging that Roosevelt would lead America into the war. "If his promise to keep our boys out of foreign wars is no better than his promise to balance the budget," Willkie declared, "they're already almost on the transports."

Roosevelt waited until the last two weeks to campaign actively, but he did a masterful job. He contrasted Willkie's endorsement of some New Deal initiatives with the Republican policies of 1932, and he felt obliged to respond to Willkie's charges. "Your boys," the president flatly stated, "are not going to be sent into any foreign wars." With the solid backing of the lower classes, Roosevelt swept to easy victory, although Willkie was able to win eight states in addition to the two that Alfred Landon had carried four years earlier. The president was genuinely fearful of some of the right-wing elements behind Willkie. After the returns were in, FDR said to Joseph Lash, "We seem to have avoided a *Putsch*, Joe."

A Third Term and a Second World War
Even before his third term officially began, Franklin Roosevelt was faced with momentous decisions. The election results appeared to be an endorsement of his policy of providing material assistance to Great Britain but also an emphatic agreement with his promise to keep American boys out of foreign wars. On the other side of the world, tension was growing between the United States and Japan. Before the election, Roosevelt had decided to increase the pressure on the Japanese to stop their war against China. The president ordered an embargo on all shipments of scrap metal to the Far Eastern empire. American oil, which was absolutely vital to the Japanese, would still be made available to them.

The British need for war supplies was becoming desperate, but American neutrality legislation required that they pay for every-

thing they received from the United States, and they were no longer able to do so. While cruising in the Caribbean in December, Roosevelt hit on an idea to break through this impasse. The result was the Lend-Lease program, by which the United States would make supplies available to the British as they needed them and would be repaid in kind when the war was over. In announcing the concept at a press conference, the president employed one of the simple illustrations for which he was famous:

> Suppose my neighbor's home catches on fire, and I have a length of garden hose four or five hundred feet away. If he can take my garden hose and connect it up with his hydrant, I may help him put out his fire. Now what do I do? I don't say to him before that operation, "Neighbor, my garden hose cost me $15, you have to pay me $15 for it." What is the transaction that goes on? I don't want $15—I want my garden hose back after the fire is over.

Lend-Lease was a brilliant stroke for furnishing aid to Britain and, later, other nations fighting the Nazis. In 1941, the United States became, in Roosevelt's words in a fireside chat, "the great arsenal for democracy." This, he told the American people, was the best way to keep the nation out of the war. The Lend-Lease program still had to be accepted by isolationists in Congress, such as Burton K. Wheeler of Montana, who declared, "The lend-lease-give program is the New Deal's triple A foreign policy; it will plow under every fourth American boy." Overcoming such venomous attacks, Roosevelt obtained congressional approval of the Lend-Lease Act in March, 1941, and immediately asked for an unprecedented appropriation of seven billion dollars to fund the program.

Roosevelt had begun 1941 by presenting his vision of a just world. In the context of an economic bill of rights, the president said the world should be based upon Four Freedoms:

freedom of speech, freedom of religion, freedom from want, and freedom from fear. Here, nearly a year before the United States entered World War II, FDR was presenting a shorthand formula for the ideals that the Allies should seek in the war. There was no longer much pretense of American neutrality. The United States had become an active nonbelligerent, clearly on the anti-Nazi side but not involved in the fighting. It was a strange situation. Roosevelt and other Americans were calling on other nations to give their all against the Nazi menace, which the Americans clearly perceived to be a threat to themselves as well as to others, while Americans remained at a safe distance three thousand miles from the fighting.

The Roosevelt and American position in the war became even more anomalous in the summer of 1941, when the president secretly went to Argentia Harbor, Newfoundland, for a conference with British prime minister Winston Churchill. The purpose of the meeting was to discuss war strategy—an odd undertaking for a country that was not supposed to be at war. As it happened, though, no important strategic decisions were reached at the Argentia Conference. Its impact came instead from a declaration of war aims, the Atlantic Charter, to which Roosevelt and Churchill agreed. The Atlantic Charter provided a general framework for the Allied vision of what the postwar world ought to be like. It was for Americans in World War II what Woodrow Wilson's Fourteen Points had been in World War I and in fact addressed some of the same ideals: equal access to world trade, freedom of the seas, "no territorial changes that do not accord with the freely expressed wishes of the peoples concerned," self-government for all nations under forms of their own choosing, a secure peace for all nations, and arms reductions. Partly reiterating Roosevelt's call for the Four Freedoms, the Atlantic Charter also looked forward to "the fullest collaboration between all Nations in the economic field with the object of securing, for all, improved labor standards, economic advancement, and social security."

Such an elaboration of war aims must surely be a prelude to American entry into the war. Not so, Roosevelt insisted. This insistence points up an important question about his leadership. As biographer James M. Burns has noted, "Roosevelt would lead—but not by more than a step. He seemed beguiled by public opinion, by its strange combinations of fickleness and rigidity, ignorance and comprehension, by rapidly shifting optimism and pessimism." Clare Booth Luce, Republican congresswoman from Connecticut and wife of *Time-Life-Fortune* publisher Henry Luce, said that the gesture that symbolized FDR was not Churchill's "V for victory" sign but a wet finger held in the air to judge the direction of the wind. Luce was no friend of Roosevelt, and her characterization may seem unduly harsh, but it was not very far from the mark. FDR's view of the role of leadership in a democracy was to stay close to public desires, to try to shape the attitudes of the people but never to alter them drastically. Far more than most people realized at the time, Roosevelt relied on scientific samplings of public opinion in reaching his decisions. Opinion analyst Hadley Cantril of Princeton University frequently provided the president with polling results. This is one of the many ways in which FDR set the tone for subsequent presidents, who have often been guided more by polls than by principles.

Roosevelt did have principles; he really believed in the Four Freedoms and the ideals stated in the Atlantic Charter. He also believed that the defeat of the Nazis was essential to the realization of those goals and that active American participation in the war would be necessary to achieve victory over the forces of evil unleashed by Hitler. In 1941, Roosevelt understood that the American people agreed with him on all of these points except the last. In the 1940 campaign, he had encouraged the belief that the United States could aid the Allies but

Franklin D. Roosevelt's address to Congress regarding the Japanese attack on Pearl Harbor, December 8, 1941:

Mr. Vice President, Mr. Speaker, Members of the Senate, and of the House of Representatives:

Yesterday, December 7th, 1941—a date which will live in infamy—the United States of America was suddenly and deliberately attacked by naval and air forces of the Empire of Japan.

The United States was at peace with that nation and, at the solicitation of Japan, was still in conversation with its government and its emperor looking toward the maintenance of peace in the Pacific.

Indeed, one hour after Japanese air squadrons had commenced bombing in the American island of Oahu, the Japanese ambassador to the United States and his colleague delivered to our Secretary of State a formal reply to a recent American message. And while this reply stated that it seemed useless to continue the existing diplomatic negotiations, it contained no threat or hint of war or of armed attack.

It will be recorded that the distance of Hawaii from Japan makes it obvious that the attack was deliberately planned many days or even weeks ago. During the intervening time, the Japanese government has deliberately sought to deceive the United States by false statements and expressions of hope for continued peace.

The attack yesterday on the Hawaiian islands has caused severe damage to American naval and military forces. I regret to tell you that very many American lives have been lost. In addition, American ships have been reported torpedoed on the high seas between San Francisco and Honolulu.

Yesterday, the Japanese government also launched an attack against Malaya.

Last night, Japanese forces attacked Hong Kong.

Last night, Japanese forces attacked Guam.

Last night, Japanese forces attacked the Philippine Islands.

Last night, the Japanese attacked Wake Island.

And this morning, the Japanese attacked Midway Island.

Japan has, therefore, undertaken a surprise offensive extending throughout the Pacific area. The facts of yesterday and today speak for themselves. The people of the United States have already formed their opinions and well understand the implications to the very life and safety of our nation.

As commander in chief of the Army and Navy, I have directed that all measures be taken for our defense. But always will our whole nation remember the character of the onslaught against us.

No matter how long it may take us to overcome this premeditated invasion, the American people in their righteous might will win through to absolute victory.

I believe that I interpret the will of the Congress and of the people when I assert that we will not only defend ourselves to the uttermost, but will make it very certain that this form of treachery shall never again endanger us.

Hostilities exist. There is no blinking at the fact that our people, our territory, and our interests are in grave danger.

With confidence in our armed forces, with the unbounding determination of our people, we will gain the inevitable triumph—so help us God.

I ask that the Congress declare that since the unprovoked and dastardly attack by Japan on Sunday, December 7th, 1941, a state of war has existed between the United States and the Japanese empire.

stay out of the war. In 1941, he continued to go along with this popular impression. By the fall of that year, Roosevelt probably could have pushed a war declaration through Congress, but it would have left the country bitterly divided, and he had no desire to lead a disunited country into war. The president would wait for events that would solidify the public behind an all-out war effort.

Such events were not long in coming. Roosevelt had given his permission for American naval vessels in the Atlantic to transmit to their British counterparts the location of German submarines they encountered. Here was another distinctly unneutral act, but Hitler was anxious to postpone American entry into the war as long as possible, and he ordered his U-boat commanders to avoid hostile actions against American ships. In September, 1941, however, an American destroyer, the USS *Greer*, trailed a German U-boat for two hours, reporting its position to a British plane, which dropped depth charges at the submarine. Finally, the U-boat launched torpedoes at the *Greer*. They missed, but Roosevelt at last had an incident that gave him a pretext for widening American efforts against the Nazis. He declared that the United States Navy would guard the western half of the Atlantic and that if any German or Italian warships entered the region, American officers had orders to shoot on sight. This amounted to a declaration of naval war in a large part of the Atlantic and freed British ships to operate in the eastern half of the ocean. American ships would guard British ships to Iceland. Roosevelt called his new policy "active defense."

Still Hitler did not make a hostile move against the United States. He had already plunged himself into a two-front war in July when he broke his nonaggression pact with the Soviet Union and launched an invasion of that country. This new Nazi aggression had presented Roosevelt with an important choice. Should Lend-Lease assistance be made available to the Soviets, whose Communist government many Americans detested almost as much as they did Hitler's regime? Senator Harry S. Truman of Missouri spoke for many when he said, "If we see that Germany is winning we ought to help Russia and if Russia is winning we ought to help Germany and in that way let them kill as many as possible."

Germany was winning, but Roosevelt had motives for extending aid to the Soviets other than that cited by Truman. Although the president had no liking for the communists, he realized that they did not at that time pose a serious threat to the United States. The Nazis did, and anyone who was fighting them deserved American assistance. Lend-Lease aid began to flow into the Soviet Union.

For all the concern over the Nazi horrors and the growing American participation in the Atlantic war, it was from the Pacific that the United States was to be drawn fully into the conflict. Roosevelt's short-term objective in the Pacific was to delay a showdown with Japan, but while Roosevelt sought to put off confrontation, time was running out for the Japanese. Militarists were insistent on bringing matters to a head. They were aware of the American military buildup, which would eventually tip the scales in favor of the United States. When Japan occupied the French colony of Indochina in July, President Roosevelt froze all Japanese credits in the United States, bringing trade between the two nations to a halt. Roosevelt also cut off shipments of high-octane gasoline to the Japanese. He was trying to blend conciliation and pressure into a policy that would bring concessions from Japan. It almost worked. Japanese prime minister Fumimaro Konoye sought a personal meeting with the president. Roosevelt would agree only if the Japanese would pledge in advance to withdraw from China. Although the civilian leaders of the island nation might have accepted this demand, they had to contend with the militarists. The latter convinced Emperor Hirohito to agree in the fall to a

The USS *West Virginia*, USS *Tennessee*, and USS *Arizona* on fire in Pearl Harbor on December 7, 1941. *(U.S. Navy/National Archives)*

timetable that placed a strict limitation on diplomacy. If the diplomats had not gained concessions from the Americans by the end of November, the military would take over and launch an attack.

Much of this was known to Roosevelt, because American cryptographers had broken the main Japanese diplomatic code. This fact has led some Roosevelt critics to charge that he knew in advance of the attack on Pearl Harbor and allowed it to occur in order to get the country into the war. This charge misses two important points. First, Roosevelt did want the United States to enter the war, but against Germany, not Japan. Second, Roosevelt knew only that the Japanese planned an attack in early December, not where that attack would take place. The assumption was that it would be against

the Dutch West Indies, British Malaya, or the American Philippines. Few thought the Japanese would venture as far east as Hawaii.

The Japanese surprise attack on Pearl Harbor on December 7, 1941, produced a unified American nation. In mid-November, Congress had passed by very narrow margins a president-sponsored bill to arm American merchant ships. In the Senate, 37 voted nay; in the House, 194 members opposed the measure. Less than four weeks later, the Senate unanimously passed a declaration of war and only one member of the House voted against it.

Although this was the wrong war, Hitler solved that problem by abiding by his treaty with Japan and declaring war on the United States on December 11. Americans were united as they had never been before.

The Home Front

The war solved some domestic problems and exacerbated others. Most significantly, it ended the Depression. The effects of the economic collapse were still evident as Roosevelt's third term began. Of the first one million men drafted for military service in 1940 and 1941, 13 percent were rejected for reasons stemming from malnutrition. Unemployment still stood at eight million in 1940 despite the early military buildup. By 1944, it had fallen to 670,000, about 1 percent of a greatly enlarged workforce. Not only had almost all of those who had been unable to find work in the 1930's obtained jobs, but also millions of people, mostly women and minorities, had entered the labor market and found employment.

Production for military purposes soared to fantastic levels. Family incomes rose rapidly, and the share of the nation's income going to lower groups on the socioeconomic scale increased, as families that had previously had no employed wage earner sent two or more members into war plants.

All of this was mainly to the good, but problems also arose. The migration of people to the locations of defense plants disrupted communities and families and created critical housing shortages. The growth of consumer incomes at a time when consumer goods were in short supply threatened to produce runaway inflation. The unprecedented spending (the incomprehensible figure of some $100 billion in fiscal 1944) that cured the Depression would at the same time swell the national debt to record levels. The demand for labor made the task of union organizers easier, and membership jumped by six million during the war, reaching 25 percent of the labor force. Yet strikes could endanger the war effort. Also, the flow of rural Southern blacks into urban areas where jobs were available led both to a growing awareness of the disparity between the antiracist rhetoric of the war against Nazism and the reality of life for African Americans and to friction between black and white workers in war industries.

Roosevelt was forced to try to deal with these domestic problems at the same time that he was engaged in the largest war in human history. Before U.S. entry into the war, African Americans, angry at discrimination in defense industries and the armed forces, threatened a massive march on Washington, D.C., in the summer of 1941. Alarmed at what such a demonstration might do to America's image abroad, Roosevelt reluctantly agreed to issue Executive Order 8802, which called on defense employers and unions to treat everyone equally and created a Fair Employment Practices Commission (FEPC). The FEPC was a toothless organization, but its creation marked a turning point in the federal attitude toward racial discrimination, and Roosevelt deserves some credit for the step, even though he took it under duress.

The needs of the wartime economy led to a new proliferation of federal agencies and far more governmental regulation than had existed in the New Deal years. The activities of the Office of Production Management and the Office of War Mobilization organized the American economy with more efficiency than it had ever known before. The Office of Price Administration had to resort to rationing of scarce commodities, but it did a remarkable job of holding down the inflationary pressures inherent in a war economy. Roosevelt would have done more along these lines had Congress been willing to go along. The president was insistent that war profiteering be checked. His attempts to impose confiscatory taxes on the highest incomes—he said that during the war no one should be allowed to have an after-tax income in excess of twenty-five thousand dollars—were rejected by Congress. Although taxes were raised substantially during the war, they did not come close to matching spending levels. That the resulting deficit produced full employment meant that an important legacy of the

Roosevelt war years would be a much greater acceptance of Keynesian economics, although no evidence exists that FDR himself ever accepted the deficit doctrine.

On the whole, organized labor was cooperative during the war, but there were exceptions. Most notable was Roosevelt's longtime adversary, John L. Lewis. In 1943, the United Mine Workers' chief attempted to defy the president's wage and price stabilization program. Roosevelt responded by seizing the coal mines and threatening to draft striking miners.

One of the most important developments on the home front during World War II was the emergence of a permanent defense industry that would be needed to construct the sophisticated weapons of modern warfare. These complex weapons also required well-trained soldiers to operate them, which meant an ominous departure from the American democratic tradition against a large standing army in peacetime. It also marked the beginning of the military-industrial complex that Dwight D. Eisenhower would warn about nearly two decades later.

The dangers that a standing army and a military-industrial linkage posed to American democracy were real but not immediate. The worst blot on American democratic practice during World War II was the treatment of Japanese Americans. In the wake of the Pearl Harbor attack, anti-Japanese actions were to be expected, but few materialized at first (although someone did cut down several Japanese cherry trees around the Tidal Basin in Washington, D.C.). Soon, however, white Californians began to turn harshly against their neighbors of Japanese ancestry. Thirty-six incidents of "violent patriotism" against Japanese Americans had been reported by March, 1942. Some "patriots" chose odd ways in which to express their love of country. Along with seven murders and nineteen assaults were two rapes of Japanese American women. To protect these citizens

against such attacks, but more to guard against the possibility of sabotage, President Roosevelt early in 1942 signed an order to evacuate all people of Japanese ancestry from the West Coast. Concern about sabotage was not based on any evidence. General John De Witt, who oversaw the removal, admitted that no fifth column activities had occurred, but said, "The very fact that no sabotage has taken place is a disturbing and confirming indication that such action will be taken." The result of these essentially racial fears was that approximately 110,000 Japanese Americans, some 70,000 of whom were native-born United States citizens, were uprooted and placed in "relocation centers," which Roosevelt more forthrightly called concentration camps. Their only crime was their race.

No similar actions were taken against German or Italian Americans, although Roosevelt was worried about the former. "I don't care so much about the Italians," the president said privately. "They are a lot of opera singers, but the Germans are different, they may be dangerous." FDR was not enthusiastic about the internment of Japanese Americans, but he went along with one of the greatest assaults on the civil liberties of a group of American citizens in the history of the United States.

President Roosevelt's openness to new ideas led him into the greatest technological undertaking of the era. In 1939, a group of physicists who were alarmed at reports that scientists in Nazi Germany were making progress in the area of nuclear fission asked Albert Einstein to write to the president and explain to him the possibility of the construction of bombs with enormous explosive power. Einstein's letter was taken to Roosevelt by Alexander Sachs, a friend of the president, who persuaded him of the urgency of the matter and of the nearly incomprehensible danger should the Nazis succeed in developing atomic weapons before the democratic nations did. Roosevelt promptly started an exploratory program in nuclear fission. After American entry into the war, it expanded rapidly.

The Manhattan Project eventually employed 150,000 people at sites around the country. The secrecy of the undertaking required that Congress appropriate vast sums of money without knowing the nature of the project on which the funds were being spent. Great Britain and the United States cooperated in atomic research from the start, but Roosevelt was reluctant to inform the Soviets. By the time of the president's death in the spring of 1945, the Manhattan Project was nearing its awful climax, but no decision about using it for postwar cooperation had been made.

The Good War

The early months of American participation in World War II were not encouraging. Japanese forces swallowed up islands across the western Pacific. American troops in the Philippines fought valiantly, but they finally had to surrender. On the other side of the world, Hitler had been unable to knock the Soviet Union out of the war or to mount an invasion of England, but the Germans were still on the offensive and both of those feats still seemed possible.

Well before Pearl Harbor, President Roosevelt had settled on an "Atlantic first" strategy. He saw the Nazis as a more formidable threat than the Japanese. The latter would be held by delaying actions while American forces were built up to defeat Germany. Throughout the war, Roosevelt's primary goal was to win a decisive military victory in the shortest possible time, with the fewest possible American casualties. He was very much concerned with achieving his objectives for the postwar world, but he did not believe that he had a right to extend the war for these purposes.

This view was not shared by the leaders of the United States' chief allies. Both Churchill and Stalin always kept an eye on their postwar goals as they made wartime decisions. Stalin's desperate need in 1942 was the opening by the western Allies of a second front that would draw German troops away from the Soviet front. Churchill was in no hurry to do this favor for his communist ally, and it was not without reason that Stalin complained that the British leader was willing to let the Soviets absorb the bulk of the Allied casualties. Roosevelt was more ready to provide relief for the hard-pressed Soviets and was also anxious to have American troops get into action against the Nazis. Churchill was adamant in insisting that the Allies did not yet have sufficient strength to risk an attack across the English Channel. The two leaders agreed on a fall, 1942, offensive in French North Africa. Operation Torch furnished little relief to the Soviets and was not of much strategic significance in winning the war, but it did give American forces a chance to engage the enemy.

As the North African campaign continued in late 1942, a more significant military development was occurring deep in the Soviet Union. The Red Army stopped the penetration of Hitler's troops at Stalingrad, held their ground in a horrible struggle, and finally began to push the Germans back. The Nazis were far from beaten, but they had ceased to advance.

In the late weeks of 1942, the tide also began to turn against the Japanese. American forces won a costly struggle with the Japanese on Guadalcanal, in the Solomon Islands. It was a long way to Tokyo, but like their Axis partners the Japanese were now on the defensive. There was cause for optimism when Roosevelt and Churchill met at Casablanca in January, 1943, to discuss strategy. In making the trip to Morocco, Roosevelt became the first American president to journey abroad during wartime and the first since Lincoln to enter a zone of war.

At Casablanca, Churchill gradually persuaded his American counterpart that a cross-channel invasion should be postponed in favor of an attack in the Mediterranean, into what the British leader termed the "soft underbelly" of the Axis. Although Roosevelt was always confident of his persuasive abilities in face-to-face meetings, it was Churchill who was usually successful in swinging the American president over to his way of thinking. Still, as the Atlantic Charter had overshadowed strategic decisions at Argentia, it was a statement at the end of the Casablanca meeting that became its most significant product. At a press conference at the conclusion of the meetings, Roosevelt said, "The elimination of German, Japanese, and Italian war power means the unconditional surrender by Germany, Italy, or Japan." This policy had not been agreed on by the leaders at Casablanca, but Roosevelt's public statement made it Allied policy. Some have questioned its wisdom, suggesting that the demand for unconditional surrender stiffened enemy resistance and hindered efforts by German military leaders to overthrow Hitler. Roosevelt, however, well remembered how the armistice that ended World War I had given Hitler an opportunity to gain a following by falsely claiming that the German military had not really been defeated. When the courses of Germany and Japan after World War II are contrasted with that of Germany after the first war, Roosevelt's insistence on unconditional surrender appears to be vindicated.

Churchill continued to oppose a "premature" invasion of France and to argue instead for further adventures in the Mediterranean. The Anglo-Americans won a fairly quick victory in Sicily, and when they landed in Italy Mussolini was overthrown. Soon the Italian government surrendered, but German troops rapidly moved in and made the soft underbelly hard. The troops of the western Allies remained bogged down on the Italian peninsula through 1943 and into 1944. Meanwhile, the Red Army slowly advanced on the long Soviet front and Stalin's anger over the repeated postponements of the cross-channel invasion grew.

Tension between the Soviets and the West was high. The alliance was one of necessity, not choice. It was held together by the cement of a common enemy. Lesser, but still significant, differences existed between Roosevelt and Churchill. The British leader favored a division of much of the postwar world into spheres of influence dominated by the three major powers. Roosevelt, an old Wilsonian, preferred a greater reliance on an international peacekeeping organization. Roosevelt understood the forces of nationalism that were rising in Asia and believed that the principles of the Atlantic Charter should be applied to colonial possessions. He was particularly anxious to keep the French from returning to Indochina and to persuade the British to take steps toward Indian independence. Churchill made his opposing position clear: "I have not become the King's First Minister in order to preside over the liquidation of the British Empire." Roosevelt was on the correct side in opposing colonialism, but he was unwilling to increase the pressure on his friend and ally.

Stalin's reluctance to travel far from the fighting in his country and his anger at the failure of the allies to open a second front in France had led him to decline previous invitations to meet with Roosevelt. The first gathering of the Big Three took place in November, 1943, at Tehran. Roosevelt's confidence in his ability to deal with people in a face-to-face meeting was put to a great test. The president tried to win Stalin over by teasing Churchill. The Soviet dictator joined in the fun but was happy with Roosevelt only when the American agreed with him in opposing Churchill's desires for further peripheral actions in the Mediterranean. It was agreed at Tehran that the Anglo-American invasion of German-held France, named Operation Overlord, would begin in the spring of 1944. Roosevelt's emphasis on quick victory had finally prevailed over Churchill's strategic hopes for the postwar world.

Great differences among the Allies remained, and out of those differences the Cold War developed during the later stages of World War II. The greatest problem areas were the disposition of Eastern Europe (especially Poland), the scope and power of the international organization to be formed, and the treatment of the defeated Germans. All of these difficult issues were left unresolved at Tehran.

As the war continued, reports of Nazi atrocities mounted. In 1942, word reached the White House that Hitler had ordered the "final solution" of what he termed the "Jewish problem": the systematic slaughter of all Jewish people the Nazis could find. At the end of that year, Rabbi Stephen Wise gave FDR a paper outlining Hitler's "Blue Print for Extermination." In the summer of 1943, *The New York Times* published a story documenting the Nazis' systematic murder of at least 1.7 million people. Roosevelt could not plead ignorance of the Holocaust as an excuse for not taking more effective steps to counteract it.

Early in 1944, Treasury Secretary Henry Morgenthau asked his department's general counsel, Randolph Paul, to write a report on the situation. Paul's "Report to the Secretary on the Acquiescence of this Government in the Murder of Jews" pulled no punches. It charged that the United States State Department had failed to do what it could to rescue Jews and in fact had stood in the way of private efforts to do so. "One of the greatest crimes in history, the slaughter of the Jewish people in Europe, is continuing unabated," Paul correctly declared. Faced with this and other evidence, Roosevelt set up a War Refugee Board, but the president never took much effective action to halt the Holocaust. He steadfastly refused to seek changes in the immigration laws, worried about angering Muslims in the Middle East, and did not order the bombing of railroad tracks leading to

The D day invasion of Normandy as seen from a landing barge. (*Coast Guard/National Archives*)

the death camps. Roosevelt maintained that the rapid defeat of Hitler would be the most effective means of stopping the horror.

The decisive step toward ending the war came with the D day invasion on the beaches of Normandy in June of 1944. Once General Dwight D. Eisenhower's forces had established themselves on the Continent, it was only a matter of time until Hitler's armies were vanquished. With the exception of a startling Nazi counteroffensive in December, 1944 (the Battle of the Bulge), the Allied vise closed steadily on the Nazis from east and west.

During these final months of war in Europe, the American political calendar called for a presidential election. Roosevelt insisted that he wanted to retire, but he was determined to see the war through to a successful conclusion. There was no pretense of a draft in 1944; the president made it plain that he was available for a fourth term. His long tenure in the White House was no longer much of an issue. As a popular joke had it, "If he was good enough for my pappy, and good enough for my grandpappy, then he's good enough for me!"

The only serious questions concerned Roosevelt's health and his running mate. The sixty-two-year-old chief executive was noticeably older and less vigorous than he had been during his previous campaigns. He was suffering from an enlarged heart and high blood pressure. These particulars were unknown to the public, but his appearance was a cause for concern.

Vice President Henry Wallace was anathema to conservative Democrats, who considered him a leftist visionary. Roosevelt had forced Wallace on a reluctant party in 1940; he could do it again. As was his wont, FDR indicated to several prospective running mates that each had his backing. In the end the choice fell on Harry S. Truman, a border state senator who had been faithful in support of the New Deal. As is the case with most decisions on vice presi-

dential candidates, this one was made with political considerations in mind, not with a thought that the person chosen might soon become president.

The Republicans chose Thomas E. Dewey, the forty-two-year-old governor of New York, who was noted for his drive and lack of humor. Roosevelt's main tasks in the 1944 race were to demonstrate his health and to get people to go to the polls. The former was accomplished with a few good speeches and a lengthy open-air motorcade through a downpour in New York. This was surely of no benefit to the president's health, but it was a great help to the image of his health.

The job of getting people to turn out on Election Day was more difficult. The people most likely to vote for Roosevelt were often those least likely to vote, especially during the war, when so many were away from home in the armed services or had moved to different voting jurisdictions in search of defense industry employment. The consequence was a low turnout and the narrowest of Roosevelt's four national victories. The margin was comfortable, though: 3.6 million popular votes and 432 to 99 in the electoral college.

One result of FDR's reelection was that the American people seemed to have endorsed United States participation in a new world organization. The structure of the United Nations was one of the major topics to be addressed when the Big Three convened at the Soviet Crimean resort of Yalta in February, 1945. The leaders did reach agreement on the United Nations. The major powers were to have vetoes over U.N. actions and resolutions, a point on which Stalin would not budge. The question of Poland was more perplexing. With a substantial number of Polish American constituents to consider, Roosevelt wanted a democratic government in Poland. Stalin, whose country had been invaded via Poland twice in less than thirty years, demanded a government in that country that would be friendly to the Soviet Union. Both positions were reasonable. Unfortunately, they were incompatible. The long history of Russian domination of Poland meant that any popularly elected Polish government would be unfriendly toward Moscow. Since the Red Army was already in possession of most of Poland, there was little that Roosevelt and Churchill could do at Yalta but try to convince Stalin that he should broaden the communist-oriented government that he had already established in the country. This the Soviet leader finally agreed to do, but in terms so loose as to be nearly meaningless.

Contrary to the later charges of his political opponents, Roosevelt did not "give Poland away" at Yalta, either intentionally or because of ill health. He never had Poland in the first place and had to accept the best deal he could get from Stalin. Moreover, Roosevelt did achieve one of his primary objectives at Yalta. Stalin agreed to declare war on Japan three months after the Germans surrendered. At the time of Yalta, American military analysts still expected the Japanese war to last a long time, and Soviet intervention was prized as a way to save tens of thousands, perhaps hundreds of thousands, of American lives.

Undoubtedly, Roosevelt was in poor health at the Crimean conference. This does not appear to have affected his judgment, but by the time he returned from the arduous journey, he was very weak. After a halting report to Congress, delivered from a seated position, the president went to Warm Springs, Georgia, for a period of recuperation. While there on the afternoon of April 12, 1945, in the company of his former mistress, Lucy Mercer Rutherfurd, the president suffered a "terrific headache." Less than three hours later, the longest presidency in American history reached its end.

FDR and the American Presidency

The man Americans mourned in the spring of 1945, less than a month before the defeat of Germany and four months before the Japanese surrender, is generally acknowledged to rank with George Washington and Abraham Lincoln as one of the greatest presidents. Circumstances helped to provide opportunities for greatness for each of these leaders: precedent setting for Washington as the first president, preserving the Union during the Civil War for Lincoln, and meeting the two greatest crises of twentieth century America—the Great Depression and World War II—for Franklin D. Roosevelt.

"If during the lifetime of a generation no crisis occurs sufficient to call out in marked manner the energies of the strongest leader," Franklin Roosevelt's cousin Theodore once said, "then of course the world does not and cannot know of the existence of such a leader; and in consequence there are long periods in the history of every nation during which no man appears who leaves an indelible mark in history." That fate may, to a degree, have befallen Theodore Roosevelt, but Franklin Roosevelt did not lack challenges. "There is," he declared in his 1936 acceptance speech, "a mysterious cycle in human events. To some generations much is given. Of other generations much is expected. This generation of Americans has a rendezvous with destiny."

Crises may furnish an opportunity for greatness, but it is left up to the individual to deal with them in such a way that he or she will be judged a great leader. This FDR did. His confidence, humanitarianism, and dedication to democracy led the nation through hard times and war during an era in which democratic beliefs were besieged. Franklin D. Roosevelt is one of the few leaders of whom it can be said without hesitation that the world would have been a greatly different place had he not lived. Had a conservative been elected in 1932, conditions might have continued to deteriorate to the point of revolution; had a radical won, he might well have taken the nation toward socialism. American democracy is strong, but it needed a great champion in the 1930's and 1940's. Roosevelt filled that role admirably.

The leaders of the Big Three (left to right): Soviet premier Joseph Stalin, FDR, and British prime minister Winston Churchill. *(Library of Congress)*

Certainly, FDR had many faults. Yet in the end what stands out about him is that he gave the United States the courage and outlook necessary for the country to survive its worst economic collapse and its largest international war and to emerge from both a stronger nation than it had been before those upheavals.

Roosevelt was not an intellectual. He always preferred to obtain information from people rather than books. He was a politician and a moralist, in the best sense of those words. His moralism grew out of his aristocratic heritage. He brought the sense of stewardship that was ingrained in people of his class to the national government. By thus blending morality with economics, responsibility with government, he met the desires of a people wracked by depression and in the process established a new role for the federal government. That role was not one of dominance but of caring.

Roosevelt's view of government was expansive. He believed that government in a democracy was an instrument of the people and should be used to meet their needs. He was certainly not a socialist, but he believed that making capitalism more humane through reform and government regulation was essential to saving the economic system.

Not only was Roosevelt not a socialist but also he was the antithesis of an ideologue. He loved to try to combine opposites, to experiment in an eclectic fashion to see what would work. He was guided by common sense rather than a coherent philosophy. Once he made a decision, he rarely looked back to second-guess it. His brand of leadership was to stay close to the wishes of the people. This can be criticized as government by opinion poll or weather vane, but it can also be praised as the essence of democratic government. Roosevelt was one of the best interpreters of public attitudes ever to sit in the White House. His personal popularity was extraordinary, even among people who were unsure of his policies. In 1938, at a time when Roosevelt's political rating had declined, polls indicated that 80 percent of all Americans liked him as a person and only 10 percent disliked him.

Roosevelt's style of administration was similar to his practice in other realms. He did not like to delegate too much authority to any one aide or administrator, preferred informal gatherings of advisers to formal use of the cabinet, and liked to draw advisers from differing perspectives and shift his favor from one to another. He also had the faults of his virtues. His practical, one-problem-at-a-time approach was helpful in resolving many issues, but it prevented long-range planning that might have been useful in dealing with both the economy and the war.

Roosevelt's failings, real though they were, pale when placed beside his accomplishments.

Just before taking office, Roosevelt said that the presidency is preeminently a place of moral leadership. So it was during his long tenure in the White House. He made the office of president far more powerful and much more the center of national attention than it had ever been before. Lincoln may have decided the question of whether the term "United States" is singular or plural, but Franklin Roosevelt gave real meaning to the unity of the country. Most Americans after Roosevelt look to the federal government as a means of solving problems and look to the White House to offer possible solutions. Every president after Franklin D. Roosevelt lives, as historian William Leuchtenberg put it, "in the shadow of FDR."

Robert S. McElvaine

Suggested Readings

Abbott, Philip. *The Exemplary Presidency: Franklin D. Roosevelt and the American Political Tradition.* Amherst: University of Massachusetts Press, 1990. Appraises the legacy of Roosevelt.

Buhite, Russell D., and David W. Levy, eds. *FDR's Fireside Chats.* Norman: University of Oklahoma Press, 1992. Gathers transcripts of thirty-one fireside chats delivered in the thirteen years of Roosevelt's presidency.

Burns, James M. *Roosevelt: The Lion and the Fox.* 1956. Reprint. New York: Smithmark, 1996. A comprehensive, two-volume biography from a preeminent presidential scholar.

Davis, Kenneth S. *FDR: Into the Storm.* New York: Random House, 1993. Davis, in this penultimate volume of his five-book biography of Roosevelt, covers Roosevelt's response to growing fascism in Europe and his 1940 campaign, among other topics.

_____. *FDR: The War President, 1940-1943.* New York: Random House, 2000. The last of Davis's five volumes on Roosevelt covers the entrance of the United States into World War II and Roosevelt's handling of war diplomacy and the domestic homefront.

Ferrell, Robert H. *The Dying President: Franklin D. Roosevelt.* Columbia: University of Missouri, 1998. Chronicles Roosevelt's decline in health and speculates on the consequences of his incapacity during the final days of World War II.

Franklin D. Roosevelt Presidential Library and Museum. http://www.fdrlibrary.marist.edu/. The Web site for Roosevelt's official library.

Freidel, Frank. *Franklin D. Roosevelt.* 4 vols. Boston: Little, Brown, 1952-1990. Four volumes cover Roosevelt's early years up to his launching of the New Deal.

_____. *Franklin D. Roosevelt: A Rendezvous with Destiny.* Boston: Back Bay Books, 1991. A single-volume biography that covers Roosevelt's life and accomplishments thoroughly.

Goodwin, Doris Kearns. *No Ordinary Time: Franklin and Eleanor Roosevelt: The Home Front in World War II.* New York: Simon & Schuster, 1994. A meticulously detailed biography, which won the Pulitzer Prize, of the Roosevelts spanning from 1940 to 1949.

Jenkins, Roy. *Franklin Delano Roosevelt.* New York: Henry Holt, 2003. Jenkins, a historian and former politician, approaches Roosevelt's biography with an emphasis on FDR's character and personality.

Lash, Joseph P. *Eleanor and Franklin.* New York: New American Library, 1971. Details the relationship between the president and the first lady based on personal papers of Mrs. Roosevelt.

Leuchtenberg, William Edward. *The FDR Years: On Roosevelt and His Legacy.* New York: Columbia University Press, 1995. A book of interpretation of the New Deal from a notable historian of FDR.

McElvaine, Robert S. *The Great Depression: America, 1929-1941.* Rev. ed. New York: Times Books, 1993. Provides interpretive essays of Roosevelt's first two terms.

Maney, Patrick J. *The Roosevelt Presence: A Biog-*

raphy of Franklin Delano Roosevelt. New York: Twayne, 1998. A biography and an analysis of Roosevelt's legacy, emphasizing that he transformed the modern-day presidency.

Miller, Nathan. *FDR: An Intimate History*. Garden City, N.Y.: Doubleday, 1983. A standard but thorough biography.

Rozell, Mark J., and William D. Peterson, eds. *FDR and the Modern Presidency: Leadership and Legacy*. Westport, Conn.: Praeger, 1997. A series of essays examine the impact of Roosevelt's administrations on the modern presidency.

Schlesinger, Arthur M., Jr. *The Age of Roosevelt*. 3 vols. Boston: Houghton Mifflin, 1957-1960. A multivolume work of the life and times of Roosevelt.

Thompson, Robert S. *A Time for War: Franklin Delano Roosevelt and the Path to Pearl Harbor*. New York: Prentice Hall Press, 1991. Argues that Roosevelt provoked war with Japan and Germany.

Ward, Geoffrey C. *Before the Trumpet: Young Franklin Roosevelt, 1882-1905*. New York: Harper and Row, 1985. A detailed account of the future president's early years.

Harry S. Truman

33d President, 1945-1953

Born: May 8, 1884
    Lamar, Missouri
Died: December 26, 1972
    Kansas City, Missouri

Political Party: Democratic
Vice President: Alben W. Barkley

Cabinet Members

Secretary of State: James F. Byrnes, George C. Marshall, Dean Acheson
Secretary of the Treasury: Fred M. Vinson, John W. Snyder
Secretary of War: Robert P. Patterson, Kenneth C. Royall
Secretary of the Navy: James V. Forrestal
Secretary of Defense: James V. Forrestal, Louis Johnson, George C. Marshall, Robert A. Lovett
Attorney General: Tom C. Clark, J. Howard McGrath, James P. McGranery
Postmaster General: R. E. Hannegan, Jesse M. Donaldson
Secretary of the Interior: Harold Ickes, Julius A. Krug, Oscar L. Chapman
Secretary of Agriculture: C. P. Anderson, C. F. Brannan
Secretary of Commerce: W. A. Harriman, Charles Sawyer
Secretary of Labor: L. B. Schwellenbach, Maurice J. Tobin

Often described as a man who was too small for the job, Harry S. Truman believed that he was an unusually successful president. Proud of his knowledge of history, he maintained that he had learned the lessons of the past and avoided the mistakes that had been made in it. To him, the most relevant lessons were those taught by the history of the 1920's and 1930's. The mistakes of that past had resulted in the tragedy of World War II. Faced with similar chal-

Truman's official portrait. *(White House Historical Society)*

lenges, Truman had, in his own view, made the decisions required to avoid World War III.

The Path to Power

The apparent harmony between Truman's personality and the situation within the Democratic Party by 1944 had much to do with Truman's rise to the White House. Franklin D. Roosevelt had helped to make the party more complex and powerful by adding a New Deal wing to the party of the South and a few Northern urban machines, thereby converting the Democrats from the minority to the majority party. By 1944, the party was troubled by intense internal conflict over policy and control, with conservatives anxious to check the ad-

vance of the New Deal pitted against liberals eager to revive it as a force for reform. To many of the liberals, the vice president, Henry A. Wallace, seemed to be especially attractive, surely as a vice president and possibly as Roosevelt's successor. To Wallace's foes, James F. Byrnes of South Carolina seemed a better choice for the vice presidency, but although the party did discard the idealist who had been serving as vice president since 1941, it did not substitute the experienced Southern politician for him. Instead, the Democrats turned to a gregarious, pragmatic border-state senator whose personality seemed to fit the conditions inside the party.

Harry S. Truman had not always been the gregarious person he was in 1944. Born in

THE FIRST LADY
BESS TRUMAN

Elizabeth Wallace "Bess" Truman, wife of the thirty-third president, was born in Independence, Missouri, on February 13, 1885. As a young girl, Bess was very athletic, excelling at baseball, horseback riding, and tennis. However, her life would change forever in 1903 when her father committed suicide. Hoping to go on to college, she instead had to care for her mother and three younger brothers. The sudden and tragic death of her father, an aspiring politician, caused Bess to disdain politics and guard her private life closely.

Bess graduated high school with Harry Truman in 1901. Truman began courting her when she was twenty-five years old, but any serious relationship seemed out of the question, as she continued to care for her widowed mother. Undaunted, Harry was determined to change her mind. After a brief courtship, he proposed marriage, but she rejected him. In 1917, she changed her mind, but the marriage had to wait until the conclusion of World War I, as Harry had enlisted and was sent to France. They were married in 1919 and had one child, Mary Margaret, born in 1924.

After Truman's election to the U.S. Senate in 1934, Bess worked in Harry's office as a clerk. She was not pleased when he was nominated for the vice presidency in 1944, fearing that the story of her father's suicide would become public. After only eighty-two days, when President Franklin Roosevelt died unexpectedly, Harry became president, leaving Bess unsure of how to handle her new role as First Lady, especially following Eleanor Roosevelt. She held only one press conference, and although she diligently performed the duties required of a First Lady, Bess preferred to stay in Independence as much as possible.

After the Truman presidency, the Trumans returned to Missouri for good. She died on October 18, 1982, at age ninety-seven and was buried in the courtyard of the Truman Library next to Harry. Although sometimes called "the reluctant First Lady," Bess Truman was admired for her down-home, simple lifestyle as well as for her sharp wit and charming personality.

Raymond Frey

Lamar, Missouri, on May 8, 1884, the oldest of three children of John Anderson and Martha Ellen (Young) Truman, and reared in Grandview and Independence, he had been rather withdrawn as a boy. His poor vision and the thick glasses he wore had hampered his feforts to join the activities that other boys enjoyed. He had drawn close to his mother and had turned to books and the piano. Although not unhappy, his early years were far from satisfying. In spite of his great appetite for books, especially histories, he failed to graduate near the top of his high school class and did not go on to college. His poor eyesight frustrated his hope for an appointment to West Point and a career in the Army.

After high school, unsure of what he should do with his life, Truman moved to Kansas City, where he worked at several jobs. Then he returned to his grandfather's farm in Grandview, where his personality began to change. The large farm provided the young Truman a rich opportunity to prove himself, and he also became active in various organizations, such as the Masons and the National Guard. During World War I, he served as captain of an artillery battery and was very popular with his men. After the war, he owned and operated a men's store in downtown Kansas City. It became for him more than a place to make money, serving as a gathering spot for his friends and a base from which he moved about the city visiting other men and encouraging them to come to the store. Such activities culminated the slow transformation of the retiring boy into a very gregarious adult.

Truman's new personality provided a foundation for his political career. Politics now became attractive to him, for such a career offered great opportunities for association with people. He in turn became attractive to politicians as his popularity with voters became clear.

Truman had been born and reared a Southern Democrat. His ancestors had migrated to Missouri from Kentucky in the 1840's and had shown Confederate sympathies during the Civil War. Like his father, he had become active in Democratic politics in independent and rural Jackson County, an area with Southern ties and customs.

Truman, however, did not remain merely a Southern Democrat. He received much of his early political education as a member of an urban Democratic machine. While living on the farm, he joined Kansas City's Pendergast organization, which was trying to spread its influence into rural Jackson County. In 1922, recognizing that he was well liked outside the city, the machine threw its weight behind him in the race for eastern district judge of the county court (an administrative post). During the next twelve years as a county official, Truman did help the organization gain strength, accepting one of the basic rules of machine politics and appointing the machine's members to offices that he controlled. In 1934, Tom Pendergast, influenced again by confidence in Truman's popularity outside the city, asked him to run for the United States Senate and furnished essential support in his successful campaign.

Also in 1934, Truman added a new dimension to his point of view. He became a New Deal Democrat. Earlier, he had participated in efforts to use government for economic purposes (especially to build roads), had supervised welfare agencies, and had promoted regional planning, but he had been closer to "old deal" groups such as the Chamber of Commerce than New Deal ones such as labor unions. Now he campaigned for the Senate as a New Dealer, endorsing what had been done and promising to support further developments.

As a senator, Truman fulfilled his promises. He voted for major measures such as Social Security and the Wagner Labor Relations Act, backed the president in his unsuccessful attempt to increase the number of justices on the Supreme Court, investigated the malpractices of financial and industrial leaders, and championed federal regulation of transportation facilities. At the same time, Truman attempted to strengthen and protect the Pendergast machine. He obtained federal patronage for it and defended the organization against the rising tide of criticism that eventually overwhelmed it.

Truman also established close ties with leading Southern Democrats in Washington, D.C., including ones who were unhappy with Roosevelt and the New Deal. The Missouri senator seemed to place a higher value on developing and maintaining good relations with the various members of his party than on promoting the point of view of one of its factions.

To move higher in American politics, Truman needed to become a national figure, and he did so during World War II as head of a senatorial investigating committee soon known as the Truman Committee. The committee, which dealt with mismanagement and corruption in war production, helped to make him popular with a multitude of groups, especially the critics of big business and big government, as his investigations and reports frequently criticized the contributions of business and government to the war effort. At the same time, his concentration on the war programs enabled him to avoid identification with any one of the contending factions of the party. While he explored the construction of army camps, the procurement of airplanes, and the like, other figures who were rising toward the top of the party, such as Henry Wallace, were taking stands on the issues that divided the party and the nation. Everyone wanted to win the war, and Truman's work clearly contributed toward that goal. Not everyone wanted to revive the New Deal.

As a consequence of the ways in which he had functioned on the national stage, Truman was acceptable to all the major factions in the Democratic Party in 1944. The leading promoter of his nomination as vice president, Robert Hannegan, who had been a major figure in the Democratic organization in St. Louis and

was now chairing the Democratic National Committee, represented the urban machine wing. He played an important part in convincing Roosevelt that the controversial Wallace would hurt the ticket, whereas Truman would not.

Although Truman's major support came from the party's urban machines, he would not have been nominated if he had not been acceptable to the other groups. The Southern faction accepted him, although its members preferred other candidates. These politicians consoled themselves with talk of Truman's Southern background and assurances that he was much more desirable than Wallace. New Dealers also accepted Truman, despite their preference for Wallace. They stressed Truman's senatorial voting record with its consistent support for the New Deal and his obvious—to them—superiority to Byrnes.

Thus Truman became president when Roosevelt died on April 12, 1945, because the Missourian had seemed to satisfy the needs of the party in 1944. As he had advanced in politics, he had not switched from being one type of Democrat to being another; rather, he had added one to another, layer by layer. By 1944, he contained within himself all three types, just as his party did, and thereby became an ideal choice to hold the parts together.

Although Truman's career so far had been dominated by domestic matters, his presidency would be controlled by foreign affairs, and he brought to his new responsibilities a distinct point of view on international matters that stressed political considerations, especially the distribution of power, the importance of the military factor, and the need to deal quickly and forcefully with aggressive nations. His own experiences as a soldier during World War I and as a reserve officer in the 1920's and 1930's, and the nation's experiences in world affairs since 1918, had shaped his fundamental ideas on American foreign policy. The nation's military weakness and its isolationism had, he was convinced, contributed significantly to the coming of World War II. Such mistakes of the past had to be avoided in the future. That was the clear lesson of history.

FDR's Successor

International affairs dominated Truman's first four months in office, a quite successful period for him. By April 12, the job of defeating Adolf Hitler's Germany was almost complete. The German armies had lost the war, but Hitler had not yet given up. On April 30, he committed suicide; on May 8, the new German government surrendered.

Determined to carry Roosevelt's projects to completion, Truman battled on behalf of a new international organization and American membership in it. On April 13, he promised that the San Francisco Conference to organize the United Nations would be held as scheduled. It was, and by June 26 it completed its work and Truman moved on to victory at home. On July 28, the Senate, by a vote of 89 to 2, rati-

fied American participation in the new organization. Building on Roosevelt's preparations, Truman had avoided a repetition of Woodrow Wilson's failure in 1919-1920.

Truman next sought victory over Japan. American forces and their allies had gained control of nearly all of the Philippine Islands and had defeated the Japanese on Iwo Jima and Okinawa. Plans had been made and approved by Truman for an invasion of Japan, but recent victories purchased at heavy cost had strengthened convictions that the invasion would also be very costly for American forces.

The administration recognized that Japan had lost the war but also knew that the nation was not ready to surrender on American terms. Strategic bombing had severely damaged Japan's industry and inflicted heavy civilian losses, and American submarines had blockaded Japan so that the people could not get enough food. Its air and sea forces were nearly destroyed, and Japan had been cut off from the vital resources of Southeast Asia. A peace fac-

---

Excerpts from a White House press release regarding the dropping of an atomic bomb on Hiroshima, Japan, August 6, 1945:

Sixteen hours ago, an American airplane dropped one bomb on Hiroshima and destroyed its usefulness to the enemy. That bomb had more power than 20,000 tons of TNT. It had more than two thousand times the blast power of the British "grand slam" which is the largest bomb ever yet used in the history of warfare.

The Japanese began the war from the air at Pearl Harbor. They have been repaid manyfold. And the end is not yet. With this bomb we have now added a new and revolutionary increase in destruction to supplement the growing power of our armed forces. In their present form these bombs are now in production and even more powerful forms are in development.

It is an atomic bomb. It is a harnessing of the basic power of the universe. The force from which the sun draws its power has been loosed against those who brought war to the Far East. . . .

We are now prepared to obliterate more rapidly and completely every productive enterprise the Japanese have above ground in any city. We shall destroy their docks, their factories, and their communications. Let there be no mistake; we shall completely destroy Japan's power to make war.

It was to spare the Japanese people from utter destruction that the ultimatum of July 26 was issued at Potsdam. Their leaders promptly rejected that ultimatum. If they do not now accept our terms they may expect a rain of ruin from the air, the like of which has never been seen on this earth. Behind this air attack will follow sea and land forces in such numbers and power as they have not yet seen and with the fighting skill of which they are already well aware.

tion with substantial political strength sought a negotiated settlement, but Washington knew that it faced significant opposition, especially within the still strong army.

American leaders not only wanted Japan to surrender but also were determined to force great changes on Japan, including removal of the wartime leaders from power, demilitarization, democratization, and liberalization of the nation and destruction of its empire. Influenced by intense hostility toward a people who had attacked Pearl Harbor and believing such changes were needed to make the world of the future a peaceful one, Washington was convinced that only massive military force could produce them.

By late July, however, an alternative to a large and costly invasion seemed to be available. The first test of an atomic device was made on July 16. The new weapon seemed capable of forcing Japan's unconditional surrender more quickly and at a much lower price than an invasion. Supplementary considerations also influ-

enced the decision to use the new weapon; above all, there was hope that the bomb would limit Soviet expansion and alter the country's behavior, which, especially in Eastern Europe, had become alarming. The bomb, in sum—not American or Soviet ground forces—might bring about the unconditional surrender of the Japanese, do so more quickly than an invasion could, and do so without such heavy loss of life and without great gains to the Soviet Union in Asia.

Informed that two atomic bombs would soon be available, President Truman, on July 24, ordered their use against Japan as soon after August 3 as weather permitted. The first bomb obliterated Hiroshima on August 6, the Soviet Union declared war on August 8 and quickly moved against the Japanese on the mainland, and the second bomb hit Nagasaki on August 9. Five days later, Japan accepted surrender terms that conformed to American specifications and opened the door to a revolution in Japan.

Truman with British prime minister Winston Churchill (left) and Soviet premier Joseph Stalin (right) at the 1945 Potsdam Conference at the end of World War II. *(NARA)*

The Beginning of the Cold War

The victories from May to August ended World War II but did not prevent the emergence of a new and different type of international conflict, a cold war between the United States and the Soviet Union. The Cold War was nonviolent—a feature that distinguished it from what is customarily meant by war but which was no less intense, so intense as to be the dominant feature of the relationship between the two nations. The Cold War also affected virtually all other nations, imposing pressure on them to take sides.

Both ideological differences and economics contributed to the emergence of the Cold War but did not fully explain it. Of other factors, World War II was especially important. It had destroyed the power of the nations that had separated the Soviet Union and the United States, giving them new opportunities to clash with each other. It had increased the power of both. The United States, its economy stimulated by the war, had developed great military strength while suffering relatively light loss of lives and had obtained new influence in crucial places, especially Western Europe and Japan. The war had a more mixed impact on Soviet power. The war did inflict serious damage on the Soviet Union, taking many more lives than in any other country and wreaking heavy damage on the economy, but victory gave the Soviets new opportunities, especially in Eastern Europe and Germany, which they eagerly seized. The war also increased the self-confidence and sense of power of both countries, for they had triumphed over strong adversaries. Finally, the war reduced the influence of isolationism in both, convincing American leaders of its folly and persuading Soviet leaders that they must control Eastern Europe and Germany to be secure.

The Cold War emerged and escalated during late 1945 and through 1946 for several reasons. The ending of World War II reduced pressures on both nations to cooperate with each other. The atomic bomb increased the American leaders' sense of strength and alarmed the Soviets. Soviet behavior in Eastern Europe and Iran, where they maintained their military presence and sought to shape political developments, troubled Americans, as it contravened their ideas for the postwar world; seemed to violate agreements that Roosevelt, Winston Churchill, and Joseph Stalin had made at Yalta in February, 1945; and suggested that the Soviet Union might continue to expand as Germany and Japan had. Soviet pressure on Turkey in 1946 also contributed to the Cold War and so did rivalry over Germany. There, the two nations were locked into a system of joint control; they had promised reunification of Germany, but they now disagreed over the terms.

In this deteriorating international situation, Truman rejected Roosevelt's efforts to cultivate Soviet friendship and instead developed a "get tough" policy, insisting that he was "tired of babying the Soviets" and that they needed to be "faced with an iron fist and strong language," as the only language they understood was "how many divisions have you." The new policy sought to liberate Eastern Europe from Soviet control. It assumed that Roosevelt's objectives there had been correct but that his methods had been inadequate. The Yalta agreements had stated that free elections would be held, but the Soviet Union had refused to allow them. Therefore, Truman assumed, the United States now had to take a new approach to the Soviet Union in order to compel that nation to honor its agreements and bring political reality in Eastern Europe into harmony with American democratic ideals.

The United States did not use the military to force the desired changes. In fact, the nation reduced its military presence in Europe very rapidly after the end of World War II and carried out a large-scale program of demobilization, even though the president and most of his aides highly valued military power. Truman be-

An atomic bomb test in 1946. *(U.S. Navy)*

lieved that the nation must have a powerful navy and air force and a strong army reserve "because only so long as we remain strong can we ensure peace in the world." The United States could not "on one day proclaim our intention to prevent unjust aggression and tyranny in the world, and on the next day call for immediate scrapping of our military might." In spite of Truman's belief that military weakness had been one of the great mistakes of the past that must not be repeated, the administration rapidly demobilized the armed forces, influenced by pressure to bring the boys home, a belief that the nation could rely on the United Nations for security, and concern, which Truman shared, about large-scale government spending. The United States retained and developed one powerful military resource, the atomic bomb, but did not threaten to use it and quickly learned that mere possession of it would not force the Soviet Union out of Eastern Europe.

The Cold War in its early stage was largely a war of words, each side employing verbal pres-

sure against the other. They clashed over Eastern Europe, Italy, Germany, Iran, Turkey, and other places, one side seeking liberation and the other control of Eastern Europe, each side trying to prevent control of Germany by the other and pursuing other objectives. Washington hurled critical speeches and diplomatic protests at Moscow, charged that the Soviets were not behaving as they had promised at Yalta, and denied recognition to some of the new regimes the Soviet Union supported in Eastern Europe. "We shall refuse to recognize any government imposed on any nation by the force of any foreign power," Truman insisted. He and his lieutenants also tried to bargain with the Soviet Union and to convince the Soviets that the United States wanted governments that would be friendly to the Soviet Union as well as representative of all "democratic" elements. The Soviet Union, however, regarded American interest in Eastern Europe as a threat to its security and another attempt at encirclement by capitalist nations. Soviet leaders charged Washington with using threats and at the same time tried to persuade American officials to accept the new situation in Eastern Europe.

Although Truman achieved a few of his objectives in 1946, he failed in Eastern Europe. Concerned but not swayed by American power, the Soviets tightened their control. They tolerated noncommunist but friendly governments that were established in several countries, including Finland, Austria, and Hungary, and pulled their troops out of pluralistic Czechoslovakia. In other countries, such as East Germany, Poland, and Romania, however, the Soviets tightened their control, using police action to remove unfriendly politicians from office and to pave the way for large Communist Party victories at the polls.

As the Cold War escalated, Truman sought to unify his administration's position on foreign policy by removing dissenters. Henry Wallace, an advocate of toleration of Soviet behavior in Eastern Europe and renewed efforts at cooperation, had warned that American hostility toward the Soviet Union was leading to war. "The tougher we get, the tougher the Russians will get," he predicted. "Our interest in establishing democracy in Eastern Europe, where democracy by and large has never existed, seems to her," he advised, "an attempt to reestablish the encirclement of unfriendly neighbors which was created after the last war and which might serve as a springboard of still another effort to destroy her." After Wallace publicized these views in September, 1946, Truman fired him from his job as secretary of commerce.

The Emergence of Containment

In 1947, the Truman administration's strategy for waging the Cold War shifted from liberation to containment, and Washington began to draw more heavily on American economic power to accomplish its objectives. This shift

---

THE VICE PRESIDENT
ALBEN W. BARKLEY

Alben William Barkley served as vice president during Harry S. Truman's second administration. The son of a tobacco farmer, Barkley was born on November 24, 1877, in Graves County, Kentucky. After his education in local public schools, he graduated from Marvin College in Kentucky in 1897. Barkley furthered his education by taking graduate courses at Emory College in Georgia and studying law at the University of Virginia.

Barkley's career began in education with a teaching position at Marvin College. After studying law with John Hendrick, Congressman John Wheeler, and Judge William Bishop in Paducah, Kentucky, he was admitted to the bar in 1901 and established a law practice in Paducah. On June 23, 1903, he married Dorothy Bower, and the couple would eventually have three children. Barkley's first position office was as prosecuting attorney for McCracken County, a position he held from 1905 to 1909. From 1909 to 1913, he served as judge of McCracken County and went on to serve in the U.S. House of Representatives from 1913 to 1927.

From the House, Barkley ran for the U.S. Senate, winning the election of 1926. He was reelected in 1932, 1938, and 1944. During his long career in politics, Barkley also attended several state Democratic conventions. He resigned his Senate seat in 1949 in order to become Truman's vice president, a position he held until 1953.

After the death of his first wife, Barkley married Jane Hadley, a widow, on November 18, 1949. On leaving the vice presidency, he was reelected to the U.S. Senate in 1954 but died on April 30, 1956.

Robert P. Watson and Richard Yon

was produced by the interaction of situations in Southern and Western Europe, including economic depression and communist pressure, and American perceptions. In spite of American aid, Europe had not recovered from the war, and the economic conditions encouraged communists to believe that they could enlarge their power and influence. In France and Italy, the large communist parties reversed their policy, established at the end of the war, of cooperation with bourgeois governments, and in Greece, communist-led revolutionaries waged a guerrilla campaign against the government. Each side in the Greek civil war received military and economic help from outsiders, the revolutionaries from Yugoslavia, Bulgaria, and Albania and the government from Great Britain. The possibility of renewed Soviet pressure on Turkey also influenced development in the area, the Soviets having indicated in 1946 that they wanted air and naval bases in Turkey and a share in control of the Dardanelles. Finally, in February, 1947, the British, weakened by World War II, announced that they would be forced to withdraw their forces from Greece by the end of March and could no longer afford to provide financial assistance to Greece and Turkey.

By then, the Truman administration had a fixed perspective through which it viewed developments in Southern and Eastern Europe. It strongly emphasized the Soviet Union's role in the world's trouble spots. To Washington, the Soviet Union appeared to have unlimited ambitions and substantial power, and it seemed eager and able to draw Southern and Western Europe into its empire by prolonging and exploiting the economic crisis that had followed the war.

In addition, the administration regarded Europe as an area of major political and economic importance to the United States. The United States could not be secure if a hostile power dominated Europe and could not prosper if political or economic conditions in Europe prevented Americans from obtaining materials, investing capital, or selling products there and in areas linked with Europe.

American leaders also assumed that economic conditions exerted a powerful influence on politics: "The seeds of totalitarian regimes are nurtured in misery and want," Truman maintained. If Europe remained depressed, he believed, communism would triumph; if Europe became prosperous, communism would lose out.

Finally, administration leaders believed that the United States had the capacity and responsibility to tackle problems such as those in Southern and Western Europe. Only the United States had the economic strength needed to help the nations there. Thus, the United States must act.

The old concept of the "American mission" reinforced Truman's perception of the lessons of history to produce this sense of responsibility. In explaining the administration's position, the president spoke in the language of that mission, interpreting world politics as a struggle between alternative ways of life:

One way of life is based upon the will of the majority, and is distinguished by free institutions, representative government, free elections, guarantees of individual liberty, freedom of speech and religion, and freedom from political oppression. The second way of life is based upon the will of a minority forcibly imposed upon the majority. It relies upon terror and oppression, and controlled press and radio, fixed elections, and the suppression of personal freedoms.

The United States had a mission to guarantee that the first way of life survived and prospered.

It would best do so, the Truman administration decided, through the containment policy, with the Truman Doctrine and the Marshall Plan as its main features in 1947-1948. In March, 1947, Truman proposed that the United States should "support free peoples who are resisting

The Truman Doctrine

March 12, 1947

At the present moment in world history nearly every nation must choose between alternative ways of life. The choice is too often not a free one.

One way of life is based upon the will of the majority, and is distinguished by free institutions, representative government, free elections, guarantees of individual liberty, freedom of speech and religion, and freedom from political oppression.

The second way of life is based upon the will of a minority forcibly imposed upon the majority. It relies upon terror and oppression, a controlled press and radio; fixed elections, and the suppression of personal freedoms.

I believe that it must be the policy of the United States to support free peoples who are resisting attempted subjugation by armed minorities or by outside pressures.

I believe that we must assist free peoples to work out their own destinies in their own way.

The world is not static, and the status quo is not sacred. But we cannot allow changes in the status quo in violation of the Charter of the United Nations by such methods as coercion, or by such subterfuges as political infiltration. In helping free and independent nations to maintain their freedom, the United States will be giving effect to the principles of the Charter of the United Nations.

---

attempted subjugation by armed minorities or outside pressure" and asked that $400 million be sent to Greece and Turkey. In June, Truman's secretary of state, General George C. Marshall, called on Europeans to get together and "draw up a program designed to place Europe on its feet economically" and suggested that the United States would supply "friendly aid in drafting a European program and later support of such a program so far as it may be practical for us to do so." The president and his top lieutenant on foreign affairs proposed that the United States play a role of crucial importance in world affairs: It should use its economic power to halt communist expansion.

Although the administration's containment policy enjoyed wide popularity, even in the Republican-controlled Congress, it did encounter some opposition. Henry Wallace was especially critical of it. Wallace attacked "the Truman-led, Wall Street-dominated, military-backed group that is blackening the name of American democracy all over the world" by supporting "kings, fascists, and reactionaries."

He charged that the Marshall Plan was "a plan to interfere in the social, economic, and political affairs of countries receiving aid" and that the administration was willing to help only those countries that would accept "our kind of government" and subordinate their economy to the American economy. Labeling it the Martial Plan, he warned that it would lead to war; he proposed that it be replaced with a program handled by the United Nations.

Senator Robert A. Taft of Ohio, the Republican leader in the Senate, was another significant critic. Reflecting his party's strong desire to reduce government spending, he argued that the administration's proposals were too costly and likely to wreck the American economy.

Several factors enabled the president to overcome the opposition of Wallace, Taft, and others and gain congressional approval of aid to Greece and Turkey in May, 1947, and of the plan for European recovery the following year. The administration employed dramatic rhetoric to argue persuasively about the dangers of the international situation and marshaled im-

The Berlin airlift. *(NARA)*

pressive evidence of the seriousness of Europe's plight, the ability of the United States to supply the required aid, and the economic and political benefits the nation would derive from it. The administration also carefully cultivated leaders in and out of Congress and gained the cooperation of some major figures, especially Senator Arthur H. Vandenberg of Michigan, chair of the Senate Foreign Relations Committee.

Although hardly intending to do so, the Soviets helped Truman win the adoption of his program. While most European nations joined together to plan a coordinated attack on their problems, the Soviet Union withdrew from these efforts and forced the Eastern Europeans to follow suit, fearing that the Marshall Plan would enable the United States to interfere in the internal affairs of European countries, gain control of their economies, and restore Germany as a strong, dangerous power. Had the Soviet Union been included in the program, Truman would surely have encountered greater difficulties in persuading Congress to finance it. In addition, Communists, with assurances of

support from the Soviet Union, seized complete control of Czechoslovakia in Feburary, 1948. This dramatic illustration of the Soviet Union's determination to tighten its control in Eastern Europe in 1947-1948 created especially great difficulties for Wallace, who claimed that liberals and Communists could work together. In Czechoslovakia, at least, they had not.

The consequences of Truman's policy of containment and economic aid were immediately apparent. The policy strengthened anti-communist groups in Southern and Western Europe and aided progress toward the establishment of a West German republic. It also encouraged the Soviets to tighten further their control of Eastern Europe, a process that encouraged Yugoslavia to rebel and establish itself as an independent communist country in 1948. Progress toward an independent West Germany persuaded the Soviets to impose a blockade on land and water traffic into Berlin, a city jointly controlled by the Soviet Union, the United States, Great Britain, and France but inside the Soviet zone of occupation, and the United States responded by airlifting supplies into the western sectors of the city, resuming the draft, enlarging the air force, and stationing two groups of long-range bombers in England and Germany.

The Cold War escalated rapidly in 1947-1948, and the United States, under Truman's leadership, took on a large role in Europe, relying heavily on economic power backed up by air power and the atomic bomb.

Avoiding Depression

Chiefly significant for his role in the history of American foreign policy, Truman did not accomplish nearly as much at home, yet he did enjoy some successes there. For one, he avoided a postwar depression, a possibility many people had anticipated and feared. Recognizing that the Great Depression was ended by the war, not by the New Deal or private enterprise, pessimists feared that by stopping massive government spending and reducing the size of foreign markets, peace would bring depressed conditions similar to those of the 1930's.

The federal government did cut spending sharply once the fighting stopped, and furthermore Truman had difficulty establishing a domestic economic program. Conflicts inside the administration hampered efforts to do so, as Truman, seeking broad support, staffed the administration with both liberals and conservatives. Clashes with Congress over economic policies were even more significant. Less than a month after the surrender of Japan, Truman delivered a major message on domestic policy that in effect called for a revival of the New Deal. In the next year, however, he failed to persuade Congress to accept his proposals for a fair employment practices committee, a housing program, and price controls. Congress did vote for the Employment Act of 1946, a response to the fear of depression. The act declared the government's responsibility for maintaining high employment and established the Council of Economic Advisors to assist the president in promoting that goal.

In November, 1946, the Republicans gained control of Congress for the first time since the early days of Herbert Hoover's presidency. The electorate's decision was influenced by the bitter struggles over prices and wages and by dissatisfaction with Truman. Dominated by Republicans determined to reduce the size and cost of the federal government as well as the power of organized labor, the Eightieth Congress clashed with the president in many economic areas, including welfare, price control, taxes, agriculture, reclamation, and labor.

In spite of the sharp cuts in spending and the difficulties in shaping economic policy, a postwar depression did not occur, and the president, as well as the federal government as a whole, deserves some credit for preventing one. Federal spending, however, remained well above prewar levels, and the government administered programs established during the Roosevelt years, especially Social Security and the G.I. Bill of Rights, that gave the unemployed money to spend and kept people out of the job market. Furthermore, the administration and the Congress agreed on a tax cut immediately after the war, and the government maintained foreign sales at a high level through overseas relief, loans, and aid, and it helped American firms gain access to raw materials abroad.

With the private sector contributing even more than government, the postwar years were quite prosperous. During the first year, the economy suffered from many strikes, shortages of consumer goods, an increase in unemployment, and inflation, but the nation avoided truly massive difficulties. After a brief transition period, the economy began to grow again and continued to do so until 1949.

An Unexpected Victory

In spite of the economic accomplishments of these years, Truman suffered many political troubles. He not only faced an apparently reviving Republican Party but also his own party

A triumphant Truman holds a copy of the early edition of the *Chicago Daily Tribune* for November 4, 1948. *(Library of Congress)*

seemed to be disintegrating. The Truman-Wallace clash over foreign policy resulted in the defection of a bloc of liberals into the Wallace camp. Late in 1947, the deposed cabinet officer announced that he would run for president in 1948 on a third-party ticket. Campaigning strenuously, Wallace emphasized several themes: Containment was a creature of Wall Street and the military, was imperialistic, and was leading to atomic war; reform at home depended on peace in the world; a return to reliance on Roosevelt's United Nations would permit a revival of his New Deal; the groups opposed to reform—big business and the big brass—also promoted international conflict, so their power had to be destroyed before policies could be changed.

While losing the support of Wallace and the Progressives, Truman also lost support in the South because of his efforts to improve race relations. He had entered the White House with an interest in this issue, as African Americans had been active participants in the politics of

Kansas City and Missouri and had educated him on some of their problems, needs, and desires and made him somewhat receptive to their demands for change. An increase in Southern white violence against blacks also affected his thinking after he became president, as did his concern about the American image in the world.

Truman's interest in the African American vote also helped make him a more active advocate of change in race relations than any of his predecessors had been. The 1946 congressional elections suggested that Northern and Western blacks, a rapidly growing group as a consequence of black immigration from the South, were moving to the Republican Party, partly because of Truman's failure to persuade Congress to pass civil rights legislation. Following the 1946 elections Truman established a Committee on Civil Rights to investigate race relations and make recommendations for government action. As the 1948 election approached, his top political adviser, Clark Clifford, told him that he must act on civil rights. African American voters held the balance of power in several key states, and no policies "initiated by the Truman administration no matter how 'liberal' could so alienate the South in the next year that it would revolt."

In the Truman period the leading proponent of change in race relations was the National Association for the Advancement of Colored People (NAACP). The organization moved into the political arena on occasion to battle for laws against lynching; discrimination in employment, housing, and public accommodations; and the poll tax. More characteristic, however, were its struggles in the judicial arena aimed at persuading judges to enforce the Fourteenth and Fifteenth Amendments to the United States Constitution. By the Truman years, the organization had acquired a large amount of experience in the courts, had developed a high degree of skill, and had enjoyed some successes. It also had greater resources than ever before as a consequence of its growth during the war from 50,000 to 450,000 members. Furthermore, in the new climate in race relations it had more friends to call on for help, some of whom filed amicus curiae, "friend of the court," briefs in NAACP-sponsored cases.

Late in 1947, Truman's Justice Department became one of the NAACP's new friends when it filed an amicus curiae brief in a restrictive covenant case brought by the NAACP. A step that had been proposed by the Committee on Civil Rights, this marked the beginning of the department's participation in the Civil Rights movement. The Supreme Court, before which the NAACP argued this and other cases in the

---

Excerpts from Harry S. Truman's message to Congress regarding civil rights, February 2, 1948:

In the State of the Union Message on January 7, 1948, I spoke of five great goals toward which we should strive in our constant effort to strengthen our democracy and improve the welfare of our people. The first of these is to secure fully our essential human rights. I am now presenting to the Congress my recommendations for legislation to carry us forward toward that goal.

This Nation was founded by men and women who sought these shores that they might enjoy greater freedom and greater opportunity than they had known before. The founders of the United States proclaimed to the world the American belief that all men are created equal, and that governments are instituted to secure the inalienable rights with which all men are endowed. In the Declaration of Independence and the Constitution of the United States, they eloquently expressed the aspirations of . . . mankind for equality and freedom. . . .

Today, the American people enjoy more freedom and opportunity than ever before. Never in our history has there been better reason to hope for the complete realization of the ideals of liberty and equality. . . .

The Federal Government has a clear duty to see that Constitutional guarantees of individual liberties and of equal protection under the laws are not denied or abridged anywhere in our Union. That duty is shared by all three branches of the Government, but it can be fulfilled only if the Congress enacts modern, comprehensive civil rights laws, adequate to the needs of the day, and demonstrating out continuing faith in the free way of life. I recommend, therefore, that the Congress enact legislation at this session directed toward the following specific objectives:

1. Establishing a permanent Commission on Civil Rights, a Joint Congressional Committee on Civil Rights, and a Civil Rights Division in the Department of Justice.
2. Strengthening existing civil rights statutes.
3. Providing Federal protection against lynching.
4. Protecting more adequately the right to vote.
5. Establishing a Fair Employment Practice Commission to prevent unfair discrimination in employment.
6. Prohibiting discrimination in interstate transportation facilities.
7. Providing home-rule and suffrage in Presidential elections for the residents of the District of Columbia.
8. Providing Statehood for Hawaii and Alaska and a greater measure of self-government for our island possessions.
9. Equalizing the opportunities for residents of the United States to become naturalized citizens.
10. Settling the evacuation claims of Japanese-Americans.

Truman years, was highly receptive to the group's arguments. It was composed of men who had been appointed by Roosevelt and Truman, who were highly critical of the tendency of the Court before 1937 to invalidate economic legislation and who inclined toward a belief that the Court should be more concerned with noneconomic issues such as civil rights. Not dominated by precedent, they were often influenced by legal theories about the need for law to reflect social and economic realities. In the spring of 1948, this sympathetic Court announced two decisions on civil rights cases. One did not attack segregation per se, but ruled that a state must provide legal education for blacks "as soon as it does for any other group." The other, the case in which the Justice Department had entered a brief, ruled that judicial enforcement of real estate contracts designed to exclude, on the basis of race and other qualities, persons from living in residential areas—in other words, restrictive covenants—constituted state action and thus violated the equal protection clause of the Fourteenth Amendment.

By the time the Court spoke on restrictive covenants Truman had taken an even larger step. In line with Clifford's advice and with the bold report of the Committee on Civil Rights, he delivered a special message to Congress on civil rights in February. He called for national action, including legislation that would give federal protection against lynching, protect the right to vote, prohibit discrimination in interstate transportation, and establish a permanent fair employment practices commission.

Leaders in the South protested more vigorously than Clifford had anticipated. They charged that Truman's proposals "would destroy the last vestige of the rights of the sovereign states," and they began to organize in the hope of forcing party leaders to behave more conservatively. Feeling betrayed by Truman, they blamed his actions on a new interest in African American votes, and they threatened to deprive him of the white Southern votes he needed for reelection. Hostility toward the civil rights proposals and toward advocates of civil rights legislation was widespread in the South; Southerners seemed divided only on the question of the steps to be taken. Although some insisted that the South must continue to work within the Democratic Party, others proposed a bolt from it. The latter group hoped their threats would restrain the Democrats and encourage them to adopt a weak civil rights plank and nominate a foe of civil rights legislation.

The administration worked to limit the scope of the Southern revolt. Advisers most fearful of the loss of black votes and the Wallace threat urged new steps in civil rights, but Truman for the moment believed that loss of white Southern votes was the biggest problem and counseled caution. At the Democratic convention of 1948, a spokesperson for the White House proposed a civil rights plank for the party platform that ignored the specific proposals Truman had made in February. Anti-Wallace liberals, with Hubert H. Humphrey of Minnesota as one of the leaders, battled successfully for a stronger civil rights plank that made the president's stand in February the official position of the party, commended his "courageous stand on the issue of civil rights," and called on lawmakers "to support our President" in guaranteeing a set of clearly defined rights.

The civil rights plank produced the Southern bolt that the administration had feared. Following its acceptance, thirty-five delegates from Mississippi and Alabama withdrew from the convention, and shortly thereafter the bolters joined other Southerners in a conference in Birmingham that nominated Governor J. Strom Thurmond of South Carolina for the presidency and adopted a declaration of principles that expressed Southern resentments and fears. The leaders of this States' Rights Party expected to obtain the South's electoral votes, defeat Truman, restore Southern influence in the Democratic Party, and use that influence to maintain the "Southern way of life."

Truman leaves the podium after having addressed the National Association for the Advancement of Colored People at the Lincoln Memorial, Washington, D.C., in June, 1947. *(NARA)*

Truman now appeared certain to lose the election. Before the Democratic convention, he had seemed so unpopular that several groups of Democrats had tried to substitute Dwight D. Eisenhower as the party's candidate, and he had been saved largely by Eisenhower's refusal to run. By midsummer, the pollsters agreed that the Republican candidate, Governor Thomas E. Dewey of New York, would win.

Truman, however, avoided defeat, largely because of the Democrats' basic strength, developed under Roosevelt, and his long and strenuous campaign. In his campaign, Truman sought chiefly to persuade Democrats not to desert him. He attacked the "do-nothing" Eightieth Congress and linked his Republican opponent with his party's congressional leadership. The president portrayed himself as a crusader rallying the people to save the gains made under the New Deal and pictured the GOP as dominated by big business and a threat to New Deal programs. To combat Wallace, he argued that the administration's foreign policy promoted peace, charged that the Progressive Party was dominated by communists, and advised liberals that they must unite to be effective. To contain defections to Thurmond, Truman reminded Southerners of their need for economic programs of the New Deal type and of the dangers of Republican rule. He seldom discussed civil rights.

Truman did discuss that subject in Harlem, however, and just before the campaign began he issued two executive orders calling for changes in race relations in the armed forces and the federal government. The Committee on Civil Rights had recommended an end to Jim Crow in the military, and Truman in his civil rights message had promised to take such action. The Southern revolt and opposition from the army had encouraged delay, but African American leaders, above all A. Philip Randolph, head of the Brotherhood of Sleeping Car Porters, demanded action and issued their own threats. The Republican platform criticized racial segregation in the armed forces, and the Democratic civil rights plank added to the pressure. In this situation, several liberal leaders advised the president to do everything he could to carry out that plank, warning that otherwise he would lose the black vote. In response, Truman ordered equality of treatment and opportunity in the armed forces, and when confusion arose about the order's purpose, he stated that it was intended to end segregation.

Truman contributed to his own victory through other uses of presidential power. In May, he had recognized the new state of Israel; in July, he called Congress into special session to demonstrate that the Republicans would not enact legislation that their party platform endorsed. Throughout the campaign period he both clashed with the Soviets and pushed for negotiations with them over Berlin.

In spite of the divisions within his own party, Truman was reelected—but by a small margin. He held on to most but not all of the states where the Democrats were traditionally strong. He was somewhat weaker in the East and South than Roosevelt had been but slightly stronger in the Midwest and Far West than Roosevelt had been in 1940 and 1944.

Truman's victory maintained Democratic control of the White House but did not demonstrate great popular support for the president himself. He received less than 50 percent of the popular vote, won by the narrowest margin— 4.5 percent—in any election since 1916, and drew a much smaller percentage of the voters to the polls than had voted in the presidential contests of the Roosevelt period. The Democrats recovered control of Congress. The result seemed to indicate voter approval of established programs but little demand for new ones, except among African Americans.

Although the campaign was waged chiefly on domestic issues, the outcome was especially significant for foreign policy. It gave added support to the administration's policy of containment. Three of the four presidential contenders—Dewey and Thurmond as well as Truman—endorsed that policy. The only one who challenged it—Wallace—was destroyed politically, receiving less than 3 percent of the popular vote.

Changes in Containment

In his second term, Truman militarized and expanded the containment policy. By 1949 the United States had substantial military power, much more of it than it had had before World War II, but it had reduced the size of the armed forces sharply since 1945—from twelve million to one and a half million persons. Truman's early defense policy relied heavily on atomic bombs and long-range bombers to deliver them—and strictly limited military spending. To increase the efficiency of the armed forces, Congress, pressed by Truman, passed the National Security Act of 1947, which partially unified the armed forces, but it turned down his proposal to build strength through a system of universal military training.

Budgetary considerations heavily influenced thinking on military policy among members of Congress as well as White House staff members and the president himself. After Louis Johnson replaced James Forrestal in the newly created position of secretary of defense in 1949, they came to dominate the Defense Department as well. The economizers assumed that the United States had a limited amount of money to devote to national purposes. They feared that if the government tried to spend too much it would hurt the American economy, and a strong economy was absolutely essential in the fight against communism. They also assumed that European economic recovery was more important than the development of a large army. Since European recovery cost several billion dollars each year, less than $15 billion appeared to be available for the development of American military power. Confidence in air power made lower defense expenditures seem acceptable. As the United States had a monopoly on atomic bombs and long-range bombers, it did not appear to need a large army. Equipped with the latest technology, the new air force could guarantee that Soviet armies would not move; Soviet leaders would not be foolish enough to provoke an American attack upon the Soviet Union.

The assumption about the limits on American economic resources also encouraged the administration to focus on Europe at the expense of Asia, even though the advance of the communists in the Chinese civil war threatened American hopes for the development of good United States-Chinese relations. Washington made several efforts to influence the Chinese revolution, including diplomacy designed to halt the civil war and establish a coalition government, but decided against massive economic aid.

Truman did not seriously consider large-scale military intervention in China either. Such intervention had no significant advocates in the United States and no significant popular support. Americans had traditionally opposed military engagements on the Asian mainland, and postwar military policy supplied an additional restraint. Furthermore, at the time the civil war reached a crisis stage, Truman simply did not have a large army to order into combat in China.

While the United States made a relatively small effort to exert its influence, the Chinese communists gained control of mainland China. Their victory greatly affected international relations, leading to closer ties between the Soviet Union and China and greater conflict between the United States and China. The communists denounced the Americans harshly for their intervention, small though it was, and the United States refused to recognize the new regime or to permit it to become a member of the United Nations.

The United States did maintain a presence in Asia, which was especially important in Japan. There, the United States monopolized the occupation, refusing to allow any other nation to participate, and used its new power in the country to reshape its life and block communist efforts to give their own form to it. Although Japan had been the most powerful country in Asia, most Americans derived little comfort from their nation's accomplishments there, and developments in China engendered a sense of great frustration.

At the end of the 1940's and the beginning of the 1950's, these developments, continuing tension in Eastern Europe, and the Berlin blockade, along with the substitution of Dean Acheson for George Marshall as secretary of state, persuaded the administration to make changes in its policies. Acheson, especially, pressed for greater reliance on military power. The North Atlantic Treaty Organization (NATO), a Western defense alliance whose members promised to cooperate militarily if the Soviet Union moved against one of them, was the first result. NATO nations did not embark on a military buildup, but rather relied heavily on American atomic power to defend the West. Nuclear weapons had come to be central to the policy of containment.

The acceptance of the NATO treaty by a wide margin in the Senate in July, 1949, illustrated the significance of Truman's defeat of Wallace. Wallace opposed the treaty; so did Taft. The administration, however, helped once again by Senator Vandenberg, triumphed over the opposition even though the treaty marked a significant departure from the nation's traditional opposition to "entangling alliances" in peacetime. The treaty's champions insisted that NATO would convince the Soviets that military moves would be too risky and thereby serve to prevent war.

Further militarization of containment followed quickly after the establishment of NATO, chiefly because of the Soviet development of the atomic bomb, which was tested by the Soviets in August, 1949, and announced by Truman the following month. Soviet possession of the atomic bomb appeared to alter the military situation fundamentally, as it challenged the West's reliance on the American monopoly of atomic weapons. Congress responded by accepting an administration request for the establishment of a military assistance program that would use American economic power to promote the military development of the nation's allies. In further response to the Soviet atomic bomb, Truman decided early in 1950 to build an even more powerful weapon of mass destruction, a hydrogen bomb, which could also be delivered by the United States Air Force.

At the same time, the administration developed a plan for a huge buildup of American forces. National Security Council-68 (NSC-68)—the bureaucratic label for the plan—called for a great increase in the defense budget, including a substantial expansion of the army. Championed by Acheson and widely endorsed inside the administration by the late spring of 1950, the plan assumed that the Soviet Union's capacity to expand its sphere of influence had been increased significantly and would become even greater if the United States and its allies did not develop more military power. The plan also assumed that the United States could afford to spend much more money on its military forces. Administration economic views, as well as the conception of the importance of military power, had also changed, at least for the champions of NSC-68.

By June, 1950, however, Truman had not yet decided to press for a greatly increased program of military spending and the development of an expanded military establishment including a large army as well as a powerful air force. Restrained largely by political considerations, by his doubts that the people and the Congress were ready to endorse the spending envisioned in the plan, he did not make the decision to implement NSC-68.

The Korean War

In the last week of June, 1950, Truman clearly extended containment to the Asian mainland. He decided to intervene militarily after the forces of North Korea invaded South Korea. Truman's interpretation of history dictated his decision. Viewing North Korea as a puppet of the Soviets, he saw the invasion as a Soviet-backed move against the free world. The attack, he maintained, demonstrated that "communism had passed beyond the use of subversion to conquer independent nations and will now use armed invasion and war." This view encouraged him to see the Korean situation as similar to ones in the 1930's, such as the Japanese invasion of Manchuria, not as a civil war or as an attack by one small country on another. He was convinced that he must avoid the great American mistake of the 1930's: the refusal to get involved significantly at an early stage in the development of aggression. United States intervention would halt aggression, discourage communist moves in other places, reassure America's allies about its reliability, and avoid a larger war. The fact that he had not avoided the mistake of military weakness did not inhibit him. The president believed that success in Korea would not require great effort. Thus, although the United States was not well prepared for the kind of ground war that was raging in Korea, Truman decided to intervene. He secured United Nations sponsorship for the police action in Korea and then intervened first with air and sea power and then with ground forces as the South Korean army fell back before the forces from the North.

Truman's doubts about the wisdom of a military buildup and popular and congressional opposition to it quickly disappeared. Although Washington limited the war to the Korean peninsula, the war became the largest military effort that United States had yet made in Asia. The war grew in a step-by-step fashion, but still involved heavy losses on both sides. Soon after the fighting began, the United States engaged in a military buildup along the lines that had been laid out in NSC-68. Annual expenditures on defense were pushed above $50 billion by 1952, and the armed forces grew to more than three million men. The army, which played the largest role in the war, experienced the most substantial growth. American military policy no longer emphasized budgetary restrictions or placed heavy reliance on the new weapons.

The Korean War led to an expansion of American involvement elsewhere in Asia, including American economic aid to the French to help them win their battle against revolution in Indochina. The administration, however, continued to regard Europe as more important than Asia to its containment policy. The decision to intervene in Korea had, in fact, been influenced by Truman's desire to demonstrate to his European allies that the United States could be relied on for Europe's defense and to convince the Soviets that they dare not move against any allies of the United States.

At the same time the Americans fought in Korea, the Truman administration stepped up its efforts to develop Europe's military strength, hoping thereby to restrain the Soviets. The United States pushed plans for a great expansion of NATO forces, enlarged the military assistance program, and sent additional American troops and an American commander, General Dwight D. Eisenhower, to Europe.

Truman's view that the Korean War was part of a larger picture, and far from the most important part, led him to reject a proposal for

U.S. troops in Korea in 1950. *(U.S. Marine Corps)*

a much larger effort in the Korea-China theater, a rejection that contributed to a major civil-military clash.

American forces, led by General Douglas MacArthur, won a spectacular victory over North Korea in September, 1950. Rather than stop after enemy forces had been driven out of South Korea, Truman, eager to take advantage of an opportunity to destroy a communist regime and unite the peninsula under a noncommunist government, sent his armies north to liberate the entire country from communism. MacArthur advised him that the Soviets and Chinese would not intervene, at least not effectively, but as American forces advanced toward the Chinese border, the Chinese, seeing the American advance as a threat to their security, attacked with a heavy concentration of troops and pushed the American and Korean troops away from China and out of North Korea before the end of the year.

MacArthur now proposed a much greater military effort. He urged the administration to throw more force against the Chinese in Korea and to carry the war into China itself, using American air and naval power and the troops of Chiang Kai-shek in Formosa. The United States should seek a decisive victory that would liberate North Korea, reunify the peninsula, cripple China, and prevent it from seizing other areas. He had confidence that the United States could succeed in these efforts and that it should and could defend every place in the world that was threatened by communism. To him, the administration placed too little value on Asia.

Truman rejected MacArthur's proposals, regarding them as costly, dangerous, and unnecessary. The potential dangers included all-out war with China and even the Soviet Union as well, should it conclude that it must come to the defense of China. "We are trying to prevent a world war—not to start one," Truman explained. Furthermore, MacArthur's proposal could tie the United States down in an area of secondary importance and furnish the Soviets with new opportunities for expansion in Asia, which, the administration assumed, was the Soviet objective. MacArthur did not accept Truman's rejection of his proposal; rather, he appealed directly to the public and the Republicans in Congress for support. The president considered this action a threat to his authority as commander in chief as well as to his foreign policy and, in April, 1951, removed MacArthur from all of his commands. As Truman explained, he considered it "essential to relieve General MacArthur so that there would be no doubt or confusion as to the real purpose and aim of our policy."

The administration had returned to the original goal of the war, containment. Washington now sought a negotiated settlement, limited American military operations to Korea, and employed no more force than seemed necessary to gain terms it could accept. In spite of public discontent with the conduct of the war, which grew as the fighting became stalemated in 1951 and efforts at negotiation failed to produce a settlement, the administration persisted in pursuit of its goal, confident that the defense of South Korea had many desirable consequences. "The attack on Korea was part of a greater plan for conquering all of Asia," Truman insisted, but the enemy had "found out that aggression is not cheap or easy," and "men all over the world who want to remain free . . . know now that the champion of freedom can stand up and fight and that they will stand up and fight."

The Fair Deal

As the Truman administration changed American foreign and military policies from 1949 to 1953, Truman battled for a Fair Deal at home. Although based on the New Deal's assumption that the government should promote desirable social and economic change, the Fair Deal was more than a mere continuation of the New Deal. It sought to strengthen the labor movement; to expand benefits and coverage under

Social Security; to raise the minimum wage; to increase public housing, slum clearance, public power, and reclamation; and to institute federal aid to education and national health insurance. Finally, the Fair Deal envisioned changes in the farm program that would serve the interests of consumers and provide the basis for a farmer-labor alliance, and it expressed more concern about civil rights than had the New Deal.

In his fight for the Fair Deal, Truman enjoyed victories but also suffered defeats. His major success was the Housing Act of 1949, which included a public housing provision and slum clearance. Congress also enacted legislation to expand public power, soil conservation, reclamation, and flood control; increased the number of people covered and the benefits paid by Social Security; and raised the minimum wage. Congress did not, however, enact the new farm program, federal aid to education, national health insurance, Truman's labor program, or the civil rights proposals.

The Truman administration did influence Supreme Court decisions in the area of civil rights. Continuing to cooperate with the NAACP, the Justice Department submitted "friend of the court" briefs that helped to persuade the Court to hand down decisions in 1950 attacking segregation in interstate commerce and higher education and coming close to ruling that separate educational facilities could never be equal. Two and a half years later, Truman's Justice Department, in one of its last acts, filed a brief that advised the Court to overrule the separate-but-equal doctrine as it applied to elementary and secondary schools.

As commander in chief, Truman had a much larger role in the desegregation of the armed forces than he did in the judicial attacks on discrimination and segregation. In 1949, however, he learned that a directive from the commander in chief was not enough. His earlier order had led the Navy and Air Force to adopt a policy of integration, but the Army offered strong resistance, arguing that it must conform to the customs of the larger society to be effective and that African Americans were not well suited for combat. This resistance forced the president to apply pressure on the Army to persuade it to adopt integration as a policy, but even that pressure did not end the practice of segregation. Rather, the high casualties of the Korean War, compelled the Army to send blacks into combat alongside whites to replace other whites who had been killed or wounded. Integration worked. Whites and blacks in combat units got along well together, and the blacks fought more effectively than they had in segregated units. The experience changed the minds of army officers and key Southern congressmen.

Several factors prevented Truman from enacting more of his Fair Deal legislation. He was not as interested in domestic matters as he was in foreign affairs, he was not as articulate and skillful in managing Congress as Roosevelt had been, and he relied quite heavily on conservative advisers and administrators who resisted his reform proposals.

Truman also worked in a situation that posed major difficulties for a reformer. Depression had generated support for innovation in Roosevelt's early years, whereas Truman functioned in a relatively prosperous period. He faced a powerful conservative coalition in Congress that had already demonstrated that it could frustrate a president, even one as skillful as Roosevelt. Furthermore, as an advocate of change in race relations, Truman had to contend with the filibuster. It was used by Southern senators who took advantage of the interest that Truman and other advocates of civil rights legislation had in other areas as well. Pro-civil rights senators could tolerate inaction by the Senate for only so long before they felt compelled to give up on their efforts on behalf of civil rights in order to move forward in other areas. Powerful pressure groups, such as the American Farm Bureau Federation and the

American Medical Association, only added to Truman's frustrations.

The Korean War proved an additional obstacle to reform efforts. It commanded the attention of the president and the Congress. They believed that no matter was more deserving of their time and energy. Also, it increased the importance of Southern Democrats, many of whom occupied major positions in the congressional committees concerned with military and foreign affairs. Furthermore, as a far-from-popular war, it helped the Republicans gain seats in the congressional elections of 1950.

The Red Scare

An escalating Red Scare, generated by a widely held belief that communists inside the United States constituted a serious threat to the nation, was another obstacle in the Fair Deal's path. The scare distracted attention from reform, put Truman on the defensive against charges that his administration had been seriously infected by the "Communist conspiracy" and was "soft on communism," completed the destruction of the radical Left, thereby depriving reformers of helpful support, and raised doubts about the loyalty of liberals. Anyone who suggested that American life needed to be changed in important ways seemed un-American to many people in the early 1950's.

Communist penetration of the federal government had been insignificant, but communism in American life nevertheless became a large issue. Some historians have blamed Truman and his aides for McCarthyism, the extreme version of the Red Scare. Truman did make contributions, but they were hardly the crucial factor in the rise of McCarthyism.

The Truman administration responded to an already developing phenomenon and contributed to its further growth. In 1947, the president established a loyalty-security program for the federal government, and the next year, the Justice Department moved against the leaders of the American Communist Party, obtaining

their conviction for conspiring to overthrow the government by force and violence. Three years later, the United States Supreme Court upheld the convictions.

During the 1948 campaign, Truman sought to exploit the communist issue to his own advantage. He presented his party as the effective foe of communism and charged that the Republicans were "unwittingly the ally of the Communists in this country." In support of his claim about vigorous Democratic opposition to communism, he pointed to the "strong foreign policy" that he had developed and that checked the "Communist tide," the domestic programs of the Roosevelt-Truman administration that prevented the communists from making "any progress whatever in this country," and his loyalty program that made certain "that Communists and other disloyal persons are not employed by the Federal Government." On the other hand, he listed "considerable opposition" from Republicans in Congress to his foreign aid program and to his efforts "to strengthen democracy at home," and he charged that Republican investigations of communism lacked "the democratic safeguards of the loyalty program." He also contended that the communists backed Wallace because they wanted a Republican victory. A Republican administration's "reactionary policies" would "lead to the confusion and strife on which communism thrives." Truman's rhetoric and actions distressed civil libertarians.

In the early 1950's, Truman became much more critical of those who fomented the Red Scare, believing that it had taken on dangerous proportions. The anticommunist crusade had in fact turned on him.

If Truman's earlier behavior contributed to the Red Scare, clearly other factors were more important to its growth. A series of frustrating developments after 1948, including the communist victory in China, the development of the Soviet atomic bomb, and the Korean War, stimulated its growth. It also was influenced by

Senator Joseph McCarthy. *(Library of Congress)*

to American freedom. "Instead of striking blows at communism," the provisions of the McCarran bill would, he maintained, "strike blows at our own liberties and at our position in the forefront of those working for freedom in the world." He referred to the deportation provisions of the McCarran-Walter bill as "worse than the infamous Alien Act of 1798" and "inconsistent with our democratic ideals." Congress overrode the vetoes; its ability to do so testified to the great strength of the Red Scare.

Early in 1950, a Republican senator from Wisconsin, Joseph R. McCarthy, had emerged as the most promising figure in the crusade against domestic communists, and his needs and skills contributed to the rise of the movement that he came to personify. He supplied the American people with a conspiracy theory to explain recent history that pinned the blame for apparent communist successes on disloyal men in the Democratic administration, especially the State Department. Hurling such charges, he made himself into a major figure in American politics.

McCarthy successfully identified himself with frustrated conservatives. He expressed in his own way a view that had long had adherents in conservative circles and was now more widely endorsed as a consequence of the American struggle against the Soviet Union and China. It held that radicals constituted a serious threat to American institutions. He did not create this view, but he made it his own. Conservative Republicans rallied to his cause, supplying much of his active support.

McCarthy encountered opponents, including Truman, but they did not check his rise. McCarthy and others like him, according to the president, were "chipping away our basic freedoms just as insidiously and far more effectively than the Communists have ever been

several spy cases, by the unhappiness of many conservatives, and by the needs of Republicans. Conservatives, especially conservative Republicans, were opposed to the domestic changes of the Roosevelt-Truman period and recent developments in foreign affairs. Feeling cheated of deserved victories in the last three presidential elections, they employed their substantial power in Congress against the executive branch.

By the early 1950's, Congress led the anticommunist crusade and had passed several pieces of anticommunist legislation. The lawmakers enacted the McCarran Internal Security Act of 1950, which supplied the government with a battery of weapons to use against communists and other radicals. In 1952, Congress passed the McCarran-Walter Immigration and Nationality Act, with provisions barring the immigration of "subversives" and permitting the attorney general to deport immigrants with communist affiliations even after they had become citizens.

Truman vetoed these bills, convinced that the anticommunist crusade had become a threat able to do," and they had "created such a wave of fear and uncertainty that their attacks upon our liberties go almost unchallenged." Such arguments failed to rally the public behind Truman, perhaps because he and his aides had so frequently preached the dangers of communists themselves. Still, given the forces working against him now, Truman might have been even less successful in rallying support if he had not had an anticommunist record to which he could point. He would surely have accomplished more if the Senate had supplied strong opposition to McCarthy. Only a minority of senators, however, opposed their Wisconsin colleague, many of the Democrats were quite tolerant of him, and some senators feared him, as he participated strenuously in the congressional elections of 1950 and gained a reputation for great political effectiveness. Most of the active senatorial opposition came from a small band of liberals, most of whom were new to the Senate and incapable of leading it.

The Loss of Power
By 1952, another presidential election year, Truman had become an unusually unpopular president. Only 23 percent of the people, according to a public opinion poll in late 1951, approved of his performance. This was the lowest presidential rating in the history of scientific polling, then nearly two decades old, and would not be surpassed by any president, not even Richard Nixon in 1974, until Jimmy Carter in 1980. Along with his other problems, Truman faced mounting public criticism over the scandals in his administration. During his second term, officials in various federal agencies had been charged with corruption, and in April, 1952, Truman forced Attorney General J. Howard McGrath to resign because of lack of zeal in investigating these charges. That same month, Truman further undermined his popularity when he seized major American steel mills in order to prevent a strike. The president had become frustrated both with labor's de-

mands for wage increases, which threatened his wartime efforts to curb inflation, and what he considered management's intransigence. Therefore, he placed the mills under federal control. When the Supreme Court ruled, in *Youngstown v. Sawyer*, that Truman's action exceeded presidential authority, he returned the mills to private control and acquiesced in an eventual rise in wages and steel prices that he thought inflationary.

In such a situation Truman felt compelled to withdraw as a candidate for reelection. He was not prevented by the Constitution from running again, but he concluded that he should take himself out of the race. Later, he would suggest that he would have won if he had run, just as he had in 1948. The situation, however, was much more difficult than in 1948, only in part because it now included a famous opponent with a very attractive personality, Dwight D. Eisenhower.

Truman's plight was illustrated by the difficulties he had in finding someone who would go before the country as his successor. Early in 1952, he turned to the governor of Illinois, Adlai Stevenson, but found him reluctant to make the race. Stevenson's reluctance was not a reflection of weaknesses in his personality but of political shrewdness. Stevenson did not want to be Truman's handpicked successor, and he tried as much as possible to avoid having that label pinned on him. This act testified dramatically to Truman's lack of success as a political leader. He had not demonstrated the skill in coalition politics that had been anticipated for him by his champions eight years before.

When Stevenson finally accepted the Democratic nomination, Truman worked hard for him even though he had grown unhappy with the Illinois Democrat. The president's vigorous efforts in the campaign duplicated what he had done in 1948, but this time they failed. Truman could not maintain Democratic control of the White House.

Eisenhower swept to victory by a wide margin in an election in which an unusually large percentage of the eligible voters went to the polls and in which many Democrats voted for him. Each of the major candidates attracted many more voters than had Truman four years earlier. Supported by all classes, Eisenhower made a breakthrough in the traditionally Democratic South, made significant gains in the large Northern cities where Democrats had dominated since 1928, swept the suburbs, and restored Republican domination of the towns and rural areas in the Middle and Far West. Unhappiness with the course of American foreign policy and the war, fears of communism, and concern about corruption and inflation influenced the outcome. A positive factor was the confidence in and affection for Eisenhower.

Discontent with Truman contributed to the outcome. Just before he left office to return to his home in Independence, Missouri, only 31 percent of the people approved of his performance in the White House. He, however, looked upon himself as having been an unusually successful president.

A Sense of Success

In his farewell address to the American people on January 15, 1953, Truman expressed a feeling of success, not failure as president. Describing the president's job as big and hard, he emphasized his role as decision maker. "The greatest part of the President's job is to make decisions.... The President...has to decide. He can't pass the buck to anybody. No one else can do the deciding for him. That's his job." To Truman, it seemed, he had played that demanding role well. "We feel we have done our best in the public service," he continued. "I hope and believe we have contributed to the welfare of this Nation and to the peace of the world."

Dealing only briefly with domestic accomplishments, he emphasized economic success, maintaining that "we in America have learned how to attain real prosperity for our people."

He also pointed with pride to his civil rights record. "We have made great progress in spreading the blessings of American life to all of our people," he insisted. "There has been a tremendous awakening of the American conscience on the great issues of civil rights—equal economic opportunities, equal rights of citizenship, and equal educational opportunities for all our people, whatever their race or religion or status of birth."

The chief significance of his presidency, Truman asserted, lay in foreign affairs. "The menace of Communism—and our fight against it" he called "the overriding issue of our time." Then he added, "I suppose history will remember my term in office as years when the 'cold war' began to overshadow our lives. I have had hardly a day in office that has not been dominated by this all-embracing struggle—this conflict between those who love freedom and those who would lead the world back into slavery and darkness."

Truman was proud of the manner in which he had dealt with the Soviet challenge, as he saw it, regarding his moves as "great and historic...." He listed his accomplishments as the withdrawal of Soviet troops from Iran after the United States took a firm stand, the freedom and independence of Greece and Turkey as a result of American aid, "the Marshall Plan which saved Europe, the heroic Berlin airlift,... our military aid program," and the defense pacts in the North Atlantic region and elsewhere. "Most important of all," he insisted, "we acted in Korea." That decision was, he believed, "the most important in my time as president," and the right one. Referring to the invasion of South Korea as a "test," he argued, "We met it firmly. We met it successfully. The aggression has been repelled. The Communists have seen their hopes of easy conquest go down the drain. The determination of a free people to defend themselves has been made clear to the Kremlin." Truman maintained that the policies which he had inaugurated had "set the course" that would "win" the Cold War and that the sign of victory would be the ultimate breakup of the communist system. There was, he argued, a "fatal flaw" in the communist world. "Theirs is a godless system, a system of slavery; there is no freedom in it, no consent. The Iron Curtain, the secret police, the constant purges, all of these are symptoms of a great basic weakness—the rulers' fear of their own people." This weakness guaranteed victory. "As the free world grows stronger, more united, more attractive to men on both sides of the Iron Curtain and as the Soviet hopes for easy expansion are blocked—then there will have to come a time of change in the Soviet world."

For his own time, however, Truman did not claim that "liberation" was at hand. Yet he did claim that his policies "averted World War III up to now, and we may already have succeeded

in establishing conditions which can keep that war from happening as far ahead as man can see." He declared that the "whole purpose of what we are doing is to prevent World War III."

Truman believed that war had been a real possibility during his years as president and that he had successfully avoided it because he had learned the lessons of history and had not repeated the mistakes of the past. Those lessons and mistakes were found in the years between the two world wars.

Truman divided the interwar period into two eras, each with different lessons. The first period was the 1920's, which taught the need for cooperation and trade with other nations. The second period was the 1930's, which demonstrated the need to respond to aggressors. During the 1930's, Truman reminded his listeners, "the Japanese moved into Manchuria, and

Truman in the Oval Office with Adlai Stevenson, the defeated Democratic candidate for president in the 1952 election, on December 4, 1952. *(NARA)*

free men did not act. The Nazis marched into the Rhineland, into Austria, into Czechoslovakia, and free men were paralyzed for lack of strength and unity and will." These were "years of weakness and indecision," and World War II was the "evil result." Americans, he said, should compare the indecision and inaction of the 1930's with "the speed and courage and decisiveness with which we have moved against the Communist threat since World War II."

Truman pointed particularly to the situation in Korea. "Here was history repeating itself," he maintained, comparing the invasion of South Korea "to the 1930's—to Manchuria, to Ethiopia, the Rhineland, Austria, and finally to Munich." The invasion was "another probing action, another testing action." If he had behaved as leaders had in the 1930's and had "let the Republic of Korea go under, some other country would be next, and then another." The evil consequences would grow: "The courage and confidence of the free world would be ebbing away, just as it did in the 1930's. And the United Nations would go the way of the League of Nations." Finally, the United States would be forced to fight a large-scale war as it had from 1941 to 1945. The lessons, however, had been learned. "Where free men failed the test before, this time we met the test."

Truman had not behaved as had Hoover, Roosevelt, and other Western leaders. He, like them, had faced the threat of world war. Their actions had contributed to the coming of such a war, but his had avoided one. Because he had learned the lessons of history and avoided the mistakes of the past, he had been forced to fight only a limited war even though his situation had been as dangerous as theirs—even more dangerous, as he was the first president to serve in the atomic age and a third world war would be even more destructive than the first and second.

The significance of the Truman period and the Truman presidency was to be found, Truman suggested, chiefly in its contrast with the years between the great wars. His incumbency as president would have been enormously important, he implied, even if nothing of importance had taken place at home. Failure and frustrations, it appears, could have been tolerated there, but not in international affairs. Mistakes there could have been fatal. International affairs were paramount in the Truman presidency, and they had been well conducted.

Richard S. Kirkendall

Suggested Readings

Beschloss, Michael R. *The Conquerors: Roosevelt, Truman, and the Destruction of Hitler's Germany, 1941-1945*. New York: Simon & Schuster, 2002. Using archives opened in the late twentieth century, Beschloss traces how Roosevelt arrived at, and Truman instituted, a plan for the reconstruction of postwar Germany.

Burns, Richard D. *Harry S. Truman: A Bibliography of His Times and Presidency*. Wilmington, Del.: Scholarly Resources, 1984. A comprehensive list of primary and secondary sources for further study.

Donaldson, Gary. *Truman Defeats Dewey*. Lexington: University Press of Kentucky, 1999. An analysis of the presidential election of 1948.

Donovan, Robert J. *Conflict and Crisis: The Presidency of Harry S. Truman*. New York: Norton, 1977.

_____. *Tumultuous Years: The Presidency of Harry S. Truman, 1949-1953*. New York: Norton, 1982. Donovan's two volumes offer a complete examination of Truman's presidency.

Ferrell, Robert H. *Harry S. Truman: A Life*. Columbia: University of Missouri Press, 1994. One of the preeminent historians on Truman examines key episodes of Truman's career.

_____. *Harry S. Truman and the Modern American Presidency*. New York: Longman, 1983. Reflects the view of Truman as national hero, a perspective that emerged during the 1970's.

_____, ed. *Harry S. Truman and the Bomb.* Worland, Wyo.: High Plains, 1996. Gives insights into Truman's decision to drop the atomic bomb on Japan.

Gosnell, Harold F. *Truman's Crises.* Westport, Conn.: Greenwood Press, 1980. A substantial biography.

Gullan, Harold I. *The Upset That Wasn't: Harry S. Truman and the Crucial Election of 1948.* Chicago: Ivan R. Dee, 1998. Details the events of the 1948 election.

Hamby, Alonzo L. *Man of the People: The Life of Harry S. Truman.* New York: Oxford University Press, 1995. A balanced portrait of Truman's complex personality.

Harry S. Truman Presidential Museum and Library. http://www.trumanlibrary.org/. The Web site of Truman's official library.

Kirkendall, Richard S., ed. *The Harry S. Truman Encyclopedia.* Boston: G. K. Hall, 1989. Brings together more than three hundred topical articles about the Truman presidency.

McCullough, David G. *Truman.* New York: Simon & Schuster, 1992. A substantial Pulitzer Prize-winning biography that explores Truman's rise from humble roots to the presidency, examines the key decisions of his administration, and emphasizes Truman's character and integrity.

Neal, Steve. *Harry and Ike: The Partnership That Remade the Postwar World.* New York: Scribner, 2001. Examines the unusually close relationship and political collaboration between Truman and Dwight D. Eisenhower.

Truman, Harry S. *Memoirs.* Garden City, N.Y.: Doubleday, 1955-1956. Truman's autobiography.

_____. *Off the Record: The Private Papers of Harry S. Truman.* Edited by Robert H. Ferrell. New York: Harper & Row, 1980. Writings of Truman that span from 1945 to 1971.

_____. *Talking with Harry: Candid Conversations with President Harry S. Truman.* Edited by Ralph E. Weber. Wilmington, Del.: SR Books, 2001. In a series of interviews that took place in 1959, Truman reflected on history, the office of the presidency, partisan politics, and Cold War issues.

Truman, Margaret. *Harry S. Truman.* New York: Morrow, 1973. The first lady published this biography the year after Truman's death.

Wainstock, Dennis. *The Decision to Drop the Atomic Bomb.* Westport, Conn.: Praeger, 1996. An account of the political, military, and diplomatic events that led to the Japan bombings.

Walker, Samuel J. *Prompt and Utter Destruction: Truman and the Use of Atomic Bombs Against Japan.* 1997. Rev. ed. Chapel Hill: University of North Carolina Press, 2004. Walker evaluates the roles of U.S.-Soviet relations and of American domestic politics, among other factors, on the decision to drop the atomic bombs on Japan.

Dwight D. Eisenhower

34th President, 1953-1961

Born: October 14, 1890
    Denison, Texas
Died: March 28, 1969
    Washington, D.C.

Political Party: Republican
Vice President: Richard M. Nixon

Cabinet Members

Secretary of State: John Foster Dulles,
    Christian A. Herter
Secretary of the Treasury: George Humphrey,
    Robert B. Anderson
Secretary of Defense: Charles E. Wilson, Neil H.
    McElroy, Thomas S. Gates
Attorney General: H. Brownell, Jr., William P.
    Rogers
Postmaster General: A. E. Summerfield
Secretary of the Interior: Douglas McKay, Fred
    Seaton
Secretary of Agriculture: Ezra T. Benton
Secretary of Commerce: Sinclair Weeks,
    Lewis L. Strauss
Secretary of Labor: Martin Durkin, James P.
    Mitchell
Secretary of Health, Education, and Welfare:
    Oveta Culp Hobby, Marion B. Folsom,
    Arthur S. Flemming

During his administration, Dwight David Eisenhower, the thirty-fourth president of the United States, was much criticized by news commentators, political pundits, and students of the presidency. Critics attacked him for his alleged blunders, blandness, and laziness in office. A common image of the president depicted him as a mumbling, bumbling, stumbling, fumbling leader who preferred a game of golf or a bridge foursome to the duties of his office. A series of stories and jokes, at Eisenhower's expense, circulated even while he was in office. One story claimed that if Eisenhower

Eisenhower's official portrait. *(White House Historical Society)*

609

died, then Vice President Richard Nixon would become president, but if Sherman Adams (Eisenhower's chief of staff, who supposedly ran the administration) died, then Eisenhower would become president. Another story described an Eisenhower doll as one that, when wound, did nothing for four years. One of Eisenhower's own speechwriters described the president as a "walking debate" and an "oaf."

Yet to the majority of Americans in the 1950's, Eisenhower was known simply as Ike, and, having elected him to office in 1952 by a comfortable margin, they reelected him in 1956 by an even greater margin and would probably have reelected him to a third term if the Constitution did not prohibit his running again. Politically, he was the most powerful president of the postwar era.

What accounted for Eisenhower's immense popularity in the 1950's, even as some critics, including the majority of professional historians, held him in such low esteem? Undoubtedly, one reason was that he was a national hero, a poor boy of humble origins from Abilene, Kansas, who had led the Allied armies to victory over Germany in World War II. Another reason was almost certainly Eisenhower's famous grin and winning personality, which of-

THE FIRST LADY
MAMIE EISENHOWER

Mary "Mamie" Geneva Doud was born on November 14, 1896, in Boone, Iowa. One of four daughters of a wealthy businessman, Mamie grew up in a loving family in comfortable homes with summers in Denver, Colorado, her studies culminated by completing Miss Walcott's Fashionable School in Denver. She married Dwight D. "Ike" Eisenhower, an Army lieutenant, in 1916 after a brief courtship.

Mamie entered the White House in January, 1953, with a wealth of experience in meeting and entertaining prominent and powerful national and international leaders. She had been the hostess of numerous informal and formal gatherings while Eisenhower was president of Columbia University and a North Atlantic Treaty Organization (NATO) commander. She quickly established a reputation for running the White House in a firm, efficient, and yet benevolent manner.

Her view of being First Lady clearly was to remain largely in the background and provide her husband with personal, but not policy, support. Mamie was unquestionably successful at this, maintaining high public opinion levels throughout Eisenhower's eight years in office. She became famous for her "Mamie bangs" hairstyle and for favoring pink clothing. However, Mamie fought to overcome personal health problems. Particularly troublesome were a weak heart and an inner-ear malady which made her light-headed and caused her to stagger while walking. This symptom led to gossip that she had a drinking problem. Mamie fought this rumor by declining to drink alcohol in public and withdrawing to her bedroom during bouts of dizziness.

The strength of Mamie's support for her husband was evident during the several medical crises that he suffered during his presidency. Aides noted that she remained at his side and played a key yet private role in ensuring that his recovery progressed according to the physicians' plan.

Mamie left the White House with Eisenhower in 1960 for their retirement home in a farmhouse near Gettysburg, Pennsylvania. She and Ike enjoyed a quiet life there entertaining family and friends until his death on March 28, 1969. Mamie maintained as many family traditions as her health permitted until her death on November 1, 1979.

Robert Dewhirst

ten masked his short and fiery temper. The "I Like Ike" buttons of the 1952 and 1956 campaigns expressed the genuine sentiment of most Americans.

Equally important was the fact that his administration reflected many of the broad undercurrents and overarching themes of American life in the 1950's. It is too simplistic to dismiss the 1950's as a serene, rather passive, decade much akin to the 1920's in its political apathy, conformity, and materialism. Much more complex than that, the 1950's witnessed the escalation of the Civil Rights movement, the start of the space age, and the beginnings of America's involvement in Vietnam. The 1950's was also an anxious period when Americans, haunted by the fear of nuclear holocaust, seriously considered a proposal to build an air raid shelter for every family in the United States and when schoolchildren were instructed in the event of a nuclear attack to protect themselves by hiding their faces and assuming a fetal position under their desks.

Yet those who characterize the 1950's in terms of its crassness, mediocrity, and political conservatism would not be entirely wrong. The 1950's was above all a period of unprecedented prosperity, mass consumption, and planned obsolescence, when consumers, encouraged by mass advertising, chose from a seemingly endless variety of goods and gadgets, many of questionable durability. It was also a period of mass culture, when television invaded the homes of even America's poorest families (some still without indoor plumbing) and, along with radio and motion pictures, produced forms of entertainment characterized by their drabness and humdrum quality. Finally, the 1950's was a decade whose political leaders generally accepted the political goals, programs, and policies of the previous twenty years but who took few political initiatives or showed little imagination of their own.

The Eisenhower administration mirrored the climate of the times. As later historians have shown, President Eisenhower was not the indifferent, ineffectual leader that his contemporaries often accused him of being. He was an activist president and a shrewd organizer and coordinator of men and women. He had a keen and often penetrating intellect, and although he preferred to operate quietly behind the scenes, he was fully informed and completely in charge of his administration. The common image of Eisenhower, even when he was president, as an essentially inarticulate and incoherent leader who was controlled and manipulated by his cabinet is simply false.

Yet Eisenhower was not an original thinker or an intellect. "Eisenhower's mind is, like his personality, standard-American," one observer noted. "It is unschematic, distrustful of fine distinctions into the realm of matter and things, concerned with the effect of ideas rather than their validity." Also, Eisenhower was almost a father figure in the 1950's, a president who stood above the political fray and a leader whose purpose was to watch over and assure continuation of the status quo affluence. His was a middle-of-the-road presidency designed to assure the good life at a time when it seemed obtainable to the great majority of Americans. (African Americans, Latinos, other ethnic minorities, and the most destitute were largely ignored—African Americans until the end of the 1950's, and the others until the 1960's.) Advocating moderate policies and an economy of abundance, Eisenhower rejected both orthodox Republicanism and New Deal statism. Instead, he sought an authentic American center, which would assure freedom and security by accepting the basic economic and social tenets of the New Deal, even as he remained a fiscal conservative in most matters. At the same time, Eisenhower was a strident anticommunist who continued the nation's basic foreign policy of containment, with the added flourish of threatening massive retaliation in case of communist aggression, but who nevertheless followed policies in many ways more restrained than those of subsequent administrations. In short, Eisenhower reflected perfectly the temper of the times even as he led the country with good sense and much prudence.

A Midwestern Boyhood

The future president was born in Denison, Texas, on October 14, 1890, the third son of David and Ida Eisenhower. Both his parents were members of the River Brethren Protestant sect, descendants of German-born farmers who had first come to Pennsylvania in the eighteenth century and later migrated to the Middle West. They had met while students at Lane University, a small school in Lecompton, Kansas, operated by the River Brethren. They were married at the college chapel on September 23, 1885.

A family quickly followed. In 1886, Ida gave birth to the first of her six sons, Arthur. A second son, Edgar, was born in 1889, followed by David Dwight (Ida later reversed the names to avoid having two first-name Davids in the family), Roy in 1892, Paul (who died in infancy) in 1894, Earl in 1898, and Milton in 1899. Times were hard for the Eisenhowers. As a wedding gift, David's father, Jacob, a successful farmer from Abilene, Kansas, had given his son a 160-acre farm and two thousand dollars, but David lost everything in a business he had started after his partner absconded with all of his cash. Bankrupt after he had paid off his creditors, David found a ten-dollar-a-week job with the Cotton Belt Railroad in Denison, where Dwight was born. With three sons, little money, and few prospects, however, David was persuaded by his family in 1891 to return to Abilene, where he found work with a local creamery and later with a gas plant.

Making hardly more than he had in Texas, David Eisenhower's financial problems multiplied as his family grew, but the family managed. Although Dwight wore clothes handed down from his older brothers and sold vegetables to more prosperous families on the north

side of town (his family lived in the poorer south side of Abilene) to make some pocket money, his younger years were generally typical of boys growing up in a small Midwestern town at the turn of the century. Dwight enjoyed listening to the old-timers tell about the days when Abilene, the northern terminus of the Chisholm Trail, had been a wild frontier town, which probably explains his later love for Western novels. He was also a natural athlete who loved sports, fishing, and hunting. At Abilene High School, he played football and baseball and was regarded as something of a football hero. It was in sports that he first displayed some of his later talent as a leader. He organized Saturday afternoon games of baseball or football and helped form the Abilene High School Athletic Association to purchase athletic equipment for the baseball and football teams. He also arranged camping and hunting trips with his friends, taking charge of their money and purchasing necessary food and supplies.

In school, Dwight was a good student, particularly in history. His class prophecy was that he would become a Yale University history professor, whereas his brother Edgar would become president of the United States. As a sophomore at Abilene High, Dwight first met Swede Hazlett, the son of a physician and pharmacist who lived in the more affluent north side of town. The two boys would later become lifelong friends. Even as president, Eisenhower would write Hazlett long, introspective letters in which he would lay out his most private thoughts on pressing issues before him.

At the time that Eisenhower was graduated from high school in 1909, he stood about 6 feet tall and weighed approximately 150 pounds, having blue eyes and light brown hair that had not yet begun to thin. He had the coordination and gait of an athlete. Sometimes shy with girls, he was, for the most part, popular, poised, and remarkably self-confident. From his father, a stern disciplinarian who sometimes displayed a fierce temper, he had acquired his own short

The Vice President
Richard M. Nixon

Richard M. Nixon was born on January 9, 1913, in Yorba Linda, California, the son of a citrus farmer and store owner. While attending public schools, he worked in his father's grocery store and gasoline station. Nixon graduated from Whittier College in California in 1934 and from Duke University Law School in 1937. He was then admitted to the bar and began practicing law in the firm Winger and Beasley in Whittier, but he soon joined as partner the firm Beasley, Kroop, and Nixon. On June 21, 1940, Nixon married Thelma "Pat" Ryan. They had two daughters.

During World War II, Nixon was an attorney in the Office of Emergency Management in Washington, D.C. He was then commissioned as a lieutenant junior grade in the Navy and ended his service in 1946 at the rank of lieutenant commander. Nixon was elected to the U.S. House of Representatives in 1946, serving in the chamber from 1947 until 1950, when he campaigned successfully for the U.S. Senate, where he served from 1951 until 1953. Nixon was a part of Dwight D. Eisenhower's successful presidential campaign, serving as his vice president from 1953 to 1961. Nixon became one of the nation's most active vice presidents, traveling worldwide on behalf of Eisenhower and often filling in on assignments when Eisenhower's health waned.

Nixon sought the presidency in 1960 but was defeated by John F. Kennedy in one of the closest elections in American history. After his defeat, Nixon joined the law firm of Adams, Duque, and Hazeltine, then ran unsuccessfully for governor of California in 1962. Although he announced his retirement from politics, Nixon remained active as an author, penning several books and practicing law with the New York City-based firm of Mudge, Stern, Baldwin, and Todd.

In 1968, Nixon won the presidency, serving from 1969 until his disgraced exit from office in August of 1974 as a result of the Watergate scandal. In his postpresidential years, he moved back to New York City and continued to write until his death on April 22, 1994.

Robert P. Watson and Richard Yon

---

temper, but his mother had passed on to her son her warm personality and ingratiating smile and, perhaps, Ike's later concern for organization. Ida was a born organizer, who had established a regular routine of chores for her sons that included cooking, cleaning, caring for the family chickens, and tending to the family garden.

From West Point to the White House

In 1911, Eisenhower entered the United States Military Academy at West Point after working for a year to help put his brother Edgar through his first year of college. He had been persuaded to apply to both West Point and the United States Naval Academy at Annapolis by Swede Hazlett, who himself had been appointed to the

naval academy. Although the two young men intended that Ike (Dwight's nickname since childhood) would join Hazlett at Annapolis, when Eisenhower was offered an appointment at West Point, he jumped at the opportunity. In June, he left Abilene to enter West Point as a member of the class of 1915, "the class on which the stars fell" (fifty-nine of the 164 graduates of the class of 1915 would rise to the rank of brigadier general or higher).

Eisenhower's career at the military academy was undistinguished. Although he did manage to graduate in the top third of his class in 1915, he was known more for his skill at coaching football than for anything else. He had planned to play football as a cadet, but he injured his knee in 1912 and had to leave the team. Instead, he became a cheerleader and a coach of the junior varsity team. Evaluations of his potential as an officer were mixed. One instructor recorded that Eisenhower would enjoy army life but not excel, whereas another wrote that he "was born to command." His career as a cadet, however, made a lasting impression on him. At West Point he had learned the importance of discipline and dedication, had been taught about the structure of command and the responsibilities of leadership, and had come to appreciate even more the value of teamwork, something he had already learned from playing and coaching football.

Commissioned a second lieutenant in the infantry, Eisenhower was assigned to Fort Sam Houston in San Antonio, Texas. There he met Mary Geneva Doud (nicknamed Mamie), the daughter of a well-to-do Denver couple, who was spending the fall and winter in Texas. Following a whirlwind courtship, Ike and Mamie were married in Denver on July 1, 1916. Fourteen months later, Mamie gave birth to a boy, Doud Dwight, whom she and Ike called Icky.

During the next few years, Eisenhower was assigned to various army posts in the United States. The new officer was greatly disappointed that he did not see service in Europe during World War I. Instead, he became an instructor in the use of a new weapon, the tank. In 1920, he and Mamie suffered a personal tragedy when Icky died following a bout of scarlet fever. Still grief stricken over the loss of his son, Eisenhower was assigned in 1922 to Camp Gaillard at the Panama Canal. Ike's two years at Camp Gaillard were important ones for him, primarily because he was greatly influenced by his superior, General Fox Conner, a man versed in military history and theory, who passed on to his young subordinate much of his own considerable knowledge about tactics, logistics, reconnaissance, and intelligence. Later, Eisenhower would refer to Conner as one who "held a place in [his] affections that no other, not a relative, could obtain."

In 1925, Eisenhower was selected to the Command and General Staff School (C&GS) at Fort Leavenworth, Kansas, generally considered an essential step for high command. Although he was graduated first in a class of 275 and was later appointed to the Army War College (another step toward higher command), his major posting during this period was as a member of the American Battle Monuments Commission from 1927 to 1929, hardly a choice assignment for an ambitious officer. Furthermore, having reached the age of forty in 1930, he still held only a major's rank.

In the war game exercises at C&GS and in his work for the Battle Monuments Commission, Ike displayed a mastery of detail, a capacity to work under pressure and as part of a team, and a talent for translating concepts and ideas into action. These abilities did not go unnoticed by his superiors or by such senior officers as General John Pershing, who headed the Battle Monuments Commission and who even asked Eisenhower to help him with his memoirs. This task brought him into contact for the first time with Colonel George C. Marshall, who as chair of the Joint Chiefs of Staff during World War II would help catapult him upward in his career.

In 1929, Eisenhower was assigned to the War Department in Washington, D.C., where he served under the army's chief of staff, General Douglas MacArthur. Ike's three years in the War Department afforded him excellent training in administration and personal diplomacy, which would be extremely important to him later. He worked closely with MacArthur, writing many of the general's speeches, reports, and press releases. He also lobbied Congress and helped prepare a national economic mobilization plan, during the course of which he visited industrial plants and met with business leaders throughout the country. He also had major responsibility for organizing the Industrial War College to train officers in supply, and he worked with a combined executive-congressional committee organized to determine "how to take the profits out of war."

Eisenhower impressed MacArthur enough that when he left for the Philippine Islands in 1935 he took Ike with him. Eisenhower's four years in the Philippines were generally not pleasant for him. Mamie and his son, John, who had been born in 1922, remained behind in Washington, D.C., for a year, and then when they joined him, Mamie frequently became ill. Moreover, Ike was anxious to serve with American troops, and his personal relationship with MacArthur, which had been close in Washington, became increasingly strained as he clashed more and more with the general over MacArthur's grandiose, but financially unrealistic, plans for building a Filipino army. By the time he returned home in 1939, each man was glad to be rid of the other.

While serving in the Philippines, Eisenhower was promoted to the rank of lieutenant colonel, but as he told his son after returning home, he did not expect to be made a full colonel until 1950, at which time he would be sixty years old and unlikely to make general. Yet within five years he would be a four-star general and an internationally known figure. What changed Eisenhower's destiny was World War II.

Events moved rapidly for Eisenhower as the army expanded following the outbreak of war in Europe in 1939. In 1941, he was promoted to the rank of colonel. Three months later, he was made chief of staff of the Third Army, which soon thereafter participated in large-scale maneuvers in Louisiana. Ike's tactical skills in these maneuvers won for him a promotion to the rank of brigadier general and brought him to the attention of General Marshall, now the army chief of staff, who in March, 1942, passed over 350 senior officers to promote Ike to major general. Two months later, Marshall appointed

Eisenhower gives orders to his troops on D day, June 6, 1944. *(Library of Congress)*

him commander of the European theater of operations (ETO) and, shortly thereafter, put him in charge of the invasion of North Africa, America's first major combat mission in the war. Following victory in North Africa, Ike was put in command of the May, 1943, invasion of Sicily and then the invasion of Italy. Finally, in December, 1943, before the Italian campaign had been concluded, he was named commander of Operation Overlord, the invasion of Europe across the English Channel. By this time, Eisenhower had already attained the rank of full general.

Several reasons accounted for Eisenhower's meteoric rise in less than four years from a relatively obscure brigadier general to commander of the largest military operation ever conceived. These were, for example, Ike's relatively young age, his unbounded energy, his poise under pressure, and his ability to take command of a situation and make hard decisions. When Marshall first recommended Eisenhower for promotion to major general in 1942, he was looking for relatively young and energetic commanders with considerable initiative. Ike seemed to display these qualities, as well as those of geniality and supreme self-confidence. Almost everyone whom Eisenhower met liked him and trusted him implicitly. Even more important, Ike emphasized teamwork and was able to bring together and work successfully with military and political leaders from all the Allied nations. He was comfortable with world leaders, and he had shown in North Africa that he could run a combined British-American operation. President Franklin D. Roosevelt, who chose Eisenhower for Overlord, appreciated these qualities of leadership.

The successful invasion of Europe on June 6, 1944 (D day), and the victory over Germany less than a year later turned Eisenhower into a world celebrity. He enjoyed overwhelmingly favorable press coverage. More than any other person, except perhaps Prime Minister Winston Churchill of Great Britain, he was associated with victory in Europe. Returning to the United States from Europe in June, 1945, he made a round of triumphant appearances. Everywhere he received a hero's welcome, and the first talk began to be heard of Ike as future presidential candidate.

At that time, however, Eisenhower had no interest in politics. Indeed, he shared the military's general bias against politicians and claimed to be apolitical. "Your conclusions concerning my attitude toward politics are 100 percent correct," he wrote Swede Hazlett in March, 1946. "I cannot conceive of any set of circumstances that could ever drag out of me permission to consider me for any political post." Instead, he accepted an appointment by President Harry S. Truman in November, 1945, as army chief of staff, a position he held until 1948 when he retired from the Army to become president of Columbia University. As chief of staff, he advocated a universal military training and unification of the armed forces. While at Columbia, he opposed loyalty oaths for faculty members, and he instituted several new programs, including an Institute of War and Peace Studies.

As Eisenhower confessed to Hazlett before accepting the position at Columbia, however, he knew "nothing about the workings of a great University," and after moving to Columbia, he found himself increasingly isolated from the faculty, many of whom had opposed his appointment because he had no advanced degree. At the same time, war had broken out in Korea in June of 1950, the world appeared in crisis, and Eisenhower felt secluded at Columbia. When President Truman asked him in the fall of 1950 to assume the command of the newly formed North Atlantic Treaty Organization (NATO), he readily accepted, taking an indefinite leave of absence from Columbia.

Eisenhower served as commander of NATO from 1951 to June, 1952, when he returned to the United States to run for president. As the military commander who had directed the liberation of Europe during World War II, he was a staunch proponent of a strong Atlantic alliance, and as head of NATO, he worked relentlessly in the cause of collective security. Indeed, had Senator Robert A. Taft of Ohio, the likely Republican nominee for president in 1952, supported NATO, he might not have opposed him for the presidency. In June, 1951, Eisenhower met with Taft to discuss the European alliance. Dismayed by the senator's talk of limiting the number of divisions in NATO and by what he sensed as growing isolationism in Congress, Eisenhower concluded that Taft's advocacy of such a "Fortress America" foreign policy indicated an ignorance of world affairs. He later claimed that, had Taft indicated any commitment to collective security, he, Eisenhower, would have withdrawn his own name as a candidate for the Republican nomination.

Eisenhower had been under growing pressure for several years to make a bid for president. Although he continued to deny any interest in the office, he left his options open, meeting politically influential people and making public appearances that only increased the demand that he run. He had never declared a political preference, but his own conservative views on most domestic issues inclined him toward the Republican Party. He was finally persuaded to seek the office in 1952 by a group of moderate Republicans, led by Senator Henry Cabot Lodge of Massachusetts, that was determined to prevent the right wing of the party from gaining the nomination for Taft and that saw in General Eisenhower an extremely popular alternative whose international orientation coincided with its own. Resigning from the army in June, Eisenhower returned home to campaign against the Ohio senator, and at the Republican National Convention in July, he was nominated on the first ballot. As his running mate, he selected Richard Nixon, a conservative senator from California favored by the Taft wing of the party. Focusing on the issues

of Korea, communism, and corruption, and promising to go to Korea if elected, he easily defeated his Democratic opponent, Governor Adlai Stevenson of Illinois, in the November elections.

Cabinet and Staff: An Organizational Approach to the Presidency

Eisenhower took the oath of office on January 20, 1953. During his first administration, American society was, for the most part, affluent, complacent, and self-satisfied. The journalist Marquis Childs described what he perceived to be the national mood at mid-decade: "No American boy was being shot at anywhere, our taxes had been cut, and we were on our way to making eight million automobiles in a single year." Although undercurrents of change in both foreign and domestic policy were already present, the widespread mood in the nation was to leave matters pretty much as they had evolved since the New Deal of the 1930's. For domestic issues, this meant retaining the broad outlines of the social welfare state developed under Franklin D. Roosevelt and Harry S. Truman but not going much beyond that. In foreign affairs, it meant continuing the essential policy of containing Soviet aggression developed after World War II, although the great majority of Americans were anxious to end the no-win war in Korea.

The new administration was committed to these basic principles, although President Eisenhower thought it essential that government spending be cut and a cheaper way be found to limit Soviet expansion than by relying on large military forces. Eisenhower was a fiscal conservative who had long believed in the need to limit government spending and authority. Even as a young military officer, he had expressed occasional disagreement with his younger brother Milton, then rising through the ranks of federal bureaucracy, who saw a much more positive role for government than he did. After Ike returned to the United States from Europe in 1945, he became good friends with many of the nation's richest and most powerful business leaders, whose staunch conservative views on fiscal and other issues he found congenial. Increasingly, he inveighed against statism and talked about the importance of following a middle course.

President Eisenhower characterized his domestic programs as dynamic conservatism, by which he meant that he would be "conservative when it comes to money and liberal when it comes to human beings." To help carry out his programs, the new president picked for his cabinet a group of successful businessmen. (One journalist quipped that Eisenhower's cabinet consisted of "eight millionaires and a plumber," the latter referring to Secretary of Labor Mar-

tin Durkin, former head of the Plumbers and Steamfitters Union.)

Unquestionably, the two most influential members of the cabinet were Secretary of State John Foster Dulles and Treasury Secretary George Humphrey. The former, a senior partner in the prestigious law firm of Sullivan and Cromwell, was a longtime spokesperson for the Republican Party on foreign policy. Articulate and strong-willed, Dulles rejected the Truman administration's strategy of containment in favor of a new and bolder stance in world affairs that included the "liberation" of "captive peoples" under communist control. Such a program would include the threat of nuclear retaliation against aggression at places of America's own choosing. Commonly referred to as mas-

Eisenhower reacts to cheers during his inauguration ceremony, while Harry S. Truman stands behind him, on January 20, 1953. *(Library of Congress)*

sive retaliation, or brinkmanship (going to the brink of nuclear war), Dulles's program really represented a variant of containment, which was supposed to reduce defense costs by relying on American air power instead of costly conventional forces. In fact, the policy of massive retaliation was tempered by the unlikelihood of atomic warfare in situations of local conflict, whose relation to Soviet expansion was not always apparent. Eisenhower, however, shared Dulles's view of the Soviet threat to the West, and the two men developed a close working relationship.

Much the same was true with Treasury Secretary Humphrey. An Ohio industrialist who had supported Taft in 1952, Humphrey quickly became one of Eisenhower's closest and most trusted advisers. Friendly and gregarious like the president, he was extremely bright and conversant on most policy issues. On fiscal matters, he was even more conservative than Eisenhower. As Treasury secretary, he made the reduction of federal spending and the balancing of the budget his overriding concerns.

In addition to his cabinet, Eisenhower depended heavily on his White House advisers and developed an elaborate staff system and chain of command very much along the lines of a military command structure. To head his staff, he named Sherman Adams, a former governor of New Hampshire. A tireless administrator, Adams determined more or less who got to see the president and what was placed before him for his perusal. In 1958, Adams was forced to resign his position as a result of a scandal involving the peddling of influence on behalf of a Boston industrialist, Bernard Goldfine, in exchange for several gifts. Eisenhower would later refer to the Adams affair as the saddest event of his administration.

Eisenhower also looked to his brother Milton as an unofficial adviser. The intellectual of the family and president of The Johns Hopkins University, Milton normally spent three or four days a week at the White House. He

Eisenhower's secretary of state, John Foster Dulles. *(Library of Congress)*

was held in complete trust by his older brother, who regarded him as his possible successor. Generally more liberal than the president in economic and domestic affairs, Milton also played an important role in foreign affairs, especially in cultivating closer relations with Latin America.

Domestic Affairs: Limiting the Role of the Federal Government

The basic conservatism of the new administration became clear soon after Eisenhower took office. The president believed that federal involvement in developing electric power and natural resources amounted to "creeping socialism," which he was determined to end. One of his early acts as president, therefore, was to sign a Submerged Lands Act, pushed through by a coalition of Republicans and Southern

Democrats, which turned over offshore oil rights to the seaboard states. Eisenhower also jettisoned a Republican proposal for the federal construction and operation of a huge hydroelectric complex in the Hell's Canyon area of the Snake River in favor of a project by the privately owned Idaho Power Company.

The most sensational episode in Eisenhower's attempts to limit the federal role in the development of electric power involved a proposal by Edgar Dixon and Eugene Yates to build a privately owned and operated generating plant to supply the power needs of the city of Memphis. This would allow the federally operated Tennessee Valley Authority (TVA), which provided power to Memphis, to divert electricity to a plant of the Atomic Energy Commission (AEC) in Paducah, Kentucky. Eisenhower preferred this option to the construction by the TVA of an additional facility to supply the AEC's needs. In 1954, Eisenhower instructed the AEC to negotiate a contract with Dixon and Yates. The opposition by public power adherents to the contract was immense, however, and became even more so when discrepancies in awarding the contract became public, including a conflict of interest and the failure to let out the contract for public bidding.

The Dixon-Yates issue played a role in the 1954 elections when the Democrats employed the slogan "Nixon, Dixon and Yates" to embarrass the administration. They might have embarrassed the White House even more had not Memphis announced that it would build its own power plant. Claiming that he favored this type of municipal initiative in the first place, the president ordered the AEC to cancel its contract with the Dixon-Yates combine. When Dixon-Yates sued to recoup its losses, the administration was placed in the uncomfortable position of having to state that the contract was invalid because of a possible conflict of interest in awarding it. Public power advocates could find satisfaction at the defeat of this alleged threat to the TVA.

Besides his opposition to federal public works projects, Eisenhower's basic conservatism was evident in other respects as well. He tried, for example, to overturn Democratic farm policy, based on price supports for certain agricultural commodities, through a flexible farm-price support program, but this proved a costly failure. In his first State of the Union message, he announced that he would soon end all controls on prices and wages and then proceeded to carry out that pledge. He also abolished the Reconstruction Finance Corporation, established during the Hoover administration to make loans to banks, railroads, and other businesses. He refused to sign a construction measure, believing that it interfered with local autonomy, and he opposed amendments to Social Security providing for medical insurance.

Yet Eisenhower thought of himself and his administration as belonging in the middle of the road, and he accepted the basic outline of the welfare state that had developed in the last twenty years. Thus he signed into law a measure providing for the biggest single expansion of the Social Security system in history, which brought the self-employed into the system. He also fought successfully for an increase in the minimum wage from seventy-five cents to one dollar an hour, and he favored limited expansion of federal activity in housing, medical care, and education. In 1955, he signed into law a measure providing for construction of forty-five thousand housing units over the following four years, and he pushed unsuccessfully for plans to subsidize private health insurance programs and to make federal grants to the states for school construction. In addition, his administration established the Department of Health, Education, and Welfare (HEW), and it obtained legislation providing for the construction with Canada of the St. Lawrence Seaway and for the building of a forty-two-thousand-mile interstate highway system, the largest program of its kind in the nation's history.

Excerpts from Dwight D. Eisenhower's "Atoms for Peace" address to the United Nations General Assembly, December 8, 1953:

The United States knows that if the fearful trend of atomic military buildup can be reversed, this greatest of destructive forces can be developed into a great boon, for the benefit of all mankind.

The United States knows that peaceful power from atomic energy is no dream of the future. That capability, already proved, is here—now—today. Who can doubt, if the entire body of the world's scientists and engineers had adequate amounts of fissionable material with which to test and develop their ideas, that this capability would rapidly be transformed into universal, efficient, and economic usage.

To hasten the day when fear of the atom will begin to disappear from the minds of people, and the governments of the East and West, there are certain steps that can be taken now.

I therefore make the following proposals:

The Governments principally involved, to the extent permitted by elementary prudence, to begin now and continue to make joint contributions from their stockpiles of normal uranium and fissionable materials to an International Atomic Energy Agency. We would expect that such an agency would be set up under the aegis of the United Nations. . . .

I would be prepared to submit to the Congress of the United States, and with every expectation of approval, any such plan that would:

First, encourage worldwide investigation into the most effective peacetime uses of fissionable material, and with the certainty that they had all the material needed for the conduct of all experiments that were appropriate;

Second, begin to diminish the potential destructive power of the world's atomic stockpiles;

Third, allow all peoples of all nations to see that, in this enlightened age, the great powers of the earth, both of the East and of the West, are interested in human aspirations first, rather than in building up the armaments of war;

Fourth, open up a new channel for peaceful discussion, and initiate at least a new approach to the many difficult problems that must be solved in both private and public conversations, if the world is to shake off the inertia imposed by fear, and is to make positive progress toward peace.

Against the dark background of the atomic bomb, the United States does not wish merely to present strength, but also the desire and the hope for peace.

McCarthyism

One matter left over from the Truman administration, which caused Eisenhower considerable anguish during his first term, was the so-called Red Scare, or the national alarm over alleged communists in government, charges that were most closely associated with the name of Senator Joseph McCarthy of Wisconsin. On this issue, the president's record was less than admirable. Although Eisenhower detested McCarthy personally, he and other White House leaders shared the common belief that Soviet espionage in the United States had jeopardized national security. For this reason, the president allowed Julius and Ethel Rosenberg, convicted of giving atomic secrets to Soviet agents, to be executed as spies on June 13, 1953, despite worldwide pleas for clemency. He also issued an executive order permitting the firing of seven thousand federal employees as security risks, and he forced the Atomic Energy Commission to withdraw its security clearance from J. Robert Oppenheimer, often referred to as the father of the atomic bomb, even though no evidence existed to show that he was disloyal to the country.

Central High School in Little Rock, Arkansas, in September, 1957. *(Library of Congress)*

By his own actions, therefore, Eisenhower seemed to give substance to Senator McCarthy's charges that the United States was faced with an internal communist conspiracy. As a result of the 1952 elections, which gave Republicans control of Congress, McCarthy was in a position to promote his accusations. Appointed chair of the Permanent Investigations Subcommittee on Government Operations, McCarthy intensified his hunt for alleged subversives in the executive branch. In doing so, he seemed to ignore the fact that a president and administration of his own party were in office.

McCarthy objected to the appointment of Charles Bohlen as ambassador to the Soviet Union because he had been Franklin D. Roosevelt's interpreter at the Yalta Conference of 1945 during which, the Wisconsin senator charged, the United States "handed over" Eastern Europe to the Soviets. He attacked the Voice of America because, he claimed, Communist

Party sympathizers had schemed to locate two transmitters where their signals could easily be jammed by the Soviets. He sent two aides, Roy Cohn and G. David Schine, to Europe to locate and destroy "subversive" books (such as the works of Ralph Waldo Emerson and Henry David Thoreau) at the libraries of the United States Information Service. He accused the army of "being soft on Communism" by promoting to major and then giving an honorable discharge to a dentist, Irving Peress, who had once pleaded the Fifth Amendment when questioned about communist connections. Calling before his committee General Ralph Zweicker, Peress's commanding officer, McCarthy told the general that he was not fit to wear his uniform. He also summoned Army Secretary Ted Stevens to answer questions before his subcommittee.

Eisenhower was outraged by McCarthy's charges. At Dartmouth College in June, he spoke out against book burners. Also, when a McCarthy aide, J. B. Matthews, accused the Protestant clergy of communist leanings, Eisenhower released a telegram to the National Conference of Christians and Jews objecting to Matthews's article. For the most part, however, the president took the position that he would not denigrate his office by getting "into the gutter with that guy." He also did not want to cause a break with the Republican right wing.

In the end, Senator McCarthy brought about his own undoing. In response to McCarthy's accusations that the Army was coddling communists, the Army brought charges of its own against McCarthy, the most sensational of which was that McCarthy had tried to blackmail it into giving preferential treatment to McCarthy's aide, Schine, who had been recently inducted into the service. The subsequent Army-McCarthy hearings, which were televised nationally, showed McCarthy to be a bully and a bore who evaded issues and constantly pleaded points of order. Thereafter, the tide of opinion turned against McCarthy. On December 2, 1954, the Senate voted to condemn him for "conduct unbecoming a senator." Three years later, with little public support left, he died. As a result of his activities, a new word, "McCarthyism," was added to the English language to describe unsupported, demogogic accusations of disloyalty.

As for the Eisenhower administration, it felt vindicated in its policy of generally ignoring McCarthy until time and circumstances brought about his downfall. Still, like Truman before him, President Eisenhower by his own actions and timidity, bore some of the responsibility for the climate of fear that sustained McCarthy as long as it did.

Brown v. Topeka: Beginnings of the Civil Rights Movement

On the issue of civil rights, the White House's record was substantially better, but not all that it might have been. As a general proposition,

Eisenhower believed that every American citizen was entitled to vote and to equal protection under the law. As a military commander in World War II, he had experimented with integrating several army units toward the end of the war, and one of his first acts as president was to order desegregation of facilities in federal offices and on military bases. At the same time, however, the president thought that responsibility for civil rights should be left to the individual states, and in his memoirs he later made clear that he had little regard for those who "believed that legislation could institute instant morality."

In 1954, the Supreme Court under Earl Warren, whom Eisenhower had appointed as chief justice eight months earlier, concluded unanimously in a landmark case, *Brown v. Board of Education of Topeka, Kansas*, that "in the field of public education the doctrine of 'separate but equal' had no place. Separate educational facilities are inherently unequal." A year later, the Supreme Court ordered federal district courts to speed up the process of desegregation of public schools. By 1957, several Southern states and the District of Columbia had complied with the desegregation order, but many others, including Arkansas, had not. When several African American students tried to integrate Central High School in Little Rock in September, 1957, Governor Orville Faubus ordered the National Guard to block their entry. Faubus maintained that his order was necessary to prevent violence on the part of an unruly crowd of whites who had gathered in front of the school. When violence erupted after the National Guard had been removed in response to an order by a federal judge, Eisenhower, who was vacationing in Newport, Rhode Island, federalized the National Guard and sent in army troops to reopen the school, which had been closed. This was the first time since Reconstruction that the federal government had used military force to protect the rights of African Americans. Even so, two years would pass before Central High School was finally desegregated.

Throughout most of the crisis, Eisenhower had displayed a singular lack of leadership. Privately, he deplored the Supreme Court decision of 1954, and he later called his appointment of Earl Warren as chief justice "the biggest damn fool mistake I ever made." In the summer of 1954, he told a newsman that he could not "imagine any set of circumstances that would ever induce me to send federal troops . . . into any area to enforce the orders of a federal court," causing opponents of desegregation to believe that they could resist desegregation orders without fear of federal intervention. Despite the crisis (the most serious domestic matter of his administration), Eisenhower had continued to vacation in Newport instead of returning to Washington, D.C., to underscore the seriousness of this confrontation between federal and state authority. Even his decision to confer with Governor Faubus in Newport while the turmoil in Little Rock was building was probably unwise. The meeting settled nothing, for after Faubus returned to Little Rock from Newport, he made further efforts to delay school desegregation. Meanwhile, he and his cause received national attention, and Faubus became something of a hero among forces resisting desegregation.

Even before the events in Little Rock, the Civil Rights movement, encouraged by the *Brown* decision of 1954, had begun to gather momentum. In 1957, Congress approved, and the president signed, a civil rights bill establishing a Civil Rights Commission and a Civil Rights Division within the Justice Department and empowering the federal district courts to hear cases involving violations of a person's voting rights. Although a much-amended and weak measure, it was the first such civil rights legislation in eighty-two years. In 1960, Congress passed, and the president quickly signed, a second and stronger civil rights act authorizing the appointment of federal referees to investigate voting rights violations and providing for stiff fines and prison terms for those violating a person's voting rights or threatening to obstruct a court order.

Even more important than this legislation was the fact that African Americans themselves had begun to mobilize in nonviolent protests to gain their civil rights in the South. In 1955, in Montgomery, Alabama, a black woman, Rosa Parks, refused to give up her seat to a white man on a city bus as required by state law and local ordinances. After her arrest, African Americans in Montgomery, led by a twenty-five-year-old minister, Martin Luther King, Jr., began a successful boycott against the bus line, which cut patronage by a third and attracted nationwide attention. In 1956, the Supreme Court declared the Alabama laws unconstitutional.

The Montgomery boycott was only the first chapter in the direct protest movement. In 1960, a group of African American students from North Carolina Agricultural and Technical College staged a sit-in at a Woolworth store in Greensboro when they were refused service at the lunch counter. The technique caught on immediately, and within the next few months, similar demonstrations took place in cities throughout the South involving, by the end of the year, fifty thousand blacks and white supporters and leading to partial or total integration of public accommodations in 126 Southern cities. By this time, Martin Luther King, Jr., had emerged as the undisputed leader in the campaign of passive resistance.

The Civil Rights movement extended over the two terms of Eisenhower's administration. The civil rights measures of 1957 and 1960 were passed by a Democratic-controlled Congress and would not have become law had it not been for the efforts of Senate Majority Leader Lyndon B. Johnson, who, probably more than any other individual, was responsible for getting the two bills through the Senate despite strong opposition from Southern legislators.

The Democrats had captured both houses of Congress in the 1954 elections and increased their majority in the Senate and the House of Representatives in 1956 and again in 1958. Yet Eisenhower and his middle-of-the-road policies remained popular among the electorate. In 1956, he easily defeated Adlai Stevenson, who had been renominated by the Democrats, by an even greater margin than in 1952, despite the fact that Eisenhower had suffered a serious heart attack a year earlier. In the November elections, Eisenhower received more than 57 percent of the popular vote and 457 electoral votes to Stevenson's 73 electoral votes.

Foreign Policy

If Eisenhower accepted the basic tenets of the New Deal and Fair Deal in social welfare legislation during his two terms in office and practiced a policy of what he regarded as dynamic conservatism, so too did he follow an internationalist foreign policy much along the lines that had developed after World War II. The president, however, was a consummate Cold Warrior and a strident anti-Communist, an attitude he shared fully with Secretary of State Dulles. Together, these two men raised the pitch of the Cold War rhetoric and followed a policy of confrontation with the Soviet Union.

Eisenhower's most pressing problem after he took office in 1953 was to end the Korean War, which had been stalemated for almost two years. To break the deadlock in the armistice negotiations over the repatriation of prisoners of war (POWs), which alone prevented an end to the war, the president issued a threat to the Chinese Communists that the United States would not be held responsible for failing to withhold atomic weapons if a truce could not be arranged. Whether it was because they responded to this threat of nuclear war, the Communist negotiators in Panmunjom agreed to the United Nations position on POWs, which provided for the return of prisoners on a voluntary basis only. With this issue settled, an armistice was signed on July 27, 1953, establishing a demilitarized buffer zone between North and South Korea roughly along the thirty-eighth parallel.

As Secretary of State Dulles explained in a 1956 article in *Life* magazine, the threat of nuclear war was the type of brinkmanship that was sometimes necessary to prevent—or, in the case of Korea, to end—war. "You have to take some chances for peace, just as you must take chances in war," he stated.

Vietnam: The Background to American Intervention

In his *Life* article, Dulles cited two other instances besides Korea in which the Eisenhower administration had resorted to brinkmanship, both in Asia. The first of these came in Indochina (Vietnam), where the French had been waging war against communist guerrillas, known as the Vietminh and led by Ho Chi Minh, a Vietnamese communist and nationalist. At the end of 1952, the lame duck Truman administration had approved $60 million in support for the French effort. By 1954, the United States was paying almost four-fifths of the cost of the war. Still, Ho Chi Minh's forces had gained the upper hand and controlled more than half the country. In a last desperate effort to salvage victory, the French sent their best troops into an isolated garrison north of Hanoi called Dienbienphu and dared the Vietminh to come after them. The French were convinced that in a conventional battle they could defeat the guerrillas. The Vietminh, however, brought heavy artillery up the mountains that surrounded Dienbienphu and began to inflict heavy losses on the garrison. By this time, the French were tired of the war, and it was clear that the fall of Dienbienphu would mean the withdrawal of French troops from Vietnam.

President Eisenhower believed that the fall of Vietnam would mean a victory for communist aggression and the failure of containment. The president compared the fall of Vietnam to a row of dominoes. "You have a row of dominoes set up, and you knock over the first one, and what would happen to the last one was certainly that it would go over quickly. So you have a beginning of integration that would have the most profound influence." Eventually, Eisenhower implied, all of Southeast Asia might fall to the Communists if they were not stopped in Vietnam.

What to do? In the end, the administration did nothing, but not before giving serious consideration to American military intervention in the war. Several of Eisenhower's advisers, including Admiral Arthur Radford, chair of the Joint Chiefs of Staff, and Vice President Richard Nixon, recommended an air strike, including the use of atomic weapons, to relieve the garrison in Dienbienphu. Admiral Radford's plan, known as Operation Vulture, called for a strike employing tactical atomic bombs by sixty American B-298's stationed in the Philippines, supported by 150 American carrier-based fighters. The attack against the forces besieging Dienbienphu would devastate the enemy, Radford believed, and rescue the French from certain defeat.

Both Eisenhower and Secretary of State Dulles rejected the use of atomic weapons in Vietnam but considered a conventional air strike. Eisenhower, however, established certain preconditions without which he would not intervene. These included the support of Congress and the backing of America's allies in Europe. Congress itself would not approve American intervention, so soon after the end of the Korean War, without the firm support of the NATO allies, especially Great Britain. Eisenhower and Dulles also insisted that any American intervention in Vietnam be preconditioned on the French promise to give the states of Indochina their independence. None of these preconditions were met. Prime Minister Winston Churchill of Great Britain told Eisenhower that he was unable to obtain his cabinet's approval of military participation, and the French re-

fused to state that independence would follow the success of its armed forces against the Communists. Without the support of America's allies, Congress also refused to give its approval to military intervention. As a result, Dienbienphu fell to the Communists on May 8, without American intervention.

Following the fall of Dienbienphu, a new government came into power in France led by Pierre Mendès-France, who was committed to ending the war in Indochina. At a conference in Geneva that had been meeting since February to discuss Far Eastern questions, the French agreed to a truce and a temporary partition of Vietnam at the seventeenth parallel, with the French withdrawing south of that line. National elections were to be held within two years to elect a government for all of Vietnam. The French would administer the elections in the South, and the elections would be supervised by an international commission. Neither part of Vietnam was to join a military alliance or to allow foreign bases in its territory.

The United States regarded the Geneva accords, which it did not sign (although it did promise to support free elections for the unification of Vietnam), as a major setback for the West. Before Dienbienphu fell, the Eisenhower administration had gone to the brink of a war to save that outpost. Eisenhower had resisted unilateral involvement precisely because he was determined to avoid a second Korea, but he would have considered using nuclear weapons if the Chinese had intervened in the war and if Congress and America's European allies had consented. On May 26, the president approved recommendations by the Joint Chiefs of Staff that called for "employing atomic weapons, whenever advantageous . . . against those military targets in China, Hainan and other Communist-held offshore islands" in case of Chinese intervention in Indochina. The threat of atomic warfare if the Chinese should expand the conflict or attempt to spread their control throughout Southeast Asia was transmitted to the Chinese through John Foster Dulles.

To forestall the possibility of further communist expansion in Southeast Asia, Dulles helped organize the Southeast Asia Treaty Organization (SEATO), an Asiatic defense community that included Pakistan, Thailand, and the Philippines, as well as the United States, Great Britain, France, Australia, and New Zealand. Although the organization existed only on paper and its members had no obligations except to consult in the event of threatened subversion, the United States included Cambodia, Laos, and Vietnam under its umbrella in violation of the Geneva accords. Also, the United States began dealing directly with South Vietnam instead of through the French and sent huge amounts of military and economic assistance to bolster the government of Ngo Dinh Diem, a member of the Catholic minority and a staunch anticommunist who had spent several years in exile in the United States.

In effect, the United States replaced France as the principal guardian of Southeast Asia against communist expansion. By the summer of 1955, the French had left Vietnam. Ngo Dinh Diem announced that elections would not be held in 1956, realizing that he would lose a fair election against Ho Chi Minh. The United States fully supported Ngo in this decision, for the fact was that, although Eisenhower had avoided American intervention in Vietnam, he had made a commitment to a separate South Vietnam and to the Ngo Dinh Diem government that would shackle subsequent administrations.

Cold War Crises: Quemoy, the Suez, and the Hungarian Uprising

No sooner had the armistice in Vietnam been arranged than the administration was faced with another crisis, this time involving a threat by the Chinese Communists to "liberate" the small offshore islands of Quemoy (Jinmen) and Matsu, controlled by the Chinese Nationalists.

The crisis began in September, 1954, when the Chinese Communists started to shell the island of Quemoy, killing two Americans and raising the threat of an invasion. The Communists also talked about an early liberation of Taiwan (Formosa). In January, 1955, the shelling of Quemoy and Matsu intensified. In response, Eisenhower asked for and received from Congress the Formosa Resolution, which was virtually a blank check authorizing Eisenhower to take whatever steps were necessary to protect Formosa and the Pescadore Islands against attack, including the protection "of closely related localities."

Intermittent bombardment of Quemoy continued, and a major war scare ensued. In March, Secretary Dulles informed Eisenhower that the situation in the Formosa Strait was "far more serious" than he had realized. The administration gave serious consideration to using nuclear weapons against mainland China and might have done so had the Chinese actually launched an invasion of the islands. On March 12, Dulles went public with his threat of atomic reprisal. In a statement, the secretary spoke of "new and powerful weapons of precision which can utterly destroy military targets without endangering unrelated civilian centers." At a press conference a few days later, President Eisenhower said much the same thing.

These warnings evidently had a sobering effect on the Chinese Communists, for on April 23, Foreign Minister Chou En-lai spoke of Chinese friendship with the Americans and suggested a conference to discuss Far Eastern matters, "especially the question of relaxing tensions in the Taiwan area." In August, negotiations got under way in Geneva between American and Chinese diplomats. Although the conference settled none of the outstanding differences between the two countries, Chinese pressure on Quemoy and Matsu lessened, and the crisis subsided.

A similar crisis developed in 1958, after Chiang Kai-shek, the Chinese Nationalist leader, reinforced Quemoy and Matsu with one hundred thousand men, and the Chinese Communists began shelling the islands once more. At first, Eisenhower pledged to defend the islands, but under heavy criticism at home and abroad from those who did not believe that the islands were worth the risk of war, the administration backed down and compelled Chiang to renounce publically the use of force to regain control of the mainland of China. In return, the Beijing government agreed to a de facto cease-fire.

The Eisenhower Doctrine

January 5, 1957

We have these simple and indisputable facts:

1. The Middle East, which has always been coveted by Russia, would today be prized more than ever by International Communism.
2. The Soviet rulers continue to show that they do not scruple to use any instance to gain their ends.
3. The free nations of the Middle East need, and for the most part want, added strength to assure their continued independence. . . .

There is general recognition in the Middle East, as elsewhere, that the United States does not seek either political or economic domination over any other people. Our desire is a world environment of freedom, not servitude. On the other hand many, if not all, of the nations of the Middle East are aware of the danger that stems from International Communism and welcome closer cooperation with the United States to realize for themselves the United Nations goals of independence, economic well-being and spiritual growth. . . . Under these circumstances I deem it necessary to seek the cooperation of the Congress . . . The action which I propose would have the following features.

It would, first of all, authorize the United States to cooperate with and assist any nation or group of nations in the general area of the Middle East in the development of economic strength dedicated to the maintenance of national independence.

It would, in the second place, authorize the Executive to undertake in the same region programs of military assistance and cooperation with any nation or group of nations which desires such aid.

It would, in the third place, authorize such assistance and cooperation to include the employment of the armed forces of the United States to secure and protect the territorial integrity and political independence of such nations, requesting such aid, against overt armed aggression from any nation controlled by International Communism.

These measures would have to be consonant with the treaty obligations of the United States, including the Charter of the United Nations and with any action or recommendations of the United Nations. They would also, if armed attack occurs, be subject to the overriding authority of the United Nations Security Council in accordance with the Charter.

The present proposal would, in the fourth place, authorize the President to employ, for economic and defensive military purposes, sums available under the Mutual Security Act of 1954, as amended, without regard to existing limitations . . . .

The occasion has come for us to manifest again our national unity in support of freedom and to show our deep respect for the rights and independence of every nation—however great, however small. We seek, not violence, but peace. To this purpose we must now devote our energies, our determination, ourselves.

Despite the policy of brinkmanship that the administration had followed in the Korean War, Vietnam, and the Quemoy and Matsu crisis, Eisenhower feared a nuclear war and sought to avoid conflict with the communist world. Also, the president was alarmed at the high cost of the Cold War. In a speech in 1953, he remarked, "Every gun that is made, every warship launched, every rocket signifies, in the final sense, a theft from those who hunger and are not fed. . . . The cost of one heavy bomber is this: a modern brick school in more than 30 cities."

Eisenhower sought therefore to reduce tensions with the Soviet Union, and for that purpose he agreed to meet with the Soviet leaders in Geneva in July, 1955. Winston Churchill had urged such a conference after the death of Joseph Stalin in 1953, and a series of conciliatory gestures by the Soviet Union, most notably an agreement to end its military occupation of Austria, convinced Eisenhower to go to Geneva. Meeting from July 18 to 23, delegations from the United States, Great Britain, France, and the Soviet Union discussed the issues of German reunification, European security, disarmament, and East-West trade. None of these issues was resolved, and the main accomplishment of the meeting was an agreement to have each country's foreign minister consider these same questions at a meeting in the fall. Reporters, however, talked of a "spirit of Geneva," and the meeting did seem to represent a thaw in the Cold War, at least until October, when the foreign ministers' meeting ended in deadlock.

Indeed, relations between Moscow and Washington reached another low point in the fall of 1956 as a result of a new crisis, this time in the Middle East, and a revolution against Soviet control in Hungary. The crisis in the Middle East developed in July, 1956, when Gamel Abdel Nasser of Egypt nationalized the Suez Canal following the cancellation of American, British, and French pledges of aid to Egypt for the construction of the huge Aswan Dam on the Nile River. Nasser seized the canal partly to pay for the dam. About the same time, Nasser, an Arab nationalist, made threatening gestures against Israel. Great Britain and France, both large stockholders in the canal company, plotted with Israel, which wanted to launch a preemptive attack against Egypt, to retake the canal. On October 29, Israel attacked across the Sinai Desert toward the Suez. As prearranged, Great Britain and France demanded that Egypt and Israel stop fighting and withdraw from the area of the canal. When Nasser refused, they destroyed what remained of the Egyptian air force and occupied the northern third of the waterway.

Furious that the allies had not consulted with him before launching their attack and anxious that it might cause the Arab states to move closer to the Soviet Union, Eisenhower went to the United Nations. Along with the Soviet Union, the United States introduced a resolution condemning the action of its own allies. It also applied pressure against Great Britain and France to stop the fighting by cutting off badly needed oil supplies from Latin America. (Mideast oil could no longer reach Europe through the Suez Canal.) Humiliated and resentful toward the United States, Great Britain and France had little choice but to agree to withdraw their forces from Egypt. As a result, Egypt maintained control of the canal, for which it paid $81 million. Nasser became a hero throughout the Arab world, and the Soviets increased their influence in the Middle East, even agreeing to build the Aswan Dam.

One reason Eisenhower had been so upset by the developments in the Middle East was that they distracted world attention from Eastern Europe, where the Soviet Union was putting down a revolution by Hungarian students and workers against its control. At the Twentieth Party Congress in February, Nikita Khrushchev, the new leader of the Soviet Union, had shocked the world by attacking Joseph Stalin for his crimes against the Soviet people and by indicating a liberalization of Stalinist restrictions. Several months later, riots broke out in Poland against the ruling Politburo, and leadership was transferred to Wladyslaw Gomulka, an independent Communist. News of Gomulka's success spread to Hungary, and the students and workers took to the streets, demanding that longtime Stalinist leader Erno Gero be replaced by Imre Nagy. The Soviets gave in to these demands, but when Nagy announced that Hungary was withdrawing from the Warsaw military pact, which bound it to the Soviet Union, this proved too much for Moscow. Khrushchev sent tanks into Budapest and brutally crushed the revolution.

President Eisenhower hailed the Hungarian uprising as "the dawning of a new day" in Eastern Europe, and frequent talk by Secretary Dulles and others about "liberating" the captive countries of Eastern Europe and "rolling back" communism had given some leaders of the revolution cause to believe that they could depend on the United States for military assistance. There was never a chance, however, that Eisenhower would risk World War III by giving military support to the Hungarians, even if the United States had been militarily able to do so, which it was not. Talk about liberation was nothing more than that—talk. Taken together, the disarray among the Western allies caused by the Suez crisis and the failure of the United States—indeed its military incapacity—to come to the aid of the Hungarians made the fall of 1956 one of the bleakest for the United States in the history of the Cold War.

The Suez crisis revealed also the potency of Third World nationalism and the danger of growing Soviet influence among Third World nations. For the remainder of his administration, therefore, Eisenhower made the containment of communist expansion in the Third World one of his highest priorities. This meant continuing attention to developments in

Soviet tanks in the streets of Budapest, Hungary, in 1952. (*Library of Congress*)

the Middle East and new emphasis on relations with Latin America.

As a result of the Suez crisis and the Soviet Union's expanded influence in the Middle East, Dulles and Eisenhower managed to get through Congress, in 1957, legislation authorizing the president to use military forces if deemed necessary to defend Middle Eastern nations that requested such aid from overt Communist-inspired aggression. This became known as the Eisenhower Doctrine. Employing the doctrine, Eisenhower in April gave

Fidel Castro at the United Nations on September 22, 1960. *(United Nations)*

King Hussein of Jordan $10 million and shifted the Sixth Fleet to the eastern Mediterranean in order to prop up Hussein's government during a period of political and economic instability.

The next year, the president sent American troops into Lebanon under the provisions of the Eisenhower Doctrine to forestall a threatened communist coup similar to one in Iraq. Actually, the unrest in Lebanon was internal, but in a television address, Eisenhower suggested to the American people that Lebanon was about to become a victim of indirect communist aggression. Eventually, fourteen thousand troops were landed in Lebanon, but their activity was restricted to Beirut and the adjoining airport. When the coup failed to materialize, the administration was subjected to criticism at home and to further complications in the Middle East, largely as a result of the fact that the Eisenhower Doctrine took little account of Arab nationalism.

Revolution in Cuba

After 1958, President Eisenhower showed increased concern about developments in Latin America. Largely ignored by the United States during Eisenhower's first term in office, Latin America had been almost totally excluded from such programs as economic assistance under the United States' foreign aid program. A series of developments culminating with a riot during Vice President Nixon's visit to Venezuela caused the administration to review its Latin American policy. In 1958, the White House came out in support of regional economic aid for Latin America, central to which was the establishment of an Inter-American Development Bank. The basis for the Alliance for Progress program of the Kennedy administration was traceable to the Eisenhower administration.

Yet the administration's new sense of urgency in Latin America came too late to prevent a revolution in Cuba, led by Fidel Castro, from turning bitterly anti-American. Cuba had long been a haven for American investment and a playground for American tourists, but the president of Cuba, Fulgencio Batista, was a cruel dictator, and in 1959, Castro overthrew the Batista regime. Washington extended prompt recognition to the new Cuban government and made several friendly gestures. Castro, however, would not forgive the United States for its support of Batista and other dictators in Latin America. Relations between Havana and Washington deteriorated after Castro began to confiscate land and other properties owned by American citizens, conducted kangaroo courts and mass executions of former Batista officials, and leaned closer and closer to views held by communist supporters. By 1960, Eisenhower determined that Castro was a communist (which he certainly was by this time if not earlier) and gave the Central Intelligence Agency permission to plan for an invasion of Cuba by a group of anti-Castro exiles with the purpose of overthrowing the Castro regime. Preparations for the invasion were still incomplete when Eisenhower left office in 1961, but by this time Khrushchev could boast that the Monroe Doctrine had "died a natural death." As one of its final acts, the Eisenhower administration severed diplomatic relations with Cuba in 1961.

The U-2 Affair

Eisenhower's administration ended on a somber note in another way as well. In November, 1958, the Soviets precipitated a crisis over Berlin by stating that negotiations on European security, a nuclear-free Germany, and the end of four-power occupation of Berlin had to begin within the next six months or Moscow would conclude a separate peace treaty with East Germany, which would then control access routes into West Berlin. The status of that city had posed a dilemma for the Soviet Union for many years. An estimated three million East Germans had escaped into and through West Berlin since the end of World War II. The glowing prosperity and glittering life of West Berlin was in marked contrast to the depressed state of affairs in East Berlin. Also, West Berlin was a center of espionage activity directed against the Communist world. What made Khrushchev

In 1958, Eisenhower watches as the six members of the President's Commission on Civil Rights are sworn in. *(Library of Congress)*

decide to move against West Berlin in late 1958, however, was the placement in West Germany of American bombers capable of carrying nuclear warheads and the knowledge that American forces in Germany were equipped with tactical nuclear weapons.

In the United States, some in the administration wanted to increase the armed services and prepare for war against the Soviet Union. Eisenhower rejected such advice but held firm against the Soviet ultimatum. Fearful of provoking a nuclear war, Khrushchev began to back down. He extended the deadline in stages until the end of 1961. He also visited the United States in September, 1959, and arranged with Eisenhower for a summit meeting in Paris, scheduled for May, 1960.

The summit meeting never took place. On the eve of the conference, an American U-2 spy plane was shot down over Soviet territory. At first, the United States denied that it was a spy plane, but when the Soviet Union released details of the flight and displayed the pilot, who had been captured alive, the American government was caught in a lie. Although Khrushchev, who wanted the Paris summit to take place, gave Eisenhower every opportunity to dismiss the U-2 incident, Eisenhower made full disclosure of the spy flights and implied they would continue. Furious, Khrushchev canceled the meeting.

It is perhaps not surprising, therefore, that the Democratic candidate for president in 1960, John F. Kennedy, harped on the accusation that the United States had lost much of its prestige and influence under Eisenhower. The Democratic candidate also accused Eisenhower of letting the United States fall behind in the development of intercontinental ballistic missiles (ICBMs). As Kennedy would find out after he took office, a missile gap existed, but it involved the Soviets lagging far behind the Americans.

Soviet premier Nikita Khrushchev examines the wreckage of the U-2 spy plane shot down over the Soviet Union in May, 1960. *(Library of Congress)*

To a large number of Americans, however, the time was right to put a younger man in office, one who promised to revitalize the United States and bring it back to its paramount position in the world.

Yet the Eisenhower administration was not the do-nothing, standpat administration that some had accused it of being, and the 1950's was not the dull, dreary, and uneventful decade that others charged. Each of these accusations contained an element of truth but not the whole truth. Eisenhower had accepted and, in some respects, extended, the basic tenets of the social welfare state that had been established since the 1930's, and although he did not go much beyond the Cold War clichés of the previous administration, he was guided by the policy of containment with its burden of international responsibilities. Also, if relations with the Soviet Union were not much better when Eisenhower left office than when he entered in

1953, neither were they worse. It is also to Eisenhower's credit that he ended one war (Korea) and prevented the United States from becoming militarily involved in another (Vietnam) when many of his advisers were urging such a course. The Eisenhower administration gave the United States seven and a half years of relative peace, more than his predecessor and successor.

The Last Years

In January, 1961, Eisenhower, the oldest president in the nation's history up to that time, was succeeded in office by John F. Kennedy, then the nation's youngest elected president, after Kennedy narrowly defeated Vice President Nixon. Retiring to his farm in Gettysburg, Pennsylvania, Eisenhower continued to be consulted on foreign policy questions by the new president and then by his successor, Lyndon Johnson. He also lived to see his former vice president elected to the presidency in 1968. Eisenhower appears to have become somewhat politically more conservative during the last years of his life, and he continued to advocate a strong anticommunist foreign policy. At the 1964 Republican National Convention, which nominated the right-wing Barry Goldwater for president, Eisenhower joined the right-wing extremists in excoriating the media for allegedly biased political reporting. He also supported the expansion of America's involvement in Vietnam after 1965 as essential to prevent further communist aggression. At the same time, he preferred Governor William Scranton of Pennsylvania or some more moderate Republican to Goldwater in 1964, and he remained committed to a broad internationalist foreign policy, which included considerable sympathy for the political and economic aspirations of Third World nations and an expanded program of American foreign aid for less developed countries.

In 1968, the former president's health deteriorated rapidly after he suffered two major heart attacks, the second on the day after he ad-

dressed the Republican National Convention in August from his suite at Walter Reed Hospital. Although Eisenhower managed to live another seven months, he died peacefully on March 28, 1969, after giving his final command: "I want to go; God take me."

Burton I. Kaufman

Suggested Readings

Alexander, Charles C. *Holding the Line: The Eisenhower Era, 1952-1961*. Bloomington: Indiana University Press, 1975. A standard treatment of the Eisenhower presidency.

Ambrose, Stephen E. *Eisenhower*. 2 vols. New York: Simon & Schuster, 1983-1984. Considered by many to be the definitive biography on Eisenhower.

_____. *Ike's Spies: Eisenhower and the Espionage Establishment*. Jackson: University Press of Mississippi, 1999. Details Eisenhower's successes and failures at world espionage.

Beschloss, Michael R. *Eisenhower: A Centennial Life*. New York: Harper, 1990. An illustrated biography with photographs by Vincent Virga.

Bowie, Robert R., and Richard H. Immerman. *Waging Peace: How Eisenhower Shaped an Enduring Cold War Strategy*. New York: Oxford University Press, 1998. Evaluates the long-term effect that Eisenhower's New Look strategy has had on American foreign policy.

Boyle, Peter G. *Eisenhower*. New York: Pearson/Longman, 2005. Examines such issues as Eisenhower's role both in the Cold War and in establishing the United States as a superpower.

Cook, Blanche. *The Declassified Eisenhower: A Divided Legacy*. Garden City, N.Y.: Doubleday, 1981. A critical analysis of Eisenhower's foreign policy.

D'Este, Carlo. *Eisenhower: A Soldier's Life*. New York: Henry Holt, 2002. Focuses on Eisenhower's military career and gives insight into the development of his leadership characteristics.

Divine, Robert A. *Eisenhower and the Cold War.* New York: Oxford University Press, 1981. A brief evaluation of Eisenhower's foreign policy.

Dwight D. Eisenhower Library and Museum. http://www.eisenhower.utexas.edu/ddehp.htm. The Web site of the official Eisenhower presidential library.

Eisenhower, Dwight D. *Ike's Letters to a Friend, 1941-1958.* Edited and annotated by Robert W. Griffith. Lawrence: University Press of Kansas, 1984. Brings together Eisenhower's correspondence with longtime friend Swede Hazlett.

Greenstein, Fred I. *The Hidden-Hand Presidency: Eisenhower as Leader.* New York: Basic Books, 1982. A highly acclaimed evaluation of Eisenhower's leadership style.

Hold, Daniel D., and James W. Leyerzapf, eds. *Eisenhower: The Prewar Diaries and Selected Papers, 1905-1941.* Baltimore: Johns Hopkins University Press, 1998. Gives insight into Eisenhower's development as a military and political leader.

Kinnard, Douglas. *Ike, 1890-1990: A Pictorial History.* Washington, D.C.: Brassey's, 1990. An engaging illustrated biography.

Lee, Alton R. *Dwight D. Eisenhower: A Bibliography of His Times and Presidency.* Wilmington, Del.: Scholarly Resources, 1991. A comprehensive list of primary and secondary sources for further study.

Lyon, Peter. *Eisenhower: Portrait of the Hero.* Boston: Little, Brown, 1974. Gives detailed coverage of Eisenhower's foreign policy.

Neal, Steve. *The Eisenhowers.* Lawrence: University Press of Kansas, 1984. A fine study of the Eisenhower family.

Pach, Chester J. *The Presidency of Dwight D. Eisenhower.* Lawrence: University Press of Kansas, 1979. Rev. ed. 1991. A good survey of the Eisenhower presidency.

Parmet, Herbert S. *Eisenhower and the American Crusades.* 1972. Rev. ed. New Brunswick, N.J.: Transaction, 1999. Examines the domestic policies of Eisenhower.

Warshaw, Shirley Anne, ed. *Reexamining the Eisenhower Presidency.* Westport, Conn.: Greenwood Press, 1993. A revisionist view of Eisenhower, arguing that he was more involved with policymaking than he was previously credited.

Wicker, Tom. *Dwight D. Eisenhower.* New York: Henry Holt, 2002. A slim volume that nonetheless discusses key events of the Eisenhower presidency and ultimately concludes that Eisenhower was a great man but not a great president.

John F. Kennedy

35th President, 1961-1963

Born: May 29, 1917
    Brookline, Massachusetts
Died: November 22, 1963
    Dallas, Texas

Political Party: Democratic
Vice President: Lyndon B. Johnson

Cabinet Members
Secretary of State: Dean Rusk
Secretary of the Treasury: Douglas Dillon
Secretary of Defense: Robert McNamara
Attorney General: Robert F. Kennedy
Postmaster General: J. Edward Day, John A.
    Gronouski
Secretary of the Interior: Stewart L. Udall
Secretary of Agriculture: Orville Freeman
Secretary of Commerce: Luther Hodges
Secretary of Labor: Arthur Goldberg,
    W. Willard Wirtz
Secretary of Health, Education, and Welfare:
    Abraham Ribicoff, Anthony Celebrezze

John Fitzgerald Kennedy, the thirty-fifth president of the United States, was the first Roman Catholic to occupy the White House and the first president born in the twentieth century. With his victory in 1960 at the age of forty-three, he became the youngest American elected to the presidency. A native of Boston and a 1940 graduate of Harvard University, he saw combat as a naval officer in the South Pacific during World War II. Elected in 1946 to the U.S. House of Representatives from Boston's Eleventh Congressional District, he served three terms and was elected to the Senate in 1952, where he served until his presidential victory in 1960.

Kennedy's official portrait. *(White House Historical Society)*

The Kennedy administration was noted for its atmosphere of youthful vigor and intellectual sophistication, which inspired comparisons with the popular Arthurian myth of Camelot. Its foreign relations were early dominated by the disastrous Bay of Pigs invasion of Cuba in 1961 and then by the Cuban Missile Crisis of 1962, wherein Kennedy successfully confronted the Soviet threat of Caribbean-based nuclear rockets. Domestic issues were characterized by a summons to a New Frontier of change, symbolized by such dramatic initiatives as the Peace Corps, but characterized more by a series of reform proposals, most of which failed to pass the Congress—such as federal aid to education, Medicare, civil rights laws, and tax reduction. Kennedy's presidential victory over Republican Richard Nixon in 1960 had been so narrow that he lacked a working majority for his programs in Congress. His administration's hopes for a major reelection victory in 1964, with a strong congressional mandate, were shattered by his assassination in Dallas on November 22, 1963.

Childhood to Manhood

John Fitzgerald "Jack" Kennedy was born near Boston, Massachusetts, on May 29, 1917, the second of the nine children of Joseph P. and Rose Fitzgerald Kennedy. Grandson of a poor Irish immigrant, Joseph represented the emergence of the successful third generation, whose family fortunes had prospered through a shrewd and industrious combination of tavern keeping, banking, and Democratic machine politics. Joseph himself considerably multiplied the family wealth while acquiring a deserved reputation for shrewd intelligence, creative enterprise, and political savvy as well as for unprincipled self-aggrandizement and ruthless manipulation. In 1937, he became President Franklin D. Roosevelt's ambassador to the Court of St. James, but he had an even greater ambition: The office of the president for his firstborn, Joseph P. Kennedy, Jr.

When Joseph, Jr., died in combat during World War II, John Kennedy became heir apparent to the Kennedy clan's political ambition. Unlike his athletic, gregarious older brother, Jack was a sickly, quiet, and shy child. Struck by scarlet fever when he was three, Jack remained a frail boy whose athletic contribution to the robust Kennedy image took the less physical forms of sailing and swimming. The Kennedy boys attended mostly elite, Protestant-affiliated boarding schools, the better to equip them for the challenge of Harvard and the Yankee-dominated world beyond. Young Jack attended Dexter, Riverdale Country Day, Canterbury, and Choate, prestigious prep schools where he was frequently ill and a mediocre student at best. Yet if he was more of a loner, less pushy and calculating than the favored older brother with whom he was invariably compared, Jack's introspection took a more subtle, thoughtful form. His illnesses reinforced a bookish tendency, and his lack of brilliance disguised a persistent and wide-ranging intellectual curiosity.

At Harvard, after Joe was graduated, Jack emerged toward his own mature individualism, his career there culminating in a published honors thesis that illustrated many of the attributes of the mature man's character. Originally titled "Appeasement at Munich," his senior thesis was awarded magna cum laude and then was quickly published as a book that achieved considerable celebrity, selling eighty thousand copies under the Churchillian title *Why England Slept* (1940). Its analysis was grounded in the lessons of history and reflected a Whiggish cast of mind that lamented the slowness and uncertainty of democracies when threatened by authoritarian regimes.

Kennedy's assessment in *Why England Slept* of the danger of unpreparedness was widely praised as balanced and objective rather than argumentative and as clearly independent of his father's more rigid isolationism (and alleged anti-Semitic tendencies). The Harvard se-

The Kennedy family at Hyannisport in 1963: JFK, John, Jr., Jackie, and Caroline. *(NARA)*

Stanford School of Business Administration, and then took an aimless tour through Latin America. American entry into the war, however, brought an ensign's commission and, through Ambassador Kennedy's timely and typical intervention with Admiral James V. Forrestal and Massachusetts Senator David Walsh, a stint in naval intelligence in Washington followed by assignment to PT boat training and combat duty in the South Pacific. On the night of August 2, 1943, commanding officer Kennedy's *PT 109* was rammed at night and sunk by the Japanese destroyer *Amigari*. Throughout the ensuing week of shipwreck and suffering, during which two of his crew died, the young lieutenant showed an extraordinary combination of courage, determination, stamina, and cool leadership that merited the intense loyalty of his men and a mantle of wartime heroism that even his subsequent detractors could not tarnish. During this ordeal, he also caught malaria, and his terrible night of swimming, towing wounded comrades with the towrope in his teeth, compounded both his chronic back problem and an old adrenal insufficiency that dangerously weakened his resistance to disease throughout his life.

nior's thesis also reflected Kennedy's elite advantages, including professional stenographic dictation and typing, and editorial assistance from such journalistic notables as Arthur Krock and Henry Luce. His father provided personal access to such leaders as Sir Winston Churchill, the duke and duchess of Kent, Cordell Hull, Harold Ickes, William Bullitt, Herbert Feis, and Charles ("Chip") Bohlen. His thesis research in Harvard's Widener Library was reinforced by well-connected travels through Europe, the Soviet Union, the Balkans, Turkey, and Palestine. Being the wealthy son of Ambassador Kennedy had pronounced advantages, and Jack was beginning to enjoy the limelight.

World War II

Graduated from Harvard in the spring of 1940 with his career goals uncertain, Kennedy considered Yale Law School, briefly attended the

Congressman Kennedy

Ambassador Kennedy once explained to his biographer with characteristic bluntness the necessary transfer of presidential ambitions from Joe to Jack: "I got Jack into politics, I was the one. I told him Joe was dead and that it was therefore his responsibility to run for Congress. He didn't want it. He felt he didn't have the ability and he still feels that way. But I told him he had to." As President Kennedy recalled to journalist Bob Considine, "I was drafted. My father wanted his eldest son in politics. 'Wanted' isn't the right word. He demanded it. You know my father." Both the ambassador's claim and his son's deference underestimated Jack's ambition, but the patriarch's drive was a major determinant of the extraordinary family's political fortunes.

Jack Kennedy's path to the White House was marked from the beginning by a unique combination of advantage, tragedy, and luck— the latter taking the form in 1946 of Congressman (and former Massachusetts Governor) James Michael Curley's decision to relinquish his safe Democratic seat in the blue-collar Eleventh Congressional District and run for mayor of Boston. The formidable Kennedy campaign discouraged all serious opposition, and freshman Representative Kennedy entered the Republican-controlled Eightieth Congress with no plarticular mandate on the issues and with little discernible program beyond a call for federal housing assistance for veterans.

Congressman Kennedy's three terms in the House were curiously aimless and lackluster for a dashing wartime hero with alleged presidential ambitions. On domestic issues his voting record reflected an unimaginative, bread-and-butter New Dealism that befitted his blue-collar constituency. This included support for such standard items of the liberal Democratic agenda as the closed shop, an increased minimum

---

THE FIRST LADY
JACQUELINE KENNEDY

Despite entering the White House when she was only thirty-one years old and serving merely three years, Jacqueline Kennedy nevertheless became one of America's most influential first ladies. Born on July 28, 1929, in Southampton, New York, Jacqueline Lee Bouvier was a well-bred, well-educated Roman Catholic, like her future husband. Jackie married Senator John F. Kennedy on September 12, 1953, before newsreel cameras and fourteen hundred guests. A daughter, Caroline, was born in November, 1957, and a son, John F. Kennedy, Jr., was born in December, 1960, barely three weeks after Kennedy's presidential victory.

John Kennedy initially feared that his wife had too much "status" and not enough "quo" to be popular. Jackie Kennedy proved him wrong. Overcoming her distaste for mass politics, Jackie helped shape John Kennedy's image as a vigorous, glamorous leader for a new generation. In the White House, playing to the masses and not the matrons, she helped spearhead the postwar generations's heady rush into consumerism, while also giving it an arts-oriented, aristocratic imprimatur. Her White House restoration project inspired great pride throughout Cold War America and provoked remarkably little vocal dissent about the costs or the project's frivolous nature. Jackie Kennedy's televised tour of the White House in 1962 was a ratings triumph, further feeding the Kennedy legend.

All of this provided an essential backdrop to the profound and tragic role Jackie Kennedy played after John Kennedy's assassination in November, 1963. In labeling his administration—and their time in the White House—"Camelot," the young widow captured the extraordinary way in which Americans focused their hopes and dreams on the presidential couple. Jackie's comment may have been the most influential phrase a First Lady ever uttered, as it shaped Kennedy's reputation for decades. Jackie Kennedy remained an American icon, mysteriously alluring yet somehow familiar, until her death from cancer on May 19, 1994.

Gil Troy

wage, continued price and rent controls, and public housing. His major committee appointment was to Education and Labor, where he cordially joined fellow freshman and war veteran Richard Nixon. Foreshadowing their presidential rivalry to come, and also Kennedy's dilemma as a Catholic president, Kennedy supported federal aid to education, but only if it included such auxiliary services for parochial schools as school transportation, lunch, textbooks, and health care.

Democrat Kennedy dutifully opposed the Republican Eightieth Congress's Taft-Hartley Act to counterattack the New Deal's empowerment of organized labor, including support for President Truman's unsuccessful veto. Kennedy, however, sympathized with much of the Republican stir over "industrial communism," which mainstream Democrats called Red-baiting the unions, and he shared with Nixon and Wisconsin's Joe McCarthy an anticommunist fervor that was muted in his rhetoric, unlike theirs, but that found resonance among his constituency of ethnic Catholics.

To liberal Democratic loyalists, Jack Kennedy was an intriguing disappointment. They were troubled by his obliviousness to the demagogic danger they saw in McCarthyism, and they were irritated by his cronyism with fellow Irish Catholic McCarthy and by his and his father's poorly concealed support in 1948 of Nixon's successful challenge to California's liberal senator, Helen Gahagan Douglas. Furthermore, Kennedy's abiding intellectual interests were in foreign affairs, where the House provided little outlet. He appeared to be a part-time congressman, compiling one of the poorest attendance records in the House.

Not content to work as part of his party's minority team in Congress, he seemed a self-centered loner, noted for escorting beautiful women to elite social affairs. He was also notable for his extremely gaunt, sallow appearance and the crutches he used to ease the constant pain of an unforgiving back. If he often appeared lethargic and bored, the public was unaware of the terrible diagnosis made in 1950 that he had Addison's disease, a debilitating adrenocortical insufficiency that required daily injections of the steroid deoxycorticosterone (DOCA) through pellet implantation in his thighs. Kennedy told Joseph Alsop that he expected to die in his forties.

Senator Kennedy

Political prudence had dictated in 1948 that freshman congressman Kennedy not run against the formidable Senator Leverett Saltonstall when the Yankee Republican sought reelection from Massachusetts. Yet in 1952 Kennedy did challenge the reelection of the aristocratic Republican Henry Cabot Lodge, Jr. In spite of the massive Eisenhower tide that year, Kennedy still defeated Lodge in a race determined less by sharply contested political issues than by Kennedy's maturing appeal as a candidate and the superiority of the Kennedy political organization. This victory marked a transition in the Kennedy staff from Joseph Kennedy's political operatives to Jack's own younger loyalists. The new, able lieutenants, most of whom remained with Kennedy through the White House years and came to be known as the Irish Mafia, included younger brother Robert, Lawrence O'Brien, Kenneth O'Donnell, and, after his recruitment as the new senator's legislative assistant in Washington, Nebraskan Theodore Sorensen.

Kennedy's Senate career began auspiciously in 1953 with his marriage to the elegant Jacqueline Lee Bouvier. Physically, however, his back miseries dangerously incapacitated him, and politically his refusal to take a stand on the Senate censure of Joe McCarthy in 1954 alienated the dominant liberal wing of his party. In 1955, he published *Profiles in Courage*, a collection of essays that celebrated courageous statesmen in American history and that captured for Kennedy the Pulitzer Prize in biography the following year. Although Kennedy clearly bore responsibility for the original concept and ultimate content of the book, *Profiles in Courage* was primarily researched and written by an eclectic group of aides and consultant academics, most significantly the gifted Sorensen. Moreover, the Pulitzer committee had overridden its jury for biography, which had not even ranked *Profiles in Courage*. Nevertheless, the book was widely read and praised, and Kennedy's reputation as an eloquent and visionary young statesman was greatly enhanced.

In 1956, the Democrats renominated Adlai Stevenson to challenge the popular Dwight Eisenhower, who had suffered a heart attack in 1955. In retrospect it was fortunate for Kennedy's ambitions that his hard run for the vice presidential nomination, which Stevenson had thrown open to his party, was blocked by Senator Estes Kefauver of Tennessee. With a recovered Eisenhower presiding over peace and prosperity in 1956, Kennedy tried to aid his party's doomed ticket by making a nationwide speech-making tour, effectively promoting his expertise in foreign affairs. In 1957, he won a coveted seat on the Senate Foreign Relations Committee, where he attracted international attention for his anticolonialism, including criticism of French policies in Algeria and Indochina, as well as for his traditional Cold War appeals for a stronger defense against Soviet imperialism.

The year 1957 was a watershed one for Jack Kennedy's presidential ambitions. With Eisenhower ineligible to run for a third term in 1960, the Republican administration was jarred by a sharp recession, by corruption scandals centering on senior presidential adviser Sherman Adams, and by the Soviet launch of *Sputnik*. In the 1958 congressional elections, Kennedy easily defeated a weak Republican candidate, and nationally the Democratic Party tightened its congressional control with a stunning gain of fifteen seats in the Senate and forty-eight in the House.

By 1959, Kennedy was strategically positioned for the presidential contest ahead. He possessed not only a beautiful wife and a growing family but also a compelling public style and a striking persona in the new age of television. Cortisone treatments had greatly improved his health and spirits, and a minor side effect of facial puffiness had also transformed the old gauntness into a handsome visage. His talented staff continued to produce a cascade of speeches and essays that were published under his signature.

Moreover, as a sure-handed and now-veteran politician, Kennedy had skillfully neutralized the more dangerous domestic issues. On civil rights, he supported Senate Majority Leader Lyndon Johnson's leadership toward a centrist compromise in the Civil Rights Act of 1957. He thereby earned surprising support among Southern Democrats, who preferred his moderation to the strident liberalism of his Senate colleague, Hubert Humphrey of Minnesota. On labor, although his brother Robert had aggressively led the Senate staff investigation of labor racketeering, Jack Kennedy demonstrated expert command of the issues on the Senate's labor subcommittee. He steered a safe path between attacks on labor bossism to protect union members and the Republican administration's antiunionism, as embodied in the Landrum-Griffin Act of 1959. To reassure liberal Democrats, Kennedy fought the loyalty oath provision of the National Defense and Education Act of 1958. To reassure Protestants, he opposed general aid to parochial schools as a violation of constitutional separation between church and state.

Early in 1959, Kennedy quietly authorized Sorensen to begin organizing an academic brain trust out of Cambridge, Massachusetts, including Paul Samuelson, Arthur Schlesinger, John Kenneth Galbraith, Archibald Cox, Walt Rostow, and Jerome Wiesner. He also flatly rejected considering the vice presidency and opened his files to James M. Burns, the Pulitzer Prize-winning biographer of Franklin D. Roosevelt, whose sympathetic campaign biography of Kennedy pointed toward the presidential contest of 1960.

The Presidential Campaign and Election of 1960

Because President Eisenhower was barred from a third term in 1960 by the Twenty-second Amendment, the Republican standard fell to Vice President Richard M. Nixon. The Democratic field, in contrast, was wide open, with Governor Stevenson, the party's titular leader, having been twice defeated. American voters had historically turned to their governors for presidential candidates, but by 1960 the growth of federal authority since the New Deal, along with the postwar prominence of foreign affairs, had focused the nation's political attention increasingly on Washington and especially on the Senate, with its treaty authority and international jurisdiction. For the Republicans, both Nixon and his ultimate running mate, Henry Cabot Lodge, Jr., had been senators (Lodge, Kennedy's victim in 1952, had been appointed by Eisenhower as ambassador to the United Nations). Among the Democrats, four senators vied for their party's presidential nomination.

First to announce his candidacy was Hubert Humphrey, the liberal champion, who was promptly challenged by Kennedy in a string of state primaries during the spring of 1960. The other two, Stuart Symington of Missouri and Majority Leader Lyndon Johnson of Texas, avoided the primary battles, hoping to bargain in a deadlocked convention. The amply financed and well-organized Kennedy organization, however, crushed Humphrey in a series of primaries beginning with Wisconsin on April 5, where the Catholic-Protestant voter split was salient, and running through Illinois, Massachusetts, Pennsylvania, Indiana, and Nebraska. The primary battle culminated in heavily Protestant West Virginia, where Kennedy forcefully declared his political independence from religious obligations and drove Humphrey from the contest with an impressive majority of 60.8 percent of the primary vote. By July, when the Democratic nominating convention met in Los Angeles, Kennedy's momentum was unstoppable. He climaxed his first-ballot victory with a surprise announcement that Johnson would be his running mate. (It was a dual surprise, with political veterans expressing astonishment that Johnson would relinquish the powerful majority leadership for the vice presidency.) On July 15 Kennedy's acceptance speech proclaimed a New Frontier of challenge to "get America moving again."

In the ensuing campaign against the Nixon-Lodge ticket, Kennedy stressed economic stagnation at home and declining U.S. prestige abroad. He especially criticized the incumbent Republican administration for allowing a "missile gap" to develop between the Soviet and American arsenals (current intelligence reports supported the alleged gap, but subsequent evidence has disproved it), and he chided the administration for allowing the transformation of Cuba into a Soviet base. The fall campaign featured four televised debates between Nixon and Kennedy, in which Kennedy performed impressively, especially in the first debate on September 26, when Nixon appeared tentative and insecure.

Kennedy met the religious issue head-on, opposing "unconstitutional" federal aid to parochial schools and telling the Houston Ministerial Association on September 12 that "I believe in an America where the separation of church and state is absolute—where no Catholic prelate would tell the President (should he be a Catholic) how to act and no Protestant minister would tell his parishioners for whom to vote." He met the medical issue head-on also, falsely denying that he had Addison's disease but legitimately displaying a healthy constitution that bore up well under the punishing campaign.

President John F. Kennedy (right) poses with his brothers, attorney general Robert Kennedy (left), and Senator Ted Kennedy in August, 1963. *(AP/Wide World Photos)*

On Election Day, a record 68,838,979 Americans cast presidential ballots, and Kennedy emerged with a tiny plurality of just over 110,000. Nixon had carried twenty-six states to Kennedy's twenty-three, but Kennedy still won in the electoral college with a substantial margin of 303 to 219. The Catholic issue that had doomed Democrat Al Smith in 1928 had cost Kennedy an estimated one and a half million votes, but his huge Catholic majorities in the urban-industrial states had given him narrow pluralities there and hence large electoral totals. Also, Lyndon Johnson's tireless railroad campaign across the South—the train was nicknamed the "Cornpone Special"—had helped hold losses from the more conservative and Protestant South to such border states as Ten-

nessee, Kentucky, and Oklahoma. Although Kennedy's campaign had largely avoided the controversial issues of labor and civil rights reform, he had successfully courted the African American vote, telephoning Martin Luther King, Jr.'s wife to express his sympathy when King was jailed in Georgia in October.

The overall result of the campaign was a shrewdly orchestrated presidential victory that kept intact the Democrats' classic but volatile post-New Deal coalition of labor, liberals, Catholics, African Americans, and Southerners. Kennedy's victory did little to help other Democrats; the party lost two seats in the Senate and twenty in the House. In many cases, these losses resulted from a recapture of normally Republican seats lost in the Democratic tide of 1958, although the Democrats were still left with safe margins in both the House (263 to 174) and the Senate (64 to 36). Such partisan majorities, however, did not easily translate into legislative program majorities, especially when such controversial issues as desegregation and civil rights divided the old Roosevelt coalition down the middle.

Presidential Transition: The Kennedy Team, Style, and Agenda

Kennedy aide Adam Yarmolinsky referred to the president's new cabinet as consisting of "nine strangers and a brother." The brother was, of course, thirty-six-year-old Robert Kennedy, who had finished the University of Virginia Law School but had never practiced law. Bobby's appointment as attorney general embarrassed senior Democrats but satisfied the demands of Ambassador Kennedy, who also

The Vice President
Lyndon B. Johnson

Lyndon B. Johnson was born on August 27, 1908, near Stonewall, Texas. His father was a rancher and member of the Texas state legislature who moved the family to Johnson City, Texas, and back again to Stonewall during Lyndon's youth. After graduating from a public school, Lyndon Johnson spent two years in California working various jobs and then enrolled in Southwest Texas State Teacher's College, graduating in 1930.

Johnson's foray into politics came early. After a brief stint teaching in Texas, he accepted a position as an aide to Congressman Richard Kleberg in 1931. While in Washington, D.C., Johnson studied law at Georgetown but was disinterested in the topic and never graduated. While back visiting Texas, he met Claudia "Lady Bird" Taylor, whom he married on November 17, 1934, after a brief courtship. The Johnsons had two daughters. In 1936, President Franklin D. Roosevelt appointed Johnson as the Texas state administrator for the National Youth Administration. A year later, he was elected to the U.S. House of Representatives to fill the vacancy of a recently deceased congressman. Johnson served in the House from 1937 to 1949.

In 1941, Johnson made an unsuccessful bid for the U.S. Senate when a seat opened after the death of the incumbent. During World War II, Johnson was commissioned as lieutenant commander in the Navy, serving in the South Pacific. When Roosevelt recalled members of Congress serving in the armed forces, Johnson returned to Washington in 1942. Johnson finally gained a seat in the U.S. Senate in 1948, ultimately serving from 1949 to 1961 in the capacity of party whip and later, party leader. During this time, he was a delegate to the Democratic National Convention and chaired the Texas delegation. He was, however, unsuccessful in his effort to secure the presidency in 1960 but accepted the vice presidential spot on the ticket with John F. Kennedy. After Kennedy's assassination in November, 1963, Johnson was elevated to the presidency, where he was elected to his own term in 1964 and served until 1969, when he chose not to seek reelection because of the controversy surrounding the Vietnam War.

After his presidency, Johnson retired to his ranch in Texas. He died on January 22, 1973.

Robert P. Watson and Richard Yon

engineered in Massachusetts the appointment of a seat warmer to hold Jack's vacated Senate seat for Edward "Teddy" Kennedy in 1964. The leading stranger was Dean Rusk, whose appointment as secretary of state surprised a nation that had for the most part never heard of him and revealed many of the determining characteristics of the Kennedy style of leadership.

Popular speculation for secretary of state had centered on Adlai Stevenson, but Kennedy had little belief in Stevenson's political acumen and toughness, and he offered him instead what the disappointed Stevenson privately called the "errand boy" position of ambassador to the United Nations. Kennedy's early favorite for secretary of state was Senator J. William Fulbright of Arkansas, the intellectually formidable chair of the Senate Foreign Relations Committee. When Fulbright's appointment was blocked by opposition from a combination of labor and civil rights forces who objected to the Southerner's support for right-to-work laws and racial segregation, and by Jewish insistence on a more stalwart ally of Israel, Kennedy turned to the little-known Rusk of the Rockefeller Foundation, who was a competent and loyal professional. President Kennedy, in effect, had chosen to become his own secretary of state.

The other cabinet "strangers" served political and constituent needs in the modern fashion, in which presidents attempt to govern primarily through their expanded and loyalist White House staffs, and "cabinet government" becomes a myth served largely through rhetoric. Orville Freeman for Agriculture, Luther Hodges for Commerce, Arthur Goldberg for Labor, Abraham Ribicoff for Health, Education, and Welfare (HEW)—all were visible Democrats who were politically well matched to their constituencies. For Treasury, Kennedy picked an Eisenhower Republican, Douglas Dillon, to reassure the business community. Kennedy's major new find was Ford Motor Company president Robert McNamara, who promised to get a grip on defense, was a Republican, and was not a Catholic.

Kennedy's cabinet reflected the tenor of the new administration. The secretaries were not liberal ideologues but rather safe, competent, elite men of influence. Together with Kennedy's energetic young lieutenants on the informally structured White House staff—Sorensen, O'Donnell, O'Brien, and Myer Feldman—who radiated (and cherished) a self-conscious toughness to lend muscle and respect to the romantic myth of Camelot, they made a formidable team.

When President Kennedy took the oath of office on January 20, 1961, his moving inaugural address, which owed a heavy debt to the talented pen of Theodore Sorensen, intoned the new litanies:

> Let the word go forth from this time and place, to friend and foe alike, that the torch has been passed to a new generation of Americans—born in this century, tempered by war, disciplined by a hard and bitter peace, proud of our ancient heritage. . . . Let every nation know . . . that we shall pay any price, bear any burden, meet any hardship, support any friend, oppose any foe, to insure the survival and the success of liberty. . . .

> So let us begin anew—Let us never negotiate out of fear. But let us never fear to negotiate. . . . And so, my fellow Americans: ask not what your country can do for you—ask what you can do for your country.

The New Frontier and the Eighty-seventh Congress

The New Frontier that nominee Kennedy had proclaimed in Los Angeles and that President Kennedy enunciated in his inaugural address and state messages in early 1961 reflected far more a tone and spirit than a specific legislative program. Kennedy's first one hundred days were characterized by superbly performed press conferences, where the charismatic young president with the arresting Boston accent charmed millions of television viewers with his crisp sense of command and his witty spontaneity. Not legislative bills and congressional lobbying but executive orders set the tone: appoint more African Americans, launch the Peace Corps, negotiate on nuclear arms control. Jacqueline Kennedy redecorated the White House, and the Kennedys graced it with Nobel laureates and artists of world renown.

Given his executive style and weak political margin in the Eighty-seventh Congress, Kennedy was generally successful on Capitol Hill in exercising his presidential prerogatives in foreign affairs and unsuccessful in his domestic initiatives. His early victories included establishing the Peace Corps and the Alliance for Progress, creating the U.S. Arms Control and Disarmament Agency, achieving five-year loans for developing nations, and gaining U.S. membership in the Organization for Economic Cooperation and Development. Kennedy also greatly increased the budget appropriations of the National Aeronautics and Space Administration (NASA) for the moon-shot race with the Soviets (from $915 million in fiscal 1961 to $3.7 billion in fiscal 1963) and especially for the Pentagon (topping $48 billion by fiscal 1963, an increase of $8 billion since fiscal 1961). An

instinctive fiscal conservative, he nevertheless pursued expansionist fiscal and monetary
policies, increasing federal expenditures from
$81.5 billion in fiscal 1961 to $94.3 billion in fiscal 1963. In the second congressional session he
added the major Trade Expansion Act of 1962
and a United Nations bond authorization.

In domestic policy, Kennedy's successes
were largely confined to incremental increases
in traditional New Deal programs that held
special appeal to an overwhelmingly Democratic Congress, whose new public works
projects and federal appointments would be
controlled by a Democratic president and traditional patronage arrangements. These achievements included raising the minimum wage to
$1.25 an hour, aiding depressed areas (as prom-
ised in the crucial West Virginia primary), increasing Social Security benefits, expanding
the interstate highway and water antipollution
programs, creating seventy-three new federal
judgeships, and passing a $4.9 billion omnibus
housing bill. Kennedy's congressional achievements also included the 1962 establishment of
the Communications Satellite Corporation, the
legislation for which was passed by invoking
the first cloture on a Senate filibuster since 1927
(the administration ironically sought cloture
against filibustering Senate liberals, who were
objecting to a "giveaway" of the public's air-
wave rights).

Still, Kennedy failed to make a major breakthrough in domestic legislation, and by the end
of the Eighty-seventh Congress routine defeats
of his major program initiatives were becoming
embarrassing. These included such key initiatives as federal aid to education, a Department
of Urban Affairs (which promised to the cabinet the first African American, Housing and
Home Finance Administrator Robert Weaver),
Medicare, urban mass transit, youth unemployment programs, and a change in Senate
Rule 22 to make filibusters easier to terminate.
In 1961 and 1962, Kennedy submitted nine executive reorganization plans, and Congress re-

jected four of them. In the face of a burgeoning
Civil Rights movement with increasingly explosive potential, Kennedy did not even offer
the country a civil rights bill; he merely mildly
endorsed efforts to ban the poll tax and reduce
the disfranchising effects of literacy tests in federal elections.

The explanation for these failures lies in a
combination of Kennedy's beliefs and style,
congressional circumstances, and public opinion. Given the president's dominant interest in
foreign affairs, his lack of interest in liberal domestic reform, and his tendency to offer and explain programs to Congress but not to lobby
hard for them, the senior congressmen's powerful committees felt free to ignore his more
controversial importunings. The White House
legislative staff under Sorensen and O'Brien
was superior, but Kennedy withheld from the
congressional fray both himself and his re-
doubtable vice president and former legislative
wizard, Lyndon Johnson. Yet his selection of
Johnson, so crucial to his narrow victory, had
led to the appointment of the mild-mannered
Mike Mansfield of Montana as Senate majority
leader. In the more troublesome House, where
the conservative coalition between Republicans and Southern Democrats was stronger,
Kennedy persuaded the powerful speaker,
"Mr. Sam" Rayburn of Texas, to pack the
twelve-member House Rules Committee by
adding two Democrats and one Republican,
loosening the obstructionist grip of the gate-
way committee's conservative chair, Democrat
Howard Smith of Virginia. Rayburn, however,
died of cancer in November, 1961, and the new
speaker was John W. McCormack of Massachusetts, whose coolness toward the Kennedys
was stronger than his grip on the House.

The classic example of Kennedy's dilemma
in domestic politics was his repeated and embarrassing failure to secure passage of his
promised bill to aid education. Despite the
pressures of *Sputnik* and the baby boom, the
Kennedy administration was unable to over-

come the whiplash of opposition generated by three interlocked issues: religion, school desegregation, and federal control. This translated politically into fear of taxpayer support of parochial (especially Catholic) schools, financial coercion in school desegregation, and control of local school curricula by federal bureaucrats. Such fears created an unlikely coalition of Roman Catholics, Southern Democrats, and conservative Republicans that blocked all efforts at federal school aid throughout the Kennedy administration and symbolized the administration's fecklessness in domestic affairs.

The Bay of Pigs, the Berlin Wall, and the Cuban Missile Crisis

Kennedy's early performance as an untested world leader was judged less by what he formally proposed to the American people and to Congress than by the consequences of his covert initiatives and the aggressive probings of the Soviet Union. The first international crisis broke early and disastrously when on April 17, 1961, a force of twelve hundred anti-Castro refugees trained by the Central Intelligence Agency (CIA) invaded Cuba at the Bay of Pigs. Despite Kennedy's insistence on a covert operation, American participation was widely known even before the invasion. Partly for that reason, Kennedy reduced the three air strikes planned for the operation to one (and cut the number of planes in it) and refused to approve additional air support once the invasion began. Fidel Castro's army and militia of two hundred thousand men easily crushed and captured the inept invaders and humiliated the new American president. Kennedy had inherited the project from Eisenhower and had yielded to the

JFK examines the combat flag of the 2506th Cuban Landing Brigade from their mission during the Bay of Pigs invasion in April, 1961. *(NARA)*

assurances of CIA Director Allen Dulles that Castro could be overthrown as easily as the Arbenz Communists in Guatemala in 1954. Kennedy cut his losses by an early admission of defeat and responsibility, and paradoxically his popularity rating soared in the face of the Cuban debacle. He had, however, executed the implausible invasion plan, formally denied U.S. complicity, misled Ambassador Stevenson, and resisted not only the warnings of such liberal advisers as Stevenson, Chester Bowles, and Arthur Schlesinger but also the cautions of such old-school statesmen as Dean Acheson, Fulbright, and Rusk. Thus humiliated by the despised Castro, Kennedy replaced Dulles at the CIA with another Republican conservative,

---

Excerpt from John F. Kennedy's speech in West Berlin, June 26, 1963:

Two thousand years ago, the proudest boast was *civis Romanus sum*. Today, in the world of freedom, the proudest boast is *Ich bin ein Berliner*.

There are many people in the world who really don't understand, or say they don't, what is the great issue between the free world and the Communist world. Let them come to Berlin.

There are some who say that communism is the wave of the future. Let them come to Berlin.

And there are some who say, in Europe and elsewhere, we can work with the Communists. Let them come to Berlin.

And there are even a few who say that it is true that communism is an evil system, but it permits us to make economic progress. *Lass' sie nach Berlin kommen*. Let them come to Berlin.

Freedom has many difficulties and democracy is not perfect. But we have never had to put a wall up to keep our people in—to prevent them from leaving us. I want to say on behalf of my countrymen who live many miles away on the other side of the Atlantic, who are far distant from you, that they take the greatest pride, that they have been able to share with you, even from a distance, the story of the last eighteen years. I know of no town, no city, that has been besieged for eighteen years that still lives with the vitality and the force, and the hope, and the determination of the city of West Berlin.

While the wall is the most obvious and vivid demonstration of the failures of the Communist system—for all the world to see—we take no satisfaction in it; for it is, as your Mayor has said, an offense not only against history but an offense against humanity, separating families, dividing husbands and wives and brothers and sisters, and dividing a people who wish to be joined together.

What is true of this city is true of Germany: Real, lasting peace in Europe can never be assured as long as one German out of four is denied the elementary right of free men, and that is to make a free choice. In eighteen years of peace and good faith, this generation of Germans has earned the right to be free, including the right to unite their families and their nation in lasting peace, with good will to all people.

You live in a defended island of freedom, but your life is part of the main. So let me ask you, as I close, to lift your eyes beyond the dangers of today, to the hopes of tomorrow, beyond the freedom merely of this city of Berlin, or your country of Germany, to the advance of freedom everywhere, beyond the wall to the day of peace with justice, beyond yourselves and ourselves to all mankind.

Freedom is indivisible, and when one man is enslaved, all are not free. When all are free, then we can look forward to that day when this city will be joined as one and this country and this great Continent of Europe in a peaceful and hopeful globe. When that day finally comes, as it will, the people of West Berlin can take sober satisfaction in the fact that they were in the front lines for almost two decades.

All free men, wherever they may live, are citizens of Berlin. And, therefore, as a free man, I take pride in the words *Ich bin ein Berliner*.

JFK at the Berlin Wall on June 6, 1963. *(AP/Wide World Photos)*

John A. McCone, and approved a clandestine anti-Castro operation code named Mongoose, which included bizarre attempts to assassinate the Cuban leader using Mafia hit men and exploding cigars.

The Soviet probes began at a summit meeting between Kennedy and Communist Party Chairman Nikita Khrushchev at Vienna in early June, 1961, and then tested the unity and will of the North Atlantic Treaty Organization (NATO) at vulnerable Berlin. Kennedy responded with a firm statement of American resolve to defend West Berlin, a call for civil defense measures in the United States, and an increase in U.S. and NATO readiness. In early August, Khrushchev boasted of a new 100-megaton nuclear warhead, and the Communists erected a barbed-wire fence, which was quickly replaced by a concrete wall, along the border between East and West Berlin, effectively stopping the flow of refugees out of the East. The president then sent fifteen hundred American troops along the autobahn from West Germany to West Berlin in order to demonstrate American commitment to the city. The Soviets did not challenge the convoy, and the crisis eased without any real resolution of the issues.

Another Soviet probe involved the placement of Soviet missiles in Cuba. On October 22, 1962, Kennedy told the American people that offensive missile sites were being prepared in Cuba "to provide a nuclear strike capacity against the Western Hemisphere." He then boldly announced a naval blockade of offensive weapons into Cuba. Khrushchev broke the tension on October 27 by agreeing to remove the missiles under U.N. supervision (which the angry Castro blocked) in return for a U.S. pledge not to invade Cuba, which Kennedy agreed to but never formalized. Kennedy also terminated Operation Mongoose.

In facing the crisis and publicly facing down Khrushchev, Kennedy had resisted pressure from his military advisers to bomb the missile sites. His intelligence sources had convinced him that Khrushchev's main goal was to prevent an American invasion of Cuba, and that the Soviets had neither the intention nor the preparedness to risk nuclear war over such an issue.

Kennedy's prestige soared in the wake of his bold and successful maneuver, which removed much of the sting from the Bay of Pigs fiasco and the subsequent need to pay ransom for Castro's 1,113 prisoners. In the congressional elections of November, the Democrats evenly traded four lost seats in the House for four gains in the Senate and were quick to claim the lightest midterm losses since 1934. Republicans had counted heavily on the Cuban issue and complained bitterly that Kennedy's timing in announcing the missile site discovery was politically targeted toward the fall elections. As the Kennedy administration entered 1963 and the Eighty-eighth Congress, the Soviets had been faced down by a determined and sure-handed young president, the economy was quickening, and renewed Democratic majorities dominated the Congress.

Soviet Détente and the Indochinese Quagmire

In 1963, Kennedy was to reverse dramatically the deteriorating relations with the Soviet Union that had occasioned such dangerous confrontations over Berlin and Cuba. At the same time, however, U.S. efforts to prevent the communist takeover of Laos continued to falter. By the end of 1963, the American client regime in Vietnam was collapsing, despite the in-

fusion of ten thousand American military personnel as "advisers."

Kennedy's inaugural address had been criticized as an eloquent but saber-rattling Cold War challenge, and the combination in 1962 of Khrushchev's new 100-megaton warheads and Kennedy's missile blockade had alarmed Western leaders. In 1963, hardening relations with Peking inclined Moscow to a more conciliatory attitude toward Washington, which was then reciprocated. On June 10, President Kennedy expressed a new and less bellicose tone in a speech at American University: "Let us reexamine our attitude toward the Cold War," he said. "We must deal with the world as it is, and not as it might have been had the history of the last eighteen years been different. We must, therefore, persevere in the search for peace in the hope that constructive changes within the Communist bloc might bring within reach solutions which now seem beyond us."

In that speech he announced that the United States, the Soviet Union, and Great Britain would begin new talks on a nuclear test ban. On July 25, a limited agreement was initialed in Moscow, and the Senate ratified the Nuclear Test Ban Treaty on September 24. It pledged the signatory nations not to conduct tests of nuclear weapons underwater, in the atmosphere, or in outer space. That summer a hot line was installed linking the White House and the Kremlin. In addition, President Kennedy proposed a joint U.S.-Soviet manned flight to the moon and authorized negotiations for the private sale of $250 million in surplus wheat to the Soviet Union.

In Southeast Asia, however, conditions continued to deteriorate. Attention had concentrated primarily on Laos during 1961 and 1962. Kennedy chose not to take a military stand against communist insurgents there but instead agreed to negotiations that led to a neutral government. The agreement soon collapsed, however, as the Communist-backed Pathet Lao pummeled the neutralist forces of

Premier Souvanna Phouma, and the United States and China exchanged heated charges. In neighboring South Vietnam, Kennedy rejected the idea of negotiations but also refused to commit American forces to a direct combat role. Instead he sought a "limited partnership" in the defense of that nation against communist insurgency and invasion from North Vietnam. Nevertheless he continued and even escalated American involvement there. During his administration, the number of American military advisers in South Vietnam increased from about three thousand to more than sixteen thousand.

In 1963, South Vietnam began to dominate the news, as the Catholic regime of Premier Ngo Dinh Diem cracked down hard on protesting Buddhists, and grisly scenes of self-immolating Buddhist priests appeared on American television. Protests broke out across the United States against the widely reported repression and corruption associated with Ngo; his brother

and secret police chief, Ngo Dinh Nhu; and his wife, Madame Nhu—the infamous "Dragon Lady." This coincided with a marked cooling in U.S.-South Vietnam relations and led to a military coup on November 1, in which Diem and Nhu were killed. Frustrated by America's inability to move South Vietnam toward political and social reforms, the Kennedy administration actively abetted the plotters, then was unable to prevent the murder of the Ngo brothers. The military junta that replaced Ngo Dinh Diem was short-lived, and local Viet Cong successes continued in the countryside. This was the crumbling legacy that Lyndon Johnson was to inherit.

The Belated Commitment to Civil Rights Reform

When campaigning for president against Nixon in 1960, Kennedy was quick to accuse the Eisenhower administration of failing to bar racial

Civil rights leaders Fred L. Shuttlesworth, Dr. Martin Luther King, Jr., and Ralph D. Abernathy hold a press conference in Birmingham, Alabama, in May, 1963. *(Library of Congress)*

discrimination in federally assisted housing "with the stroke of a pen." Once elected, however, Kennedy avoided the pen stroke for almost two years, until safely after the elections of 1962. Like Franklin D. Roosevelt, he saw his high-priority legislation held potentially hostage by powerful Southern Democrats in Congress. Such key bills as the trade and tax measures, federal aid to education, and Medicare were too important to risk with a civil rights fight that would invite the enmity of such powerful Southern legislators as James Eastland of Mississippi and Robert Kerr of Oklahoma in the Senate and Wilbur Mills of Arkansas and Howard Smith of Virginia in the House.

During the fall of 1962, the turmoil associated with the admission of a black law student, James Meredith, to the all-white University of Mississippi taught both Jack and Bobby Kennedy the necessity of dealing firmly with bitter resistance by such defiant Southern politicians as Governors Ross Barnett of Mississippi and George Wallace of Alabama. On February 28, 1963, Kennedy proposed his first civil rights bill, which concentrated on voting and excluded controversial provisions for equal employment machinery or open public accommodations. In early April, in Birmingham, peaceful demonstrators led by the Reverend Martin Luther King, Jr., were shown on television being attacked by police dogs and fire hoses under the aggressive direction of police chief Eugene ("Bull") Connor. The demonstrations spread to hundreds of towns and cities throughout the spring and summer of 1963, and on June 11, in a nationwide television address, President Kennedy said, "We are confronted primarily with a moral issue." He called for an omnibus civil rights bill, including a ban on segregated restaurants, hotels, and other public accommodations.

On August 28, more than 200,000 black and white Americans converged peacefully in the March on Washington for Jobs and Freedom. Kennedy had crossed the Rubicon on civil rights, as had a bipartisan coalition in the House, where the Judiciary Committee with strong administration support reported out a comprehensive civil rights bill in early November. The main test lay ahead in the Senate, where a conservative and Southern-led filibuster was certain—and had never failed in the past.

John F. Kennedy and the Eighty-eighth Congress

President Kennedy's decisive commitment to civil rights was paralleled by a major initiative for an economy-boosting tax cut. In January, 1963, he called for an "urgent" and politically unorthodox $10.3 billion cut in personal and corporate taxes, even though the administration budget projected a deficit of $8.3 billion for fiscal 1964. Kennedy's Keynesian tax cut bill, shorn of its earlier tax reform initiatives but increased to $11.1 billion, was reported out by the House Ways and Means Committee on September 13, and it passed the House on September 25. Senate passage was hoped for early in 1964.

These major Kennedy initiatives, however, pointing as they did toward the harvest of the Kennedy legacy by President Lyndon Johnson in 1964, should not obscure a further deterioration in Kennedy's record with the Congress. Except for his initiatives in civil rights and the tax cut, Kennedy's accomplishments remained few and marginal. They included a new federal program supporting community treatment centers for the mentally ill, grants and loans for college and medical school construction, and modest expansion of air pollution and manpower retraining programs. Both the tempo and the output of Congress in response to administration proposals was further reduced in the Eighty-eighth Congress. Although the first session ran through December 30, 1963, for a near record 356 days, it completed only four of twelve annual appropriations bill (even though the fiscal year had ended the previous July). Its adoption of 44.3 percent of administra-

JFK signs a nuclear test ban treaty on October 7, 1963. *(NARA)*

campaign would provide Kennedy with an opportunity to argue the issues sharply and enter the Eighty-ninth Congress with a clear mandate and strong program majority. To do this he needed first to patch and mend the tattered Democratic coalition, where his drives for education aid and civil rights reform had especially rent the political fabric.

It was such a mending trip that took him to Dallas, Texas, on November 22, 1963, where an assassin gunned him down. The assassination investigatory commission, headed by Chief Justice Earl Warren, concluded that President Kennedy had been murdered by Lee Harvey Oswald acting alone—a finding that has been much disputed by competing conspiracy theories but that stands as a formal and public judgment in the absence of conclusive evidence to the contrary.

tion proposals in 1962 dropped sharply to 27.2 percent in 1963.

In foreign affairs, President Kennedy, by the fall of 1963, had achieved a measure of balanced firmness and détente with the Soviets that had earned for him high regard in American and indeed world opinion. His belated commitment to civil rights followed an apparently irresistible tide of domestic opinion, fueled by the televised brutality of Southern all-white police forces. Yet like all controversial measures, the civil rights bill had a polarizing effect that drove Kennedy's Gallup ratings downward markedly. He was already gearing up for the reelection campaign in 1964, hoping for the Republicans to nominate hard-line conservative Senator Barry Goldwater rather than a more centrist candidate such as Governor Nelson Rockefeller of New York or Governor George Romney of Michigan. A rightist Goldwater

Camelot and Martyrdom: The Kennedy Legacy

Martyrdom powerfully ennobled the memory of Abraham Lincoln, and its impact on the reputation of the captivating young Kennedy was equally stunning. The world naturally views his presidential legacy through the mythic prism of a Camelot whose hero had fallen—and in truth the martyred leader was uncommonly blessed with youth, grace, and charm; an ironic and spontaneous wit; and a probing political intelligence that was enriched by a superior education. The courage and character he had demonstrated in war bore the hallmark of genuine heroism. His ability to master the new political demands of the age of television was matched only by Franklin D. Roosevelt's command of radio, and it was unsurpassed in his own time. The profound loyalty, respect, and affection that he commanded from his able

The Kennedys' open limousine makes its way through crowds on a Dallas street moments before the president is assassinated on November 22, 1963. *(AP/Wide World Photos)*

even through the White House years, with consorts ranging over a wide spectrum. Also, Kennedy had lied to the American people about his Addison's disease.

Beyond Camelot and the alleged contradictions of the personal character of its hero, what were the unique and lasting contributions of President Kennedy's thousand days in office? Clearly, high rank must be accorded to his effective destruction of the powerful myth that a Roman Catholic is unfit for the American presidency. His consistent opposition to direct federal aid to parochial schools helped to doom his education bill, but it confirmed the historic primacy of a secular presidency.

In Kennedy's preferred domain of foreign affairs, one may compare the adventuresome fiasco at the Bay of Pigs with the subsequent triumph over Khrushchev in the Cuban Missile Crisis, and also the hawkish ring of his inaugural address with his conciliatory American University speech, and conclude that his growth as president ultimately moved the republic away from the brink of nuclear war. His Arms Control and Disarmament Agency and Nuclear Test Ban Treaty nourished a successful legacy of détente, especially in Europe. Throughout his thousand days, the United States kept the peace, however uneasily.

In contrast, Kennedy's fascination with counterinsurgency, his early approval of the Cuban invasion and Operation Mongoose, and later his military escalation in Vietnam and his involvement in the toppling of Ngo Dinh Diem all left a legacy that led toward the disastrous American war in Vietnam. The overthrow and

lieutenants signaled a rare devotion and was reflected in the worldwide grief that marked his untimely passing. That same grief was echoed thirty-six years later, in 1999, with the tragic crash of a small plane piloted by the charismatic John F. Kennedy, Jr., who many had hoped would continue his father's political legacy.

Romantic myths such as Camelot reinforce their darker underside by implicitly denying it. Critics charged that the nation's charmed intellectuals and captivated media practiced a double standard—they blinked at character flaws in John Kennedy that they would savage with relish in a Johnson or a Nixon. Kennedy's inherited wealth and his father's connections bought his career, they said, and ghosted and helped publish his books and essays. His sexual and marital indiscretions were reputedly sustained murder of Ngo fundamentally changed America's Vietnam commitment. The president and his senior administrators were appalled by the assassinations, but their role in the coup assigned to them a heavy measure of responsibility for what followed. It seemed as if the military-dominated governments that ruled South Vietnam for the rest of the war were inherited by the United States—unruly American offspring to whose fate and ultimate defeat Kennedy's successors remained tightly and tragically bound.

In domestic policy Kennedy has generally been accorded high marks for promoting economic growth through the expansion of world trade and the pump-priming tax cut. The latter achievement was signed by President Lyndon Johnson, and its economic impact was even greater than its proposers had hoped. It constituted the first of a triple harvest that Johnson freely acknowledged as fulfilling the Kennedy promise: the tax cut and the civil rights bill of 1964, and federal aid to education in 1965. Yet Johnson achieved the first two, in addition to launching his War on Poverty, with essentially the same Congress that had so consistently defeated most of Kennedy's legislative proposals throughout his administration.

It was Johnson, of course, who enjoyed the landslide over Goldwater and who translated those majorities into the extraordinary burst of new Great Society programs that so dwarfed Kennedy's legislative achievements for the New Frontier. To speculate how Kennedy might have fared with a Goldwater challenge and beyond is to engage in dreams of what might have been. Perhaps it is best that Kennedy is most singularly and warmly associated in the public memory with the concrete achievement of the Peace Corps—whose meaning, like that of its mentor, is derived less from its demonstrable impact than from an abiding spirit of youth and hope.

Hugh Davis Graham

Suggested Readings

Benson, Michael. *Who's Who in the JFK Assassination: An A to Z Encyclopedia*. London: Kensington, 1993. An excellent compendium of the characters and events related to the assassination.

Brauer, Carl M. *John F. Kennedy and the Second Reconstruction*. New York: Columbia University, 1977. A good case study of Kennedy and the civil rights crisis.

Chomsky, Noam. *Rethinking Camelot: JFK, the Vietnam War, and U.S. Political Culture*. Boston: South End Press, 1993. A reassessment of Kennedy's presidency.

Duffy, James P., and Vincent L. Ricci. *The Assassination of John F. Kennedy: A Complete Book of Facts*. New York: Thunder's Mouth Press, 1992. Discusses the evidence, theories, characters, investigations, conflicting testimony, and controversies of the assassination.

Giglio, James N. *John F. Kennedy: A Bibliography*. Westport, Conn.: Greenwood Press, 1995. A comprehensive bibliographic overview of the Kennedy years.

_____. *The Presidency of John F. Kennedy*. 2d rev. ed. Lawrence: University Press of Kansas, 2006. A balanced portrait of Kennedy's term.

John Fitzgerald Kennedy Library and Museum. http://www.jfklibrary.org/. The Web site of Kennedy's official presidential library and museum.

Kennedy, John F. *Let the Word Go Forth: The Speeches, Statements, and Writings of John F. Kennedy*. Compiled by Theodore C. Sorensen. New York: Delacourt Press, 1988. Several key writings and speeches are included as well as numerous photographs.

O'Brien, Michael. *John F. Kennedy: A Biography*. New York: St. Martin's Press, 2005. A lengthy biography that also serves well as a survey of other sources about Kennedy.

Parmet, Herbert S. *Jack: The Struggles of John F. Kennedy*. 2 vols. New York: Dial Press, 1980. A standard scholarly biography.

_____. *JFK: The Presidency of John F. Kennedy*. New York: Dial Press, 1983. A standard assessment of the Kennedy White House.

Posner, Gerald. *Case Closed: Lee Harvey Oswald and the Assassination of JFK*. New York: Random House, 1993. Argues that Oswald acted alone in the assassination.

Rust, William J. *Kennedy in Vietnam*. New York: Scribner, 1985. Provides good analysis of Kennedy's role in the escalation in Southeast Asia.

Salinger, Pierre. *John F. Kennedy, Commander in Chief: A Profile in Leadership*. New York: Penguin Studio, 1997. Kennedy's press secretary discusses Kennedy's political career.

Schlesinger, Arthur M., Jr. *A Thousand Days: John F. Kennedy in the White House*. Boston: Houghton Mifflin, 1965. Eminent presidential historian Schlesinger brings together photographs and documents to chronicle Kennedy's tenure as president.

Schwab, Orrin. *Defending the Free World: John F. Kennedy, Lyndon Johnson, and the Vietnam War*. Westport, Conn: Praeger, 1998. Using a blend of diplomatic, political, and institutional evidence, Schwab examines the resolve of U.S. leaders to take a stand in Vietnam.

Scott, William E. *November 22, 1963: A Reference Guide to the JFK Assassination*. Lanham, Md.: University Press of America, 1999. The expertise of medical and ballistic experts, government officials, and law enforcement is consulted, and an extensive bibliography is included.

Sorensen, Theodore C. *Kennedy*. 1965. Reprint. New York: Perennial Library, 1988. A comprehensive memoir written by Kennedy's White House chief of staff.

_____. *The Kennedy Legacy*. New York: Macmillan, 1993. An evaluation of Kennedy's impact.

Thompson, Robert S. *The Missiles of October: The Declassified Story of John F. Kennedy and the Cuban Missile Crisis*. New York: Simon & Schuster, 1992. A detailed examination of the Cuban Missile Crisis.

Wills, Garry. *The Kennedy Imprisonment*. Boston: Little, Brown. 1982. Provides a wide-ranging, sometimes savage critique of the Kennedy legend.

Lyndon B. Johnson

36th President, 1963-1968

Born: August 27, 1908
    Gillespie County, Texas
Died: January 22, 1973
    near Stonewall, en route to San
    Antonio, Texas

Political Party: Democratic
Vice President: Hubert H. Humphrey

Cabinet Members

Secretary of State: Dean Rusk
Secretary of the Treasury: Douglas Dillon,
    Henry H. Fowler, Joseph W. Barr
Secretary of Defense: Robert McNamara, Clark
    Clifford
Attorney General: Robert F. Kennedy, N. de B.
    Katzenbach, Ramsey Clark
Postmaster General: John A. Gronouski,
    Lawrence F. O'Brien, W. Marvin Watson
Secretary of the Interior: Stewart L. Udall
Secretary of Agriculture: Orville Freeman
Secretary of Commerce: Luther Hodges, John T.
    Connor, Alexander B. Trowbridge, C. R.
    Smith
Secretary of Labor: W. Willard Wirtz
Secretary of Health, Education, and Welfare:
    Anthony Celebrezze, John W. Gardner,
    Wilbur J. Cohen
Secretary of Housing and Urban Development:
    Robert C. Weaver, Robert C. Wood
Secretary of Transportation: Alan S. Boyd

At one o'clock on the afternoon of November 22, 1963, John F. Kennedy died from gunshot wounds received while riding in a motorcade through Dallas, Texas. Lyndon Baines Johnson became the thirty-sixth president of the United States. A little more than two and a half hours later, aboard *Air Force One* on a runway at a Dallas airport, Johnson took the oath of office. Immediately thereafter, the plane took off for the flight back to Washington, D.C., carrying the new president as well as the body of the slain one. During the next four days, amid the ceremonies marking Kennedy's burial, a Kennedy legend was born that, for some people, would cast a shadow over Lyndon Johnson's presidency. For them, Johnson remained always the usurper, the unsophisticated Texan who never matched the glamour, vigor, and promise of Kennedy. The man who flew back to assume the power of the presidency, however, had first left Texas for Washington a long time before, and his experience in the capital had shaped his attitudes and goals.

Rise to Power

Lyndon Johnson's life began in Texas, southwest of Dallas in the hill country, a beautiful but deceptively rugged land. There he was born on August 27, 1908, to Rebekah Baines and Sam Ealy Johnson, Jr. Sam Johnson owned a fairly prosperous farm and served the people against the special interests in the Texas state legisla-

Johnson's official portrait. *(White House Historical Society)*

Mexican American community south of San Antonio. He dedicated enormous energy to his job and exercised a demanding paternalism, but still became exceedingly popular with his students and the community. Years later, when he was president, Johnson cited his year among the poor of Cotulla as the origin of his commitment to oppose racism and eradicate poverty. After graduation, Johnson returned to teaching, this time in Houston, but soon quit to become assistant to the newly elected congressman from Texas's Fourteenth District, Richard M. Kleberg.

In December, 1931, at the age of only twenty-three, Lyndon Johnson arrived in Washington, D.C., for the first time. He never severed his ties to Texas nor lost his love for the hill country, but except for a two-year stint as director of a federal agency in Texas, neither did he live there again until he left the White House in 1969. He never ran for state office. The capital served as his escape from the hill country and became the stage upon which he played out his ambitions. His life as a Texan in Washington, a provincial in the capital, only exacerbated his insecurities. Johnson at once envied and felt patronized by the better-educated, more sophisticated residents of the capital, especially the intellectuals from the Northeast.

As a young congressional aide, Johnson worked incredibly hard and quickly mastered his job. He cajoled the conservative Kleberg into voting for much of the New Deal, excelled at constituent services, learned everything he could about how the government worked, and cultivated people in high and low places within it, especially a friend of his father, Congressman Sam T. Rayburn. While still working for Kleberg, in 1934, Johnson met Claudia Alta Taylor, a recent graduate of the University of Texas, daughter of a well-to-do merchant from

ture. Johnson served only a few terms in the legislature, however, and went broke at farming in the early 1920's. He then moved his family to nearby Johnson City, where Lyndon grew up. Except for displaying an intense interest in his father's political activities, Lyndon had a not-uncommon small-town Texas childhood. He did, however, develop a fierce determination to succeed and to escape the rigors of the hill country. The young Lyndon also acquired a deep sense of insecurity, perhaps because of his relations with his parents or the embarrassment of his father's financial difficulties.

After high school, Lyndon left for California, but a little more than a year later, he returned to Texas and took a job on a Johnson City road crew. Soon he enrolled at Southwest State Teachers College in nearby San Marcos, where he was graduated in 1930. Johnson had to work his way through school and took a year off to teach in Cotulla, Texas, a small, poor, primarily

Karnack, and descendant of Alabama gentility. . The young aide courted Lady Bird, as she was already known, with the same intensity with which he had taught school and managed Kleberg's office. Within a few months, she agreed to marry him. A woman of great consideration for others and considerable business and political acumen, Lady Bird Johnson displayed unquestioning loyalty to and unending patience with her husband.

After a year of marriage, the young couple returned to Texas. Johnson had used his connections in Washington, D.C., to secure the post of Texas state director of the newly created National Youth Administration (NYA). He did an excellent job of administering this New Deal relief program, some said the best job of any state director. After only two years, Johnson resigned in order to run for the Tenth Congressional District seat when the incumbent died. He campaigned as a devoted disciple of Franklin D. Roosevelt and his New Deal, stressing that he would vote for the president's then-controversial plan to add members to the Supreme Court. In a ten-man race, Johnson won a plurality of the votes, all that was necessary in a special election. Shortly after Johnson's victory, Roosevelt visited Texas, and Johnson took

---

THE FIRST LADY
LADY BIRD JOHNSON

An instrumental voice in Lyndon Baines Johnson's long political career, Lady Bird Johnson is remembered as one of the most active First Ladies ever to reside in the White House. Claudia Alta Taylor was born on December 22, 1912, in the small community of Karnack, Texas. The family's cook and nursemaid, Alice Tittle, remarked that the young girl was as pretty as a "lady bird," and the nickname stuck. Her father, Thomas "T. J." Taylor, owned a store and sold land, while her mother, Minnie, enjoyed a variety of intellectual and artistic pursuits. Tragically, when Lady Bird was only six years old, her mother fell down a staircase while pregnant with her fourth child, suffering a miscarriage and ultimately dying from her injuries.

Lady Bird attended St. Mary's in Dallas and later graduated from the University of Texas with degrees in history and journalism. She also wrote for the campus newspaper. After a brief and intense courtship, Lady Bird married Lyndon Johnson in San Antonio on November 17, 1934. In the early years of their marriage, the couple suffered miscarriages but eventually had two daughters, Lynda in 1944 and Luci in 1947.

Despite her initial disinterest in politics, Lady Bird Johnson eventually helped fund her husband's first campaign, worked in his congressional office, and became an effective campaigner for the Kennedy-Johnson ticket in 1960. Lady Bird was one of the most active vice presidential spouses, filling in for Jacqueline Kennedy on many events when the First Lady was either disinterested or occupied with two infant children.

As First Lady, Lady Bird Johnson edited her husband's speeches, hosted "Women Doer Luncheons" at the White House, supported Head Start for children, and gained fame for her "beautification" effort, which not only advocated planting greenery and limiting unsightly billboards but also promoted a broad array of conservation programs. After the White House, Lady Bird continued her advocacy for conservation and served on the boards of the National Geographic Society and University of Texas. For her many achievements, she was awarded the Presidential Medal of Freedom in 1977 and a Congressional Gold Medal in 1988.

Robert P. Watson

the opportunity to ingratiate himself with the president. Roosevelt naturally welcomed such a loyal supporter, and he soon developed a real fondness for him.

In 1937, Lyndon Johnson returned to Washington as congressman from the Tenth District of Texas, which included the hill country and the capital of Austin. With his experience in Washington, the tutelage of influential House member Rayburn, and, most important, the favor of President Roosevelt and the assistance of his influential aides, the young Texan quickly became a very effective congressman. Most of the measures of the New Deal had already passed, though Johnson arrived in time to cast a vote for the first minimum wage law. Johnson's success, however, came not from his voting record or his role in floor debates—in fact, he rarely made speeches or introduced bills—but rather from his skill at serving constituents and at securing federal benefits for his district: millions of dollars in Works Progress Administration and Public Works Administration construction, one of the first four federal housing projects, and, after Roosevelt's intervention, a Rural Electrification Administration loan that at least brought electricity to the Texas hill country. Johnson ran unopposed in the next two elections.

In 1941, Johnson lost a special election for a vacated Senate seat but remained in the House, where he became, under Roosevelt's influence, an avid supporter of military preparedness and of an activist foreign policy. Except for seven months in uniform, Johnson remained in Congress during World War II. After the war, he became a bit more conservative than he had been in the 1930's. Roosevelt, his liberal hero and patron, had died. The nation as a whole had become more conservative. Most important, Johnson had begun to position himself for a statewide race and realized that postwar Texas would accept less liberalism than had the Depression-struck Tenth District. Although he supported President Harry S. Tru-

man on most foreign policy matters, he sometimes voted against him on domestic issues, most prominently in voting for the Taft-Hartley Act designed to limit the influence of organized labor.

In 1948, Johnson ran again for the Senate. Campaigning by helicopter, he waged a determined race in the Democratic primary that stressed his anticommunist credentials and opposition to unions. He won a runoff by only 87 votes, and his opponent and others charged that voting irregularities in South Texas accounted for the margin. Indisputably, one voting box had been stuffed and its ballots burned before investigators could check them. Whether Johnson stole the election or whether

LBJ with Lady Bird Johnson in 1936. *(LBJ Library)*

it was stolen for him by others unconnected to him or even whether the stealing on his side only balanced theft by the other side remains unclear. In any case, a close vote in the state executive committee placed Johnson's name on the ballot as the Democratic nominee, and therefore at that time in Texas as the winner, and clever arguments by Johnson's lawyers in federal courts defeated his opponent's attempt to overthrow that decision.

Lyndon B. Johnson—teased as "Landslide Lyndon" because of the closeness of the vote and tainted by the accusations of fraud—joined the Senate in 1949. He very quickly became an influential member through the same means he had employed in the House: incredibly hard work, mastery of the system, and cultivation of an influential elder, in this case Senate leader Richard Russell of Georgia. Johnson kept the voters of Texas happy, again through dedicated constituent services but also by his opposition to civil rights and organized labor and by his unswerving support of oil and gas interests. While protecting his position in Texas, he moved rapidly into a leadership position within the Senate. In 1951, he became Democratic whip, and in 1953, after the defeat of the incumbent, he became minority leader. In 1955, when the Democrats regained control of the Senate, Johnson became majority leader. By 1958, he had established himself as one of the ablest majority leaders in Senate history.

His success owed something to his use of money and influence. As early as 1940, Johnson served as a conduit of campaign contributions to national politicians from the oilmen and other wealthy individuals of Texas. As majority leader, he craftily built support through his control of committee assignments and office space. He also performed various personal favors and kindnesses. Ultimately, however, his power in the Senate rested on two things: his ability to convince individual senators to vote with him and his masterful use of legislative tactics.

Johnson rarely moved his colleagues through inspiring oratory. The majority leader never won an argument on the floor, one observer commented, and never lost one in the cloakroom. His method in the latter place came to be called the Johnson "Treatment," best described by newspapermen Rowland Evans and Robert Novak:

> Its tone could be supplication, accusation, cajolery, exuberance, scorn, tears, complaint, the hint of threat. It was all of these together. It ran the gamut of human emotions. Its velocity was breathtaking, and it was all in one direction. Interjections from the target were rare. Johnson anticipated them before they could be spoken. He moved in close, his face a scant millimeter from his target, his eyes widening and narrowing, his eyebrows rising and falling. From his pockets poured clippings, memos, statistics. Mimicry, humor, and the genius of analogy made The Treatment an almost hypnotic experience and rendered the target stunned and helpless.

Critics called such efforts "arm twisting"; Johnson rightly preferred the term "seduction." He rarely asked a senator to vote against his constituents on an issue important to them and always tailored his argument to the political or personal needs of the man or woman he confronted. Along with the amazing force of his presentation, therefore, his success owed much to his awesome ability to understand what the object of his seduction desired, needed, or responded to—an ability derived partly from instinct, partly from the hard work of intelligence gathering that produced an accurate profile of each of the senators.

That intelligence system also provided the majority leader remarkably accurate vote counts. The Senate rarely surprised him, and he had a sure sense of when and how to present a bill. Johnson himself kept his own counsel, rarely making speeches or even publicly explaining his position. In fact, he often emphasized a bill's conservative nature with Southerners and its progressive intent with liberals. Such an approach allowed him to build the diverse coalitions central to his success. It also helped that he worked with a phenomenally popular Republican president, Dwight D. Eisenhower. Johnson usually supported Eisenhower on foreign affairs and occasionally on domestic matters as well. He especially delighted in portraying himself and his party as allied with the president in a fight against the ultraconservatives of the president's own party.

Johnson, in short, excelled as a legislative tactician rather than as a strategist, as his aide George Reedy put it. The majority leader never tried to establish a Democratic agenda. Indeed, he scorned senators who sought to do so through impassioned public or Senate speeches—"show horses" he called them. He preferred "workhorses," senators of whatever ideological belief or party affiliation who worked quietly and steadily to pass legislation. He and his workhorses passed a number of measures, many of them surprisingly liberal for the conservative 1950's: an increase in housing subsidies for the poor, a moderate (more moderate than the liberals wanted) rise in the minimum wage, and an expansion of Social Security coverage, including the establishment of benefits for the disabled. Johnson was also instrumental in the start of the space program, and he played a major role in the censure of Senator Joseph McCarthy and the passage of the 1957 Civil Rights Act.

Beginning in 1950, but exploiting an already widespread and intense fear of internal communist subversion, McCarthy commanded national attention with reckless attacks on the loyalty and patriotism of many individuals within and outside government. Only in 1954 did the majority leader decide that the popular McCarthy had become vulnerable and then quietly mobilize the Senate establishment against him. The Senate soon voted to censure McCarthy, and under Johnson's leadership every Democrat voted in favor. McCarthy's influence and career quickly declined.

The majority leader's role in the passage of the Civil Rights Act of 1957 proved more public than his role in the fall of McCarthy. Until that time Johnson's record on racial issues had resembled that of many Southern moderates of the era. He only occasionally resorted to race-baiting and aided African Americans when he could do so without attracting public attention, but he never attacked segregation and consistently voted against federal intervention in Southern race relations. By 1957, though, Johnson figured the time had come for federal legislation. The Supreme Court decision against school segregation and the Montgomery bus boycott had created a climate for action. Many African Americans had voted Republican in 1956, and Johnson believed that the Democratic Party had to woo them back. Moreover, he knew that he himself needed to escape his identification with Southern racial practices if he were to realize his growing ambition to be president.

In 1957, Johnson set out to pass a civil rights bill without provoking a Southern filibuster that had blocked earlier civil rights legislation and that he feared would divide his party. Working from a strong bill proposed by the Eisenhower administration, Johnson made significant concessions to the Southerners to convince them to allow a vote (though they still voted against the bill) and yet persuaded enough senators to agree to the compromise to pass the act in what some described as a "legislative miracle." Although weak and ineffective, the Civil Rights Act of 1957 was the first federal civil rights law since Reconstruction, it placed the federal government on record as supporting black voting rights, and it opened the way for the far more effective legislation enacted during Johnson's presidency. Finally, the bill passed without a seriously divisive confrontation over a filibuster and therefore with minimal damage to the Democratic Party and sectional relations.

Response to Johnson's role in both the McCarthy censure and the passage of the Civil

Rights Act typified opinions held about the majority leader. Many observers considered both major successes and praised Johnson as a master tactician who secured legislation few could have passed. Others, particularly in the liberal wing of the Democratic Party, questioned why he had waited so long to attack McCarthy and condemned the Civil Rights Act as a sellout to Southern racists. They minimized Johnson's legislative accomplishments and believed that he refused to take a valiant liberal stand in the face of sure defeat because of his own conservatism. Their antipathy limited Johnson's chances of securing the Democratic nomination for president just as surely as his success as majority leader made him a likely candidate.

Exactly when Johnson decided that he wanted to be president remains unclear. Some seem to believe that he reached the decision in his mother's womb. Clearly, the thought had crossed his mind as early as 1940 and never entirely passed from it. He always minimized his chances, though, because he believed that no Southerner could be elected. Nevertheless, from 1955 on, he thought of it more and more, and in 1960 he made a halfhearted, poorly conceived attempt to secure the Democratic nomination. He failed; John F. Kennedy easily won nomination on the first ballot at the convention. The new nominee then offered Johnson the vice presidency.

Some maintained that Kennedy offered the majority leader the second spot on the ticket only because he expected him to say no. More likely, the tough-minded politician realized that Johnson could help him in the crucial state of Texas as well as in the rest of the South. In either case, when the liberals heard of Kennedy's offer, many balked at the idea of Johnson on the ticket, and Kennedy wavered in his decision. During that period, Robert Kennedy, the nominee's younger brother, went to Johnson and asked him to withdraw. Johnson then called John Kennedy, who told him that Bobby was out of touch and reassured him that he was the nominee. Out of the confusion and Bobby's visit, however, emerged animosity between Johnson and the younger Kennedy, which only grew with time.

If some observers could not believe that Kennedy had offered the job to Johnson, others were astonished that Johnson accepted it. The vice presidency offered no challenge and less real power than the post of majority leader. Johnson believed that he could help the ticket, and as a loyal Democrat may have felt a duty to do so. Johnson may also have seen the vice presidency as a means to free himself of his sometimes troublesome ties to conservative Texas and thereby enhance his chance for a later run for the presidency. Moreover, with his astute sense of political timing, Johnson may have realized that he would not retain the power that he had as majority leader if either Kennedy, an activist within his own party, or his opponent, Richard M. Nixon, a very different Republican from Eisenhower, became president. Perhaps, too, Johnson believed that he could invest the office with real power.

That fall, Johnson campaigned very hard for the ticket and clearly helped Kennedy carry Texas and possibly other states as well. Once in office, Johnson did try to increase the power of the vice president, sending a memo to the White House outlining considerable authority for himself and seeking a role in the Senate Democratic caucus. Summarily rebuffed in both attempts, Johnson found himself becoming a typical vice president. Kennedy, who always treated him well, asked Johnson to chair the President's Committee on Equal Employment Opportunity and the National Aeronautics and Space Council. As head of the latter, Johnson urged Kennedy to undertake the program to land an American on the moon. Kennedy also sent Johnson on eleven trips abroad, during which he visited thirty-three countries. On a courageous trip to West Berlin during a Soviet-American crisis over access and on a fact-finding mission to South Vietnam, Johnson performed well and served a useful function. He turned many other trips into American-style campaign stops, sometimes winning friends for the United States but often generating unflattering press reports of his folksy ways and unreasonable demands on the diplomatic staff. Such stories only increased the derision of Johnson as "Uncle Cornpone" by many within the Kennedy camp. By 1963, rumors circulated, which Johnson apparently believed, that he would be dropped from the ticket in 1964. They were untrue, but the powerlessness and ignominy of the vice presidency took their toll. In what was for him an amazing act of self-restraint, Johnson never publicly aired his resentments or criticized Kennedy. He remained a most loyal vice president but an increasingly miserable one.

Assuming Power

With the assassination, Johnson escaped his exile in the vice presidency and assumed the awesome burdens of the presidency at a most difficult time. As he flew back from Dallas, the new president realized that he had to reassure the nation and the world that the government would continue. He also knew that he had to convince both of the legitimacy of his power. His career thus far had left LBJ, as he was often called during his presidency, particularly suited to do so. He knew the ways of Washington, D.C., and the means of power as well as anyone. Using his experience, Johnson quickly established his control over the government and his intention of carrying out Kennedy's goals. Turning on The Treatment, he convinced the Kennedy cabinet and staff to remain with him, though he began bringing in his own advisers as well. Two days after Kennedy's burial, Johnson delivered a sentimental but hugely successful televised address to a joint session of Congress. He began by saying, "All I have I would have given gladly not to be standing here today" and closed by quoting from "America the Beautiful." In between, he promised to carry out Kennedy's plans for the nation and, echoing Kennedy's inaugural rhetoric of "let us begin," urged "let us continue."

To ease public concern over a possible plot against the government, Johnson appointed a panel of distinguished Americans, headed by Chief Justice Earl Warren, to investigate the Kennedy assassination. The Warren Commission, as it came to be called, in September, 1964, issued a reassuring report that Lee Harvey Oswald had acted alone in killing Kennedy. That conclusion has not been disproven, although critics have established the commission's lack of thoroughness and have raised serious questions about its findings.

Throughout the transition, Johnson performed masterfully. He calmed the nation's fears and reassured people of the continuity in government. LBJ also quickly moved to enact two measures that Kennedy had proposed but failed to convince Congress to pass, a tax cut and a civil rights bill. In doing so, Johnson sometimes invoked Kennedy's memory but always relied on the skills that he had developed in Congress. The old legislative wizard advised his aides on how to manipulate the Congress and used his telephone, a favorite instrument, to administer The Treatment to wavering congress members. As he had in the Senate, he often compromised, but as president LBJ displayed a greater willingness—to use his analogy—to push in his whole stack. He soon won more than a few pots.

Kennedy's Keynesian advisers had recommended a tax cut, despite a budget deficit, in order to stimulate a stagnant economy. Johnson concluded that to pass the tax cut he would have to reduce the proposed budget, thus lowering the potential deficit and making the cut easier for fiscal conservatives to accept. He ordered a rigorous review of the already planned budget and pared it significantly, primarily through cuts in defense spending. By the end of February, 1964, Congress had passed a substantial reduction in personal and business taxes, which, most economists contend, provided the desired stimulus to the economy.

Congress moved more slowly on the civil rights bill. From the first, Johnson made clear his determination not to compromise the strength of the bill. Unlike in 1957, he knew a filibuster could not be avoided and resolved to wait it out. Violent white Southern response to nonviolent black protest, particularly in demonstrations in Birmingham, Alabama, led by Martin Luther King, Jr., had helped create a national consensus that something had to be done. LBJ used that consensus, the Kennedy legacy, and whatever else he could think of to pass the bill. He worked especially hard to create a "hero's niche" for Senate Republican leader Everett Dirksen, whose support Johnson realized would be crucial in invoking cloture as well as in passing the bill. Dirksen admirably filled the niche, though only after securing certain compromises that the Republicans wanted. With his and other Republican support, the Senate voted cloture and then passed the bill. On July 2, 1964, Johnson signed the Civil Rights Act of 1964 outlawing segregation in public accommodations and discrimination in employment as well as authorizing federal suits to ensure school desegregation. A strong measure, it served as the legal basis for the destruction of the rigid system of segregation that had ruled the South for seventy years or more.

In addition to the tax bill and Civil Rights Act, Johnson worked for passage of a comprehensive antipoverty bill. The idea for such legislation originated in the Kennedy White House, though Kennedy had not finally decided or publicly declared his intention to seek it. Shortly after Kennedy's assassination, his

Johnson is sworn in as president following the assassination of Kennedy. *(LBJ Library)*

economic advisers approached Johnson with their ideas and received quick approval to proceed, no doubt partly because LBJ believed, given Kennedy's lack of public comment, that he could make the poverty program his own. In his State of the Union address that January, the president announced, with typical understatement, "This administration today, here and now, declares unconditional war on poverty in America." At first LBJ left planning to the White House economists, but he later created an independent agency, the Office of Economic Opportunity, to oversee the battle. The bill it presented to Congress had something for everyone: work study, financial aid for college students; the Job Corps, a training program for the unemployed; Volunteers in Service to America (VISTA), an agency to sponsor volunteers to work in depressed areas; and loans for small businessmen and farmers. The measure also included the Community Action Program (CAP). Johnson later claimed that he envisioned a system of local involvement not unlike what he had seen in the National Youth Administration (NYA) of his early Texas days. The plan's authors, though, saw community action agencies as a means of local control and coordination of antipoverty programs and of "maximum feasible participation," in the words of the act, for the poor themselves. CAP would later become very controversial, but at the time neither it nor anything else stopped Johnson as he maneuvered the Economic Opportunity Act through Congress. To make it easier for congress members to support the bill, LBJ funded the act at a little less than $1 billion, enough for a skirmish, not a war, but planned to increase its appropriations later.

The tax cut, the Civil Rights Act, and the Economic Opportunity Act constituted an impressive legislative achievement, particularly since under Kennedy's leadership the first two had been stalled in Congress. Yet they only whetted Johnson's appetite for accomplishment, and during the spring of 1964, he began to define a larger domestic vision. His speech-

writers had begun slipping the phrase Great Society into his speeches, and Johnson slowly adopted it as a label, like the New Deal used by his hero Franklin D. Roosevelt, for his domestic reform agenda. On May 22, in a commencement address at the University of Michigan, the president outlined what he meant by the slogan. "The challenge of the next half century," the president contended, is whether Americans have the wisdom to use their "wealth to enrich and elevate our national life, and to advance the quality of American civilization. . . . For in your time we have the opportunity to move not only toward the rich society and the powerful society, but upward to the Great Society." Such a society, he explained, would provide abundance for all, end poverty, establish racial justice, educate children, revive the cities, and beautify the environment. It would not, Johnson added, be "a safe harbor, a resting place, a final objective, a finished work. It is a challenge constantly renewed, beckoning us toward a destiny where the meaning of our

Johnson meets with civil rights leader Dr. Martin Luther King, Jr. *(Library of Congress)*

lives matches the marvelous products of our labor."

That summer, LBJ established task forces, extragovernmental study groups composed of experts from various fields. They proposed much of what became the Great Society legislation, but such an undertaking would involve more than laws. In enunciating his goal, Johnson had moved beyond public opinion. He would not only have to convince Congress to enact legislation but also have to define his vision and create wide public support for it. He would have to be, in other words, not simply the tactician he had been in the Senate but also a strategist, not simply the master of Congress but mentor for the nation as well. Whether he could do this remained to be seen. Thus far, though, Johnson had performed extremely well at managing the nation. He had secured passage of important legislation, had begun to define a broader vision for the country, and—just for good measure—in April had prevented a major rail strike through highly publicized personal intervention.

Johnson had devoted considerably less time to foreign affairs than to these domestic matters. The major foreign policy issue that he faced when he took office, and the problem that would haunt his administration, was Vietnam. Building on a commitment dating to the late 1940's, Johnson's predecessor had increased American involvement in Vietnam by providing more economic and military aid, by increasing the number of American troops there to more than sixteen thousand, and by acquiescing in, if not supporting, a coup against the president of South Vietnam. Faced with the deteriorating situation in the wake of the coup, LBJ, no doubt following his instincts as well as continuing Kennedy's policy, in his first months in office resolved "to do more of the same but do it more efficiently and effectively." He pledged to preserve an independent, noncommunist South Vietnam, raised the number of U.S. advisers in Vietnam to more than

twenty-three thousand, and provided another fifty million dollars in economic aid. The Joint Chiefs of Staff pushed for a bombing campaign against the North as well, but Johnson only authorized them to prepare contingency studies. He also approved covert operations along the North Vietnamese coast and considered asking Congress for a resolution of support.

On August 2, 1964, the destroyer *Maddox*, conducting electronic espionage off the coast of North Vietnam, fired warning shots at rapidly approaching North Vietnamese patrol boats. The boats fired torpedoes at the *Maddox*. When informed of the incident, Johnson ordered the destroyer C. *Turner Joy* to join the *Maddox*, and two nights later North Vietnamese patrol boats again allegedly fired on the U.S. ships. A few observers at the time, and more since, doubted whether the second attack ever occurred, suspecting that problems with sonar and panic by its operators yielded false readings. At the time, Johnson did not convey such doubts to the American people; nor did he inform them that the night of the first incident the South Vietnamese had conducted attacks against the North that the North Vietnamese could easily have assumed the *Maddox* was supporting. Instead, LBJ portrayed the incident as an unprovoked attack on American ships. He ordered air reprisals against the North and sought a resolution of support from Congress. After limited debate and with only two dissenting votes, Congress obliged with the Southeast Asia Resolution, or Tonkin Gulf Resolution, which authorized the president to do whatever necessary, including armed intervention, to protect Americans and defend freedom in Southeast Asia. "Like grandma's nightgown," Johnson observed, "it covered everything." The president had not decided to send American troops or to bomb the North; indeed, he still hoped to avoid doing both. LBJ wanted a broad statement of congressional approval that would allow him to keep his options open. Moreover, his show of determination protected him from

THE VICE PRESIDENT
HUBERT H. HUMPHREY

Hubert H. Humphrey served as vice president in the second administration of Lyndon Johnson. Humphrey was born in Wallace, South Dakota, on May 27, 1911. His father was a pharmacist and, after attending public schools, Hubert Humphrey attended the University of Minnesota and the Denver College of Pharmacy. Following in his father's footsteps, he worked in the family drugstore from 1933 to 1937. On September 3, 1936, Humphrey married Muriel Fay Buck, and they eventually would have four children.

Humphrey tired of the pharmacy business and returned to the University of Minnesota in order to complete his degree, which he did in 1939. He then enrolled in graduate school at Louisiana State University, where he also taught briefly. Humphrey intended to become a professor and pursued his Ph.D. in political science at the University of Minnesota, where he also taught.

Beginning in 1941 and through World War II, Humphrey served in several administrative positions with the Works Progress Administration. He also taught at Macalester College in Minnesota. Humphrey grew increasingly passionate about politics and managed President Franklin D. Roosevelt's reelection effort in Minnesota in 1944. From 1945 to 1948, he served as mayor of Minneapolis, and he was elected to the U.S. Senate in 1948, earning reelection in 1954 and 1960. From 1956 to 1958, he was picked as a U.S. delegate to the United Nations, and in 1961, he became majority whip of his party in the Senate.

President Lyndon B. Johnson picked Humphrey as his vice presidential nominee in 1964, and Humphrey served in this capacity from 1965 until the end of Johnson's presidency in 1969. Humphrey was unsuccessful in his own campaign for the presidency in 1968 and, later in 1976, declined an effort to run for the White House. After his vice presidency ended in 1969, Humphrey was elected again to the U.S. Senate in 1970 and was reelected in 1976. Humphrey died on January 13, 1978, leaving behind a legacy that included championing civil rights and equal opportunity, publishing books including *War on Poverty* (1964), and serving on the board of the Smithsonian Institution.

Robert P. Watson and Richard Yon

Republican charges of "softness." The 1964 presidential campaign had just begun.

Johnson's success in office had eliminated all doubt that he would receive the Democratic nomination. Only the question of who would be his running mate remained. Johnson clumsily eliminated many people's sentimental choice, Robert Kennedy, believing that Bobby would not help the ticket and wanting to escape the shadow of the Kennedys. Perhaps trying to build suspense for the convention, the president then turned the process of choosing a running mate into a public guessing game. Finally, as he left for the convention, he announced that

he had selected Hubert H. Humphrey, a former Senate ally, a dedicated liberal, and a longtime champion of civil rights.

At the convention, the sole major dispute concerned the seating of the Mississippi delegation. Only a minor incident in the Johnson administration, it nevertheless offered an epiphonal moment for understanding the gulf between the president and those who sought reform outside the system. Mississippi civil rights workers, despite the murder of some of their colleagues and the imprisonment or beating of many more, succeeded in organizing a political party and selecting convention delegates according to Democratic Party rules. Calling themselves the Mississippi Freedom Democratic Party (MFDP), these reformers asked the convention to seat their delegates rather than the regular Mississippi delegation selected without African American participation. Fearing that a floor fight over the issue would mar his convention and endanger the Democrats' chances in the South, LBJ forced through a compromise that sat the regulars if they pledged to support the ticket, allowed two representatives of the MFDP to vote in the convention, and prohibited seating in all future conventions any delegation for a state that disfranchised African Americans. Many of the civil rights workers reacted bitterly and staged a protest on the convention floor. They believed that Johnson and the liberal establishment had sold them out despite the moral authority of their cause; Johnson and his supporters thought that a politically realistic compromise had been reached that advanced the African American cause in the future. Both were cor-

rect; neither comprehended the position of the other.

The fight over the seating of the Mississippi delegation did little to disrupt LBJ's well-orchestrated celebration of his nomination. The campaign went nearly as smoothly. In the campaign, Johnson faced Republican Barry M. Goldwater of Arizona. Goldwater had publicly expressed opposition to Social Security, had voted against the Civil Rights Act, had talked of lobbing a nuclear round into the Kremlin, and generally appeared outside the mainstream of American politics. He wanted to repeal the present and veto the future, Johnson quipped at one point in the campaign. Johnson and the Democrats shrewdly and sometimes savagely exploited Goldwater's image as a warmonger while they themselves ran on the vague promise of peace and prosperity. Vietnam never became a major issue, by agreement between the candidates, although Johnson occasionally talked about it. He emphasized his hope for a peaceful settlement, usually adding the caveat

LBJ signs the Civil Rights Act of 1964. *(NARA)*

that peace depended on an end to aggression. Many of his listeners apparently missed the qualification, but the public did hear and remember when LBJ proclaimed that he had no intention of sending American boys to fight Asian wars. The only major threat to Johnson's campaign occurred in October, when Walter Jenkins, a close and longtime aide, was arrested in a Washington restroom for "disorderly conduct" with an old man. Jenkins quickly resigned, major world events soon pushed the scandal off the front pages, and it did little to damage Johnson's chances. The crowds greeting Johnson on his campaign stops were still large and enthusiastic, and in November he won one of the greatest electoral victories ever. LBJ carried forty-four states with more than 61 percent of the popular vote.

Problems of Public Perception

For a time, Johnson basked in the adulation of the campaign crowds and the magnitude of his victory. The satisfaction proved short-lived, however, as older insecurities and ambitions reemerged. Johnson resolved to become the greatest president ever but also questioned whether the people really liked him. Although his victory reflected public approval of LBJ's assumption of power after Kennedy's assassination, it constituted as much a rejection of Goldwater as an endorsement of Johnson. Support for Johnson was, to use his image, like a Texas river, mighty wide but awfully shallow. The shallowness resulted partly from the fact that the public did not really know, like, or trust Lyndon Johnson. Many Americans considered him simply a Texas boor, given to wheeling and dealing, shady if not corrupt, obsessed with power and unburdened by political principles. The image—not altogether unfair—emerged from the complexity of Johnson's personality and politics. His inability to overcome it and to convey the depth and sincerity of his political philosophy proved very important to his presidency, especially during the second term.

The real Lyndon Johnson is surprisingly elusive. Even more than most politicians, Johnson remained constantly onstage, playing whatever role, political or personal, he believed the situation demanded. The fact that he presented different images to different people at different times makes it almost impossible for the historian to decide which, if any, constituted the true Johnson. Indeed, as George Reedy has suggested, he probably remained "an enigma even to himself." Most observers tried to describe him by listing numerous, often contradictory adjectives or simply by saying that he was very complex or by maintaining that he combined all that was human.

At times Johnson seemed more than merely human. He stood over 6 feet, 3 inches tall, weighed more than two hundred pounds (how much more depended on the success of his latest diet), and wore a shirt with a 17.5-inch neck and 37-inch sleeves. Many people who knew him commented on the long arms and huge hands that drew people to him. Not only his size but also his searching eyes, phenomenal intensity, and tremendous energy allowed him to dominate individuals or small groups. The "guy's just got extra glands," his friend Abe Fortas explained. Johnson also had an impressive memory and, according to many, a very agile and able mind. He turned it to little save politics. The only other consistent interest in his life was cattle breeding, both the economics and the mechanics of it. Even in politics, his mind attacked only practical matters. He gave no thought to intellectual abstractions or theories, rendering him even more than most men a product, sometimes a prisoner, of his experience.

A few aides and friends who loved his company despite his narrow interests remained devotedly loyal. Johnson could be amazingly generous and thoughtful, inviting members of the White House staff to presidential parties, bestowing gifts, or even quietly paying the unexpected expenses of a staff member. Even some of the loyal friends, though, admitted that Johnson could also be very unpleasant. Once when LBJ himself wondered aloud why people did not like him, former Secretary of State Dean Acheson replied, "Let's face it, Mr. President, you just aren't a likable man." Johnson bullied his staff and flew into a rage over the most inconsequential matters. He almost never apologized for his outbursts, though Lady Bird often tried to make amends and Johnson himself occasionally indirectly compensated through some great kindness. In addition to indulging his temper, Johnson apparently had a need to humiliate—at any rate, he seemed to enjoy it. Hubert Humphrey became perhaps the most prominent victim. Johnson had admirably selected a man of considerable stature as his vice president, but he toyed with him in announcing his choice, once dressed him in an oversized cowboy suit on a visit to the Johnson ranch, and inflicted many petty humiliations.

Other aspects of LBJ's public and private behavior in the White House did little to counteract stories of his attempts to humiliate and his temper. Early in his presidency, the press reported that he drank beer as he raced his Lincoln Continental around the ranch. Later, he pulled one of his beagles up by its ears, and on another occasion he pulled up his own shirt to display his gallbladder surgery scar—in both instances for the cameras. He bullied visitors into skinny-dipping with him in the White House pool and held conferences while he received a rubdown, sat on the toilet, or had an enema. Surely in doing so he sought not only to save time but also to intimidate and degrade. The flaunting of such behavior even suggests that the provincial enjoyed making the capital, indeed the world, aware that he had not abandoned his "country" ways. For most Americans, though, it only raised doubts about what sort of man ran the country.

LBJ's reputation as a wheeler-dealer tainted by corruption raised doubts as well. Johnson had become a very rich man while receiving only a small salary from the government. The accumulation of the Johnson fortune, estimated at anywhere from $3 million to $14 million or more when he entered the White House, began in 1943 when Lady Bird used part of her inheritance to purchase an unprofitable Austin radio station, KTBC. With occasional help from Lyndon and some of his staff as well as favorable rulings by the Federal Communications Commission, she transformed the station into a very profitable enterprise. In 1948, the FCC awarded it Austin's only television channel. Without any significant competition, KTBC television became phenomenally lucrative. With its profits and some shrewd business maneuvers, the Johnsons purchased interest in other stations and, by 1964, five thousand acres of Texas land to supplement the more than three thousand acres in Alabama that Lady Bird inherited. No one has produced evidence that Johnson overtly employed his influence to secure the favorable FCC rulings that helped make possible KTBC's success. Many have questioned the ethical propriety of a government official responsible for overseeing a regulatory agency profiting so handsomely in a regulated industry.

Just before Johnson became president, charges surfaced of financial corruption and influence peddling by Bobby Baker, secretary to Senate Democrats and former Johnson protégé. Many observers believed that Baker's problems began only after Johnson left the Senate, but instead of saying so, LBJ announced, to much incredulity, that he and Baker had never been close. Soon the public learned that in 1957 an insurance company paid Baker a sizable commission for writing two policies on the life of Lyndon Johnson, that the president of the company had then bought time on Johnson's television station, and that later its vice president had given the Johnsons an expensive television set. Johnson, by then president, maintained that the families frequently exchanged gifts, and the press let the matter drop. Baker, though, eventually served time on other charges. After the Baker affair and Jenkins's arrest, however, the Johnson administration proved remarkably free of scandal. Yet many Americans continued to think of Johnson as at least tainted by corruption.

Johnson's seemingly shady past and unattractive personality contributed to a larger problem—a public perception of LBJ as a man obsessed with power. Johnson did have, as one friend remarked, an instinct for power "as primordial as a salmon's going upstream to spawn." He sought it all his life and in the White House reveled in its attainment. Fearing his wrath, the White House staff tried to anticipate his whims by stocking gargantuan quantities of ice cream or Fresca or whatever he fancied at the moment. Johnson dispensed presidential souvenirs to almost everyone with whom he came in contact, particularly favoring an electric toothbrush bearing the presidential seal because its recipient would think of Lyndon Johnson first thing in the morning and last thing at night. He turned bill-signing ceremonies into virtual royal displays, using numerous pens and bestowing them on the honored many. On one occasion, as Johnson ran toward a group of waiting helicopters, his military guide pointed to one and suggested, "That's your helicopter, Mr. President." Johnson stopped in his tracks and replied, "Son, they're all my helicopters."

Because of his enjoyment of the excesses of power, because of his tendency to bully and humiliate, but most especially because he sometimes appeared such a political opportunist, many Americans believed that Johnson sought power for its own sake, not to employ it to some larger public purpose. Yet Johnson's career testified to his desire to govern and, despite shifts here and there, displayed his commitment to certain basic political beliefs. They did not, however, fit easily into the traditional categories of liberal or conservative. They rested first and foremost on a faith in and

fondness for "the system," in other words, for the nation's political and business establishments.

Johnson accepted, indeed relished, the cumbersome, imperfect system of politics that ruled in Washington, D.C. He talked so much of consensus and used his favorite biblical quotation, "Come, then, let us reason together," so often during his presidency that people began to snicker at the words. LBJ, however, believed in them. He considered a consensus reached by reasoning together—and maneuvering and trading—a perfectly honorable and proper way to pass legislation and therefore to govern—and he sought to govern. "I have never believed," he wrote in his memoirs, "that those who are governed least are governed best. We *are* the people, as Franklin Roosevelt said. And the proper function of a government of the people, by the people, and for the people is to make it possible for all citizens to experience a better, more secure, and more rewarding life." LBJ wanted to use government to foster economic abundance and to improve the physical and social environment, but most of all, wrote George Reedy, he had "a burning desire to make life easier for those who had to struggle up from the bottom."

Johnson did not seek to ease the rise of those at the bottom by tearing down or radically restructuring the economic establishment. He had no quarrel with American capitalism; after all, it had been good to him. Throughout his career, only his advocacy of public power constituted a challenge to private ownership. As president he sponsored a tax cut that benefited business, and he rarely attacked business leaders. Some Great Society programs, particularly environmental and safety legislation, increased government regulation, but the Johnson administration did less to foster central planning or government intervention in the economy than had the New Deal. "I never wanted to demagogue against business, Wall Street, or the power companies," Johnson once

In a ceremony on Ellis Island in 1965, LBJ signs an immigration bill ending the discriminatory quota system. *(Yoichi R. Okamoto, LBJ Library Collection)*

said in rare criticism of his hero Roosevelt. "I thought FDR was wrong."

Rather than attacking or changing the system, Johnson sought to ease the rise of the people at the bottom by bringing them into it—and changing them, if necessary, to do so. Education always remained the reform closest to his heart, and Johnson considered it primarily a means by which the poor and disadvantaged could improve their lot in life by learning the skills of the system. When he taught in Cotulla, Johnson strove to instill in his Mexican American students the ways of the Anglo world in which, he realized, they would have to make their way. Many of OEO's programs took much the same approach. Head Start, a prekindergarten program for the disadvantaged added to OEO in 1965, and the Job Corps developed in participants the skills needed to fit into and succeed in the educational and business systems. The scholars who planned the Great Society may have operated from theories designed to

overcome a "culture of poverty," but Johnson, never one for abstractions, conceived the purpose simply as teaching the poor, just as he had done in Cotulla, what they needed to enter and to advance in the business world.

Johnson also favored, though far less enthusiastically or consistently than he did programs to bring poor people into the system, government aid to those deprived of a basic standard of living. He often said that in so rich a nation no one should be without food or medical care. In the Senate he fought to expand Social Security benefits to the disabled; in his second term he worked for medical insurance programs for the needy and elderly. Only late in his administration, however, did he support expansion of the food stamp program. Funding for these and other existing entitlement programs did rise during his years in office, but public aid as a percentage of the gross national product would be far higher at the end of the Nixon and Ford administrations than at the end of Johnson's.

Johnson, in sum, consistently, or at least as consistently as most politicians, endeavored to use his power in behalf of certain beliefs. He accepted the economic and political systems of the nation but sought to use government to increase the abundance that they produced, to improve the environment, and to bring more people into the economic mainstream. His vision of a Great Society emerged out of these principles, but the public never completely perceived his purpose. For some people the reality and image of the president's personality—what journalists Evans and Novak called the private Johnson—overwhelmed what he did in government—the public Johnson. For others, Johnson's political craftiness led them to consider everything he did as "only politics." Especially in the White House, the fault lay with Johnson, not simply the public's perception of him. The president failed to communicate his sincerity or purpose and larger vision to the nation.

He always blamed, sometimes in incredible displays of temper and self-pity, the northeastern intellectuals and the press. Indeed, neither group liked him very much: some intellectuals and reporters because he was not John Kennedy, others because of the private Johnson. With journalists, the more important of the two groups, Johnson made matters worse. The man whose Senate success rested on his amazing ability to read the wants and desires of others never fathomed the goals or needs of the press. His constant changes in schedule inconvenienced them; his nearly pathological insistence on secrecy made their work difficult. As he had in the Senate, Johnson wanted to keep his options open to the very last minute and abhorred leaks that would curtail them, a reasonable attitude that he took to irrational extremes. At times LBJ changed an appointment if it was reported in the press before he announced it; on other occasions he denied any intention of doing what he then proceeded to do. Not surprisingly, the press came to distrust him and, more important, accused Johnson of creating a so-called credibility gap.

Though his poor relations with the press did not help, Johnson's problem in projecting his vision went deeper. He performed poorly on television, appearing and sounding listless. Despite repeated attempts to improve, LBJ never mastered the medium. Americans rarely saw the compelling figure described by those who met him personally or received The Treatment. Television, however, was only part of the problem; Johnson had never excelled as a formal orator. He always thought "private negotiations and compromise" more important than "public rhetoric" and, according to Reedy, considered a speech merely a "crowd pleaser" in which he had not really given his word. As president, Johnson's speaking style relied heavily on sentimentality and, part of his Southwestern style of storytelling, hyperbole. ("Hyperbole was to Lyndon Johnson," Bill Moyers once observed, "what oxygen is to life.") Sometimes the sentimentality succeeded, as in Johnson's address to Congress right after the Kennedy assassination, but more often it resulted in Johnson being labeled corny or insincere. Surely his exaggerations and numerous superlatives contributed to the credibility gap. His difficulties in public oratory, magnified by television, hindered his ability to communicate his vision of how he wanted to use his power to shape the country.

Yet Johnson had been reelected, despite these problems of personality and perception. Perhaps they would have remained, as they were in 1964, decidedly secondary to Johnson's accomplishments, but in 1965, Johnson expanded the Great Society and became embroiled in Vietnam. In undertaking both crusades, Johnson needed the full trust and support of the American people and considerable skill in shaping public opinion. His unattractive image and poor public oratory, therefore, became a greater handicap in his second term. Moreover, people angered by his crusades, particularly the war in Vietnam, often seized on and exaggerated the image of Lyndon Johnson as a boor and bully.

1965: Two Crusades

In January, 1965, aware of the dangers of overconfidence bred by his landslide victory but also of the limited lifespan of his popular mandate, Johnson went to Congress with proposals for major domestic reforms, most of them generated by the task forces established in 1964. Since his landslide victory had helped elect a large number of new liberal Democratic congressmen, his party had a more comfortable working margin over the Republicans—68 to 32 in the Senate and 295 to 140 in the House—than it had the year before. Using this majority and his legislative skills, LBJ pushed through Congress several bills, which, along with the three major ones passed in 1964, constituted the heart of his Great Society program.

First to be enacted was the $1.3 billion Elementary and Secondary Education Act. For many years Congress had debated but failed to pass a program of federal aid to primary and secondary education. This time a compromise that allowed federal aid to students in parochial schools, but not to the schools themselves, secured the support of the Roman Catholic hierarchy, which during the Kennedy administration had helped block passage of a similar measure with no aid for parochial schools. Even with the compromise and the heavy Democratic majority, the bill constituted a Johnson triumph. Congress had passed, historian and Johnson aide Eric Goldman observed, "a billion-dollar law, deeply affecting a fundamental institution of the nation, in a breathtaking eighty-seven days. The House approved it with no amendment that mattered; the Senate had voted it through literally without a comma changed."

Next, Congress passed an expanded version of a health insurance bill submitted by Johnson. It created Medicare, a program to help pay medical costs for the elderly, and Medicaid, a similar program for the poor. Other legislation followed: college scholarships, more money for housing for the needy, rent supplements, an end to the discriminatory quota system for immigrants, and the creation of the Department of Housing and Urban Development. Johnson also asked for, and Congress created, the National Endowments for the Arts and for the Humanities to enhance the cultural environment and stronger air and water quality acts to improve the physical environment, as well as a highway beautification program that was a personal campaign of Lady Bird.

That same spring, Johnson helped secure the passage of another major civil rights bill. The 1964 act had not satisfied the president, and later that year he ordered the attorney general to draft a voting rights bill. The "right to vote with no ifs, ands, or buts" was the key to achieving African American rights, Vice President Humphrey recalled LBJ saying. "When the Negroes get that, they'll have every politician, north and south, east and west, kissing their ass, begging for their support." In early 1965, Johnson did not believe that the time was right to pass such legislation, but after violent police attacks on demonstrators demanding the right to vote in Selma, Alabama, and the murder of a Northern minister there—a situation so bad that Johnson finally nationalized the Alabama National Guard to protect the protesters—Johnson decided that the time had come to enact a voting rights law.

To urge Congress to do so, Johnson delivered one of the most moving addresses of his career to a joint session and, through television, to the nation. In unequivocal language, he demanded the passage of a voting rights bill and also made the strongest statement in behalf of black equality ever offered by a president. "What happened in Selma is part of a far larger movement which reaches into every section and State of America. It is the effort of American Negroes to secure for themselves the full blessings of American life. Their cause must be our cause too. Because it is not just Negroes, but really it is all of us, who must overcome the crippling legacy of bigotry and injustice." Then he added, borrowing a line from the unofficial anthem of the Civil Rights movement, "And we shall overcome." Four months later, Congress passed the Voting Rights Act of 1965, arguably the most important civil rights legislation ever enacted in the United States. It eliminated literacy tests for voting and authorized federal supervision of elections in states or voting districts where such tests had been used and fewer than half the voting age population voted or were registered to vote. Johnson's Justice Department eventually placed all or part of seven Southern states under the jurisdiction of the act, and by the end of the decade, black voter registration and office holding had risen dramatically.

In the same spring that Congress passed the Voting Rights Act and other Great Society measures, Johnson took a series of steps that substantially altered American involvement in Vietnam and rendered the war there as large a part of his legacy as domestic reform. Since the incident in the Gulf of Tonkin, Viet Cong activity and infiltration of troops and supplies from the North had increased. By December, 1964, military planners concluded that the situation was perilous and recommended a bombing campaign against the North. LBJ hesitated to

---

Excerpts from Lyndon B. Johnson's address to Congress regarding the Voting Rights Act of 1965, March 15, 1965:

I will send to Congress a law designed to eliminate illegal barriers to the right to vote.... This bill will strike down restrictions to voting in all elections—Federal, State, and local—which have been used to deny Negroes the right to vote. This bill will establish a simple, uniform standard which cannot be used, however ingenious the effort, to flout our Constitution. It will provide for citizens to be registered by officials of the United States Government, if the State officials refuse to register them. It will eliminate tedious, unnecessary lawsuits which delay the right to vote. Finally, this legislation will ensure that properly registered individuals are not prohibited from voting. . . .

To those who seek to avoid action by their National Government in their own communities, who want to and who seek to maintain purely local control over elections, the answer is simple: open your polling places to all your people. Allow men and women to register and vote whatever the color of their skin. Extend the rights of citizenship to every citizen of this land.

There is no constitutional issue here. The command of the Constitution is plain. There is no moral issue. It is wrong—deadly wrong—to deny any of your fellow Americans the right to vote in this country. There is no issue of States' rights or national rights. There is only the struggle for human rights. I have not the slightest doubt what will be your answer. . . .

But even if we pass this bill, the battle will not be over. What happened in Selma is part of a far larger movement which reaches into every section and State of America. It is the effort of American Negroes to secure for themselves the full blessings of American life. Their cause must be our cause too. Because it's not just Negroes, but really it's all of us, who must overcome the crippling legacy of bigotry and injustice.

And we shall overcome.

This great, rich, restless country can offer opportunity and education and hope to all, all black and white, all North and South, sharecropper and city dweller. These are the enemies: poverty, ignorance, disease. They're our enemies, not our fellow man, not our neighbor. And these enemies too—poverty, disease, and ignorance: we shall overcome.

undertake such an expansion of the war. He only increased economic aid and expanded various pacification programs designed to "win the hearts and minds" of the people of South Vietnam. When the situation continued to deteriorate, in early 1965 Johnson decided that a bombing campaign against the North had become necessary. Using the enemy's attack on American troops in South Vietnam as a reason, the United States in early February began an air war against North Vietnam. Soon General William Westmoreland, whom Johnson had appointed commander of American forces in Vietnam, requested troops to guard air bases there, and in March thirty-five hundred marines arrived in Vietnam. By April, Johnson had approved their employment in offensive operations. In July, after the Viet Cong had taken control of parts of the country and the fall of the government in Saigon appeared a very real possibility, the president approved sending fifty thousand more troops to Vietnam to undertake combat missions. Johnson also committed himself to send additional troops if they were needed.

Between February and July, 1965, then, Johnson had begun an air war against North Vietnam, committed American troops to a direct combat role in the South, and dramatically increased the number of Americans fighting there. Perhaps one scholar exaggerated when he referred to the decisions of this period as "the Americanization of the war," for the South Vietnamese still did much of the fighting and bore much of the brunt of the war, but surely the United States had gone to war in Vietnam.

LBJ's goal in Vietnam, the survival of a stable, secure, noncommunist government in the South, was that of his predecessors Eisenhower and Kennedy. Faced with the likelihood that the government of South Vietnam would fall, however, a prospect the others had not faced, Johnson decided to use American air power and combat troops to prevent it and to inflict enough suffering, through the destruction of

certain targets in the North and search-and-destroy tactics against enemy forces in the South, to force the North Vietnamese and Viet Cong to seek a negotiated settlement. Phased escalation of both the bombing and the number of American troops, Johnson and his advisers believed, would allow the United States to increase the pressure until the enemy sought peace. Few of Johnson's advisers talked of "winning" the war in any other terms. Johnson rejected an all-out bombing campaign or an invasion of the North.

The president did not decide on a policy of phased escalation in a fit of jingoistic enthusiasm or out of some innate love of battle; however, although he listened to a wide variety of opinions, he never seriously considered any other course. He rejected dramatic escalation or an all-out attack on the North because either might lead to Soviet, or more likely Chinese, intervention, a wider war, and possible nuclear confrontation. He wanted to avoid World War III at all cost; indeed, he believed that the course he chose did exactly that. Johnson's view of foreign policy had been formed in the late 1930's when, following Roosevelt, he adopted an activist view of America's role in the world. Like so many others of his generation, he looked back on the appeasement of Adolf Hitler as the cause of World War II. He therefore concluded that either aggression must be stopped or a greater danger surely encountered later. In the years after World War II, such thinking led him and much of official Washington, in which his attitudes were shaped, to the containment doctrine, which centered U.S. foreign policy on stopping Soviet and communist expansion and to the subsequent interventions in Greece and Korea. Johnson saw the war in Vietnam as another case of communist aggression, which had to be faced there or in some other place or some larger war.

Johnson also feared the domestic consequences if he abandoned South Vietnam to communism. In so many ways the product of his own political experience, he remembered well the McCarthy era. He worried that the loss of South Vietnam to communism would set off a similar period of hysteria that would be detrimental to his and the Democratic Party's political future as well as to the country. As the war continued, Johnson deeply resented his liberal critics and the young protesters, but he appeared always to fear more the wrath of the Right if he failed to keep the anticommunist faith.

Having decided that the war was necessary, however, Johnson did little to rally the American people to the cause. Instead, he took the nation to war by indirection. He sought no congressional declaration of war beyond the Tonkin Gulf Resolution and refused to call up the reserves. He did not at the time announce the April shift of U.S. soldiers to an offensive role and told the nation of the July decision for escalation during an afternoon press conference. Johnson apparently feared that a fervent embrace of the war would lead to an abandonment of his first love, the Great Society. He even tried to hide the cost of the war lest it lead to a reduction in spending on reform programs. LBJ also realized that he had to mobilize people for a limited war. If he summoned them too heartily, they might demand the very wider war that he sought to avoid. To convince them to fight only the small conflict he thought appropriate demanded considerable skill in shaping public opinion. Little of Johnson's career or his political talents fitted him for the task. To make matters worse, his decision to send American troops, after he had declared in the 1964 campaign that he would not do so, left many Americans distrustful of his intentions from the start. As a result of all these factors, Johnson failed to summon and sustain the national will to support his course in Vietnam, although perhaps no other president could have either.

As LBJ expanded U.S. commitments in Vietnam, he also ordered American troops into the Dominican Republic. That Caribbean nation had experienced a succession of governments after the 1961 assassination of longtime dictator Rafael Trujillo. In April, 1965, a military junta seized power, but it soon faced armed rebellion by leftists and constitutional forces. As the fighting in the streets increased, the U.S. ambassador requested that troops be sent to protect American lives. LBJ immediately dispatched four hundred marines. Later the same day, April 28, fearing disorder and a communist takeover, Johnson decided on armed intervention. U.S. troops, eventually numbering twenty-two thousand, went to the Dominican Republic, stabilized the situation, and by August secured a U.S.-supported government. The following year the Dominican Republic held free elections, and in May the last American troops went home.

Some praised Johnson for restoring order and ensuring elections. Others criticized the president for undermining the only chance for noncommunist revolutionary change. They believed the intervention to be part of a larger administration policy of supporting the status quo and fostering a climate for American economic interests throughout Latin America. Even many Americans who did not go that far in their criticism remained unconvinced by Johnson's claim of communist influence among the rebels and felt misled by his early, hyperbolic accounts of the danger to Americans. His performance in the Dominican crisis reinforced the doubts of those who believed that Johnson had raced unthinkingly into Vietnam and fed growing public perception of a Johnson credibility gap.

1966 and 1967: Time of Trial

The intervention in the Dominican Republic and the escalation of the war in Vietnam marked a major turning point in the presidency of Lyndon Johnson. In 1966 and 1967, Johnson's presidency increasingly came under siege. Many Americans believed that Johnson failed to fight the Vietnam War with sufficient vigor.

More vocal intellectuals and young protesters criticized him for fighting it at all. Influenced partly by this antiwar sentiment, but also by more complex factors beyond LBJ's control, some college students and other young Americans rebelled against the "establishment"—their term for an amorphous evil reaching from the suburbs through the universities and corporations to the government. As the chief symbol and proponent of the establishment, Johnson evoked their special wrath. Many African Americans embraced their own form of radicalism as black power replaced nonviolence as the tactic of some in the Civil Rights movement. Both white and black radicals denounced American values and took to the streets, as did many in the nation's ghettos when rioting erupted in several cities. Many more Americans, appalled by the disorder and criticism, blamed Johnson for it, as Herbert Hoover had been blamed for the Depression. They believed that reform had gone far enough, and a few suspected that the Great Society programs contributed to the disquiet. The community action agencies, which in some cities had brought the radicalized poor into the administration of the War on Poverty, came in for special criticism.

Though he later claimed that he had already perceived the shift in public mood, in 1966 Johnson decided not to abandon domestic reform despite the turmoil and the financial demands of the war in Vietnam. He spoke of the Great Society as frequently as he had the year before and asked Congress for "guns and butter," funding for both the war and domestic reform. In 1966, Congress did enact the Model Cities Program, a major part of the Great Society. It established demonstration projects in sixty-three cities to provide slum renewal, area redevelopment, and other improvements to the urban environment. LBJ's other legislative victories that year proved more modest: a high-

The Detroit riot of July, 1967. *(Archive Photos)*

way and automobile safety law, a rise in the minimum wage, and the creation of the Department of Transportation. In fact, Congress passed considerably fewer of Johnson's proposals than it had the year before. His legislative wizardry worked far less well as the public's willingness to support reform and the government's ability to finance it declined.

Nowhere were the changed circumstances in which the president operated more apparent than in the field of civil rights. In 1967, Johnson made an important symbolic statement when he appointed Thurgood Marshall, the lawyer who had led the fight for school desegregation, the first African American justice of the Supreme Court. In general, though, in 1966-1967, Johnson found himself less often promoting black advancement and more often reacting to black violence as summer riots in the urban centers, which had begun in 1964, became more numerous. In his public discussion of the disorders, Johnson tried to deplore the violence without endorsing reaction or abandoning his support for black equality. During the summer of 1967, he sent army troops into Detroit to reestablish order after a riot but also created a commission to study the causes of such civil disturbances. The Kerner Commission, as it came to be called after its chairman Otto Kerner, in 1968 reported severe problems in the ghettos and a fundamental division between whites and blacks in American society. Johnson simply accepted the report and did not respond to its recommendations for new programs. He did not believe that he could secure the necessary appropriations. By then, LBJ no longer urged Congress to pass new reform initiatives but rather appealed for it to levy new taxes to curtail inflation.

As early as 1966, Johnson's economic advisers warned him of the inflationary potential of his attempt to have both guns and butter. At that time he told some congressmen that no rise in personal taxes would be necessary, though he asked for and received an increase in automobile and telephone excise taxes. When, later in the year, Johnson requested an additional increase in taxes, Congress balked. Johnson settled for a policy of budgetary restraint and appeals to business and labor to hold down prices and wages. In 1967, Johnson sought first a 6 percent and then, when the economy continued to heat up, a 10 percent tax surcharge. LBJ failed to work out a compromise with congressmen who wanted major reductions in spending to accompany the surcharge, and his bill never got out of committee. The failure to limit the

President Johnson greets U.S. troops in Vietnam in 1966. *(Yoichi R. Okamoto/NARA)*

federal budget deficit because of spending for both the Great Society and the Vietnam War, many economists contend, provided the initial impetus for the devastating inflation of the 1970's.

Johnson's increasing difficulties with Congress resulted not only from changing domestic and budgetary realities but also from growing opposition to his foreign policy and perhaps his own increasing involvement in world affairs. In his first two years in office, Johnson never left the continental United States; from 1966 through 1968, he made twelve trips outside it, several of them to Vietnam, Guam, or Honolulu to confer on Vietnam. The war, however, was not his only foreign policy concern.

In 1967, a crisis erupted in the Middle East. In May, Egypt moved troops into the Sinai and closed Israel's vital water route through the Gulf of Aqaba. Johnson publicly defended Israel's right of access but also worked behind the scenes to prevent war. Some critics contended that he did not send the Israelis a strong enough signal of American opposition, but in any case, Israel, feeling threatened by the Egyptian moves, on June 5 launched a very successful attack against its old enemy. The Johnson administration announced the United States' neutrality but hastily added that it continued to support the existence and rights of Israel. The latter statement especially angered several Arab states, which quickly broke diplomatic relations with the United States. After six days, though, Israel, which had already conquered sizable amounts of Egyptian territory, signed a cease-fire. During this Six-Day War, the Israelis sank the USS *Liberty*, an intelligence-gathering ship plainly marked and clearly in international waters. Casualties included 34 dead and 171 wounded. Neither Johnson nor anyone else made much of the incident, and Israel paid indemnities to the families of the casualties. Labeled an accident by the Israelis, the sinking has never been fully explained.

During the Six-Day War, Johnson and Aleksey Kosygin, chair of the Council of Ministers of the Soviet Union, talked frequently on the hot line, thereby helping to avoid an expansion of the conflict into a larger war. Although Johnson adhered to the containment doctrine, as he demonstrated in Vietnam and the Dominican Republic as well as by his attempts to strengthen the North Atlantic Treaty Organization, he still sought to reduce Cold War tensions. He avoided unnecessary verbal attacks on the Soviet Union and kept open channels of communication. During his administration the United States and the Soviet Union signed a new consular convention and, along with other countries, a treaty banning weapons of mass destruction from outer space. In June, 1967, Johnson and Kosygin held at Glassboro, New Jersey, a hastily arranged and not particularly successful summit conference. The two leaders discussed ongoing negotiations toward arms reduction but reached no agreements.

Neither relations with the Soviets nor the Six-Day War ever absorbed the president's attention or undermined his popularity the way the Vietnam War did. It came to consume his administration. By the end of 1965, 185,000 American troops were serving in Vietnam, and the war and its casualties clearly troubled Johnson. Over the Christmas holidays, he instituted a bombing halt and a well-publicized peace initiative. They failed to achieve results, and on January 31, 1966, Johnson resumed the bombing. In February, the Senate Foreign Relations Committee held televised hearings on the war, which helped fuel the growing opposition to Johnson's policy.

Johnson tried to rally popular support with bellicose patriotism and affirmations of American resolve. He held firmly to his strategy of phased escalation to prevent the overthrow of the government in the South and to force the North to negotiate. He gradually expanded the list of targets to be bombed in North Vietnam and increased the number of American troops in the South to more than 500,000. The military situation had improved since 1965, and the fall of South Vietnam no longer appeared imminent, owing more to the larger American presence than to any dramatic improvement in the strength or popular support of the South Vietnamese government. The expectation that the gradual increase in pressure on the North would force it to the bargaining table proved false: With Soviet and Chinese aid, the North had met each U.S. escalation with one of its own.

Nevertheless, Johnson continued to seek a negotiated settlement. He ordered fifteen different bombing pauses in hopes of spurring negotiations and, according to a list in his memoirs, pursued seventy-two peace overtures. Critics questioned how seriously he pursued them, and clearly the difficulties of fine-tuning military pressure and peace initiatives undermined these efforts. In the final analysis, though, the problem was that neither side was willing to make the concessions necessary to get negotiations started. Through most of his administration, LBJ insisted on a prior agreement on mutual deescalation before talks could begin and objected to any role for the Viet Cong. In late 1967, his position softened to insistence that the North would not take advantage of a bombing halt before discussions could begin. The North Vietnamese, whom Johnson probably rightly believed had little if any interest in talks, insisted on an unconditional, permanent end to the bombing before they would negotiate.

By the end of 1967, therefore, both the search for peace and the war itself seemed condemned to stalemate. Lyndon Johnson's administration did too. In 1966 and 1967, Johnson had managed to push few new reforms through Congress and worried as much about curtailing inflation as transforming America. In 1967, he rarely even used the term Great Society. His own personal popularity reached a new low that October. Protesters followed him everywhere, some chanting, "Hey, Hey, LBJ, How

many kids have you killed today?" The press criticized him harshly, especially because of his credibility gap. The personal failings overlooked in 1964 now seemed so much more important. One well-known cartoon, which made fun of both his boorishness and his problems in Vietnam, pictured a saddened LBJ pulling up his shirt to show not the scar from his gallbladder operation but one in the shape of Vietnam.

In private and occasionally in public, LBJ lashed out at his critics. He always suspected, according to one confidant, a conspiracy by "the intellectuals, the press, the liberals, and the Kennedys" to destroy him. When Secretary of Defense Robert McNamara, an early architect of the Vietnam policy, began to work within the administration for a change of course, Johnson quickly nominated him to be president of the World Bank. Unlike McNamara, the president in late 1967 believed that the situation in Vietnam had improved and orchestrated another campaign to convince Americans that the war was being won.

1968: Abdicating Power

In January, 1968, matters became worse rather than better. Prospects that Congress would pass the tax surcharge still did not appear good, and a British devaluation of the pound in November, 1967, had led to a drain on U.S. gold reserves that was not stopped until March. On January 23, North Korea captured the intelligence ship USS *Pueblo* and its crew of eighty-three men outside North Korea's twenty-five-mile limit. Johnson expressed his outrage and mobilized fourteen thousand members of the Air Force and Navy reserves, but he did little else except begin negotiations for the return of the ship's crew. They did not succeed until the following December. Worst of all, on January 30-31, during Tet, the Vietnamese New Year, the Viet Cong and the North Vietnamese launched a major offensive.

Catching American and South Vietnamese forces off guard, the enemy attacked many hamlets, most major cities, and almost every provincial and district capital. A Viet Cong squad even penetrated the grounds of the U.S. embassy in Saigon. The American and South Vietnamese armies quickly recovered and inflicted heavy casualties on the enemy. Johnson pronounced Tet a victory, but the press had emphasized the failures, and a public grown suspicious of LBJ's pronouncements on Vietnam doubted his assessment. Many people wondered how, if the war had been going so well at the end of 1967, the enemy had launched such an extensive offensive in January. The Tet Offensive crystallized growing frustration with both Johnson and the war among those who sought to expand it as well as among those opposed to it.

The Tet Offensive also catalyzed a reassessment of Vietnam policy within the administration. Some critics of the new policy offer what amounts to a "stab in the back" thesis. They argue that the press turned the Tet victory into defeat, mobilizing public opinion against the war and forcing Johnson to abandon the escalation that would at last have won it. Such an interpretation has weaknesses. As historian George Herring observes, "That victory was within grasp," even with an increase in troops, "remains quite doubtful." Moreover, Johnson clearly listened to voices within government rather than to critics in the streets or the press. Secretary of State Dean Rusk suggested a

bombing halt as a means to defuse criticism. Newly appointed Secretary of Defense Clark Clifford, formerly an ardent supporter of escalation, a group of civilians within the Defense Department, and a few close aides began to work for an end to escalation. The Wise Men, a group of establishment leaders assembled by Clifford and briefed by important officials, also urged Johnson to change his policy.

Responding to these insiders and probably to his congressional contacts as well, Johnson in March, 1968, decided on a new policy, although he did not abandon his commitment to the war. Johnson rejected Westmoreland's request for 200,000 additional troops (and soon replaced him as commander in Vietnam) and agreed to an increase of only 13,500 soldiers. He sought instead to strengthen the South Vietnamese army, initiating a program later expanded by his successor. He halted bombing over all of North Vietnam except a small strip just above the demilitarized zone where he believed it necessary to continue attacks in order to protect American troops below the zone. Finally, he resolved to undertake a new peace initiative and named a high-ranking representative to meet with the North Vietnamese.

On March 31, the president announced these measures during a nationally televised address. At its end, he linked them to a startling announcement: "I shall not seek, and I will not accept, the nomination of my party for another

Excerpt from Lyndon B. Johnson's "renunciation speech" regarding the 1968 presidential race, March 31, 1968:

With American sons in the fields far away, with America's future under challenge right here at home, with our hopes and the world's hopes for peace in the balance every day, I do not believe that I should devote an hour or a day of my time to any personal partisan causes or to any duties other than the awesome duties of this office—the Presidency of your country.

Accordingly, I shall not seek, and I will not accept, the nomination of my party for another term as your President. But let men everywhere know, however, that a strong and a confident and a vigilant America stands ready tonight to seek an honorable peace; and stands ready tonight to defend an honored cause, whatever the price, whatever the burden, whatever the sacrifice that duty may require.

Protesters at the 1968 Democratic National Convention, Chicago. *(Library of Congress)*

less unify, a divided nation. Armed with the power of incumbency, not to mention the ability to influence the election through dramatic initiatives in Vietnam, Johnson conceivably could have retained power. Yet, realizing he could no longer use that power to govern, to accomplish what he believed needed to be done, he declined to make the effort to do so. His abdication of the presidency may offer the most convincing evidence that he did not want power only in and for itself.

When he removed himself from the presidential race, Johnson became a lame duck president who watched others fight for the right to succeed him. His administration still managed a few victories. After the assassination of civil rights leader Martin Luther King, Jr., and the rioting that followed it, Congress passed LBJ's last major civil rights legislation, a strong open housing law that banned discrimination in the sale and rental of most real estate. Congress also approved a Safe Streets Act that Johnson had sought since early 1967, a truth-in-lending law, and more money for housing and conservation. It even, finally, passed the tax surcharge. In July, the United States, the Soviet Union, and many other nations signed the Nuclear Nonproliferation Treaty.

Frustrations and failures, however, continued. Johnson suffered an embarrassing defeat over nominations to the Supreme Court. In 1965, Johnson had convinced Kennedy appointee and liberal Arthur Goldberg to resign from the Court in order to serve as ambassador to the United Nations. Apparently, Johnson appealed to Goldberg's patriotism, suggested that he might help bring peace in Vietnam, and

term as your president." Almost no one had expected it; Johnson had decided to withdraw from the coming presidential race. The debate over why he chose to do so continues. One student of the Johnson administration argues that because of his health—he had had a major heart attack in 1955 and underwent two operations while in the White House—Johnson never intended to run and had made that decision in 1965. Popular lore has it that LBJ fled from office in the face of antiwar pressure, particularly the surprisingly strong showing of peace candidate Eugene F. McCarthy in the New Hampshire primary and the subsequent announcement by Johnson's nemesis Bobby Kennedy that he, too, would challenge the president's renomination. It seems likely, however, that Johnson based his decision on more complex reasons. Sometime in early 1968, frustrated by his inability to conclude the war in Vietnam, haunted by its casualties, aware especially after New Hampshire of his unpopularity, and stymied in his efforts to pass the tax surcharge, Johnson decided that he could not govern, much hinted that he could expect to return to the Court. In Goldberg's place, LBJ appointed Abe Fortas, a very able lawyer who happened to be a very old friend. In June, 1968, Chief Justice Earl Warren offered to resign, and the president decided to elevate Fortas to chief justice. He also announced that he would appoint Homer Thornberry, a federal judge and Johnson associate, to Fortas's seat. Many in Congress, upset by Fortas's liberal record on the Court and his ill-advised conduct off the bench—including continuing to advise the president—and aghast at the cronyism implied by the Thornberry nomination, blocked Fortas's nomination with a filibuster. Johnson finally withdrew it and did not make another. His successor got to pick the next chief justice and also a replacement for Fortas, who had to resign in 1969 when it became public that while on the Court he had accepted, though later returned, a large fee from a foundation. It is difficult not to conclude that Johnson had squandered his chance to help shape the Supreme Court for the next decade.

Johnson's greatest frustration remained, as it had since 1965, Vietnam. The North Vietnamese responded to the president's March 31 proposals, but for a time nothing came of the discussions. Heavy fighting continued in the South as Johnson sought to ensure a strong bargaining position. Finally, in October the United States and North Vietnam reached an understanding by which the United States would stop all bombing of the North and North Vietnam would exercise restraint in the South and limit infiltration from the North. The plan also included a complex "your side-our side" formula to finesse the refusal of the South Vietnamese to negotiate with the Viet Cong and of the North Vietnamese and Viet Cong to talk with the government of the South. When the agreement was announced, the South Vietnamese refused to participate, probably assuming that the next administration would be more supportive. Johnson decided to proceed anyway and on October 31 announced a total

bombing halt over North Vietnam, which remained in effect throughout the remainder of his term. Two weeks later, South Vietnam agreed to join the talks. By the time they began, Johnson was about to leave office. He had failed to bring peace to Vietnam.

By then his successor had been elected. During the summer the Democratic Party met in Chicago, with Lyndon Johnson not in attendance. Violent confrontations between antiwar protesters and police outside the convention hall and deep divisions within the party disrupted the convention. With Robert Kennedy having been assassinated that June and Eugene McCarthy far from popular with the party regulars, the delegates nominated Vice President Humphrey. Hurt by the discord within his party, tainted by his support for Johnson's war effort, and, for the most part, unaided by the president, Humphrey lost a very close race to Republican Richard Nixon. After a smooth transition, in January, 1969, Johnson turned over power to Nixon.

Johnson returned to the ranch near Johnson City that he had visited so often as president. The provincial had come home. According to some accounts, LBJ had trouble adjusting to life without power and went through a period of withdrawal. Soon, however, he turned his tremendous energies to the management of the ranch. He also worked with a staff writing his memoirs and closely monitored the operation of the Lyndon Baines Johnson Library and the Lyndon Baines Johnson School of Public Affairs at the University of Texas. His interest in politics eventually revived, but the former president rarely made public appearances and did not attend, and may not have been wanted at, the 1972 Democratic Convention. He spent more time with his family than he had during his career. He especially enjoyed his grandchildren; both of his daughters had married while he occupied the White House. During a visit to one of his daughters in 1972, Johnson suffered another heart attack.

Never very healthy after that, Johnson began to get his financial affairs in order. At a December, 1972, conference held at the Johnson Library, he made one last rousing speech in favor of the rights of African Americans. When a group of black radicals interrupted the scheduled program to protest, Johnson heard them out, went back to the podium, and offered a vigorous discussion of how they could make the system work. Johnson died the following month, on January 22, 1973, one day before Richard Nixon announced a cease-fire in Vietnam.

Even before Johnson died, journalists and historians had begun to describe the Johnson presidency using words such as "irony" and "tragedy." Lyndon Johnson had held office at a time of unusual turmoil in American life, a period of rebellion by some among the young and black and poor. His administration certainly did not single-handedly foment this rebellion, but Johnson's style and the war he waged in Vietnam certainly fueled it. Both the rebels and those who resented their rebellion began to lose faith in the "system" and especially in the ability of government to meet people's needs and respond to their wishes. Perhaps the greatest irony of Johnson's presidency rested in this fact, that the man with such love for the system, who as a legislative leader could make it work so well, presided over a period in American history when so many lost faith in it. The greatest tragedy was that the style and skills that Johnson acquired within the system, in the Congress where he first learned how to make it work, poorly equipped him for the task that he faced as president. He had learned how to maneuver in secret, how to build legislative coalitions, how to pass bills. He had not learned how to be a moral leader or how to mobilize a nation. All presidents need to be able to do these things, but times of turmoil especially demand such leadership.

Even so, the skills he had acquired helped Johnson leave a legacy of domestic reform second only to that of Franklin D. Roosevelt. During Johnson's years in office, Congress passed more than two hundred pieces of legislation that created more than five hundred social programs. His attempt to create a Great Society has been rightly criticized. He may have pushed for too much too fast. He never devoted the attention to administering programs that he did to enacting them. Certainly, bringing the disadvantaged into the system proved more difficult than LBJ and many of the social theorists who staffed his task forces believed. Funding never matched promises, either. One of the major difficulties of his crusade for a Great Society, as in other aspects of his presidency, arose out of Johnson's failure to shape a national commitment to it. He talked of the Great Society with such hyperbole that many in the middle class believed that the country had been given to the poor. The poor, in contrast, heard the rhetoric but saw only the meager results of low funding and decided that the government could not or would not help them. Consequently, people in both groups turned against the president and his programs.

Despite such shortcomings, however, Johnson and his Great Society legislation made real and important contributions. Doubtless, the southern-born Johnson did more to promote the integration of African Americans into U.S. society and government than any other president, though his programs probably were more successful in dismantling the legalized biracial system in the South than in ending de facto segregation throughout the nation. He had a commendable record on environmental legislation and indeed played an important role in putting the environment on the national agenda. Finally, though the War on Poverty was far from a battle to the death, the number of poor people in the nation declined during his administration. Medicaid meant that almost everyone who needed one saw a doctor, and Medicare protected many older members of the middle class from financial ruin from repeated illnesses.

Alongside the record of domestic reform, and in the minds of many people overshadowing it, Vietnam constituted the other part of Johnson's legacy. The architects of the containment doctrine that led the United States into Southeast Asia, Johnson's three predecessors who expanded involvement in Vietnam, and his successor who fought the war four more years all shared in the responsibility for the war. Yet Johnson alone decided to bomb the North and to assume a full combat role in the South. He thereby took the nation into a war that cost more than fifty-five thousand American lives (more than thirty thousand of them during Johnson's years in office) and incredible sums of money, left the nation divided, and failed in its goal of establishing a stable, secure, noncommunist South Vietnam. Though perhaps adopted for the best of motives, his policy of phased escalation simply did not achieve the desired results. Also, Johnson was not able to sustain a national commitment to the cause. Historians in the future will almost certainly criticize him for his Vietnam policy, though, like his contemporaries, some may decry his failure to fight it more aggressively whereas others may condemn his decision to fight it at all.

An accurate and fair evaluation of Johnson's record in the White House acknowledges the failure in Vietnam but also incorporates his skillful handling of the transition after Kennedy's assassination, his legislative record, his major accomplishments in the field of civil rights, and his contributions to the bettering of the lot of the poor and elderly. Something of an American original, a fascinating provincial in the capital, Johnson offers a larger-than-life reminder of the complexity of history.

Gaines M. Foster

Suggested Readings

Andrew, John A. *Lyndon Johnson and the Great Society*. Chicago: I. R. Dee, 1998. Discusses the underlying principles and objectives of the Great Society as well as its successes and failures.

Bernstein, Irving. *Guns or Butter: The Presidency of Lyndon B. Johnson*. New York: Oxford University Press, 1996. Analyzes Johnson's decision to pursue domestic initiatives of the Great Society while the Vietnam War escalated.

Bornet, Vaughn D. *The Presidency of Lyndon B. Johnson*. Lawrence: University Press of Kansas, 1983. Remains an essential volume for understanding the events of Johnson's presidency.

Caro, Robert A. *The Years of Lyndon Johnson: Means of Ascent*. New York: Knopf, 1990. Covers the years between 1941 and 1948, including an excellent account of the contentious 1948 senatorial election.

_____. *The Years of Lyndon Johnson: The Path to Power*. New York: Knopf, 1982. A lengthy biography of Johnson's early years, ending its account in 1941.

Dallek, Robert. *Flawed Giant: Lyndon Johnson and His Times, 1961-1973*. New York: Oxford University Press, 1998. Chronicles Johnson's White House years and after, with information drawn from interviews with close associates and tapes released late in the twentieth century.

_____. *Lone Star Rising: Lyndon Johnson and His Times, 1908-1960*. New York: Oxford University Press, 1991. A scholarly biography that covers Johnson's early years and rise to political prominence.

Divine, Robert A., ed. *The Johnson Years*. 2 vols. Lawrence: University Press of Kansas, 1987. Gives a good analysis of the Johnson presidency.

Dugger, Ronnie. *The Politician: The Life and Times of Lyndon Johnson*. New York: Norton, 1982. Emphasizes the influence of Johnson's Texas and frontier heritage on his decisions on Vietnam.

Evans, Rowland, and Robert Novak. *Lyndon B. Johnson: The Exercise of Power*. New York:

New American Library, 1966. Provides good coverage of Johnson's Senate years.

Goldman, Eric F. *The Tragedy of Lyndon Johnson*. New York: Knopf, 1969. A former aide contributes his memories of the White House years.

Hunt, Michael H. *Lyndon Johnson's War: America's Cold War Crusade in Vietnam, 1945-1969*. New York: Hill and Wang, 1996. A spare, direct telling of the Vietnam crisis especially valuable for the general reader.

Johnson, Lady Bird. *A White House Diary*. New York: Holt, Rinehart and Winston, 1970. The memoirs of the First Lady.

Johnson, Lyndon B. *The Vantage Point: Perspectives of the Presidency, 1963-1969*. New York: Holt, Rinehart and Winston, 1971. Aides wrote much of the book, and Johnson reportedly refused to let them use the most fascinating and personal of his reminiscences. The book therefore has little of the private Johnson, though it does offer a useful compendium of his interpretation of events.

Kearns, Doris. *Lyndon Johnson and the American Dream*. New York: Harper & Row, 1976. Kearns takes a psychologically interpretive approach to her biography.

Kotz, Nick. *Judgment Days: Lyndon Baines Johnson, Martin Luther King, Jr. , and the Laws That Changed America*. Boston: Houghton Mifflin, 2005. Examines Johnson's role in the Civil Rights movement and American race relations.

Lyndon Baines Johnson Library and Museum. http://www.lbjlib.utexas.edu/. The Web site of the official presidential library of Johnson.

Reedy, George. *Lyndon B. Johnson: A Memoir*. New York: Andrews and McMeal, 1982. A former aide combines history, biography, memoir, and musings for an engaging read on Johnson.

Schulman, Bruce. *Lyndon B. Johnson and American Liberalism*. Boston: Bedford Books of St. Martin's Press, 1995. A biography that focuses on his role as the emblematic figure in the rise and fall of postwar American liberalism.

VanDemark, Brian. *Into the Quagmire: Lyndon Johnson and the Escalation of the Vietnam War*. New York: Oxford University Press, 1991. A close, almost day-to-day examination of Johnson's Vietnam policy.

Richard M. Nixon

37th President, 1969-1974

Born: January 9, 1913
    Yorba Linda, California
Died: April 22, 1994
    New York, New York

Political Party: Republican
Vice Presidents: Spiro T. Agnew,
    Gerald R. Ford

Cabinet Members

Secretary of State: William P. Rogers, Henry
    Kissinger
Secretary of the Treasury: David M. Kennedy,
    John Connally, George Shultz, William
    Simon

Secretary of Defense: Melvin Laird, Elliot
    Richardson, James R. Schlesinger
Attorney General: John Mitchell, Jr., Richard G.
    Kleindienst, Elliot Richardson, William B.
    Saxbe
Postmaster General: Winton M. Blount
Secretary of the Interior: Walter J. Hickel,
    Rogers C. B. Morton
Secretary of Agriculture: Clifford M. Hardin,
    Earl L. Butz
Secretary of Commerce: Maurice H. Stans,
    Peter G. Peterson, Frederick B. Dent
Secretary of Labor: George Shultz, James D.
    Hodgson, Peter J. Brennan
Secretary of Health, Education, and Welfare:
    Robert Finch, Elliot Richardson, Caspar
    Weinberger
Secretary of Housing and Urban Development:
    George W. Romney, James T. Lynn
Secretary of Transportation: John A. Volpe,
    Claude S. Brinegar

Nixon's official portrait. *(White House Historical Society)*

Richard Milhous Nixon, born in Yorba Linda, California, on January 9, 1913, became the thirty-seventh president of the United States in 1969. On August 9, 1974, as a result of the Watergate scandal, he resigned during his second administration, becoming the first president in the country's history to leave office in this manner. The 2,026 days he spent as president were marked not only by significant achievements in domestic and foreign policy but also by a constitutional crisis of unprecedented proportions. His resignation culminated a political career plagued by controversy from its inception.

Formative Influences: Correcting Popular Misconceptions

Contrary to what most psychological historians have asserted, Nixon's formative years were not particularly traumatic or unusual for someone growing up in two small California towns near Los Angeles. The Irish ancestors of

---

THE FIRST LADY
PAT NIXON

Thelma Catherine Ryan was born in Ely, Nevada, on March 16, 1912, but was raised on a farm outside Los Angeles, California. Her mother, Kate Halberstadt Bender Ryan, died when Pat was thirteen, so she took over the housekeeping responsibilities for her father. Her father, William Ryan, gave her the nickname of "Pat," preferring this to Thelma.

At the age of seventeen, Pat lost her father. She worked to put herself through the University of Southern California, graduating in 1937 with a degree in merchandising. After graduation, she accepted a teaching job at Whittier High School, near Los Angeles. At the school, through a theatrical group, she met Richard Nixon, a young lawyer, who had just graduated from Duke University. Pat and Richard became engaged and were married on June 21, 1940, in Riverside, California.

Shortly after they married, World War II began, and Nixon spent almost all the war years away, serving in the Navy in the Pacific Theater. During this time, Pat continued teaching at Whittier. In 1946, the first of their two daughters, Patricia, was born, and Nixon entered politics, winning election to the U.S. House of Representatives. In 1948, their second daughter Julie, was born.

In 1950, Nixon was elected to the U.S. Senate, and two years later, he was tapped as Dwight Eisenhower's vice presidential running mate. During the campaign, Nixon was accused of improprieties involving campaign funds. Despite pressure to step down from the ticket, Nixon insisted on addressing the issue on national television. During his famous "Checkers" speech, with Pat by his side, he referred to the "cloth coat" she was wearing as evidence of the couple's frugal lifestyle. The ploy worked, and Nixon stayed on the ticket. He served as vice president for eight years and ran for the presidency in 1960, narrowly losing to John F. Kennedy.

Nixon's election to the presidency in 1968 was a remarkable political comeback. Upon entering the White House, Pat redecorated it in European style, replacing the classical restorations of Jackie Kennedy. She also gave extravagant parties and receptions, her most famous being the wedding reception for her daughter Tricia in the White House Rose Garden. She also represented the president on numerous occasions, including the relief effort for victims of an earthquake in Peru in 1970, and she was involved in numerous charities.

Disaster came in 1973 as evidence unfolded about Nixon's involvement in the Watergate scandal. Pat's close relationship with her husband was strained during this time, since he refused to talk about the incident with her.

In August, 1974, Nixon resigned rather then face impeachment. The couple retired to their homes, traveling between San Clemente, California, and New Jersey. Pat died at their home in Park Ridge, New Jersey, on June 22, 1993, ten months before her husband.

Dean M. Shapiro

both his mother and his father dated back to the colonial period, and both parents grew up in the Midwest before migrating to California. Although Frank Nixon became a Quaker upon marrying Hannah Milhous in 1908, Nixon commented in his *Memoirs* (1978) that the type of Quakerism his family practiced—first in Yorba Linda and then in Whittier—resembled the Protestantism of the churches in the area rather than the stricter version the Milhous family had known in Butlerville, Indiana.

His father being neither a particularly good nor a lucky businessman, Nixon grew up as many boys of his generation did, poor but by no means impoverished, and imbued with the 1920's ethos which combined hard work with the dream of unlimited opportunity. Although much has been made of the deaths of his two brothers Arthur and Harold, they occurred eight years apart, when Nixon was twelve and twenty years old, respectively. While he naturally commented on their deaths, neither seemed to have negatively affected his personality or psyche. Early loss of siblings was not uncommon for Nixon's generation, nor was small-town Republicanism or the close-knit rural environment in which he was reared.

A good student and hard worker, Nixon excelled scholastically at Whittier High School and Whittier College, earning a scholarship to Duke University Law School in 1934. Although he worked equally hard in law school, graduating third in his class, he did not obtain a suitable offer from a prestigious law firm upon graduation. Instead, Nixon returned to Whittier to practice law from 1937 until 1942. Perhaps his meeting, courtship, and marriage to Thelma Catherine (Pat) Ryan between 1938 and 1940 constituted the most memorable episode in Nixon's life before he entered politics in 1946.

If anyone experienced a harsh, poverty-stricken childhood, it was Pat Ryan, not Richard Nixon. Shortly after her birth on March 16, 1912, her miner father moved the family from

Ely, Nevada, to Artesia, California, to become a truck farmer. By the time she was eighteen, both her parents had died. After trying several different jobs on both coasts, she returned to California to work her way through the University of Southern California. She did not complete her undergraduate education until 1937—the year Nixon finished law school. The same age as Nixon, she met him during the rehearsal of a play after she moved to Whittier to teach high school commercial subjects. Apparently Nixon impulsively decided he wanted to marry her after their first date. Even though as a young, successful lawyer he was one of Whittier's most eligible bachelors, they did not become engaged or married until three years later, in 1940.

Subsequently, World War II brought the newlyweds to Washington, D.C., where Nixon worked in the tire-rationing section of the Office of Price Administration (OPA). Quickly disillusioned with the red tape of government bureaucracy, Nixon obtained a commission and served in the South Pacific between 1942 and 1946, rising to the rank of lieutenant commander. There was nothing particularly distinguished about either his civilian or his military career during these years, and those who knew him best did not perceive any overt political ambition.

Like most American politicians, Nixon's views on government, and on domestic as well as foreign policies, appeared to be more influenced by his adult experiences beginning with World War II than with any unresolved childhood psychological crises or ideological influences which he may have experienced as a young man while going to school or establishing himself as a lawyer. As Nixon himself later said:

I came out of college more liberal than I am today, more liberal in the sense that I thought it was possible for government to do more than I later found it was practical to do. I became more conservative first, after my experience with OPA. . . . I also became greatly disillusioned about bureaucracy and about what the government could do because I saw the terrible paper work that people had to go through. I also saw the mediocrity of so many civil servants.

In contrast to his rather nondescript background, Nixon's political career prior to assuming the presidency proved as controversial as it was meteoric. Elected to the Eightieth Congress in 1946 at the age of thirty-three, he served two terms, then ran successfully for the U.S. Senate in 1950. By 1952, at thirty-nine, he was elected vice president of the United States, and he only narrowly missed being elected president in 1960 at forty-seven. Eight years later, Nixon won the presidency in an almost equally close contest.

Preparation for the Presidency: Hard Lessons

Nixon's twenty-three years as a politician before becoming president were peppered with controversy, beginning in 1946 when he defeated the five-term liberal Democratic congressman, Jerry Voorhis, and later in 1950 when he defeated equally liberal Democrat Helen Gahagan Douglas for a Senate seat. In both campaigns, Nixon charged his opponents with having left-wing political views. In retrospect, he probably would have defeated Voorhis and Douglas, whose government careers were basically undistinguished, without any Red-baiting because of the increasing postwar conservatism. Both remain better known for running against Nixon than for any other political achievements.

Under the direction of Murray Chotiner, a lawyer-turned-campaign-consultant for such Republican luminaries as Earl Warren and William Knowland, Nixon mounted Hollywood-style media campaigns and employed political packaging techniques (now considered commonplace) complete with innuendoes about

his opponents' presumed Communist Party affiliations. Such tactics in 1946 and 1950 immediately earned for him the reputation among liberal Democrats as an opportunistic product of the Cold War and a "political polarizer" who would do anything to win an election. In 1948 Nixon, as a member of the House Committee on Un-American Activities, initiated the successful attempt to end the diplomatic and governmental career of Alger Hiss by exposing his connections with the Communist Party in the 1930's. In the same year, he proposed the Mundt-Nixon bill, which would have required individual communists and communist organizations to register with the federal government. These actions forever identified him in the American mind as a hard-line anticommunist, despite the facts that he neither became involved with the 1950's McCarthy anticommunist campaign nor made the single-minded pursuit of domestic communists a major goal of his public life.

During his years as Dwight D. "Ike" Eisenhower's vice president, from 1953 until 1961, Nixon campaigned widely for Republican candidates and in the process obtained the unenviable reputation as the party hatchet man, especially for his attacks on Adlai Stevenson, twice the Democratic presidential candidate in the 1950's. As a result, elements within the press, many academics, and liberals in general found it easier to criticize the conservatism of the Eisenhower administrations—not by attacking a popular president, but by concentrating on the politics and personality of his vice president.

Otherwise, the 1950's were relatively quiet years for the country and for Nixon politically, despite the fact that he later placed five of his *Six Crises* (1962) in that decade. Of these, probably only one—the 1952 charge that he had created a slush fund of a little more than $18,000 to further his political career—constituted a real crisis. By going on nationwide television on September 23, 1952, Nixon successfully defended himself and forced Eisenhower to keep him on the Republican ticket as vice president. In this broadcast, he presented embarrassingly detailed information about his family's finances, including the fact that his wife, Pat, did not own a fur coat like so many Democratic politicians' wives but only "a respectable Republican cloth coat." This speech is best remembered, however, because of his emotional statement that his children would keep a dog named Checkers although the cocker spaniel had been a political gift.

In addition to the 1952 Checkers speech, two other media events at the end of the decade enhanced Nixon's political fortunes and popularity with the general public: the stoning of his car by an anti-American mob in Caracas, Venezuela, in 1958, and his 1959 "kitchen" encounter with Soviet leader Nikita Khrushchev in which Nixon championed the American way of life during their conversations at an American home building display in Moscow. The three events did not add up to a common pattern of constant controversy or crises as much as they represented sporadic and potentially negative incidents which Nixon turned into politically profitable opportunities in the valuable, but often discouraging, learning process he underwent during his two terms as vice president. Always outside the president's private group of advisers, and occasionally humiliated by Ike in public, Nixon bided his time and mended his own political fences by courting both moderate and conservative Republicans in order to ensure his presidential nomination in 1960.

Although Eisenhower gave him few formal responsibilities, in eight years Nixon permanently upgraded the office of vice president and gave it a much more meaningful and insti-

Soviet premier Nikita Khrushchev and Vice President Nixon hold the "kitchen debate" in 1959. *(AP/Wide World Photos)*

tutionalized role than it had ever had before. In part he accomplished this feat through several well-publicized trips abroad on behalf of the president in the 1950's. (Nixon nostalgically repeated the 1953 trip to Asia and the Far East in 1985.) The vice presidency also assumed greater importance because Eisenhower suffered a heart attack in 1955, a bout with ileitis in 1956, and a stroke in 1957. Throughout all these illnesses, Nixon handled himself with considerable tact and self-effacement, while presiding over nineteen cabinet sessions and twenty-six meetings of the National Security Council (NSC).

Following his stroke, President Eisenhower worked out a plan with Nixon, Secretary of State John Foster Dulles, and Attorney General William Rogers to create the office of acting president in the event he became incapacitated from illness. This formal agreement substituted under Presidents Eisenhower and Kennedy for a constitutional amendment (which was not ratified until 1967) granting the vice president full authority to govern when the president could not discharge the powers and duties of his office.

Nixon's unsuccessful campaign against John F. Kennedy was fraught with ironies and political lessons he never forgot. Repeatedly, the press described Kennedy as a "youthful front-runner" representing a new generation, when in fact both men came from approximately the same age cohort, Nixon being only four years older than his forty-three-year-old Democratic opponent. In addition, Nixon's congressional and vice presidential records on civil rights and foreign policy were more liberal than Kennedy's, yet the press perceived them

The Vice President
Spiro T. Agnew

Spiro T. Agnew was born on November 9, 1918, in Baltimore, Maryland, as Spiros Anagnostopoulos. His family was of Greek ancestry and eventually shortened or "Americanized" their last name. After graduating from public schools, Agnew attended the Johns Hopkins University, earning a degree in 1940, and then Baltimore Law School. During this time and in his early career, Agnew worked in an array of jobs, including supermarket manager, claims adjuster, and clerk with a casualty company. He spent the duration of World War II in the U.S. Army, serving in the European Theater of operations for part of that time. On May 27, 1942, Agnew married Elinor Esabel Judefind, and they had four children.

After the war, Agnew returned to Baltimore and finished the law degree he started prior to enlisting, graduating in 1947. Agnew joined the law firm of Karl Steinmann, then established his own practice in Towson, Maryland. Agnew's entrance into politics came in 1957 when he was named to the Baltimore County Zoning Board of Appeals, which he chaired from 1958 to 1961. In 1961, he became the executive for Baltimore County, serving until 1967. During the 1966 elections, Agnew won his race for governor of Maryland. Two years later, he was in the number two spot on Richard M. Nixon's presidential ticket. Agnew served as vice president from 1969 until he was forced to resign on October 10, 1973, because of a scandal involving his misuse of campaign funds and income tax evasion. Agnew pleaded "no contest" to the charges and was fined ten thousand dollars.

After his vice presidency, Agnew worked as an international trade executive and split his time between homes in Maryland and California. He died on September 17, 1996, near his home in Towson, Maryland.

Robert P. Watson and Richard Yon

The Kennedy-Nixon debates in 1960. *(AP/Wide World Photos)*

as less so. Finally, Nixon learned the hard way that television would play a most significant role in the 1960 election—the closest one in United States history since Grover Cleveland defeated James G. Blaine in 1884. As a result, Nixon perfected a television campaign style of his own in 1968 and 1972 in direct reaction to his loss of four nationally televised debates with Kennedy in September and October—losses based not on debating or substantive points but on style and image.

To his credit, Nixon did not challenge this 1960 election, which he lost to Kennedy by only 112,000 popular votes, though there was every indication that the Democrats did not legally win in either Illinois or Texas, whose combined electoral college tally tipped the election in the Democrats' favor, 303 to 219. "Our country can't afford the agony of a constitutional crisis," Nixon remarked in an unconsciously prescient moment to one reporter who had unearthed a number of voting irregularities in both states, "and I damn well will not be a party to creating one just to become President or anything else." Nevertheless, after 1960 Nixon resolved never again to take any preelection lead for granted— not in 1968 or even in 1972. All campaigns became "no holds barred" contests to him.

Temporarily retiring to private life, he wrote his first book and best-seller, *Six Crises*, in 1961, and decided to run for governor of California in 1962. Defeat in this election prompted his much-quoted remark to reporters that they would not "have Nixon to kick around anymore." It spurred him to move to New York, where at long last he joined the prestigious law firm of his earlier dreams and continued to build bridges between moderate and conservative factions within the Republican Party, especially after Barry Goldwater's defeat by

Lyndon B. Johnson in 1964. By 1968, Richard Nixon was once again positioned to win his party's nomination for the presidency of the United States.

Unlike 1960, he faced a Democratic Party hopelessly divided over the war in Indochina and haplessly led by Hubert Humphrey in the wake of LBJ's unexpected refusal to run again, Robert Kennedy's assassination, and a strong third-party bid by George C. Wallace. Also unlike 1960, his opponent had no intrinsically better television image than he did. Instead of debating Humphrey, Nixon and his aides began perfecting thirty-second and one-minute television commercials—an innovation which eventually transformed U.S. presidential primaries and campaigns into media events rather than substantive discussions of issues—the opposite of what Nixon intended.

A Time of Transition
Richard Milhous Nixon became president at a critical juncture in American history. Following World War II, popular and official opinion in the United States had generally agreed on two things: the effectiveness of most New Deal domestic policies and the necessity of most Cold War foreign policies. The consensus on these two crucial postwar issues began to break down during the 1960's. The war in Indochina hastened the disintegration of both consensual constructs because of its disruptive impact on the nation's political economy. By 1968, the traditional Cold War, bipartisan approach to the conduct of foreign affairs had been seriously undermined. Similarly, the "bigger and better" New Deal approach to the modern welfare state seemed to many, even many liberals, to have reached a point of diminishing returns.

When Nixon finally captured the highest office in the land, he inherited not only Johnson's Vietnam War but also LBJ's Great Society. This transfer of power occurred at the very moment when both endeavors had lost substantial support among the people at large and—most

important—among a significant number of decision makers and opinion leaders across the country. On previous occasions when such a breakdown occurred within policy and opinion-making circles, drastic things happened. One such period preceded the Civil War; another, shorter one, occurred just before the Spanish-American War; another during the early years of the Great Depression; and another in the course of the 1960's.

A man less in tune with popular as well as elite attitudes might not have responded so quickly to manifestations of domestic discontent over the war and welfare. Nixon's sense of timing was all the more acute in 1968 and 1972 as a result of his close loss to John F. Kennedy in 1960 and his overwhelming defeat in California in 1962. By 1968, he realized that old Republican campaign slogans and traditional anticommunist shibboleths would not suffice. He deliberately kept his statements about domestic policy vague but quite palatable to the masses by talking about dispersing power. On foreign policy, however, as early as 1967, in a widely cited article, he gave notice to the tiny elite who dominated policy formulation that he had begun to question certain Cold War assumptions, such as nonrecognition of China.

Unlike the 1960 campaign, in 1968 the Democratic candidate, Hubert Humphrey, was clearly more liberal than Nixon except on one issue. Humphrey, the Democrat, appeared to be defending past American efforts to win the war in Vietnam more than did Nixon, the Republican many considered to be an original Cold Warrior. Thus, Nixon stressed victory in Vietnam less than Humphrey, implying that he had a "secret plan" for ending the war based on more diplomacy and less military escalation. This left Humphrey wearing the very tarnished military mantle of LBJ. Had President Johnson halted the bombing of North Vietnam and renewed peace talks in Paris before the end of October, Humphrey might have been able to squeeze by Nixon because the election results proved almost as close as in 1960. Nixon won by 500,000 popular votes and received 301 electoral votes, compared to 191 for Humphrey and 46 for Wallace.

Sensing the transitional mood of the country as it drifted away from consensus, and convinced that presidents can accomplish significant deeds only in their first administration, Nixon moved quickly on several fronts even before his inauguration. For example, he gave his approval to the reopening of the Warsaw talks with China, privately decided upon a gradual and unilateral withdrawal of American troops from Vietnam, made Henry Kissinger his national security adviser, approved a plan for reorganizing the NSC system, and concluded that Roy Ash, president of Litton Industries, should initiate a massive reorganization of the executive branch. Yet at the same time president-elect Nixon contacted Arthur Burns about becoming his deputy for domestic affairs

while simultaneously deciding that Daniel Patrick (Pat) Moynihan would become head of a new Urban Affairs Council (UAC) to formulate domestic policy, even though Burns and Moynihan were at opposite ends of the political and economic spectrum. These early private actions before his inauguration clearly indicated that Nixon intended to restructure the office of the president to accomplish his domestic and foreign goals.

Nixon's Advisers

One cannot look to the 1968 campaign for much advance warning about the structural and substantive changes Nixon later advocated when he called for a "decade of reform." As it turned out, he came to rely on two quite different sets of advisers: "free-thinking" outsiders who brainstormed with him on major issues, and "political broker" insiders who worked to draft and implement his legislative and administra-

Presidential candidate Nixon at a Republican campaign rally in 1968. *(NARA)*

tive priorities. Initially, for example, momentum for change on most domestic and foreign affairs came after the election from such free-thinking outsiders as Robert Finch, Richard Nathan, Pat Moynihan, Henry Kissinger, and later John Connally. All these men appealed to Nixon's preference for bold action, and with the exception of Finch, Nixon had not been closely associated with any of them before being elected president.

Moynihan and Kissinger, in particular, influenced certain crucial details, but not usually the broad outlines, of domestic and foreign policies during the first administration by supporting ideas based on the concept of "linkage." Once convinced by these two men that "everything relates to everything," Nixon personally began to "preside over a more rapid evolution toward planning than any other President since FDR," according to historian Otis L. Graham in *Toward a Planned Society: From Roosevelt to Nixon* (1976). During his first two years in office, Nixon embarked on a planned risk-taking course in both foreign and domestic policy resulting in attempted reversals of traditional American positions on government reorganization, the idea of a guaranteed annual income, environmental considerations, revenue sharing (including block grants), the value of the dollar, the bombing of Cambodia, rapprochement with China, and détente with the Soviet Union. Thus, concepts about foreign policy as well as welfare, social service spending, the environment, economic relations between the federal government and the states, and structural reform of the executive branch all changed significantly under Nixon.

The impact of the free-thinking outsiders on Nixonian policies is easy to trace. Moynihan, Finch, and Nathan greatly influenced specific legislation on welfare; Kissinger carried out the president's foreign policy first as national security adviser and later as secretary of state; and Connally, whom Nixon appointed secretary of the treasury in 1971, single-handedly talked the president into imposing wage and price controls and devaluating the dollar. Connally also played a crucial role in two of Nixon's most important environmental decisions, favoring the creation of the Environmental Protection Agency and a Department of Natural Resources—both against the wishes of the farm bloc. Perhaps of all the free-thinking outsiders who advised him, Nixon was most impressed by Connally, whom he wanted for his vice president in 1968, when Connally was still a Democrat and governor of Texas; whom he wanted to succeed him had he completed his second term; and whom he favored for the vice presidency after Spiro T. Agnew resigned on October 10, 1973, when publication of information indicating that Agnew had accepted payoffs while governor of Maryland led him to plead *nolo contendere* to a single charge of federal income tax evasion. "Only three men in America understand the use of power," Nixon confided to Arthur Burns. "I do. John does. And," he grudgingly added, "I guess Nelson [Rockefeller] does."

Nevertheless, political broker insiders increasingly gained ascendancy over the flamboyant outsiders within the first Nixon administration, and his plans to reorganize the executive branch became more corporate in nature and more central to his thinking. Gray-flannel types such as John Ehrlichman and H. R. Haldeman, the president's two closest aides; Arthur Burns, counselor to the president and later head of the Federal Reserve Board; Melvin Laird, secretary of defense; George Shultz, secretary of labor and later head of the Office of Management and Budget; and businessman Roy Ash, chair of the President's Council on Executive Reorganization, all played the role of political broker insiders. In Nixon's first years in office, Ehrlichman, Shultz (who later became Ronald Reagan's secretary of state), and Laird became dominant insiders on policy, while Haldeman and Ash concentrated on organizational matters.

THE VICE PRESIDENT
GERALD R. FORD

Gerald R. Ford served as vice president in the second administration of Richard M. Nixon. Ford was born Leslie King on July 14, 1913, in Omaha, Nebraska. His parents divorced while their son was an infant and, after his mother married Gerald Ford, he was adopted by his stepfather and given the name Gerald R. Ford, Jr. Ford was raised in Grand Rapids, Michigan, attending public schools and distinguishing himself as a football player. He graduated from the University of Michigan in 1935, where he played football. From Michigan, Ford attended law school at Yale, completing his degree in 1941.

After completing his education, Ford established the law practice of Busten and Ford but enlisted in the Navy in 1942. He was promoted to lieutenant commander and discharged in 1946. After the war, Ford returned to his law practice and married Elizabeth Bloomer on October 15, 1948. The Fords had four children. Ford started his political career in 1948 when he was elected to the U.S. House of Representatives, where he served from 1949 to 1973, rising to the rank of minority leader in 1965. During this time Ford also served as a delegate to conferences in Europe.

After the October, 1973, resignation of Vice President Spiro Agnew, Ford was named and then confirmed as vice president on December 6, 1973. In less than one year, on August 9, 1974, President Nixon resigned from office disgraced by the Watergate scandal. Ford became president. He attempted to win election in his own right in 1976 but was defeated. In retirement, Ford split his time between homes in California and Michigan and remained active in swimming, golf, and tennis.

Robert P. Watson and Richard Yon

Ehrlichman, for example, aided by John Whitaker, significantly influenced the content of Nixon's welfare and environmental legislation especially in connection with land-use policies. Ehrlichman was described by one forest conservation specialist as "the most effective environmentalist since Gifford Pinchot." Burns became the unexpected champion of revenue sharing within the administration. Shultz confined his advice largely to economics and labor but proved surprisingly influential in desegregation matters. Before Kissinger's ascendancy, Laird could be seen brokering on a wide variety of topics from foreign policy to such diverse issues as the volunteer draft, revenue sharing, governmental reorganization, and the situation in Vietnam. If there is a single underestimated, understudied influential figure in the first Nixon administration, it is the most diffident of the honest broker insiders, Melvin Laird.

At the same time that Nixon began relying on certain free-thinking personalities who encouraged him to make sweeping policy recommendations, he also began experimenting with changes in the decision-making process with the reorganization of the NSC and the creation of the UAC, precursor of the Domestic Council. Although he has been called a "management conscious president," Nixon had little previous management experience. In fact, his interest in establishing orderly procedures appears as much rooted in a characteristic desire to avoid personal confrontation as it was in his "preoccupation with the technology of management." From the very beginning, therefore, a tendency existed within his administration for process to become policy; for organizational reform to become a substitute for substantive considerations; for effectiveness to become more important than morality or constitutionality.

In fact, these rigid organizational expectations which characterized the Nixon administration isolated the president from opposing points of view and produced a "results at any price approach," or, at the very least, exaggerated expectations about effectiveness of structural reform. Not surprisingly, Nixon and many of his unelected top advisers began to exhibit a callous and cavalier attitude toward party politics and constitutional government. After five Republican-hired burglars were arrested on June 17, 1972, for breaking into the Watergate headquarters of the Democratic Party, the illegal and unconstitutional tendencies inherent in Nixonian attitudes about politics and government began to pollute the White House atmosphere.

Nixon once said that he thought the "mark of a leader is whether he gives history a nudge." There is no doubt that he accomplished this goal as president, but in ways he did not anticipate. Whether relying on flamboyant outsiders

President Nixon and the First Lady in Washington, D.C., in April, 1969. *(NARA)*

or honest broker insiders, he essentially took the initiative and made many of his own decisions, particularly in foreign affairs. While he and his closest advisers later disagreed on who influenced whom most, Nixon came to the Oval Office with innovative diplomatic ideas which cannot be "Kissingerized" even by Kissinger. In addition, to the dismay of many liberals and conservatives in Congress, he moved quickly into domestic reform. Given the fact that he and Bill Clinton were the only twentieth century presidents to be elected without their party having control over either house of Congress, Nixon's positive historical "nudges" in both foreign and domestic matters were truly impressive. Yet so were the negative ones.

Nixon as Domestic Reformer

Despite predictions by the media that Nixon would be a cautious, if not actually a "do-nothing," president, he proclaimed that the 1970's should become a "decade of government reform," and he actively pursued six areas of domestic reform: welfare, civil rights, growth policy, economic policy, environmental policy, and reorganization of the federal bureaucracy. These domestic programs may ultimately outlive his better-known activities in the realm of foreign policy and even transcend his negative Watergate image.

All of Nixon's attempted changes in domestic and foreign policy were aimed at establishing a conservative, yet modern, public policy. In domestic affairs, for example, faced with a jumbled, pluralist set of federal-state relations, Nixon pointed the way toward a conservative public policy to which his speechwriters and advisers later gave the name New Federalism. To understand Nixon's New Federalism, it is necessary to know how he defined a federal, as opposed to a state or local, function. Nixon applied a rule of thumb which distinguished between those activities requiring larger cash transactions and those primarily involving services. Thus, he attempted to return to the states some power over service issues (what social scientists call distributive issues) such as education, manpower training, and public health, while retaining control at the national level over cash transfers or nondistributive issues such as welfare, energy, and the environment. Above all, Nixon's New Federalism was not intended to cut federal spending programs.

Presidents usually achieve their domestic objectives in three basic ways: legislation, appeals in the mass media, and administrative actions. Nixon offered extensive legislative programs to Congress during his first administration, and when he encountered difficulty obtaining passage, resorted more and more to reform by administrative change, especially at the beginning of his abortive second term in office. His intent with most of these domestic reforms was to address national problems by redistributing federal power away from Congress and the bureaucracy. Consequently, all Nixonian domestic reforms between 1969 and 1971 were ultimately linked under the rubric of New Federalism and by overlapping personnel on various policy-making committees. All competed for attention with his well-known interest in foreign affairs. All involved a degree of boldness which he thought necessary for a successful presidency. All increased federal regulation of nondistributive public policies. All were made possible in part because he was a Republican president who took advantage of acting in the Disraeli tradition of enlightened conservatism. All offended liberals (and many conservatives), especially when it came to implementing certain controversial policies with legislation. Yet by the 1980's, many liberals wished they had Nixon's domestic legislation on environmental issues and social service spending "to kick around" again. Most important, both his failures and his successes with domestic reform ultimately made Nixon determined to reorganize the executive branch of government with or without congressional approval.

Popular and academic opinion held that Nixon would not recommend any noteworthy social reform. Yet by the end of his first term as president, Nixon had succeeded in several major domestic reform areas, including that of civil rights. Although he was strongly criticized by liberals for employing delaying tactics and not extending busing to Northern cities, his administration achieved impressive results in the area of desegregation. In 1968, 68 percent of all African American children in the South and 40 percent in the entire nation attended all-black schools. By the end of 1972, less than 8 percent of southern African American children attended all-black schools and less than 12 percent nationwide. President Johnson expended $911 million for civil rights activities, including $75 million for civil rights enforcement during the 1969 fiscal year. For the fiscal year 1973, the Nixon administration's budget called for $2.6 billion in total civil rights outlays, of which $602 million was earmarked for enforcement through a substantially strengthened Equal Employment Opportunity Commission (EEOC).

During his first administration, with the aid of George Shultz, President Nixon also initiated the Philadelphia Plan, which set specific numerical goals for minority employment in the construction industry and extended this plan to nine other cities. While Presidents Kennedy and Johnson had employed the term "affirmative action," it "did not have much bite" until the Nixon administration required federal contractors to hire a certain number of minority workers under the Philadelphia Plan. Finally, Nixon made a special effort to encourage African American entrepreneurship by creating the Office of Minority Business Enterprise in 1969.

The Nixon administration was also attentive to the economic status of women and publicized its appointments of women to high government positions. Partially as a result of a 1970 report of a Task Force on Women's Rights and Responsibilities appointed by Nixon, Congress approved the Equal Rights Amendment (ERA) for women and submitted it to the states for ratification in 1972. Nixon's support for the ERA dated back to the beginning of his political career in 1946, and he cosponsored ERA bills as a congressman and senator and continued to support them as vice president. After the passage of the Equal Pay Act in 1963, however, he was not as enthusiastic about the ERA because he believed equality in the workplace had been guaranteed by this legislation. Nevertheless, in March, 1972, he endorsed the ERA as president of the United States.

In addition, Nixon endorsed a surprisingly enlightened rights policy for American Indians. Since World War II, white integrationists and Indian self-determinationists had debated whether American Indians had a "unique dual relationship" with the government of the United States because they were both individual citizens of the country and members of federally recognized sovereign tribes. Until the Nixon administration, the national policy had followed primarily an integrationist approach aimed at terminating tribal ties. After appointing Louis R. Bruce, a Mohawk in favor of self-determination, as commissioner of Indian affairs, Nixon quickly moved to change federal policy by declaring in a special message to Congress on July 8, 1970, that the federal government would assist American Indians in pursuing "Self-Determination without Termination." In this address the president assured "the Indian that he [could] assume control over his own life without being separated involuntarily from the tribal groups."

Nixon's determination to strengthen American Indians' sense of autonomy without threatening their sense of community became even more evident when he asked Congress to repeal the 1953 House Concurrent Resolution

"You Were Saying That You Saw A Western Movie The Other Day . . ."

A 1970 political cartoon in *The Washington Post* comments on Nixon's difficult relationship with the press. *(Library of Congress)*

which had endorsed integration at the expense of self-determination. Ironically, this legislation dated from the time Nixon had been vice president. As president, however, he effectively ended the policy of forced termination of tribal status and turned over more decisions about American Indian policies to the elected tribal governments.

Thus, beginning in 1969 the Nixon administration increased the budget of the Bureau of Indian Affairs by 214 percent and requested a total, all-agency budget of $1.2 billion for Indian affairs in fiscal year 1973, an increase of $300 million in two years. Funds for improving the health of American Indians doubled under

Nixon. In addition, Congress, with Nixon's approval, passed legislation strengthening existing tribal governments, restoring previously terminated tribal status, and financing tribal commercial development. With the passage of the 1975 Indian Self-Determination and Educational Assistance Act, headlines across the country declared it to be the most significant piece of American Indian legislation since 1934, and credited Nixon with having initiated his own "New Deal" for American Indians. Indeed, by 1975, Nixon appeared to have lived up to earlier praise from Bruce Willkie, the executive director of the National Congress of American Indians (NCAI), who said in 1970 that he was "the first U.S. President since George Washington to pledge that the government will honor obligations to the Indian tribes."

Nixon and Welfare

Nixon set an unexpectedly fast pace on the issue of welfare reform, in part because both Health, Education, and Welfare (HEW) Secretary Finch and UAC head Moynihan became early advocates of what came to be known as the Family Assistance Program (FAP). Had this legislation succeeded in Congress it would have changed the emphasis of American welfare from providing services to providing income; thus, it would have replaced the Aid to Families with Dependent Children (AFDC) program, whose payments varied widely from state to state, with direct payments to families from $1,600 (initially proposed in 1969) to $2,500 (proposed in 1971) for a family of four. States were expected to supplement this amount and, in addition, all able-bodied heads of recipient families (except mothers with preschool children) would be required to "accept work or training." If such a parent refused to accept work or training, however, only the parent's payment would be withheld. In essence, FAP unconditionally guaranteed children an annual income and would have tripled the number of children then being aided by AFDC.

As the most comprehensive welfare reform ever proposed by a United States president, FAP's dramatic reversal of thirty-five years of incremental welfare legislation probably contributed more to its defeat than Nixon's loss of interest with the approach of the 1972 presidential election. The fundamental switch from services to income payment which FAP represented proved too much for liberals and conservatives alike in Congress, and they formed an unlikely alliance to vote it down. FAP's final defeat in the Senate in 1972 ironically led to some very impressive examples of incremental legislation that may not have come to pass had it not been for the original boldness of FAP. Congress approved, for example, Supplementary Security Income (SSI) on October 17, 1972. This measure constituted a guaranteed annual income for the aged, blind, and disabled.

The demise of FAP also led Nixon to support the uniform application of the food stamp program across the United States, better health insurance programs for low-income families, and automatic cost-of-living adjustments (COLA) for Social Security recipients to help them cope with inflation. From the first to the last budget for which his administration was responsible, that is, from 1971 through 1975, spending on all human resource programs exceeded spending for defense for the first time since World War II. All in all, there was a sevenfold increase in funding for social services under Nixon, making him, not Johnson, the "last of the big spenders" on domestic programs.

Mixing Economics and Politics

Nixon appeared to reverse himself when he became president from views he held before, or at least, from views others attributed to him. Nowhere is this more evident than on domestic and foreign economic issues. The president dramatically announced his New Economic Policy (NEP) on August 15, 1971, at the close of a secret Camp David meeting with sixteen economic advisers. His failure to obtain more revenue through tax reform legislation in 1969, along with rising unemployment and inflation rates in 1970, precipitated Nixon's NEP, which tried to balance U.S. domestic concerns with wage and price controls and international ones by devaluing the dollar.

As president, Nixon did not make balancing the budget a major object of policy when faced with inflation. First he tried to deal with it in typically conservative fashion by tightening the money supply. When this monetary approach did not work and the economy appeared to be heading into a recession by 1970, the administration had to turn to fiscal policy solutions. On the advice of his Council of Economic Advisors (CEA), headed by Paul McCracken, Nixon became the first president to submit a budget based on "the high-employment budget standard." As he said in his 1971 State of the Union Message, his full-employment budget was "designed to be in balance if the economy were operating at its peak potential. By spending as if we were at full employment, we will help to bring about full employment." This full-employment budget actually justified an "acceptable" amount of deficit spending; specifically, that amount which would result if expenditures did not exceed the hypothetical revenue which would accrue if full employment existed. By setting such a limit on fine-tuning the economy and on expansion, Nixon proclaimed himself a conservative Keynesian.

Unfortunately, the business and financial communities did not endorse the president's full-employment budget. By 1971, they were more worried about the breakdown of the international economic system established in 1944 with the Bretton Woods agreement. For the first time, therefore, they were ready to consider variable rates for international currencies. Since ending gold convertibility and allowing the dollar "to float" on international markets would cause even more inflation in the United States, such a move had to be offset by some deflationary action. Under Treasury Secretary

Connally's influence, Nixon agreed that if foreign countries continued to demand ever-increasing amounts of gold for the U.S. dollars that they held, the United States would go off the gold standard, but would at the same time impose wage and price controls to curb inflation. The president's NEP perfectly reflected the "grand gesture" that Connally thought he should make on economic problems, and the post-Camp David television broadcast simply added drama to economic issues most Americans thought boring.

Although the high-handedness of the NEP with respect to traditional U.S. trading partners, especially Japan, left long-term scars, it was a short-term domestic success. The NEP initially worked so well that by early 1972, output rose sharply, unemployment fell, and inflation remained low, making Nixon the first president since World War II to bring about an economic upturn in a presidential election year—something he believed essential for solidifying a new coalition of Republican voters throughout the country. Since the Democrats remained even more disorganized behind the leadership of peace candidate George McGovern than they had been under Humphrey, Nixon's economic policies added to, but were not entirely responsible for, his victory margin of 18 million votes or 60.8 percent of the popular vote.

Long-term implementation of wage and price controls, however, revealed not only how politically motivated Nixon's commitment had been, but also how impossible it was to abandon them without exacerbating inflationary trends within the economy. Consequently one legacy of Nixon's NEP was more inflation and more federal regulation of the economy than during any other presidency since the New Deal. The administration extended federal regulation in four major areas: energy (specifically oil prices), the environment, occupational health and safety, and consumer production safety. In each instance, especially with respect to environmental legislation, Nixon tried to establish limits on the amount and expense of regulation, but he usually failed to convince enough members of Congress, who also mixed politics and economics without always anticipating long-range consequences.

When he was not trying to act before Congress could upstage him on regulatory issues, Nixon proposed deregulation based on free market assumptions which were more traditionally in keeping with conservative Republicanism. The administration not only devalued the dollar but also made deregulatory recommendations for the production of food crops, for the reduction of tariff and other barriers to international trade, and for interest rates paid by various financial institutions. By and large, however, politics made Nixon more liberal on economic matters, confounding both his friends and enemies.

Governmental Reorganization Along Corporate Lines

Nixon had inherited a White House staff and executive office badly in need of reorganization because of burgeoning personnel and the fact that major departments resembled diversified holding companies more than single-function divisions. That he turned to corporate management techniques is not surprising when one considers that his Council on Executive Reorganization (known as the Ash Commission) consisted of four top corporate executives and John Connally. Nevertheless, his failure to obtain welfare reform from Congress propelled him toward a corporate presidency more quickly than otherwise would have been the case.

Nixon received recommendations based on some of the most advanced corporate theories from the Ash Commission. Acting on its advice, he introduced management by objectives into government operating procedures for the first time and mounted several major attempts to reorganize the executive branch. His suc-

cesses in these areas constitute some of his most lasting achievements. By the time he resigned from office, Nixon had replaced the Post Office Department with a public corporation less subject to political patronage, merged the Peace Corps and Volunteers in Service to America (VISTA), into one agency called ACTION, and created five new domestic advisory boards: first, the UAC, which became the Domestic Council; the Council on Environmental Quality (established at the initiative of Congress, but effectively utilized by Nixon); the Rural Affairs Council; a Council on Executive Reorganization; and a Council on International Economic Policy (CIEP).

Nixon established the Environmental Protection Agency (EPA) and recommended that the functions of the Atomic Energy Commission (AEC) be divided into two new agencies, the Nuclear Regulatory Commission and the Energy Research and Development Administration—both of which came into existence under President Ford. He also created the Office of Child Development and the National Oceanic and Atmospheric Administration. During the Nixon administration, the Bureau of the Budget was transformed into the Office of Management and Budget, whose monitoring and investigatory powers gave it greater influence than ever before on the budgets of all government agencies and departments.

When Nixon tried to implement certain reorganizational (and ideological) ideas by impounding federal funds and eliminating the Office of Economic Opportunity (OEO), the agency established under President Johnson to aid the poor, he antagonized liberals in Congress and the country at large. Believing that the functions of OEO "should be spun off into other departments," the president first appointed Donald Rumsfeld as OEO director. For nineteen months, Rumsfeld succeeded in reorganizing the bureaucracy of the agency without unnecessarily antagonizing either moderate liberals or conservatives. He accomplished this primarily by streamlining OEO into a more efficient bureaucracy; merging, farming out, or transferring some of its programs into other cabinet departments or government agencies; lowering its public profile; and weeding out the most obvious "advocate types," such as Terry Lenzer, the head of OEO's Legal Services Division. Nixon was so pleased with Rumsfeld's performance at OEO that in December, 1970, he appointed him as counselor to the president, leaving the ultimate dismantling of OEO to Howard Phillips, who as acting director ruined his own career in the process by alienating Republican as well as Democratic supporters of the agency.

While Nixon ultimately succeeded in abolishing OEO, federal courts ruled against most of the administration's attempts to impound funds earmarked by Congress for projects which the administration either opposed or viewed as exceeding the president's recommended budget ceilings. By 1973, Nixon had withheld eighteen billion dollars of appropriated congressional funds. In 1974, the Ninety-third Congress created the Budget Reform Act which gave itself, not the president, ultimate control over spending ceilings.

There is every indication that most of Nixon's recommendations for government reorganization encouraged a blurring or merging of functions between cabinet officers and members of his executive office. Although both sets of officials were appointed, not elected, the former did require congressional approval, while the latter did not. Therefore, after Congress delayed or turned down several of his major proposals for reorganizing the executive branch, Nixon decided following his landslide election in 1972 to call for the resignation of his entire cabinet and to create a set of four special counselors to the president, or "super-secretaries," to take charge of certain domestic bureaucracies; for example, the heads of Housing and Urban Development (HUD), HEW, the Treasury, and the Agriculture Department were to be given responsibility for Community Development, Human Resources, Economic Affairs, and Natural Resources, respectively. These super-secretaries would have had direct and frequent access to Nixon and his White House staff. In addition, he wanted to create a second line of subcabinet officials consisting largely of former or current White House aides to act as presidential assistants responsible for such broad functional areas as domestic affairs, economic affairs, foreign affairs, executive management, and White House coordination. This last Nixon reorganization plan also called for these super-secretaries or counselors and presidential assistants to operate as a "super-cabinet" in order to enhance White House control over the bureaucracy.

By the end of his first administration, Nixon had also clearly decided that he needed loyal "politician managers" in these key super-secretariat positions and in many of the more than two thousand appointed "plum" managerial jobs within the executive branch. Through his appointment powers he hoped to place loyalists throughout the top levels of government to ensure the implementation of the decentralized aspects of his New Federalism such as sharing with states and local communities, welfare reform, and the impounding of federal funds earmarked for projects in excess of the president's recommended ceiling. Yet all aspects of this comprehensive reorganization, announced following the 1972 election, failed to become institutionalized as details about Watergate began to emerge in 1973 and to occupy Nixon's attention for most of his truncated second term in office.

Foreign Policy: The Geopolitics of Nixon and Kissinger

At first glance, Nixon and Kissinger, his principal foreign policy adviser, appear to be an odd couple—an American Quaker and a German Jew. In fact, however, by the time they met in 1968, they shared many similar viewpoints and similar operational styles. Both of them thrived on covert activity and decisions reached in private, both distrusted the federal bureaucracy, and both agreed that the United States could impose order and stability in foreign affairs primarily through appearing and acting tough. Neither man had previously headed any complex organizational structure, but both thought that "personalized executive control" and formalistic procedures and structures would enable them to succeed in the area of their greatest combined experiences; namely, foreign policy. Finally, each had a history of previous failure and

Secretary of State Henry Kissinger meets with Chinese premier Chou En-lai in 1971. *(National Archives/Nixon Project)*

rejection by peer or government officials which made them very sensitive to protecting themselves and their positions of power from public and private criticism. Often their concern for self-protection was reflected in their obsession with all types of eavesdropping, whether in the form of wiretaps or reconnaissance flights over communist territory. They even eavesdropped on themselves: Nixon by installing an automatic taping system at the White House and Kissinger by having all of his phone conversations either taped or transcribed from notes.

With Nixon's approval, Kissinger quickly transformed the National Security Council system into a personal foreign policy secretariat. By subordinating the Senior Interdepartmental Group, formerly chaired by a representative of the State Department, to the Review Group, which he chaired, Kissinger effectively undercut the State Department's influence over policy making. Ultimately, he chaired six special committees operating out of the NSC. Moreover, he created interdepartmental committees that prepared policy studies which were submitted directly to his Review Group before

they were presented to the NSC or to the president. He also tried to provide a "conceptual framework" for American diplomacy by establishing a series of National Security Study Memoranda (NSSM). These were drafted by the NSC staff and signed by Kissinger on behalf of Nixon. They directed various agencies and groups within the government to prepare detailed policy options, not policy recommendations, which were then passed on by Kissinger to the NSC and argued out in front of the president.

The NSSM system was designed to prevent respondents, the State Department, and other executive departments from becoming advocates. By relegating them to analysis, the new NSC system supposedly put the bureaucrats in their "proper places." Even this elaborate restructuring did not completely satisfy the desire of the president and his secretary of state to control the process of foreign policy formulation. Most covert foreign policies of the Nixon administration, for example, bypassed the NSC. This says something quite significant about policy making under Nixon and the legacy he left in foreign affairs. When a decision could be carried out which did not rely upon the civilian or military bureaucracy for implementation, the NSC was ignored, regardless of whether the action was covert. It was utilized, however, whenever the covert or overt policy required bureaucratic support.

Using this guideline, it can be determined when the NSC system was employed as a debating forum for presenting options to the president, and when it was not. The NSC did not debate the concept of Vietnamization, the Nixon Doctrine, the secret Kissinger negotiations with North Vietnam, the international aspects of Nixon's New Economic Policy announced in August, 1970, the various attempts by the Central Intelligence Agency (CIA) to undermine the elected Marxist government of Salvador Allende of Chile, or the planning of Nixon's historic trip to China to redirect U.S. Asian policy vis-à-vis the Soviet Union. All these policies or actions were presented to the NSC, if at all, as faits accomplis. Yet, the NSC did debate and approve of the secret bombing of Cambodia and the mild response of the United States to the EC-121 incident in the first year of the Nixon administration. Later it played a role in such policy decisions as the attempt to keep Taiwan in the United Nations with a "two China" policy, the decision to conduct incursions into Cambodia and Laos, the détente agreements with the Soviet Union, and Middle Eastern diplomacy before the 1973 Yom Kippur War. The key to understanding this varied track record of the NSC rests in the amount of bureaucratic support at home and abroad necessary to carry out each of the policies. Nixon not only sought greater presidential control over the process of foreign policy formulation but also wanted to alter the basic assumptions of that policy.

In Kansas City, on July 6, 1971, Nixon laid down a five-power strategy which he hoped would replace the bipolar, confrontational aspects of the Cold War since 1945. Instead of continuing to deal bilaterally with the Soviet Union, Nixon hoped to bring the five great economic regions of the world—the United States, the Soviet Union, mainland China, Japan, and Western Europe—into constructive negotiation and mutually profitable economic competition. Admitting that the United States could not long maintain its post-World War II position of "complete preeminence or predominance," Nixon outlined a "pentagonal strategy" which would promote peace and economic progress among the major superpowers.

This meant that from the beginning of the Nixon administration entire areas of the world such as southern Asia, the Middle East, Africa, and Latin America—areas commonly referred to as the Third World—occupied a secondary place in the president's (and his secretary of state's) geopolitical approach to foreign policy. In particular, Nixon and Kissinger largely ignored economic foreign policy considerations in dealing with the Third World. This neglect accounts for the seemingly erratic aspects of U.S. foreign policy in Third World areas which fell outside the parameters of pentagonal strategy. Nixon was more interested in maintaining American spheres of influence in the Third World than in the economic needs of individual countries falling within this designation. Thus, the United States promoted the overthrow of Allende in Chile, restrained Egyptian and Syrian aggression in the Middle East while ignoring the potential instability of the Shah's regime in Iran and indirectly encouraging the rise of Organization of Petroleum Exporting Countries (OPEC) oil prices, continued to oppose Fidel Castro in Cuba, and supported Pakistan against India. The grand design may have been "grand" by superpower standards, but it remained ineffectually grandiose with respect to the Third World.

Vietnam: Too Little, Too Late

Nevertheless, the first and in many ways foremost problem that Nixon faced in foreign affairs involved the Third World. He had inherited from his predecessor a war in Southeast Asia in which the United States fought to prevent the fall of the government of South Vietnam to internal communist subversion and an attack from North Vietnam which had the support of China and the Soviet Union. Although Nixon had talked in his campaign of a secret plan to end the war, he still thought the noncommunist government in the South could be, and should be, preserved even though growing domestic opposition to the war meant that he had to reduce the American role in the conflict. Nixon therefore followed a policy which came to be called Vietnamization in which greater efforts were made to strengthen the South Vietnamese army and to turn over to it more of the ground combat operations. This then allowed Nixon to reduce the number of American troops in Vietnam. Even as he pursued Vietnamization, however, Nixon still sought to prevent a communist victory in South Vietnam and soon adopted dramatic means to avoid one.

Nixon's Secretary of Defense Melvin Laird, on the other hand, had two primary goals: to end the war and to end the draft. While neither of these goals turned Laird into a dove, they made him one of the few true believers in the policy of Vietnamization—a term he coined—and the behind-the-scenes architect of the Nixon Doctrine. Vietnamization and the Nixon Doctrine are logical extensions of each other because the former called for South Vietnamese troops to replace Americans, while the latter called for American allies in general to be prepared to undertake their own ground fighting in the future. These views made him question the extension of the war into Cambodia and Laos. Unlike Nixon and Kissinger, Laird was more interested in ending the war in Vietnam than in winning it at any cost.

The Nixon Doctrine represents the internationalization of the policy of Vietnamization or, at the very least, its blanket application to the Far East. As such, its purpose was

to provide a shield if a nuclear power threatens the freedom of any nation allied with us . . . in cases involving other types of aggression we shall furnish military and economic assistance when requested in accordance with our treaty commitments. But we shall look to the nation directly threatened to assume the primary responsibility for the manpower for its defense.

Clearly, the subsequent invasions of Cambodia and Laos violated the intent if not the letter of the Nixon Doctrine. Laird and others pointed out this contradiction at NSC meetings, while Kissinger reportedly insisted: "We wrote the goddam doctrine, we can change it."

The guarded secret decision to bomb Cambodia and the general widening of the war to include Laos also can be understood only in relation to other actions which were undertaken around the same time. These included Vietnamization, the unilateral withdrawal of American troops, and stepped up negotiations with the Viet Cong in Paris. In December, 1968, under President Johnson, the Joint Chiefs of Staff had originally requested "standby authority . . . to pursue North Vietnam Army/Viet Cong (NVA/VC) Forces into Cambodia following major enemy offensives mounted and supported in Cambodia" in December, 1968. The Joint Chiefs of Staff simply reiterated this position to the new Nixon administration when asked on January 21, 1969 (NSSM no. 1), to provide a "study of the feasibility and utility of quarantining Cambodia."

Since 1966, LBJ had refused to consider a mutual, let alone a unilateral, withdrawal of American troops from Vietnam. (Whether they realized it or not, the Joint Chiefs of Staff had more bargaining power on the questions of whether to bomb and/or invade Cambodia because of Vietnamization, Nixon's private commitment to a gradual pullout of U.S. soldiers and, above all, his desire for better relations with China which precluded bombing enemy sanctuaries there.) Early attempts at rapprochement with China automatically made

Cambodian sanctuaries ideal substitutes with which to placate the Joint Chiefs of Staff, who did not approve of rapid Vietnamization and troop withdrawal.

Laird, however, insisted that "because of the political implications of bombing Cambodia, the entire NSC should review the policy." This review took place on March 16, 1969, and the secret sorties began two days later under the general code name MENU with the exact target areas given the unsavory titles BREAKFAST, LUNCH, DINNER, SUPPER, DESSERT, and SNACK. From March 18, 1969, to May 1, 1970, these bombings remained secret. Thus the bombing of Cambodia was one of the few truly covert foreign policy undertakings of the Nixon administration which received full NSC consideration.

Although Nixon came to office committed to ending the war in Vietnam through negotiations, he ended up expanding and prolonging the conflict. As a result, he could never build the domestic consensus he needed to continue the escalated air and ground war, even with dramatically reduced U.S. troop involvement, and to ensure passage of some of his domestic programs. For Nixon (and Kissinger), Vietnam became a symbol of influence in the Third World which, in turn, was but one part of their geopolitical or grand design approach to international relations. Thus the war in Southeast Asia had to be settled as soon as possible so as not to endanger other elements of Nixonian diplomacy and domestic policy.

According to his book *No More Vietnams* (1985), the president viewed that conflict as military, moral, and global. Consequently, he first sought to bring military pressure to bear on the North Vietnamese in order to speed up the negotiating process. There is little indication, however, that this approach succeeded, because the Viet Cong correctly counted on opposition in the United States to the announced bombing and invasion of Cambodia in April, 1970, and of Laos in February, 1971. In like manner, Nixon's commitment to the war as a "moral cause" did not ring true, as the carnage in that civil war increased despite American troop withdrawals. Finally, the president never succeeded in convincing the country that quick withdrawal from Vietnam would "damage American strategic interests" all over the world. Congress did abolish the draft, and Nixon continued to bring U.S. troops home. These actions

---

Excerpts from Richard M. Nixon's speech regarding the invasion of Cambodia by American and South Vietnamese forces, April 30, 1970:

If, when the chips are down, the world's most powerful nation, the United States of America, acts like a pitiful, helpless giant, the forces of totalitarianism and anarchy will threaten free nations and free institutions throughout the world.

It is not our power but our will and character that is being tested tonight. The question all Americans must ask and answer tonight is this: Does the richest and strongest nation in the history of the world have the character to meet a direct challenge by a group which rejects every effort to win a just peace, ignores our warning, tramples on solemn agreements, violates the neutrality of an unarmed people, and uses our prisoners as hostages?

If we fail to meet this challenge, all other nations will be on notice that despite its overwhelming power the United States, when a real crisis comes, will be found wanting. . . .

I would rather be a one-term President and do what is right than to be a two-term President at the cost of seeing America become a second-rate power and to see this Nation accept the first defeat in its proud 190-year history.

---

diminished the size of antiwar demonstrations beginning in 1971, but opposition to the war in Vietnam continued in Congress. Nixon had failed to convince many of its members and their constituents that the conflict in this tiny Third World country warranted the military, moral, and global importance he attributed to it.

Instead, the president allowed his secretary of state to become involved in secret negotiations with the North Vietnamese from August 4, 1969, to January 25, 1972 (when they were made public). As a result, only marginally better terms were finally reached in 1973 which had not been agreed to in 1969. The trade-off between Hanoi's agreement that President Nguyen Van Thieu could remain in power in return for allowing Hanoi's troops to remain in place in South Vietnam pales when compared to the additional twenty thousand American lives lost during this three-year period—especially when the inherent weaknesses of the Saigon government by 1973 are taken into consideration.

On the tenth anniversary of the peace treaty ending the war in Vietnam, Nixon acknowledged that "Kissinger believed more in the power of negotiation than I did." He also said that he "would not have temporized as long" with the negotiating process had he not been "needlessly" concerned with what the Soviets and Chinese might think if the United States pulled out of Vietnam precipitately. Because Nixon saw no way to end the war quickly in 1969 except through overt, massive bombing attacks which the public demonstrated it would not tolerate in 1970 and 1971, there was neither peace nor honor in Vietnam by the time that war was finally concluded on January 27, 1973.

Shuttle Diplomacy: The Middle East

A long overdue full-scale NSC debate over American Middle East policy took place in an all-day session on February 1, 1969. This meeting established the basic goals of the United States for the 1970's; namely, substantial Israeli withdrawal from occupied territory in exchange for contractual and practical security arrangements with Egypt. Unfortunately, however, it adopted the least successful means of the entire decade for achieving these goals, the Rogers Plan, which called for American-Soviet agreement on a comprehensive peace settlement in the Middle East and for a more "evenhanded" public posture toward both the Israelis and the Arabs. This policy of evenhandedness had been tentatively proposed by Governor William Scranton, Nixon's special, preinauguration envoy to the Middle East.

Until President Reagan and his Secretary of State George Shultz affirmed a joint military-political cooperation with Israel at the end of 1983, no American president or secretary of state formally disavowed the general principle of evenhandedness established at the February, 1969, NSC meeting. Yet these principles had been breached more than honored in the intervening fourteen years. Even the original attempt to obtain them through the Rogers Plan lasted only a year.

There are several reasons why the plan of Nixon's first secretary of state would probably have failed even if it had not been sabotaged by Henry Kissinger. From the beginning, the Rogers Plan was based on two untenable assumptions: that the Soviet Union would agree to become a joint peacemaker with the United States and would pressure Gamel Abdel Nasser of Egypt into accepting a compromise peace based on U.N. Resolution 242, which had been adopted in 1967 and called for an Israeli withdrawal from lands it had occupied, but also for peace and the recognition of the right of every state in the area to a peaceful existence; and that a publicly impartial stance toward Israel and the Arabs would enhance the American bargaining position with both sides in a way that previous pro-Israeli statements had not. Israel and Egypt both opposed the Rogers Plan when it became public at the end of 1969 because it was an obvious attempt by the Big Two (or in this case the Big One) to impose a settlement.

Aside from the Nixon Doctrine, the new Republican administration did not appear to have a positive alternative to the Rogers Plan, which was rejected by the Soviet Union in October, 1969, until after the Yom Kippur War. From the time of the 1970 crisis in Jordan through the 1973 war, the United States appeared to pursue a policy of stalemate. At the most, the stalemate policy seemed to consist of using sporadic behavior modification techniques on Israel beginning in the spring and summer of 1970. For example, on two occasions promises to Israel of more military equipment were deferred in an attempt to prevent any untoward actions against Jordan when that country appeared on the verge of falling apart.

The years from 1969 to 1973 can be considered an incubation period for the Nixon administration's Middle East policy. At the end of the Yom Kippur War, Kissinger's step-by-step disengagement policy, otherwise known as shuttle diplomacy, emerged full-blown. This approach was not only piecemeal and stopgap in nature but also essentially bilateral, although Kissinger's frantic shuttling about gave the false impression of creating multilateral arrangements. He soon fell into the post-Yom Kippur War habit of telling the Israelis and Arabs what they wanted to hear, sometimes exceeding both congressional and White House intentions. Finally, in the wake of the Yom Kippur War, Kissinger no longer called for expulsion of the Soviet Union from the area. Instead, Anwar el-Sadat's independent expulsion of Soviet personnel was viewed as a hopeful model. Rather than further polarize the Arabs into moderate and militant camps, the administration deemed it possible that Arab nationalism would assert itself against Soviet imperialism.

The 1973 Yom Kippur War broke the stalemate that since 1969 had substituted for American policy in the Middle East. "It took the war to unfreeze the positions" on both sides, Kissinger later told an aide. By the time this breakthrough occurred, the stalemate had cost the United States more than Kissinger could ever gain back, even though it freed him to play hopscotch diplomacy among Middle Eastern countries. Seyom Brown in *The Crisis of Power* (1979) and others have documented that there was little substance to show for all of Kissinger's shuttling.

Détente with China and the Soviet Union

Nixon's most lasting foreign policy achievements remain improved relations with China and the Soviet Union, including a strategic arms limitation agreement with the latter. Détente is the term most often used to describe the results of his overtures to both countries. Détente literally means "the relaxing or easing of tensions between nations." Normalization of U.S. relations with China was part of the president's grand design to bring this giant communist nation into the ranks of the superpowers. Long before Nixon sent Kissinger on a secret mission to Peking in July, 1971, to arrange the details of his visit there the following year, the administration had been indicating to the Chinese through various unilateral gestures of reconciliation that it wanted to make fundamental improvements in economic and scholarly exchanges.

Although various government officials publicly denied that Nixon courted China in order to bring pressure to bear on the Soviet Union, the president's highly publicized visit to the People's Republic of China in February, 1972 (with its attendant joint communique), did not go unnoticed by Soviet leaders. The China trip is, therefore, indirectly linked to the success of negotiations leading to the ten formal agreements between the United States and the Soviet Union in May, 1972. The most important of these agreements provided for

Nixon tours the Great Wall of China in 1972. *(National Archives/Nixon Project)*

Union which the Senate approved. The agreement included a treaty limiting the deployment of antiballistic missiles (ABMs) to two for each country, and it froze the number of offensive intercontinental ballistic missiles (ICBMs) at the level of those then under production or deployed. SALT I, in essence, established a rough balance between the nuclear arsenals of the two superpowers, despite the "missiles gaps" which continued to exist between them in specific weapons. For example, when Nixon signed SALT I, the United States had a total of 1,710 missiles: 1,054 land-based ICBMs and 656 on submarines. The Soviet Union had a total of 2,358 missiles: 1,618 land-based ICBMs and 740 on submarines. SALT I by no means stopped the nuclear arms race, but it recognized that unregulated weapons competition between the two superpowers could no longer be rationally condoned.

prevention of military incidents at sea and in the air; scholarly cooperation and exchange in the fields of science and technology; cooperation in health research; cooperation in environmental matters; cooperation in the exploration of outer space; facilitation of commercial and economic relations; and, most important, arms control.

In the area of arms control, Nixon's détente strategy contained the potential not only to substitute for containment, the central premise of United States foreign policy since the 1940's which was directed at stopping Soviet expansion in the world, but also to transcend the Procrustean ideological constraints which were at the very heart of the post-World War II conflict between these two nations. This potential was never fully realized, in part because Nixon's successors proved unable to build upon the delicate balance between containment and détente which he left behind.

Nevertheless, the Strategic Arms Limitation Talks (SALT) conducted in Helsinki in 1969 and in Vienna in 1970 led to the two arms control agreements which Nixon signed in Moscow in 1972. SALT I was the only arms control agreement between the United States and the Soviet

Watergate

Despite his obvious achievements in foreign and domestic policy, a 1982 national poll of U.S. specialists rated the thirty-seventh president of the United States a failure, along with Andrew Johnson, James Buchanan, Ulysses S. Grant, and Warren G. Harding. There was one reason for this overwhelmingly negative evaluation—Watergate—a word which will forever be associated with the presidency of Richard Milhous Nixon, although not with the same emotional fervor. Watergate swept the country in 1973 and 1974 as no scandal involving the highest officials of government had since the Teapot Dome scandal in the 1920's, and for good reason.

The cover-up by the president and his top aides of the original break-in at Democratic National Committee Headquarters in Washington, D.C., on June 17, 1972, and of related corrupt or criminal political activities ultimately resulted in the indictment, conviction, and sentencing of fifteen men, including the top White House aides to Nixon (Ehrlichman and Haldeman), the White House counsel (John W. Dean III), a special assistant to the president (Charles Colson), one former cabinet member (Attorney General John Mitchell, Jr.), and ten others who worked for the Committee for the Re-election of the President (CREEP) or the White House "plumbers'" unit which was engaged in break-ins before Watergate occurred. In addition to these men in whom public trust had been placed, four Cubans arrested in the Watergate complex also served time for their participation in the original crime.

At one level, therefore, Watergate can be viewed as dirty politics, carried to its logical and, in this instance, illegal extreme. At another level, however, Watergate is inextricably related to the war in Indochina, in particular, and in general to the wartime standards of behavior which had prevailed since the onset of the Cold War. This quasi-war atmosphere had slowly eroded public sensitivity to moral and ethical issues in foreign policy. The first wiretaps of the Nixon administration on the friends, acquaintances, and employees of Henry Kissinger were all undertaken in the name of national security. Likewise, the first break-in by the plumbers' unit at the office of Daniel Ellsberg's psychiatrist had nothing to do with partisan politics, but with the release of the Pentagon Papers (which Ellsberg had leaked to the press) in June, 1971.

Until the mid-1960's, only a few knowledgeable Americans knew about constitutional violations incurred in the battle against communism under various presidents since World War II, and they were, for the most part, either indifferent or curiously enthusiastic. Most Americans, however, remained largely ignorant of the escalating illegal activities of the CIA, the increased spying on United States citizens by the Federal Bureau of Investigation (FBI), and the clandestine plans for overthrowing governments or assassinating their leaders under presidents Truman, Eisenhower, Kennedy, and Johnson. As the war in Vietnam dragged on with no clear-cut victory in sight, more and more Americans became aware of the inherent dangers to the Constitution in the methods for conducting U.S. foreign policy which had evolved during the decades of Cold War.

The United States has never fought a war without violating the constitutional rights of its citizens. Vietnam was no exception. What was exceptional was the increased sensitivity of people toward violations of the Constitution in the conduct of foreign and domestic policy. Many people had their consciousnesses raised about such violations because of their association with the Civil Rights movement of the late 1950's and the 1960's. When Nixon assumed office, he did so as a wartime president. As far as the White House was concerned, a wartime atmosphere prevailed that warranted traditional wartime violations of the Constitution.

By 1969, the fighting had been going on inconsequentially for too many years. Thus a significant and vocal portion of the population began to question the White House and Congress about the conduct of the war. The scattered, often regionally isolated cases of antiwar protests begun during the Johnson administration became nationally coordinated and epidemic under the Nixon administration. More important than the demonstrations, however, was the fact that public-opinion leaders across the country and the elite group of opinion makers during the second Johnson administration began to disagree with one another.

It would prove easier to unite the American people behind his efforts to end the war, and even behind certain domestic policies, than it would be to reunite the elite opinion makers as he wound down the war. Nixon's real problem and the reason that he could not get away with wartime actions which disregarded the Constitution, as presidents had in the past, was that a substantial group of influential bureaucrats, policy makers, opinion leaders, and numerous students opposed him. Largely white and middle class with draft-exempt status, these students constituted an important elite group of future American leaders.

If he ever intended to deal successfully with a divided elite, Nixon had to reestablish consensus at both the public and elite levels. His election victory in 1972 represented a partial success with the former, but it did nothing to bring around the disaffected elite groups which every president must have behind him, especially in time of war. As Nicholas Hoffman has said, "Nixon was the first American President since Lincoln to guide the nation through a war that fundamentally divided the ruling classes." Abraham Lincoln, after all, had closed down newspapers and suspended writs of habeas corpus to keep Copperheads in jail during the Civil War. Nixon did not have the luxury of such direct unconstitutional actions because the civil war he faced was in Vietnam, not in the United States. Yet his paranoia about antiwar activists was no less than Lincoln's, and some would claim that Nixon acted as though those in opposition to the war were fomenting another civil war in the United States. At least he probably came to believe it was easier to fight an incipient civil war at home than the real one in Vietnam.

Indeed, there was a civil war going on among the American opinion leaders. Wartime presidents had traditionally silenced dissent and attacked with impunity such powerless

The Watergate complex in Washington, D.C., in 1971. (Copyright Washington Post. Reprinted by permission of D.C. Public Library)

715

groups as Japanese Americans, self-proclaimed socialists and communists, or assorted first- and second-generation European immigrants. Nixon, in contrast, had no choice but to take on the so-called best and brightest among the policy-making elite. His unique dilemma raises the very interesting question: What realistic avenues are open to any president who challenges an influential segment of the establishment? It was in Nixon's political and psychic self-interest to end a war that fundamentally divided many of the best and brightest.

Clearly, his aides came to the conclusion that this monumental task could be undertaken only by what has been called a "pickup team of greedy amateurs and romantics." In other words, they decided that the best and the brightest had to be defeated by the middling and the mediocre. G. Gordon Liddy and E. Howard Hunt were, at best, "second-rate second-story" men. The "third-rate" burglaries they planned and ineptly executed are a testimony to their incompetence. Apparently, Hunt and Liddy did not realize that Larry O'Brien and other Democratic Party officials had already moved the bulk of their campaign operation to Florida by the time of the second break-in on June 17. Moreover, because no strong potential candidate had emerged to oppose Nixon, the Democratic Party was in such a state of disarray by the summer of 1972 that some implied there was nothing to find out, let alone expose, at Democratic National Headquarters. All that men such as Liddy and Hunt knew how to do was to break in, photograph, and bug, however counterproductive such acts had proven previously with Ellsberg's psychiatrist.

Although Jim Hougan suggests in *Secret Agenda: Watergate, Deep Throat and the CIA* (1984) that both James W. McCord, Jr., and Hunt were still working for the CIA to expose a sex-ring operation which would have compromised certain prominent Democrats, there is no conclusive proof that this was the case. A possible connection between Howard Hughes and Nixon—namely, $100,000 purportedly paid to the president's friend Charles (Bebe) Rebozo— still appears to be the most likely reason for the May and June break-ins because of the fear that O'Brien had knowledge of this transaction. No reason put forth to date satisfactorily explains the criminal break-in at the Watergate complex.

The arrest of McCord, Bernard Baker, Virgilio Gonzalez, Eugenio Martinez, and Frank Sturgis after Frank Wills, the night watchman at the Watergate, discovered adhesive tape not once, but twice, on basement doors of the expensive office and apartment complex in Washington, D.C., set off a series of events and investigations unprecedented in U.S. history. This burglary culminated a series of political dirty tricks authorized by CREEP beginning in the fall of 1971. Most of these activities, including two Watergate break-ins (the first had occurred over Memorial Day weekend), were approved by Attorney General Mitchell and presidential counsel Dean. President Nixon learned of the burglars' connections with CREEP and White House personnel on June 20, 1972, and on June 23 he agreed with the recommendations of Mitchell, Dean, and Haldeman that the CIA should prevent an FBI investigation of the Watergate break-in on grounds of national security. The CIA did not comply with the president's attempt to obstruct justice in a criminal matter and the investigation moved forward, but not until after the 1972 presidential election.

Even before the release of the "smoking gun" tape of June 23 on August 5, 1974, which revealed how early Nixon had been involved in the cover-up, the Watergate Special Prosecution Task Force headed by Texas attorney Leon Jaworski had concluded by the end of June, 1974, that

beginning no later than March 21, 1973, the President joined an ongoing criminal conspiracy to obstruct justice, obstruct a criminal investigation, and commit perjury (which included pay-

President Nixon during the press conference releasing the transcripts of the Watergate tapes on April 29, 1974. *(NARA)*

ment of cash to Watergate defendants to influence their testimony, making and causing to be made false statements and declarations, making offers of clemency and leniency, and obtaining information from the Justice Department to thwart its investigation) and that the President is also liable for substantive violations of various criminal statutes.

All these actions had taken place in the space of two years—from the summer of 1972 to the summer of 1974. Early in 1973, Federal Judge John J. Sirica used heavy-handed legal tactics by threatening the Watergate defendants with tough sentences unless they told the truth. As McCord and others began to talk about payoffs from the White House, illegal campaign contribution evidence began to surface. Nixon fired Haldeman, Ehrlichman, Dean, and Mitchell by formally accepting their resignations of April 30, after he admitted on May 22

that they had been involved in a White House cover-up without his knowledge. Dean then decided to testify before the Senate Select Committee on Presidential Campaign Activities (the Ervin Committee), and from June 25 to 29 he accused the president of being involved. Among other things, testimony before this committee disclosed the existence of a White House "enemies list" of prominent politicians, journalists, academics, and entertainers, who had been singled out for various types of harassment, including Internal Revenue Service (IRS) audits. In July, Alexander Butterfield, a former White House assistant, revealed, almost inadvertently, in responding to questions from the Ervin Committee, that Nixon had a voice-activated taping system in the Oval Office.

From this point forward, various attempts to obtain these tapes from the White House failed until July 24, 1974, when the Supreme

Court ruled in *United States v. Nixon* that the president could not retain subpoenaed tapes by claiming executive privilege. During this protracted struggle, Archibald Cox, the first special prosecutor appointed to investigate Watergate, acting on behalf of a federal grand jury, also tried to gain access to the tapes. When Cox rejected a compromise proposed by Nixon, the president ordered both Attorney General Elliot Richardson and Deputy Attorney General William D. Ruckelshaus to fire the special prosecutor. Refusing to do so, they resigned. On October 20, 1973, an acting attorney general finally carried out Nixon's order, but this "Saturday Night Massacre" was subsequently ruled an illegal violation of Justice Department procedures in *Nader v. Bork*. This incident also created such negative public opinion that the president agreed to turn over nine subpoenaed tapes to Judge Sirica, only to announce on October 31 that two of the tapes did not exist and on November 26 that a third had an unexplained eighteen-and-a-half minute gap in it—an erasure which remains unexplained.

Finally, on October 30, 1973, the House Judiciary Committee, headed by Peter Rodino, began preliminary investigations. In April, 1974, it launched a full-scale impeachment inquiry which led on July 27 to a vote recommending the impeachment of the president. Nixon resigned from office on August 9, rather than face an impeachment trial. On September 8, President Gerald Ford (whom Nixon had appointed after Vice President Agnew resigned in the midst of, but for reasons unrelated to, Watergate on October 10, 1973) unconditionally pardoned the former president for all federal crimes he may have committed or been a party to, freeing Nixon from any criminal or civil liability in the Watergate affair. Questions about whether a deal had been struck between Ford and Nixon over this pardon before the latter resigned contributed to Ford's defeat by Democrat Jimmy Carter in the 1976 election.

The legacy of Watergate lies in the fact that it precipitated a demand for accountability on the part of government officials and a demand for greater public access to government informa-

---

Excerpt from Richard M. Nixon's resignation speech, August 8, 1974:

In all the decisions I have made in my public life, I have always tried to do what was best for the nation. Throughout the long and difficult period of Watergate, I have felt it was my duty to persevere, to make every possible effort to complete the term of office to which you elected me. . . .

I would have preferred to carry through to the finish whatever the personal agony it would have involved, and my family unanimously urged me to do so. But the interest of the nation must always come before any personal considerations. From the discussions I have had with congressional and other leaders, I have concluded that because of the Watergate matter I might not have the support of the Congress that I would consider necessary to back the very difficult decisions and carry out the duties of this office in the way the interests of the nation would require. I have never been a quitter. To leave office before my term is completed is abhorrent to every instinct in my body. But as president, I must put the interest of America first. America needs a full-time president and a full-time Congress, particularly at this time with problems we face at home and abroad.

To continue to fight through the months ahead for my personal vindication would almost totally absorb the time and attention of both the president and the Congress in a period when our entire focus should be on the great issues of peace abroad and prosperity without inflation at home.

Therefore, I shall resign the presidency effective at noon tomorrow. Vice President Ford will be sworn in as president at that hour in this office.

tion. Thus, Watergate directly or indirectly produced a series of reforms for elections, financing political campaigns, and ensuring greater public access to secret or classified documents. These reforms specifically included the establishment of the Federal Election Commission, the Congressional Budget Office, the War Powers Act, the 1974 and 1978 Presidential Materials and Preservation Acts, and the 1974 amendments to the Freedom of Information Act. In addition, Congress agreed to open conference committees to public scrutiny and the Democratic Party continued its efforts (which had begun before Watergate) to reform the primary system, with the Republican Party following suit. Unfortunately, most of these congressional acts and reforms have since been violated, watered down, or contradicted by presidential actions. Some have created unforeseen additional problems, such as the uncontrolled financing of candidates by political action committees (PACs), overly complicated ethical standard requirements, and the automatic triggering of special prosecutor investigations in response to trivial incidents.

The break-in itself was a disaster looking for a place to happen—given the decline in political ethics over many years prior to Nixon's presidency. Nixon obstructed justice thereafter for two years and got away with it as president of the United States, a dramatic performance if ever there was one. It was hoped that Watergate's legacy would be the prevention of unconstitutional and unethical behavior. The impeachment trial of President Bill Clinton twenty-five years later raised many of the same concerns—obstruction of justice, misuse of executive power—in the context of sexual scandal. Some tried to establish direct links between the two cases, finding common ethical issues, while others pointed to differences in criminal action and scope. Whether such comparisons are valid, the Clinton impeachment led many people to revisit the "national nightmare" called Watergate.

Nixon's reputation was revisited during the 1980's and especially following his death on April 22, 1994, in New York City, at the age of eighty-one. Clinton and former presidents Ford, Carter, and George Bush were all in attendance at his funeral (Reagan was too ill to attend), and the nation seemed ready to look at the whole picture of his political career, not merely its ignominious end.

Joan Hoff-Wilson

Suggested Readings

Aitken, Jonathan. *Nixon: A Life*. Washington, D.C.: Regnery, 1993. Written with full cooperation of Nixon, who granted the author interviews and access to his diaries.

Colodny, Len, and Robert Gettlin. *Silent Coup: The Removal of a President*. New York: St. Martin's Press, 1991. A solid reevaluation of the Watergate era.

Genovese, Michael A. *The Nixon Presidency: Power and Politics in Turbulent Times*. Westport, Conn.: Greenwood Press, 1991. Gives an overview of the legacy of the Nixon presidency.

Kimball, Jeffrey P. *The Vietnam War Files: Uncovering the Secret History of Nixon-Era Strategy*. Lawrence: University Press of Kansas, 2004. Draws on more than 140 print documents and taped White House conversations bearing on Nixon-era strategy in order to provide an in-depth study of Nixon's war policy.

Kutler, Stanley I., ed. *Abuse of Power: The New Nixon Tapes*. New York: Free Press, 1997. A good distillation of more than two hundred hours of secret Nixon tapes released in 1996.

Litwak, Robert. *Détente and the Nixon Doctrine: American Foreign Policy and the Pursuit of Strategy*. New York: Cambridge University Press, 1984. Provides good detail on the relationship between the two concepts.

Lukas, J. Anthony. *Nightmare: The Underside of the Nixon Years*. New York: Viking, 1976. Among the best-documented accounts of Watergate.

Matthews, Christopher. *Kennedy and Nixon: The Rivalry That Shaped Postwar America*. New York: Simon & Schuster, 1996. A fascinating study of the rivalry that began between the two men with their elections to the House of Representatives in 1946.

Morris, Roger. *Richard Milhous Nixon: The Rise of an American Politician*. New York: Holt, 1990. Details the years from Nixon's birth in 1913 to his vice presidential campaign of 1952.

Nixon, Richard M. *RN: The Memoirs of Richard Nixon*. 1978. Reprint. New York: Grosset & Dunlap, 1990. Nixon's autobiography.

Reeves, Richard. *President Nixon: Alone in the White House*. New York: Simon & Schuster, 2001. Uses thousands of interviews and declassified documents and tapes to detail the isolation that Nixon fostered both for himself and for his administration.

Safire, William. *Before the Fall*. Garden City, N.Y.: Doubleday, 1975. Safire, who served as a speechwriter for Nixon, writes a valuable insider's account.

Schoenebaum, Eleanor W. *Profiles of an Era: The Nixon-Ford Years*. New York: Harcourt, 1979. A short, straightforward biographical account of Nixon as well as 450 biographical sketches of key figures in his administration.

Shawcross, William. *Sideshow: Kissinger, Nixon, and the Destruction of Cambodia*. 1979. Rev. ed. New York: Cooper Square Press, 2002. A valuable interpretation of Nixon's expansion of the war in Indochina.

Small, Melvin. *Presidency of Richard Nixon*. Lawrence: University Press of Kansas, 1999. A balanced biography that takes a topical approach to the critical domestic and foreign policy initiatives of the Nixon administration.

Strober, Gerald S., and Deborah H. Strober. *Nixon: An Oral History of His Presidency*. New York: HarperCollins, 1994. Based on interviews of key figures in the administration, journalists, opponents, and more, the book focuses on the entire Nixon presidency.

Walker, Anne Collins. *China Calls: Paving the Way for Nixon's Historic Journey to China*. Lanham, Md.: Madison Books, 1992. A fascinating behind-the-scenes account of how the trip to China came together, based on telephone transcripts of the White House team and Chinese officials.

Wicker, Tom. *One of Us: Richard Nixon and the American Dream*. New York: Random House, 1991. Examines the people, places, and events that shaped Nixon's character.

Wills, Garry. *Nixon Agonistes: The Crisis of the Self-Made Man*. 1970. Reprint. Boston: Houghton Mifflin, 2002. One of the most enduring interpretative accounts of Nixon's political life.

Witcher, Russ, ed. *Articles, Interviews, and Book Excerpts (1976-2000) on Richard Nixon's Legacy*. Lewiston, N.Y.: Edwin Mellen Press, 2003. A collection of twenty excerpts from American journalism between 1976 and 2000 that examine the Nixon legacy.

Gerald R. Ford

38th President, 1974-1977

Born: July 14, 1913
     Omaha, Nebraska

Political Party: Republican
Vice President: Nelson A. Rockefeller

Cabinet Members

Secretary of State: Henry Kissinger
Secretary of the Treasury: William Simon
Secretary of Defense: James R. Schlesinger,
    Donald H. Rumsfeld
Attorney General: William B. Saxbe, Edward H.
    Levi
Secretary of the Interior: Rogers C. B. Morton,
    Stanley K. Hathaway, Thomas D. Kleppe
Secretary of Agriculture: Earl L. Butz, John
    Knebel
Secretary of Commerce: Frederick B. Dent,
    Rogers C. B. Morton, Elliot Richardson
Secretary of Labor: Peter J. Brennan, John T.
    Dunlop, W. J. Usery
Secretary of Health, Education, and Welfare:
    Caspar Weinberger, Forrest D. Mathews
Secretary of Housing and Urban Development:
    James T. Lynn, Carla A. Hills
Secretary of Transportation: Claude S. Brinegar,
    William T. Coleman

The first person to occupy both the presidency and the vice presidency without being elected to either office, Gerald Rudolph Ford, Jr., succeeded the first president to resign, fellow Republican Richard M. Nixon. Ford's unelected (and somewhat unexpected) appearance in the White House occurred in troubled times for many Americans. The domestic economy suffered from increasing unemployment and in-

flation. In Southeast Asia, the Saigon regime neared collapse following the almost total withdrawal of American forces from a war in Vietnam that had become equally costly, futile, and unpopular. At home, with the national bicentennial less than two years away, Ameri-

Ford's official portrait. *(White House Historical Society)*

721

cans were stunned and dismayed by the rapid decline in the credibility, and subsequent resignation under threat of impeachment, of President Nixon, who had only recently been reelected by a landslide.

Initially popular if not popularly chosen, President Ford brought with him to the White House a quarter century of experience in the House of Representatives. He also addressed his presidential responsibilities with energy, knowledge, and determination. Ford, however, retained from the discredited Nixon administration many White House advisers and cabinet officers from whom he never established sufficient independence and over whom he did not adequately impose his own initiatives and authority. Consequently, Ford himself was largely responsible for the frag-

mentation and turbulence of his staff, whose effectiveness was diminished by constant infighting between Nixon and Ford loyalists.

Problems soon surfaced. Less than a month after becoming president, Ford granted a "full, free and absolute pardon" to his afflicted and vulnerable predecessor, confirming the suspicions of many that Ford had concocted a deal with former president Nixon before the latter's resignation. These realities led to Democratic insinuations in 1976 that the Ford administration was an extension of the unsavory Watergate era rather than its resolution.

Two later mishaps contributed to President Ford's loss of public confidence and his ultimate failure to win the 1976 election. After his aircraft landed in Salzburg, Austria, in June, 1975, Ford slipped on a wet, rubberless metal

The Ford family in 1960. *(Gerald R. Ford Library)*

THE FIRST LADY
BETTY FORD

Elizabeth Ann "Betty" Bloomer was born on April 8, 1918, and married Gerald R. Ford on October 15, 1948. The marriage would mark the second one for her and the first for him. While being a divorcée was an uncommon trait for a First Lady, Betty Ford would prove to be a nontraditional First Lady in other ways.

Betty Ford is often looked to as the bridge to the modern First Lady because of her public stance on controversial topics and her willingness to be open and frank at all times. She thought that her office could be a platform for forcing change in substantive areas. Most notably, she decided to work toward achieving greater rights for women. Not only did she become a vocal supporter of the Supreme Court abortion rights decision in *Roe v. Wade* but she also aggressively campaigned for the Equal Rights Amendment (ERA). Although Betty Ford is remembered for her outspoken advocacy of causes that mattered to her, she is also remembered for her ability to give of herself openly in order to help others.

On September 26, 1974, Betty Ford was diagnosed with breast cancer. Rather than keep this a secret, as many families tended to do, she went public and disclosed her disease and her treatment, a mastectomy. Letting the public know about this very private incident made it more acceptable for other women to get check-ups for cancer, get treatment if needed, and handle the pain of the disease. Betty Ford was given credit for saving countless lives with this single act, which helped to establish her reputation as being honest and forthright. Toward the end of the Ford presidency, her attitude and candor left her with approval ratings that surpassed those of her husband.

Unlike many other First Ladies, Betty Ford continued to make her mark after leaving office. In 1978, she disclosed that she had developed an addiction problem and was undergoing treatment. Once again, her public disclosure of a personal problem made it possible for others to seek help—many felt that if Betty Ford could do it, so could they. She went on to establish the famous Betty Ford Center for alcohol and drug treatment and remained active in the day-to-day operations of it.

Jeffrey S. Ashley

---

boarding ramp, almost falling at the feet of welcoming Austrian Chancellor Bruno Kreisky. Anyone else might have taken an identical spill. A cameraman photographed the incident, and immediately newspaper cartoonists joined television comics in ridiculing the president as an uncoordinated, drink-dropping stumblebum. In reality, Ford had been a star college athlete, was an avid skier and swimmer, and remained one of the most physically coordinated and fit of all presidents. The stumblebum image was greatly exaggerated if not false, but many Americans apparently believed it, including at least one professional historian, Irwin Unger, who still described Ford, in a 1982 textbook, as "physically awkward."

The second unfortunate event, according to one of Ford's inner circle, Robert Hartmann, writing in *Palace Politics* (1980), "was just as accidental and explicable" but one for which the president himself "must bear some of the blame." This was Ford's "incredible conclusion" in the second televised debate with 1976 Democratic presidential opponent Jimmy Carter that "there is no Soviet domination of Eastern Europe." Apparently, Ford had not meant to convey the message that his own chosen words in fact conveyed, but the remark stood and the damage was done, establishing the fear that an already bumbling Ford had also become a dangerous wanderer in a foreign affairs fantasyland.

Hartmann insists that the president's brief administration was not without substantial accomplishments but concedes that Ford may be remembered only "for never having been elected, for healing our land, for falling down steps, and for pardoning Richard Nixon." Succeeded by Democratic president Jimmy Carter in January, 1977, Ford joined in history only four previous chief executives whose terms had been shorter than his: William H. Harrison (1841), Zachary Taylor (1849-1850), James A. Garfield (1881), and Warren G. Harding (1921-1923).

Self-Discipline and Achievement

The thirty-eighth president of the United States was born in Omaha, Nebraska, on July 14, 1913. He was originally named Leslie King, Jr., but when Ford was two years old, his parents were divorced and his mother took him with her to Grand Rapids, Michigan. There, in 1916, Dorothy King married Gerald Rudolph Ford, who adopted Leslie and renamed him Gerald Rudolph Ford, Jr. His mother's second marriage gave Ford three younger half brothers—Thomas, Richard, and James. The Ford family was well balanced, close, and loving. The elder Ford was a hardworking and prosperous owner of a local paint and varnish company. Dorothy Ford actively involved herself in numerous church and community projects, in addition to being an apparently devoted mother to her four sons. The future president enjoyed a healthy, positive childhood, learning to give, take, share, win, and lose. He also learned always to do his best and to become an achiever rather than a wishful thinker. In high school, Ford played center on the football team, joined the Boy Scouts, served on the student council, and was well liked. During the early years of the Great Depression, he worked at various part-time jobs to help his family get through the

hard times. From this background, together with his Episcopalian upbringing, came Ford's widely respected honesty, openness, and reliability. He seems, finally, to have developed as a mature person with a deep sense of purpose and self-worth.

In 1931, Ford entered the University of Michigan on a football scholarship, but he had to continue working part-time in order to pay all of his expenses. He joined the Delta Kappa Epsilon social fraternity and made two lifelong friends at the university—John R. Stiles, who was later Ford's congressional campaign manager, and Philip Buchen, who became Ford's law partner and eventually a member of President Ford's White House staff. Ford was named to the college all-star team after his senior season and received professional offers from both the Detroit Lions and the Green Bay Packers. He declined these invitations and instead pursued legal studies at Yale University, where he also coached the undergraduate boxing team and served as an assistant football coach.

Throughout high school, college, and law school, Ford was a consistently bright, above-average student. Future critics who delighted in pointing out that President Ford had never been a profound thinker or a straight-A student forgot that several solid presidents—Harry S. Truman and Dwight Eisenhower among them—had not excelled academically, and that from some points of view one of the great White House disappointments, Woodrow Wilson, had been a history professor and that mediocre president Chester A. Arthur had belonged to Phi Beta Kappa.

Several months after Ford's graduation from Yale Law School in 1940, the Japanese attacked Hawaii, bringing the United States formally into World War II and Ford into the United States Navy. As an ensign he trained recruits in North Carolina for a year and then served for the remainder of the war on the aircraft carrier USS *Monterey* in the Pacific theater. By 1946, Ford had risen to the rank of lieutenant commander and wore ten battle stars; he therefore had more combat experience than many of the war veterans who became national political figures.

Entry into Politics: A Team Player

Returning to his Grand Rapids law practice after the war, Ford became one of the young reformers of local Republican politics and in 1948 ran for the Fifth District congressional seat of Bartel C. Jonkman, an isolationist and member of the entrenched and reactionary Grand Rapids Republican establishment. A fresh and vigorous Ford campaign upset the complacent and unpopular Jonkman handily, and later in the year, on the same national Election Day that underdog Democratic President Harry S. Truman defeated Republican contender Thomas E.

Dewey, Ford outpolled a Democratic congressional challenger. During the 1948 campaign Ford married Elizabeth "Betty" Bloomer. They subsequently had four children—Michael Gerald (born 1950), John Gardner (born 1952), Steven Meigs (born 1956), and Susan Elizabeth (born 1957).

From 1949 to 1973, Ford served as a diligent and loyal member of the House Republican "team," first as an apprentice congressman and after 1963 as a party leader. He did his homework conscientiously, rarely missing sessions or committee meetings. Unlike other congressional contemporaries who used their positions in the House as a means to advance to the executive branch, Ford concentrated on his House duties and responsibilities. Ford never displayed "presidential fever" and only once

In March, 1952, Congressmen Ford, Robert Kean, and Norris Cotton (left to right) read a letter from General Dwight D. Eisenhower announcing that he does not plan to leave his European assignment to seek the Republican presidential nomination. *(AP/Wide World Photos)*

permitted his name to be mentioned for the vice presidency. At the 1960 Republican convention, Michigan supporters staged a brief Ford boomlet, but presidential nominee Richard Nixon chose instead Massachusetts senator Henry Cabot Lodge, Jr., as his running mate.

Ford remained in Congress, to which his admiring Fifth District constituents reelected him repeatedly, never giving Ford less than 60 percent of their votes. Chosen Republican conference chair in 1963 and House minority leader two years later, "Jerry" Ford was as much a "House man" by 1973

As House Republican leader, Ford displays a huge gavel in September, 1968, as a symbol of the party's fight to win control of the House in the elections that fall. *(AP/Wide World Photos)*

as Sir Winston Churchill remained a "Commons man" throughout his long and distinguished career. Whereas Michigan's Fifth District was a virtual Republican "pocket borough," as it provided Ford a secure House seat for twenty-four years, the United States was not a parliamentary democracy. The future president never had to develop or sustain a pluralistic national constituency until 1976, by which time he was the White House incumbent defending a frayed and suspect administration against a spirited attack by the nominee of the national majority party.

Hardly any Americans outside Michigan knew of Ford at all, or even what he looked like, until he and Senate Minority Leader Everett Dirksen of Illinois appeared together on the so-called Ev and Jerry Show, a series of televised press conferences during the late 1960's in which Ford and the more oratorical Dirksen (who did most of the talking) criticized the Great Society programs of Democratic President Lyndon B. Johnson. Although Johnson had thought enough of Ford, or of his status within the Republican Party, to appoint the Michigan congressman to the Warren Com-

mission to investigate President John F. Kennedy's assassination, Johnson was "the source of savage wisecracks that have plagued Ford to this day"—crudities such as "Jerry's a nice guy, but he played football too long without a helmet." Johnson later directly apologized to Ford for such insensitive statements, but many Washington insiders largely agreed with them and considered Ford a person of little significance or, worse, a "lightweight."

Ford was not a lightweight. He was in fact an experienced and widely respected House minority leader among few other responsible personages in an unusually cynical and demoralized Washington. It was not Ford who publicly used abusive language to describe colleagues, peddled influence, sought to cover up felonies, or tape-recorded visitors' comments in his office without their knowledge, as his presidential predecessor had. The only blemish on Ford's entire pre-vice presidential record was his ill-considered attempt in 1969, loyally undertaken at the behest of Nixon's White House, to impeach liberal Supreme Court Justice William O. Douglas. The movement fizzled and Ford repented. It is possible to serve honestly, intelligently, and constructively as a congressional leader without having presidential aspirations or even being "presidential timber." Dozens of persons have done so since 1789. Most of them have been forgotten by all but historians because they were only briefly, if ever, in the national spotlight. Without a presidential constitutency and lacking the presidential aura, these individuals did not seek the presidency and were not seriously considered by their parties as viable presidential contenders. Democratic House speaker Sam Rayburn was one modern example of the type; Republican House minority leader Gerald Ford was another. Neither of these men was a lightweight.

An Accidental President

Ford made history by becoming the nation's first accidental vice president when, on October 12, 1973, President Nixon nominated him to succeed Vice President Spiro T. Agnew, whose resignation two days earlier had become necessary because of his involvement in a Maryland bribery scandal. (One previous vice president had resigned and others had died in office, but no constitutional mechanism existed for filling vice presidential vacancies until the Twenty-fifth Amendment to the Constitution was ratified in 1967.) Why did Nixon choose Ford to succeed Agnew? He chose him, first and foremost, because the Twenty-fifth Amendment required congressional confirmation of a president's vice presidential nominee, and Nixon knew that the Democratic congressional majority would confirm a "respectable" but not a "presidential" Republican. Ford was solidly respectable and equally unpresidential, a factor Ford himself was apparently compelled to reemphasize by promising Nixon that he would not seek the 1976 Republican presidential nomination. Although President Nixon was already in difficulty with Watergate in the fall of 1973, no one could predict the events that were to follow. Nixon, Ford, and almost every-

one else assumed that the president would complete his term; the Republican presidential nomination would be won by John Connally, George Bush, or perhaps Ronald Reagan; and that Vice President Ford would at last return to private life. In addition, President Nixon obviously preferred a loyal, low-profile vice president who would not attempt to overshadow or upstage his chief in the White House. No inexperienced politician could fill such a role, which required a respectable and reliable team player—Gerald R. Ford.

Two months of congressional hearings and investigations into Ford's background and qualifications followed his nomination. Having passed congressional scrutiny, Ford took office on December 6, 1973. In his inaugural remarks that day, he said, "I am a Ford, not a Lincoln." This unpretentious, car-culture metaphor suggested that although Ford recognized his limitations when compared with the greatest of Republican presidents, the new vice president was nevertheless a durable and dependable leader in his own way. Adhering predictably to his established reputation as a team player, Ford remained in the background, permitting the White House to establish his agenda and itinerary. Until President Nixon was forced to admit that he had lied about his knowledge of the Watergate cover-up, Vice President Ford continued loyally to believe that Nixon had done nothing wrong and would complete his presidential term. It was therefore with genuinely troubled feelings that Ford beheld the rapid disintegration of Nixon's defense and personal credibility as, between December, 1973, and early August, 1974, the odds that Ford would become president rose steadily from possible to probable to certain.

On August 9, 1974, the second accident that propelled Ford into the White House occurred: Richard M. Nixon, under threat of impeachment, resigned. Before 1974, eight American vice presidents had reached the White House because their chiefs had died in office, through natural causes or assassination. Writing in 1966, Stanford professor Thomas A. Bailey described the eight as our "accidental Presidents." (In less formal classroom presentations, Bailey referred to them as "their Accidentcies.") Unlike his eight predecessors, however, Ford had not been elected to the vice presidency.

Despite having never faced the national electorate, Ford impressed the nation favorably during his first moments as chief executive. The most noteworthy of his remarks after taking the presidential oath was his since frequently quoted reference to the past agonies of Watergate: "Our long national nightmare is over," he declared, conveying a message that many Americans had been longing to hear, and to believe. (The phrase was not a Ford inspiration, although he said it convincingly; Robert Hartmann, a Ford adviser, had suggested it.) In the same speech, Ford asked fellow Americans to pray that former President Nixon, a man "who brought peace to millions," could "find it for himself." Hartmann later recalled in *Palace Politics* that "no president ever started off with more friends and fewer enemies" than Ford.

A Pardon for Richard M. Nixon

President Ford's honeymoon with the American press and public, however, lasted barely a month, for on September 8 Ford announced his "full, free and absolute pardon" of former President Nixon for all crimes that he had committed, or may have committed, during his tenure in the White House. The pardon meant that Nixon would never be indicted, tried, and convicted (or acquitted) in connection with Watergate or anything else that took place during his presidency; nor would the former president lose any of the perquisites of a retired chief executive—pension, staff allowances, or Secret Service protection.

Ford insisted that his reasons for pardoning Nixon were sound and valid—"It was the right

---

Excerpt from Gerald R. Ford's remarks on signing a proclamation pardoning Richard M. Nixon, September 8, 1974:

It is not the ultimate fate of Richard Nixon that most concerns me, though surely it deeply troubles every decent and every compassionate person. My concern is the immediate future of this great country. In this, I dare not depend upon my personal sympathy as a long-time friend of the former President, nor my professional judgment as a lawyer, and I do not.

As President, my primary concern must always be the greatest good of all the people of the United States whose servant I am. As a man, my first consideration is to be true to my own convictions and my own conscience. My conscience tells me clearly and certainly that I cannot prolong the bad dreams that continue to reopen a chapter that is closed. My conscience tells me that only I, as President, have the constitutional power to firmly shut and seal this book. My conscience tells me it is my duty, not merely to proclaim domestic tranquillity but to use every means that I have to insure it.

I do believe that the buck stops here, that I cannot rely upon public opinion polls to tell me what is right.

I do believe that right makes might and that if I am wrong, ten angels swearing I was right would make no difference.

I do believe, with all my heart and mind and spirit, that I, not as President but as a humble servant of God, will receive justice without mercy if I fail to show mercy.

Finally, I feel that Richard Nixon and his loved ones have suffered enough and will continue to suffer, no matter what I do, no matter what we, as a great and good nation, can do together to make his goal of peace come true.

---

thing to do." First, he felt that Nixon had suffered enough and had paid dearly for whatever he may have done. Second, Ford was sincerely concerned about Nixon's physical and mental condition at the time, believing that further criminal proceedings might break the former president altogether or even harass him into committing suicide. Third, criminal proceedings against Nixon would likely go on for months, perhaps even years, and require the reappearance as witnesses of all the Watergate participants. Such a prolonged and lurid public spectacle, Ford believed, would only add to the American people's feelings of turmoil. Finally, criminal proceedings against the former president would affect the White House itself, within which many of Nixon's tapes and papers remained stored. Having to locate, sort out, copy, and furnish these materials to attorneys for both sides could paralyze Ford's presidential staff.

President Ford addresses the nation on his pardon of Richard M. Nixon. *(Gerald R. Ford Library)*

Unfortunately, few persons beyond Ford's intimate entourage fully accepted the president's reasons for pardoning Nixon. Many immediately concluded that the pardon was Ford's part of a deal made either directly with Nixon or through Nixon's White House chief of staff, General Alexander Haig. (Nixon, Ford, and Haig all subsequently denied that a deal was made.) Among those who continued to believe that an understanding had been reached before Nixon's resignation was former Nixon aide John Ehrlichman. Writing in *Witness to Power* (1982), Ehrlichman recalled how President Nixon might have weighed the relative advantages and liabilities of resignation and impeachment as the end drew near. A pardon, he believed Nixon concluded, would terminate "*all* the risk and would make possible a gradual rehabilitation of Nixon's influence and image.

If one cared about one's place in history, the pardon route was the best. And Richard Nixon cared deeply about his place in history."

What did Ford (who could not have been oblivious to his own place in history) stand to gain by pardoning Nixon? Getting Nixon out of the White House and himself into it could not have been Ford's motive. By late July of 1974, all three men who were involved—Ford, Nixon, and Haig—must have realized that Nixon would leave the presidency, either voluntarily or by the impeachment process. If Ford agreed to pardon Nixon after he had resigned, his motives undoubtedly were, as Ford said they were, to spare both the afflicted president and the nation the agonies of both an impeachment trial and further criminal proceedings.

President Ford's controversial pardon of Nixon caused the first crisis within his own White House staff. White House press secretary Jerald F. TerHorst resigned at once, charging that it was improper to let Nixon go free while many of the former president's loyal subordinates remained in prison for doing his bidding. According to Hartmann's assessment,

"TerHorst's abrupt exit immeasurably compounded the damage done by Ford's pardon decision. . . . With his defection, the tiny phalanx of Ford people [within a White House still controlled by Nixon staffers] was weakened and Ford's own shining image was dimmed."

A Crippled Administration

Certainly, President Ford commenced his administration with a White House staff composed overwhelmingly of Nixon people. A transition team did not succeed in replacing Nixon holdovers with a majority of Ford's own people. The holdovers included cabinet members as well as many middle- and lower-rung staffers. Even at the end of his term, Ford's own appointees remained in the minority. Hartmann believed, indeed, that the "fatal" weakness in Ford's presidency was not the Nixon pardon and the public resentment of it but, as Hartmann had warned the president in a November, 1975, memorandum, "your retention of and reliance on Nixon Administration figures from a past you are trying to put behind you." The Nixonites (the more offensive of whom Hartmann called the "Praetorians" without naming them specifically) were convinced that "it was *their* White House, not Ford's. They honestly believed the new President needed them more than they needed him, and that he was incapable of running the place without them."

Ford never even responded to Hartmann's memorandum, and disloyal Nixonites remained in the White House, undercutting such Ford ideas as the WIN (Whip Inflation Now) program and ensuring repeatedly bland, punchless Ford speeches by keeping presidential speechwriters confused and edgy. One of Ford's most conscientious writers was John J. Casserly, who had come to the White House from the Commerce Department. On January 23, 1976, Casserly resigned, having reached the limit of his toleration and finding himself on bad terms with other Ford staffers. Casserly liked and admired President Ford, whom he called a "decent and good man" in his 1977 *The Ford White House*, but concluded that Ford lacked "the firmness to run the White House or the leadership to be President."

Hartmann, however, later concluded that Ford had demonstrated great leadership through his career, including the presidential years, but was deficient in command:

Much has [been] written on Presidential leadership, but command is what the Presidency is all about. . . . To put it bluntly, a President must be something of an SOB. It is not enough to surround himself with them. He must at times be *the* SOB and he must, however secretly, rather relish this role. Ford was simply too nice a guy; he boasted that he had adversaries but no enemies, and he really meant it. Sometimes he hurt people, but he hated it. Not for nothing was he called "good old Jerry." But nobody ever called our first President "good old George." A commander must be capable of shooting his own mutinous troops.

"Good old Jerry" was the joint product of a decent, religious family background and of twenty-four years within the congressional system as a team player in the minority party. Only from 1953 to 1955 were Ford and his House Republican colleagues able to initiate and push majority party legislation. From 1949 to 1953 and from 1955 to 1973, they had either to defend the programs of Republican presidents against congressional Democratic onslaughts or to oppose congressional Democratic initiatives ordered by Democratic presidents. Ford thus early in his political career developed a work mentality of compromise and adjustment, which meshed compatibly with his own personal, team-player athletic experiences. Compromise and adjustment well suit a minority member of Congress but can be lethal if maintained by an occupant of the presidency, which demands aggressive and decisive leadership at all times, as well as the ruthlessness of an

THE VICE PRESIDENT
NELSON A. ROCKEFELLER

Nelson Rockefeller was born on July 8, 1908, in Bar Harbor, Maine. His father was John D. Rockefeller, whose dynastic family had amassed a fortune in the oil industry. Nelson was educated at the Lincoln School in New York City and then attended Dartmouth College, graduating in 1930. On June 23, 1930, he married Mary Todhunter Clark. The couple eventually had five children, although one died in infancy.

Rockefeller served from 1931 to 1958 as the director of the Rockefeller Center and as its president from 1938 to 1945. In addition, he was a principal figure with the Museum of Modern Art from 1932 to 1953, serving as both trustee and president. Rockefeller's involvement in politics included service as the coordinator of Inter-American Affairs in the U.S. State Department from 1940 to 1944 and as assistant secretary of state from 1944 to 1945. In the administration of Dwight D. Eisenhower, Rockefeller was appointed as undersecretary of Health, Education, and Welfare from 1953 to 1954 and special assistant to the president from 1954 to 1955. In 1958, Rockefeller was successful in his bid for governor of New York, serving from 1959 to 1973. After divorcing his wife in 1962, he married Margaretta "Happy" Murphy on May 4, 1963, and had two children with his second wife.

During this time, Rockefeller gained national notoriety not only for his family connections but also as the recipient of numerous distinguished awards for his service and philanthropy. He also published several books. Rockefeller was a candidate for the presidency in 1960, 1964, and 1968 but was unsuccessful in securing his party's nomination. However, after Gerald R. Ford ascended to the presidency, he nominated Rockefeller to be his vice president, and Rockefeller was sworn in on December 19, 1974. Questions arose as to whether he would remain on the ticket during Ford's 1976 campaign, but Rockefeller resigned after a mutual decision with Ford. Rockefeller died on January 26, 1979.

Robert P. Watson and Richard Yon

"SOB," as Hartmann (and others) have observed.

Even in the Oval Office, President Ford remained essentially Congressman Ford, and "good old Jerry" seemingly did not become sufficiently skeptical, thick-skinned, or brutal to handle either the White House staff or the lonely responsibilities of presidential command. Trusting, open, optimistic, unwilling to hurt anyone's feelings—and expecting similar behavior from other White House employees—President Ford continued to do his best while a divided and unruled staff progressively subverted his authority and goals.

Perhaps the most successful piece of Praetorian subversion involved the man Ford appointed vice president, former New York governor Nelson A. Rockefeller, who assumed his duties on December 19, 1974. The wealthy and multitalented Rockefeller, dean of the party's liberal and cosmopolitan eastern wing, had long been disliked if not despised by conservative Republicans from the hinterland. White House hinterlanders continually downgraded Rockefeller, kept him isolated from the president whenever possible, and sought to neutralize whatever influence he possessed. After President Ford decided to seek another term in 1976, he apparently succumbed to conservative and Praetorian pressure and in November, 1975, obtained from his vice president a statement that Rockefeller would not be on the Republican ticket during the forthcoming campaign. (The eventual Republican vice presidential nominee in 1976 was a conservative midwesterner, Senator Bob Dole of Kansas. Hartmann believed several years later that Ford would have been "unbeatable" in 1976 had his vice president been George Bush, his defense secretary Ronald Reagan, and his secretary of state Nelson A. Rockefeller.)

Domestic Legislation and Foreign Policy

Although President Ford remained ill served by a staff he failed to command, the Ford administration went dutifully and doggedly on. Among the major items of legislation Ford signed in 1974 were a $25 billion federal aid to education act (which included a restriction on busing) and the Federal Campaign Reform Act, providing public funding for the campaigns of serious presidential contenders and establishing spending limits for presidential and congressional candidates. The reform legislation had grown out of Watergate-related disclosures of illegal contributions made to President Nixon's 1972 reelection effort. As a result of the 1974 law, President Ford and his 1976 Democratic opponent, Jimmy Carter, became the first presidential candidates whose campaigns were funded largely by taxpayers. Ford also signed in 1974 a $4.8 billion federal commitment to improve public mass transit facilities. Responding to rising national unemployment which by mid-1975 had reached 9.2 percent of the workforce, the president, on June 30, approved a measure extending unemployment benefits for a maximum of sixty-five weeks.

The conservative Ford also vetoed fifty-three bills during his two-year administration, of which the Democratic Congress was able to override only nine. (Hartmann applauded the forty-four vetoes that stood, claiming they saved the taxpayers $9.2 billion and helped cut the growth rate in federal spending by one-half "for the first time in decades.") Among the measures that became law without Ford's approval were a $7.9 billion educational appropriation in 1975, plus two welfare-social services appropriations and a job bill in 1976. In opposing further federal aid to education and assistance to lower-income groups during recession, Ford may have pleased conservative Republicans, but he did so at the cost of support among voters in 1976. Not only did Ford's many vetoes likely add to his subsequent opposition but also the president's 1976 budget was, in Hartmann's view, "politically . . . suicidal" in an election year. At the same time that he supported a $28 billion cut in government spending programs already on the books, Ford proposed to reduce taxes on individuals and corporations by $28 billion. Treasury Secretary William Simon and Council of Economic Advisors Chairman Alan Greenspan energetically urged Ford to adopt this politically risky policy of economic retrenchment. (Hartmann described these Nixon holdovers as possessing two of "the best economic minds of the eighteenth century.")

Even less spectacular than Ford's domestic accomplishments were his achievements in foreign affairs. The president retained Nixon's flamboyant and brilliant secretary of state, Henry Kissinger, and Ford's foreign policy became in effect an extension of the Nixon-Kissinger policy. Peace among the superpowers was maintained, and both Ford and Kissinger traveled extensively to confer with foreign dignitaries, but few solid or workable new initiatives emerged. A qualified exception was Kissinger's success at bringing about an Israeli-Egyptian interim peace in the Middle East in October, 1975.

Ford also had to cope with the aftermath of the Nixon-Kissinger "peace" in Vietnam—though congressional action had eliminated any further military intervention. Ford's most painful duty was to oversee the evacuation of American personnel from Saigon when the South Vietnamese regime collapsed in April of 1975. The president's most dramatic foreign policy endeavor, however, followed a month later when Cambodians of the Khmer Rouge seized the American merchant ship *Mayaguez* in the Gulf of Siam. Ford successfully used naval and military forces to rescue the crewmen. At home, President Ford attempted to heal the domestic wounds of the Southeast Asian war by offering, on September 16, 1974, a clemency work program for Vietnam draft evaders and military deserters. To receive amnesty under the plan, they had to perform two years of public service work and to take an oath of allegiance. About 22,500 out of 124,000 eligibles applied for the program. Many draft evaders and deserters criticized the plan because, by not offering unconditional amnesty, it implied guilt, whereas some veterans' groups felt the president's approach was "soft."

Ford's presidency, like that of Ronald Reagan several years later, almost ended tragically. On September, 5, 1975, Manson Family member Lynette "Squeaky" Fromme pointed a gun at Ford in Sacramento, California, but was quickly apprehended. Then, on September 22, 1975, political activist Sarah Jane Moore shot at Ford as he emerged from the St. Francis Hotel in San Francisco. A bystander deflected Moore's hand as she fired, and fortunately Ford, unlike Reagan, was not injured. Ford's luck in seeking reelection would not be as good. Almost as soon as he took office, he had to begin preparations for the race, and ill omens and difficulties burdened his efforts from the first.

The Election of 1976

Thirty-eight Republican incumbents had already met defeat in the 1974 congressional elections, enabling the Democrats to increase their House majority to 291 of the 435 members and their Senate lead to 61 of 100. Lingering disaffection over Watergate, Ford's Nixon pardon, and prevailing economic conditions were blamed for Republican losses. The Ford administration was also threatened from within. A strong challenge for the Republican presidential nomination by former California governor

Ronald Reagan jeopardized the party's fragile unity and irritated Ford. Nevertheless, the convention nominated the president by a narrow margin.

Ford's Democratic opponent, former Georgia governor Jimmy Carter, had swept through the primaries, eliminating one better-known Democrat after another, until his nomination had become a certainty even before the party's national convention. Carter attracted voters because he was an outsider with no previous civilian experience in the federal government. No one could connect him with, or blame him for, the ongoing confusion in Washington, D.C. When Carter stressed his own personal honesty and promised "never to lie," he gained the support of many suspicious, resentful, and disenchanted Americans. Although President Ford was Carter's actual rival, former President Nixon was the implicit target of the Georgian's moralistic slogans and promises. Because Ford had pardoned Nixon and had retained many Nixon appointees, Carter sought to connect the two in as many voters' minds as possible.

Probably because he had perceived Carter's strategy at the time, Hartmann remained all the more convinced that it was Ford's failure to get rid of the White House Nixonites that finally brought about the president's defeat:

> I believe President Ford could have survived his sudden pardon of former President Nixon if he had coupled it with the dismissal of Nixon's court and constituted one of his own choosing. Everybody expected him to do so; it is the first thing a new President does. He had the clear precedents of Harry Truman, who got rid of FDR's Praetorian Guard in short order, and of Lyndon Johnson, who hung onto Kennedy's and lived to regret it. As President, Ford boldly took the first step—and I believe pardoning Nixon was right and spared the country endless agony—but not the second step, which would have put Watergate behind us where the American people wanted it to be.

Hartmann's verdict is supported by the relatively close margin of Carter's 1976 victory—40.3 million popular votes to Ford's 38.5 million, with an edge in electoral votes of only 297 to 240. Of the six previous presidential incumbents who had been defeated in seeking reelection, only John Adams in 1800 and Grover Cleveland in 1888 lost by a smaller margin in the electoral count than Ford. Also, both Adams and Cleveland had been elected before, whereas Ford had not.

Ford's Presidency: An Assessment

Gerald R. Ford had been an able congressman and a respected House minority leader. His personal integrity, genuine commitment to public service, and forthright confrontation of critical issues restored much-needed respect to a tarnished presidency. His administration reduced the inflation rate from slightly above 12 percent to below 5 percent and "reversed the recessionary trend and increased total employment to a record high," as Hartmann recalled. President Ford also launched the nation's inner rehabilitation from the trauma of Vietnam and engaged in stabilizing discussions with the major communist powers. His administration laid the groundwork for future Middle East accords as well. He also greatly underestimated the destructive consequences of the Nixon pardon ("right" though it may have been), however, and failed either to reconstitute or to command the White House staff. Ford was, finally, one of many recent victims of media imagery, which substitutes judgment by appearance for judgment of performance. Had he been more experienced in using visual media, as was his 1976 rival and second successor, Ronald Reagan, President Ford might have remained in the White House for the next four years.

Ford has been described as an "adequate" but "undistinguished" president. Assessments that emerged in the early twenty-first century began to be slightly more favorable as the documented record of the 1970's became more established and permitted closer and less impressionistic comparisons with the administrations of both his predecessor and successor. President Bill Clinton helped this reassessment by honoring Ford with the Presidential Medal of Freedom in 1999. In 2001, Ford was honored with a John F. Kennedy Profile in Courage Award, in recognition for the political courage it took to pardon Richard Nixon.

Mark T. Carleton

Suggested Readings

Cannon, James M. *Time and Chance: Gerald Ford's Appointment with History*. New York: HarperCollins, 1994. An admiring biography of Ford.

Casserly, John J. *The Ford White House: The Diary of a Speechwriter*. Boulder: Colorado Associated University Press, 1977. Presents a vivid day-by-day account of a frustrated Ford staffer.

Firestone, Bernard J., and Alexj Ugrinsky, eds. *Gerald R. Ford and the Politics of Post-Watergate America*. Westport, Conn.: Greenwood Press, 1993. A collection of essays and transcripts of panel discussions, prepared by political scientists, historians, and members of the Ford administration, that discusses issues such as the pardon of Richard Nixon, Middle East diplomacy, economic policy, and Ford's relations with the press.

Ford, Betty, with Chris Chase. *The Times of My Life*. New York: Harper & Row, 1978. The First Lady chronicles her life and her perspectives of the Ford presidency.

Ford, Gerald R. *A Time to Heal: The Autobiography of Gerald R. Ford*. New York: Harper & Row, 1979. The president's memoirs.

Gerald R. Ford Presidential Library and Museum. http://www.ford.utexas.edu/. The Web site of Ford's official presidential library.

Greene, John R. *Gerald R. Ford: A Bibliography*. Westport, Conn.: Greenwood Press, 1994. A comprehensive bibliographic overview of the Ford years.

_____. *The Presidency of Gerald R. Ford*. Lawrence: University Press of Kansas, 1995. Gives a balanced portrait of Ford's term.

Hartmann, Robert. *Palace Politics: An Inside Account of the Ford Years*. New York: McGraw-Hill, 1980. A thorough and critical assessment of Ford's presidency, written by a man who served on Ford's House, vice presidential, and presidential staffs.

Lee, Edward. *Nixon, Ford, and the Abandonment of South Vietnam*. Jefferson, N.C.: McFarland, 2002. Discusses world events that distracted Nixon and Ford from the events in Vietnam and argues that the administrations abandoned the cause in that region.

Mieczkowski, Yanek. *Gerald Ford and the Challenges of the 1970's*. Lexington: University Press of Kentucky, 2005. A reexamination of the Ford presidency that argues Ford's administration successfully confronted some of the most troubling crises of the postwar era.

Rozell, Mark J. *The Press and the Ford Presidency*. Ann Arbor: University of Michigan Press, 1992. Uses the case of the Ford administration to analyze the complicated relationship between what presidents say and do and how their words and deeds are portrayed in the elite press.

Thompson, Kenneth W. *The Ford Presidency: Twenty-two Intimate Perspectives of Gerald R. Ford*. Lanham, Md.: University Press of America, 1988. An issues-oriented collection of essays on the Ford presidency.

Wetterhahn, Ralph. *Last Battle: The Mayaguez, the Lost Fire Team, and the End of the Vietnam War*. New York: Carroll & Graf, 2001. Examines one of the most critical foreign policy issues that Ford had to deal with during his administration.

Jimmy Carter

39th President, 1977-1981

Born: October 1, 1924
Plains, Georgia

Political Party: Democratic
Vice President: Walter Mondale

Cabinet Members

Secretary of State: Cyrus Vance, Edmund Muskie
Secretary of the Treasury: W. Michael Blumenthal, G. William Miller
Secretary of Defense: Harold Brown
Attorney General: Griffin Bell, Benjamin R. Civiletti
Secretary of the Interior: Cecil D. Andrus
Secretary of Agriculture: Bob S. Bergland
Secretary of Commerce: Juanita M. Kreps, Philip M. Klutznick
Secretary of Labor: F. Ray Marshall
Secretary of Health and Human Services: Joseph A. Califano, Jr., Patricia Roberts Harris
Secretary of Housing and Urban Development: Patricia Roberts Harris, Moon Landrieu
Secretary of Transportation: Brock Adams, Neil E. Goldschmidt
Secretary of Energy: James Schlesinger, Charles W. Duncan, Jr.
Secretary of Education: Shirley Hufstedler

Campaigning for the presidency in 1976, Jimmy Carter described himself as a farmer, a Southerner, a born-again Christian, and a nuclear physicist. Although somewhat misleading, his description provided a fair index of the character and career of the man who sought to become the thirty-ninth president of the United States.

Spokesman for the New South

James Earl Carter, Jr., was born October 1, 1924, in Plains, Georgia, the first son of Lillian Gordy and James Earl Carter. Lillian was a registered nurse, Earl a prosperous businessman and farmer. Both parents stressed the importance of

Carter's official portrait. *(White House Historical Society)*

education to Jimmy and their other children, Ruth, Gloria, and Billy. An obedient, hardworking, enterprising youth, their eldest son not only excelled in his studies at school but also earned enough money from a boiled peanut business to invest in cotton and real estate. He was graduated from Plains High School as valedictorian of the class of 1941, spent a year each at Georgia Southwestern College and the Georgia Institute of Technology, received a coveted appointment to the United States Naval Academy, and was graduated from Annapolis in 1946, fifty-ninth in a class of 820.

Though he had none of the credentials of a nuclear physicist, in the early 1950's as a young lieutenant in the Navy he worked for Captain Hyman G. Rickover on the *Seawolf*, one of the prototypes for the nuclear submarine. In 1953, when his father died, Carter resigned from the Navy and returned to Plains to run the by-then-failing family business. In partnership with his wife, Rosalynn, whom he had married in 1946, he not only revived but also expanded the enterprise and became a wealthy agribusinessman. A deacon and Sunday school teacher in the Plains Baptist Church, in 1967 he experienced a "new birth" which intensified his commitment to Christianity. Carter also gradually became involved in politics, first at the local level, where he served on the Sumter County School Board, then at the state level, where he served two terms in the Georgia Senate from 1963 to 1966.

In 1966, Carter made his first attempt to win the Georgia governorship. Campaigning as a moderate progressive, he lost to Lester Maddox, a conservative segregationist. Carter then spent the next four years campaigning for the 1970 gubernatorial election. His experience as state senator and his 1966 congressional campaign (at the last minute he had forfeited a likely seat in the House of Representatives in order to run for the governorship) had whetted his desire for higher public office. He had become what James Wooten called the "existen-tial politician," committed to an endless cycle of holding one office while preparing to run for another, caught up in "a process of always becoming something else."

In 1970, Carter's chief opponent was the liberal former governor Carl Sanders, rather than an extreme segregationist. With the help of political aides Jody Powell, Hamilton Jordan, Charles Kirbo, and Gerald Rafshoon, Carter mounted a grassroots campaign geared to rural, conservative, white Georgians. Although the *Atlanta Constitution* opposed him as an "ignorant, racist, backward, ultra-conservative, redneck South Georgia peanut farmer," he defeated Sanders handily in the Democratic primary runoff and went on to win over his Republican opponent in the general election, winning 60 percent of the vote.

On Inauguration Day, he surprised many of his supporters by unequivocally pledging to work against racial discrimination. "I say to you quite frankly that the time for racial discrimination is over," he declared in his inaugural address. "No poor, rural, weak, or black person should ever again have to bear the additional burden of being deprived of the opportunity for an education, a job, or simple justice." Presumably, he sought to dispel the segregationist image his campaign had fostered. If so, it worked, for the address won for him national publicity as a leading voice of the "new" South. *Time* magazine featured him on its cover with the caption "Dixie Whistles a Different Tune: Georgia Governor Jimmy Carter" and proclaimed him one of a new breed of racial moderates flourishing below the Mason-Dixon line.

Carter carried out his pledge to fight racial discrimination in Georgia. Among other things, he increased state government employment of African Americans (from 4,850 when he took office to 6,684 when he left) and proclaimed Martin Luther King, Jr., Day on January 15, 1973. As governor he also worked for environmental protection, education, and tax and welfare reform. His main effort, however—and

THE FIRST LADY
ROSALYNN CARTER

Eleanor Rosalynn Smith was born on August 18, 1927, in Plains, Georgia, the daughter of Allie Murray Smith and Edgar Smith. She grew up in Plains and was a friend of Ruth Carter, her classmate and sister of Jimmy Carter. The Carter family had a prosperous peanut-growing business in Plains. When Jimmy was home on leave from the United States Naval Academy in the summer of 1945, he and Rosalynn went out on a date. They were married on July 7, 1946, shortly after his graduation from the Naval Academy, in the Plains Methodist Church.

Between 1947 and 1952, while Jimmy was still in the Navy, their three sons were born: John William "Jack" in Portsmouth, Virginia, in 1947; James Earl III "Chip" in Honolulu, Hawaii, in 1950; and Donnel Jeffrey in New London, Connecticut, in 1952.

When Jimmy's father died in 1953, the Carters moved back to Plains to run the family business. For the first year they lived in public housing. Jimmy ran the warehouse, and Rosalynn kept the books. While in Plains, the couple's only daughter, Amy Lynn, was born in 1967.

As governor of Georgia in the early 1970's, Jimmy Carter was one of the most enlightened Southern leaders of the post-civil rights era. By the end of his term, he set his sights on becoming the first president of the United States to be elected from the Deep South since before the Civil War. Rosalynn proved to be a tireless, articulate campaigner in support of her husband. She campaigned alone on his behalf in forty-one of the fifty states.

While her husband was in office, she was dedicated to helping those with mental illness. Her efforts resulted in the Mental Health Systems Act of 1980. Also during her years in the White House, Rosalynn received two honorary degrees as First Lady: a Doctor of Humanities degree from Tift College of Mercer University and a Doctor of Humane Letters degree from Morehouse College in Atlanta.

Following her husband's defeat by Ronald Reagan in the 1980 election, Rosalynn continued to stay active in various charitable causes. In 1991, she launched a nationwide campaign called "Every Child by Two," which was dedicated to promoting early childhood immunizations. In 2001, she was inducted into the National Women's Hall of Fame.

Dean M. Shapiro

---

perhaps his major achievement—was the reorganization of state government. Stormy relations with the Georgia legislature made it and other legislative goals difficult to achieve. Disdaining the conventional swapping and trading, Carter frequently resorted to the veto or threat of a veto to maintain the integrity of proposed legislation. Legislators regarded him as self-righteous and stubborn. "Like a south Georgia turtle," one of them was quoted by Wooten. "He just keeps moving in the direction he's headed and it doesn't matter what you do to him. You can step on him or hit him with a stick or run over him with a pickup truck, and it doesn't faze him a bit. He just keeps on going in the way he wants to go." Another difficulty Carter faced, especially in his crusade for state reorganization, was mustering public support for rather abstract, intangible reforms. Despite such problems, he generally succeeded in streamlining the state government and in some cases saving money through zero-based budgeting. He did not win great popularity as governor, but he has been praised for helping Georgians adjust, as painlessly as possible, to necessary economic and social changes, especially in the area of civil rights.

The Campaign of 1976: An Appeal to Idealism

On December 12, 1974, shortly before his term as governor expired, Carter announced his candidacy for the presidency of the United States. He had already begun campaigning, having taken the job of chair of the 1974 Democratic Campaign Committee. It offered an ideal opportunity to meet people throughout the country while making fund-raising speeches for Democratic congressional candidates, as well as a means of enhancing his status in the national Democratic Party. Carter had also accepted an invitation to join the Trilateral Commission, a private international foreign policy organization formed in 1973 by the chairman of Chase Manhattan Bank, David Rockefeller. Later, in the presidential campaign, Carter cited his association with the commission to establish his foreign policy credentials. In his 1975 autobiography *Why Not the Best?*, he said that membership on the commission had given him "an excellent opportunity to know national and international leaders in many fields of study concerning foreign affairs" and had provided "a splendid learning opportunity. . . . " Indeed, Carter's connection with the Trilateral Commission supplied him with more than information about foreign affairs. As Laurence Shoup has noted, it also provided or at least reinforced a major element of his campaign strategy: In a key Trilateral Commission document published in 1975, Samuel P. Huntington observed that the political history of the 1960's and 1970's showed that "the 'outsider' in politics, or the candidate who could make himself or herself appear to be an outsider, had the inside road to political office." The commission even furnished campaign support by putting Carter in touch with fund-raisers and wealthy contributors, the mass media, and various interest groups.

Carter won the Democratic nomination in 1976 because he worked longer and harder than any of the nine other candidates and, some observers said, because he wanted to be president more than any of the others did. In 1975, he spent 250 days on the road, visiting nearly every state to secure media attention and popular support. In twenty-two months of campaigning for the presidency, he made 1,495 speeches in 1,029 cities and traveled 461,240 miles. During the primaries and in the general election, he and his key aides—the foursome who had helped engineer the 1970 campaign for the governorship, plus a newcomer, pollster Patrick Caddell—devised a campaign strategy to exploit popular distrust of and alienation from government in the wake of Vietnam and Watergate. They promoted Carter as an outsider and antipolitician in their campaign against "the Washington establishment." They presented Carter's limited political experience as a state senator and one-term governor as a major asset

Carter at home with his brother Billy the day before the presidential election in 1976. *(Archive Photos)*

Amy and Jimmy Carter at the White House in February, 1977. *(NARA)*

and touted his abhorrence of political horse-trading as a virtue. Perhaps recalling his relations with the Georgia legislature, Carter said during the campaign that he had "always been inclined on a matter of principle or importance not to compromise unless it's absolutely necessary." He also said, however, that he was not disposed "to twist arms or force people to vote different from what they thought." He indicated that he might try to appeal beyond the legislature to the people. "There is a final forum that even transcends the inclination of the legislative body," he declared. "That's the people themselves."

On the campaign trail, Carter's vigor and youthfulness, even the similar shock of hair, reminded many of the late John F. Kennedy, but it was the wide, toothy grin that quickly became the Carter hallmark. Although lampooned by political cartoonists, it seemed to convey his feeling of goodwill toward others,

while at the same time masking a basic shyness or, some would say, remoteness. One journalist interpreted the grin as an indication that the candidate might have a sense of humor about himself. Certainly it provided a welcome change from Richard Nixon's dour looks and Gerald Ford's blandness. Carter's soft-spoken, down-home style also contributed to his appeal as a candidate pledged to serve the people rather than the special interests.

As Elizabeth Drew observed in *American Journal: The Events of 1976* (1977), Carter combined his anti-government message with one of hope. Whereas the antigovernment message was grounded in an apparent enmity toward politicians, the hopeful message was based on a populistic faith in the American people. There was nothing wrong with them, Carter insisted—or, for that matter, with the system of government in the United States, which he declared to be "the best on earth." Thus at the same time that he condemned the government, he held out the possibility of redemption, of having "once again a nation with a government that is as honest and decent and fair and competent and truthful and idealistic as are the American people."

Carter promised to restore trust and pride in the government. He told the American people that he would never lie to them, never mislead them, never betray their trust. Throughout his campaign, he emphasized character over ideology or issues. He refused to be categorized as a conservative, liberal, or moderate, and when critics complained that he was "fuzzy" on the issues, he answered by making a distinction between what he called two levels of the campaign. One level was "the tangible issues" such as unemployment, inflation, the environment, health, education and welfare, taxation, agriculture, and nuclear proliferation. The other level was "the intangibles" such as integrity, compassion, and competence. Carter obviously felt more comfortable and thought it was more important—and presumably more conducive to electoral victory—talking about the intangibles than the tangible issues. When he did touch on the latter, he promised solutions without providing many details.

On November 4, Carter won the election. The vote, however, indicated no great surge of confidence on the part of the American people but rather continued apathy and skepticism. In one of the closest elections in United States history, Carter received 40,827,394 popular votes against Gerald Ford's 39,145,977. Voter turnout had declined from 62.8 percent in 1960 to 54.3 percent in 1976, which meant that fewer than three out of ten Americans registered to vote had cast their ballots for Carter. The close victory posed the challenge of Carter's presidency—to win the trust of the American people and prove his leadership ability.

Embattled: Carter vs. the Washington Establishment

In the area of domestic affairs, Carter accomplished a number of objectives in education, transportation, conservation, and energy. At his behest, Congress created a separate Department of Education; deregulated the airline, trucking, and railroad industries; established a billion-dollar "superfund" to clean up abandoned chemical waste sites; and instituted a comprehensive national energy policy. Nevertheless, Carter's relations with Congress were difficult, even acrimonious at times. This situation was partly a result of the power relationship that existed between the White House and

Capitol Hill. Carter's narrow election victory weakened his hand; he could hardly point to a broad popular mandate for his proposals. At the same time, Congress continued to seek ways of regaining the power it had lost during the imperial presidencies of Lyndon Johnson and Richard Nixon.

Carter's difficulties with Congress also stemmed from his dislike of pork-barrel legislation. This led to an early confrontation with the Congress in mid-February, 1977, when Carter announced a plan to eliminate nineteen water projects around the country from the federal budget. He said he considered them a waste of taxpayers' money and threatened to take his case to the people; however, when the Congress held firm and when Carter realized that his stand on the water projects was jeopardizing other parts of his legislative program, he backed down. Later he wrote in his memoirs that the water projects battle had caused "the deepest breach" between him and the Democratic leadership in the Congress, but he continued to believe that he had been right in opposing the projects. The next year he vetoed the annual public works bill because it included some of the same projects.

Carter's fiscal conservatism also alienated some congressmen, particularly liberal members of his own party. Carter admitted feeling more comfortable with conservative Democrats and Republicans than with liberals. During the campaign he had called for comprehensive programs to create jobs and aid cities, to provide national health insurance, and to initiate welfare and tax reform. Once in office, however, he decided that inflation posed a greater threat than recession or unemployment and frequently allowed his determination to balance the budget by 1981 to take precedence over social programs. Thus he scrapped a program of significant welfare reform when Joseph Califano, the secretary of health, education, and welfare, reported that it would cost billions more than the existing program.

Carter attributed many of his difficulties with Congress to the influence that special interests wielded among the legislators. It seemed to him that members of Congress were much more vulnerable to such influence than was the president, partly because of the erosion of party discipline and consensus. "One branch of the government must stand fast on a particular issue to prevent the triumph of self-interest at the expense of the public," he declared in his memoirs. In the case of tax reform, Carter admitted that as president he had failed to marshal sufficient support among the American people to counteract the influence of the special interests. As a result, the administration's tax package had fallen victim to what he called "a pack of powerful and ravenous wolves, determined to secure for themselves additional benefits at the expense of other Americans." He thought he was much more successful standing up to another lobby, which he termed "the most formidable ever evolved in the military-industrial community," when he made the decision not to build the B-1 bomber.

The Energy Crisis: "The Moral Equivalent of War"

More than any other, the energy problem revealed the difficulties Carter encountered in working with Congress. On the president's instructions, James Schlesinger, secretary of the newly created Department of Energy, drew up a comprehensive energy program to submit to the Congress. While it was in the planning stage, Carter and Schlesinger kept the details from congressmen as well as high administration officials, fearing that if parts of it were revealed, it would be destroyed by special interest groups and lobbyists even before it reached Capitol Hill. Not surprisingly, the secrecy irritated legislators who thought they should be consulted about energy policy.

Carter unveiled his program in a speech in April, 1977, in which, borrowing a phrase from William James, he termed solving the energy crisis "the moral equivalent of war." Besides urging the American people to enlist in a voluntary conservation effort, he sent to Congress a package of energy bills he wanted passed. Like tax reform, the energy program immediately drew fire from a wide range of special interest groups, including the oil lobby, automobile companies, consumer groups, and environmentalists. After a long struggle, the Congress passed legislation that, among other things, eliminated waste and promoted conservation of oil and gas, in some cases through tax incentives; encouraged development and use of other sources of energy such as coal and solar power; decontrolled oil prices; and levied a windfall profits tax on oil companies. Carter termed the struggle for a national energy policy "a bruising fight" that led to "no final clear-cut victory." He insisted, however, that overall the energy program was "a good compromise" and well worth the effort it entailed.

Carter's inability to prevent Congress and the special interests from battering his legislative proposals hurt his standing in the public opinion polls. The Bert Lance affair, involving an old friend whom Carter had appointed director of the Office of Management and Budget, proved even more damaging. Early in the summer of 1977, the press, the Senate Governmental Affairs Committee, and the comptroller of the currency began raising questions about the propriety of Lance's business dealings before coming to Washington, D.C. Carter believed Lance innocent of wrongdoing, but as new findings and allegations surfaced, he became increasingly aware of the damage the charges inflicted on him and his administration. Caught between loyalty to a friend and concern for the presidency, Carter at first gave Lance an unequivocal endorsement. "Bert, I'm proud of you," Carter told him at a nationally televised press conference in August. Then, after he thought Lance had had an opportunity to exonerate himself in Senate committee hearings, he encouraged him to resign. Late in Sep-

THE VICE PRESIDENT
WALTER MONDALE

Walter Mondale was born on January 5, 1928, in Ceylon, Minnesota. His father was a preacher, and the family had little money. After graduating from the local public school in nearby Elmore, Mondale attended Macalester College. His involvement in politics began as a college student, when he worked for Democratic candidates and organizations, including a stint in Washington, D.C. Mondale returned to Macalester and graduated cum laude in 1951. During the Korean War, he joined the U.S. Army, then went to law school at the University of Minnesota. On December 27, 1955, he married Joan Adams.

Mondale completed his law degree in 1956, was admitted to the bar that same year, and joined a prestigious firm that included Minnesota's governor, Orville Freeman. Shortly thereafter, he established his own law firm. Then, in 1959, Mondale was appointed attorney general of Minnesota; he was elected in his own right the following year. In 1964, he was appointed to the U.S. Senate to fill a vacated seat, then was elected to that seat in 1966. He was reelected in 1972.

Mondale was selected as Jimmy Carter's vice presidential candidate in 1976. After the victory, Mondale served as one of the most active and influential vice presidents in American history. However, the Carter-Mondale ticket lost their reelection in 1980. After gaining the party's nomination for president in 1984, Mondale was handily defeated by Ronald Reagan.

After the defeat, Mondale returned to the practice of law until he was appointed as U.S. ambassador to Japan during the Clinton administration. Popular Minnesota senator Paul Wellstone was campaigning for reelection in 2002 when he was killed in a tragic plane wreck. The party recruited a reluctant Mondale out of retirement to finish the campaign for Wellstone, which he did. Even though Mondale lost what would be his final campaign, he remained well respected for his distinguished public career.

Robert P. Watson and Richard Yon

tember he accepted with regret Lance's resignation.

Many observers regarded the Lance affair as a turning point in the Carter presidency. Raising the specter of Watergate, it cast a pall of suspicion over Carter and his administration. That in itself would have hurt any presidency, but it was especially damaging to Carter because he had campaigned as a man of high moral and ethical standards and had promised to restore integrity to government. The Lance affair raised the question whether Carter and his people were any more trustworthy than other politicians. The answer seemed to be that they were not, even though Lance was never convicted of any illegal activity during the Carter years. The struggles with Congress over legislation had already tarnished Carter's image by revealing his weakness in obtaining implementation of his programs. The Lance affair generated skepticism about his character as well as his competence.

Following the Lance affair, Carter began turning his attention away from domestic needs and concentrating on international affairs. In that area, he established a more impressive record, despite his lack of experience, although there, also, questions about his leadership ability dogged his efforts.

The Panama Canal Treaties

One of the most urgent foreign policy issues Carter confronted when he assumed office was the Panama Canal. Since 1964, the United States and Panama had been renegotiating the Panama Canal Treaty. Formidable opposition to any new treaty had developed in the United States, however, opposition which former California governor Ronald Reagan, among others, successfully tapped during the 1976 presidential primaries. "When it comes to the Canal, we built it, we paid for it, it's ours and we should tell Torrijos and Company that we are going to keep it!" Reagan declared, and most Americans apparently agreed with him. As late as the fall of 1977, polls showed that 78 percent of the American people did not wish to "give up" the canal; only 8 percent approved the idea. Moreover, a large number of senators had gone on record opposing any new treaty.

After six months of negotiations with Panamanian officials, Special Representative Sol Linowitz and Chief Negotiator Ellsworth Bunker succeeded in framing two treaties which were signed by President Carter and General Omar Torrijos, the leader of Panama. The treaties provided for joint operation and defense of the canal by the two countries for the rest of the century, with the United States retaining the right to use military force if necessary to keep the canal open and operating, and guaranteed the neutrality of the canal after it was turned over to Panama at the end of 1999. After the signing of the treaties, the Carter administration mounted a concerted lobbying effort to secure Senate approval. The strategy was not to try to persuade a majority of the American people to favor the treaties but, as Carter explained in his memoirs, to convince key elected officials, public opinion leaders, campaign contributors, and other influential people to give their senators "running room" on the treaty. Carter also encouraged undecided senators to visit the Canal Zone and talk with military leaders there, as well as with

Carter and Alejandro Orfila (center), the president of the Organization of American States, watch as Panamanian president Omar Torrijos signs the Panama Canal Treaty in September, 1977. *(AP/Wide World Photos)*

General Torrijos, and he met privately with all but a few senators to persuade them to approve the treaties. On one occasion, Carter admitted in his memoirs, he even told a white lie in the hope of obtaining the vote of Republican senator S. I. Hayakawa. It was the day the Senate was to vote on one of the treaties. Carter got a call from some Senate leaders who were conferring with Hayakawa. "I knew he was listening when they asked me if I needed to meet occasionally with the California semanticist to get his advice on African affairs. I gulped, thought for a few seconds, and replied, 'Yes, I really do!' hoping God would forgive me." After almost two months of debate, the Senate confirmed the two treaties by a very close margin, on March 16 and April 18, 1978, voting in each case 68 in favor and 32 opposed. The ratification process was finally completed in September, 1979, when, after another massive lobbying effort by the administration—this time in both the House and Senate—laws implementing the treaties gained approval.

Ratification of the Panama Canal treaties was a signal victory for Carter and largely the result of the kind of successful congressional lobbying he failed to muster on behalf of other programs. In the long run, however, it may have been politically damaging. Carter maintained that it "left deep and serious political wounds," and he attributed his own reelection defeat, as well as that of eighteen senators, to his and their support of the Panama Canal treaties.

The Camp David Accords

Carter's most impressive foreign policy achievement was the peace treaty ending thirty-one years of hostility between Israel and Egypt. In April, 1977, Carter began talking with the leaders of the two countries, Israeli prime minister Menachem Begin and Egyptian president Anwar el-Sadat. The culmination of the mediating process came in September, 1978, when the three men conferred at Camp David for thirteen days, during which Begin and Sadat reached final agreement on a framework for peace. That served as a basis for the peace treaty signed on March 26, 1979, in which, among other things, the two countries agreed to establish normal and friendly relations and to start negotiations on Palestinian self-rule on the West Bank and the Gaza Strip; Israel agreed to a phased withdrawal from the Sinai; and Egypt agreed to end its economic boycott of Israel and allow Israeli ships and cargoes through the Suez Canal.

As Haynes Johnson and Hedley Donovan have observed, Carter's success in facilitating peace between Israel and Egypt was in large measure a personal triumph. His aptitude for problem solving and absorption in detail, his religious faith and knowledge of biblical history, his sensitivity to personality differences between Begin and Sadat, and his patience and stamina all paid off in his negotiations with the two Middle East leaders. His efforts, however, did little to raise his standing in the public opinion polls, and whatever luster Carter acquired upon the signing of the Egyptian-Israeli treaty dimmed when, shortly afterward, Israel began establishing new settlements on the West Bank.

Carter scored two foreign policy successes with the Panama Canal treaties and the Egyptian-Israeli Peace Treaty. He also normalized United States relations with the People's Republic of China, completing the process begun by President Richard Nixon. Relations with the Soviet Union, however, proved troublesome. Early in his presidency Carter vowed to continue détente, but toward the end of his term he sounded and acted like a Cold Warrior. Events in places such as Cuba, Africa, and Afghanistan had much to do with his shift in policy. So did the different outlooks of his two foreign policy advisers, the pugnacious Zbigniew Brzezinski, national security adviser, and the more conciliatory Cyrus Vance, secretary of state. Even early in his term Carter seemed torn between Brzezinski's advocacy of a get-tough policy

Anwar el-Sadat, Carter, and Menachem Begin at Camp David. *(NARA)*

and Vance's emphasis on diplomatic accommodation. On one hand, he denounced Soviet treatment of dissidents such as Andrei Sakharov and Soviet backing of Cuban troops in Africa as well as the presence of a Soviet brigade in Cuba; he also approved construction of the MX missile system. On the other hand, he encouraged the negotiations that produced the Strategic Arms Limitation Talks (SALT) II Treaty, limiting the United States and the Soviet Union to 2,250 strategic weapons each and imposing limits on the number of warheads and the development of new kinds of nuclear weapons.

After Carter and Soviet president Leonid Brezhnev signed the SALT II Treaty on June 18, 1979, the already fragile relations between the two countries deteriorated. When Soviet troops invaded Afghanistan in December of that year, Carter decided that "verbal condemnation" was not enough, that the Soviets "must pay a concrete price for their aggression." He requested the Senate to delay consideration

of SALT II (which by then had little chance of passing), announced an embargo on high-technology equipment and grain sales to the Soviet Union, and organized an international boycott of the 1980 Summer Olympics in Moscow. Then, on January 23, 1980, in his State of the Union address to Congress, he announced what became known as the Carter Doctrine. Declaring that the Soviet presence in Afghanistan posed "a grave threat" to the region containing more than two-thirds of the world's exportable oil, he warned that "an attempt by any outside force to gain control of the Persian Gulf region will be regarded as an assault on the vital interests of the United States of America, and such an assault will be repelled by any means necessary, including military force." In the same address, Carter requested an increase in military spending and the resumption of draft registration. Nevertheless, Carter's sanctions and tough language failed to persuade the Soviet Union to withdraw its troops from Afghanistan. At home Carter's efforts elicited little public enthusiasm, some criticism—from George Kennan and Senator Edward Kennedy, for example—and, in the case of the grain embargo, considerable resentment among American farmers.

Foreign Policy Initiatives: The Primacy of Human Rights

Carter's denunciation of Soviet treatment of dissidents was part of a larger program of championing human rights around the world. In an address at Notre Dame University in May, 1977, Carter declared that a commitment to human rights was "a fundamental tenet" of his foreign policy. His administration not only protested the torture and execution of political prisoners but also sought to eliminate discrimination based on race, sex, religion, or ethnic origin and to promote freedom of travel and emigration, freedom of religion, and the right to vote, work, and be given a fair trial. In asserting the primacy of human rights, Carter repudiated the pragmatic approach associated with former presidents Richard Nixon and Gerald Ford and former secretary of state Henry Kissinger. Carter defended the idea of basing American foreign policy on moral principle as "a practical and realistic approach to foreign affairs." Inducing authoritarian right-wing allies and friends of the United States to protect human rights would help prevent the outbreak of leftist revolutions, he argued; championing human rights would also strengthen American influence among the unaligned nations in the Third World. Perhaps the most important reason, however, for launching the human rights campaign, at least in Carter's view, was that "it was the right thing to do."

Except for the release of a few political prisoners, Carter was unable to win much success in his crusade. Like so many of his domestic and foreign policy initiatives, it failed to fire the imagination of the American people. Perhaps Vietnam had made them wary of grandiose appeals to moral principle. Critics faulted the human rights campaign on various grounds. Some dismissed it as another instance of substituting rhetoric for action. Others criticized the administration for applying the human rights test selectively, exempting certain allies such as Iran under Mohammad Reza Shah Pahlavi (known as the shah), the Philippines, and South Korea. Still others thought the denunciations of Soviet human rights violations jeopardized a new arms limitation treaty. In his memoirs, Carter admitted that his human rights pronouncements had caused tension between the United States and the Soviet Union, but he doubted they had ever been directly responsible for any failure to reach accord on matters of common interest. "Even if our human-rights policy had been a much more serious point of contention in Soviet-American relations, I would not have been inclined to accommodate Soviet objections," he wrote. "We have a fundamental difference in philosophy concerning human freedoms, and it does not benefit us to cover it up. The respect for human rights is one of the most significant advantages of a free and democratic nation in the peaceful struggle for influence, and we should use this good weapon as effectively as possible."

Iran and the Hostage Crisis

The Iranian seizure of American hostages in November, 1979, proved to be Carter's toughest foreign policy problem. Even more than the Soviet invasion of Afghanistan, the hostage crisis made Carter appear weak and ineffectual. Upon taking office he had reaffirmed United States support of the shah, the leader of Iran. Early in 1979, the shah was overthrown by a religious, antimodern, popular revolution led by Ayatollah Ruhollah Khomeini. Then on November 4, militant Iranians overran the United States embassy in Tehran, took some sixty Americans hostage, and vowed not to release them until the shah, who was in New York City for medical treatment, was returned by the United States to stand trial in Iran. After a few weeks of holding the hostages, the Iranians released the women and blacks among them, leaving a total of fifty-two men in captivity; they also put forth additional demands that the United States apologize for "crimes against the Iranian people," pay financial damages, and turn over the shah's assets to Iran.

Carter refused all such demands and, when the ayatollah threatened to try some of the hostages as spies, warned that if any of the Americans were tried or harmed the United States would inflict severe punishment on Iran, including military action. Early in the hostage crisis Carter ordered a suspension of oil imports from Iran and froze billions of dollars of Iranian assets in American banks. His initial response evoked an upsurge of popular support. In the month after the crisis began, his approval rating in the polls soared from 32 to 61 percent. On December 4, he announced that he would run for a second term as president. He observed, however, that for the next few months he would not campaign, in order to devote full attention to the hostage situation.

In his memoirs, Carter wrote that during the hostage crisis he listened to every recommendation offered him, no matter how absurd, from returning the shah for trial in Iran to dropping an atomic bomb on Tehran. His administration was divided over the proper response, with Secretary of State Vance advocating reliance on diplomatic means and National Security Adviser Brzezinski favoring a military solution. Ultimately, Brzezinski won the debate when Carter and his advisers agreed to attempt the ill-fated military rescue operation of April 24 and 25, 1980. Of all Carter's advisers, only Vance opposed the mission, and he offered his resignation as secretary of state three days before the operation was launched, although it was not made public until afterward. In his memoirs, Carter wrote that he decided on the rescue mission only when intelligence information indicated there was almost no chance of the hostages being released within five or six

months. No doubt Carter and his advisers had also become impatient with diplomatic efforts and economic sanctions, which had proven unavailing. Another reason that Carter and his advisers agreed to the rescue operation has been suggested by Gary Sick, the staff member on Iran in the National Security Council during the Carter presidency. As fellow government workers, they tended to identify with the imprisoned Americans and felt guilty for having left them exposed at the embassy in Tehran. Such feelings, Sick argues, encouraged "a strong impulse to do something, almost as if action was a necessary end in itself."

On April 25, Carter went on television to announce that the rescue operation had failed, with the loss of eight of the rescue team in a helicopter crash. In his brief statement, he took full responsibility for the mission and praised the courage of the volunteers who had participated in it. Five days later, on April 30, he declared that his responsibilities were now "manageable enough" for him to travel again and begin to campaign in the Democratic primaries. It seems likely that Carter and his aides were looking for an opportunity to abandon the Rose Garden strategy because it had begun to work against him politically. Critics were charging him with hiding behind the hostages to avoid debating his principal rival for the Democratic nomination, Edward Kennedy. In a sense Carter had himself become a hostage to the crisis—he had painted himself into a corner, Patrick Caddell later remarked. Having declared that he would not travel or campaign in order to devote full attention to the hostage situation, he could not change his position lest he be thought to have lost interest in the hostages or hope for their release. Although it failed, the rescue operation seemed to provide a convenient terminus to one phase of the crisis, freeing Carter to resume a more normal schedule.

The crisis dragged on for 444 days. Not until January 20, 1981, some thirty minutes after a new president, Ronald Reagan, had taken the

One of the hostages is displayed to the crowd outside the U.S. embassy in Tehran, Iran, on November 9, 1979. *(AP/ Wide World Photos)*

oath of office, did the Iranians release the fifty-two Americans. The timing was seen as one last humiliation for Carter.

Carter thought later that one of the reasons he was defeated for a second term stemmed from the "cautious and prudent policy" he had followed in the hostage crisis. Although not a disaster, his handling of the Iranian situation certainly did little to enhance his reputation as president and contrasts sharply with his remarkably successful mediation of the Camp David accords between Egypt and Israel. Why was he successful in the one case and judged to have failed in the other? As Hedley Donovan has pointed out, in the case of the Camp David talks, both Carter's abilities and the circumstances in which he operated were conducive to success. He had studied the situation in the Middle East intensively; he admired Sadat ("more than any other leaders," he wrote in his memoirs) and respected Begin. The Camp Da-

vid talks were focused in time and held in a setting where Carter was in control, where the participants were isolated from the outside world, and from which the press was excluded. Although he wanted the talks to succeed, Carter could be somewhat detached since the safety of no American lives hinged on the outcome. Finally, the Camp David talks took the form of orderly, rational discourse among three men who had entered into them voluntarily and with some hope, even determination, of reaching accord. In such a situation, Carter's patient mediation facilitated the development of understanding and trust essential to any agreement between Begin and Sadat.

The Iranian hostage situation presented an entirely different situation. Carter was thrust into a potentially violent confrontation, not only with the Ayatollah Khomeini but also with the fanatic anti-American militants who demonstrated outside the United States embassy in Tehran. He had to deal with a seizure of American hostages and with a revolution as well—what one historian has described as a "man-made hurricane" that the United States, despite its might, was powerless to control. As the leader of the revolution, Khomeini pursued a policy of deliberate intransigence, against which Carter's aptitude for patient, rational negotiation proved unavailing. Patience was the wisest policy, since release of the hostages depended finally on internal developments in Iran. Once the crisis reached an impasse, however, Carter became increasingly vulnerable to criticism for not acting to free the hostages. Saturation coverage by the media may have exacerbated popular frustration with what was seen as a weak, do-nothing policy. A few days before the 1980 presidential election, voting in the Iranian Parliament seemed to signal a breakthrough in the crisis. Nothing came of it, and it served mainly to highlight Carter's inability to secure the release of the Americans. In the end, the Iranians underscored their own control of the situation—and Carter's lack of control—by delaying the release of the hostages, after months of negotiation with the Carter administration, until just after President Reagan took office.

The questions the hostage crisis raised about Carter's leadership ability were not new. They had dogged him almost since the beginning of his presidency, but they seemed to acquire special significance in the context of the hostage situation. Not surprisingly, they dominated the 1980 presidential campaign, and voter disenchantment with Carter's performance combined with a shift toward conservatism to deny his bid for a second term.

The Carter Presidency: The Question of Leadership

The question of leadership has also been the focus of evaluations of the Carter presidency. Most of the journalists and historians who have written about Carter have judged him an intel-

ligent, industrious, honest man who lacked the leadership ability required of an effective president. Arriving in Washington as a self-proclaimed outsider and antipolitician, he failed to develop the good working relationship with Congress he needed to implement his programs. This failure was partly because of his thinly veiled scorn for the legislators and the special interests he thought manipulated them, partly because of the inexperience of his White House staff, and partly because of his estrangement from the Democratic Party leadership. Even after four years in office he had not made any strong alliances on Capitol Hill or provided effective leadership for members of his staff. In an article titled "The Passionless Presidency," James Fallows, chief White House speechwriter during Carter's first two years as president, observed that Carter failed to induce or inspire his staff to come up with new ideas, goals, or policies. Carter ran the White House like a bureaucracy, Fallows noted, with the result that "the White House took on the spirit of a bureaucracy, drained of zeal, obsessed with form, full of people attracted by the side-dressings of the work rather than the work itself."

Finally, Carter proved unable to lead the nation as a whole. He claimed to feel a personal, almost mystical bond with the American people, but they did not reciprocate. Although he thought of the people as "a final forum," he was not successful in appealing to them for support. His famous "crisis of confidence" speech of July 15, 1979, is the best illustration of this fact. Carter delivered the speech in the midst of increasing public anger and frustration provoked by a severe gasoline shortage, long lines at filling stations, and huge price increases for oil and gas. Instead of focusing on the domestic energy crisis and proposing legislative remedies, Carter decided to broaden the scope of his speech. In it he contended that the problems of the nation went much deeper than gasoline lines or shortages, or inflation or recession. The true problem was "a crisis of confidence" among the American people. To solve it he called on Americans to engage in a collective act of will. Sounding not unlike Norman Vincent Peale proclaiming the "power of positive thinking," Carter declared, "We simply must have faith in each other, faith in our ability to govern ourselves, and faith in the future of this Nation." To revive that faith, he urged Americans to rally around the "standard" of energy. "On the battlefield of energy we can win for our Nation a new confidence, and we can seize control again of our common destiny." Unfortunately, what Carter had earlier called "the moral equivalent of war" had already demonstrated scant potential for exciting enthusiasm or unity among the American people, and the July call to arms was unlikely to change matters. To be sure, after the speech Carter's approval rating in the opinion polls rose slightly, but he undermined whatever positive results

the address had produced by suddenly announcing the resignation of high officials in the cabinet and White House, thereby calling attention once again to the weaknesses of his administration. In that context, the statement that had appeared to be a successful bid for support ("I realize more than ever that as President I need your help") now looked like a confession of inability to lead.

Fallows attributed Carter's inability to inspire his staff or the American people to his style of thought. Carter believed "fifty things, but no one thing," Fallows argued, noting that although Carter had well-reasoned positions on various issues, he had no "large view" of their priority or the relations among them. Fallows, and more recently Haynes Johnson, Robert Shogan, and Hedley Donovan, agreed in attributing Carter's inability to lead to the absence of an overall political philosophy or ideology capable of inspiring loyalty to something

Rosalynn and Jimmy Carter help build a home as volunteers for Habitat for Humanity in 1992. *(Reuters/Steve Jaffe/Archive Photos)*

Excerpts from Jimmy Carter's speech "Energy and the National Goals—A Crisis of Confidence," July 15, 1979

I know, of course, being President, that government actions and legislation can be very important. That's why I've worked hard to put my campaign promises into law, and I have to admit, with just mixed success. But after listening to the American people, I have been reminded again that all the legislation in the world can't fix what's wrong with America. So, I want to speak to you first tonight about a subject even more serious than energy or inflation. I want to talk to you right now about a fundamental threat to American democracy.

I do not mean our political and civil liberties. They will endure. And I do not refer to the outward strength of America, a nation that is at peace tonight everywhere in the world, with unmatched economic power and military might.

The threat is nearly invisible in ordinary ways. It is a crisis of confidence. It is a crisis that strikes at the very heart and soul and spirit of our national will. We can see this crisis in the growing doubt about the meaning of our own lives and in the loss of a unity of purpose for our nation.

The erosion of our confidence in the future is threatening to destroy the social and the political fabric of America.

The confidence that we have always had as a people is not simply some romantic dream or a proverb in a dusty book that we read just on the Fourth of July.

It is the idea which founded our Nation and has guided our development as a people. Confidence in the future has supported everything else—public institutions and private enterprise, our own families, and the very Constitution of the United States. Confidence has defined our course and has served as a link between generations. We've always believed in something called progress. We've always had a faith that the days of our children would be better than our own.

Our people are losing that faith, not only in government itself but in the ability as citizens to serve as the ultimate rulers and shapers of our democracy. . . . In a nation that was proud of hard work, strong families, close-knit communities, and our faith in God, too many of us now tend to worship self-indulgence and consumption. Human identity is no longer defined by what one does, but by what one owns. But we've discovered that owning things and consuming things does not satisfy our longing for meaning. We've learned that piling up material goods cannot fill the emptiness of lives which have no confidence or purpose.

larger than himself. In the 1980 campaign, he successfully dodged questions about ideology, and during his presidency he tried to substitute moralism and exhortation for ideology. During the 1980 campaign, Adam Clymer of *The New York Times* reported that although Carter had a list of goals he wanted to pursue in his second term, he still lacked any overriding vision or philosophy. That lack of vision and the resultant inability to lead gave Carter the reputation as one of the less effective presidents of the twentieth century.

Nevertheless, Carter continued to be a presence on the national and international scenes after leaving office. He became an advocate for the group Habitat for Humanity, which builds houses for poor families, and even helped construct some of them himself. He wrote books about morality and the experience of aging. He offered his talents as a peace negotiator in times of international crisis in the Middle East and elsewhere. His strong moral stance and humanitarian record came to be regarded with nostalgia in an increasingly cynical world. In 1999, he and Rosalynn were awarded the Presidential Medal of Freedom, while in 2002, Carter won the Nobel Peace Prize for, among other things, his extensive humanitarian and peace negotiation efforts. In many ways, Jimmy Carter earned the respect that had eluded him in the White House.

Anne C. Loveland

Suggested Readings

Anderson, Patrick. *Electing Jimmy Carter: The Campaign of 1976.* Baton Rouge: Louisiana State University Press, 1994. A memoir of the presidential election by one of Carter's former speechwriters.

Biven, W. Carl. *Jimmy Carter's Economy: Policy in an Age of Limits.* Chapel Hill: University of North Carolina Press, 2002. Traces how the Carter administration developed and implemented economic policy and how its approach paved the way for a new direction for the Democratic Party.

Bourne, Peter G. *Jimmy Carter: A Comprehensive Biography from Plains to Post-Presidency.* New York: Scribner, 1997. An admiring biography by a close personal friend of the Carters.

Brinkley, Douglas. *The Unfinished Presidency: Jimmy Carter's Journey Beyond the White House.* New York: Viking, 1998. Discusses Carter's postpresidential life and his efforts toward international peace and social justice.

Carter, Jimmy. *Keeping Faith.* Toronto: Bantam Books, 1982. Carter's presidential memoirs.

_____. *Why Not the Best?* Nashville, Tenn.: Broadman Press, 1975. A brief autobiography describing his early life, education, and business and political activities before the 1976 election.

Donovan, Hedley. *Roosevelt to Reagan.* New York: Harper & Row, 1985. The former *Time* editor and insider in the Carter administration describes his "encounters" with Carter and with eight other presidents.

Dumbrell, John. *The Carter Presidency: A Reevaluation.* New York: St. Martin's Press, 1993. Discusses the successes and failures of the Carter presidency from the perspective that a decade of new analysis affords.

Fink, Gary M. *Prelude to the Presidency.* Westport, Conn.: Greenwood Press, 1980. Examines Carter's days as governor of Georgia.

Jimmy Carter Library and Museum. http://www.jimmycarterlibrary.org/. The Web site of Carter's official presidential library.

Johnson, Haynes. *In the Absence of Power.* New York: Viking Press, 1980. An assessment of Carter and his presidency written before he left office.

Kaufman, Burton I. *The Presidency of James Earl Carter, Jr.* Lawrence: University Press of Kansas, 1993. Part of the University of Kansas's American Presidency series, this volume details the highs and lows of the Carter administration.

Morris, Kenneth E. *Jimmy Carter: American Moralist.* Athens: University of Georgia Press, 1996. A full-scale biography that explores the link between Carter's moral values and his policy decisions.

Shogan, Robert. *None of the Above.* New York: New American Library, 1982. An insightful comparative analysis of Carter and his predecessors and successor.

Shoup, Laurence H. *The Carter Presidency and Beyond.* Palo Alto, Calif.: Ramparts Press, 1980. An interesting perspective on the sources of Carter's domestic and foreign policy.

Sick, Gary. *All Fall Down.* New York: Random House, 1985. An analysis of the Carter administration's handling of the Iranian hostage crisis.

Slavicek, Louise Chipley. *Jimmy Carter.* New York: Chelsea House, 2003. A standard biography.

Thornton, Richard C. *The Carter Years: Toward a New Global Order.* New York: Paragon House, 1991. Provides a balanced overview of the Carter presidency.

Troester, Rod. *Jimmy Carter as Peacemaker: A Post-presidential Biography.* Westport, Conn.: Praeger, 1996. An examination of Carter's postpresidential role as peace negotiator and humanitarian.

Ronald Reagan

40th President, 1981-1989

Born: February 6, 1911
    Tampico, Illinois
Died: June 5, 2004
    Los Angeles, California

Political Party: Republican
Vice President: George H. W. Bush

Cabinet Members

Secretary of State: Alexander Haig, George
    Shultz
Secretary of the Treasury: Donald Regan,
    James A. Baker III, Nicholas Brady
Secretary of Defense: Caspar Weinberger,
    Frank C. Carlucci
Attorney General: William French Smith,
    Edwin Meese III, Dick Thornburgh
Secretary of the Interior: James Watt, William P.
    Clark, Donald P. Hodel
Secretary of Agriculture: John R. Block,
    Richard E. Lyng
Secretary of Commerce: Malcolm Baldrige,
    C. William Verity, Jr.
Secretary of Labor: Raymond J. Donovan,
    William E. Brock, Ann Dore
    McLaughlin
Secretary of Health and Human Services:
    Richard S. Schweiker, Margaret Heckler,
    Otis R. Bowen
Secretary of Housing and Urban Development:
    Samuel Pierce
Secretary of Transportation: Andrew L. Lewis,
    Jr., Elizabeth Dole, James H. Burnley IV
Secretary of Energy: James B. Edwards,
    Donald P. Hodel, John S. Herrington
Secretary of Education: T. H. Bell, William J.
    Bennett, Lauro F. Cavazos

Reagan's official portrait. *(White House Historical Society)*

Ronald Reagan became the fortieth president of the United States on January 20, 1981. After serving two full terms in office, the first president since Dwight D. Eisenhower to do so, he was succeeded by his vice president, George H. W. Bush, in 1989.

The eight years of the Reagan administration represent a period of unprecedented domestic economic prosperity, as well as peaceful interaction between the United States and other nations. This was a period of transition, as Reagan began his administration amid growing East-West tensions, which increased with his accusations about the "evil empire" of the Soviet Union. He left office after signing the first major arms control agreement between the United States and the Soviet Union in almost a decade. In those eight years, the United States regained a forceful role internationally, an image fostered by events such as the bombing of Libya in April, 1986, in response to a terrorist bombing in Berlin that took the life of a member of the U.S. military.

Concomitantly, however, the Reagan legacy also included the largest deficit in the history of the country, a balance of payments skewed in favor of the United States' trading partners, and a marked shift in domestic political priorities.

The Early Years

Ronald Wilson Reagan was born on February 6, 1911, in Tampico, Illinois. His father, John Edward Reagan, was a New Deal Democrat who had been head of the Works Project Administration in Dixon, Illinois. His mother, born Nelle Wilson, was more conservative, a very religious woman who spent much of her time engaged in works of charity. The family moved often in Reagan's youth, but these early years were the ones that seemed to have imbued in Reagan his commitment to the American ideals of hard work, charity toward those less fortunate, and patriotism. After completing his preparatory schooling, Reagan entered Eureka College, graduating in 1932 with a major in economics.

His media career began with a job as a sports announcer with radio station WOO in Davenport, Iowa, followed by a job with station WHO in Des Moines, Iowa. In 1937, at the age of twenty-six, during a trip to California to cover baseball spring training, he was signed by an agent for the Warner Bros. studio for a film part in which he played a radio announcer. He went on to act in more than fifty films, including *Knute Rockne—All American* (1940) and *Bedtime for Bonzo* (1951). He made his last film, *The Killers*, in 1964. In many ways, it can be argued that Reagan's early career as an actor was excellent preparation for his later political career. At ease in front of the camera, he developed a style to which the American public responded very positively, thereby earning for himself the title the "Great Communicator."

It was also during this early period in Hollywood that Reagan first became politically active: During the 1930's and 1940's, he worked for or was a member of Americans for Democratic Action, the American Veterans Committee, the United World Federalists, and the Hollywood Independent Citizens Committee of the Arts, Sciences, and Professions. He also became involved in Hollywood politics when he was elected president of the Screen Actors Guild (SAG) in 1947. He was reelected to serve five additional one-year terms. One of his primary responsibilities in his capacity as president of SAG was to represent the interests of members of the guild in negotiating union contracts and in other labor disputes. These were often bitter battles, and they contributed directly to his rethinking of many of his political and ideological convictions. As a result of his experiences in Hollywood during those early years, Reagan was converted, politically and ideologically, from a New Deal Democrat to a conservative Republican.

During this period, Reagan was married for nine years to actress Jane Wyman, with whom

Reagan in a scene from the film *Knute Rockne—All American*. (Museum of Modern Art/Film Stills Archive)

eral, during this period Reagan's reputation was that of a respected and also moderate force in the anticommunist movement. These activities and events, especially against the backdrop of the Cold War, contributed to Reagan's further reevaluation of his assumptions about politics and the role of government in the United States.

In 1954, Reagan became spokesperson for the General Electric Company and host of its weekly television show. He traveled around the country on behalf of GE, preaching the corporate philosophy, which blended well with his own. He spoke of the need for a strong military as the only means of assuring the nation's security, and he warned of the dangers of big government. Both these themes would figure prominently in his own political campaigns in later years. He remained as spokesperson for GE until 1962, at which point he resigned in order to devote himself to the Republican Party and his own political career.

The Governor of California

Especially following Barry Goldwater's overwhelming defeat in his bid for the presidency in 1964, Reagan became increasingly active in Republican Party politics in California. Although he had little political experience beyond his activities in Hollywood, a group of California businessmen suggested that he run for the governorship of the state. He did so, and in 1966 he defeated two-term Governor Edmund G. (Pat) Brown by a margin of nearly one million votes. Reagan served two terms in the office, altering the complexion of California politics as a result. The experience also introduced him to the political realities that would help him considerably in his bid for the presidency and, subsequently, in his eight years in that office.

he had two children: a daughter, Maureen, and an adopted son, Michael. The couple divorced in 1948, and in 1952, Reagan married Nancy Davis, the daughter of a prominent physician. Reagan's bride, Nancy, was also politically conservative, and her orientation further encouraged the political and ideological metamorphosis of her husband. Nancy's direct influence on her husband in any number of different areas persisted through the White House years.

During Reagan's tenure in Hollywood in the 1940's and 1950's, it is possible to see the development of the themes that would later be central to his administration as president. The Cold War then being waged between the United States and the Soviet Union strengthened his anticommunist convictions. When McCarthyism and anticommunist feelings swept Hollywood in the early 1950's, Reagan became one of the leading figures in purging the alleged communists from the Screen Actors Guild. At that time, he also resigned from any liberal organization of which he was a member. In gen-

The three cornerstones of his administration were taxes and government spending, welfare reform, and higher education in the state. He did have an impact on all three areas, although the final outcomes were not necessarily the ones that he had initially sought. As he worked to implement changes in these areas, for six of his eight years as governor he did so with an unfriendly Democratic majority in the state legislature, a situation that would be replicated during his second term as president. Hence, his years as governor provided both the political experience that he would take to the office of president of the United States and the opportunity to see at first hand the differences between the theory and reality in first creating policies and then implementing them.

During his initial term as governor, Reagan, having inherited from Pat Brown a large state budget deficit, secured the largest tax increase in the history of the state. The increases were for corporate, personal income, and sales tax; he

THE FIRST LADY
NANCY REAGAN

As First Lady, Nancy Reagan was known for her elegance and style. Prior to marrying Ronald Reagan, Nancy Davis was a successful actress, appearing in eleven motion pictures, including *Hellcats of the Navy* (1957), in which she played opposite her husband. Nevertheless, she often said that her life really began when "I married the man I loved." Nancy Reagan became her husband's biggest supporter as he went from president of the Screen Actors Guild to president of the United States.

Nancy was born Anne Frances Robbins in New York City on July 6, 1921. Her mother, Edith, was an actress who later married a prominent neurosurgeon, Dr. Loyal Davis. Dr. Davis moved the family to Chicago and adopted young Nancy. She attended Smith College in Massachusetts as a theater major and went to New York following graduation. Eventually, well-connected friends of her mother helped Nancy launch her career. She soon won a studio contract and was bound for Hollywood.

Nancy chose to give up her film career when she married Reagan in 1952. She soon had children to care for—Patricia Ann "Patti" and Ronald Prescott "Ron"—and was also a part-time mother to Reagan's two children from his first marriage to actress Jane Wyman. When Reagan became governor of California in 1967, his wife easily assumed the duties of official hostess. She devoted herself to her husband's career and was one of his best advisers. She was proud when Reagan's political ambitions turned into a successful run for the White House in 1980.

As First Lady, Nancy Reagan brought an almost royal feel to the White House. She was criticized for her lavish redecorating of the family quarters and for accepting gifts of designer clothing. However, others felt that the good done by her involvement with the "Just Say No" drug prevention campaign more than offset the negative criticisms. She was also a notable patron of the arts and author of *My Turn*, a 1989 account of her years in the White House.

As president, Ronald Reagan served two complete terms (1981-1989), the first president to do so since Dwight Eisenhower. When the Reagans left the White House, they had the satisfaction of seeing their vice president, George H. W. Bush, assume the presidency.

Reagan was diagnosed with Alzheimer's disease several years after leaving the White House. Nancy lovingly cared for him until his death in 2004. She became active in the struggle for better understanding of the disease.

Dean M. Shapiro

actually lowered property taxes. During his two terms as governor, the state budget grew from $4.6 billion to $10.2 billion, a significant portion of which was then allocated to local governments for welfare and education.

Following his victory over Democratic candidate Jesse Unruh in 1970, Reagan turned his attention to the issue of welfare, focusing on the fact that approximately one out of nine people in the state were receiving some form of welfare benefit. Reagan proposed a major welfare reform package, including the introduction of Medi-Cal, a variant of the federal Medicare program. Versions of his proposed reforms were finally adopted after lengthy debates within the state legislature.

In the area of higher education, Reagan responded to the turmoil and unrest prevalent among many college students protesting the war in Vietnam: He reduced university funding by 27 percent during his first two years in office. Once the protest movement subsided, as the war came to a halt, he reversed his position and increased funding to higher education within the state. By the time he left office in 1974, funding for higher education had more than doubled over what it had been when he took office.

Also emerging during Reagan's tenure as governor was the social agenda that he would pursue as president, including his outspoken opposition to abortion on demand and his support for capital punishment.

The Run for the Presidency

As Reagan became more prominent nationally, his name was mentioned as a possible Republican candidate for president—first in 1968, when he did relatively well, although not well enough to secure the nomination against Richard Nixon. To become the Republican candidate in 1976, Reagan had to face incumbent

Nancy and Ronald Reagan wave to the crowd at a campaign stop in 1980. *(Ronald Reagan Library)*

president Gerald Ford, who had become president following the resignation of Nixon in August, 1974. At that time, Reagan had campaigned actively for the support needed to run as the Republican Party candidate. He fell 60 votes short of defeating President Ford for the nomination.

Reagan had another opportunity to run in 1980. He had spent the time between the election of 1976 and 1980 working on his campaign, and he reaped the rewards when he was officially nominated to be his party's candidate at the Republican National Convention in Detroit, defeating his closest rival, George H. W. Bush, by an overwhelming margin of 1,939 to 55.

In the 1980 presidential campaign against incumbent Democratic president Jimmy Carter, Reagan focused on Carter's failures during his four years in office, including an inflation rate exceeding 12 percent, the concomitantly high unemployment rates, and the apparent decline in the United States' international prestige. His campaign seemed to touch the American public: Reagan won an overwhelming victory of 489 electoral votes to Carter's 49 and about 51 percent of the popular vote to Carter's 42 percent. (The third-party candidate, John Anderson, received most of the remaining 7 percent.) Reagan declared this overwhelming victory to be his "mandate" by the American public to govern according to the policies and programs that he had outlined during the campaign.

The New Conservatism

Ronald Reagan came into the office of president of the United States determined to change the country's policies and priorities and with the strong belief that his overwhelming margin of victory gave him the support of the American public necessary to achieve those goals. Domestically, he pledged to reduce the size of the national government, strengthen the role of the states within the framework of the federal system of government, reduce government expenditures through massive budget cuts, and lower taxes and inflation. He also sought to restructure foreign policy to make the United States more assertive and forceful internationally, to enable the nation to regain its lost power and prestige, and to achieve "peace through strength." During his first term, Reagan was aided in the pursuit of his goals by a Republican majority in the Senate, the first since 1954, and by a number of Southern Democrats who supported Reagan's conservative agenda.

Reagan's key cabinet appointments, such as his appointment of Alexander Haig, former commander of the North Atlantic Treaty Organization (NATO), as secretary of state, and of former budget director Caspar Weinberger as secretary of defense, reaffirmed his commitment to a strong defense and to the perception that the United States would not yield to the Soviet Union. Donald Regan, chairman of brokerage house Merrill Lynch, was made secretary of the treasury. William French Smith, a longtime personal friend of Reagan, was named to the post of attorney general. These and the other appointments Reagan made during his first term supported his commitment to a conservative political and social agenda for the duration of his administration.

Reagan's personal popularity and his "honeymoon" period were, ironically, extended well into his first term in office when he was shot by John Hinckley, Jr., a psychotic young man, outside a hotel in Washington, D.C., in March of 1981. The incident had the effect of rallying Congress and the public behind the new president, strengthening his political position and support for his programs.

Reagan's Domestic Agenda

Reagan approached the presidency with his own conservative social, political, and economic agenda. These were articulated during his campaign in 1980 against Carter, and Reagan remained committed to them for his eight years in office. Many of the principles that he advocated were extensions of those he put forward and worked for as governor of California, and they reflected Reagan's conservatism. His two terms as president are considered among the most ideological in recent history.

Reagan came to office with a number of assumptions regarding the relationship between the economy and government. One of the primary goals that he hoped to accomplish was to "get the government off the people's backs." Specifically, Reagan's desire was to reduce government intervention in the economy, allowing government decisions to be made by business operating in a free market economy rather than by bureaucrats in government agencies in Washington, D.C. The core of this principle can be found in Reagan's belief that, when left alone to work freely, people will design, produce, and sell more because they know that they will make money by doing so. This tendency results in a cycle that creates jobs, extends prosperity to others, and benefits society on the whole by increasing productivity and creating more income through taxes. Conversely, if constricted by government by high taxes and excessive regulation, individuals will not derive the full benefits of their achievements. Investment then dwindles, production drops, and the entire economy slumps.

In theory, according to supply-side economics as advocated by economist Arthur Laffer and others, the key to low inflation, high

---

THE VICE PRESIDENT
GEORGE H. W. BUSH

George H. W. Bush was born on June 12, 1924, in Milton, Massachusetts. Both sides of his family had amassed great fortunes, and Bush's father would go on to serve in the U.S. Senate. The younger Bush grew up in Greenwich, Connecticut, attending such exclusive prep schools as Greenwich County Day School and Phillips Academy. The family summered at their home in Kennebunkport, Maine.

Bush joined the U.S. Navy in 1942 as the youngest naval combat pilot. After several missions in World War II, he was shot down but rescued by a U.S. submarine crew. He married Barbara Pierce on January 6, 1945. The couple had six children, one of whom died at a young age. Bush attended Yale after being discharged from the military. Although his family had extensive business contacts and opportunities, Bush decided to move his family to Odessa, Texas, after graduating in 1948 in order to enter the oil industry. Later, he moved to Midland, Texas.

Bush entered politics in 1966, gaining a seat in the U.S. House of Representatives, where he served from 1967 to 1971. After a failed bid for the U.S. Senate, Bush's career was advanced by a number of choice political appointments by Presidents Richard M. Nixon and Gerald R. Ford, including ambassador to the United Nations, U.S. liaison to China, chair of the Republican National Committee, and Central Intelligence Agency (CIA) director.

Bush ran for president in 1980 and failed to win the party nomination, but he was selected to be Ronald Reagan's vice presidential nominee. After eight years as vice president, Bush ran a successful campaign for president in 1988. His reelection effort in 1992, however, proved unsuccessful. Although Bush was less active in public affairs than most contemporary former presidents, he supported the successful gubernatorial campaigns of two of his sons and became only the second person in American history to be both president and father of a president. In his retirement, Bush split his time between Houston and Kennebunkport.

Robert P. Watson and Richard Yon

economic growth, low unemployment, and a balanced federal budget lies in cutting taxes and limiting government interference. The supply-siders argued that, if those things were accomplished, the economy would boom, thereby leading to an increase in revenues as more people and corporations could pay more in taxes.

This theory was adopted and implemented during Reagan's first term in office and became known as Reaganomics. Upon taking office, Reagan wanted to achieve three economic goals: reduce the size of the federal government, stimulate economic growth, and increase military spending. What Reagan discovered was that these three objectives were not totally compatible. He began by assigning a high priority to cutting taxes and keeping them cut. In his first few years in office, he worked with Congress to achieve limited tax cuts. He continued to push for tax reform, which he finally achieved with the passage of the 1986 Tax Reform Act. This bill altered the traditional approach to taxation by "tax brackets," simplifying the more than two dozen into two basic categories. It eliminated those individuals in the lowest income brackets, so that they paid no taxes at all. It increased the size of standard deductions and exemptions for individuals and couples while eliminating certain deductions for other areas. In effect, it gave the average individual lower tax rates with lower deductions, while closing many of the corporate loopholes—thereby shifting a greater portion of the tax burden onto the shoulders of the corporations.

The effect of these tax cuts was, as predicted, to stimulate the economy, which resulted in a drop in the unemployment rate and an increase in business activity. The tax cuts also contributed to an increase in the budget deficit, however—which Reagan had been determined to reduce. One of the major dilemmas facing the Reagan administration, and one which was not resolved during his eight years in office, was how to reduce the size of the deficit and balance the federal budget.

In keeping with his own priorities of building the military, starting in 1981 Reagan authorized an increase in spending for defense, resulting in a 50 percent increase in constant dollars over the next six years. While Reagan came into office determined to increase spending for the military, he was equally determined to cut or totally eliminate many domestic programs. In addition to helping to reduce the budget deficit, he claimed, such programs were detrimental because they were expensive and little benefit was derived from the investment in them. Furthermore, they contributed to the growth of large government, which Reagan also opposed, and they made people dependent on society rather than contributors to it.

While Reagan was not willing to eliminate all types of domestic social welfare programs, he made a distinction between "the truly needy," those who could not support themselves, and "the working poor," those who could support themselves if they wished but who chose not to do so. Reagan claimed that government has an obligation to the former to ensure that they do not starve, but government is not obligated to guarantee support for those who can provide for themselves but choose not to do so.

Reagan's proposals to cut some of these programs were controversial from the beginning; specifically, controversy centered on whether many of the cuts proposed allowed the government to retain an adequate "safety net" for those individuals who needed government assistance. What was unclear is where that net should be. The final outcome was that there were no cuts in such publicly accepted programs as Social Security and Medicare. The biggest cuts in domestic welfare were in means-tested programs, such as Aid to Families with Dependent Children (AFDC), job training programs, Medicaid, and student loans. Even though Reagan had come into office proclaim-

Supreme Court Justice Sandra Day O'Connor. *(Library of Congress)*

ing the need to reduce federal spending and balance the budget, it soon became apparent that, politically, the best he could accomplish was to reduce the rate of increase of federal spending for certain programs.

When he entered the White House, Reagan inherited a projected budget deficit of well over $200 billion, a number that continued to grow as the amount spent every year far exceeded the income of the government. The size of the federal deficit grew large enough for members of Congress to enact legislation in 1985, the Gramm-Rudman Balanced Budget Act, specifically to create a plan to eliminate the deficit and balance the budget. The bill was signed into law by President Reagan, who had been advocating, unsuccessfully, the need for an amendment to the Constitution to balance the federal budget. During his tenure in office, however, Reagan discovered how difficult it is

to bring a budget into line when only a limited number of items can be cut and when taxes cannot be raised.

As president, Reagan advocated a conservative social agenda that supported the notion of government as responsible for legislating morality and religion. Throughout his eight years in office, Reagan supported the idea of prayer in schools and promoted the return to "old-fashioned values." He campaigned actively for the overturn of the 1973 Supreme Court decision of *Roe v. Wade*, which made abortion legal, and advocated federal legislation to ban abortion on demand. Despite the appeal that these ideas held for some Americans, Reagan was not successful in implementing any of them.

One of the legacies of the Reagan years is the change that he made in the makeup of the Supreme Court. In 1981, Reagan stunned many with his appointment of Sandra Day O'Connor to serve as the first female justice of the Supreme Court. Her impeccable credentials and record, as well as the fact that she was a woman, contributed to her relatively easy confirmation by the Senate. Five years later, Reagan made his second appointment to the Court when he nominated Antonin Scalia to be an associate justice. He, too, won Senate approval, and the orientation of the Court started to shift dramatically.

Shortly thereafter, in 1987, Reagan recommended Robert Bork to fill the next vacancy. By this time, the political climate had changed considerably, and the Senate began a very difficult and politically charged series of confirmation hearings. The verdict of the Senate was not to confirm Bork, which was seen as a major defeat for Reagan, who finally submitted the name of Anthony Kennedy to fill the vacant post on the Court. Kennedy was confirmed by the Senate and took his seat in 1988. In addition, Reagan appointed then-Associate Justice William Rehnquist as chief justice of the United States, an appointment that also was confirmed by the Senate.

These critical appointments altered the character of the Supreme Court considerably, reflecting the conservative orientation of Reagan and members of his administration.

The First Term: Foreign Policy

One of the primary goals of the Reagan administration was to restore the international power and prestige of the United States. Reagan believed that the United States had declined in power internationally, thereby clearing the way for events such as the Soviet invasion of Afghanistan in December, 1979, and the taking of the fifty-two hostages from the U.S. embassy in Tehran, Iran. Even though Reagan came into office pledging to pursue arms control negotiations with the Soviet Union, he also believed that such negotiations would be pointless unless the United States could deal from a position of strength. Further, he reiterated many of the themes, heard years earlier, of the need for a strong military to deter the aggression of the Soviet Union. To accomplish these goals, the president authorized a real increase in the defense budget, increased the size of the U.S. Navy (moving toward the goal of a "600 ship navy"), and supported the creation and deployment of new and more sophisticated weapons for the military. In conjunction with these real increases in the size and capabilities of the military, Reagan also advocated the need for the United States to be more assertive in exercising its own power in the world. Public opinion polls indicated that most American citizens were backing him at every step.

The Soviet Union was the driving force behind Reagan's foreign and national security

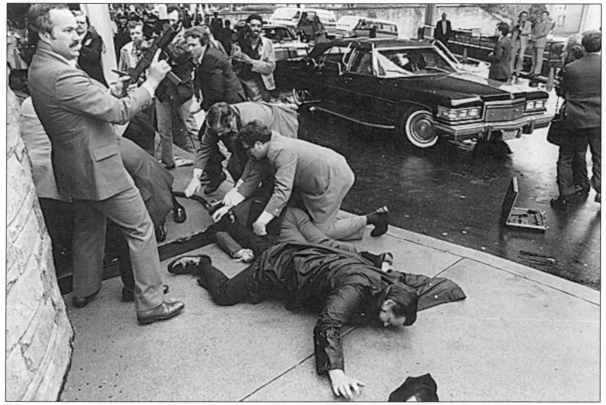

Bystanders and security personnel dive to the ground during the assassination attempt on President Reagan's life on March 30, 1981, outside the Washington Hilton Hotel. *(NARA)*

policy. Reagan was determined to achieve a position of parity with, if not superiority to, the Soviet Union. To achieve this goal, he actively pushed for the deployment of the MX intercontinental ballistic missile, reversed Jimmy Carter's stand and agreed to the development of the B-1 bomber, and authorized research into the creation of another new long-range plane known as the Stealth bomber. This aircraft was reputed to have a highly sophisticated design that made it virtually invisible to radar. The development of two new strategic bombers was justified by the need to update the aging B-52 force.

U.S.-Soviet Relations

U.S.-Soviet relations, which started to cool under Carter, deteriorated still further during the first years of the Reagan administration. Reagan's "evil empire" rhetoric about the Soviet Union, coupled with the signals sent by his appointments of hard-line advisers, made clear the direction that his administration would take. Tensions between the two superpowers threatened to escalate following an incident occurring on September 1, 1983, when the Soviet Union shot down a routine passenger flight of a Korean Air Lines 747. Among the passengers who perished were several Americans, including a congressman.

This incident was followed two months later by the first deployment of the new intermediate-range nuclear missiles in Europe as part of NATO forces. That deployment provided the impetus for the Soviet delegation to walk out of the ongoing arms control talks in Geneva. Under the terms of the NATO agreement, signed in December, 1979, the United States was committed to pursue the dual tracks of development and deployment of the nuclear missiles while simultaneously pursuing arms control. Although Reagan was bound to uphold that decision, he also made clear his conviction that force deployment was a necessary prerequisite to arms control.

Although Reagan was personally skeptical of the value of arms control, he also believed that the time was not appropriate for reaching an agreement, given political uncertainty with the Soviet Union. The rapid succession of leaders taking office in the Soviet Union made it difficult for the Reagan administration to conduct negotiations and virtually impossible for the Soviets to formulate any consistent policy positions. When Reagan had assumed office in January of 1981, Leonid Brezhnev was premier of the Soviet Union. His illness and then death on November 10, 1982, ushered in a "succession crisis" within the Soviet Union. Brezhnev was succeeded by Yuri Andropov, who died only a year later, on February 9, 1984. He was succeeded by Konstantin Chernenko, who died on March 10, 1985, at which time Mikhail Gorbachev came to power. It was only after Gorbachev took office and introduced his policies of *glasnost* (openness) and *perestroika* (restructuring), accompanied by the dramatic arms buildup of the United States, that U.S.-Soviet relations started to ease.

The Strategic Defense Initiative

On March 23, 1983, at the end of a nationally televised speech on the defense budget, Reagan unveiled his plan for a new defense program "to counter the awesome Soviet missile threat with measures that are defensive." Reagan surprised the world by calling upon the U.S. scientific community to turn its attention to the creation of a new weapon system that would render nuclear weapons "impotent and obsolete." The Strategic Defense Initiative (SDI), or "Star Wars," as it came to be popularly known, provided a real symbolic victory in the fight to surpass the Soviet Union militarily. It also became one of the major stumbling blocks in the arms control negotiations: The Soviet Union demanded that plans for the development of SDI not go forward, claiming that it was in violation of the terms of the Antiballistic Missile Treaty of 1972 and thereby calling into question

Excerpts from Ronald Reagan's televised speech regarding the Strategic Defense Initiative, March 23, 1983:

Let me share with you a vision of the future which offers hope. It is that we embark on a program to counter the awesome Soviet missile threat with measures that are defensive. Let us turn to the very strengths in technology that spawned our great industrial base and that have given us the quality of life we enjoy today.

What if free people could live secure in the knowledge that their security did not rest upon the threat of instant U.S. retaliation to deter a Soviet attack, that we could intercept and destroy strategic ballistic missiles before they reached our own soil or that of our allies?

I know this is a formidable, technical task, one that may not be accomplished before the end of the century. Yet, current technology has attained a level of sophistication where it's reasonable for us to begin this effort. It will take years, probably decades of efforts on many fronts. There will be failures and setbacks, just as there will be successes and breakthroughs. And as we proceed, we must remain constant in preserving the nuclear deterrent and maintaining a solid capability for flexible response. But isn't it worth every investment necessary to free the world from the threat of nuclear war? We know it is. . . .

I call upon the scientific community in our country, those who gave us nuclear weapons, to turn their great talents now to the cause of mankind and world peace, to give us the means of rendering these nuclear weapons impotent and obsolete.

Tonight, . . . I am directing a comprehensive and intensive effort to define a long-term research and development program to begin to achieve our ultimate goal of eliminating the threat posed by strategic nuclear missiles. This could pave the way for arms control measures to eliminate the weapons themselves. We seek neither military superiority nor political advantage. Our only purpose—one all people share—is to search for ways to reduce the danger of nuclear war.

My fellow Americans, tonight we're launching an effort which holds the promise of changing the course of human history. There will be risks, and results take time. But I believe we can do it.

the sincerity with which the United States could enter into any new agreement.

Later that year, in October, Reagan sent another forceful signal about the power of the United States and the role that the United States would be playing globally when he ordered a surprise military attack on the Caribbean island of Grenada. Following the assassination of the prime minister of Grenada, Maurice Bishop, on October 19, a new government had been created that had strong ties to the Soviet Union and Cuba. President Reagan justified the attack, at least in part, by pointing to the need to assure the safety of American students in a medical school on the island, who, he believed, were endangered by the possibility of a communist takeover. After meeting minimal resistance, the U.S. invasion force of almost two thousand Marines and Army rangers took control of the island, deported the Cubans, and helped establish a pro-American government.

This military operation was met by criticism by some of the United States' allies, who had not been consulted in advance. The majority of Americans, however, rallied behind Reagan, and the limited military operation sent a clear signal to the Soviet Union regarding communist presence in the Western Hemisphere. Furthermore, the invasion of Grenada occurred only two days after a Muslim terrorist had driven a truck into the U.S. Marine headquarters in Beirut, Lebanon, killing 241 Americans. In the wake of that act of aggression, Reagan's decision enjoyed full public support, proving that he could, and would, act decisively in time of crisis.

Middle East Policy

The Middle East was another region that plagued Reagan during his first term in office. U.S. policy toward the Middle East during the Reagan years was in accord with his desire to revive U.S. power internationally as well as to limit Soviet influence globally. Since the creation of the state of Israel in 1948, U.S. interests in the Middle East had been tied directly to the security of Israel, as well as the need to assure free passage of oil through the Persian Gulf. The war between Iraq and Iran, which had begun in 1980, threatened the balance of power in the region and became a direct threat to the interests of the United States when both countries began attacking tankers in the Persian Gulf and endangering oil refineries. Furthermore, sometime in 1982, the United States had become aware of evidence that suggested that Iran was supporting terrorist groups in the Middle East, including groups engaged in the taking of American hostages. Subse-

quently, Reagan pointed to Iran as a sponsor of international terrorism, and the United States led the fight to stop all arms shipments to Iran.

While the Iran-Iraq war raged, Lebanon continued to be a major trouble spot. Reagan's fear was that the longer the war in Lebanon continued, the greater was the possibility that the Soviet Union would gain a stronghold in the region, at the expense of the United States and to the immediate peril of Israel. Israel's primary concern at this time was Palestinian statehood, represented by the Palestine Liberation Organization (PLO), and guarantees of the future security of Israel. The Reagan administration tacitly supported the creation of some sort of Palestinian state on the West Bank. Israel, however, sought to establish Jewish settlements on the West Bank, while Syria, Lebanon, Jordan, and the PLO could not agree as to whether a Palestinian state should exist and, if so, what form it should take.

U.S. Marines in Beirut, Lebanon, in December, 1983. *(U.S. Navy)*

In June, 1982, with the tacit approval of the United States, Israel invaded Lebanon, drove out the PLO, and attempted to establish a friendly Christian government. This new government soon collapsed and Reagan, fearful of the outcome if Israel withdrew from Lebanon, authorized the continued presence of U.S. Marines. In April, 1983, a powerful bomb exploded in the U.S. embassy in Beirut, killing forty-six people, including sixteen Americans. In September, 1983, Reagan stated the need for continued U.S. presence in the region and stationed naval forces off the coast of Lebanon. Then, in October of 1983, Muslim terrorists drove a truckful of explosives into the Marines' barracks, killing 241 Americans.

Reagan continued to talk about how "the United States will not be intimidated by terrorists" and announced that the United States would not "cut and run." Nevertheless, pressure at home was mounting against Reagan's policy in Lebanon. Members of Congress threatened to invoke the War Powers Act over what they saw as the increasing U.S. military buildup in the region, as well as the dangers to the members of the U.S. armed forces serving in the area. The tide of public opinion had turned as well, and, facing a reelection campaign, Reagan authorized the withdrawal of the troops by the end of February, 1984.

Policy Toward Latin America

The other major area that concerned Reagan was Latin America, specifically Nicaragua. The overthrow of Anastasio Somoza García and the subsequent rise to power of the Sandinista government raised many of the old fears of a Soviet stronghold in the region and the concomitant fear that, if not stopped, Nicaragua would become the base for exporting revolution throughout Latin America. Almost immediately upon taking office, Reagan terminated all economic assistance to Nicaragua and began a campaign to extend military and economic support to the Contras fighting to overthrow the Sandinista

government. For the remainder of his term of office, Reagan would fight an ongoing battle with Congress over the issue of support for the Contras, or "freedom fighters," as Reagan preferred to call them.

What was not anticipated during Reagan's first term was the link between his policy toward Nicaragua and the Middle East that would emerge to plague him during his second term, in what became known as the Iran-Contra affair.

Foreign Policy: The Second Term

In many ways, Reagan's foreign policy in his second four years in office differed markedly from that of the first term. The arms buildup that had started during the first term had enabled Reagan to achieve his goal of asserting U.S. military and political power once again. Although American Marines had died in Beirut, the United States was not in a position of direct combat anywhere in the world. As the Republicans pointed out during the 1984 election campaign, "not an inch of territory had been seized by the Communists during the Reagan Administration." Although public support for the large defense buildup and the more bellicose foreign policies was eroding, part of the reason was that Reagan's policies during his first term in office had succeeded. The White House and the American people believed that the United States was strong once again.

As he approached his second term, Reagan did so as the first American president since Herbert Hoover not to meet with his Soviet counterpart. Polls indicated that the American public wanted an arms control agreement, which in 1984 seemed a pipe dream. Yet Reagan approached the 1984 election as one of the most popular presidents in recent history. Regardless of the number of people who disagreed with his policies, Reagan himself was able to retain his popularity and the political advantage that went with that because of this appeal to the American people.

Reagan signs the Japanese American Internment Compensation Bill in 1988. *(Ronald Reagan Library)*

Reagan swept the 1984 election, defeating Democratic candidate Walter Mondale by an overwhelming margin, with a 59 percent plurality in the popular vote, and a sweep of 525 to 13 electoral votes. With that degree of support, as well as the belief that the United States had regained a position of strength internationally, Reagan was able to alter some of his policies dramatically from the first term to the second.

Although Reagan's foreign policy remained focused on the Soviet Union, one of the major changes was in the type of relations that the two countries would pursue, especially after Mikhail Gorbachev came to power in March, 1985. This event was coupled with a change in Reagan's own perceptions regarding the ability of the United States to negotiate with the Soviet Union from a position of strength for the first time in many years, as well as Reagan's strong desire to achieve a permanent agreement with the Soviet Union. The result was Reagan's de-

sire to meet with the new Soviet leader personally and to see the resumption of serious arms control negotiations.

In November, 1984, only a few weeks after Reagan's reelection, the announcement was made that arms control talks would resume the next year, and U.S. and Soviet negotiators met once again in Geneva in March, 1985. In November, Reagan and Gorbachev met for the first of what would be an annual summit meeting between the two heads of state. In the space of a few years, the course of U.S.-Soviet relations had been altered dramatically, moving from an atmosphere of hostility and Cold War to one of cooperation leading to a resurgence of détente.

The first summit meeting resulted primarily in the settlement of secondary issues, such as cultural exchanges and the resumption of air flights between the two countries, rather than any major substantive agreement. At that meeting, however, the two leaders agreed in principle to an Intermediate-Range Nuclear Forces (INF) agreement. Reagan and Gorbachev followed the first summit one year later with another held in Reykjavik, Iceland, in October, 1986. In the course of this meeting, progress seemed to be made toward the goal of achieving a verifiable arms control agreement. Movement toward this goal was thwarted shortly thereafter, when Gorbachev announced that he wanted to link an INF treaty with limits on SDI. Reagan was steadfast in his refusal to compromise on SDI, and the arms control talks collapsed again.

Early in 1987, Gorbachev dropped his insistence on the linkage between SDI and INF, and both sides agreed in principle to a "double-zero option," that is, the total elimination of both intermediate-range (600-3,400 miles) and short-range (300-600 miles) missiles from Europe. In addition, both sides also agreed to historic measures that were necessary to verify compliance with the agreement. These measures included

not only provisions for surveillance by "national technical means," primarily spy satellites, but also, for the first time, a provision for officials and scientists to visit highly sensitive military and scientific installations on the other side to make sure that the weapons were being dismantled as agreed.

At a third summit in Washington, D.C., in December, 1987, Reagan and Gorbachev signed the INF Treaty. This agreement was the first to result in the reduction of the actual number of nuclear missiles (about 4 percent), and it marked the first time that an entire class of nuclear weapons was eliminated. The INF Treaty was ratified by the U.S. Senate in 1988.

The final summit meeting between Reagan and Gorbachev took place in Moscow in May, 1988. Although both leaders talked of the need to build upon the arms control momentum started with the INF Treaty, leading toward the signing of a strategic arms agreement, nothing substantive resulted from this final summit. Nevertheless, it helped confirm the belief that

---

Excerpt from Ronald Reagan's remarks at the Brandenburg Gate in West Berlin, Germany, June 12, 1987:

In the 1950's, Khrushchev predicted: "We will bury you." But in the West today, we see a free world that has achieved a level of prosperity and well-being unprecedented in all human history. In the Communist world, we see failure, technological backwardness, declining standards of health, even want of the most basic kind—too little food. Even today, the Soviet Union still cannot feed itself. After these four decades, then, there stands before the entire world one great and inescapable conclusion: Freedom leads to prosperity. Freedom replaces the ancient hatreds among the nations with comity and peace. Freedom is the victor.

And now the Soviets themselves may, in a limited way, be coming to understand the importance of freedom. We hear much from Moscow about a new policy of reform and openness. Some political prisoners have been released. Certain foreign news broadcasts are no longer being jammed. Some economic enterprises have been permitted to operate with greater freedom from state control.

Are these the beginnings of profound changes in the Soviet state? Or are they token gestures, intended to raise false hopes in the West, or to strengthen the Soviet system without changing it? We welcome change and openness; for we believe that freedom and security go together, that the advance of human liberty can only strengthen the cause of world peace. There is one sign the Soviets can make that would be unmistakable, that would advance dramatically the cause of freedom and peace.

General Secretary Gorbachev, if you seek peace, if you seek prosperity for the Soviet Union and Eastern Europe, if you seek liberalization: Come here to this gate! Mr. Gorbachev, open this gate! Mr. Gorbachev, tear down this wall!

relations between the two superpowers had changed considerably during Reagan's tenure in office.

The Bombing of Libya

While progress was being made in the area of arms control and U.S.-Soviet relations during Reagan's second term in office, other incidents occurred that, at times, seemed to overshadow the progress between the superpowers. In the area of U.S. foreign policy, one of the most dramatic took place in April, 1986, when Reagan authorized the U.S. military to bomb Libya in retaliation for a Libyan-backed terrorist bombing of a discotheque in West Berlin earlier in the month. Reagan previously had made the decision for, and had given approval in principle to, a U.S. military strike against suspected terrorist targets. The bombing of the discotheque, which resulted in the death of one American and a Turkish citizen, provided the reason to implement these plans.

Two U.S. flyers and at least thirty-seven Libyans, including one of dictator Muammar al-Qaddafi's daughters, were killed in the raid. In the short term, the raid caused great strife between the United States and its NATO allies, who were, with the exception of the United Kingdom, unsupportive of the raid. In fact, one of the U.S. bombs inadvertently hit and damaged the French embassy in Tripoli. In the longer term, however, it appears that Reagan's strategy paid off. Subsequent to the attack, the European countries increased their own anti-terrorist activism and diminished their relationship with Libya. The action, moreover, seemed to undermine the leadership of Qaddafi, who remained relatively silent after the episode.

Trouble Spots

One of Reagan's greatest foreign policy successes was not fully recognized until he was out of office and George H. W. Bush was inaugurated as the forty-first president. The Soviet invasion of Afghanistan in December, 1979, had renewed fears of Soviet expansion. Soviet involvement in Afghanistan had continued throughout the years of the Reagan administration, with the Soviets suffering more than forty thousand casualties in their fight against the *mujahadeen* rebels. In keeping with his anti-communist perspective and his belief that the Soviets had committed an act of aggression, Reagan backed the *mujahadeen*, extending economic and military aid. On the whole, the Congress supported Reagan's policy in Afghanistan. In early 1988, following discussions with the United States on the issue, Gorbachev announced a plan to withdraw Soviet troops from Afghanistan by February 15, 1989.

Through the end of the Reagan administration, the Middle East continued to be a major trouble spot. In early 1987, Reagan concluded that Iran had endangered the oil exports of Kuwait, a pro-Iraq country in the Iran-Iraq War, by threatening the free movement of the Kuwaiti tankers through the Persian Gulf. To counter this threat, Reagan put the tankers under the U.S. flag and then authorized the use of U.S. naval vessels to protect them against attack by Iranian gunboats. In 1987, an Iraqi missile struck the USS *Stark*, killing thirty-seven sailors. Then, in mid-1988, a U.S. naval commander mistook an Iranian passenger airplane for a military plane and had it shot down, killing 290 civilians. Throughout these months, members of Congress called for the need to invoke the 1973 War Powers Act and withdraw all American forces, but this did not occur. As a result of the U.S. military actions, the Persian Gulf did remain open for passage, and the U.S. Navy successfully completed its mission. Critics questioned both the wisdom and the necessity of the policies, however, given the costs. The Persian Gulf region would erupt into a larger conflict during the Bush administration following Iraq's invasion of Kuwait.

Reagan had to confront a number of other trouble spots during his second term in office.

In 1986, after fourteen years of dictatorship, Ferdinand Marcos was deposed as president of the Philippines, to be replaced by Corazon Aquino, the widow of one of his murdered opponents. The United States had been formally linked to the Philippines through the Treaty of Mutual Defense, which entered into force in 1952. These ties were strengthened by the agreement to lease to the United States a naval base at Subic Bay and an Air Force base, Clark Field, for an annual rent of $500 million.

Even in the face of mounting opposition to Marcos and continued U.S. presence in the Philippines, Reagan continued to support the dictator. In February, 1986, Marcos bowed under domestic pressure and called for elections, which he won, although under questionable circumstances. Pressure from within the Philippines and finally from Reagan forced Marcos to leave the country to be replaced officially by Aquino.

The Iran-Contra Affair
Much of Reagan's success in the area of foreign policy threatened to be overshadowed by events in Central America, specifically the link between Iran and Nicaragua that unfolded as the Iran-Contra affair. While the Iran-Contra affair never had the impact on Reagan that Watergate had on Richard Nixon, it nevertheless cast some shadows on the Reagan administration and raised some very basic questions about the responsibilities of the president and the extent of the independent authority of his staff.

The event started to unfold in 1985, when it became known that Iranian-backed terrorists had seized a number of U.S. hostages in the Middle East, including some members of the State Department and the Central Intelligence Agency (CIA). Even though Reagan had often stated that he would never negotiate with terrorists, in August and September of 1985, the president worked through Israel to send anti-tank missiles and other military equipment to Iran. For the next fourteen months, shipments

of weapons were sent to Iran in a highly secret operation. Simultaneously, several hostages were released, although others were seized. Reagan's national security adviser, Robert McFarlane, under Reagan's orders secretly went to Tehran to negotiate with the Iranians.

In November, 1986, this information was disclosed publicly, and Reagan told the American public that his policy was designed with the hope of opening contact with some of the Iranian "moderates." This policy was implemented despite strong protests from both Secretary of State George Shultz and Secretary of Defense Caspar Weinberger.

Approximately three weeks later, Attorney General Edwin Meese III announced that the money obtained from the arms sales to Iran had been secretly diverted to help the Contras in Nicaragua. This had occurred in 1985-1986, in direct conflict with the congressional ban on sending lethal aid to the Contras.

During the summer of 1987, joint Senate and House committees conducted nationally televised hearings on the Iran-Contra connection. In addition, Reagan assembled a special commission chaired by former Texas senator John Tower and including former secretary of state and Democratic senator Edmund Muskie and Brent Scowcroft, a retired Air Force lieutenant general and Henry Kissinger's deputy on the National Security Council. The Tower Commission was empowered to investigate the role of the White House in the Iran-Contra affair. The Tower Commission concluded that "the primary responsibility for the formulation and implementation of national security policy falls on the president." It also concluded that, in this case, the staff of the National Security Council was responsible for the policies that were implemented and that President Reagan was too far removed from the policies enacted by the members of his staff. Following the revelation in 1994 of Reagan's diagnosis of Alzheimer's disease, some wondered whether this debilitating condition had begun to affect his

Lieutenant Colonel Oliver North testifies on July 7, 1987, about the Iran-Contra affair. *(AP/Wide World Photos)*

memory and his ability to lead during his years in office.

The congressional investigation supported many of the conclusions of the Tower Commission report. Lieutenant Colonel Oliver North, an aide at the National Security Council, emerged as one of the central figures. He testified that he had worked largely under the direction of William Casey, the head of the CIA, who had died of a brain tumor months earlier. North became a hero to many Americans for his devotion to his country and president, even if that meant breaking the law.

By the end of the Iran-Contra investigations, it seemed apparent that Reagan had been unaware of much that had been done in the name of American foreign policy and the Reagan Doctrine. The incident raised important questions about who really does make policy and how much knowledge or control the president really has over a very large staff that is supposed to act in his behalf.

The Reagan Legacy

When Ronald Reagan took office in January, 1981, the presidency of the United States was in a state of decline. Humiliation over the Vietnam War, the Watergate scandal and its culmination in the resignation of Richard Nixon, and the perception of a series of weak leaders and poor political decisions all combined to undermine the role of the president, the power of the office, and the prestige of the United States. No president since Dwight D. Eisenhower had been able to overcome these obstacles to be elected to serve two full terms in the office. The eight years of the Reagan administration reversed many of these trends.

From the start of his first term in office, Ronald Reagan was the "Great Communicator," able to reach the American people, who believed in and supported him. With the backing of a Republican Senate during his first term in office, he could implement policies and convey a sense of leadership that enabled him to restore to the office a prestige and sense of power that had been absent for many years. Although a social conservative, he appointed Sandra Day O'Connor to serve as the first female justice of the Supreme Court, Jeane Kirkpatrick as his ambassador to the United Nations, and Elizabeth Dole as his secretary of transportation.

Domestically, Reagan promised the American people that he would get the economy moving, once again reversing the trends that had undermined the nation. He was able to control inflation and bring down unemployment, and the economy of the United States did thrive. Tied directly to this was a marked alteration in the priorities of the country, as reflected in the budget. A dramatic increase in spending for the military reflected Reagan's firm belief in the need for "peace through strength." The size of the armed forces grew dramatically, as did the readiness of those forces. Many argue that it was this increase that allowed the United States to be as successful as it was in dealing with the Soviets and in regaining its position as global leader. Some also argue that this increase was a major factor in precipitating the economic crisis tied to the breakup of the Soviet Union in 1991.

Also reflected in the budget was the need to cut domestic programs that were not deemed essential to the United States. The cuts in many of the welfare programs illustrate clearly Reagan's conservative orientation and his belief in the need to shrink the size of the federal government. While these programs were cut amid some controversy, Reagan was able to sustain his popularity throughout the eight years in which he served as president.

In reassigning his budget priorities, Reagan also presided over the growth and acceleration of the largest budget deficit in the history of the country, which many believe led to the 1990 recession that brought down George H. W. Bush and swept Bill Clinton into office. Although critics feared that the deficit would have a disastrous impact on the future economic situation in the country, continued fiscal reform led to a balanced budget and a surplus by 1998.

During the Reagan years, another potentially dangerous trend emerged: For the first time, the United States was importing more than it exported, thereby altering the balance of payments. For the first time, the United States became a debtor nation, which would have a direct impact not only on the domestic economic situation but also on foreign policy options. Clearly, the short-term impact of Reagan's economic policies was beneficial, and the Reagan Revolution seemed to have worked.

Former president Reagan and former Soviet president Mikhail Gorbachev relax at Reagan's California ranch in 1992. *(AP/Wide World Photos)*

Most people had to answer "yes" in response to the question Reagan asked the American people in 1984: whether they were better off than they had been four years earlier.

In the area of foreign policy, the Reagan administration began under the cloud of diminishing U.S. global prestige, another perception that Reagan was able to reverse in eight years. He believed in the importance of military might and in the need to negotiate from a position of strength. His national security and foreign policies were designed to underscore these points. A combination of a military buildup and an assertive policy sent unambiguous signals to the world about the resolve of the United States. By the end of his two terms in office, the result was the resurgence of the U.S. role internationally and the beginning of a new era of cooperation between the United States and the Soviet Union. This change was exemplified in the signing and ratification of the INF Treaty by the United States and Soviet Union in December, 1987, along with the commitment to pursue a more cooperative course of action in the future.

For eight years, Ronald and First Lady Nancy Reagan imposed a sense of dignity and conveyed a positive image of the United States, which in turn was reflected in the way the United States was viewed by other countries. Even after leaving office, Reagan continued to be a role model through public disclosure of his struggle with Alzheimer's disease. The "Reagan image" was especially important in boosting the pride that many Americans took in themselves and their country. To many Americans, this change in attitude was long overdue, and it represents one of the most important legacies of the Reagan years.

Joyce P. Kaufman

Suggested Readings

Abrams, Herbert L. *"The President Has Been Shot": Confusion, Disability, and the Twenty-fifth Amendment in the Aftermath of the Attempted Assassination of Ronald Reagan*. New York: W. W. Norton, 1992. A detailed account of the attempt on Reagan's life.

Bosch, Adrian. *Reagan: An American Story*. New York: TV Books, 1998. The companion volume to the documentary on Reagan's life for the Public Broadcasting Service (PBS) network series *The American Experience*.

Cannon, Lou. *President Reagan: The Role of a Lifetime*. Rev. ed. New York: Public Affairs, 1991. Cannon, a journalist who covered Reagan for a quarter of a century, uses interviews (three with Reagan himself) to analyze Reagan's successes and failures and to reveal how Reagan's acting career shaped his presidency.

_____. *Reagan*. New York: Putnam, 1982. One of the standard sources on the early Reagan years.

Cardigan, J. H. *Ronald Reagan: A Remarkable Life*. Kansas City, Mo.: Andrews McMeel, 1995. Chronicles Reagan's life from his radio broadcasting days to the presidency.

Dallek, Robert. *Ronald Reagan: The Politics of Symbolism*. 1984. Rev. ed. Cambridge, Mass.: Harvard University Press, 1999. Offers a critical interpretation of the first term of the Reagan administration.

D'Souza, Dinesh. *Ronald Reagan: How an Ordinary Man Became an Extraordinary Leader*. New York: Free Press, 1997. D'Souza, a former Reagan senior domestic policy adviser, argues that Reagan was a visionary who laid the groundwork for the robust economy of the 1990's.

Hannaford, Peter, ed. *Recollections of Reagan: A Portrait of Ronald Reagan*. New York: William Morrow, 1997. An illuminating collection of fifty-one essays by political associates and acquaintances.

Kengor, Paul, and Peter Schweizer, eds. *The Reagan Presidency: Assessing the Man and His Legacy*. Lanham, Md.: Rowman & Littlefield, 2005. A series of essays explores Reagan's impact on the American presidency.

LaFeber, Walter. *The American Age: United States Foreign Policy at Home and Abroad: 1750 to the Present*. New York: W. W. Norton, 1989. An unbiased overview of U.S. foreign policy during the Reagan administration.

Levy, Peter B. *Encyclopedia of the Reagan-Bush Years*. Westport, Conn.: Greenwood Press, 1996. Details the social trends, world events, popular culture, and political climate of the Reagan-Bush administrations.

Mervin, David. *Ronald Reagan and the American Presidency*. New York: Longman, 1990. A standard evaluation of Reagan's presidency.

Morris, Edmund. *Dutch: A Memoir of Ronald Reagan*. New York: Random House, 1999. A biography written in the form of a first-person narrative.

Noonan, Peggy. *When Character Was King: A Story of Ronald Reagan*. New York: Viking, 2001. Noonan, a former speechwriter for Reagan, argues Reagan's popularity and power as a president emanated from his strength of character.

Pemberton, William E. *Exit with Honor: The Life and Presidency of Ronald Reagan*. Armonk, N.Y.: M. E. Sharpe, 1998. A balanced biography that also includes an evaluation the Reagan presidency.

Reagan, Ronald. *An American Life*. New York: Simon & Schuster, 1990. The president's memoirs.

Ronald Reagan Presidential Library and Foundation. http://www.reaganlibrary.com/welcome.asp. The Web site of Reagan's official presidential library.

Stockman, David A. *The Triumph of Politics*. New York: Harper & Row, 1986. An insider's perspective on the formulation of Reagan's economic policies.

Strober, Deborah H., and Gerald S. Strober. *Reagan: The Man and His Presidency*. Boston: Houghton and Mifflin, 1992. A single narrative of Reagan's presidency and impact, drawn from countless interviews with friends and associates.

Talbott, Strobe. *Deadly Gambits*. New York: Knopf, 1984. Analyzes the Reagan administration's approach to arms control.

The Tower Commission Report. New York: Bantam Books, 1987. In-depth information on the events leading up to and surrounding the Iran-Contra affair.

George H. W. Bush
41st President, 1989-1993

Born: June 12, 1924
    Milton, Massachusetts

Political Party: Republican
Vice President: Dan Quayle

Cabinet Members
Secretary of State: James A. Baker III,
    Lawrence Eagleburger
Secretary of the Treasury: Nicholas Brady
Secretary of Defense: Dick Cheney
Attorney General: Dick Thornburgh, William P.
    Barr
Secretary of the Interior: Manuel Lujan, Jr.
Secretary of Agriculture: Clayton K. Yeutter,
    Edward Matigan
Secretary of Commerce: Robert A. Mosbacher,
    Barbara H. Franklin
Secretary of Labor: Elizabeth Dole, Lynn
    Martin
Secretary of Health and Human Services:
    Louis W. Sullivan
Secretary of Housing and Urban Development:
    Jack Kemp
Secretary of Transportation: Samuel K. Skinner,
    Andrew Card
Secretary of Energy: James D. Watkins
Secretary of Education: Lauro F. Cavazos,
    Lamar Alexander
Secretary of Veterans Affairs: Edward J.
    Derwinski

George Herbert Walker Bush won the presidency at a time of transformation, at home and abroad. The Cold War was coming to an end, and for the first time in almost fifty years, people dared to dream of a genuine peace. Domestic politics was in flux; Ronald Reagan had shaken traditional electoral coalitions and had mastered the vagaries of television to pioneer a new politics of image and "character." An old-fashioned man, Bush offered voters the security of the past, and they responded by electing

Bush's official portrait. *(White House Historical Society)*

him president of the United States. As chief executive, Bush delivered the stability he had promised. He skillfully managed U.S. foreign policy and endeavored to put a "kinder and gentler" face on the social and economic conservatism that he inherited from his predecessor. Unfortunately for Bush, his success in liquidating the Cold War made him dispensable in an era seeking a New World Order, and his caution at home left him vulnerable to charges of indifference as the economy slipped into recession. By 1992, Bush had become an anachronism, visibly uncomfortable in an electoral realm where his opponent played the saxophone on the *Arsenio Hall Show* and bantered easily with youth on Music Television (MTV). This time, voters rejected the solidity of the past for new directions. In defeat, George H. W. Bush, the last American president to have fought in World War II, gave way gracefully to William Jefferson Clinton, the first president of the baby boom generation.

Privilege, the Pacific, and Petroleum

George H. W. Bush was born into a patrician class that generally eschewed the hurly-burly of politics for the more refined strife of board rooms and country clubs. Only occasionally would a member of this elite break with convention and run for elective office. One other such individual was Franklin Delano Roosevelt. Another, significantly, was Bush's father, Prescott Bush, Sr.

The elder Bush was born in Ohio into a local manufacturing family. Upon graduation from Yale University, he saw action as a captain in the field artillery during World War I. Following the war, Prescott Bush returned home and was married to Dorothy Walker of St. Louis, Missouri, daughter of a prominent businessman. Bush then embarked upon a successful career in business, which culminated in his becoming a partner in the powerful investment banking firm of Brown Brothers, Harriman and Company. Bush believed that money was not

an end in itself; for him, responsibility followed wealth. As a contemporary wrote, "Pres had an old-fashioned idea that the more advantages a man has, the greater his obligation to do public service." For two decades, Bush labored as a representative to the Greenwich, Connecticut, town meeting. In 1950, at the age of fifty-five, Prescott Bush entered the race for United States senator in Connecticut, running as a member of the internationalist (later Eisenhower) wing of the Republican Party. He lost by a narrow margin, 1,000 votes of 860,000 cast. Vindication came two years later, when Bush triumphantly captured the state's other senate seat, vacated by the incumbent's sudden death. In 1956, he won reelection, and he served until his retirement in 1963. Prescott Bush's career would be a powerful example and stimulus for his son.

George H. W. Bush was born on June 12, 1924. One of five children, Bush enjoyed what was in many ways an idyllic childhood. He grew up in Connecticut, his summers punctuated by trips to the family's vacation home at Kennebunkport, Maine. Prescott and Dorothy Bush saw to it that affluence did not spoil their children. They inculcated in George and his siblings the Puritan work ethic and a strict code of conduct. Dorothy Bush, in particular, rooted out any signs of arrogance or boastfulness that arose in her children because of their birth or their accomplishments. A keen sportswoman, she chastised her children for any signs of vaunting behavior in victory. From this background, the future president developed the mixed traits of hard work and aristocratic restraint, competitiveness and loyalty, and ambition and self-effacement that would characterize his political career.

Bush's first chance to test himself against the high standards set by his parents came with the Japanese attack on Pearl Harbor in 1941. The seventeen-year-old Bush wanted to enlist as soon as he was graduated from Phillips Academy, Andover. His parents opposed his plans, urging him instead to join his older

THE FIRST LADY
BARBARA BUSH

Barbara Bush became the first woman since Abigail Adams to be both the wife and the mother of a president. She was born Barbara Pierce on June 8, 1925. Her parents were Pauline and Marvin Pierce. Her father became the president of the McCall Corporation, which published *Redbook* and other magazines. Barbara grew up in Rye, New York, and attended private schools. In 1941, she met George Herbert Walker Bush at a dance during Christmas vacation. War kept Barbara and George apart for years. George joined the Navy and flew torpedo bombers in the Pacific. Barbara finished high school and enrolled for a time at Smith College. They were engaged while George was on leave in 1943 and married when he returned from his tour of duty, on January 6, 1945.

During Bush's business and political careers, Barbara Bush supervised twenty-nine moves. The Bushes had six children: George, Robin, John "Jeb," Neil, Marvin, and Dorothy. Robin Bush died of leukemia at the age of three. The loss devastated Barbara. She later wrote, "Because of Robin, George and I love every living human more." Barbara was a valuable asset to her husband in his political career because of her speaking ability and sharp sense of humor. When the Bushes entered the White House in 1989, she became a popular and effective First Lady. She performed her official duties with a wry sense of perspective. She also made jokes about her figure, fake pearls, and white hair, and she admitted that she looked like "everybody's grandmother." As First Lady, Barbara Bush devoted herself to the cause of family literacy. She wrote a best-selling book for children, donating the proceeds to literacy programs. The Bushes settled in Houston in 1993. Barbara Bush wrote her memoirs and actively supported a number of charities.

Daniel P. Murphy

brother at Yale. The secretary of war, Henry Lewis Stimson, delivered the commencement address at Bush's school in the spring of 1942. The venerable soldier and statesman told the graduating class that the war would be a long one and that they would do their country a service by getting more schooling before joining the military. Following this address, Prescott Bush asked his son if the secretary's words had had any effect. "No, sir," was the reply, "I'm going in." The elder Bush said no more and shook his son's hand.

As soon as he came of age, George Bush joined the Navy and began a course in naval aviation. For a time, Bush at eighteen was the youngest flyer in the Navy. During World War II, he flew fifty-eight combat missions in the Pacific. His most notable exploit came on September 2, 1944, while piloting a Grumman Avenger torpedo bomber based on the carrier USS *San Jacinto*. His squadron received orders to attack a radio-communications center on Chichi Jima, an island in the Bonins chain, which included Iwo Jima. Enemy antiaircraft fire hit Bush's plane as he dived in to strike. Bush completed his bombing run, then ordered the other two men in the plane to bail out. Bush abandoned his plane last, successfully parachuting into the ocean. Both of his crewmen died. Floating in the Pacific, Bush experienced some frightening moments as a Japanese boat from the island raced to pick him up. Fortunately, planes from his squadron chased the Japanese away. Soon an American submarine surfaced and rescued the downed flyer. Bush then spent an adventurous month aboard the submarine before being reunited with his ship and squadron. He received a Distinguished Flying Cross for his conduct at Chichi Jima. Bush was rotated back to the United States in December, 1944. In January, he married Barbara Pierce, the beautiful daughter of an executive of the McCall Publishing Company, whom he had met at a dance during the Christmas holidays of 1941. The young war hero and newlywed was training for the expected invasion of Japan when the conflict ended in August, 1945.

Demobilized, Bush attended Yale University, majoring in economics and acting as captain of the baseball team. Already able to combine a winning amiability with a formidable capacity for work, Bush made Skull and Bones, the most prestigious and secretive club on campus, and also earned a Phi Beta Kappa key. Bush was graduated in 1948 and promptly moved his family to Texas, where he hoped to make his way in the oil industry. He began as an equipment clerk for Dresser Industries, an oil supply company in which his father had an interest. There Bush learned the rudiments of the oil business. In 1951, with the help of seed money from relatives, Bush and a friend formed the Bush-Overbey Development Company. For two years, Bush thrived as an independent oilman, seeking oil across the country, from Montana to the Gulf of Mexico. He helped found the Zapata Petroleum Corporation in 1953. The next year, he became president of a spin-off enterprise, Zapata Off-Shore Company, with its headquarters at Houston. Bush's domestic happiness matched his business success until he and Barbara were dealt a devastating blow by the loss of their three-year-old daughter Robin to leukemia. They consoled themselves in the warm relationship they maintained with their other five children. In later years, Bush would declare that he and Barbara considered their greatest accomplishment to be the fact that their children still came home.

Into Politics

Bush developed an interest in politics just as his business brought him to the threshold of wealth. Unfortunately, his ambition seemed doomed to frustration. A Republican, he lived in a state that had been resolutely Democratic since the days of Reconstruction. However, by the time Bush began to contemplate a political career, change appeared in the offing. Dwight D. Eisenhower had carried Texas in 1952 and 1956. Richard M. Nixon only narrowly lost the state to John Fitzgerald Kennedy in 1960. Texas was exhibiting early signs of the political realignment in the South that would challenge the traditional dominance of the Democratic Party.

Bush took advantage of this moment of opportunity. In 1962, he became chair of the Harris County Republican Party. For two years, he worked to build a Republican organization in the Houston area. He began what would become a lifelong task of seeking common ground between conservative and more moderate Republicans. Bush made a run for elective office in 1964, challenging Senator Ralph Yarborough. He campaigned effectively, but with Lyndon B. Johnson at the head of the Democratic ticket, it was a bad year for Republicans in Texas. Bush won the largest Republican vote in Texas history, but it was not enough to defeat the incumbent. Despite his loss, Bush enjoyed this new sphere of activity. In 1966, he resigned from Zapata to campaign for a newly created congressional seat in Houston. That fall, Bush enjoyed his first victory in a general election.

In Washington, D.C., Bush represented the opinions of his constituency, ranking as one of the most conservative members of the House of Representatives. In the area of civil rights, however, Bush braved the displeasure of his supporters. He voted for the Civil Rights Act of 1968, with its controversial provisions for open housing. Bush went home, explained his stand to the voters, and was triumphantly reelected. In his second, and final, term in the House, his most notable act was his support for the creation of the Environmental Protection Agency (EPA). In 1970, Yarborough stood for reelection. Because of his liberal voting record, the senator seemed vulnerable to a Republican challenge. Bush sacrificed his safe congressional seat and declared his candidacy in the Senate race. Unfortunately for Bush, Lloyd Bentsen, a conservative Democrat, eliminated Yarborough in the primary election. Bentsen went on to defeat Bush in November.

Utility Man

As Bush closed his congressional office, doors opened for him elsewhere. Party leaders had marked Bush as a "comer." At the 1968 Republican Convention, he had been mentioned as a possible running mate for Nixon. The president himself believed that this promising political figure deserved some recognition for his effort against Bentsen. In December, 1970, Nixon nominated the lame duck congressman for the position of ambassador to the United Nations. The nomination came under attack because of Bush's unfamiliarity with foreign relations. Despite the criticism, the Senate confirmed Bush in February, 1971. At the United Nations, Bush began to earn his reputation as a "good soldier" by loyally supporting the administration's "two China policy." Bush fought valiantly to keep Taiwan in the United Nations, even as the Nixon administration's diplomacy with the People's Republic of China doomed his efforts.

President Nixon rewarded Bush for his service in this thankless position by asking him, in December, 1972, to take the job of chair of the Republican National Committee. Bush moved into his new office early in 1973, in time to be caught up in the storm of the Watergate scandal. Nixon assured him that he had done nothing wrong. So once again, Bush faithfully waged a hopeless battle for the administration, even as new revelations rendered such support increasingly untenable. Only at the end, in the summer of 1974, when he became convinced that Nixon had lied to him and that the party could not survive an impeachment crisis, did Bush take the lead amongst Republicans in suggesting that the president resign.

Gerald R. Ford considered Bush for the vice presidency, but ultimately picked Nelson A. Rockefeller. In compensation, Ford offered Bush a choice of diplomatic posts. Bush agreed to head the United States Liaison Office in Beijing. This position held the allure of being far from the soured political atmosphere of Washington, D.C., required no senatorial confirmation, and presented the challenge of involvement in one of the most sensitive areas of American foreign policy. Bush's sojourn in China produced no significant diplomatic initiatives, but he did take advantage of the opportunity to cultivate relationships with Chinese leaders that would in time prove to have important consequences.

In November, 1975, President Ford called Bush back to Washington, D.C. In the so-called Halloween Massacre, Ford had reorganized his administration in preparation for the presidential campaign of 1976. Many Nixon appointees were asked to resign or were fired, among them William Colby, head of the Central Intelligence Agency (CIA). Ford asked Bush to take the position of director of central intelligence. Bush accepted, though reluctantly. He enjoyed China and did not relish a return to Capitol Hill, fearing that the job of running the CIA would prove a political dead end. The process of winning confirmation in the Senate reinforced the unpalatability of the job. Critics charged that his appointment politicized a nonpartisan post. These attacks reflected concerns that Bush might be chosen to be Ford's running mate in 1976. To quiet such fears, the president issued a statement announcing that Bush would not be considered for the Republican vice presidential nomination. His estimate of the political cost of the post borne out by events, Bush duly received his confirmation as director of central intelligence.

Bush inherited an agency riven by scandal. Congressional investigating committees had uncovered evidence that the CIA had plotted to assassinate Cuban leader Fidel Castro and had sponsored other disreputable activities. It fell to Bush to protect, reform, and heal the intelligence establishment. During the year that Bush headed the CIA, he replaced most of the top managers of the agency and worked to restore its tarnished public image. Although Bush served too brief a time to build a permanent institutional legacy, as he left office with the Ford administration in early 1977, he generally received high marks for his performance in a difficult job. Veteran intelligence officers praised Bush for his success in improving agency morale.

The Election of 1980

Bush's relegation to the sideline in 1976 proved a blessing in disguise. He was not forced to choose between Ford and Reagan in the bruising primary campaign of that year and escaped any blame for the defeat in November. As a student, rather than a participant, in the election of 1976, Bush learned valuable lessons. He admired the way Jimmy Carter manipulated the primary system to transform himself from a dark horse candidate into the presidential nominee of the Democratic Party. Back home in Houston, working as the chairman of a local bank, Bush continued to watch Carter. He found less to admire in Carter's leadership as president. Bush's hopes rose with the president's political difficulties. A survey of potential Republican presidential candidates convinced Bush that he was the best man for the race. The essence of Carter's 1976 strategy had been to start early and target the first primaries. Victories in these contests would generate recognition, bringing in money and thereby more victories. Emulating Carter, Bush began early and moved fast. He started organizing a campaign and raising money in 1978, officially declaring his candidacy on May 1, 1979.

Up to a point, Bush's strategy worked. Months of diligent campaigning paid off in late 1979 as he began to win nonbinding straw polls at Republican Party gatherings. In the most im-

portant of these, in Maine, Bush upset Senator Howard Baker of Tennessee. Baker had been sufficiently confident of victory that he had flown in several reporters to record the event. Instead, they described the triumph of Bush, giving his campaign much-needed publicity. Then, in January, 1980, Bush stunned the political world by defeating Reagan, the Republican front-runner, in the Iowa caucuses. Suddenly Bush became Reagan's leading challenger. For a few heady weeks, Bush seemed capable of overtaking the popular Californian. In a famous formulation, Bush talked of his "Big Mo," or the newfound momentum behind his campaign.

The collapse of Bush's hopes came about as rapidly as their inflation. Reagan campaigned vigorously in New Hampshire, the next state to hold a primary. At a debate scheduled between Bush and Reagan at Nashua High School, the other Republican candidates demanded seats on the stage. Reagan proved amenable to this arrangement. Bush demurred. He wanted to establish himself in the public mind as the only alternative to Reagan. An embarrassing scene ensued at the high school, as the other candidates followed Reagan and Bush to the platform. When the moderator attempted to shut down the debate because of this irregularity, Reagan uttered a telling protest, remembered from an old film: "I paid for this microphone, Mr. Green." Reagan appeared a magnanimous populist. Bush, on the other hand, seemed pettily legalistic. Reagan won a commanding victory in the primary. Bush finished second but well behind. Thereafter, Reagan's march to the Republican presidential nomination proceeded inexorably. Bush remained in the race, suffering many defeats and gaining a few victories. Ironically, on the evening of Bush's greatest success, winning the Michigan primary in May, the television networks forecast that elsewhere Reagan had captured enough delegates to ensure his nomination. Bush withdrew his candidacy ten days later.

Bush still aspired to the secondary post that had eluded him so many times in the past. At the Republican Convention in Detroit, a highly publicized flirtation between Reagan and Gerald Ford seemed likely to dash Bush's prospects once again, but the nominee's rapprochement with the former president collapsed. Reagan then asked Bush to become his running mate, and Bush accepted. That fall he shared in Reagan's electoral triumph.

Vice President

Bush served President Reagan with his customary loyalty. He embraced Reagan's robust conservatism, despite his well-known criticisms of aspects of it during the 1980 primaries. Most notably, then-candidate Bush had branded Reagan's supply-side fiscal ideas "voodoo economics." Bush's ready adaptation to the good-soldiering role of the vice presidency contributed to a reputation for intellectual elasticity that would later haunt him as he campaigned in 1988. Bush's unswerving adherence to the administration line also did not mollify certain hard-core conservatives in the Reagan entourage, who regarded the vice president as an ideological opportunist whose right-wing rhetoric merely camouflaged incipient apostasy. In fact, Bush came by his conservatism honestly. Adjusting to Reagan's positions on the budget, taxes, and abortion did not demand a grave distortion of his convictions. His differences with the Reaganites would always lie more in the realm of style rather than substance.

Bush's troubles with some of Reagan's acolytes did not extend to the man himself. Bush and Reagan developed a friendly working relationship. The vice president's position in the administration was solidified by his dignified and deferential conduct following the attempt by John Hinckley, Jr., to assassinate President Reagan on March 30, 1981. The president early on demonstrated his confidence in Bush by asking him to head a special Task Force on Regulatory Relief, charged with a mission dear to Reagan's heart. Ultimately, Bush's task force recommended the elimination of hundreds of federal regulations in an effort to cut the red tape associated with the federal bureaucracy. The vice president received other important and well-publicized responsibilities. Bush led the South Florida Task Force, and later the National Narcotics Border Interdiction System, which attempted, unsuccessfully, to stem the flow of illegal drugs into the country. He also acted as the chair of the National Security Council's crisis management team.

The president employed Bush on a number of diplomatic missions, including one to El Salvador, in order to warn the leaders of that nation about human rights abuses, and one to India, in order to improve relations with that important power. Bush played a leading role in extricating the Marines from Beirut after the debacle of American policy in Lebanon. Perhaps the vice president's greatest achievement was his tour of European capitals in February, 1983, when he helped persuade allied governments to accept the deployment of American intermediate-range nuclear missiles, a show of strength that led eventually to the Intermediate-Range Nuclear Forces (INF) Treaty with the Soviet Union. Bush also was kept busy in the early 1980's attending the funerals of aged Soviet leaders: Leonid Brezhnev in 1982, Yuri Andropov in 1984, and Konstantin Chernenko in 1985. Significantly for the future, this last funeral gave Bush the opportunity to be the first high-ranking American official to meet the ambitious and reform-minded Mikhail Gorbachev after his accession to power.

Bush's activist role as vice president nearly brought him political ruin when the Reagan administration became embroiled in the Iran-Contra scandal. As controversy erupted concerning American arms sales to Iran, Bush steadfastly maintained that he was unaware that this was part of a deal to release American hostages held in Lebanon. He insisted that he was "out of the loop" concerning Oliver

North's diversion of funds from these arms sales to support the Nicaraguan Contras. The vice president's claims were met with some skepticism, both because of his presence at meetings where the sales of weapons to Iran was discussed and because some of his aides were linked to fund raising for the Contras. Though no definitive evidence ever appeared to refute his defense, questions about the Iran-Contra affair would haunt Bush for the rest of his political career.

The Election of 1988

Despite his accomplishments as vice president, Bush failed to emerge from the shadow of Ronald Reagan. He had won a reputation as the "perfect staff man" rather than as a leader. His preparatory-school mannerisms inspired a major newsmagazine to term him a "wimp." An indifferent public speaker, he was dismissed by some Democratic politicians as a man born with a "silver foot in his mouth." Consequently, Bush faced severe challenges as he prepared to run for the presidency in 1988. Even in his own party, many were unwilling to acknowledge him as the successor of Reagan. A number of Republicans entered the race for the presidential nomination, the most formidable of them being Senator Bob Dole of Kansas. When Dole inflicted an embarrassing defeat on Bush in the Iowa caucuses, it appeared as if Dole might impose on Bush the fate he had hoped to administer to Reagan in 1980. Instead, history repeated itself, with Bush's role reversed. After intense campaigning, he turned back Dole's challenge in New Hampshire. Following this decisive victory, Bush went on to sweep the primaries in the South, driving Dole out of the race and securing the Republican nomination.

Nevertheless, Bush's chances to prevail in the fall seemed slim. Polling indicated that he still suffered from high "negatives" with a dismayingly large percentage of the electorate. At a triumphant convention in July, the Democrats nominated Governor Michael Dukakis of Massachusetts. Dukakis emphasized his managerial expertise, noting that his competence would prove a decisive weapon against a man presumed to be an ineffectual time-server. At this point in the campaign, Bush trailed Dukakis by seventeen points in the polls.

Bush, however, had advantages. The Reagan administration, despite setbacks and scandals, remained popular. The economy stayed strong, and bold diplomacy with the Soviets reduced tensions abroad. The vice president could rely on an experienced and highly skilled campaign staff, including his longtime friend James Baker and a brilliant young political strategist named Lee Atwater. Bush himself was a veteran of two presidential campaigns and beneath his patrician manner and old-school affability was a shrewd politician. The vice president and his staff devised a campaign strategy that possessed the merit of simplicity as well as effectiveness. To counteract Bush's weaknesses, they would create weaknesses for Dukakis. Since Bush had no developed agenda, other than becoming president and continuing the Reagan era of prosperity, they decided to wage a campaign on the character and values of the candidates, concentrating on a victory rather than a mandate.

Bush presented two faces to the public. On one hand, there was the reassuring and comfortable Bush who stood foursquare for traditional American values. This Bush, in campaign appearances and television commercials, demonstrated his sympathy with the aspirations and concerns of ordinary Americans. He extolled the family and the old moral code. He spoke of love of country and flag. He expressed his hatred of criminals and called for the death penalty for drug kingpins. He pointed with pride to his military service and called for a strong nation. He sang the praises of hard work and promised "no new taxes" that might eat away at workers' earnings. This Bush was a man of the people. On the other hand, there was the combative Bush, who aggressively attacked

Excerpt from George H. W. Bush's acceptance speech at the Republican National Convention, August, 1988:

I'm the one who will not raise taxes. My opponent says he'll raise them as a last resort, or a third resort. But when a politician talks like that, you know that's one resort he'll be checking into. My opponent won't rule out raising taxes. But I will. And the Congress will push me to raise taxes and I'll say no. And they'll push, and I'll say no, and they'll push again, and all I can say to them is "Read my lips: No new taxes."

Dukakis for his liberalism, his membership in the American Civil Liberties Union (ACLU), and his stands on prison furloughs and school recitation of the Pledge of Allegiance. This Bush simultaneously exposed Dukakis as a man out of touch with popular opinion and proved himself tough enough for the presidency.

Governor Dukakis and his associates never developed an effective response to the Bush strategy. The politics of character became a trap for a man who either would not or could not fight Bush on Bush's terms. For most of the campaign, Dukakis dared not embrace liberalism for fear of alienating voters, while at the same time he refused to renounce his own political roots. Instead, he waffled, vainly attempting to regain the initiative he had lost to Bush. Only at the end of the campaign did Dukakis acknowledge his pride in liberalism, and by then it was too late.

Steadily over the summer and into the fall, Bush ate into Dukakis's lead and built his own. Only one misstep marred Bush's progress. His choice of Senator J. Danforth Quayle of Indiana as his running mate caused controversy. Dan Quayle was perceived as dull and inexperienced. The senator's military record came under fire, as it was charged that he had used his wealthy family's influence to win a slot in the National Guard and avoid the draft during the Vietnam War. Bush defended his running mate and refused to drop him. This liability, however, was more than made up for by the assistance of President Reagan, who campaigned energetically for Bush. In the end, Bush won a commanding victory, defeating Dukakis in the popular vote by a margin of 54 percent to 46 percent and in the electoral college by 426 votes to 111.

Into the White House

George H. W. Bush entered the presidency determined to make the office his own. He and Barbara Bush brought a simpler, more easygoing style to the White House after the opulence of the Reagan years. On their first day of residence, they personally welcomed tourists to their new home. Bush made a point of playing ball with his grandchildren on the White House lawn. In an act symbolizing his independence, Bush removed the portrait of Calvin Coolidge that Ronald Reagan had placed in the Cabinet Room and replaced it with one of Theodore Roosevelt, an aristocratic statesman who served as an inspiration for the new president.

Bush filled his administration with old friends and experienced Washington operators. James A. Baker III became secretary of state. Another close associate, Nicholas Brady, became secretary of the treasury. Brent Scowcroft, who had served Gerald Ford as National Security Adviser, returned to the same post for Bush. Other familiar faces in the cabinet included Elizabeth Dole, the wife of Bush's rival in the primaries, and former congressman Jack Kemp. Bush nominated a former senator from Texas, John Tower, for the position of secretary of defense. Despite Tower's many years in the Senate and acknowledged expertise in defense matters, the nomination came under heavy attack because of Tower's alleged drinking, womanizing, and financial ties to defense contractors. Bush loyally defended his nominee, but the Senate Armed Services Committee rejected Tower. The president responded by successfully nominating Congressman Dick Cheney, a widely respected legislator and another veteran of the Ford administration.

The fight over the Tower nomination signaled that the brief honeymoon was over between Bush and the Democrats, who controlled both houses of Congress. At his inauguration, Bush called for a renewal of bipartisanship. Early in his presidency, Bush took steps to distance his administration from the ideologically confrontational style of his predecessor. He wanted to find moderate ground with Congress, on which a consensus could be built, but Bush was swimming against the tide. The intense partisan political warfare that had accompanied the Reagan Revolution continued unabated. Both parties had their grievances and

martyrs. The Republicans remembered the liberal assault on Reagan's unsuccessful Supreme Court nominee Robert Bork, an event that had transformed the unfortunate judge's surname into a verb. The Democrats remembered the ruthlessness of Bush's presidential campaign. In addition, 1989 was a traumatic year for the Democratic House leadership. Majority Whip Tony Coelho resigned after being accused of financial irregularities in the purchase of a $100,000 junk bond. Jim Wright, the speaker of the House, was also forced into retirement after being found guilty of violating House ethics rules. Republican representative Newt Gingrich, who had orchestrated the campaign against Speaker Wright, soon found himself in turn the subject of an ethics investigation.

Thus the vicious edge to Washington politics, which would persist through the 1990's, was solidly in place as Bush took office. His

THE VICE PRESIDENT
DAN QUAYLE

J. Danforth Quayle was born in Indianapolis on February 4, 1947. The family moved to Huntington, Indiana, when Quayle was a child, and he attended public schools. Later, the family moved again to Phoenix but, prior to his graduation from high school, moved back to Huntington, where Quayle graduated. He attended DePauw University in Indiana, graduating in 1969, then joined the National Guard during the Vietnam War and worked on the Guard's newspaper. During this period he also attended the law school at Indiana University/Purdue University and, in 1972, married Marilyn Tucker. The Quayles opened a law firm together in 1974 and had three children.

Quayle's family owned a successful newspaper, and Quayle soon changed careers, serving as general manager and later as associated editor of the *Herald-Press*. His foray into politics started when he was elected to the U.S. House of Representatives in 1976, serving two terms before winning a seat in the U.S. Senate in 1980. Quayle was reelected in 1986. In 1988, George H. W. Bush selected Quayle as his vice presidential nominee, and the ticket was a success.

Quayle's vice presidency is remembered largely for the widespread criticism and ridicule he received from the media for his frequent gaffes while speaking. In fact, there was much speculation that he would be dropped in the 1992 reelection bid. However, Bush kept Quayle on the ticket. After the Bush-Quayle team lost in 1992, Quayle remained somewhat active in politics, speaking publicly and writing newspaper columns. He declined to run for president in 1996 because of an illness but did make an unsuccessful run for the office in 2000.

Robert P. Watson and Richard Yon

hopes for bipartisanship withered in this poisoned atmosphere. Bush's relations with Congress would be rocky throughout his presidency. The president would watch cherished pieces of legislation, such as a reduction in the capital gains tax, die inglorious deaths at the hands of Capitol Hill Democrats. For his part, he stymied the legislative program of the Democrats through what the press termed the "veto strategy," exercising his veto power forty-four times. The result was gridlock and a growing sense that change was needed if pressing national business was to be addressed.

Domestic Initiatives

As Ronald Reagan's legatee and without a clear mandate of his own, Bush pursued no Roose-veltian Hundred Days early in his presidency. His native caution, a conservative distrust of "big government," and a growing sensitivity to the budget deficit all helped preclude sweeping legislative gestures. When the president talked of a "thousand points of light" revitalizing American life, he was referring to private initiatives. Many, in both parties, criticized Bush for lacking a coherent program for his administration; the "vision thing" plagued Bush throughout his term. He repeatedly emphasized his conservative stance on taxes, trade, and government regulation, but Bush never found the rhetorical magic that had invigorated the Reagan presidency. He wanted his actions to speak for him. Ultimately this proved inadequate, and many Americans became con-

Bush signs the Americans with Disabilities Act of 1990. *(White House)*

Excerpts from George H. W. Bush's inaugural address, January 20, 1989:

I have spoken of a thousand points of light, of all the community organizations that are spread like stars throughout the Nation, doing good. We will work hand in hand, encouraging, sometimes leading, sometimes being led, rewarding. We will work on this in the White House, in the cabinet agencies. I will go to the people and the programs that are the brighter points of light, and I will ask every member of my government to become involved. The old ideas are new again because they are not old, they are timeless: duty, sacrifice, commitment, and a patriotism that finds its expression in taking part and pitching in. . . .

Some see leadership as high drama, and the sound of trumpets calling, and sometimes it is that. But I see history as a book with many pages, and each day we fill a page with acts of hopefulness and meaning. The new breeze blows, a page turns, the story unfolds. And so today a chapter begins, a small and stately story of unity, diversity, and generosity—shared, and written, together.

vinced that Bush was not interested in domestic policy.

Despite this public perception, Bush's domestic record was not devoid of accomplishment. Soon after taking office, he proposed a plan to save the savings and loan industry, which had come to the brink of collapse as a result of bad loans made during the halcyon days of deregulation during the 1980's. Bush sponsored proposals to increase federal aid for child care and education. He professed a desire to be known as the "education president" and worked to focus attention on American schools. After sparring with Congress, Bush signed a bill raising the minimum wage to $4.25 and creating a special training wage for younger workers. He disappointed some conservative backers by forbidding the importation of certain types of automatic weapons favored by drug dealers. He also ended the Reagan administration's expansion of the military, cutting spending on defense as the dangers of the Cold War receded. Two of the most significant pieces of legislation enacted with Bush's support were the Americans with Disabilities Act, which enforced new protections for citizens living with a wide range of disabilities, and the Clean Air Act, which set vigorous new standards on emissions from automobiles, utilities, and industrial plants.

Winds of Change

George Bush's greatest achievements would come in the realm of foreign policy. He successfully presided over the end of the Cold War and inaugurated the era when the United States stood alone as the world's sole superpower. If Bush did not launch the New World Order that he proclaimed in more expansive moments, he helped shape a period of extraordinary ferment and left the United States more secure than it had been in more than a half a century.

Bush brought a distinctive style to his diplomacy. Long an assiduous networker and famous in Washington for his Christmas card list, he cultivated strong personal ties to other world leaders. Through summits and frequent phone calls, he created bonds of trust and respect in foreign capitals that would serve American interests well in times of crisis. One of the most consequential relationships Bush developed was that with Soviet leader Mikhail Gorbachev.

In the first months of his presidency, Bush proceeded very cautiously in dealing with the Soviet Union. He was waiting for the completion of a policy review before taking a definitive stand on Gorbachev's efforts to reform Soviet society. Within the administration, opinion was divided between those who believed that Gorbachev was merely attempting to retool the

Berliners celebrate atop the dismantled Berlin Wall in November, 1989. (*AP/Wide World Photos*)

viet empire. This made it easier for Gorbachev to acquiesce to the rapid collapse of the communist regimes in Eastern Europe.

First in Poland and Hungary, then in Czechoslovakia and Bulgaria, communist officials were forced to give way to newly invigorated democratic movements. Revolution came violently to Romania in December, culminating in the televised execution of the former dictator Nicolae Ceausescu and his wife on Christmas Day. The most remarkable scenes of change came in East Germany. On November 9, the East German government, reeling from internal protests, opened the Berlin Wall. The breaching of this symbol of communist tyranny electrified the world. Young Germans from both sides of the divide celebrated atop what became merely an obsolescent stretch of concrete. The dissolution of the East German state followed in short order. Sustained diplomacy by Bush and James Baker persuaded Gorbachev to accept the reunification of Germany and its membership in the North Atlantic Treaty Organization (NATO). In return, Bush counseled moderation to the victorious democrats in former Soviet satellite states. He initially refused to recognize Lithuania's declaration of independence from the Soviet Union, fearing that the Baltic republic's attempt at succession might undermine Gorbachev's position.

Bush received scathing criticism for his refusal to back the Lithuanians. He defended his stand by arguing that he was acting in the best interests of the United States and that he was adjusting his policy to the "overall relationship" with the Soviet Union. Bush found himself making the same sort of case regard-

Soviet Union for more effective competition with the United States and those who were convinced that he was genuinely trying to create a more open polity. In the summer of 1989, Bush put an end to this period of irresolution and began making overtures to Gorbachev. He invited the Soviet leader to a summit on Malta, which proved enormously important in forging an active partnership between the two leaders. Support of Gorbachev now became the heart of Bush's strategy for winding down the Cold War. He labored to bolster the Soviet leader against the possibility of a coup by his many internal opponents. He assured Gorbachev that the United States would not take advantage of the growing troubles within the So-ing China. As a former envoy to China, Bush was deeply committed to the policy of improving relations with Beijing. He believed closer ties between the United States and China would promote international security. He also was deeply interested in encouraging Sino-American trade, convinced that it would provide U.S. jobs and prepare the way for democracy in China. Unfortunately, the growing friendliness between the American and Chinese governments was brought into question on June 4, 1989, when Chinese authorities used force to disperse prodemocracy demonstrators in Tiananmen Square. Hundreds, and possibly thousands, of the demonstrators were killed. In the wake of this massacre, many more dissidents were rounded up and imprisoned. President Bush joined in the international condemnation of this brutal repression, but he refused to impose significant sanctions on the Chinese regime, despite an outcry for strong measures

from Capitol Hill. Bush held that American relations with China were too important to be sacrificed to a moment of outrage. He secretly sent Brent Scowcroft and Deputy Secretary of State Lawrence Eagleburger to Beijing to explain American concerns and to urge an end to the crackdown on dissent. In coming years, Bush would successfully lobby Congress to grant China most-favored-nation (MFN) trade status.

Change came to other parts of the world as well. In 1989, F. W. de Klerk became prime minister of South Africa. De Klerk soon freed Nelson Mandela, the leader of the African National Congress (ANC). President Bush met with both De Klerk and Mandela and supported sanctions against South Africa until apartheid, its system of racial separation, was abolished. In 1991, with reform well under way, Bush lifted these sanctions. Moreover, with American encouragement, Augusto Pinochet, the right-

Graffiti in Panama City in January, 1990, following the U.S. invasion to overthrow General Manuel Noriega. *(Reuters/Santiago Lyon/Archive Photos)*

wing dictator of Chile, stepped aside in 1989, to be replaced by an elected government. In Nicaragua, Bush abandoned efforts to bring down the Sandinista government through the Contras' armed insurrection. Instead he worked for a political solution to the Nicaraguan problem and was rewarded in 1990 when an anti-Sandinista coalition won an upset victory in free elections. In neighboring El Salvador, patient diplomacy finally bore fruit, and in 1992, a guerrilla war that had raged for twelve years came to an end. The government and the guerrillas agreed to a package of reforms and made the commitment to resolve future difficulties through the ballot box.

Bush used less peaceful means to overthrow Manuel Noriega, the dictatorial ruler of Panama. Noriega had once been on the CIA's payroll, but by the late 1980's, he had shifted his fealty from the United States to the Medellín drug cartel. He was wanted in the United States on charges of drug trafficking, gun running, and money laundering. His increasingly reckless behavior culminated in an incident in which an American soldier from the Canal Zone was killed. Noriega compounded crime with folly by threatening further actions against Americans. On December 20, 1989, Bush responded by invading Panama with twenty-five thousand troops. The Americans made short work of Noriega's forces and, after a manhunt, captured the former strongman and carried him off for trial in Miami. Twenty-three Americans died. Some five hundred Panamanians, many of them civilians, also perished. The invasion proved to be overwhelmingly popular in the United States, and even most Panamanians welcomed the Americans as liberators.

The Gulf War

Throughout the Iraq-Iran War that raged from 1980 to 1988, the United States tilted toward Iraq as a bulwark against the revolutionary Islamic fundamentalism of Iran. The American government provided the Iraqi dictator Saddam Hussein with valuable intelligence and military hardware. Even after Hussein made peace with Iran, American policymakers continued to regard Iraq as a force for stability in the Middle East. They failed to weigh adequately Hussein's well-known brutality, his militarism, and his growing economic desperation. Hence the Bush administration was taken by surprise when, on August 2, 1990, Iraqi forces invaded and occupied the neighboring principality of Kuwait, a tiny state richly endowed with oil. By taking Kuwait, Hussein was making a bold bid for international influence. His army, the fourth largest in the world, now sat poised to strike at Saudi Arabian oil fields that made up 20 percent of the world's oil reserves.

President Bush refused to accept the Iraqi aggression as a fait accompli. He declared, "This will not stand." He immediately began arranging a vigorous response. Within a week of the fall of Kuwait, Bush had ordered 100,000 American troops and a fleet of warplanes to Saudi Arabia to defend the desert kingdom against any further adventuring by Saddam Hussein. He persuaded the United Nations Security Council to demand an Iraqi withdrawal from Kuwait. The Security Council imposed severe economic sanctions on Iraq as a means of pressuring the Iraqis to comply. Here Bush's patient diplomacy with China and the Soviet Union paid off handsomely. Neither former Cold War rival stood in Bush's way as he rallied international opinion against Hussein. The Soviets in particular proved cooperative. Bush met with Gorbachev in Helsinki, Finland, on September 9 to discuss Kuwait. Though the Soviets would later express deep reservations about the American military effort, Gorbachev never broke ranks on the fundamental principle that Iraq had to leave Kuwait.

Bush early on became convinced that Hussein's army would have to be ejected from Kuwait by force. He began building a grand alliance of nations committed to the liberation of

Excerpts from George H. W. Bush's address at the start of the Persian Gulf War, January 16, 1991:

While the world waited, Saddam Hussein systematically raped, pillaged, and plundered a tiny nation no threat to his own. He subjected the people of Kuwait to unspeakable atrocities, and among those maimed and murdered, innocent children.

While the world waited, Saddam sought to add to the chemical weapons arsenal he now possesses, an infinitely more dangerous weapon of mass destruction—a nuclear weapon. And while the world waited, while the world talked peace and withdrawal, Saddam Hussein dug in and moved massive forces into Kuwait.

While the world waited, while Saddam stalled, more damage was being done to the fragile economies of the Third World, emerging democracies of Eastern Europe, to the entire world, including to our own economy.

The United States, together with the United Nations, exhausted every means at our disposal to bring this crisis to a peaceful end. However, Saddam clearly felt that by stalling and threatening and defying the United Nations, he could weaken the forces arrayed against him.

While the world waited, Saddam Hussein met every overture of peace with open contempt. While the world prayed for peace, Saddam prepared for war. . . .

This is an historic moment. We have in this past year made great progress in ending the long era of conflict and Cold War. We have before us the opportunity to forge for ourselves and for future generations a new world order, a world where the rule of law, not the law of jungle, governs the conduct of nations.

When we are successful, and we will be, we have a real chance at this new world order, an order in which a credible United Nations can use its peacekeeping role to fulfill the promise and vision of the U.N.'s founders. We have no argument with the people of Iraq. Indeed, for the innocents caught in this conflict, I pray for their safety.

Our goal is not the conquest of Iraq. It is the liberation of Kuwait. It is my hope that somehow the Iraqi people can, even now, convince their dictator that he must lay down his arms, leave Kuwait and let Iraq itself rejoin the family of peace-loving nations.

. . . But even as planes of the multinational forces attack Iraq, I prefer to think of peace, not war. I am convinced not only that we will prevail, but that out of the horror of combat will come the recognition that no nation can stand against a world united. No nation will be permitted to brutally assault its neighbor.

Kuwait. By the time Bush was through, military units from twenty-seven countries were part of the coalition force gathering in Saudi Arabia. Other nations, including Germany and Japan, pledged financial support. In November, Bush ordered American commanders to begin planning an offensive to drive back the Iraqis. The United Nations set January 15, 1991, as a deadline for Hussein to pull his forces from Kuwait. At home, Bush faced a debate over war powers. He believed that he had the authority to launch a military offensive against Iraq. Many in Congress disputed this. A number of Democrats on Capitol Hill were convinced that the president was moving too precipitously and not giving economic sanctions enough time to work. In the end, Bush asked Congress for a resolution authorizing military action in the Persian Gulf, if necessary. The resolution passed on January 12, by a comfortable margin in the House and much more narrowly in the Senate.

Last-minute talks with Hussein's envoys failed to resolve the crisis. The January 15 deadline passed with no movement by the Iraqis. On January 16, President Bush ordered Operation Desert Storm to begin. For five weeks, Allied forces pounded the Iraqis from the air, unleashing a devastating arsenal of high-tech, precision weaponry. On February 23, General Norman Schwarzkopf ordered a ground assault. He commanded 700,000 troops, nearly 500,000 of them Americans; 200,000 of these wheeled in a great armored arc to trap and crush retreating Iraqi formations. Within four days, Kuwait had been cleared of the Iraqi invaders. As the punishment coalition forces were inflicting on the retreating Iraqis began to look like a massacre, Bush ordered an end to the war.

The Persian Gulf War was a personal triumph for Bush. Through diplomatic skill, he had overcome a number of obstacles and struck a mighty blow for the forces of international order. Only 128 American lives were lost in battle. Iraqi casualties numbered in the tens of thousands. Critics called the victory hollow, because Saddam Hussein remained in power and even was able to crush uprisings by Shiite Muslims in the south and Kurds in the north. Bush answered by arguing that the coalition forces had no mandate to invade Iraq. Bush's extraordinary diplomatic success in building the coalition limited his options. Many coalition partners actively opposed fighting on to Baghdad. Bush was also concerned that a crusade against the Iraqi dictator could result in a bloody quagmire. It would be left to Bush's son, President George W. Bush, to overthrow Saddam Hussein in 2003 and also to fight a long guerrilla

In 1990, President Bush shares Thanksgiving dinner with troops from Operation Desert Shield serving in Saudi Arabia. *(NARA)*

war with Iraqi insurgents. However, in 1991, the terrorist attacks of September, 2001, had yet to occur. The threat posed by Hussein was conventional, and Bush responded with conventional methods. He fenced in what was left of Hussein's military machine with no-fly zones in the north and south of Iraq and created a refuge for the Kurds in the north. U.N. sanctions and inspections were imposed on Iraq to prevent Hussein from rearming. Bush took advantage of the momentum created by the Gulf War to encourage a peace conference between Israel and its Arab neighbors. Months of negotiating resulted in formal talks in the fall of 1991, and the beginning of a peace process.

A Time of Troubles

In the immediate aftermath of the Gulf War, President Bush enjoyed unprecedented popularity. However, his poll numbers soon began to falter, as Americans focused on domestic problems. In the fall of 1990, the economy slipped into a recession. Bush was slow to acknowledge the turnaround in the economy, and when he did take steps to combat the recession, these were seen as too little, too late. The nation's economic woes focused attention on the continuing burden of the budget deficit. Facing acrimonious budget negotiations with congressional leaders, Bush decided to accept a compromise deficit reduction plan that included some tax increases. In the short run, the legislation failed to revive the economy. This and the fact that Bush had reneged on his promise to never raise taxes infuriated conservative Republicans. They had always doubted his commitment to Reaganite principles. Their readiness to defect from the president's camp would prove politically crippling.

In 1990, Bush had easily replaced retiring Supreme Court justice William Brennan with David Souter, a little-known federal judge from New Hampshire. The retirement of the legendary African American jurist Thurgood Marshall in 1991 presented Bush with a more delicate

political problem. He responded by nominating Clarence Thomas, a conservative African American judge who had headed Reagan's Equal Opportunity Commission. The Thomas nomination precipitated an unexpected political firestorm when a former employee of Thomas's named Anita Hill charged that he had sexually harassed her in the early 1980's. Bush stood behind Thomas, who won a narrow confirmation, but the ugly dispute between Thomas and Hill aggravated the polarization of American politics and created the impression that Bush was insensitive to the concerns of women. In 1990, Bush had vetoed a bill making it easier for women and minorities to sue employers for discrimination. In the wake of the Thomas scandal, he signed a new version of the bill, but this gesture failed to mollify his critics and further disgusted conservatives.

At the end of July, 1991, Bush and Mikhail Gorbachev met in Washington to sign a treaty formalizing steep reductions in American and Soviet stockpiles of nuclear weapons. A few weeks later, on August 19, Gorbachev was deposed in a coup organized by Soviet leaders frightened by his reforms. Bush initially reacted cautiously to the news. However, once it became clear that Boris Yeltsin, the president of the Russian Federation, was successfully resisting the coup, Bush began to rally international support for the charismatic Russian leader. The coup attempt collapsed, and Gorbachev briefly returned to office, but his authority had become a shadow. Real power now lay with Yeltsin, who decided to liquidate the Soviet Union in December, 1991, replacing it with a new Commonwealth of Independent States. Bush and Gorbachev had their last telephone conversation as leaders on Christmas Day, 1991. They expressed their mutual esteem. In retrospect, Bush's role in the winding down of the Cold War would often be described as that of a passive witness to a largely peaceful process. In fact, the president's skillful diplomacy helped ensure that the breakup of the Soviet Empire did not take a different and more dangerous turn. Bush moved quickly to build a relationship with Yeltsin. He arranged financial assistance for the new regime and signed an agreement between the United States and Russia calling for even deeper cuts in their nuclear arsenals.

The Election of 1992

In the fall of 1991, Bush pondered retirement. He was beginning to suffer from some minor ailments and was clearly tired. In the end, though, the allure of the presidency was too much, and Bush decided to grasp at the brass ring of a second term. Despite his decision to run, it quickly became clear that Bush had lost the fire of 1988. His political advisers urged Bush to launch his campaign in 1991, but he put them off until 1992. When he did at last organize his reelection effort, it displayed little of the energy and skill that had won him the presidency. Key members of his earlier team were gone. Lee Atwater had died, and James Baker was still at the State Department.

The economy continued to bedevil the president. Though it slowly began to pick up speed in 1992, the public remained more impressed with its weaknesses than its strengths. Bush devoted more time to economic issues, but he never found a program that sparked enthusiasm with voters. Characteristically, Bush's most significant initiative to stimulate the economy was an effort to encourage free trade agreements around the world. The most enduring result of this push was the North American Free Trade Agreement (NAFTA) with Canada and Mexico. Bush negotiated the treaty; it would be ratified under his successor.

Bush faced a challenge from the Right during the primary season. Patrick Buchanan, a conservative political commentator, rallied Republicans dissatisfied with Bush's lapses from Reaganite orthodoxy. Buchanan also expressed a populist distrust of big business and free trade that played well to voters concerned about their jobs. Though Buchanan never posed a serious threat to Bush's renomination, his presence in the race embarrassed the president and forced him to make unavailing gestures to the Right at a time when he needed to be reassuring moderate swing voters. The conservative coalition that had triumphed in 1980, 1984, and 1988 was collapsing.

The Democrats nominated Governor William Jefferson Clinton of Arkansas. Bill Clinton skillfully positioned himself as a moderate and hammered away at the importance of the economy. A relatively youthful man and an exuberant campaigner, Clinton promised renewed energy and purpose for government at a time when Americans recognized themselves to be at a historical crossroads. The race between Bush and Clinton became a three-way contest when H. Ross Perot, an eccentric Texas businessman and billionaire, threw his hat into the ring. Amply funded by his immense fortune, Perot ran as a populist, capitalizing on widespread distrust of the major parties by offering "commonsense" solutions to America's problems.

Bush searched in vain for an effective message to take to the people. He returned to the tactics of 1988, raising questions about Governor Clinton's character and attacking him for his equivocal behavior in avoiding the draft during the Vietnam War. In the end, Bush's attempt to resurrect the politics of character failed. The Clinton team responded energetically, raising questions about the Iran-Contra scandal. The decision of Iran-Contra prosecutor Lawrence Walsh to indict former secretary of defense Caspar Weinberger in October reminded the public of Bush's ambiguous role in the scandal and took away whatever wind there was behind his campaign. The American people were looking for new directions, and George Bush had none to offer. Clinton handily won the election, taking 43 percent of the vote to Bush's 38 percent and Perot's 19 percent.

President Bush's last months in office were busy. He launched air raids against a recalcitrant Saddam Hussein and sent thirty thousand American troops to assist famine relief in Somalia. He worked hard to ensure a smooth transfer of authority to the new administration. The transition from George H. W. Bush to Bill Clinton was widely seen as symbolic, a passing of power, and mission, from one generation to the next. Bush had ably ended the Cold War. Younger hands would guide America to the millennium.

Postpresidential Years

Bush retired to his homes in Houston and Kennebunkport. He devoted himself to his family. He watched with pride as two of his sons continued the Bush tradition of public service. George W. Bush was elected governor of Texas in 1994 and then U.S. president in 2000, while Jeb Bush was elected Governor of Florida in 1998. Bush also nursed his historical legacy. He published memoirs defending his approach to foreign policy and a volume of letters and other documents. He dedicated the George H. W. Bush Presidential Library and Museum in 1997. Bush remained physically vigorous. He delighted the press and public when he celebrated his seventy-fifth birthday by skydiving from a plane.

The election of George W. Bush to the presidency in 2000 made Bush the first man since John Adams to see his son also attain the highest office in the land. In January, 2005, President Bush asked his father and Bill Clinton to lead a fund-raising effort for victims of a tsunami that had ravaged coastlines along the Indian Ocean. So successful was this presidential pairing that in September, 2005, Bush and Clinton were again asked to spearhead the relief efforts for Americans displaced by Hurricane Katrina. George H. W. Bush, even in his eighties, was respected as an elder statesman and continued to be valued as a public servant. He could take satisfaction from being the paterfamilias of the

most significant political dynasty in modern American history.

Daniel P. Murphy

Suggested Readings

Barilleaux, Ryan J., and Mark J. Rozell. *Power and Prudence: The Presidency of George H. W. Bush.* College Station: Texas A&M University Press, 2004. Argues that the unique circumstances of Bush's presidency may have limited his opportunities to achieve far-reaching policy objectives.

Beschloss, Michael, and Strobe Talbot. *At the Highest Levels.* Boston: Little, Brown, 1993. A diplomatic history that focuses on Bush's relationship with Mikhail Gorbachev.

Bose, Meena, and Rosanna Perotti. *From Cold War to New World Order.* Westport, Conn.: Greenwood Press, 2002. Analysis of Bush's foreign policy from participants, journalists, and academics.

Bush, Barbara. *Barbara Bush: A Memoir.* New York: Scribner, 1994. An engaging autobiography from the first lady.

Bush, George H. W. *All the Best, George Bush.* New York: Scribner, 1999. Organized chronologically, the book begins when Bush is eighteen and includes diary entries, letters, and memos, all accompanied by Bush's commentary.

Bush, George H. W., and Victor Gold. *Looking Forward.* New York: Doubleday, 1987. A campaign biography useful for Bush's early life.

Bush, George H. W., and Brent Scowcroft. *A World Transformed.* New York: Knopf, 1998. Bush and his former national security adviser look back on the foreign policy of the Bush administration.

George Bush Presidential Library. http://www.georgebushfoundation.org/bush/. The Web site of the official Bush presidential library.

Greene, John Robert. *The Presidency of George Bush.* Lawrence: University Press of Kansas,

2000. A sympathetic account of Bush's presidency from a distinguished scholar.

Himelfarb, Richard, and Rosana Perotti, eds. *Principle Over Politics? The Domestic Policy of the George H. W. Bush Presidency.* Westport, Conn.: Praeger, 2004. Journalists, cabinet members, and associates of Bush examine his record on such issues as the economy and national budget, disabled and civil rights, and health, science, and technology.

Mervin, David. *George Bush and the Guardianship Presidency.* New York: St. Martin's Press, 1998. An analytical study of Bush's presidency by a British academic.

Parmet, Herbert. *George Bush.* New York: Scribner, 1997. One of the best biographies of Bush.

Phillips, Kevin P. *American Dynasty.* New York: Viking, 2004. A highly critical account of the political rise of the Bush family.

Thompson, Kenneth. *The Bush Presidency.* Lanham, Md.: University Press of America, 1997. Reminiscences by members of the Bush administration.

Wicker, Tom. *George Herbert Walker Bush.* New York: Lipper/Viking, 2004. A critical analysis of Bush's career by a liberal journalist.

Bill Clinton

42d President, 1993-2001

Born: August 19, 1946
Hope, Arkansas

Political Party: Democratic
Vice President: Al Gore, Jr.

Cabinet Members

Secretary of State: Warren Christopher,
Madeleine Albright
Secretary of the Treasury: Lloyd Bentsen,
Robert E. Rubin, Lawrence H. Summers
Secretary of Defense: Les Aspin, William J.
Perry, William Cohen
Secretary of the Interior: Bruce Babbitt
Attorney General: Janet Reno
Secretary of Agriculture: Mike Espy, Dan
Glickman
Secretary of Commerce: Ron Brown, Mickey
Kantor, William Daley, Norman Y. Mineta
Secretary of Labor: Robert B. Reich, Alexis
Herman
Secretary of Health and Human Services: Donna
Shalala
Secretary of Housing and Urban Development:
Henry Cisneros, Andrew Cuomo
Secretary of Transportation: Federico Peña,
Rodney Slater
Secretary of Energy: Hazel O'Leary, Federico
Peña, Bill Richardson
Secretary of Education: Richard E. Riley
Secretary of Veterans Affairs: Jesse Brown,
Togo D. West, Jr., Hershel Gober

William "Bill" Jefferson Clinton is the son of
Virginia Cassidy, a nurse, and William Jeffer-
son Blythe III, an automobile parts salesman.
Born in Hope, Arkansas, on August 19, 1946,

Clinton never knew his father. His parents,
who married in Shreveport, Louisiana, in 1946,
were forced to live apart during most of World
War II, while Clinton's father was in military
service. On his return to civilian life, the best job
he was able to find was in Chicago, so he moved

Clinton's official portrait. *(White House Historical Society)*

797

there, coming to Arkansas as frequently as he could to be with his wife.

On one of these trip home, Blythe, driving through a heavy rain storm in Missouri, had a blowout, crashed his car into a flooded ditch, and drowned. Three months later, his son was born. Virginia named the baby William Jefferson Blythe IV. In need of providing for herself and her infant son, Virginia set out to improve her credentials by going to New Orleans, where she trained to become a nurse-anesthetist.

Billy, as he was then called, was left with his maternal grandparents in Hope. Although they had little formal education, the grandparents valued learning and education. They taught their grandson to read and to count when he was still quite young. By the time he was six, he was able to read the newspaper with a high degree of comprehension.

Early Years

Billy left his grandparents' home when he was seven. His mother, having completed her training program in New Orleans, returned to Arkansas, where she married Roger Clinton who, like her first husband, was a car salesman. She moved to Hot Springs, Arkansas, taking her young son with her. He attended elementary school in Hot Springs, where he was known as Bill Clinton rather than Billy Blythe. He used the name Clinton but did not change it legally until he was in his teens. He attended public schools save for two years between ages seven and nine when, despite coming from a Southern Baptist family, he was a student in a Roman Catholic elementary school.

Bill Clinton was a precocious youth. He loved learning and was so eager a student that he once received a "D" grade in deportment because the nun who was his teacher felt he did not give other students an opportunity to respond to questions. If he knew the answers, as he usually did, he blurted them out.

Life at home was far from ideal. Roger Clinton, although basically a kind and caring man, drank too much. When he was intoxicated, he sometimes struck his wife or Roger, Jr., the child he and Virginia had when Bill was ten years old. In fact, Roger, Sr. was so out of control at one point that he fired a gun in the house.

By the time Bill was fourteen, he had lost patience with his stepfather's antics. When Roger, quite drunk, began upbraiding his wife and young son, Roger, Jr., Bill took control of the situation, stepping between his stepfather and his mother and warning Roger never to hit her or Roger, Jr. again. He told him that if he wanted to do anything to them, he would have to go through him. Although Virginia and Roger's marriage was often strained and Virginia was separated from Roger several times, they were always reunited.

The Emergence of a Leader

People soon began to recognize that Bill Clinton had a palpable charisma that made him a natural leader. He was elected president of his junior high school class. He was a leader in his school's band and played the saxophone in a three-member band that called itself the Three Blind Mice. His involvement in extra-curricular activities in no way diminished his scholastic achievement. He was a finalist for a National Merit Scholarship and graduated fourth in his high school class of 323 students.

When he was seventeen, Clinton attended Boys' State, a camp where outstanding students learn about the political process. At Boys' State, he was elected to go to Boys' Nation in Washington, D. C. as a delegate from Arkansas.

This trip was perhaps the most crucial one Clinton would ever take. In Washington, the young Arkansas delegate met and shook the hand of President John F. Kennedy, who had long been one of Clinton's heroes and was a distinct role model for the young man. The trip to Washington convinced Bill that a life of public service was the life he wanted for himself.

THE FIRST LADY
HILLARY RODHAM CLINTON

Perhaps the most controversial First Lady of the second half of the twentieth century, Hillary Diane Rodham was born in Chicago, Illinois, on October 26, 1947. She graduated from Wellesley College and Yale University's School of Law. At Yale, she met fellow law student Bill Clinton, whom she married in 1975.

After five terms as governor of Arkansas, Bill was elected the U.S. president. His wife, a prominent lawyer and political activist, was appointed to head the President's Task Force on National Health Care Reform. The task force presented a complex plan that seemed unviable to many. Hillary Rodham Clinton rejected compromises with Congress that might have assured passage of some provisions of the plan, and health care reform was defeated in August, 1994.

There were additional problems. Questions were raised about Hillary's role in Whitewater, an Arkansas land deal; in "Travelgate," the firing of employees in the White House Travel Office; and in the suicide of Vincent Foster, her former Rose Law Firm partner and deputy White House counsel. She seemed to be the lightning rod for the administration and saw her popularity ratings take a significant dip.

Though she retreated for a time, Hillary learned from her mistakes, changed tactics, and conducted some of her activities out of the media spotlight. She was involved in welfare reform, chaired the President's Committee on the Arts and Humanities, and worked for change with a number of government departments. She assisted in founding the Department of Justice's Violence Against Women Office. She also drew wide praise both for her speeches about human rights at the United Nations Fourth World Conference on Women in Beijing, China, in 1995 and for the publication of her 1996 book *It Takes a Village*.

After enduring the revelations of her husband's affair with White House intern Monica Lewinsky, Hillary Rodham Clinton was persuaded to run for a United States Senate seat from New York. On November 8, 2000, she became the first sitting First Lady to be elected to public office.

The object of unending media scrutiny and controversy, Hillary demonstrated that the office of First Lady was flexible when she moved away from more traditional First Lady concerns into issues of public policy. Her decision to run for elective office further enlarged the potential scope of the position. Many political analysts consider her a potential candidate for president.

Myra G. Gutin

Upon his graduation from high school, Clinton won a scholarship to study music in Arkansas. He opted, however, to go to Washington to attend Georgetown University as an international affairs major, even though this decision was financially very difficult for him. Georgetown, with its cosmopolitan and multiethnic student body and politically savvy professors, opened new worlds to Clinton. Staying in school was not easy for him because of the expense, but he was determined to complete his studies at Georgetown no matter what personal sacrifices he had to make to do so.

Clinton's Initial Involvement in Politics
Faced with the necessity of earning money to stay in school, Clinton found part-time jobs to pay some of his college expenses. One summer he returned to Arkansas to work for Frank Holt, who was then running for governor. Although Holt lost the election, Clinton's involvement in his campaign paid dividends

for him. Holt's nephew, a justice in the Arkansas Supreme Court, recommended Clinton to Arkansas senator J. William Fulbright, who hired him to work part-time in his Washington office.

His work outside the University in no way impeded Clinton from being a fully involved student on campus. He was elected president of both his freshman and his sophomore classes at Georgetown, where his fellow students recognized his extraordinary devotion to his studies and appreciated his political acumen.

In 1967, while Clinton was still a student at Georgetown, Roger Clinton became seriously ill with cancer and was obviously dying. Bill, eager to show his stepfather that, despite their differences, he valued and loved him, drove for four hours every weekend until Roger died at the Duke Medical Center in Durham, North Carolina.

Clinton had never quite come to grips with the loss of his own father, and he now was again faced with the death of someone he loved. This made him increasingly aware of his own mortality and forced him to the realization that he should do as much as he could as soon as he could. Life, in his eyes, was an uncertain affair, but a major purpose in life, he believed, is to leave one's mark upon the world in some positive way.

Clinton impressed some of his Georgetown professors enough that they urged him to apply for a Rhodes scholarship, which would, following graduation, enable him to spend two years studying at Oxford University in England. Clinton held little hope of receiving this award, one of the most competitive and prestigious available to new college graduates. Despite his apprehensions, he applied and, much to his astonishment, was appointed a Rhodes scholar.

The Oxford Experience

Completing his studies at Georgetown in 1968, Clinton soon set out for England where, for the first time in his life, he could devote his full attention to his studies. The Rhodes scholarship covered all of his expenses, making it unnecessary for him to earn money to support himself and pay his tuition.

At Oxford, Clinton was in a totally new world. He had time to explore his extensive diversity of interests. He read a book almost every day, rejoicing in the opportunity that had been afforded him. He found the pace at Oxford much more relaxed than he had experienced at Georgetown, but he drove himself to accomplish as much as he could in the time he was there. His self-motivation and academic discipline were exceptional.

However, while Clinton was studying at Oxford, storm clouds were gathering at home. The United States, in an attempt to halt the incursion of communism in southeast Asia, was waging war in Vietnam. The war was an extremely controversial and generally unpopular one. Many American youth refused to fight in it, some defecting to Canada to avoid being drafted into military services. Those who refused to serve were placed in legal jeopardy. Clinton, however, was not in any immediate danger of being drafted because he had a student deferment that would be good until he completed his studies.

Upon carefully considering the validity of this war, Clinton concluded that it was an unjust conflict. He helped to organize protests against the war during his stay in Britain, an act that would return to haunt him as his political career progressed to the national arena.

When his student deferment finally expired, Clinton took his chances in the draft lottery, in which the birth dates of eligible young men were drawn at random. Clinton's birth date was low on the list of those to be drafted, so he was in little danger of being called for military service.

Attending Yale University's Law School

At the end of his second year at Oxford, Clinton could well have stayed on and continued work for a doctorate. Such a course, however, did not coincide with his long-term plans to enter politics. He realized that the best entree into a political career was a law degree. He applied and was admitted to the Yale University Law School, a number of whose professors had been in government service during the John F. Kennedy presidency.

Early in his days at Yale, Clinton was smitten by a fellow classmate, Hillary Rodham, but he was too diffident to approach her and introduce himself. Rather, he stared at her in class until one day she approached him and told him that if he was going to keep staring at her, she was going to keep staring back. She told him her name, and the two became fast friends.

Clinton soon acknowledged that Rodham was the brightest person he had ever known. The two were inseparable. During the 1972 presidential election, both of them took leaves of absence from Yale to work in the presidential campaign of George McGovern, a Democrat, who was soundly defeated by Richard M. Nixon, the Republican candidate.

Upon graduation from Yale, both Clinton and Rodham were offered jobs in Washington, D.C., to work on the staff of the House Judiciary Committee that was investigating Nixon's possible involvement in what soon came to be known as the Watergate scandal. Rodham accepted the job offer that was proffered, but Clinton wanted instead to return to his home state, Arkansas, and enter the political arena there.

The Return to Arkansas

Many people would have considered Clinton's rejection of the offer to work on the House Judiciary Committee shortsighted and downright foolish given his expectation of devoting his life to public service. In returning to Arkansas, he was going back to one of the poorest, least progressive states in the country. Perhaps his work with Senator J. William Fulbright during his

years at Georgetown had inspired him to attempt to build on the liberal, progressive outlook of this notable senator. Clinton, upon relocating in Arkansas, set as his primary goal the task of working to bring a new prosperity to his state.

Learning that the University of Arkansas at Fayetteville was about to appoint another law professor, Clinton applied for the job. Still a few months shy of his twenty-ninth birthday, Clinton's application was not taken seriously by the dean of the law school, who considered Clinton too young for the job.

Clinton, learning of this, informed the dean that he had been too young for everything he ever tried to do. The dean was persuaded and hired the young applicant. Clinton moved to Fayetteville, a sleepy town in the Ozark Mountains, where he could have settled into an unhurried and uncomplicated life had he so desired.

Three months into his first year of teaching, he filed to run for a seat in Congress against the popular Republican incumbent, John Hammerschmidt, who had the advantage of incumbency and of name recognition.

At this point, few Arkansans had any idea who Bill Clinton was. This anonymity, however, was short lived: Clinton got into his car and drove all over the state, speaking to any group he could find and making such a favorable impression that he came within a hair's breadth of winning the election. Hammerschmidt commanded 51.5 percent of the vote, which was nothing short of amazing.

Clinton had not anticipated winning the election. Rather, he had set out to determine how well he could do considering the many disadvantages he had to overcome. By the beginning of 1975, many savvy Arkansans were referring to Clinton as a boy wonder who could in time transform Arkansas politics.

Early in his campaign, Hillary Rodham came to Arkansas to take a job at the University of Arkansas Law School. Her chief reason for leaving Washington, however, was to help Clinton run for public office, which she did with unswerving dedication and impressive intelligence. Although she was a Yankee in a southern state, a definite outsider, she soon came to understand the people of that state and to realize what it would take to win them over to Clinton and to his often heterodox positions. Clinton was far from being the "good old boy" type of southern politician that had held sway for many years in much of the South.

Once the campaign was over, Rodham expressed doubts about remaining in Arkansas. She had at one point remarked that she liked a house in Fayetteville that she and Clinton had sometimes passed on their daily walks. Clinton, not wanting her to leave the state, bought the house. Before the ink was dry on the sales contract, he told Hillary what he had done, saying that now she had to stay and marry him. Shocked at first by Clinton's impetuousness, she stayed in Arkansas and within two months became Clinton's wife.

Winning Elective Office

The year after he was defeated in his bid for Congress, Clinton, who had impressed the electorate with his near victory in the race against Hammerschmidt, ran for the office of Arkansas attorney general. By this time, he had gained sufficient popularity that the Republicans, acknowledging his invincibility, did not nominate anyone to run against him. Clinton, therefore, won his first elective office with a resounding victory.

As attorney general, Clinton was tireless in pursuing controversial issues that many politicians would have avoided. His doggedness and his incredibly sound preparation for cases that he had to take before the court attracted the attention of influential politicians throughout the state and, indeed, elsewhere in the South. In 1978, they nominated him to run for governor, a position that he won handily. At age thirty-two, he was the youngest governor in the United States, a fact that was not lost on political mavens in Washington. It now appeared to many that Bill Clinton was potentially presidential material.

Clinton's First Term as Governor

When Clinton began his first term as governor in 1979, Arkansas governors did not have the usual four years in which to prove themselves. They served a two-year term. At an annual salary of thirty-five thousand dollars, they were also the lowest paid governors in the United States.

Clinton had a concrete vision of what he needed to achieve as governor. High on his list of priorities was the reform of public education in his state, which ranked close to the bottom on all national measurements of educational excellence. Clinton was convinced that the people of Arkansas were as bright as people in any other state, but that Arkansas students did not perform well on national tests because the state was not putting enough money into education.

He proposed hiring more teachers and increasing teachers' salaries, at that time among the lowest in the United States. Linked to this proposal was one, threatening to many of his constituents, that all new teachers would have to pass competency tests to ensure that those who were employed to teach were capable of doing their jobs well. Even more threatening was his proposal to consolidate many of the state's 382 school districts into more manageable and efficient administrative entities.

Although consolidation would improve the resources of many districts, combining four existing districts into one consolidated district would necessarily leave three superintendents of schools without their superintendencies. School administrators across the state balked at Clinton's proposals, and the state legislature declined to approve the budget for hiring more teachers and increasing teacher salaries.

Clinton also embarked on a much-needed road building program, raising money to fi-

Bill Clinton shown in 1979 during his first term as governor of Arkansas. *(AP/Wide World Photos)*

was sufficiently great to make him reassess what he was doing and to use his defeat as a learning opportunity.

As he thought through his two years as governor, he realized that he had tried to do too much too soon. He knew what he wanted to accomplish, and he had a solid vision of how he could accomplish his ends. What he had failed to do was to keep his constituency informed about the measures he wished to enact.

He now knew that he had to run again for public office but, that before he could do so, he had to get out and meet as many voters as possible. He needed to outline for the voters what he hoped to achieve, but he realized that it was even more important to ask questions and find out what was paramount in the voters' minds.

It was fortunate for him that Governor White was not up to the task of running the state and was making so many obvious blunders that many voters referred to him as Governor Goofy. Clinton announced his candidacy for the governorship in February, 1982, and in a humble, self-deprecating speech, told the voters that he knew he had made mistakes but that he had learned from them. He also pointed out some of the more egregious errors Frank White had made as governor.

nance it by increasing license fees on motorized vehicles. This measure was highly unpopular with most citizens. Despite public resistance to many of Clinton's policies, however, it appeared that Clinton would surely be elected for a second term when he ran for reelection in 1980. Much to his surprise and to the surprise of many Arkansans, the victory went not to Clinton but to his Republican opponent, Frank White, who defeated him by a narrow margin.

The Lessons Learned from Defeat

Losing the election left Clinton somewhat dismayed and, for a time, disheartened. Never one to give up in difficult times, he was determined to continue his political career. Many people in his situation would have abandoned all thoughts of continuing to seek a career in politics, but Clinton's devotion to public service

Governor White proved unequal to the task of running a successful campaign and lost to Clinton, who ran on a platform that emphasized educational reform, going even further than he had during his first term, this time proposing that all teachers, those about to be hired and those who had been teaching for years, be required to pass competency tests if they were to continue teaching.

When the teaching profession complained loudly about this proposal, Clinton appointed

The Vice President
Al Gore, Jr.

Al Gore, Jr., was born in Carthage, Tennessee, on March 31, 1948. He grew up splitting time between the family farm in Tennessee and a residence in the nation's capital city. Gore's father was a member of the U.S. Congress, and young Al attended the prestigious St. Albans School in Washington, D.C. Gore graduated cum laude from Harvard in 1969 and married Mary "Tipper" Elizabeth Atchison on May 19, 1970. The Gores had three daughters and one son.

During the Vietnam War, Gore enlisted and served as a reporter at a fort in Alabama and in Vietnam. After the war, Gore attended divinity school at Vanderbilt, then enrolled in its law school, but he did not finish either program. Instead, Gore accepted a position with the *Tennessean*, serving as a reporter for three years.

Gore followed in his father's footsteps, securing a seat in the U.S. House of Representatives in 1976, and was reelected several times until winning his race for the U.S. Senate in 1984. During his first term in the Senate, Gore ran unsuccessfully for president in 1988. Gore remained in the U.S. Senate and penned a successful book titled *Earth in the Balance: Ecology and the Human Spirit* (1992).

In 1992, Bill Clinton selected Gore as his running mate, and they were successful in winning the White House, where Gore served as vice president for two terms. Al Gore was one of the most active and influential vice presidents in the country's history. Gore won his party's nomination for president in 2000 but lost a contested election to George W. Bush by a mere 527 votes in Florida amid a number of controversies involving voting irregularities. Gore declined to run again in 2004 but remained active in public life.

Robert P. Watson and Richard Yon

Hillary Rodham Clinton to chair a committee on educational standards, and she helped to persuade legislators and much of the citizenry that the kind of educational reform Clinton proposed was vitally necessary in the State. The legislature this time voted in favor of implementing Clinton's educational proposals.

Because of a change in the law, the term of the Arkansas governor had been extended from two to four years, so with his election in 1982 and his inauguration as governor in 1983, he was assured of being in office until 1987. He again won reelection to the governorship in the election of 1986.

Moving Toward the Presidency

It was clear that as he gained increasing national recognition, Bill Clinton was viewed as someone who stood a good chance of winning the presidency for the Democratic Party, which

had been out of office since 1981. Many expected him to declare his candidacy in 1988, but he considered such an announcement premature. At the National Democratic Convention in Atlanta, Clinton was chosen to give the nominating speech for Michael Dukakis, providing him with his first national presentation to a mass political audience.

The speech turned out to be a disaster. The lights in the auditorium were not dimmed as they should have been. The delegates were disorderly and showed no signs of listening to Clinton's speech. Rather they chanted, "We want Mike!" Clinton's speech was much longer than it should have been. When it ended, people applauded not in approval but in relief.

Johnny Carson called Clinton a windbag, but two nights later, Clinton was on Carson's *Tonight Show* demonstrating his quick wit, his humor, and his magnanimity by overlooking what Carson had said about him. He even played the saxophone. This time the audience applauded in approval and in recognition that he was a remarkable person, big enough to overlook slights such as Carson had aimed at him.

In 1989, President George H. W. Bush appointed Clinton co-chair of a national meeting of governors to discuss educational matters. This appointment again thrust the young governor into the national spotlight and added greatly to his national image.

Eyeing the Presidency

In 1990, now quite secure in his position as Arkansas's governor, Clinton ran for another term in that office. Many voters were concerned that he would serve for half his term and then resign to run for the presidency. Clinton assured them that he anticipated completing his term, which would end in 1994, two years after the presidential election.

He was, nevertheless, engaging in activities that seemed destined to result in his candidacy at the Democratic National Convention in 1992. He was named chair of the Democratic Leadership Council, a group of party leaders, mostly from the South, who were deeply concerned about the course their party was taking. There had not been a Democratic president for ten years, and, with George H. W. Bush, the incumbent, sure to run in 1992, it seemed doubtful that a Democrat could wrest the office away from the Republicans. In 1991, President Bush's popularity was considerable as a result of the United States' victory in the Persian Gulf War against Iraq.

Clinton, always a persuasive speaker, was quickly becoming a seasoned politician. He convinced the delegates to the Democratic Leadership Council that a drastic shift in emphasis was needed if the Democrats were to have any chance of regaining the presidency and of carrying the Congress. His colleagues re-alized the wisdom and the immediate necessity of the drastic changes he proposed.

The Ronald Reagan presidency had gained ascendancy by a landslide in 1980. The Republicans portrayed the Democrats as big spenders and supporters of big government. Reagan promised lower taxes and smaller government. At the end of Reagan's two terms as president, George H. W. Bush was elected in 1988 by carrying through on Reagan's promises.

Asked about raising taxes, Bush mouthed the famous words, "Read my lips. No new taxes." By 1991, this proved to be a promise on which Bush could not deliver. Bush had indeed cut taxes, but he did so mostly for the well-to-do, following the trickle-down policy that Reagan had articulated but that most voters viewed with cynicism and contempt.

The time was obviously ripe for someone like Bill Clinton to bring about the kinds of changes that many voters demanded. Whereas the likely Republican candidate in 1992 was linked in people's minds to the eastern establishment and to big business, Clinton was the populist candidate, almost the log-cabin underdog who had risen by his own hard-won achievements to a position of considerable prominence.

Candidate Clinton

During 1991, Clinton ventured away from Arkansas to make speeches throughout the United States and to confer with party leaders. He continually denied the rumors that he was about to announce his candidacy for president. In July, 1991, however, he admitted that he was considering a run for the nation's highest office. Many Arkansans were incensed that Clinton, who had promised them to serve out his term, was now doing exactly what they had initially feared he would do.

In typical Clinton style, the governor went out among the people asking that they release him from his promise because, in the long run, he told them, he would serve both Arkansas and the United States better as president than as governor. Most of the Arkansans who listened as Clinton made his case sided with him and agreed that he should be released from his promise.

On October 3, 1991, speaking from the Old State House in Little Rock, Arkansas, Clinton announced his intention to become a candidate for the presidency. He struck many a responsive chord when he suggested that the United States, after eleven years of Republican leadership, was moving in a disastrous direction. The country, he contended, was losing its place as a major world power. He vowed that if he were elected, he would impose higher taxes on the rich, making possible lower taxes for the middle class and the poor. He proposed tax benefits for people who invested in ways that would create jobs and resolve some of the daunting problems brought about by massive unemployment.

Under the Reagan-Bush administrations, the nation had taken in less tax money than it spent. It had built up a staggering four-trillion-dollar debt by 1991. Faced with this reality, President Bush was forced to renege on his promise of no new taxes, thereby giving Clinton a decided advantage. He promised that he would work strenuously to reduce the national debt and the ruinous interest payments required to service that debt. He also vowed to put the Social Security and Medicare systems, both of which were in serious jeopardy, on a firmer financial footing.

Dealing with Scandal

The first stop on the campaign trail for Bill Clinton was necessarily New Hampshire, which holds the earliest national primaries in the United States. Clinton, who was not well known in New England, was on the Democratic ballot with five other candidates, including Paul Tsongas, former senator from Massachusetts was was clearly the favorite in this contest.

Although Clinton did not win the primary, he finished second, which was quite remarkable in light of his opposition and especially in light of the fact that two scandals involving him surfaced during the primary. When these revelations were made public, many voters wrote Clinton off, remembering how previous politicians had been destroyed by similar allegations.

The first allegation was that Clinton, while governor of Arkansas, had been involved in a prolonged sexual affair with Gennifer Flowers. He countered these accusations by going on national television with his wife, admitting that there had been problems in their marriage but claiming that those problems were behind them. His candor in addressing the problem satisfied both the press and the public.

The second allegation involved a letter he had written while he was a college student in an effort to avoid being drafted. When this letter came to light, Clinton was vilified as a draft dodger. Again, Clinton approached the public and explained away the evidence that had been presented. Although these two scandals, which might have ruined any other candidate, cast a pall over the campaign and raised serious questions about Clinton's moral fiber, the public was sufficiently forgiving to give him a near-victory in New Hampshire.

Winning the Nomination

Although the 1992 election was a race between two major candidates, George H. W. Bush and Bill Clinton, a third candidate, businessman H. Ross Perot, declared his candidacy as an independent, which somewhat muddied the electoral waters. Essentially more conservative than either of the front-runners, Perot posed a threat to the two major parties, both of which were convinced that he would emerge as a spoiler.

After New Hampshire, the Clinton campaign was one of notable victories. Clinton easily won primaries in most of the southern states, as well as in Illinois, New York, Michigan, and Pennsylvania, all states with large numbers of electoral votes. By June, he had won California, whose electoral votes, combined with the others he had accumulated, spelled a clear victory for him at the Democratic Convention later in the summer.

The voters had qualms about Clinton because of the scandals associated with him, but they had greater qualms about President Bush because the national economy was weakening as unemployment increased and the national debt rose to new highs. Ross Perot capitalized on Bush's economic woes, entering the race as a practical businessman whose lack of governmental experience would, he hoped, work to his advantage. He gambled that voter uncertainties about his inexperience would be overcome by his common sense.

Perot appeared frequently on television, but when asked pointed questions about how he would deal with specific economic problems, he always hedged, usually saying that he wished he had known he was going to be asked such a question because he had charts he could

have brought with him that would have clarified his answer.

Perot withdrew his candidacy on the last day of the Democratic National Convention, only to reenter the race in October, shortly before the election, declaring that he had made a mistake to withdraw. Clinton had judiciously selected Al Gore, Jr., of Tennessee as his running mate. An expert on environmental issues and defense, Gore was viewed as someone who could run the country adequately if Clinton should, for any reason, be unable to complete his term.

The 1992 Presidential Election

Shortly before the election, Clinton, Bush, and Perot engaged in a debate on national television. At this point, the election seemed to be anybody's race, although a Perot victory seemed doubtful. Perot had taken votes from Bush, who was more conservative than Clinton but not conservative enough for many Republicans on the far right.

The final tally showed Clinton with 43 percent of the vote, Bush with 38 percent, and Perot

---

Excerpt from Bill Clinton's acceptance speech at the Democratic National Convention, July, 1992:

We need a new approach to government, a government that offers more empowerment and less entitlement, more choices for young people in the schools they attend—in the public schools they attend. And more choices for the elderly and for people with disabilities and the long-term care they receive. A government that is leaner, not meaner; a government that expands opportunity, not bureaucracy; a government that understands that jobs must come from growth in a vibrant and vital system of free enterprise.

I call this approach a "New Covenant," a solemn agreement between the people and their government based not simply on what each of us can take but what all of us must give to our nation.

We offer our people a new choice based on old values. We offer opportunity. We demand responsibility. We will build an American community again. The choice we offer is not conservative or liberal. In many ways, it's not even Republican or Democratic. It's different. It's new. And it will work. It will work because it is rooted in the vision and the values of the American people.

Of all the things George Bush has ever said that I disagree with, perhaps the thing that bothers me most, is how he derides and degrades the American tradition of seeing and seeking a better future. He mocks it as the "vision thing."

But just remember what the Scripture says: "Where there is no vision, the people perish."

trailing with 19 percent. Clinton had won in thirty-two states, Bush in eighteen. Clinton became the second-youngest president of the United States, only a little older on the day of his inauguration than Theodore Roosevelt had been when he was first elected.

Clinton was also the first president to be born after World War II, making him a part of the baby-boom generation. The American public had spoken, and its voice called for a new era in government, a fresh start after twelve years of Republican rule.

President George H. W. Bush (bottom center), Independent candidate H. Ross Perot (center), and Democratic candidate Bill Clinton (top) during the second presidential debate at the University of Richmond on October 15, 1992. (AP/Wide World Photos)

Clinton's Promises

Like all candidates, Bill Clinton had promised the American people a great deal of what they wanted. Now, after his inauguration as president on January 20, 1993, he had to begin to fulfill the promises that had gotten him into office. He had vowed to bolster the nation's economy, to support gun control and crime prevention, to overhaul the health care and welfare systems, to make the federal government more efficient, and to sign the North American Free Trade Agreement (NAFTA) and other agreements that would promote America's trade relations with other nations, particularly those in North America.

The first two years of the Clinton administration were active and productive. The president made significant progress in his attempts to fulfill all of his major promises. Fortunately, the economy began to show a renewed vigor and finally to expand in ways that affected nearly all Americans. Inflation was coming under control, free enterprise seemed to be flourishing, and unemployment was decidedly declining.

On February 5, 1993, Clinton signed the Family and Medical Leave Act into law, and on November 30, he signed the Brady bill, which imposed a five-day waiting period on those wishing to buy handguns. On December 8, 1993, he signed the highly controversial NAFTA into law.

One dark cloud that hung over American society concerned health care. Many American families had no health insurance and little access to the medical care that one might expect to take for granted in a society as rich as that of the United States.

Ten of Clinton's closest aides testify in the public hearings on the Whitewater investigation in July, 1994. *(Reuters/Richard Clement/Archive Photos)*

In order to get health reform under way, the president appointed Hillary Rodham Clinton to head a task force to investigate how the health care system in the United States could and should be altered. This appointment, although it carried no salary, raised cries of impropriety, and the final report of the task force was harshly criticized in many quarters. Nevertheless, this report opened needed dialogue about a pressing national problem and might have led to positive outcomes had not another scandal, Whitewater, erupted at about the same time the report was released.

The Whitewater Problem

During their time in Arkansas's executive mansion, Bill and Hillary Clinton had taken a financial interest in a land development project called Whitewater. The Clintons were friends of James and Susan McDougal, who were principals in the Whitewater project. James MacDougal was accused of misappropriating funds, and it appeared that the Clintons might have been involved in questionable activities relating to the Whitewater project. The right wing of the Republican Party called for an investigation by Congress, but the Democratic majority scuttled the investigation.

Vince Foster, the Clinton's attorney, who had come to Washington with them and had an office in the White House, was under suspicion for illegal dealings relating to Whitewater. On July 20, 1993, his body was found in Fort Marcy Park near Alexandria, Virginia, with a single bullet hole in the head.

Foster's death, which was ruled a suicide, set the White House into turmoil. Rumors flew in every direction. Some suspected that Foster had been murdered to keep him quiet. Hillary Clinton was accused of removing crucial pa-

---

Excerpt from Bill Clinton's acceptance speech at the Democratic National Convention, August, 1996:

We do not need to build a bridge to the past. We need to build a bridge to the future.... Tonight, my fellow Americans, I ask all of our fellow citizens to join me and to join you in building that bridge to the 21st century. Four years from now, just four years from now—think of it—we begin a new century, full of enormous possibilities. We have to give the American people the tools they need to make the most of their God-given potential. We must make the basic bargain of opportunity and responsibility available to all Americans, not just a few. That is the promise of the Democratic Party. That is the promise of America. . . .

If we want to build that bridge to the 21st century we have to be willing to say loud and clear, if you believe in the values of the Constitution, the Bill of Rights, the Declaration of Independence, if you're willing to work hard and play by the rules, you are part of our family and we're proud to be with you. We still have too many Americans who give in to their fears of those who are different from them....

Look around here, look around here—old or young, healthy as a horse or a person with a disability that hasn't kept you down, man or woman, Native American, native born, immigrant, straight or gay—whatever; the test ought to be I believe in the Constitution, the Bill of Rights, and the Declaration of Independence. I believe in religious liberty. I believe in freedom of speech. I believe in working hard and playing by the rules. I'm showing up for work tomorrow. I'm building that bridge to the 21st century. That ought to be the test. . . .

Let us commit ourselves this night to rise up and build the bridge we know we ought to build all the way to the 21st century. Let us have faith . . . that we are not leaving our greatness behind. We're going to carry it right on with us into that new century—a century of new challenge and unlimited promise.

---

pers from his office as soon as she heard of his death. Although these rumors were unsubstantiated, they raised embarrassing questions for the president and the first lady.

Although no immediate action was taken regarding Whitewater, sentiment for an investigation was growing, and in time, Attorney General Janet Reno appointed an independent counsel, Kenneth Starr, to investigate Whitewater. Starr was so dogged in his attempt to find evidence about presidential misconduct that many people thought he had a vendetta against the Clintons, who did not cooperate fully with Starr. When he subpoenaed documents from the first lady regarding billing practices at the Rose Law Firm in Little Rock, with which she was associated during her husband's governorship, she claimed that the documents were misplaced and did not get them to Starr until months later when they mysteriously surfaced.

The Paula Jones Controversy

Another scandal erupted shortly after the Whitewater problems began to surface. Two Arkansas state troopers who had worked for Clinton during his terms as governor admitted to reporters that when Clinton was governor, they had arranged assignations for him in hotel rooms. This revelation generated a lawsuit against Clinton by Paula Jones, who claimed that the then-governor had lured her into a hotel room where he proposed that they commit a sex act.

A legal question now arose as to whether a sitting president could be required to defend himself against such an accusation while he still held office. It was finally ruled that the suit could proceed, with the president giving a deposition under oath in answer to questions posed by the prosecuting attorney. The president, despite such distractions as these, had such a great power of concentration that he continued to attend to affairs of state in such a satisfactory manner that the public gave him one of the highest approval ratings ever accorded a United States president.

Paula Jones received financial assistance in her lawsuit from the Rutherford Foundation, a conservative think-tank that was fierce in its opposition to Clinton and all that he stood for. The upshot of the Paula Jones lawsuit was that Clinton eventually paid a substantial financial settlement to Jones in order to close the case and keep it out of court.

The 1996 Presidential Election

The Paula Jones case broke in May, 1994, and the press covered it quite fully. This scandal and others, which were broadly reported, were partly responsible for the Democrats' losing their majorities in both the House and the Senate in the off-year election in 1994. Neverthe-

less, the American people acknowledged that Clinton was an effective president even though he might not have been considered a good role model. His approval ratings remained high.

By the time that the 1996 elections were held, the public had apparently been able to separate Clinton's private life from his professional life. Running against Republican senator Bob Dole, Clinton won the election by a landslide.

Voters were aware that he had performed heroic feats politically, such as bringing together the leaders of Israel and Jordan in September, 1994, to meet at the the White House for peace talks. As genocidal wars threatened the very existence of Bosnia, Clinton and Warren Christopher, his secretary of state, brought the opponents together and worked out a peace agreement. Clinton won a second term handily in the face of odds that would have been daunting to most politicians.

Clinton and Vice President Al Gore celebrate in Little Rock, Arkansas, on election night in 1996. *(AP/Wide World Photos)*

The Monica Lewinsky Affair

The Paula Jones case was important in many ways. In order to establish his client's credibility, Jones's lawyer sought to find patterns of sexual misconduct by the president. Before long, it was revealed through an anonymous telephone call to Jones's lawyers that Kathleen Willey, a former White House volunteer and Clinton campaign worker, had apparently been forced to fend off President Clinton's advances to her in the Oval Office on the very day her husband committed suicide.

A former White House worker, Linda Tripp, who had been transferred to the Pentagon and who apparently held a personal grudge against Clinton, had become the friend and confidante of a twenty-one-year-old White House aide, Monica Lewinsky. Lewinsky was an appealing young lady who had gone out of her way to ingratiate herself to the president.

Soon, Lewinsky had greater access to Clinton's White House office than aides generally are permitted. She revealed to Tripp that she was sexually involved with Clinton. The story broke on January 21, 1998, after Tripp had gone to Independent Counsel Kenneth Starr with tapes of Lewinsky's late-night telephone calls to her detailing her sexual adventures in the pantry off the Oval Office.

Clinton soon went before the nation on television and denied categorically that he had had sexual relations "with that woman, Ms. Lewinsky." Starr persisted in his investigation, which now extended far beyond his original charge to investigate Whitewater. He had spent some forty million dollars of taxpayers' money in his dogged pursuit of the investigation.

When the Lewinsky story hit the press, few in the White House thought that the president could survive the accusations and continue in office. His protestations of innocence were received skeptically, but he was finally backed into a corner when Lewinsky produced a blue dress stained with semen that she claimed was from the president. She had told Tripp about this dress, and Tripp had urged her to preserve

---

Excerpts from Bill Clinton's address regarding his relationship with Monica Lewinsky, August 18, 1998:

This afternoon in this room, from this chair, I testified before the Office of Independent Counsel and the grand jury. I answered their questions truthfully, including questions about my private life, questions no American citizen would ever want to answer.

Still, I must take complete responsibility for all my actions, both public and private. And that is why I am speaking to you tonight.

As you know, in a deposition in January, I was asked questions about my relationship with Monica Lewinsky. While my answers were legally accurate, I did not volunteer information.

Indeed, I did have a relationship with Ms. Lewinsky that was not appropriate. In fact, it was wrong. It constituted a critical lapse in judgment and a personal failure on my part for which I am solely and completely responsible.

But I told the grand jury today and I say to you now that at no time did I ask anyone to lie, to hide or destroy evidence or to take any other unlawful action.

I know that my public comments and my silence about this matter gave a false impression. I misled people, including even my wife. I deeply regret that. . . .

Even presidents have private lives. It is time to stop the pursuit of personal destruction and the prying into private lives and get on with our national life. . . .

And so tonight, I ask you to turn away from the spectacle of the past seven months, to repair the fabric of our national discourse, and to return our attention to all the challenges and all the promise of the next American century.

A ticket to Clinton's impeachment trial in the Senate. *(AP/Wide World Photos)*

it. Clinton was forced to submit to DNA testing, which proved conclusively that the semen was indeed his.

Refusing to admit defeat, Clinton again took to the airwaves and in most somber tones admitted to the public that he had acted inappropriately with Lewinsky. When he was deposed regarding this dalliance, he quibbled about what constitutes sexual contact and about ambiguities of language, but it was clear that he was guilty of the conduct of which he had been accused. Impeachment seemed all but certain.

Impeaching the President

The last and only president to be impeached before 1998 was Andrew Johnson shortly after the assassination of President Abraham Lincoln. Richard M. Nixon avoided impeachment by resigning from the presidency when it became clear to him that he could not emerge victorious from an impeachment hearing.

The House of Representatives, with its Republican majority, listened to several days of testimony and read *The Starr Report*, which outlined in specific detail exactly what the relationship between the president and Lewinsky had been. The House voted to bring the matter before the Senate, although, because a two-thirds vote was required for conviction, it seemed certain that the president would be vindicated. The Senate had enough Democrats to ensure acquittal unless some of them defected, as a small number appeared ready to do.

After anguished hearings that dragged out for several days, the Senate on February 12, 1999, voted on the two articles of impeachment lodged against the president: perjury and obstruction of justice. In the final vote, fifty-five senators, including forty-five Democrats and ten Republicans, one of whom abstained, voted against convicting the president of perjury, while forty-five, all Republicans, voted for conviction, giving the president not only the thirty-four votes that he needed for acquittal but also a numerical majority.

On the charge of obstruction of justice, the president did not fare quite so well. He received a simple majority of votes for acquittal. Fifty senators, including five Republicans who jumped ship, voted against conviction, and fifty voted for conviction. A conviction on either charge would have resulted in the president's removal from office, something that few savvy politicians wished to see happen given Clinton's high approval ratings.

Aftermath of the Impeachment Proceedings

Some people feared that Clinton would emerge from the impeachment hearings as a toothless tiger, a president who would be quite unable to perform effectively for the remainder of his term. Such was hardly the case: Clinton bounced back from adversity. His strong intellect and his ability to work persuasively with the voters permitted him to complete his term of office with a degree of distinction.

The greatest crisis he faced during this period was the Kosovo situation in which ethnic Albanians living in the southern part of Serbia were being systematically exterminated, much as Jews had been during the Hitler regime in Germany during the mid- and late 1930's. The United States, working within the framework of the North Atlantic Treaty Organization (NATO), joined other countries in forcing the hand of the Serbian dictator, Slobodan Milošević, by bombing Serbia relentlessly to destroy its infrastructure.

Meanwhile, the United Nations' World Court indicted Milošević on charges of genocide, making him a criminal in the eyes of the United Nations. Ironically, just as President Clinton was gather-ing the Joint Chiefs of Staff to discuss waging a ground war in Serbia, Milošević capitulated, handing Clinton just the victory that he most needed.

The Post-White House Days

On January 21, 2001, Bill Clinton began his life as a former president of the United States. Soon he was busy establishing himself in his office complex in New York City's Harlem district. He took up residence in Chappaqua, New York, the home that he and Hillary had bought in anticipation of Clinton's retirement and of Hillary's run for New York's Senate seat in the elections of 2000.

President Clinton and Secretary of State Madeleine Albright—the first woman to hold that office—listen to proceedings of the U.N. Security Council in September, 2000. *(AP/Wide World Photos)*

He approached his postpresidency life with his characteristic high energy. At age fifty-five, he was in great demand as a speaker and consultant. The immediate task to which he turned when he left Washington was to write a book that he had under contract to the Alfred A. Knopf Publishing Company and for which he had received a multimillion dollar advance.

He set about writing this book with single-minded determination and completed the manuscript in less than a year, making possible a 2004 publication date. The initial press run of a million and a half copies sold out quickly. The 957-page book, titled *My Life*, covers the entire span of Clinton's life up to shortly before the book's publication and provides a remarkable psychologically penetrating insight into how Clinton developed into the man he is.

Plans were afoot even before Clinton left office to create the William J. Clinton Presidential Library and Museum in Little Rock, Arkansas. Clinton became fully involved in the planning stages of this monument to his presidency.

Less than a year after he left the presidency and shortly after he had completed his manuscript for Knopf, Clinton began to experience a tightness in his chest and shortness of breath. Tests revealed significant plaque accumulations in his arteries that made quadruple bypass surgery mandatory. This surgery, performed on September 5, 2004, was successful. Within five days, Clinton was able to walk short distances and to return to his home in Chappaqua, New York. Before long, he was walking four miles a day.

The surgery severely limited his participation in the 2004 presidential campaign, in which he supported Democrat John Kerry and had anticipated being actively involved in promoting his candidacy. Clinton gave what support he could, but heavy campaigning was out of the question for him. There was some question about whether he would be able to attend the ceremonies connected with the opening of his presidential library in November, but the opening of that facility seemed to energize him.

The library contains some eighty million pages of official presidential records and almost two million photographs. It also houses seventy-nine thousand museum items. Although only a small number of these items are on display, they are available to scholars and researchers who request them.

On December 26, 2004, many Asian nations on the Indian Ocean were obliterated by a massive tsunami that killed hundreds of thousands of people. President George W. Bush appointed his father, George H. W. Bush, and Clinton to lead the U.S. fund-raising efforts for survivors of the tsunami. Clinton approached his task with considerable energy although his health was in question. In traveling and working with the elder Bush, Clinton formed a close bond with the Bush family, whose members seemed genuinely well disposed toward their former adversary. George and Barbara Bush even had Clinton visit them and stay in their vacation house in Kennebunkport, Maine, for several days during the summer of 2005.

Clinton's Future

There has been considerable speculation about what the future might hold for the former president. Some political analysts have speculated that when the post becomes vacant, Bill Clinton would be a strong candidate to serve as secretary-general of the United Nations. Because of his great concern with the health crises in Africa and his association with the World Health Organization (WHO), he was also thought of as a possible executive of that organization.

Bill Clinton's career is very much tied to that of his wife, who made a most favorable impression as the freshman senator from New York State. Hillary Rodham Clinton announced her intention to run for reelection in 2006. She was also considered among the front-runners to be the Democratic Party's candidate for the presidency of the United States in the 2008 election.

Former presidents Clinton (left) and George H. W. Bush (second from right) tour Ban Nam Khem village in southern Thailand on February 19, 2005, to view rebuilding efforts after the tsunami that occurred on December 26, 2004. *(AP/ Wide World Photos)*

Were Hillary to run and be elected, Bill Clinton would be left in a quite ambiguous situation. Presidential spouses are not expected to wield political power in any direct way, although many such spouses appear to have influenced political policy in indirect ways. No American presidential spouse, however, has been male, much less a former two-term president.

How History Will Judge Bill Clinton

It is too early to know how history will judge Bill Clinton. Many feel that he is among the most remarkable presidents the United States has ever had. Clearly an intellectual, he also has the ability to deal directly with people and to persuade them to his way of thinking. Just as President Nixon's reputation, which was firmly established by his strong international policies, has been sullied by Watergate and by his subsequent resignation, so might Bill Clinton's reputation be associated more with the Paula Jones and Monica Lewinsky scandals than with the more positive aspects of his administration.

For all its blemishes, most people think that the Clinton presidency greatly benefited the United States. The country prospered under his leadership. Unemployment was controlled, as were taxes. The budget was balanced, and the national debt was substantially reduced. The Social Security and Medicare programs were reformed in ways that should ensure their viability for years to come.

It is not easy to speculate on what will be said of Clinton one hundred years from now. It is perhaps enough to say that had it been possible for Clinton to run for a third term as president of the United States, he would have stood a good chance of being reelected.

R. Baird Shuman

Suggested Readings

Bennett, William J. *The Death of Outrage.* New York: Free Press, 1998. Bennett makes moral judgments about Clinton without considering in a balanced way the positive contributions of his administration.

Clinton, Bill. *My Life.* New York: Alfred A. Knopf, 2004. Clinton's own frank and detailed account of his life, from its earliest days through his two terms as president. A remarkably acute, well-written, and objective assessment of his presidency.

Clinton, Hillary. *Living History.* New York: Simon & Schuster, 2003. The former first lady's account of her life with Bill Clinton, this book delves into some of the more sensational aspects of his presidency but is best for its accounts of the Clintons' rise to power and of how Bill wielded that power as president of the United States.

Cwiklik, Robert. *Bill Clinton: President of the '90's.* Brookfield, Conn.: The Millbrook Press, 1997. Accurate, readable, and informative, this book is directed toward a young adult audience.

Esterhas, Joe. *American Rhapsody.* New York: Alfred A. Knopf, 2000. An exploration of the political culture in which the Clinton administration functioned. Offers a frank discussion of the grounds for impeachment.

Evans-Pritchard, Ambrose. *The Secret Life of Bill Clinton: The Unreported Story.* Washington, D.C.: Regnery, 1997. A one-sided book that emphasizes the scandals of the Clinton administration without acknowledging its positive aspects. A journalist, Evans-Pritchard is sometimes credited with disseminating anti-Clinton rumors during the late 1990's.

Hamilton, Nigel. *Bill Clinton: An American Journey: Great Expectations.* New York: Random House, 2003. An intelligent presentation that views the Clinton administration in the light of past administrations. Much valuable biographical information.

Harris, John F. *The Survivor: Bill Clinton in the White House.* New York: Random House, 2005. A nonpartisan view of Clinton's presidency.

Landau, Elaine. *Bill Clinton.* New York: Franklin Watts, 1993. One of the most effective brief biographies of Bill Clinton for young-adult readers.

Martin, Gene L., and Aaron Boyd. *Bill Clinton: President from Arkansas.* Greensboro, N.C.: Tudor, 1993. A straightforward presentation, well written and accurate, about Clinton's election and the first year of the Clinton presidency.

Morris, Dick. *Because He Could/Dick Morris and Eileen McGann.* New York: ReganBooks, 2004. Although a staunch Clinton supporter during the 1992 campaign and on into the administration, Morris is not blinded to some of the weaknesses and missteps that the administration and that Clinton himself made.

_____. *Behind the Oval Office: Winning the Presidency in the Nineties.* New York: Random House, 1997. A fine, three-dimensional portrait of the president by a man who was his stalwart adviser during the presidential campaign of 1992 and during Clinton's early years in the White House.

Tyrell, R. Emmett, Jr. *Boy Clinton: President of the '90's.* Washington, D.C.: Regnery, 1996. Although Tyrell presents valuable biographical information about Clinton, the book is slanted toward discrediting him by dwelling on his moral indiscretions.

George W. Bush

43d President, 2001-

Born: July 6, 1946
   New Haven, Connecticut

Political Party: Republican
Vice President: Dick Cheney

Cabinet Members

Secretary of State: Colin Powell, Condoleezza
   Rice
Secretary of the Treasury: Paul H. O'Neill, John
   Snow
Secretary of Defense: Donald Rumsfeld
Attorney General: John Ashcroft, Alberto
   Gonzales
Secretary of the Interior: Gale A. Norton
Secretary of Agriculture: Ann M. Veneman,
   Mike Johanns
Secretary of Commerce: Don Evans, Carlos
   Gutierrez
Secretary of Labor: Elaine Chao
Secretary of Health and Human Services:
   Tommy G. Thompson, Michael O. Leavitt
Secretary of Housing and Urban Development:
   Mel Martinez, Alphonso Jackson
Secretary of Transportation: Norman Y. Mineta
Secretary of Energy: Spencer Abraham, Samuel
   Bodman
Secretary of Education: Rod Paige, Margaret
   Spellings
Secretary of Veterans Affairs: Anthony Principi,
   Jim Nicholson
Secretary of Homeland Security: Tom Ridge,
   Michael Chertoff

George W. Bush was the first American president of the twenty-first century. He joined John Quincy Adams as only the second son of a for-

mer president in U.S. history to be elected to the presidency in his own right. Like Adams, he came to office after a controversial election. Initially, few thought much of the prospects for his administration. He could claim no political mandate. Many questioned his electoral legiti-

George W. Bush. *(AP/Wide World Photos)*

macy. Though his Republican Party controlled Congress, the margin was very narrow—only six votes in the House and the tie-breaking vote of Vice President Dick Cheney in the Senate.

Bush came to office at a time of diminished expectations for the presidency. During the 1990's, gridlock had become the norm in Washington. The president and Congress checked each other's partisan ambitions. The public tolerated this political equilibrium because for most of the decade, the United States prospered. Americans could indulge in the self-absorbed pleasures of a second Gilded Age. This tendency was reinforced by the collapse of the Soviet Union and the end of the Cold War. Scholars debated the "end of history" and the inevitable triumph of capitalism and liberal democracy. Americans banked on a "peace dividend." War and massacre still haunted the world, but it seemed far away. If this foreign ugliness did impinge on America's consciousness and interests, it seemed as if the remote-control warfare of precision munitions could settle the issue without the loss of American life. Because of this complacent sense of peace and prosperity in the second half of the 1990's, the majority of the electorate seemed simultaneously to enjoy and excuse the scandals of President Bill Clinton.

Bush did surprisingly well in his first months, passing tax cuts and pushing an education bill. On September 10, 2001, some could argue that it looked as if Bush's presidency was settling into the pattern set by his predecessors—a gritty contest with congressional opponents for incremental results. The terrorist attacks of September 11 on the World Trade Center and the U.S. Pentagon by Islamic fundamentalists changed this outlook, and Americans were brutally reintroduced to history. The 1990's suddenly looked like an escape from reality, rather than the opening of a brave new era. George W. Bush himself was transformed. His resolute response to the crisis gave him a popular legitimacy and moral authority that he had not possessed be-

fore September 11. His sense of mission was drastically redefined. He became a war president. His father, George Herbert Walker Bush, had presided over the end of the Cold War, concluding a half century of conflict with the Soviet Union and its allies. George W. Bush would launch an open-ended and costly struggle against the multifaceted threat of Islamic terrorism.

Early Years

George W. Bush was born on July 6, 1946, in New Haven, Connecticut. He was the first child of George H. W. Bush and Barbara Pierce Bush. His father, who had served with distinction as a Navy pilot in World War II was earning a degree in economics at Yale University. When Bush was two, the family moved to Texas so that his father could pursue a career in the oil business. Five siblings arrived in due course: Robin, John (Jeb), Neil, Marvin, and Dorothy.

Though it would take time for him to realize it, Bush grew up in a privileged family. His grandfather, Prescott Bush, was a partner in the powerful Wall Street investment banking firm of Brown Brothers, Harriman and Company. In 1952, Prescott Bush was elected United States senator for Connecticut. Bush's father attended the best schools, including Phillips Academy, Andover, before volunteering for the military. His postwar matriculation at Yale carried on a family tradition. The foray into the Texas oil industry was eased and financed through family connections.

George W. Bush would encounter this blue-blooded world on family visits back to New England. There he was awed by his imposing grandfather and impressed by the rule that one always appeared at dinner in coat and tie. However, this was not his life in Midland, Texas. There the family first lived in a development called Easter Egg Row, where each tract house was painted a different vibrant color and cost eight thousand dollars. Later they moved

An undated photograph of George W. Bush during his time in the Texas Air National Guard, 1968-1973. *(AP/Wide World Photos)*

Many of the fathers in Bush's neighborhood worked for oil companies and often were away on the road. The mothers were a constant presence, keeping a watchful eye both on their own children and those of neighbors. No one locked their doors; groups of children wandered freely, playing from yard to yard until their mothers summoned them to dinner at dusk. In later years, this comparatively typical childhood probably gave Bush a political edge over his more patrician father; it made it easier for him to understand and connect with ordinary voters.

George W. Bush's boyhood was warm and secure, but it was not idyllic. In 1953, Bush's family was devastated when his sister Robin died of leukemia at the age of three. His parents had concealed the seriousness of Robin's condition from their seven-year-old son. This made the shock of the loss all the more powerful. Bush tried to console his mother and tried to cheer his parents with jokes and stories. Weeks after his sister's death, at a football game, Bush startled his parents by declaring that he wished that he was Robin. When his father asked why, he replied, "Because she can probably see better from up there than we can from down here." Years later, in his campaign autobiography, Bush declared that Robin's death was the "starkest memory of my childhood." He wrote that this tragedy taught him that life was not something to be taken for granted. From this time forward, through all the years that he sought out good times, and beyond, Bush would be conscious of the inevitable fragility of existence.

When Bush was in the seventh grade, his family moved from Midland to Houston. George H. W. Bush operated oil rigs in the Gulf

a short distance away to a somewhat bigger house. The west Texas winds kept the town covered in dusty sand, and tumbleweeds blew through the yard. Midland was a small town, and the Bushes lived in a tight-knit community. There were children everywhere, and Bush had friends up and down his street. He had been born at the outset of the great postwar baby boom.

In Midland, Bush would share the experience of a generation of middle-class children growing up in the American suburbs of the 1950's. He played Little League baseball, the beginning of a lifelong attraction to the sport.

of Mexico and was prospering. For the first time, Bush enrolled in a private school. He settled into what he later called a "comfortable" life. This was disrupted by his parents' decision to send him, at age fifteen, to his father's old preparatory school at Andover. Bush had never lived away from home; now he was very far away. He gradually adapted to life on his own. Although he did not excel academically, he learned that he easily made friends. From Andover, Bush went on to Yale. His father had captained the varsity baseball team and made Phi Beta Kappa. In baseball, Bush did not make varsity, and his grade point average hung in the C range. He distinguished himself instead through an active social life. He joined a fraternity, was elected its president, and was popular on campus. One achievement he would share with his father was making the elite secret society Skull and Bones.

Finding a Place

In 1968, Bush graduated from Yale with a degree in history. The Vietnam War was at its height, and the draft compelled hard choices of young men. Bush's father had volunteered for service in World War II straight out of prep school. For a time, he was the youngest pilot in the Navy. Such an example prodded George W. Bush onto a military path. He did not, however, choose to enlist in one of the regular military services. Instead, he joined the Texas Air National Guard. Bush would later be criticized for this, because National Guard service was widely seen as a way out of combat duty in Vietnam. In fact, enlistment in the Air Na-

---

THE FIRST LADY
LAURA BUSH

Only the second First Lady in U.S. history to be married to the son of a former president, this reserved school librarian would prove to be a major force in her husband's life and political career. Laura Welch was born on November 4, 1946. As the only child of a home builder in the small town of Midland, Texas, Laura had an upbringing that was distinctly middle class, quiet, and content, with the exception of a tragic car accident in which she was involved that claimed the life of her then-boyfriend.

During her formative years, Laura developed a love of reading, which would become both her vocation and her avocation. She graduated from Southern Methodist University in Dallas with a degree in education and completed a master's degree in library science from the University of Texas. From 1968 until 1977, she worked as a teacher and school librarian in Austin, Dallas, and Houston. Then, in 1977, friends introduced her to George W. Bush. After a short courtship, the couple was married on November 5, 1977, in Midland. After a difficult bout with toxemia, Laura gave birth to twins, Jenna and Barbara, in 1981.

Laura is widely credited with helping her husband overcome a rather irresponsible and directionless early adulthood and bout with alcoholism. Although she was never a highly visible political spouse, her significance remained during George W. Bush's Texas gubernatorial campaign and ensuing two terms in the governor's mansion, where she became an advocate for literacy and established the Texas Book Festival.

Indeed, hers has been a surprising political journey. A shy girl with no interest in politics, who married into one of America's most powerful political families, Laura Bush would become an asset to her husband's public image, an independent advocate for several social causes, and one of the country's more popular First Ladies.

Robert P. Watson

tional Guard did not preclude tours in Southeast Asia.

After earning his wings as a fighter pilot in December, 1969, Bush volunteered for a program that sent Air National Guard flyers to Vietnam. He was told that the program was being closed down and that he did not have enough flying time to make the final cut.

Though Bush never went to Vietnam, his position was no safe sinecure. Service in the Air National Guard was dangerous. The men flew superannuated jets that had been retired by the Air Force. Two men in Bush's unit died in flying accidents. Despite this, Bush enjoyed being a pilot. He liked the sense of mastery over a complicated and powerful machine. He liked the excitement of testing himself in an environment where a mistake could mean death. Bush would retain something of the cocksure flyboy about him for the rest of his life, a trait infuriating to his political critics. More consequentially, he would also demonstrate the same readiness to take calculated risks; this too would often confound his opponents.

After nearly two years of training as a fighter pilot, Bush worked at a variety of jobs as he served out his commitment to the Air National Guard. Among these was a stint helping run a program that addressed poverty in the inner city. He also volunteered his services to political campaigns, including his father's unsuccessful run for the United States Senate in 1970. Bush seemed not to have a plan for his life. However, Harvard Business School changed that, which he was admitted to after he applied for admission at a friend's suggestion as he neared the end of his military service.

Once arrived in Cambridge, Bush found the atmosphere of the business school stimulating. Somewhat older than his classmates, Bush flourished as a student as he never had before. At Harvard he eagerly imbibed the latest theory on finance, marketing, and management. Bush graduated in 1975 and returned to Texas, brimming with enthusiasm for the market. Midland was benefiting from the stimulus provided the oil industry by the Arab oil embargo of 1973. High prices made oil a precious commodity, sparking a boom in new exploration. Bush eagerly threw himself into his father's old business. He began as a landman, rooting through records in Texas court houses to determine the ownership of mineral rights beneath the soil. Once he had a feel for the business, Bush used the remains of a fund that his parents had established for his education to invest in new wells. After an initial failure, his investments produced a comfortable income.

Settling Down

Friends introduced Bush to Laura Welch, a public school teacher and librarian. For Bush, it was love at first sight. The two had both grown up in Midland, living a half-mile from each other. They attended the same middle school. For a time in the early 1970's, they lived in the same Houston apartment complex, though Laura did not, like Bush, join the loud and frolicsome set that played volleyball in the pool long into the night. Bush proposed a few months after their meeting, and Laura accepted. The Bushes were married November 5, 1977. They spent their first year of marriage in a campaign for Congress.

Public service was a tradition in the Bush family. Working on his father's campaigns had introduced Bush to the world of electoral politics. When the congressman in his district decided to retire in 1977, Bush set out to replace him. He had already come to the conclusion that government was playing too great a role in the marketplace. He was offended by two laws that put price controls and further regulations on natural gas. Bush won the Republican primary, but was defeated in the general election by Kent Hance, a conservative Democrat. Hance campaigned effectively against Bush, criticizing his New England roots and education and characterizing him as an outsider to

Texas. Bush carried Midland and the neighboring counties, but that was not enough.

After the election, Bush went back into the oil business and started his own oil exploration company. In 1980, he took some time out to help his father. The senior Bush made a good showing in the Republican presidential primaries and was picked by Ronald Reagan to be his running mate. Bush was present when his father was sworn in as vice president in 1981. He met Reagan at the inauguration. The president made a great impression on Bush, who agreed completely with Reagan's call for limiting government and stimulating growth through tax cuts. He shared Reagan's conservative stance on social issues and his support for a strong national defense. Bush also admired the new president's governing style. Unlike his predecessor, Jimmy Carter, Reagan emphasized the positive. A warm and genial man in private, Reagan exuded optimism about the nation in public. In later years, Bush would be seen by many as the public policy heir of Ronald Reagan rather than of his own father. Bush's relentless emphasis on the affirmative as president was also seen as an homage to the Great Communicator, as Reagan had been known.

The 1980's were a time of transformation for Bush. He became a father in 1981 when Laura Bush gave birth to twin daughters, Jenna and Barbara. The Bushes had wanted children for some time and had been considering adoption. The pregnancy was high risk and difficult for Laura. Once the girls arrived, Bush became a "modern dad," changing diapers and later helping with homework. During these years, he had to wrestle with business difficulties as a slide in oil prices threatened the existence of Bush's company. In 1986, he saved himself and his investors by selling out to the Harken Energy Corporation. Bush then worked as a consultant to Harken and served on its board of directors.

The mid-1980's also saw a new direction in his religious life. Bush had been raised an Episcopalian. Upon his return to Midland, he attended a Presbyterian church and taught Sunday school. When he married, he became an active member of a Methodist congregation. In 1985, a conversation with the evangelist Billy Graham at the family vacation home at Kennebunkport, Maine, quickened and intensified Bush's faith. He began to study the Bible and reexamine the meaning of his religious commitment. His faith increasingly became a sustaining and steadying influence.

The following year, at the age of forty, Bush gave up drinking. Waking up the morning after a dinner party with a hangover, Bush decided that he had had enough. Always a stickler for physical fitness, Bush did not like the way he dragged during his regular three-mile run. Bush never admitted to having a problem with alcohol, though in 1976, he was arrested and fined for driving while under the influence near Kennebunkport, an episode that would haunt him during the 2000 campaign. He saw his decision to give up alcohol as part of the larger process of growth and change that he was undergoing during this period. Bush was developing into the intensely disciplined man who would become president.

Return to Politics
In 1987, Bush moved to Washington, D.C., to work on his father's presidential campaign. His father valued his assistance. Bush acted as a liaison and doorkeeper with the press. He also acted as an ambassador to conservative Republican factions suspicious of his father's reputation as a moderate. During the course of the campaign, Bush became friends with Lee Atwater, the chief political strategist of his father's campaign. The experience was a graduate course in American politics at the highest level. Following his father's victory, Bush stayed on for a while to assist in the staffing of the new administration.

With his father in the White House, Bush moved back to Texas. The sale of the Texas

Rangers baseball franchise allowed him to realize a dream. Bush put together a group of investors to purchase the team. Though he had little money to contribute himself, he became one of two managing partners. Bush thoroughly enjoyed helping run the business affairs of the Texas Rangers. He was able to mix with players and fans and became the most visible face in the Rangers management. He successfully promoted the building of a new stadium. When his partnership sold the team in 1998, Bush's investment of $600,000 returned him $15,000,000.

Bush loyally campaigned for his father in 1992. The elder Bush was defeated because he had alienated part of his conservative base and because his most formidable opponent, Bill Clinton, successfully portrayed him as unresponsive to an economic downturn. Bush learned valuable political lessons from this hard experience. He realized that political capital must be spent—his father had huge approval ratings after the Persian Gulf War but let them dissipate over months of economic bad news. Bush also learned that a political leader could not let his opponents define him—the economy had recovered from recession in 1992, but his father never found an effective response to Clinton's criticisms that problems with the economy mandated a new leader.

Bush would make good use of his political experience when he decided to run for governor of Texas in 1994. He faced a popular incumbent, Ann Richards, who possessed a gift for colorful rhetoric. In 1988, she had famously insulted Bush's often inarticulate father, saying that he was "born with a silver foot in his mouth." However, in 1994, Richards was vulnerable. She had sponsored a failed initiative to redistribute school tax money, and the conservative groundswell that would elect the first Republican Congress in fifty years could already be felt in Texas. Bush had name recognition, a formidable array of contacts, and plenty of money. He improved upon these advantages by putting together a highly capable campaign staff, some of whom, such as strategist Karl Rove and communications director Karen Hughes, would stay with him into the presidency. Remembering his defeat in 1978, Bush identified himself with conservative Texan values. He promised to get tougher on crime, to reform welfare, and to improve education. He traveled up and down Texas, appealing to Democrats who had voted for Reagan. On election day, Bush upset Governor Richards, winning more than 53 percent of the vote.

As governor, Bush worked hard to build cooperative relationships with Democrats in the legislature. He earned the confidence and respect of Bob Bullock, the Democratic lieutenant governor and a cagey veteran of Texas politics. Bullock would later endorse Bush for president. Thanks to his ability to reach across the partisan aisle, Bush achieved a number of legislative successes. He cut taxes, added work requirements to welfare, and passed tort reform. Bush was especially interested in improving the schools in Texas. He reduced state regulatory authority over local school districts, while increasing state spending on education. He encouraged school accountability through a testing program and authorized charter schools.

Bush received national attention for his defense of the death penalty; Texas executed more prisoners than any other state. In 1998, despite calls for clemency from the pope, evangelist Pat Robertson, and other luminaries, Bush upheld the death sentence of Karla Faye Tucker, a double-murderer who had become a born-again Christian in prison and who was the first woman to be executed in Texas since the Civil War. That year Bush was challenged for reelection by Garry Mauro, the Texas land commissioner. Bush won a resounding victory, getting 69 percent of the vote.

The Election of 2000

Bush was now seen as a likely contender for the Republican presidential nomination in 2000. Conventional wisdom favored the Democrats

THE VICE PRESIDENT
DICK CHENEY

Richard Cheney was born on January 30, 1941, in Lincoln, Nebraska, but grew up in Casper, Wyoming. His father, a registered Democrat, worked for the U.S. Department of Agriculture. "Dick," as he was nicknamed, was class president in high school. Cheney attended Yale in 1959 but withdrew from school after only three semesters. He returned to Yale shortly thereafter but again withdrew, in part because of poor grades.

After working in dead-end jobs and after two arrests, Cheney decided to return to school, attending Casper Community College in Wyoming and then graduating from the University of Wyoming in 1965. Cheney continued his education, earning a master's degree in 1965 from the University of Wyoming and, although he never graduated, did complete course work toward a Ph.D. in political science at the University of Wisconsin at Madison. In 1964, Cheney married his high school sweetheart, Lynne Vincent, and the couple had two daughters.

Cheney served in a number of positions in Gerald R. Ford's presidency while in his thirties, including assistant to the president and chief of staff—the youngest person ever to hold that position. In 1976, Cheney managed Ford's unsuccessful reelection effort but was elected to the U.S. House of Representatives from Wyoming two years later. Cheney served in the House from 1979 to 1989, rising to the rank of minority whip in 1988. During the administration of George H. W. Bush, Cheney was appointed secretary of defense from 1989 to 1993 and was awarded the Presidential Medal of Freedom in 1991 for his role in the Gulf War.

After leaving the White House, Cheney served with the conservative American Enterprise Institute from 1995 to 2000 and held positions on the boards of several Fortune 500 firms and as CEO of the Haliburton Corporation. In 2000, he was asked by George W. Bush to head an effort to select a vice president, but it was Cheney who was eventually selected. Cheney served as Bush's vice president from 2001 and remained on the ticket for the successful reelection in 2004.

Robert P. Watson and Richard Yon

in the next presidential election. The country was prospering. Though Bill Clinton could not run again, it was likely that his political heir would benefit from the national sense of well-being. Such had been the case with Bush's father when he succeeded Ronald Reagan. However, Clinton's scandals had taken a political toll. Though the Republican attempt to force Clinton from office had failed, the impeachment process had left the president disgraced. Many Americans were disturbed by the moral tone in Washington. They were looking for a change.

Bush began exploring a run for the presidency in early 1999 and declared himself a candidate in June. He enjoyed a number of advantages in his quest for the Republican nomination. He was a proven vote-getter in a large and diverse state. He could count on the support of a wide range of Republican party officials and officeholders. His connections gave him access to ready supplies of money. However, he had liabilities as well. The name recognition that he derived from his father was held against him. He had only held elective office since 1995. He was accused of being an inexperienced lightweight, trading on his close ties to the Republican establishment.

Thus, Bush had to fight for the nomination. He organized an experienced and highly professional political machine, bringing with him from Texas such stalwart campaigners as Rove

Republican presidential candidate Bush and Vice President Al Gore during their third and final debate at Washington University in St. Louis on October 17, 2000. *(AP/Wide World Photos)*

Cheney was a political veteran who had served in Congress, as President Gerald R. Ford's White House chief of staff, and as Bush's father's secretary of defense. The addition of Cheney to the ticket partially blunted the charges that Bush lacked the "gravitas" to govern.

The Democrats nominated Vice President Al Gore. Gore's background resembled that of Bush. He was the son of a United States senator and had lived a privileged existence in his youth. Also in the race were Patrick Buchanan, who led H. Ross Perot's Reform Party to the right (and, arguably, to obscurity), and Ralph Nader, whose Green Party candidacy would deprive Gore of a small but decisive number of votes in closely contested states.

Bush ran as a "compassionate conservative." His platform was Reaganesque, calling for reducing government, cutting taxes, and bolstering defense. It supported gun rights and opposed abortion. However, Bush argued that government did have a role to play in bettering the lives of citizens. He promoted government funding of faith-based organizations that more efficiently combated poverty and addiction. He promised more support for America's struggling schools. Finally, he deplored the moral failings of the Clinton administration, demanding an ethical standard in Washington more in line with American values. Bush's kinder and gentler Republicanism seemed to be working as the campaign neared its close. Despite a tendency to malapropisms, Bush did well in his nationally televised debates with Gore. The vice president probably made a mistake in dis-

and Hughes. He raised so much money that he became the first candidate to turn down federal matching funds in the primaries. The race quickly boiled down to a contest between Bush and Senator John McCain of Arizona. McCain was a charismatic war hero with a reputation as a political maverick. He capitalized on a good relationship with the press, and in open primaries drew the votes of many Democrats and independents. This helped McCain defeat Bush in the New Hampshire primary. However, Bush came back in conservative South Carolina. From then on, his superior organization and funding assured him the Republican nomination. Bush picked Dick Cheney as his running mate.

tancing himself from Clinton. He ran a more populist campaign that edged left of Clinton's carefully honed centrism.

Bush's slight lead in the polls was undermined in the last weekend before voting when Democratic operatives revealed Bush's hitherto unacknowledged 1976 driving-under-the-influence (DUI) citation. To many, the DUI made Bush's criticism of Clinton seem hypocritical. It also reinforced the stereotype of Bush as a frivolous playboy.

The 2000 election proved to be one of the closest in American history. Bush won twenty-nine states, including Arkansas and Tennessee, the home states of President Clinton and Vice President Gore. However, victory hinged on winning a handful of closely contested states, including Florida. So close was the election that the exit-polling media was confounded. Errors

intensified the mess. Because of a mistake over time zones, the networks called Florida a victory for Gore before the Republican panhandle had finished voting. For a while it looked as if Gore had won the election. Then the networks retracted. Late that night, they projected Bush as the winner in Florida. This gave him the presidency with a narrow electoral college victory, 271 votes to 266, despite the fact that Gore had won a plurality of 500,000 in the popular vote. However, so slim was Bush's lead in Florida that state law made a recount automatic. Because of allegations of voting irregularities, the Gore campaign immediately dispatched a small army of lawyers to Florida to contest the results. The Republicans soon responded. A disheartening legal and political battle ensued, calling into question the integrity of America's electoral process. During this period, Bush

Protesters demonstrate in front of the Supreme Court in Washington, D.C., on December 11, 2000, as the Court prepares to hear arguments on an appeal by George W. Bush to stop the hand recount of presidential ballots in Florida. (AP/Wide World Photos)

benefited from being the presumptive winner. He remained at his ranch in Crawford, Texas, and sent former secretary of state James A. Baker III to oversee his interests in Florida.

Bush won the first recount with a margin of around three hundred votes. Gore's lawyers then asked for a manual recount in four heavily Democratic counties, in one of which there were complaints about problems with punch card ballots. The Bush camp tried to stop this move, arguing that manual recounts invited human error. The Republican secretary of state of Florida tried to enforce a statutory deadline for the recounts but was overruled by a judgment of the Florida Supreme Court that set a later date for the counties to report. These results were certified by the state of Florida on November 26, giving Bush a 537 vote plurality. Gore appealed again, and this time the Florida Supreme Court ordered a statewide manual recount. Bush then took his case to the United States Supreme Court. The Supreme Court had already vacated the first intervention of the Florida Court and had asked for a clarification of its constitutional reasoning. On December 12, the Supreme Court ruled 7-2 that the Florida recount violated the equal protection clause of the Constitution, because there was no single standard for manual recounts in Florida's various counties. Then, in a 5-4 ruling, the Court ruled that time had run out on the recounts. Vice President Gore conceded the election the next day.

The 2000 election and its aftermath engendered enormous controversy. Bush's brother Jeb had been elected governor of Florida in 1998. Many Democrats claimed that he and the Republican Party in Florida tried to rig the election in favor of his brother. Republicans in turn believed that the push for repeated recounts was an attempt to provide local Democratic election officials the opportunity to "fish" for enough votes to give Gore the election. Democrats accused the largely Republican Supreme Court of giving the election to Bush. Republi-

cans countered by accusing the Democratic Supreme Court of Florida of partisan judicial activism. In 2001, two media consortiums conducted an extensive survey of Florida's ballots. They concluded that had the recounts continued, under the standards set at the time, Bush would still have emerged the narrow winner.

First Months in Office

The election crisis had abbreviated the period Bush had available to put together his new administration. Efficient management of the process enabled him to assemble a cabinet and make key appointments in record time. Colin Powell, his secretary of state, and Condoleezza Rice, his national security adviser, had both worked with his father. Donald Rumsfeld, his secretary of defense, had served in the same post during the Ford administration. Former senator John Ashcroft, Bush's nominee for attorney general, proved a political lightning rod because of his association with the Christian Right. As a gesture of goodwill, Bush named the Democrat Norman Y. Mineta as secretary of transportation. Taken together, Bush's cabinet was the most diverse in American history, including five women, three African Americans, two Asians, and one Latino.

When Bush was inaugurated in January, 2001, polls showed that most Americans were willing to accept him as the lawful president. However, many political commentators saw Bush as a deeply wounded chief executive. Democrats openly called on him to accept his status as a "minority" president and govern from the political center. Bush, however, refused to accept this prescribed role. He had been elected, and in his mind, that was mandate enough. He would actively pursue his agenda. As he did so, Bush wanted to move beyond the acrimonious politics of the Clinton era and introduce a new era of civility to Washington. He ran a disciplined White House that discouraged leaks and partisan gaffes. He and his administration initially benefited from the con-

President Bush speaks about his No Child Left Behind program during a stop at an elementary school in Nashville, Tennessee, on September 8, 2003. *(AP/Wide World Photos)*

the economy. He was able to get the bulk of what he wanted by gaining the Congressional support of most Republicans and a few conservative Democrats. In June, he signed a bill that cut taxes by $1.35 trillion over ten years. It lowered tax rates for all taxpayers, doubled the child tax credit, and provided some relief for married couples.

Bush was also determined to get an ambitious education bill through Congress. He worked very closely with Democratic leaders. He sacrificed provisions dear to conservatives such as school choice but kept testing and school accountability central to the legislation. He signed the No Child Left Behind Act into law early in 2002. A major blow to Bush's legislative hopes was the defection of Senator James Jeffords in May, 2001. A liberal Republican, Jeffords did not like the new administration's vigorous conservatism. He was also worried about losing a cherished committee chairmanship should one-hundred-year-old senator Strom Thurmond pass away, giving control of the chamber to the Democrats. So Jeffords became an independent and voted with the Democrats. The new Democratic leadership in the senate blocked legislation Bush favored and held up many of his judicial nominees.

Bush's chief preoccupation early in his first term was domestic politics. Compassionate conservatism was not understood to extend beyond the U.S. borders. During the 2000 campaign, Bush had been criticized for his lack of foreign policy credentials, although he did have strong convictions about international relations. He believed that a militarily strong

trast generated by news stories about questionable pardons issued by President Clinton during his last hectic days in office. But lingering ill-feeling about the election and the narrow balance of power in Washington would thwart Bush's hopes for a new political tone.

Bush moved quickly to fulfill his campaign promises. He established an Office for Faith-Based and Community Initiatives in the White House. In February, Bush submitted his first budget. He proposed a $1.6-trillion-dollar tax cut over ten years as a way of reducing the budget surplus. Instead of spending the surplus on bigger government, he wanted to return the money to the taxpayers. Democrats resisted the tax cuts, deriding them as a giveaway to the richest Americans and fiscally dubious as the economy began to slide into a recession. Bush responded by adopting the idea of a three-hundred-dollar payment to every taxpayer and promoted his plan as a stimulus to

United States was a force for peace. He criticized the Clinton administration for dissipating this strength in peacekeeping missions in the Balkans. Like Ronald Reagan, he believed that a robust program of missile defense was necessary for American security. Bush was viscerally antipathetic to much of the internationalist niche prevalent in official circles. He was unapologetically nationalist and saw no contradiction between this nationalism and American participation in the creation of a peaceful international order.

Bush acted on these ideas in the first months of his presidency. He stirred great controversy when he announced that the United States would not abide by the provisions of the Kyoto Protocol on global warming. He believed the proposed treaty would hurt the American economy. The Clinton administration had signed the agreement but had never submitted it to the senate for ratification. There the treaty had no chance of passage. The Senate expressed its displeasure with the Kyoto Protocol by a 95-0 vote in a nonbinding resolution. Thus Bush was simply acknowledging political reality. His forthrightness in doing so, however, caused resentment abroad.

Bush gave similar offense when his administration abrogated the 1972 Antiballistic Missile Treaty with the Soviet Union. This was necessary for Bush to pursue his program of missile defense. Many saw this as needlessly provocative. The Russian government, heir to the old Soviet Union, eventually acquiesced, and the United States and Russia signed a treaty sharply cutting their nuclear stockpiles. Despite the fact that Bush capably handled a potentially dangerous crisis in April, when a United States Air Force surveillance plane was forced down in China after a collision with a Chinese fighter, he managed in his first months in office to gain a reputation as a reckless player on the world stage. However unfair, this cowboy image would linger throughout his presidency.

Members of the media and Florida state officials watch television reports of the terrorist attacks on September 11, 2001, while waiting for Governor Jeb Bush to make a statement from Tallahassee. (AP/Wide World Photos)

September 11 and the War on Terror

On the morning of September 11, Bush was visiting a school in Florida promoting his education program. He was reading to a class of children when word came that two hijacked commercial airliners had struck the World Trade Center in New York City and a third had hit the Pentagon. A fourth plane crashed in Pennsyl-

President Bush (center) with New York City mayor Rudolph Giuliani (left), New York governor George Pataki (second from right), and New York City fire commissioner Thomas Van Essen (right) look toward the fallen buildings during a tour of Ground Zero, September 14, 2001. *(AP/Wide World Photos)*

vania as the passengers struggled to overpower their hijackers. Altogether, nearly three thousand people died. The United States quickly traced responsibility for the attacks to Osama Bin Laden and his al-Qaeda terrorist network. Bin Laden based himself in Afghanistan, where he ran training camps for Islamic jihadists. Bush made a crucial decision on September 11. He told his staff, "We are at war." Bush would not treat terrorism as a matter for law enforcement, as had the Clinton administration. Bush also quickly made it clear that this war would extend to regimes that sponsored terrorism. He told the nation, "We will make no distinction between the terrorists who committed these acts and those who harbor them." In the days

following September 11, Bush rallied the American people for war. "This conflict," he said, "was begun on the timing and terms of others. It will end in a way, and at an hour, of our choosing." The rest of Bush's presidency would be shaped by his new role as war leader.

The Bush administration quickly rallied international support in the war against Bin Laden, al-Qaeda, and the Taliban government in Afghanistan that gave the terrorists shelter. Steps were taken to share intelligence information, to round-up terror suspects, and to disrupt the financial networks that funded terrorist activities. At home, Bush created the Office of Homeland Security, headed by Pennsylvania governor Tom Ridge, to coordinate security

Excerpts from George W. Bush's address at the National Day of Prayer and Remembrance three days after the terrorist attacks on the World Trade Center and the Pentagon, September 14, 2001:

We are here in the middle hour of our grief. So many have suffered so great a loss, and today we express our nation's sorrow. We come before God to pray for the missing and the dead, and for those who love them. On Tuesday, our country was attacked with deliberate and massive cruelty. We have seen the images of fire and ashes, and bent steel.

Now come the names, the list of casualties we are only beginning to read. They are the names of men and women who began their day at a desk or in an airport, busy with life. They are the names of people who faced death, and in their last moments called home to say, "Be brave" and "I love you."

They are the names of passengers who defied their murderers, and prevented the murder of others on the ground. They are the names of men and women who wore the uniform of the United States, and died at their posts.

They are the names of rescuers, the ones whom death found running up the stairs and into the fires to help others. We will read all these names. We will linger over them, and learn their stories, and many Americans will weep. To the children and parents and spouses and families and friends of the lost, we offer the deepest sympathy of the nation. And I assure you, you are not alone.

Just three days removed from these events, Americans do not yet have the distance of history. But our responsibility to history is already clear: to answer these attacks and rid the world of evil. War has been waged against us by stealth and deceit and murder. This nation is peaceful, but fierce when stirred to anger. This conflict was begun on the timing and terms of others. It will end in a way, and at an hour, of our choosing. . . .

It is said that adversity introduces us to ourselves. This is true of a nation as well. In this trial, we have been reminded, and the world has seen, that our fellow Americans are generous and kind, resourceful and brave. We see our national character in rescuers working past exhaustion; in long lines of blood donors; in thousands of citizens who have asked to work and serve in any way possible. . . .

Today, we feel what Franklin Roosevelt called the warm courage of national unity. This is a unity of every faith, and every background. It has joined together political parties in both houses of Congress. It is evident in services of prayer and candlelight vigils, and American flags, which are displayed in pride, and wave in defiance. Our unity is a kinship of grief, and a steadfast resolve to prevail against our enemies. And this unity against terror is now extending across the world. . . .

In every generation, the world has produced enemies of human freedom. They have attacked America, because we are freedom's home and defender. And the commitment of our fathers is now the calling of our time.

---

efforts across the federal government. On October 26, he signed the Patriot Act, which gave the government new powers to combat terrorism. The former "wall" between intelligence and law enforcement agencies was breached, and surveillance tools that had been used against mobsters and drug lords were now deployed against suspected terrorists.

Afghanistan, remote and mountainous, had defied invaders for centuries. On October 7, American and allied forces commanded by General Tommy Franks launched a powerful and unconventional assault on Bin Laden and the Taliban regime. Air strikes pounded terrorist camps and Taliban troops. American special forces and a limited number of regular troops coordinated operations with Afghan allies. By early December, the Taliban government had collapsed. Bin Laden escaped and went into hiding, but his terrorist infrastructure in Afghanistan was destroyed. American and North Atlantic Treaty Organization (NATO) forces remained in Afghanistan to protect a new democratic government and hunt down remnant members of al-Qaeda and the Taliban.

Victory in Afghanistan did not mean the end of the war for Bush. In his State of the Union address in January, 2002, Bush warned of an "axis of evil," Iraq, Iran, and North Korea, where regimes hostile to the United States were developing nuclear and biological weapons that could be shared with terrorists. Over the next few months, he articulated what came to be known as the Bush Doctrine. The President argued that the Cold War strategy of containment was obsolete in a world where terrorists could strike with unprecedented destructiveness. Instead, the United States would follow a strategy of preemptive war, striking rogue regimes before they could share dangerous technologies. Ideally, the United States would work with allies, but if none was forthcoming, the nation would act unilaterally. Bush declared that American defense required unchallenged military superiority. He also called for the active promotion of democracy across the world as the best protection against the despair and fanaticism that fosters terrorism.

The Iraq War

Bush increasingly focused his attention on Iraq and its dictator, Saddam Hussein. Since the 1991 Persian Gulf War, when Bush's father had led an international coalition to expel Iraqi forces from Kuwait, Hussein's regime had been isolated by allied no-fly zones and international sanctions. This containment was growing increasingly threadbare by 2002. Hussein

Osama Bin Laden is seen at an undisclosed location broadcast on the Al-Jazeera network on October 7, 2001. *(AP/Wide World Photos)*

had expelled U.N. arms inspectors in 1998. He repeatedly defied U.N. resolutions. Shooting incidents between the Iraqi military and American and British planes patrolling the no-fly zones occurred almost daily. The Oil for Food program run by the United Nations was a sink of corruption. Billions of dollars intended to buy food for ordinary Iraqis instead financed palaces for Hussein. Most arms experts and intelligence agencies believed that the Iraqi government was manufacturing weapons of mass destruction. Bush declared that Iraq was a threat to international security and called for a resumption of arms inspections.

The prospect of war with Iraq alarmed many Democrats in Congress. They feared that Bush would act without congressional ap-

proval. Bush responded by asking Congress for authorization to use force in Iraq. He received it in October. Bush also went to the United Nations. He addressed the General Assembly on September 12 and challenged the world body to enforce its own resolutions. In November, the United Nations Security Council passed Resolution 1441, demanding a resumption of arms inspections and threatening "serious consequences" if the Iraqis did not fully comply. Arms inspections did resume, but the United States was not satisfied. The Iraqis continued to try to hide weapons systems, including banned missiles that were discovered by the inspectors. The United States and its ally Great Britain went back to the U.N. Security Council in order to get an explicit authorization of force against

During the Iraq War, a U.S. Marine covers the face of a statue of Saddam Hussein in downtown Baghdad with an American flag moments before the statue was toppled on April 9, 2003. *(AP/Wide World Photos)*

Excerpts from George W. Bush's speech on the deck of the USS Abraham Lincoln *regarding the Iraq War, May 1, 2003:*

Major combat operations in Iraq have ended. In the Battle of Iraq, the United States and our allies have prevailed. And now our coalition is engaged in securing and reconstructing that country.

In this battle, we have fought for the cause of liberty, and for the peace of the world. Our nation and our coalition are proud of this accomplishment—yet it is you, the members of the United States military, who achieved it. Your courage—your willingness to face danger for your country and for each other—made this day possible. Because of you, our nation is more secure. Because of you, the tyrant has fallen, and Iraq is free.

Operation Iraqi Freedom was carried out with a combination of precision, and speed, and boldness the enemy did not expect, and the world had not seen before. . . . In the images of fallen statues, we have witnessed the arrival of a new era. . . . Today, we have the greater power to free a nation by breaking a dangerous and aggressive regime. With new tactics and precision weapons, we can achieve military objectives without directing violence against civilians. No device of man can remove the tragedy from war. Yet it is a great advance when the guilty have far more to fear from war than the innocent.

In the images of celebrating Iraqis, we have also seen the ageless appeal of human freedom. Decades of lies and intimidation could not make the Iraqi people love their oppressors or desire their own enslavement. Men and women in every culture need liberty like they need food, and water, and air. Everywhere that freedom arrives, humanity rejoices. And everywhere that freedom stirs, let tyrants fear.

We have difficult work to do in Iraq. We are bringing order to parts of that country that remain dangerous. We are pursuing and finding leaders of the old regime, who will be held to account for their crimes. We have begun the search for hidden chemical and biological weapons, and already know of hundreds of sites that will be investigated. We are helping to rebuild Iraq, where the dictator built palaces for himself, instead of hospitals and schools. And we will stand with the new leaders of Iraq as they establish a government of, by, and for the Iraqi people. The transition from dictatorship to democracy will take time, but it is worth every effort. Our coalition will stay until our work is done. And then we will leave—and we will leave behind a free Iraq. . . .

The liberation of Iraq is a crucial advance in the campaign against terror. We have removed an ally of al-Qaeda and cut off a source of terrorist funding. And this much is certain: No terrorist network will gain weapons of mass destruction from the Iraqi regime, because the regime is no more.

Iraq. This was blocked in the Security Council by the governments of France, Russia, and China. Other allies such as Germany also opposed war. These states had strong business and political ties to Iraq and were benefiting economically from the Oil for Food program. The United States and Britain decided to attack anyway, working with a "coalition of the willing" that included Australia, Italy, Poland, and Spain.

Bush ordered the beginning of military operations on March 19, 2003. Forces commanded by General Tommy Franks swept into Iraq from bases in Kuwait. The Turkish government refused permission to launch an American armored assault from its territory. Instead, American special forces cooperated with Kurdish militias in the north. Iraq was overrun with surprising speed. Hussein's army melted away. The fiercest resistance came from irregular fighters. Baghdad fell on April 9, and the destruction of Hussein's regime was over by the end of the month. During the fighting, 137 American and 32 British soldiers had died.

Next began a long and difficult process of rebuilding in Iraq. Years of corruption had devastated Iraq's infrastructure and impoverished its people. The nation was divided by ethnic and religious differences. Supporters of the old regime and foreign jihadis launched an insurgency against the occupation that took a steady toll of American lives. Adding to American frustration was a long and discouraging hunt for Hussein and his weapons of mass destruction. Hussein was finally caught in December, 2003. The next month, a team of weapons inspectors led by David Kay concluded that American intelligence agencies had been wrong in asserting that Hussein had possessed weapons of mass destruction. He wanted such weapons and was indeed trying to obtain them but had failed to effectively reconstitute his earlier waepons program. Political opponents of the Bush administration now charged that the president had lied to the American people in taking them to war. Bush responded that he had acted on the best information at the time and that weapons of mass destruction had been only one reason for toppling Hussein.

The Iraq War and American postwar efforts to sponsor a democracy in the Middle East produced strong aftershocks in the region. Hoping to avoid Hussein's fate, Libyan dictator Muammar al-Qaddafi revealed and dismantled his own surprisingly advanced weapons program. The Pakistani nuclear scientist A. Q. Khan's trade in nuclear components was exposed and halted. Democratic stirrings began to be felt in the Gulf States. Popular demonstrations forced the Syrian army out of Lebanon in early 2005, and contested elections occurred in Egypt later that year.

Moreover, some hopeful signs concerning the plight of the Palestinians emerged. Early in his presidency, Bush kept his distance from the Arab-Israeli conflict. His "road map" to peace announced in May, 2003, went nowhere at first. Bush refused to deal with the Palestinian leader Yasir Arafat because he considered him an untrustworthy terrorist. When Arafat died in November, 2004, the Bush administration embraced his democratically elected successor Mahmoud Abbas, and encouraged reforms in the Palestinian Authority. A strong supporter of Israel, Bush believed that only the creation of a democratic Palestinian state could bring peace.

Domestic Politics

Democrats in the Senate blocked most of Bush's initiatives through 2002. Bush signed a campaign finance bill he did not like because he wanted the issue off the table before the next presidential election. He overrode his conservative instincts in order to deny the opposition a popular rallying cry. However, Bush decided to resist Democratic efforts to protect unionized jobs in the bill creating a new Department of Homeland Security. He took the issue to the people in the midterm elections, portraying the Democrats as out of touch with the new realities of the post-September 11 world. Bush gambled his prestige on the result and won an impressive victory, picking up six seats in the House of Representatives and two in the Senate, which returned the Senate to Republican control. Not since Franklin Delano Roosevelt had a president gained congressional seats in his first midterm elections.

Bush used his political capital to push through more tax cuts in May of 2003. Looking forward to the coming presidential contest, he solidified support in his base by signing a bill banning partial birth abortion. He also came out against gay marriage, which had become a contentious issue when the Massachusetts Supreme Court legalized gay unions. Bush ended the year by taking another issue away from the Democrats. He sponsored and then signed a bill adding prescription drug benefits to Medicare. Bush thus became the first Republican president to extend a major entitlement program.

President Bush aboard the USS *Abraham Lincoln* on May 1, 2003, where he declared the end of major combat in Iraq. *(AP/Wide World Photos)*

depicting the humiliation of Iraqi prisoners by American soldiers at the Abu Ghraib prison caused an international sensation and raised serious questions about the competence and good intentions of the American administration in Iraq. A Senate investigation of American intelligence failures prior to the Iraq War caused further embarrassment. The report of the bipartisan commission examining the events of September 11 recommended serious reforms of the United States intelligence community. Bush appointed a new director of the Central Intelligence Agency and signed legislation creating a national intelligence director to coordinate all government agencies conducting foreign and domestic intelligence.

The Election of 2004

Bush won the 2004 Republican presidential nomination without significant opposition. He led a unified Republican Party into the general election. The Democrats nominated Senator John Kerry of Massachusetts. Kerry had served as a Navy swift boat commander in the Vietnam War. During the campaign, Kerry emphasized his honorable war record while criticizing Bush's record in Iraq and with the economy. The Republicans highlighted Kerry's activities as a leader of Vietnam Veterans Against the War and his liberal voting record in the Senate. They delighted in portraying Kerry as a "flip-flopper" and repeatedly played a sound clip of Kerry's justification, on procedural grounds, of a vote against a military appropriations bill: "I actually did vote for the $87 billion before I voted against it."

By the end of 2003, the economy had begun to recover from the effects of the 2001 recession, September 11, and the run-up to the Iraq War. Bush credited the stimulating effects of his tax cuts. Democrats pointed to record budget deficits and argued that Bush's tax cuts would lead to a fiscal crisis. A lag in job creation led Democrats to criticize a "jobless recovery."

As the insurgency in Iraq continued into 2004 and American casualties rose, many Democrats began to attack Bush's management of the war. The publication of photographs

President Bush answers a question during a debate with Democratic presidential candidate John F. Kerry on October 8, 2004. *(AP/Wide World Photos)*

The presidential campaign reflected the bitter tenor of American politics since the 1990's. Both candidates were subject to vitriolic personal attacks. Given the fact that the nation was at war, most of these attacks centered on the candidates' military service. Former members of Kerry's swift boat squadron challenged his military record and denounced statements about the troops in Vietnam that he made while a leader of the antiwar movement in the early 1970's. Democrats charged that Bush had evaded service in Vietnam by joining the Air National Guard. They further accused him of shirking some of his Guard obligations. This line of accusation culminated when Dan Rather and the Columbia Broadcasting System (CBS) network news publicized supposedly damning thirty-year-old documents that proved to be crude forgeries.

On Election Day in November, Bush won a solid victory. He carried thirty-one states with 285 electoral votes. He dispelled the lingering taint of being a "minority" president by winning 51 percent of the popular vote and more votes in total than any candidate in history. Bush also continued to be an effective leader for his party. The Republicans added to their majorities in both the Senate and the House of Representatives. Not since Franklin Roosevelt's landslide of 1936 had a president gained seats in Congress when winning reelection.

A Second Term

Bush made a number of changes to his cabinet in his second term. Among his new cabinet secretaries, Condoleezza Rice became the first African American woman to serve as secretary of state, and Alberto Gonzales became the first Latino attorney general. Bush made the reform of Social Security a priority of his renewed administration. The gradual aging of the American population threatened Social Security's long-term solvency. Despite Bush's efforts, Congress and the public showed little enthusiasm for addressing distant problems with a cherished entitlement program.

Bush did enjoy some legislative successes early in his second term. Congress placed limits on bankruptcy filings and class action lawsuits. A deal in the Senate allowed some of Bush's judicial nominees hitherto blocked by the Democratic minority to receive confirmation votes. By a narrow margin, Congress passed the Central American Free Trade Agreement (CAFTA), an extension of trade liberalization that Bush strongly favored.

The economy continued to show strength in the face of a dramatic rise in the price of oil. Unemployment fell to levels that compared favorably with the prosperous 1990's. Supreme Court Justice Sandra Day O'Connor announced her retirement in July, 2005, which gave Bush his first opportunity to appoint a justice to the Supreme Court. He nominated John Roberts, a judge on the D.C. Circuit Court of Appeals. Chief Justice William Rehnquist died on September 3. Bush then nominated Judge Roberts for the vacant position of Chief Justice and pondered a second appointment to the Supreme Court. In a controversial move, he nominated his White House attorney, Harriet Miers, who had no previous experience as a judge; she withdrew after protests from both parties. Bush countered by nominating conservative judge Samuel Alito.

In Iraq, successful elections were held in January, 2005. A democratically elected Iraqi government began deliberations on a constitution. Unfortunately, this did not stop the insurgency in Iraq. By August, more than eighteen hundred American soldiers had been killed since the war began. The continuing toll of American casualties began to wear away Bush's popular support. Then came another crisis. On August 29, Hurricane Katrina ravaged the Gulf Coast of Mississippi, Alabama, and Louisiana. Floodwaters inundated New Orleans when levees gave way. Local and federal authorities struggled to address the devastating effects of the greatest natural disaster in American history.

By the fifth year of his presidency, Bush had led the United States through eventful times. He had grappled with the challenges of recession, terrorist attack, war, and natural disaster. Learning from the examples of Ronald Reagan and of his own father, he effectively pursued his goals, at home and abroad. Whatever lay in store for George W. Bush, supporters and critics alike agreed that the chief executive from whom so little had been expected had dominated the political agenda of the nation and left an indelible mark on the history of the presidency.

Daniel P. Murphy

Suggested Readings

Bruni, Frank. *Ambling into History*. New York: Perennial, 2003. A sympathetic account of Bush written by a *New York Times* reporter.

Bush, George W. *A Charge to Keep*. New York: Morrow, 1999. A campaign biography written by Bush and Karen Hughes. Useful for insights into Bush's youth and political ideals.

Frum, David. *The Right Man*. New York: Random House, 2003. A laudatory book about Bush's first year in office written by a political commentator who spent a year in the Bush White House as a speechwriter.

Gaddis, John Lewis. *Surprise, Security, and the American Experience*. Cambridge, Mass.: Harvard University Press, 2004. A distinguished historian writes approvingly of Bush's post-September 11 foreign policy and places it in historical perspective.

Ivins, Molly. *Bushwhacked*. New York: Random House, 2003. A critical commentary written by a political columnist with strong Texas roots.

Minutaglio, Bill. *First Son*. New York: Times Books, 1999. A detailed account of Bush's career before the presidency, written by a Texas journalist.

Podhoretz, John. *Bush Country*. New York: St. Martin's Press, 2004. A conservative political commentator celebrates Bush's early success in confounding his liberal opponents.

Sammons, Bill. *At Any Cost.* Washington, D.C.: Regnery, 2001. An account of the 2000 Florida recount that is sympathetic to Bush.

_____. *Misunderestimated.* New York: Harper-Collins, 2004. A friendly account of Bush covering the period from the 2002 mid-term election to early 2004.

Schier, Steven E., ed. *High Risk and Big Ambition.* Pittsburgh: University of Pittsburgh Press, 2004. Better than the average collection of scholarly articles covering the Bush presidency through most of the first term.

Thomas, Evan. *Election 2004.* New York: Public Affairs, 2004. A detailed chronicle of the election of 2004 by Thomas and the staff of *Newsweek.*

Toobin, Jeffrey. *Too Close to Call.* New York: Random House, 2001. An account of the 2000 Florida recount that is sympathetic to Gore.

U.S. Constitution

We the People of the United States, in Order to form a more perfect Union, establish Justice, insure domestic Tranquility, provide for the common defence, promote the general Welfare, and secure the Blessings of Liberty to ourselves and our Posterity, do ordain and establish this Constitution for the United States of America.

Article I.

SECTION 1. All legislative Powers herein granted shall be vested in a Congress of the United States, which shall consist of a Senate and House of Representatives.

SECTION 2. The House of Representatives shall be composed of Members chosen every second Year by the People of the several States, and the Electors in each State shall have the Qualifications requisite for Electors of the most numerous Branch of the State Legislature.

No Person shall be a Representative who shall not have attained to the Age of twenty five Years, and been seven Years a Citizen of the United States, and who shall not, when elected, be an Inhabitant of that State in which he shall be chosen.

Representatives and direct Taxes shall be apportioned among the several States which may be included within this Union, according to their respective Numbers, which shall be determined by adding to the whole Number of free Persons, including those bound to Service for a Term of Years, and excluding Indians not taxed, three fifths of all other Persons. The actual Enumeration shall be made within three Years after the first Meeting of the Congress of the United States, and within every subsequent Term of ten Years, in such Manner as they shall by Law direct. The number of Representatives shall not exceed one for every thirty Thousand, but each State shall have at Least one Representative; and until such enumeration shall be made, the State of New Hampshire shall be entitled to chuse three, Massachusetts eight, Rhode-Island and Providence Plantations one, Connecticut five, New York six, New Jersey four, Pennsylvania eight, Delaware one, Maryland six, Virginia ten, North Carolina five, South Carolina five, and Georgia three.

When vacancies happen in the Representation from any State, the Executive Authority thereof shall issue Writs of Election to fill such Vacancies.

The House of Representatives shall chuse their Speaker and other Officers; and shall have the sole Power of Impeachment.

SECTION 3. The Senate of the United States shall be composed of two Senators from each State, chosen by the Legislature thereof, for six Years; and each Senator shall have one Vote.

Immediately after they shall be assembled in Consequence of the first Election, they shall be divided as equally as may be into three Classes. The Seats of the Senators of the first Class shall be vacated at the Expiration of the second Year, of the second Class at the Expiration of the fourth Year, and of the third Class at the Expiration of the sixth Year, so that one third may be chosen every second Year; and if Vacancies happen by Resignation, or otherwise, during the Recess of the Legislature of any State, the Executive thereof may make temporary Appointments until the next Meeting of the Legislature, which shall then fill such Vacancies.

No Person shall be a Senator who shall not have attained to the Age of thirty Years, and been nine Years a Citizen of the United States, and who shall not, when elected, be an Inhabitant of that State for which he shall be chosen.

The Vice President of the United States shall be President of the Senate, but shall have no Vote, unless they be equally divided.

The Senate shall chuse their other Officers, and also a President pro tempore, in the Absence of the Vice President, or when he shall exercise the Office of President of the United States.

The Senate shall have the sole Power to try all Impeachments. When sitting for that Purpose, they shall be on Oath or Affirmation. When the President of the United States is tried, the Chief Justice shall preside: And no Person shall be convicted without the Concurrence of two thirds of the Members present.

Judgment in Cases of Impeachment shall not extend further than to removal from Office, and disqualification to hold and enjoy any Office of honor, Trust or Profit under the United States: but the Party convicted shall nevertheless be liable and subject to Indictment, Trial, Judgment and Punishment, according to Law.

SECTION 4. The Times, Places and Manner of holding Elections for Senators and Representatives, shall be prescribed in each State by the Legislature thereof; but the Congress may at any time by Law make or alter such Regulations, except as to the Places of chusing Senators.

The Congress shall assemble at least once in every Year, and such Meeting shall be on the first Monday in December, unless they shall by Law appoint a different Day.

SECTION 5. Each House shall be the Judge of the Elections, Returns and Qualifications of its own Members, and a Majority of each shall constitute a Quorum to do Business; but a smaller Number may adjourn from day to day, and may be authorized to compel the Attendance of absent Members, in such Manner, and under such Penalties as each House may provide.

Each House may determine the Rules of its Proceedings, punish its Members for disorderly Behaviour, and, with the Concurrence of two thirds, expel a Member.

Each House shall keep a Journal of its Proceedings, and from time to time publish the same, excepting such Parts as may in their Judgment require Secrecy; and the Yeas and Nays of the Members of either House on any question shall, at the Desire of one fifth of those Present, be entered on the Journal.

Neither House, during the Session of Congress, shall, without the Consent of the other, adjourn for more than three days, nor to any other Place than that in which the two Houses shall be sitting.

SECTION 6. The Senators and Representatives shall receive a Compensation for their Services, to be ascertained by Law, and paid out of the Treasury of the United States. They shall in all Cases, except Treason, Felony and Breach of the Peace, be privileged from Arrest during their Attendance at the Session of their respective Houses, and in going to and returning from the same; and for any Speech or Debate in either House, they shall not be questioned in any other Place.

No Senator or Representative shall, during the Time for which he was elected, be appointed to any civil Office under the Authority of the United States, which shall have been created, or the Emoluments whereof shall have been increased during such time; and no Person holding any Office under the United States, shall be a Member of either House during his Continuance in Office.

SECTION 7. All Bills for raising Revenue shall originate in the House of Representatives; but the Senate may propose or concur with Amendments as on other Bills.

Every Bill which shall have passed the House of Representatives and the Senate, shall, before it becomes a Law, be presented to the President of the United States; If he approve he shall sign it, but if not he shall return it, with his Objections to that House in which it shall have originated, who shall enter the Objections at large on their Journal, and proceed to reconsider it. If after such Reconsideration two thirds of that House shall agree to pass the Bill, it shall be sent, together with the Objections, to the other House, by which it shall likewise be reconsidered, and if approved by two thirds of that House, it shall become a Law. But in all such Cases the Votes of both Houses shall be determined by Yeas and Nays, and the Names of the Persons voting for and against the Bill shall be entered on the Journal of each House respectively. If any Bill shall not be returned by the President within ten Days (Sundays excepted) after it shall have been presented to him, the Same shall be a Law, in like Manner as if he had signed it, unless the Congress by their Adjournment prevent its Return, in which Case it shall not be a Law.

Every Order, Resolution, or Vote to which the Concurrence of the Senate and House of Representatives may be necessary (except on a question of Adjournment) shall be presented to the President of the United States; and before the Same shall take Effect, shall be approved by him, or being disapproved by him, shall be repassed by two thirds of the Senate and House of Representatives, according to the Rules and Limitations prescribed in the Case of a Bill.

SECTION 8. The Congress shall have Power To lay and collect Taxes, Duties, Imposts and Excises, to pay the Debts and provide for the common Defence and general Welfare of the United States; but all Duties, Imposts and Excises shall be uniform throughout the United States;

To borrow Money on the credit of the United States;

To regulate Commerce with foreign Nations, and among the several States, and with the Indian Tribes;

To establish an uniform Rule of Naturalization, and uniform Laws on the subject of Bankruptcies throughout the United States;

To coin Money, regulate the Value thereof, and of foreign Coin, and fix the Standard of Weights and Measures;

To provide for the Punishment of counterfeiting the Securities and current Coin of the United States;

To establish Post Offices and post Roads;

To promote the Progress of Science and useful Arts, by securing for limited Times to Authors and Inventors the exclusive Right to their respective Writings and Discoveries;

To constitute Tribunals inferior to the supreme Court;

To define and punish Piracies and Felonies committed on the high Seas, and Offenses against the Law of Nations;

To declare War, grant Letters of Marque and Reprisal, and make Rules concerning Captures on Land and Water;

To raise and support Armies, but no Appropriation of Money to that Use shall be for a longer Term than two Years;

To provide and maintain a Navy;

To make Rules for the Government and Regulation of the land and naval Forces;

To provide for calling forth the Militia to execute the Laws of the Union, suppress Insurrections and repel Invasions;

To provide for organizing, arming, and disciplining the Militia, and for governing such Part of them as may be employed in the Service of the United States, reserving to the States respectively, the Appointment of the Officers, and the Authority of training the Militia according to the discipline prescribed by Congress;

To exercise exclusive Legislation in all Cases whatsoever, over such District (not exceeding ten Miles square) as may, by Cession of particular States, and the Acceptance of Congress, become the Seat of the Government of the United States, and to exercise like Authority over all Places purchased by the Consent of the Legislature of the State in which the Same shall be, for the Erection of Forts, Magazines, Arsenals, dock-Yards and other needful Buildings;—And

To make all Laws which shall be necessary and proper for carrying into Execution the foregoing Powers, and all other Powers vested by this Constitution in the Government of the United States, or in any Department or Officer thereof.

SECTION 9. The Migration or Importation of such Persons as any of the States now existing shall think proper to admit, shall not be prohibited by the Congress prior to the Year one thousand eight hundred and eight, but a Tax or duty may be imposed on such Importation, not exceeding ten dollars for each Person.

The Privilege of the Writ of Habeas Corpus shall not be suspended, unless when in Cases of Rebellion or Invasion the public Safety may require it.

No Bill of Attainder or ex post facto Law shall be passed.

No Capitation, or other direct, Tax shall be laid, unless in Proportion to the Census or Enumeration herein before directed to be taken.

No Tax or Duty shall be laid on Articles exported from any State.

No Preference shall be given by any Regulation of Commerce or Revenue to the Ports of one State over those of another: nor shall Vessels bound to, or from, one State, be obliged to enter, clear, or pay Duties in another.

No Money shall be drawn from the Treasury, but in Consequence of Appropriations made by Law; and a regular Statement and Account of the Receipts and Expenditures of all public Money shall be published from time to time.

No Title of Nobility shall be granted by the United States: And no Person holding any Office of Profit or Trust under them, shall, without the Consent of the Congress, accept of any present, Emolument, Office, or Title, of any kind whatever, from any King, Prince, or foreign State.

SECTION 10. No State shall enter into any Treaty, Alliance, or Confederation; grant Letters of Marque and Reprisal; coin Money; emit Bills of Credit; make any Thing but gold and silver Coin a Tender in Payment of Debts; pass any Bill of Attainder, ex post facto Law, or Law impairing the Obligation of Contracts, or grant any Title of Nobility.

No State shall, without the Consent of the Congress, lay any Imposts or Duties on Imports or Exports, except what may be absolutely necessary for executing its inspection Laws: and the net Produce of all Duties and Imposts, laid by any State on Imports or Exports, shall be for the Use of the Treasury of the United States; and all such Laws shall be subject to the Revision and Control of the Congress.

No State shall, without the Consent of Congress, lay any Duty of Tonnage, keep Troops, or Ships of War in time of Peace, enter into any Agreement or Compact with another State, or with a foreign Power, or engage in War, unless actually invaded, or in such imminent Danger as will not admit of delay.

Article II.

SECTION 1. The executive Power shall be vested in a President of the United States of America. He shall hold his Office during the Term of four Years, and, together with the Vice President, chosen for the same Term, be elected, as follows:

Each State shall appoint, in such Manner as the Legislature thereof may direct, a Number of Electors, equal to the whole Number of Senators and Representatives to which the State may be entitled in the Congress: but no Senator or Representative, or Person holding an Office of Trust or Profit under the United States, shall be appointed an Elector.

The Electors shall meet in their respective States, and vote by Ballot for two Persons, of whom one at least shall not be an Inhabitant of the same State with themselves. And they shall make a List of all the Persons voted for, and of the Number of Votes for each; which List they shall sign and certify, and transmit sealed to the Seat of the Government of the United States, directed to the President of the Senate. The President of the Senate shall, in the Presence of the

Senate and House of Representatives, open all the Certificates, and the Votes shall then be counted. The Person having the greatest Number of Votes shall be the President, if such Number be a Majority of the whole Number of Electors appointed; and if there be more than one who have such Majority, and have an equal Number of Votes, then the House of Representatives shall immediately chuse by Ballot one of them for President; and if no Person have a Majority, then from the five highest on the List the said House shall in like manner chuse the President. But in chusing the President, the Votes shall be taken by States, the Representation from each State having one Vote; A quorum for this Purpose shall consist of a Member or Members from two thirds of the States, and a Majority of all the States shall be necessary to a Choice. In every Case, after the Choice of the President, the Person having the greatest Number of Votes of the Electors shall be the Vice President. But if there should remain two or more who have equal Votes, the Senate shall chuse from them by Ballot the Vice President.

The Congress may determine the Time of chusing the Electors, and the Day on which they shall give their Votes; which Day shall be the same throughout the United States.

No Person except a natural born Citizen, or a Citizen of the United States, at the time of the Adoption of this Constitution, shall be eligible to the Office of the President; neither shall any person be eligible to that Office who shall not have attained to the Age of thirty five Years, and been fourteen Years a Resident within the United States.

In Case of the Removal of the President from Office, or of his Death, Resignation, or Inability to discharge the Powers and Duties of the said Office, the Same shall devolve on the Vice President, and the Congress may by Law provide for the Case of Removal, Death, Resignation or Inability, both of the President and Vice President, declaring what Officer shall then act as President, and such Officer shall act accord-ingly, until the Disability be removed, or a President shall be elected.

The President shall, at stated Times, receive for his Services, a Compensation, which shall neither be increased nor diminished during the Period for which he shall have been elected, and he shall not receive within that Period any other Emolument from the United States, or any of them.

Before he enter the Execution of his Office, he shall take the following Oath or Affirmation:—"I do solemnly swear (or affirm) that I will faithfully execute the Office of President of the United States, and will to the best of my Ability, preserve, protect and defend the Constitution of the United States."

SECTION 2. The President shall be Commander in Chief of the Army and Navy of the United States, and of the Militia of the several States, when called into the actual Service of the United States; he may require the Opinion, in writing, of the principal Officer in each of the executive Departments, upon any Subject relating to the Duties of their respective Offices, and he shall have Power to grant Reprieves and Pardons for Offenses against the United States, except in Cases of Impeachment.

He shall have Power, by and with the Advice and Consent of the Senate, to make Treaties, provided two thirds of the Senators present concur; and he shall nominate, and by and with the Advice and Consent of the Senate, shall appoint Ambassadors, other public Ministers and Consuls, Judges of the supreme Court, and all other Officers of the United States, whose Appointments are not herein otherwise provided for, and which shall be established by Law: but the Congress may by Law vest the Appointment of such inferior Officers, as they think proper, in the President alone, in the Courts of Law, or in the Heads of Departments.

The President shall have Power to fill up all Vacancies that may happen during the Recess of the Senate, by granting Commissions which shall expire at the End of their next Session.

SECTION 3. He shall from time to time give to the Congress Information of the State of the Union, and recommend to their Consideration such Measures as he shall judge necessary and expedient; he may, on extraordinary Occasions, convene both Houses, or either of them, and in Case of Disagreement between them, with Respect to the Time of Adjournment, he may adjourn them to such Time as he shall think proper; he shall receive Ambassadors and other public Ministers; he shall take Care that the Laws be faithfully executed, and shall Commission all the Officers of the United States.

SECTION 4. The President, Vice President and all civil Officers of the United States, shall be removed from Office on Impeachment for, and Conviction of, Treason, Bribery, or other high Crimes and Misdemeanors.

Article III.

SECTION 1. The judicial Power of the United States, shall be vested in one supreme Court, and in such inferior Courts as the Congress may from time to time ordain and establish. The Judges, both of the supreme and inferior Courts, shall hold their Offices during good Behavior, and shall, at stated Times, receive for their Services, a Compensation, which shall not be diminished during their Continuance in Office.

SECTION 2. The judicial Power shall extend to all Cases, in Law and Equity, arising under this Constitution, the Laws of the United States, and Treaties made, or which shall be made, under their Authority;—to all Cases affecting Ambassadors, other public Ministers and Consuls;—to all Cases of admiralty and maritime Jurisdiction;—to Controversies to which the United States shall be a Party;—to Controversies between two or more States; between a State and Citizens of another State; between Citizens of different States;—between Citizens of the same State claiming Lands under Grants of different States;—and between a State, or the Citizens thereof, and foreign States, Citizens or Subjects.

In all Cases affecting Ambassadors, other public Ministers and Consuls, and those in which a State shall be Party, the supreme Court shall have original Jurisdiction. In all the other Cases before mentioned, the supreme Court shall have appellate Jurisdiction, both as to Law and Fact, with such Exceptions, and under such Regulations as the Congress shall make.

The Trial of all Crimes, except in Cases of Impeachment, shall be by Jury; and such Trial shall be held in the State where the said Crimes shall have been committed; but when not committed within any State, the Trial shall be at such Place or Places as the Congress may by Law have directed.

SECTION 3. Treason against the United States, shall consist only in levying War against them, or in adhering to their Enemies, giving them Aid and Comfort. No Person shall be convicted of Treason unless on the Testimony of two Witnesses to the same overt Act, or on Confession in open Court.

The Congress shall have Power to declare the Punishment of Treason, but no Attainder of Treason shall work Corruption of Blood, or Forfeiture except during the Life of the Person attainted.

Article IV.

SECTION 1. Full Faith and Credit shall be given in each State to the public Acts, Records, and judicial Proceedings of every other State; And the Congress may by general Laws prescribe the Manner in which such Acts, Records and Proceedings shall be proved, and the Effect thereof.

SECTION 2. The Citizens of each State shall be entitled to all Privileges and Immunities of Citizens in the several States.

A Person charged in any State with Treason, Felony, or other Crime, who shall flee from Justice, and be found in another State, shall on Demand of the executive Authority of the State from which he fled, be delivered up, to be removed to the State having Jurisdiction of the Crime.

No person held to Service or Labour in one State, under the Laws thereof, escaping into another, shall, in Consequence of any Law or Regulation therein, be discharged from such Service or Labour, but shall be delivered up on Claim of the Party to whom such Service or Labour may be due.

SECTION 3. New States may be admitted by the Congress into this Union; but no new State shall be formed or erected within the Jurisdiction of any other State; nor any State be formed by the Junction of two or more States, or parts of States, without the Consent of the Legislatures of the States concerned as well as of the Congress.

The Congress shall have Power to dispose of and make all needful Rules and Regulations respecting the Territory or other Property belonging to the United States; and nothing in this Constitution shall be so construed as to Prejudice any Claims of the United States, or of any particular State.

SECTION 4. The United States shall guarantee to every State in this Union a Republican Form of Government, and shall protect each of them against Invasion; and on Application of the Legislature, or of the Executive (when the Legislature cannot be convened) against domestic Violence.

Article V.

The Congress, whenever two thirds of both Houses shall deem it necessary, shall propose Amendments to this Constitution, or, on the Application of the Legislatures of two thirds of the several States, shall call a Convention for proposing Amendments, which, in either Case, shall be valid to all Intents and Purposes, as Part of this Constitution, when ratified by the Legislatures of three fourths of the several States, or by Conventions in three fourths thereof, as the one or the other Mode of Ratification may be proposed by the Congress; Provided that no Amendment which may be made prior to the Year One thousand eight hundred and eight shall in any Manner affect the first and fourth Clauses in the Ninth Section of the first Article; and that no State, without its Consent, shall be deprived of its equal Suffrage in the Senate.

Article VI.

All Debts contracted and Engagements entered into, before the Adoption of this Constitution, shall be as valid against the United States under this Constitution, as under the Confederation.

This Constitution, and the Laws of the United States which shall be made in Pursuance thereof; and all Treaties made, or which shall be made, under the Authority of the United States, shall be the supreme Law of the Land; and the Judges in every State shall be bound thereby, any Thing in the Constitution or Laws of any State to the Contrary notwithstanding.

The Senators and Representatives before mentioned, and the Members of the several State Legislatures, and all executive and judicial Officers, both of the United States and of the several States, shall be bound by Oath or Affirmation, to support this Constitution; but no religious Test shall ever be required as a Qualification to any Office or public Trust under the United States.

Article VII.

The Ratification of the Conventions of nine States, shall be sufficient for the Establishment of this Constitution between the States so ratifying the Same.

Done in Convention by the Unanimous Consent of the States present the Seventeenth Day of September in the Year of our Lord one thousand seven hundred and Eighty seven and of the Independence of the United States of America the Twelfth. In Witness whereof We have hereunto subscribed our Names,

Go. Washington—Presidt and deputy from Virginia

New Hampshire {
John Langdon
Nicholas Gilman

Massachusetts {
Nathaniel Gorham
Rufus King

Connecticut {
Wm Saml Johnson
Roger Sherman

New York {
John Langdon

New Jersey {
Wil Livingston
David Brearley
Wm Paterson
Jona. Dayton

New Jersey {
B Franklin
Thomas Mifflin
Robt Morris
Geo. Clymer
Thos FitzSimons
Jared Ingersoll
James Wilson
Gouv Morris

Delaware {
Geo. Read
Gunning Beford jun
John Dickinson
Richard Bassett
Jaco. Broom

Maryland {
James McHenry
Dan of St Tho. Jenifer
Danl Carroll

Virginia {
John Blair
James Madison Jr.

North Carolina {
Wm. Blount
Richd Dobbs Spaight
Hu Williamson

South Carolina {
J. Rutledge
Charles Cotesworth
  Pinckney
Charles Pinckney
Pierce Butler

Georgia {
William Few
Abr Baldwin

Attest: William Jackson, Secretary

Amendments to the U.S. Constitution

Amendment I.

Congress shall make no law respecting an establishment of religion, or prohibiting the free exercise thereof; or abridging the freedom of speech, or of the press, or the right of the people peaceably to assemble, and to petition the Government for a redress of grievances.

[ratified December, 1791]

Amendment II.

A well regulated Militia, being necessary to the security of a free State, the right of the people to keep and bear Arms, shall not be infringed.

[ratified December, 1791]

Amendment III.

No Soldier shall, in time of peace be quartered in any house, without the consent of the Owner, nor in time of war, but in a manner to be prescribed by law.

[ratified December, 1791]

Amendment IV.

The right of the people to be secure in their persons, houses, papers, and effects, against unreasonable searches and seizures, shall not be violated, and no Warrants shall issue, but upon probable cause, supported by Oath or affirmation, and particularly describing the place to be searched, and the persons or things to be seized.

[ratified December, 1791]

Amendment V.

No person shall be held to answer for a capital, or otherwise infamous crime, unless on a presentment or indictment of a Grand Jury, except in cases arising in the land or naval forces, or in the Militia, when in actual service in time of War or public danger; nor shall any person be subject for the same offence to be twice put in jeopardy of life or limb, nor shall be compelled in any criminal case to be a witness against himself, nor be deprived of life, liberty, or property, without due process of law; nor shall private property be taken for public use without just compensation.

[ratified December, 1791]

Amendment VI.

In all criminal prosecutions, the accused shall enjoy the right to a speedy and public trial, by an impartial jury of the State and district wherein the crime shall have been committed; which district shall have been previously ascertained by law, and to be informed of the nature and cause of the accusation; to be confronted with the witnesses against him; to have compulsory process for obtaining witnesses in his favor, and to have the assistance of counsel for his defence.

[ratified December, 1791]

Amendment VII.

In Suits at common law, where the value in controversy shall exceed twenty dollars, the right of trial by jury shall be preserved, and no fact tried by a jury shall be otherwise reexamined in any Court of the United States, than according to the rules of the common law.

[ratified December, 1791]

Amendment VIII.

Excessive bail shall not be required, nor excessive fines imposed, nor cruel and unusual punishments inflicted.

[ratified December, 1791]

Amendment IX.

The enumeration in the Constitution, of certain rights, shall not be construed to deny or disparage others retained by the people.

[ratified December, 1791]

Amendment X.

The powers not delegated to the United States by the Constitution, nor prohibited by it to the States, are reserved to the States respectively, or to the people.

[ratified December, 1791]

Amendment XI.

The Judicial power of the United States shall not be construed to extend to any suit in law or equity, commenced or prosecuted against one of the United States by Citizens of another State, or by Citizens or Subjects of any Foreign State.

[ratified February, 1795]

Amendment XII.

The Electors shall meet in their respective states, and vote by ballot for President and Vice President, one of whom, at least, shall not be an inhabitant of the same state with themselves; they shall name in their ballots the person voted for as President, and in distinct ballots the person voted for as Vice-President, and they shall make distinct lists of all persons voted for as President, and of all persons voted for as Vice-President, and of the number of votes for each, which lists they shall sign and certify, and transmit sealed to the seat of the government of the United States, directed to the President of the Senate;—The President of the Senate shall, in the presence of the Senate and House of Representatives, open all the certificates and the votes shall then be counted;— The person having the greatest number of votes for President, shall be the President, if such number be a majority of the whole number of Electors appointed; and if no person have such majority, then from the persons having the highest numbers not exceeding three on the list of those voted for as President, the House of Representatives shall choose immediately, by ballot, the President. But in choosing the President, the votes shall be taken by states, the representation from each state having one vote; a quorum for this purpose shall consist of a member or members from two-thirds of the states, and a majority of all the states shall be necessary to a choice. And if the House of Representatives shall not choose a President whenever the right of choice shall devolve upon them, before the fourth day of March next following, then the Vice-President shall act as President, as in the case of the death or other constitutional disability of the President.—The person having the greatest number of votes as Vice-President, shall be the Vice-President, if such number be a majority of the whole number of Electors appointed, and if no person have a majority, then from the two highest numbers on the list, the Senate shall choose the Vice-President; a quorum for the purpose shall consist of two-thirds of the whole number of Senators, and a majority of the whole number shall be necessary to a choice. But no person constitutionally ineligible to the office of President shall be eligible to that of Vice-President of the United States.

[ratified June, 1804]

Amendment XIII.

SECTION 1. Neither slavery nor involuntary servitude, except as a punishment for crime whereof the party shall have been duly convicted, shall exist within the United States, or any place subject to their jurisdiction.

SECTION 2. Congress shall have power to enforce this article by appropriate legislation.

[ratified December, 1865]

Amendment XIV.

SECTION 1. All persons born or naturalized in the United States and subject to the jurisdiction thereof, are citizens of the United States and of the State wherein they reside. No State shall make or enforce any law which shall abridge the privileges or immunities of citizens of the United States; nor shall any State deprive any person of life, liberty, or property, without due process of law; nor deny to any person within its jurisdiction the equal protection of the laws.

SECTION 2. Representatives shall be apportioned among the several States according to their respective numbers, counting the whole number of persons in each State, excluding Indians not taxed. But when the right to vote at any election for the choice of electors for President and Vice President of the United States, Representatives in Congress, the Executive and Judicial officers of a State, or the members of the Legislature thereof, is denied to any of the male inhabitants of such State, being twenty-one years of age, and citizens of the United States, or in any way abridged, except for participation in rebellion, or other crime, the basis of representation therein shall be reduced in the proportion which the number of such male citizens shall bear to the whole number of male citizens twenty-one years of age in such State.

SECTION 3. No person shall be a Senator or Representative in Congress, or elector of President and Vice President, or hold any office, civil or military, under the United States, or under any State, who, having previously taken an oath, as a member of Congress, or as an officer of the United States, or as a member of any State legislature, or as an executive or judicial officer of any State, to support the Constitution of the United States, shall have engaged in insurrection or rebellion against the same, or given aid or comfort to the enemies thereof. But Congress may by a vote of two-thirds of each House, remove such disability.

SECTION 4. The validity of the public debt of the United States, authorized by law, including debts incurred for payment of pensions and bounties for services in suppressing insurrection or rebellion, shall not be questioned. But neither the United States nor any State shall assume or pay any debt or obligation incurred in aid of insurrection or rebellion against the United States, or any claim for the loss or emancipation of any slave; but all such debts, obligations and claims shall be held illegal and void.

SECTION 5. The Congress shall have power to enforce, by appropriate legislation, the provisions of this article.

[ratified July, 1868]

Amendment XV.

SECTION 1. The right of citizens of the United States to vote shall not be denied or abridged by the United States or by any State on account of race, color, or previous condition of servitude.

SECTION 2. The Congress shall have power to enforce this article by appropriate legislation.

[ratified February, 1870]

Amendment XVI.

The Congress shall have power to lay and collect taxes on incomes, from whatever source derived, without apportionment among the several States, and without regard to any census or enumeration.

[ratified February, 1913]

Amendment XVII.

The Senate of the United States shall be composed of two Senators from each State, elected by the people thereof, for six years; and each Senator shall have one vote. The electors in each State shall have the qualifications requisite for electors of the most numerous branch of the State legislatures.

When vacancies happen in the representation of any State in the Senate, the executive authority of such State shall issue writs of election to fill such vacancies: *Provided*, That the legislature of any State may empower the executive thereof to make temporary appointments until the people fill the vacancies by election as the legislature may direct.

This amendment shall not be so construed as to affect the election or term of any Senator chosen before it becomes valid as part of the Constitution.

[ratified April, 1913]

Amendment XVIII.

SECTION 1. After one year from the ratification of this article the manufacture, sale, or transportation of intoxicating liquors within, the importation thereof into, or the exportation thereof from the United States and all territory subject to the jurisdiction thereof for beverage purposes is hereby prohibited.

SECTION 2. The Congress and the several States shall have concurrent power to enforce this article by appropriate legislation.

SECTION 3. This article shall be inoperative unless it shall have been ratified as an amendment to the Constitution by the legislatures of the several States, as provided in the Constitution, within seven years from the date of the submission hereof to the States by the Congress.

[ratified January, 1919, repealed December, 1933]

Amendment XIX.

The right of citizens of the United States to vote shall not be denied or abridged by the United States or by any State on account of sex.

Congress shall have power to enforce this article by appropriate legislation.

[ratified August, 1920]

Amendment XX.

SECTION 1. The terms of the President and Vice President shall end at noon on the 20th day of January, and the terms of Senators and Representatives at noon on the 3d day of January, of the years in which such terms would have ended if this article had not been ratified; and the terms of their successors shall then begin.

SECTION 2. The Congress shall assemble at least once in every year, and such meeting shall begin at noon on the 3d day of January, unless they shall by law appoint a different day.

SECTION 3. If, at the time fixed for the beginning of the term of the President, the President elect shall have died, the Vice President elect shall become President. If a President shall not have been chosen before the time fixed for the beginning of his term, or if the President elect shall have failed to qualify, then the Vice President elect shall act as President until a President shall have qualified; and the Congress may by law provide for the case wherein neither a President elect nor a Vice President elect shall have qualified, declaring who shall then act as President, or the manner in which one who is to act shall be selected, and such person shall act accordingly until a President or Vice President shall have qualified.

SECTION 4. The Congress may by law provide for the case of the death of any of the persons from whom the House of Representatives may choose a President whenever the right of choice shall have devolved upon them, and for the case of the death of any of the persons from whom the Senate may choose a Vice President whenever the right of choice shall have devolved upon them.

SECTION 5. Sections 1 and 2 shall take effect on the 15th day of October following the ratification of this article.

SECTION 6. This article shall be inoperative unless it shall have been ratified as an amendment to the Constitution by the legislatures of three-fourths of the several States within seven years from the date of its submission.

[ratified January, 1933]

Amendment XXI.

SECTION 1. The eighteenth article of amendment to the Constitution of the United States is hereby repealed.

SECTION 2. The transportation or importation into any State, Territory, or possession of the United States for delivery or use therein of intoxicating liquors, in violation of the laws thereof, is hereby prohibited.

SECTION 3. This article shall be inoperative unless it shall have been ratified as an amendment to the Constitution by conventions in the several States, as provided in the Constitution, within seven years from the date of the submission hereof to the States by the Congress.

[ratified December, 1933]

Amendment XXII.

SECTION 1. No person shall be elected to the office of the President more than twice, and no person who has held the office of President, or acted as President, for more than two years of a term to which some other person was elected President shall be elected to the office of the President more than once. But this Article shall not apply to any person holding the office of President when this Article was proposed by the Congress, and shall not prevent any person who may be holding the office of President, or acting as President, during the term within which this Article becomes operative from holding the office of President or acting as President during the remainder of such term.

SECTION 2. This article shall be inoperative unless it shall have been ratified as an amendment to the Constitution by the legislatures of three-fourths of the several States within seven years from the date of its submission to the States by the Congress.

[ratified February, 1951]

Amendment XXIII.

SECTION 1. The District constituting the seat of Government of the United States shall appoint in such manner as the Congress may direct:

A number of electors of President and Vice President equal to the whole number of Senators and Representatives in Congress to which the District would be entitled if it were a State, but in no event more than the least populous State; they shall be in addition to those appointed by the States, but they shall be considered, for the purposes of the election of President and Vice President, to be electors appointed by a State; and they shall meet in the District and perform such duties as provided by the twelfth article of amendment.

SECTION 2. The Congress shall have power to enforce this article by appropriate legislation.

[ratified March, 1961]

Amendment XXIV.

SECTION 1. The right of citizens of the United States to vote in any primary or other election for President or Vice President, for electors for President or Vice President, or for Senator or Representative in Congress, shall not be denied or abridged by the United States or any State by reason of failure to pay any poll tax or other tax.

SECTION 2. The Congress shall have power to enforce this article by appropriate legislation.

[ratified January, 1964]

Amendment XXV.

SECTION 1. In case of the removal of the President from office or of his death or resignation, the Vice President shall become President.

SECTION 2. Whenever there is a vacancy in the office of the Vice President, the President shall nominate a Vice President who shall take office upon confirmation by a majority vote of both Houses of Congress.

SECTION 3. Whenever the President transmits to the President pro tempore of the Senate and the Speaker of the House of Representatives his written declaration that he is unable to discharge the powers and duties of his office, and until he transmits to them a written declaration to the contrary, such powers and duties shall be discharged by the Vice President as Acting President.

SECTION 4. Whenever the Vice President and a majority of either the principal officers of the executive departments or of such other body as Congress may by law provide, transmit to the President pro tempore of the Senate and the Speaker of the House of Representatives their written declaration that the President is unable to discharge the powers and duties of his office, the Vice President shall immediately assume the powers and duties of the office as Acting President.

Thereafter, when the President transmits to the President pro tempore of the Senate and the

Speaker of the House of Representatives his written declaration that no inability exists, he shall resume the powers and duties of his office unless the Vice President and a majority of either the principal officers of the executive department or of such other body as Congress may by law provide, transmit within four days to the President pro tempore of the Senate and the Speaker of the House of Representatives their written declaration that the President is unable to discharge the powers and duties of his office. Thereupon Congress shall decide the issue, assembling within forty-eight hours for that purpose if not in session. If the Congress, within twenty-one days after receipt of the latter written declaration, or, if Congress is not in session, within twenty-one days after Congress is required to assemble, determines by two-thirds vote of both Houses that the President is unable to discharge the powers and duties of his office, the Vice President shall continue to discharge the same as Acting President; otherwise, the President shall resume the powers and duties of his office.

[ratified February, 1967]

Amendment XXVI.

SECTION 1. The right of citizens of the United States, who are eighteen years of age or older, to vote shall not be denied or abridged by the United States or by any State on account of age.

SECTION 2. The Congress shall have power to enforce this article by appropriate legislation.

[ratified July, 1971]

Amendment XXVII.

No law, varying the compensation for the services of the Senators and Representatives, shall take effect, until an election of Representatives shall have intervened.

[ratified May 7, 1992]

Law of Presidential Succession

The following legislation was first approved July 18, 1947. It was amended September 9, 1965; October 15, 1966; August 4, 1977; and September 27, 1979.

If by reason of death, resignation, removal from office, inability, or failure to qualify there is neither a president nor vice president to discharge the powers and duties of the office of president, then the speaker of the House of Representatives shall upon his resignation as speaker and as representative, act as president. The same rule shall apply in the case of the death, resignation, removal from office, or inability of an individual acting as president.

If at the time when a speaker is to begin the discharge of the powers and duties of the office of president there is no speaker, or the speaker fails to qualify as acting president, then the president pro tempore of the Senate, upon his resignation as president pro tempore and as senator, shall act as president.

An individual acting as president shall continue to act until the expiration of the then current presidential term, except that (1) if his discharge of the powers and duties of the office is founded in whole or in part in the failure of both the president-elect and the vice president-elect to qualify, then he shall act only until a president qualifies, and (2) if his discharge of the powers and duties of the office is founded in whole or in part on the inability of the president or vice president, then he shall act only until the removal of the disability of one of such individuals.

If, by reason of death, resignation, removal from office, or failure to qualify, there is no president pro tempore to act as president, then the officer of the United States who is highest on the following list, and who is not under any disability to discharge the powers and duties of president shall act as president; the secretaries of state, treasury, defense, attorney general; secretaries of interior, agriculture, commerce, labor, health and human services, housing and urban development, transportation, energy, education, veterans affairs.

Time Line

Washington

1732, February 11:	George Washington is born in Westmoreland County, Virginia.
1755, July 9:	After General Edward Braddock's defeat near Fort Duquesne, Pennsylvania, Washington withdraws his defeated army.
1759, January 6:	Washington marries Martha Dandridge Custis, the widow of Daniel Parke Custis, in New Kent County, Virginia.
1775, June 15:	Congress names Washington as general and commander in chief of the Army of the United Colonies.
1776, March 17:	Washington forces the British to evacuate Boston.
1776, August 27:	Washington is defeated at the Battle of Long Island.
1776, December 26:	Washington defeats the Hessians at the Battle of Trenton.
1777, December 19:	The Continental Army goes into winter quarters at Valley Forge.
1781, October 19:	Lord Cornwallis surrenders to Washington at Yorktown.
1783, September 3:	A peace treaty ends the Revolutionary War.
1783, December 23:	Washington resigns his commission and returns to private life.
1787, May 25:	Washington is unanimously elected president of the Constitutional Convention.
1789, February 4:	Washington is unanimously elected the first president of the United States.
1789, April 30:	Washington is inaugurated at Federal Hall in New York City.
1789, July 4:	The first tariff act places duties on imports.
1789, August 4:	The first federal bond is issued to fund domestic and state debt.
1790, March 1:	The first U.S. census is authorized.
1790, July 16:	Congress locates the national capital in the District of Columbia.
1791, March 4:	Vermont is admitted as the fourteenth state.
1791, December 15:	The first ten amendments to the Constitution (the Bill of Rights) are ratified.
1792, June 1:	Kentucky is admitted as the fifteenth state.
1792, December 5:	Washington is unanimously reelected president.
1793, March 4:	Washington is inaugurated in Philadelphia for a second term.
1794, July-November:	The Whiskey Rebellion occurs in western Pennsylvania.
1796, June 1:	Tennessee is admitted as the sixteenth state.
1796, September 17:	Washington issues his farewell address.
1799, December 14:	George Washington dies at Mount Vernon, Virginia.

J. Adams

1735, October 30:	John Adams is born in Braintree, Massachusetts.
1764, October 25:	Adams marries Abigail Smith in Weymouth, Massachusetts.

1774, September 5-1776:	Adams serves as a delegate to the First and Second Continental Congresses.
1776:	Adams serves on the committee to draft the Declaration of Independence.
1780, December 29:	Adams arrives as minister to the Netherlands, where he negotiates a loan and treaty.
1785, May 14:	Adams arrives as minister to England, where he serves until 1788.
1789, April 21:	Adams is inaugurated as vice president under George Washington in New York City.
1793, March 4:	Adams is inaugurated as vice president for a second term.
1796, November:	Adams is elected president.
1797, March 4:	Adams is inaugurated as President.
1798, June 25:	The Alien Act is passed.
1798, July 11:	The U.S. Marine Corps is established.
1798, July 14:	The Sedition Act is passed.
1800, April 24:	The Library of Congress is established.
1800, June 15:	The capital of the United States is moved to the District of Columbia.
1800, November 4:	Adams is defeated for reelection by Thomas Jefferson.
1801, March 4:	Adams retires to Quincy, Massachusetts.
1818, October 28:	Abigail Adams dies in Quincy.
1826, July 4:	John Adams dies in Quincy; Thomas Jefferson dies on the same day.

Jefferson

1743, April 13:	Thomas Jefferson is born in Shadwell, Goochland (now Albemarle) County, Virginia.
1769:	Jefferson begins building his home at Monticello, Virginia.
1769, May 11:	Jefferson begins service as a member of the Virginia House of Burgesses, where he serves until 1774.
1772, January 1:	Jefferson marries Martha Wayles Skelton, the widow of Bathurst Skelton, in Williamsburg, Virginia.
1774, August:	Jefferson publishes *A Summary View of the Rights of British America*.
1775, June-December:	Jefferson serves as a delegate to the Continental Congress.
1776, June 10-July 2:	Jefferson chairs the committee to prepare the Declaration of Independence.
1779, June 1:	Jefferson is elected governor of Virginia.
1780, June 2:	Jefferson is reelected governor of Virginia.
1782, September 6:	Martha Jefferson dies at Monticello.
1783, June:	Jefferson drafts a constitution for Virginia.
1785, March 10:	Jefferson succeeds Benjamin Franklin as minister to France.
1789, September 26:	Jefferson is confirmed by the U.S. Senate as the first secretary of state.
1800, November 4:	A presidential election is held; Jefferson and Aaron Burr tie for first place, and the election is referred to the House of Representatives.
1801, February 11:	Jefferson is elected president by the House of Representatives.
1801, March 4:	Jefferson is inaugurated as president.
1801-1805:	The United States fights a war against the Barbary pirates of Tripoli.

1802, March 16:	The first U.S. military academy is authorized; it opens on July 4, 1802, at West Point.
1803, February 24:	The Supreme Court decides the case of *Marbury v. Madison*, establishing its power to declare laws of Congress unconstitutional.
1803, March 1:	Ohio is admitted as the seventeenth state.
1803, April 30:	Jefferson purchases the Louisiana Territory from France for $15 million.
1804, May 14:	Meriwether Lewis and William Clark begin their expedition to the Pacific Ocean.
1804, September 25:	The Twelfth Amendment to the Constitution is ratified, requiring the separate election of the president and vice president.
1804, November 6:	Jefferson is reelected president.
1805, March 4:	Jefferson inaugurated as president for a second term.
1807, August 7:	Robert Fulton sails the steamboat *Clermont* on the Hudson River.
1807, December 22:	The Embargo Act forbids Americans to trade with warring European powers.
1808, January 1:	The importation of slaves from Africa is prohibited.
1826, July 4:	Thomas Jefferson dies in Charlottesville, Virginia; John Adams dies on the same day.

Madison

1751, March 16:	James Madison is born in Port Conway, Virginia.
1776:	Madison drafts Virginia's guarantee of religious liberty and helps write the state constitution.
1776-1777:	Madison is active in Virginia's revolutionary government.
1780-1783 and 1786-1788:	Madison serves as a member of the Continental Congress.
1787:	Madison is made a member of the Constitutional Convention; he writes essays for *The Federalist*.
1794, September 15:	Madison marries Dolley Dandridge Payne Todd, the widow of John Todd, in Harewood, Virginia.
1801-1809:	Madison serves as secretary of state in the Jefferson administration.
1808, November:	Madison is elected president.
1809, March 4:	Madison is inaugurated as president.
1811, November 7:	General William Henry Harrison defeats American Indians at the Battle of Tippecanoe.
1812, April 30:	Louisiana is admitted as the eighteenth state.
1812, May:	Madison is renominated for president.
1812, June 18:	War is declared against Great Britain.
1812, November:	Madison is reelected president.
1813, March 4:	Madison is inaugurated as president for a second term.
1813, September 10:	Oliver Hazard Perry wins a victory on Lake Erie.
1814, August 24:	British troops capture Washington, D.C., and burn the White House.
1814, September 13:	British troops are repulsed in an attack on Fort McHenry in Baltimore; Francis Scott Key writes "The Star-Spangled Banner."
1814, December 24:	A peace treaty is signed with Great Britain.

1815, January 8:	Andrew Jackson defeats the British at the Battle of New Orleans.
1816, December 11:	Indiana is admitted as the nineteenth state.
1836, June 28:	James Madison dies in Montpelier, Virginia.

Monroe

1758, April 28:	James Monroe is born in Westmoreland County, Virginia.
1776, December 26:	Monroe is wounded at the Battle of Trenton and promoted to captain by George Washington for bravery under fire.
1776-1778:	Monroe fights in the Battles of Brandywine, Germantown, and Monmouth.
1783-1786:	Monroe is a member of the Continental Congress.
1786, February 16:	Monroe marries Elizabeth Kortright in New York City.
1788:	Monroe is a delegate to the Constitutional Convention.
1799-1803:	Monroe serves as governor of Virginia.
1803-1808:	Monroe represents the United States in France, England, and Spain.
1811-1817:	Monroe serves as secretary of state in the Madison administration.
1816, November:	Monroe is elected president.
1817:	The Rush-Bagot Agreement with Great Britain eliminates fortifications on the U.S.-Canadian border, leading to the world's longest undefended border.
1817, March 4:	Monroe is inaugurated as president.
1817, July 4:	Construction begins on the Erie Canal.
1817, December 10:	Mississippi is admitted as the twentieth state.
1818, April 4:	Congress establishes the official flag of the United States.
1818, December 3:	Illinois is admitted as the twenty-first state.
1819:	With a decision in the case of *McCulloch v. Maryland,* the Supreme Court establishes its power to declare state laws unconstitutional.
1819, February 22:	Florida is purchased from Spain.
1819, May 22:	The SS *Savannah,* the first U.S. steamship to cross the Atlantic Ocean, leaves Savannah, Georgia.
1819, December 14:	Alabama is admitted as the twenty-second state.
1820, March 3:	The Missouri Compromise prohibits slavery in the northern portion of the Louisiana Purchase.
1820, March 15:	Maine is admitted as the twenty-third state.
1820, November:	Monroe is reelected as president.
1821, March 5:	Monroe is inaugurated as president for a second term.
1821, August 10:	Missouri is admitted as the twenty-fourth state.
1823, December 2:	The Monroe Doctrine is proclaimed.
1825, March:	Monroe retires to his farm in Loudoun County, Virginia.
1830, September 23:	Elizabeth Monroe dies in Oak Hill, Virginia.
1831, July 4:	James Monroe dies in New York City.

J. Q. Adams

1767, July 11:	John Quincy Adams is born in Braintree, Massachusetts.
1794:	George Washington appoints Adams minister to the Netherlands.

1796-1797:	Adams serves as minister to Portugal and Prussia.
1797, July 26:	Adams marries Louisa Catherine Johnson in London.
1803-1808:	Adams represents Massachusetts in the U.S. Senate.
1809-1814:	Adams serves as minister to Russia.
1814:	Adams serves on a peace commission to end the War of 1812.
1815-1817:	Adams serves as minister to England.
1817-1825:	Adams serves as secretary of state.
1824, November 2:	A presidential election is held; none of the four candidates receives a majority of the electoral votes.
1825, February 9:	House of Representatives elects Adams president.
1825, March 4:	Adams is inaugurated as president.
1825, October 25:	The Erie Canal opens.
1828, November 4:	Adams is defeated for reelection by Democratic nominee Andrew Jackson.
1831-1848:	Adams serves as a member of the U.S. House of Representatives.
1848, February 23:	John Quincy Adams has a stroke on the floor of the House of Representatives and dies in Washington, D.C.

Jackson

1767, March 15:	Andrew Jackson is born in Waxhaw area, South Carolina.
1784:	Jackson studies law in Salisbury, North Carolina.
1787:	Jackson fights his first duel, with Waightstill Avery.
1791, August:	Jackson marries Rachel Stockley Donelson, the estranged wife of Lewis Robards; Jackson and Rachel later remarry on January 17, 1794.
1796-1797:	Jackson represents Tennessee in the U.S. House of Representatives.
1797-1798:	Jackson serves in the U.S. Senate for Tennessee.
1798-1804	Jackson serves as a judge of the Tennessee Supreme Court.
1806, May 30:	Jackson kills Charles Dickinson in a duel.
1814:	Jackson leads the U.S. Army in campaigns against the Creeks.
1815, January 8:	Jackson defeats British troops at the Battle of New Orleans.
1817-1818:	Jackson fights against the Seminoles in Florida.
1823-1825:	Jackson serves in the U.S. Senate.
1824:	Jackson is an unsuccessful candidate for president.
1828, November 4:	Jackson is elected president.
1828, December 22:	Rachel Jackson dies.
1829, March 4:	Jackson is inaugurated as president.
1830:	The Webster-Hayne Debates on states' rights take place.
1832, May:	Jackson is nominated for president by the Democratic Party.
1832, November 6:	Jackson is reelected president.
1832, November 24:	South Carolina declares federal tariff acts "null and void."
1832, December:	Jackson issues the Nullification Proclamation; crisis is narrowly avoided.
1833, March 4:	Jackson is inaugurated as president for a second term.
1834, March 28:	Jackson is censured by the U.S. Senate for removing public deposits from the Bank of the United States.

1836, March 1:	Texas declares its independence from Mexico.
1836, March 6:	The Alamo falls; its defenders are slaughtered.
1836, April 21:	Texans defeat Mexican general Antonio López de Santa Anna at the Battle of San Jacinto.
1836, June 15:	Arkansas is admitted as the twenty-fifth state.
1837, January 26:	Michigan is admitted as the twenty-sixth state.
1837, March:	Jackson recognizes the independence of Texas.
1837, March 16:	The Senate expunges its 1834 censure resolution.
1845, June 8:	Andrew Jackson dies in Nashville, Tennessee.

Van Buren

1782, December 5:	Martin Van Buren is born in Kinderhook, New York.
1807, February 21:	Van Buren marries Hannah Hoes in Catskill, New York.
1813-1820:	Van Buren serves in New York State Senate.
1815-1819:	Van Buren serves as attorney general for New York.
1819, February 5:	Hannah Van Buren dies in Albany, New York.
1821-1828:	Van Buren represents New York in the U.S. Senate.
1829:	Van Buren serves as governor of New York.
1829-1831:	Van Buren is secretary of state in the Jackson administration.
1833-1837:	Van Buren serves as vice president in the Jackson administration.
1836, November 1:	Van Buren is elected president.
1837, March 4:	Van Buren is inaugurated as president.
1838-1839:	The Cherokees are removed from the South to Oklahoma on the Trail of Tears.
1840, November 3:	Van Buren is defeated for reelection by Whig nominee William Henry Harrison.
1844:	Van Buren is defeated in an attempt at renomination by the Democratic Party.
1848:	Van Buren is unsuccessful as the Free-Soil Party candidate for president; he retires from public life.
1862, July 24:	Martin Van Buren dies in Kinderhook, New York.

W. H. Harrison

1773, February 9:	William Henry Harrison is born near Charles City, Virginia.
1791, August 16:	Harrison is commissioned by General George Washington.
1794-1798:	Harrison serves as a soldier in the Northwest Territory.
1795, November 25:	Harrison marries Anna Tuthill Symmes in North Bend, Ohio.
1799-1800:	Harrison serves in the U.S. House of Representatives for the Northwest Territory.
1800-1813:	Harrison serves as territorial governor of Indiana.
1811, November 7:	Harrison wins the Battle of Tippecanoe.
1812-1814:	Harrison serves as a general during the War of 1812.
1813, October 5:	Harrison defeats British troops and American Indians in the Battle of the Thames.
1816-1819:	Harrison represents Ohio in the U.S. House of Representatives.

1825-1828:	Harrison represents Ohio in the U.S. Senate.
1829:	Harrison retires to his farm in North Bend, Ohio.
1836:	Harrison is unsuccessful as the Whig candidate for president.
1839, December 4-7:	Harrison is nominated for president by the Whig Party.
1840, November 3:	Harrison is elected president.
1841, March 4:	Harrison is inaugurated as president.
1841, April 4:	William Henry Harrison dies in the White House, Washington, D.C.

Tyler

1790, March 29:	John Tyler is born in Greenway, Charles City County, Virginia.
1811-1816:	Tyler serves as a member of the Virginia House of Delegates.
1813, March 29:	Tyler marries Letitia Christian at Cedar Grove in New Kent County, Virginia.
1817-1821:	Tyler represents Virginia in the U.S. House of Representatives.
1825-1827:	Tyler serves as governor of Virginia.
1827-1836:	Tyler represents Virginia in the U.S. Senate.
1839, December 4-7:	Tyler is nominated by the Whig Party for vice president.
1840, November 3:	Tyler is elected vice president.
1841, April 6:	Tyler takes the oath of president on the death of William Henry Harrison.
1842, September 10:	Letitia Tyler dies in the White House, Washington, D.C.
1844, June 26:	Tyler marries Julia Gardiner in New York City.
1845, March 1:	Texas is annexed by a joint resolution of Congress.
1845, March 3:	Florida is admitted as the twenty-seventh state.
1861, March 1:	Tyler serves as a member of the Virginia secession convention.
1861, July 20:	Tyler is a delegate to the Confederate Provisional Congress.
1862, January 18:	John Tyler dies in Richmond, Virginia.

Polk

1795, November 2:	James K. Polk is born in Mecklenburg County, North Carolina.
1823-1825:	Polk serves in the Tennessee House of Representatives.
1824, January 1:	Polk marries Sarah Childress in Murfreesboro, Tennessee.
1825-1839:	Polk represents Tennessee in the U.S. House of Representatives.
1835, December 7:	Polk is elected Speaker of the House of Representatives; he serves until March 3, 1839.
1839-1841:	Polk serves as governor of Tennessee.
1844, May 27-30:	The Democratic convention in Baltimore nominates Polk as the first "dark horse" candidate.
1844, November 5:	Polk is elected president.
1845, March 4:	Polk is inaugurated as president.
1845, October 10:	The U.S. Naval Academy opens in Annapolis, Maryland.
1845, December 29:	Texas is admitted as the twenty-eighth state.
1846, May 8:	The Battle of Palo Alto is fought against Mexican troops.
1846, May 13:	The United States formally declares war on Mexico.
1846, December 28:	Iowa is admitted as the twenty-ninth state.

1847:	U.S. forces conquer California.
1847, February 23:	General Zachary Taylor wins the Battle of Buena Vista.
1847, March 29:	U.S. troops under General Winfield Scott capture Vera Cruz on the Mexican coast.
1847, September 14:	General Scott captures Mexico City.
1848, January 24:	Gold is discovered in California.
1848, February 2:	The Treaty of Guadalupe Hidalgo ends the Mexican War.
1848, May 29:	Wisconsin is admitted as the thirtieth state.
1848, July 4:	Polk lays the cornerstone of the Washington Monument.
1849:	Polk declines to be a candidate for reelection; he retires to Nashville.
1849, June 15:	James K. Polk dies in Nashville, Tennessee.

Taylor

1784, November 24:	Zachary Taylor is born in Orange County, Virginia.
1808, May 3:	Taylor is commissioned a first lieutenant in the U.S. Army.
1810, June 21:	Taylor marries Margaret Mackall Smith in Louisville, Kentucky.
1812, September:	Taylor defends Fort Harrison against American Indians led by Tecumseh; he is promoted to the rank of brevet major for his gallantry.
1837, December 25:	Taylor is promoted to brevet brigadier general for distinguished service against the Seminoles.
1846, May 8:	Taylor defeats Mexican troops at the Battle of Palo Alto.
1846, May 9:	Taylor defeats Mexican troops at the Battle of Resaca de la Palma.
1846, May 18:	Taylor maneuvers the Mexican army out of Matamoros without a battle.
1846, May 28:	Taylor is promoted to brevet major general for distinguished service.
1846, June 29:	Taylor is promoted to general of the line.
1846, September 25:	Taylor captures Monterey.
1847, February 23:	Taylor defeats the Mexican army under General Antonio López de Santa Anna at the Battle of Buena Vista.
1848, July 18:	Taylor is nominated for president by the Whig Party.
1848, November 7:	Taylor is elected president.
1849, March 4:	Taylor is inaugurated as president.
1850, July 9:	Zachary Taylor dies in Washington, D.C.

Fillmore

1800, January 7:	Millard Fillmore is born in Summerhill, New York.
1826, February 5:	Fillmore marries Abigail Powers in Moravia, New York.
1829-1831:	Fillmore serves in the New York State Assembly.
1833-1835 and 1837-1843:	Fillmore represents New York in the U.S. House of Representatives.
1848, July 7-9	Fillmore is nominated for vice president by the Whig Party.
1848, November 7:	Fillmore is elected vice president.
1850, July 10:	Fillmore assumes the presidency upon the death of Zachary Taylor.
1850, September 18:	A fugitive slave law is enacted.

1852:	Harriet Beecher Stowe publishes the abolitionist novel *Uncle Tom's Cabin*.
1852, June:	Fillmore is denied nomination for president by the Whig Party.
1852, November:	Commodore Matthew C. Perry opens Japan to Western commerce.
1853, March 30:	Abigail Fillmore dies in Washington, D.C.
1856, November:	Fillmore is unsuccessful as the presidential candidate for the Know-Nothing Party.
1858, February 10:	Fillmore marries Caroline Carmichael McIntosh, the widow of Ezekiel C. McIntosh, in Albany, New York.
1874, March 8:	Millard Fillmore dies in Buffalo, New York.

Pierce

1804, November 23:	Franklin Pierce is born in Hillsborough, New Hampshire.
1829-1833:	Pierce serves in the New Hampshire House of Representatives; he serves as speaker in 1832.
1833-1837:	Pierce represents New Hampshire in the U.S. House of Representatives.
1834, November 10:	Pierce marries Jane Means Appleton in Amherst, New Hampshire.
1837-1842:	Pierce represents New Hampshire in the U.S. Senate.
1847:	Pierce enlists as a private in the Mexican War, rising to the rank of major general.
1852, June 1-5:	Pierce is nominated for president by the Democratic Party.
1852, November 2:	Pierce is elected president.
1853, March 4:	Pierce is inaugurated as president.
1854:	The Republican Party is founded.
1854, May 22:	Congress enacts the Kansas-Nebraska Act, nullifying the Missouri Compromise.
1854, June 30:	The Gadsden Purchase of border territory from Mexico is negotiated.
1856:	Pierce is denied renomination for president by the Democratic Party.
1863, December 2:	Jane Pierce dies in Andover, Massachusetts.
1869, October 8:	Franklin Pierce dies in Concord, New Hampshire.

Buchanan

1791, April 23:	James Buchanan is born in Mercerburg, Pennsylvania.
1814:	Buchanan serves in the War of 1812.
1814-1815:	Buchanan serves in the Pennsylvania House of Representatives.
1821-1831:	Buchanan represents Pennsylvania in the U.S. House of Representatives.
1832-1833:	Buchanan serves as minister to Russia.
1834-1845:	Buchanan represents Pennsylvania in the U.S. Senate.
1845-1849:	Buchanan serves as secretary of state in the Polk administration.
1856, June 2-6:	Buchanan is nominated for president by the Democratic Party.
1856, November 4:	Buchanan is elected president.
1857, March 4:	Buchanan is inaugurated as president.
1857, March 6:	The U.S. Supreme Court announces the Dred Scott decision, rendering the Missouri Compromise unconstitutional.

1858, May 11:	Minnesota is admitted as the thirty-second state.
1858, August-October:	The Lincoln-Douglas debates take place.
1859, February 14:	Oregon is admitted as the thirty-third state.
1859, October 16:	John Brown seizes the federal arsenal at Harpers Ferry, Virginia.
1860, November 6:	Abraham Lincoln is elected president.
1860, December 20:	South Carolina secedes from the Union.
1861, January-February:	Mississippi, Florida, Alabama, Georgia, Louisiana, and Texas secede.
1861, January 29:	Kansas is admitted as the thirty-fourth state.
1861, February 8:	The Confederate States of America is established.
1868, June 1:	James Buchanan dies in Lancaster, Pennsylvania.

Lincoln

1809, February 12:	Abraham Lincoln is born near Hodgenville, Kentucky.
1832:	Lincoln serves in the volunteer militia during Black Hawk's War.
1835-1836:	Lincoln serves in the Illinois General Assembly.
1842, November 4:	Lincoln marries Mary Todd in Springfield, Illinois.
1847-1849:	Lincoln represents Illinois in the U.S. House of Representatives.
1858, August-October:	Lincoln debates Stephen A. Douglas in the campaign for U.S. Senate.
1860, May 16-18:	Lincoln is nominated for president by the Republican Party.
1860, November 6:	Lincoln is elected president.
1860, December 20:	South Carolina secedes from the Union.
1861, January-February:	Mississippi, Florida, Alabama, Georgia, Louisiana, and Texas secede.
1861, February 8:	The Confederate States of America is established.
1861, March 4:	Lincoln is inaugurated as president.
1861, April-June:	Virginia, Arkansas, North Carolina, and Tennessee secede.
1861, April 12:	Confederate forces fire on Fort Sumter in Charleston harbor.
1861, April 15:	Lincoln issues call for volunteers.
1861, July 21:	The Union army is routed at the First Battle of Bull Run (Manassas).
1862, March 9:	The battle between the first ironclad warships, *Monitor* and *Virginia* (*Merrimac*) takes place.
1862, April 6-7:	The Battle of Shiloh is fought.
1862, September 17:	The Battle of Antietam ends Confederate general Robert E. Lee's first invasion of the northern states.
1862, September 22:	A preliminary Emancipation Proclamation is issued.
1863, January 1:	The Emancipation Proclamation is issued.
1863, June 19:	West Virginia is admitted as the thirty-fifth state.
1863, July 1-3:	Confederate troops under General Lee are defeated at Gettysburg.
1863, July 4:	Vicksburg surrenders to Union general Ulysses S. Grant.
1863, November 19:	Lincoln delivers the Gettysburg Address.
1864, June 7-8:	Lincoln is renominated for president by the Republican Party.
1864, September 2:	Union General William Tecumseh Sherman captures Atlanta.
1864, October 31:	Nevada is admitted as the thirty-sixth state.
1864, November 8:	Lincoln is reelected as president.
1865, March 4:	Lincoln is inaugurated as president for a second term.
1865, April 9:	Lee surrenders to Grant at Appomattox Courthouse, Virginia.

1865, April 14:	President Lincoln is shot by John Wilkes Booth at Ford's Theater in Washington, D.C.
1865, April 15:	Abraham Lincoln dies from his wounds.

A. Johnson

1808, December 29:	Andrew Johnson is born in Raleigh, North Carolina.
1827, Mary 17:	Johnson marries Eliza McCardle in Greeneville, Tennessee.
1828:	Johnson serves as leader of the Workingmen's Party in Tennessee; he is elected alderman in Greeneville.
1830-1833:	Johnson serves three terms as mayor of Greeneville.
1835-1837 and 1839:	Johnson serves in the Tennessee legislature.
1843-1853:	Johnson represents Tennessee in the U.S. House of Representatives.
1853-1855:	Johnson serves as governor of Tennessee.
1857-1862:	Johnson represents Tennessee in the U.S. Senate.
1862-1865:	Johnson serves as military governor of Tennessee.
1864, June 7-8	Democrat Johnson is nominated for vice president on the Union Party ticket with Republican Abraham Lincoln.
1864, November 8:	Johnson is elected vice president.
1865, April 15:	Johnson assumes the presidency upon the assassination of Lincoln.
1865, April 26:	Confederate general Joseph E. Johnston surrenders to Union general William Tecumseh Sherman at Durham Station, North Carolina.
1865, May 26:	Confederate general Edmund Kirby-Smith surrenders the last major Confederate army, effectively ending the Civil War.
1865, December 18:	The Thirteenth Amendment to the Constitution is ratified, abolishing slavery.
1867:	Congress passes the Reconstruction Act against Johnson's opposition.
1867, March 1:	Nebraska is admitted as the thirty-seventh state.
1867, March 30:	The United States purchases Alaska from Russia.
1868, February 21:	The U.S. House of Representatives impeaches Johnson.
1868, March 13:	The impeachment trial begins in the Senate.
1868, May 26:	Johnson is acquitted of all charges.
1868, July 28:	The Fourteenth Amendment to the Constitution is ratified, establishing the civil rights of all citizens.
1868:	Johnson is denied nomination for president by the Democratic Party.
1874-1875:	Johnson represents Tennessee in the U.S. Senate.
1875, July 31:	Andrew Johnson dies near Carter Station, Tennessee.

Grant

1822, April 27:	Ulysses S. Grant is born in Port Pleasant, Ohio.
1839-1843:	Grant attends the U.S. military academy at West Point.
1846-1847:	Grant serves in the Mexican War and is promoted for gallant and meritorious conduct.
1848, August 22:	Grant marries Julia Boggs Dent in St. Louis, Missouri.
1854, July 31:	Grant resigns from the U.S. Army.

1854-1860:	Grant works in farming, in real estate, and in his father's hardware and leather store.
1861, May 17:	Grant is commissioned a brigadier general in the U.S. Volunteers.
1862, April 6-7:	Grant wins the Battle of Shiloh, one of the bloodiest of the Civil War.
1863, July 4:	Grant captures the Confederate fortress city of Vicksburg, Mississippi.
1863, November 24-25:	Grant wins the Battle of Chattanooga.
1864, March 9:	Grant is commissioned a lieutenant general and made commander in chief of the U.S. Army.
1865, April 9:	Grant accepts the surrender of Confederate general Robert E. Lee at Appomattox Courthouse, Virginia.
1866, July 25:	Grant is commissioned General of the Army.
1868, May 20-21:	Grant is nominated for president by the Republican Party.
1868, November 3:	Grant is elected president.
1869, March 4:	Grant is inaugurated as president.
1870, March 30:	The Fifteenth Amendment to the Constitution is ratified, extending voting rights.
1872, January 1:	The Civil Service Act becomes effective.
1872, June 5-6:	Grant is renominated for president by the Republican Party.
1872, November 5:	Grant is reelected president.
1873, March 4:	Grant is inaugurated as president for a second term.
1876, March 10:	Alexander Graham Bell transmits a human voice over the telephone.
1876, June 25:	Sitting Bull and the Sioux defeat General George Armstrong Custer at the Battle of the Little Bighorn.
1876, August 1:	Colorado is admitted as the thirty-eighth state.
1884:	Grant's financial ruin results from bad investments.
1885:	Grant completes his memoirs four days before his death.
1885, July 23:	Ulysses S. Grant dies in Mount McGregor, New York.

Hayes

1822, October 4:	Rutherford B. Hayes is born in Delaware, Ohio.
1852, December 30:	Hayes marries Lucy Ware Webb in Cincinnati, Ohio.
1861-1865:	Hayes serves in the Union army, rising to the rank of brevet major general of volunteers.
1865-1867:	Hayes represents Ohio in the U.S. House of Representatives.
1868 and 1876-1877:	Hayes serves as governor of Ohio.
1876, June 14-16:	Hayes is nominated for president by the Republican Party.
1876, November 7:	Presidential elections are held; the results are in doubt.
1877, March 2:	An electoral commission declares Hayes the winner.
1877, March 4:	Hayes is inaugurated as president.
1878, February 19:	Thomas Alva Edison obtains the first phonograph patent.
1879, October 21:	Edison invents the first practical electric light.
1880:	Hayes declines to run for a second term as president.
1889, June 25:	Lucy Hayes dies in Fremont, Ohio.
1893, January 17:	Rutherford B. Hayes dies in Fremont, Ohio.

Garfield

1831, November 19:	James A. Garfield is born in Orange Township, Ohio.
1857-1861:	Garfield serves as president of the Western Reserve Eclectic Institute; he teaches Latin, Greek, higher mathematics, history, philosophy, English literature, and rhetoric.
1858, November 11:	Garfield marries Lucretia Rudolph in Hiram, Ohio.
1859:	Garfield serves in the Ohio State Senate.
1861-1863:	Garfield serves in the Union army, rising to the rank of major general of volunteers.
1863, December 5:	Garfield resigns from the army to take a seat in the U.S. House of Representatives.
1877:	Garfield serves as a member of the electoral commission that decides the disputed presidential election of 1876.
1880, June:	Garfield is nominated for president by the Republican Party.
1880, November 2:	Garfield is elected president.
1881, March 4:	Garfield is inaugurated as president.
1881, May 21:	The American Red Cross is organized.
1881, July 2:	President Garfield is shot by Charles J. Guiteau in a Washington, D.C., train station.
1881, September 19:	James A. Garfield dies in Elberon, New Jersey.

Arthur

1829, October 5:	Chester A. Arthur is born in Fairfield, Vermont.
1859, October 25:	Arthur marries Ellen Lewis Herndon in New York City.
1861-1863:	Arthur serves in the Union army.
1871-1878:	Arthur serves as collector of the Port of New York.
1880, January 12:	Ellen Arthur dies in New York City.
1880, June:	Arthur is nominated for vice president by the Republican Party.
1880, November 2:	Arthur is elected vice president.
1881, July 2:	President James Garfield is shot by Charles J. Guiteau.
1881, September 20:	Arthur assumes the presidency on the death of Garfield.
1883, March 9:	The Civil Service Commission is organized.
1884:	Arthur is the unsuccessful candidate for the Republican presidential nomination.
1885, February 21:	The Washington Monument is dedicated.
1886, November 18:	Chester A. Arthur dies in New York, New York.

Cleveland

1837, March 18:	Grover Cleveland is born in Caldwell, New Jersey.
1883-1885:	Cleveland serves as governor of New York.
1884, July 11:	Cleveland is nominated for president by the Democratic Party.
1884, November 4:	Cleveland is elected president.
1885, March 4:	Cleveland is inaugurated as president.
1886, March 22:	The first Interstate Commerce Commission is appointed.

1886, May 17:	The Haymarket Riot in Chicago leaves eleven people dead and more than one hundred wounded.
1886, June 2:	Cleveland marries Frances Folsom in Washington, D.C.
1886, October 28:	The Statue of Liberty is dedicated in New York harbor.
1886, December:	The American Federation of Labor is organized.
1887, February 4:	Congress passes the Interstate Commerce Act.
1888, June 5:	Cleveland is renominated for president by the Democratic Party.
1888, November 5:	Republican candidate Benjamin Harrison defeats Cleveland.
1892, June 2:	Cleveland is nominated for president by the Democratic Party.
1892, November 8:	Cleveland is elected president, defeating Harrison.
1893, March 4:	Cleveland is inaugurated as president for a second term.
1893, July 1:	A secret operation removes cancer from Cleveland's mouth.
1894, May:	Cleveland sends federal troops to Chicago to calm the Pullman Strike.
1894, July 4:	Hawaii declares itself a republic.
1895, February 24:	A Cuban revolt begins against Spanish rule.
1895, May 20:	The U.S. Supreme Court declares income tax to be unconstitutional.
1896, January 4:	Utah is admitted as the forty-fifth state.
1901, October 15:	Cleveland becomes trustee of Princeton University.
1908, June 24:	Grover Cleveland dies in Princeton, New Jersey.

B. Harrison

1833, August 20:	Benjamin Harrison is born in North Bend, Ohio.
1853, October 20:	Harrison marries Caroline Lavinia Scott.
1862-1865:	Harrison serves in the Union army, rising to the rank of brevet brigadier general.
1881-1887:	Harrison represents Indiana in the U.S. Senate.
1888, June 23:	Harrison is nominated for president by the Republican Party.
1888, November 6:	Harrison is elected president.
1889, March 4:	Harrison is inaugurated as president.
1889, April 22:	Oklahoma is opened for settlers.
1889, May 31:	The Great Johnstown Flood occurs in Pennsylvania.
1889, November 2:	North Dakota and South Dakota are admitted as the thirty-ninth and fortieth states.
1889, November 8:	Montana is admitted as the forty-first state.
1889, November 11:	Washington is admitted as the forty-second state.
1890, July 2:	The Sherman Antitrust Act is enacted.
1890, July 3:	Idaho is admitted as the forty-third state.
1890, July 10:	Wyoming is admitted as the forty-fourth state.
1892, June 10:	Harrison is renominated for president by the Republican Party.
1892, October 25:	Caroline Harrison dies in Washington, D.C.
1892, November 8:	Harrison is defeated for reelection by Democratic nominee Grover Cleveland.
1896, April 6:	Harrison marries Mary Scott Lord Dimmick, the widow of Walter Erskine Dimmick, in New York City.
1901, March 13:	Benjamin Harrison dies in Indianapolis, Indiana.

McKinley

1843, January 29:	William McKinley is born in Niles, Ohio.
1861, June 11-1865:	McKinley serves in the Union army, rising from private to the rank of brevet major of volunteers.
1871, January 25:	McKinley marries Ida Saxton in Canton, Ohio.
1877-1883 and	
1885-1891:	McKinley represents Ohio in the U.S. House of Representatives.
1892-1896:	McKinley serves as governor of Ohio.
1896, June 18:	McKinley is nominated for president by the Republican Party.
1896, November 3:	McKinley is elected president.
1897, March 4:	McKinley is inaugurated as president.
1898, February 15:	The battleship USS *Maine* blows up in the harbor of Havana, Cuba.
1898, April 25:	The United States declares war on Spain.
1898, May 1:	Commodore George Dewey destroys the Spanish fleet in Manila Bay, Philippines.
1898, June 10:	U.S. Marines land in Cuba.
1898, July 7:	The United States annexes Hawaii.
1898, December 10:	The Treaty of Paris ends the Spanish-American War.
1899, April 11:	The Philippines, Puerto Rico, and Guam are formally acquired by the United States.
1900, June 21:	McKinley is renominated for president by the Republican Party.
1900, November 6:	McKinley is reelected president.
1901, March 4:	McKinley is inaugurated as president for a second term.
1901, September 6:	President McKinley is shot by anarchist Leon Czolgosz in Buffalo, New York.
1901, September 14:	William McKinley dies in Buffalo, New York.

T. Roosevelt

1858, October 27:	Theodore Roosevelt is born in New York, New York.
1880, October 27:	Roosevelt marries Alice Hathaway Lee in Brookline, Massachusetts.
1882-1884:	Roosevelt serves in the New York State Assembly.
1884, February 14:	Alice Roosevelt dies in New York City.
1886, December 2:	Roosevelt marries Edith Kermit Carow in London.
1889-1895:	Roosevelt serves on the U.S. Civil Service Commission.
1889, May 6:	Roosevelt is appointed president of the New York City Board of Police Commissioners.
1897, April 19:	Roosevelt is appointed assistant secretary of the Navy.
1898:	Roosevelt resigns his position and forms a volunteer cavalry regiment, called the Rough Riders, which serves in the Spanish-American War.
1899-1901:	Roosevelt serves as governor of New York.
1900, June 21:	Roosevelt is nominated for vice president by the Republican Party.
1900, November 6:	Roosevelt is elected vice president.
1901, March 4:	Roosevelt is inaugurated as vice president.
1901, September 14:	Roosevelt succeeds to the presidency on the death of William McKinley.
1902, May 20:	Cuba becomes a republic.

1903, November 3:	Panama declares its independence from Colombia.
1903, November 18:	The newly formed Republic of Panama grants the United States land for a canal.
1903, December 17:	The Wright brothers make the first powered airplane flight at Kitty Hawk, North Carolina.
1904, June 23:	Roosevelt is nominated for president by the Republican Party.
1904, November 8:	Roosevelt is elected president.
1905, March 4:	Roosevelt is inaugurated as president.
1905, September 5:	A Russo-Japanese peace treaty is signed in Portsmouth, New Hampshire.
1906:	Roosevelt is awarded the Nobel Peace Prize for helping end the Russo-Japanese War.
1906, April 18-20:	A powerful earthquake rocks San Francisco, leaving seven hundred dead.
1907, November 16:	Oklahoma is admitted as the forty-sixth state.
1907, December 16:	The American "Great White Fleet" sets sail on an around-the-world voyage.
1912, June:	Roosevelt is denied renomination for president by the Republican Party.
1912, August:	Roosevelt is nominated for president by the Progressive Party (Bull Moose Party).
1912, November 5:	Roosevelt is defeated by Democratic nominee Woodrow Wilson.
1919, January 6:	Theodore Roosevelt dies in Oyster Bay, New York.

Taft

1857, September 15:	William Howard Taft is born in Cincinnati, Ohio.
1886, June 19:	Taft marries Helen Herron in Cincinnati.
1890-1892:	Taft serves as U.S. solicitor general.
1892-1900:	Taft serves as a federal circuit court judge.
1896-1900:	Taft serves as dean of the University of Cincinnati Law School.
1901, July 4:	Taft is appointed governor-general of the Philippines.
1904-1908:	Taft serves as secretary of war in the Roosevelt administration.
1907:	Taft is made the provisional governor of Cuba.
1908, June 19:	Taft is nominated for president by the Republican Party.
1908, November 3:	Taft is elected president.
1909, March 4:	Taft is inaugurated as president.
1909, April 6:	Robert Edwin Peary reaches the North Pole.
1910, February 8:	The Boy Scouts of America is incorporated.
1912, January 6:	New Mexico is admitted as the forty-seventh state.
1912, February 14:	Arizona is admitted as the forty-eighth state.
1912, June 22:	Taft is renominated for president by the Republican Party.
1912, November 5:	Taft is defeated for reelection by Democratic candidate Woodrow Wilson.
1913-1921:	Taft serves as a professor of law at Yale University.
1913, February 25:	The Sixteenth Amendment to the Constitution is ratified, authorizing an income tax.

1921, June 30:	Taft becomes chief justice of the United States.
1930, February 3:	Taft steps down from the Supreme Court.
1930, March 8:	William Howard Taft dies in Washington, D.C.

Wilson

1856, December 28:	Woodrow Wilson is born in Staunton, Virginia.
1870:	His family moves from Augusta, Georgia, to Columbia, South Carolina.
1885, June 24:	Wilson marries Ellen Louise Axson in Savannah, Georgia.
1890-1902:	Wilson serves as professor of jurisprudence and political economy at Princeton University.
1902, June 9:	Wilson is unanimously elected president of Princeton University.
1910, September 15:	Wilson is nominated for governor of New Jersey by the Democratic Party.
1911-1913:	Wilson serves as governor of New Jersey.
1912, July 2:	Wilson is nominated for president by the Democratic Party.
1912, November 5:	Wilson is elected president.
1913, March 4:	Wilson is inaugurated as president.
1913, May 31:	The Seventeenth Amendment to the Constitution is ratified, bringing the direct election of U.S. senators.
1913, December 23:	The Federal Reserve Act is established.
1914, August 3:	World War I begins in Europe.
1914, August 6:	Ellen Wilson dies in Washington, D.C.
1915, May 7:	A German U-boat sinks the liner *Lusitania*, with a loss of American lives.
1915, December 18:	Wilson marries Edith Bolling Galt, the widow of Norman Galt, in Washington, D.C.
1916, March:	General John Pershing pursues Mexican revolutionary leader Pancho Villa.
1916, June 16:	Wilson is renominated for president by the Democratic Party.
1916, November 7:	Wilson is reelected president.
1917, March 4:	Wilson is inaugurated as president for a second term.
1917, April 6:	The United States declares war on Germany.
1917, June 8:	The first units of the American Expeditionary Force land in England.
1918, January 8:	Wilson outlines his Fourteen Points for peace.
1918, November 11:	An armistice ends the fighting.
1919, January 29:	The Eighteenth Amendment to the Constitution is ratified, bringing Prohibition.
1919, June 28:	A peace treaty is signed with Germany at Versailles, France.
1919, September 26:	Wilson collapses in Pueblo, Colorado, while campaigning for the League of Nations.
1919, November 19:	The U.S. Senate rejects the Treaty of Versailles.
1920, January 13:	The first meeting of the League of Nations convenes with the United States not represented.
1920, August 26:	The Nineteenth Amendment to the Constitution is ratified, giving women the vote.

| 1920, December 10: | Wilson is awarded the Nobel Peace Prize. |
| 1924, February 3: | Woodrow Wilson dies in Washington, D.C. |

Harding

1865, November 2:	Warren G. Harding is born in Caledonia, Ohio.
1884, November 26:	Harding purchases part interest in the *Star* newspaper in Marion, Ohio.
1891, July 8:	Harding marries Florence Kling De Wolfe.
1899-1903:	Harding serves in the Ohio State Senate.
1904-1905:	Harding serves as Ohio lieutenant governor.
1915-1921:	Harding represents Ohio in the U.S. Senate.
1920, June 12:	Harding is nominated for president by the Republican Party.
1920, November 2:	Harding is elected president.
1921, March 4:	Harding is inaugurated as president.
1921, May 3:	West Virginia enacts the first state sales tax.
1921, May 19:	Congress passes the first act limiting immigration.
1921, November 11:	The Tomb of the Unknown Soldier is dedicated at Arlington National Cemetery.
1922, March 29:	The major naval powers agree on a limitation to naval armaments.
1922, October 3:	Rebecca L. Felton of Georgia becomes the first woman to serve in the U.S. Senate.
1923, January 23:	Mae Ella Nolan of California takes office as the first woman elected to Congress.
1923, August 2:	Warren G. Harding dies in San Francisco, California.

Coolidge

1872, July 4:	Calvin Coolidge is born in Plymouth, Vermont.
1905, October 4:	Coolidge marries Grace Anna Goodhue in Burlington, Vermont.
1907-1908:	Coolidge serves in the Massachusetts House of Representatives.
1912-1915:	Coolidge serves in the Massachusetts State Senate; he is president of the senate from 1914 to 1915.
1919:	Coolidge settles a Boston police strike.
1919-1920:	Coolidge serves as governor of Massachusetts.
1920, November 2:	Coolidge is elected vice president.
1921, March 4:	Coolidge is inaugurated as vice president.
1923-1924:	Senate investigations reveal the extent of the Teapot Dome oil scandal in the Harding administration.
1923, August 3:	Coolidge succeeds to the presidency on the death of President Warren G. Harding.
1924, June 12:	Coolidge is nominated for president by the Republican Party.
1924, November 4:	Coolidge is elected president.
1925, January 5:	Nellie Tayloe Ross of Wyoming becomes the first woman to be elected governor.
1925, March 4:	Coolidge is inaugurated as president.
1925, March 23:	Tennessee enacts a law making it illegal to teach the theory of evolution.

1927, May 20:	Charles Lindbergh flies solo across the Atlantic Ocean.
1928:	Coolidge decides not to seek renomination for the presidency.
1933, January 5:	Calvin Coolidge dies in Northampton, Massachusetts.

Hoover

1874, August 10:	Herbert Hoover is born in West Branch, Iowa.
1895-1913:	Hoover works as a mining engineer and consultant all over the world.
1899, February 10:	Hoover marries Lou Henry in Monterey, California.
1899-1900:	Hoover tours China with his wife; he helps defend the city of Tientsin during the Boxer Rebellion.
1914-1915:	Hoover serves as chair of the American Relief Committee in London.
1915-1918:	Hoover serves as chair of the Commission for Relief in Belgium.
1917, August-1919, June:	Hoover serves as a U.S. food administrator in Europe.
1919:	Hoover serves as chair of the Supreme Economic Conference in Paris.
1920:	Hoover serves as chair of the European Relief Council.
1921-1928:	Hoover acts as secretary of commerce during the Harding and Coolidge administrations.
1928, June 14:	Hoover is nominated for president by the Republican Party.
1928, November 6:	Hoover is elected president.
1929, March 4:	Hoover is inaugurated as president.
1929, March 16:	The first Academy Awards are presented.
1929, October 29:	The New York stock market crashes, beginning the Great Depression.
1931, March 3:	"The Star-Spangled Banner" is adopted as the U.S. national anthem.
1931, December 15:	Maria Norton of New Jersey becomes the first woman to chair a congressional committee.
1932, January 12:	Hattie Caraway of Arkansas becomes the first woman to serve in the U.S. Senate by election rather than appointment.
1932, May 21:	Amelia Earhart completes the first transatlantic solo flight by a woman.
1932, June 16:	Hoover is renominated for president by the Republican Party.
1932, July:	Unemployed veterans march on Washington, D.C.; they are dispersed by U.S. Army troops.
1932, November 8:	Hoover is defeated for reelection by Democratic nominee Franklin D. Roosevelt.
1933, February 6:	The Twentieth Amendment to the Constitution is ratified, changing the dates for the inauguration of the president and vice president from March 4 to January 20.
1944, January 7:	Lou Hoover dies in New York City.
1946:	President Harry S. Truman appoints Hoover coordinator of the European food program.
1947-1949 and 1953-1955:	Hoover serves as chair of the Hoover Commission on the reorganization of the executive branch of the U.S. government.
1964, October 20:	Herbert Hoover dies in New York City.

F. D. Roosevelt

1882, January 30:	Franklin D. Roosevelt is born in Hyde Park, New York.
1905, March 17:	Roosevelt marries Eleanor Roosevelt in New York City.
1910, November 8:	Roosevelt is elected to the New York State Senate.
1913-1920:	Roosevelt serves as assistant secretary of the Navy in the Wilson administration.
1920, July:	Roosevelt is nominated for vice president by the Democratic Party with James M. Cox.
1920, November:	The Cox-Roosevelt ticket is defeated.
1921, August:	Roosevelt is stricken with polio while at his summer home in Campobello, Canada.
1929-1933:	Roosevelt serves as governor of New York.
1932, July 2:	Roosevelt is nominated for president by the Democratic Party.
1932, November 8:	Roosevelt is elected president.
1933, February 15:	Giuseppi Zangara attempts to assassinate Roosevelt in Miami.
1933, March 4:	Roosevelt is inaugurated as president. He appoints Frances Perkins as secretary of labor, making her the first woman to serve in the cabinet.
1933, March 5-9:	Roosevelt declares a "bank holiday" to allow U.S. financial system to reorganize.
1933, March 9-June 16:	During this period, known as the Hundred Days, Congress enacts many of the New Deal recovery measures proposed by Roosevelt.
1933, March 31:	The Civilian Conservation Corps (CCC) is established.
1933, April 12:	Roosevelt appoints Ruth Bryan Owen, the daughter of William Jennings Bryan, as minister to Denmark, making her the first woman to represent the United States abroad.
1933, May 12:	The Agricultural Adjustment Act (AAA) and the Federal Emergency Relief Act (FERA) are passed.
1933, May 13:	The Tennessee Valley Authority (TVA) is approved.
1933, June 5:	The United States rejects the gold standard as the basis for its currency.
1933, June 16:	Congress creates the Federal Deposit Insurance Corporation (FDIC) and passes the National Industrial Recovery Act (NIRA), creating the National Recovery Administration (NRA) and the Public Works Administration (PWA).
1933, November 16:	The United States diplomatically recognizes the Soviet Union.
1933, December 3:	The Twenty-first Amendment to the Constitution repeals the Eighteenth Amendment (Prohibition).
1934, June 6:	The Securities and Exchange Commission is established to regulate the stock market.
1934, June 19:	The Federal Communications Commission (FCC) is established.
1935:	The Federal Bureau of Investigation (FBI) is established, with J. Edgar Hoover as chief.
1935, April 8:	The Works Progress Administration (WPA) is established.
1935, May 27:	The U.S. Supreme Court declares the NIRA unconstitutional.
1935, July 5:	The Wagner Labor Relations Act is enacted, strengthening labor unions.
1935, August 14:	The Social Security Act is passed.

1936, January 6:	The Supreme Court declares the AAA unconstitutional.
1936, June 27:	Roosevelt is renominated for president by the Democratic Party.
1936, November 3:	Roosevelt is reelected president in a landslide victory.
1937, January 20:	Roosevelt is inaugurated as president for a second term.
1937, July 22:	The U.S. Senate defeats Roosevelt's plan to "pack" the Supreme Court by adding new justices.
1938, June 25:	The Fair Labor Standards Act is passed.
1939, September 1:	Nazi Germany invades Poland, sparking World War II.
1939, September 5:	The United States declares neutrality in the European war.
1940, May 10:	Winston Churchill becomes prime minister of Great Britain.
1940, July 18:	Roosevelt is renominated for president by the Democratic Party.
1940, September 3:	Roosevelt announces the trade of fifty World War I destroyers to Great Britain in exchange for air and naval bases in the Western Hemisphere.
1940, September 16:	The Selective Training and Service Act (the draft) is approved.
1940, November 5:	Roosevelt is reelected president for an unprecedented third term.
1941, January 6:	Roosevelt outlines the Four Freedoms in his State of the Union address.
1941, January 20:	Roosevelt is inaugurated as president for his third term.
1941, March 11:	The Lend-Lease Act providing aid to Great Britain is passed.
1941, June 22:	Nazi Germany invades the Soviet Union.
1941, August 14:	Roosevelt and Churchill issue the Atlantic Charter, their joint statement of principles for a just and lasting peace.
1941, December 7:	In a date that "will live in infamy," Japanese forces launch a surprise attack on Pearl Harbor, Hawaii, and on Guam and the Philippines.
1941, December 8:	The United States declares war against Japan.
1941, December 11:	Germany and Italy declare war against the United States.
1941, December 12:	Japanese troops capture Guam, the first U.S. territory lost during World War II.
1942, April 9:	Japan captures the Philippines.
1942, June 3-4:	The U.S. naval victory at Midway marks a turning point in the war against Japan.
1942, August-November:	U.S. forces defeat Japanese troops in the Battle of Guadalcanal.
1942, October-December:	Allied forces invade North Africa.
1942, December 2:	The Manhattan Project creates the first self-sustained nuclear chain reaction, necessary to building the atomic bomb.
1943, January 14-24:	Roosevelt and Churchill meet at Casablanca in North Africa.
1943, September:	The Allies invade Italy.
1943, November 28-December 1:	Roosevelt, Churchill, and Soviet leader Joseph Stalin meet in Tehran, Iran.
1944, June 6:	Allied forces invade France, an event known as D day.
1944, June 22:	Congress approves the G.I. Bill of Rights.
1944, August-October:	The Dumbarton Oaks Conference lays the groundwork for the United Nations.

1944, July 21:	Roosevelt is renominated for president by the Democratic Party.
1944, November 7:	Roosevelt is reelected president for a fourth term.
1945, January 20:	Roosevelt is inaugurated as president.
1945, February 4-11:	Roosevelt, Churchill, and Stalin meet at Yalta in the Crimea.
1945, April 12:	Franklin D. Roosevelt dies in Warm Springs, Georgia.

Truman

1884, May 8:	Harry S. Truman is born in Lamar, Missouri.
1918:	Truman serves with the American Expeditionary Force in France, rising to the rank of major.
1919, June 28:	Truman marries Elizabeth Virginia "Bess" Wallace in Independence, Missouri.
1919-1921:	Truman works in a haberdashery (men's clothing) business in Kansas City, Missouri.
1922-1924:	Truman serves as a county court judge (administrative, not judicial) in Missouri.
1935-1945:	Truman represents Missouri in the U.S. Senate.
1941-1944:	Truman serves as chair of the Special Senate Committee to Investigate the National Defense Program (Truman Committee).
1944, July:	Truman is nominated for vice president by the Democratic Party.
1944, November 7:	Truman is elected vice president.
1945, April 12:	Truman succeeds to the presidency on the death of Franklin D. Roosevelt.
1945, May 7:	Germany surrenders unconditionally to the Allies, an event known as V-E Day.
1945, June 26:	The United Nations Charter is signed in San Francisco.
1945, July 17-August 2:	Truman attends the Potsdam Conference.
1945, August 6:	The United States drops an atomic bomb on Hiroshima, Japan.
1945, August 9:	The United States drops a second atomic bomb on Nagasaki, Japan.
1945, August 14:	Japan surrenders unconditionally to the Allies, an event known as V-J Day.
1947:	The Central Intelligence Agency (CIA) is established.
1947, May 15:	Congress approves the Truman Doctrine to fight communism in Turkey and Greece.
1948, April 1:	The Soviet Union blockades Berlin; the United States begins an airlift of food and supplies.
1948, April 2:	Congress passes the Marshall Plan to rebuild European economies.
1948, July 14:	Truman is nominated for president by the Democratic Party.
1948, November 2:	Truman is elected president.
1949, January 20:	Truman is inaugurated as president.
1949, April 4:	The North Atlantic Treaty Organization (NATO) is established.
1950, June 25:	North Korea invades South Korea; the United Nations supports South Korea.
1950, July 8:	General Douglas MacArthur is named commander in chief of the United Nations forces in South Korea.

1950, November 1:	Puerto Rican nationalists attempt to assassinate Truman.
1950, November 26:	Communist China enters the Korean War on the side of North Korea.
1951, February 26:	The Twenty-second Amendment to the Constitution is ratified, limiting presidents to two terms.
1951, April 11:	Truman relieves MacArthur from command for insubordination.
1972, December 26:	Harry S. Truman dies in Kansas City, Missouri.

Eisenhower

1890, October 14:	Dwight D. Eisenhower is born in Denison, Texas.
1911, June 14:	Eisenhower enters the U.S. military academy at West Point.
1916, July 1:	Eisenhower marries Marie "Mamie" Geneva Doud in Denver, Colorado.
1935-1939:	Eisenhower serves as assistant to General Douglas MacArthur in the Philippines.
1942, November 8:	Eisenhower is appointed commander in chief of the Allied forces in North Africa.
1943, July-December:	Eisenhower commands the invasion of Italy.
1944, June 6:	Eisenhower commands the D day invasion of France.
1945-1948:	Eisenhower serves as chief of staff for the U.S. Army.
1945, May 7:	Eisenhower accepts the unconditional surrender of Germany.
1950-1952:	Eisenhower commands the NATO forces in Europe.
1952, July 11:	Eisenhower is nominated for president by the Republican Party.
1952, November 4:	Eisenhower is elected president.
1953, January 20:	Eisenhower is inaugurated as president.
1953, June 19:	Julius and Ethel Rosenberg are executed for spying for the Soviet Union.
1953, July 27:	An armistice ends the Korean War.
1954, April 22-June 17:	The Army-McCarthy hearings are held.
1954, May 17:	The U.S. Supreme Court declares school segregation unconstitutional.
1955, April 12:	The Salk vaccine is approved for use in the prevention of polio.
1956, August 23:	Eisenhower is renominated for president by the Republican Party.
1956, November 6:	Eisenhower is reelected president.
1957, January 20:	Eisenhower is inaugurated as president for a second term.
1957, September 24:	Eisenhower sends federal troops to Little Rock, Arkansas, to enforce school integration.
1957, October 4:	The Soviet Union launches *Sputnik*, the first artificial satellite.
1958, January 31:	The United States launches its first satellite, *Explorer I*.
1959, January 1:	Fidel Castro seizes power in Cuba.
1959, January 3:	Alaska is admitted as the forty-ninth state.
1959, March 18:	Hawaii is admitted as the fiftieth state.
1969, March 28:	Dwight D. Eisenhower dies in Washington, D.C.

Kennedy

1917, May 29:	John F. Kennedy is born in Brookline, Massachusetts.
1943, August 2:	Kennedy's torpedo boat, *PT-109*, is rammed and sunk by a Japanese destroyer; he helps save crew members.

1946-1951:	Kennedy represents Massachusetts in the U.S. House of Representatives.
1952, November 8:	Kennedy is elected to the U.S. Senate.
1953, September 12:	Kennedy marries Jacqueline Lee Bouvier in Newport, Rhode Island.
1957, May 6:	Kennedy is awarded the Pulitzer Prize in biography for *Profiles in Courage*.
1960, July 13:	Kennedy is nominated for president by the Democratic Party.
1960, November 8:	Kennedy is elected president.
1961, January 20:	Kennedy is inaugurated as president.
1961, January 25:	Kennedy holds the first live presidential news conference.
1961, March 29:	The Twenty-third Amendment to the Constitution is ratified, giving residents of the District of Columbia the right to vote for president.
1961, April 17-20:	The Bay of Pigs invasion fails to oust Fidel Castro.
1961, May 5:	Alan Shepard becomes the first U.S. astronaut in space.
1961, August 12-13:	Communist East Germany builds the Berlin Wall.
1962, February 20:	John Glenn becomes the first American to orbit the earth.
1962, June 25:	The U.S. Supreme Court declares prayer in public schools unconstitutional.
1962, October:	Kennedy imposes a "quarantine" and forces the Soviet Union to withdraw nuclear missiles from Cuba, an event known as the Cuban Missile Crisis.
1963, June 19:	Kennedy proposes a strong civil rights bill to Congress.
1963, June 20:	The United States and the Soviet Union agree to a direct communication link (hot line).
1963, July 25:	The United States, Great Britain, and the Soviet Union agree to a limited nuclear test treaty.
1963, August 28:	Following the March on Washington in support of civil rights, Martin Luther King, Jr., gives his "I Have a Dream" speech.
1963, November 22:	John F. Kennedy is assassinated in Dallas, Texas.

L. B. Johnson

1908, August 27:	Lyndon B. Johnson is born in Gillespie County, Texas.
1934, November 17:	Johnson marries Claudia Alta "Lady Bird" Taylor.
1937, April 10:	Johnson wins a special election for a seat in the U.S. House of Representatives.
1941, December-1948:	Johnson serves in the U.S. Naval Reserve, rising to the rank of commander and winning the Silver Star.
1948-1961:	Johnson represents Texas in the U.S. Senate.
1953-1961:	Johnson serves as the Democratic leader in the Senate.
1960, July 14:	Johnson is unanimously nominated for vice president by the Democratic Party.
1960, November 8:	Johnson is elected vice president.
1961, January 20:	Johnson is inaugurated as vice president.
1963, November 22:	Johnson accompanies President John F. Kennedy on a visit to Dallas and is sworn in as president after Kennedy's assassination.

1963, November 29:	Johnson appoints a seven-member commission headed by Supreme Court Chief Justice Earl Warren to investigate the Kennedy assassination.
1964, January 23:	The Twenty-fourth Amendment to the Constitution is ratified, banning poll taxes.
1964, February 17:	The U.S. Supreme Court rules that congressional districts must be equal in population, known as the "one-man, one-vote" decision.
1964, March 16:	Johnson sends his legislative program for the War on Poverty to Congress.
1964, July 2:	Johnson signs the Civil Rights Act of 1964.
1964, July 18-21:	Race riots erupt in New York City.
1964, August 7:	Congress passes the Tonkin Gulf Resolution, giving Johnson approval to undertake military action in Vietnam.
1964, August 24:	Johnson is nominated for president by the Democratic Party.
1964, September 27:	The Warren Commission report names Lee Harvey Oswald as the lone assassin in the killing of President Kennedy.
1964, November 3:	Johnson is elected president in a landslide victory over Republican nominee Barry Goldwater.
1965-1969:	The war in Vietnam escalates.
1965, January 4:	Johnson proposes Great Society legislative programs in his State of the Union address.
1965, January 20:	Johnson is inaugurated as president.
1965, June 3:	Major Edward White becomes the first American to walk in space.
1965, July 30:	Johnson signs the Medicare bill.
1965, August 6:	Johnson signs a voting rights bill.
1965, August 11-16:	Race riots in the Watts section of Los Angeles leave thirty-five dead and more than eight hundred injured.
1966, June 13:	The Supreme Court ruling *Miranda v. Arizona* requires that arrested persons be made aware of their rights to silence and to an attorney.
1967, February 10:	The Twenty-fifth Amendment to the Constitution is ratified, establishing rules concerning presidential disability and succession.
1967, July:	During this "long hot summer," race riots flare in Newark, New Jersey, and Detroit, Michigan.
1968, January 23:	The USS *Pueblo* and its crew are seized by North Korea.
1968, March 12:	Senator Eugene McCarthy, antiwar candidate, makes a strong second place showing in the New Hampshire Democratic presidential primary.
1968, March 31:	In a nationally televised speech, Johnson announces that he will neither seek nor accept renomination for president.
1968, April 4:	Martin Luther King, Jr., is assassinated in Memphis, Tennessee; Johnson calls in federal troops to control riots in Washington, D.C.
1968, June 5-6:	Senator Robert F. Kennedy is assassinated in Los Angeles while celebrating his victory in the California Democratic presidential primary.
1968, August:	A confrontation between antiwar demonstrators and police at the Democratic National Convention leads to massive violence.

1968, October 31:	Johnson announces the complete halt to the bombing of North Vietnam.
1968, December 22:	The crew of the USS *Pueblo* is released by North Korea.
1973, January 22:	Lyndon B. Johnson dies near Stonewall, en route to San Antonio, Texas.

Nixon

1913, January 9:	Richard M. Nixon is born in Yorba Linda, California.
1940, June 21:	Nixon marries Thelma Catherine Patricia Ryan in Riverside, California.
1943-1945:	Nixon serves as a naval officer during World War II.
1946, November 6:	Nixon is elected to the U.S. House of Representatives from California.
1950, November 7:	Nixon is elected to the U.S. Senate from California.
1952, July 10:	Nixon is nominated for vice president by the Republican Party.
1952, September 23:	Nixon delivers his televised Checkers speech, in which he defends a secret fund raised by supporters and vows to keep the cocker spaniel named Checkers.
1952, November 4:	Nixon is elected vice president under Dwight D. Eisenhower.
1956, July 11:	Nixon is renominated for vice president by the Republican Party.
1956, November 6:	Nixon is reelected vice president.
1958, May:	Nixon is attacked by demonstrators while in South America on a goodwill tour.
1960, July 28:	Nixon is nominated for president by the Republican Party.
1960, November 8:	Nixon is narrowly defeated by John F. Kennedy for president.
1962:	Nixon is defeated in a bid for governor of California.
1968, August 8:	Nixon is nominated for president by the Republican Party.
1968, November 5:	Nixon is elected president.
1969, January 20:	Nixon is inaugurated as president.
1969, July 20:	Neil Armstrong, Apollo 11 astronaut, becomes the first person to walk on the moon.
1970, April 30:	Nixon announces that U.S. troops will invade Cambodia.
1970, May 1:	National Guardsmen kill four students at Kent State University in Ohio during an antiwar protest.
1970, May 14:	Police kill two students at Jackson State College in Mississippi during an antiwar protest.
1970, July 9:	Nixon proposes the creation of an independent Environmental Protection Agency.
1971, April 7:	Nixon announces the withdrawal of 100,000 U.S. troops from South Vietnam by December, 1971.
1971, May 2-5:	Massive antiwar demonstrations are held in Washington, D.C.; thousands are arrested.
1971, June 10:	Nixon lifts the trade embargo on Communist China.
1971, June 13:	*The New York Times* publishes the Pentagon Papers, revealing secrets of U.S. involvement in Vietnam.
1971, July 5:	The Twenty-sixth Amendment to the Constitution is ratified, lowering the voting age to eighteen.
1972, February:	Nixon visits Communist China.

1972, June 17:	Five men are arrested in a burglary at Democratic National Headquarters in the Watergate complex in Washington, D.C.
1972, August 23:	Nixon is renominated for president by the Republican Party.
1972, November 7:	Nixon is reelected president.
1973, January 20:	Nixon is inaugurated as president for a second term.
1973, January 22:	The U.S. Supreme Court ruling in *Roe v. Wade* upholds a woman's right to an abortion during the first six months of pregnancy.
1973, January 27:	A Vietnam cease-fire agreement is signed in Paris.
1973, February 7:	The U.S. Senate establishes a committee to investigate the Watergate break-in.
1973, April 30:	Nixon announces the resignations and dismissals of major White House staff members over Watergate.
1973, July 16:	Congress learns that Nixon taped all conversations and telephone calls in his White House office.
1973, October 10:	Vice President Spiro T. Agnew resigns, pleading nolo contendere to charges of income tax evasion and bribery.
1973, October 12:	Nixon nominates Congressman Gerald R. Ford for vice president.
1974, July 24:	The Supreme Court rules that Nixon must surrender the tape recordings.
1974, July 27-30:	The House Judiciary Committee recommends the impeachment of President Nixon for obstruction of justice, abuse of power, and contempt of Congress.
1974, August 5:	The White House tape recordings reveal that Nixon sought to obstruct the investigation of Watergate.
1974, August 8:	In a televised address to the nation, Nixon announces that he will resign the presidency, effective August 9.
1974, September 8:	Nixon accepts a full pardon from President Ford.
1994, April 22:	Richard M. Nixon dies in New York City.

Ford

1913, July 14:	Leslie Lynch King, Jr., is born in Omaha, Nebraska.
1917:	King is renamed Gerald R. Ford, Jr., after being adopted by his stepfather.
1942-1944:	Ford serves in the U.S. Naval Reserve with forty-seven months of active service and ten battle stars.
1948, October 15:	Ford marries Elizabeth "Betty" Bloomer Warren in Grand Rapids, Michigan.
1948, November 2:	Ford is elected to the U.S. House of Representatives.
1949-1973:	Ford represents Michigan in the U.S. House of Representatives.
1963-1964:	Ford serves as a member of the Warren Commission.
1965, January 4:	Ford is elected the House minority leader.
1973, December 6:	Ford is confirmed as vice president by the Senate following the resignation of Spiro T. Agnew.
1974, August 9:	Ford succeeds to the presidency upon resignation of Richard M. Nixon.
1974, September 8:	Ford issues a full pardon to former president Nixon.

1974, December 19:	Nelson A. Rockefeller is confirmed as vice president by the Senate.
1975, April 27:	Saigon, South Vietnam, falls to the North Vietnamese.
1976, August 18:	Ford is nominated for president by the Republican Party.
1976, November 2:	Ford is defeated for president by Democratic nominee Jimmy Carter.

Carter

1924, October 1:	Jimmy Carter is born in Plains, Georgia.
1946-1953:	Carter serves in the U.S. Navy, rising to the rank of lieutenant commander.
1946, July 7:	Carter marries Rosalynn Smith in Plains, Georgia.
1971-1975:	Carter serves as governor of Georgia.
1976, July 19:	Carter is nominated for president by the Democratic Party.
1976, November 2:	Carter is elected president.
1977, January 20:	Carter is inaugurated as president.
1977, January 21:	Carter pardons Vietnam War draft resisters.
1978, June 16:	The Panama Canal Treaty is signed to return the Canal Zone to Panama.
1978, September 6:	Carter meets with Israeli prime minister Menachem Begin and Egyptian president Anwar el-Sadat at Camp David to fashion peace accords.
1978, October 16:	Polish cardinal Karol Wojtyła is elected pope, taking the name John Paul II.
1979, January-February:	A revolution in Iran brings Muslim fundamentalists under Ayatollah Ruhollah Khomeini to power.
1979, March 28:	The nuclear reactor at Three Mile Island in Pennsylvania threatens a meltdown catastrophe.
1979, June:	Gasoline shortages hit nationwide.
1979, November 4:	Iranians seize the U.S. embassy in Tehran and take sixty-six U.S. citizens hostage.
1980, December 27:	The Soviet Union invades Afghanistan.
1980, April 22:	The U.S. Olympic Committee votes to boycott the 1980 Olympics in Moscow to protest the Soviet invasion.
1980, August 14:	Carter is renominated for president by the Democratic Party.
1980, November 4:	Carter is defeated for reelection by Republican nominee Ronald Reagan.
1981, January 18:	Iran releases the U.S. hostages.

Reagan

1911, February 6:	Ronald Reagan is born in Tampico, Illinois.
1932-1937:	Reagan gains a national reputation as a sportscaster on the radio.
1937-1942:	Reagan makes Hollywood films, including *Knute Rockne—All American*, in which he plays "the Gipper."
1940, January 24:	Reagan marries Jane Wyman (Sarah Jane Fulks) in Glendale, California; they will divorce in 1948.
1947-1952 and 1959:	Reagan serves as president of the Screen Actors Guild.
1952, March 4:	Reagan marries Anne Frances "Nancy" Robbins Davis in Los Angeles, California.
1967-1975:	Reagan serves as governor of California.

1980, July 16	Reagan is nominated for president by the Republican Party.
1980, November 4:	Reagan is elected president.
1981, January 20:	Reagan is inaugurated as president.
1981, March 30:	Reagan is shot in the chest during an assassination attempt by John Hinckley, Jr.
1981, July 29:	The largest tax cuts in U.S. history are approved by Congress, leading to a record deficit.
1981, September 25:	Sandra Day O'Connor becomes the first woman to be appointed a justice of the U.S. Supreme Court.
1981, October 6:	Egyptian president Anwar el-Sadat is assassinated.
1982:	Great Britain and Argentina go to war over the Falkland Islands.
1983, October 23:	Terrorists blow up the U.S. Marine Corps barracks in Beirut, Lebanon.
1983, October 25:	U.S. troops invade the Caribbean island of Grenada.
1984, August:	Reagan is renominated for president by the Republican Party.
1984, November 6:	Reagan is reelected president.
1985, January 20:	Reagan is inaugurated as president for a second term.
1985, March 11:	Mikhail S. Gorbachev becomes the general secretary of the Communist Party Central Committee, thus ruler of the Soviet Union.
1985, November 19-21:	A summit meeting between Gorbachev and Reagan takes place.
1986, January 28:	The space shuttle *Challenger* explodes; it is the worst disaster in the history of the U.S. space program.
1986, November:	The administration admits to an "arms for hostages" deal with Iran.
1987:	Colonel Oliver North, Admiral John Poindexter, and others testify at hearings investigating the Iran-Contra affair, the illegal diversion of Iranian arms money to Nicaraguan rebels.
1994:	Reagan reveals that he is suffering from Alzheimer's disease.
2004, June 5:	Ronald Reagan dies in Los Angeles.

G. H. W. Bush

1924, June 12:	George Bush is born in Milton, Massachusetts.
1942-1945:	Bush serves in the U.S. Navy during World War II; he is awarded the Distinguished Flying Cross and three air medals.
1945, January 6:	Bush marries Barbara Pierce in Rye, New York.
1967-1971:	Bush represents Texas in the U.S. House of Representatives.
1971-1972:	Bush serves as U.S. ambassador to the United Nations.
1973-1974:	Bush serves as chair of the Republican National Committee.
1974-1975:	Bush serves as chief of the U.S. liaison office to Communist China.
1980, July 17:	Bush is nominated for vice president by the Republican Party.
1980, November 4:	Bush is elected vice president under President Ronald Reagan.
1984, August 22:	Bush is nominated for vice president by the Republican Party.
1984, November 4:	Bush is reelected vice president.
1988, August 17:	Bush is nominated for president by the Republican Party.
1988, November 8:	Bush is elected president.
1989, January 20:	Bush is inaugurated as president.

1989, March 24:	The oil tanker *Exxon Valdez* runs aground in Prince William Sound in Alaska, creating the largest oil spill in U.S. history.
1989, June 3:	Chinese troops crush prodemocracy protesters in Beijing's Tiananmen Square.
1989, August 18:	The Solidarity labor party in Poland wins free elections, ousting the Communist Party.
1989, September 21:	Hurricane Hugo strikes South Carolina, causing great damage.
1989, October 17:	A powerful earthquake hits San Francisco.
1989, November 12:	The destruction of the Berlin Wall begins.
1989, December 10:	A noncommunist government takes power in Czechoslovakia.
1989, December 20:	U.S. forces invade Panama and install a new government.
1989, December 25:	A popular revolt ousts the communist government in Romania.
1990, February 11:	Nelson Mandela, the leader of the African National Congress in South Africa, is freed after twenty-seven years in prison.
1990, August 2:	Iraqi troops invade Kuwait.
1991, January-February:	Operation Desert Storm pushes Iraqi forces out of Kuwait but stops short of ending the dictatorship of Saddam Hussein.
1991, September 6:	Estonia, Latvia, and Lithuania are recognized as independent states by the Soviet Union.
1991, December 25:	The Soviet Union is dissolved and the Commonwealth of Independent States is created, with Boris Yeltsin as president of the Russian Republic.
1992, February 1:	Bush and Yeltsin meet at Camp David and declare a formal end to the Cold War.
1992, April 29:	The acquittal of four white police officers accused of the brutal beating of African American motorist Rodney King sparks rioting in Los Angeles; Bush blames the policies of Lyndon B. Johnson's Great Society for the riots.
1992, August 19:	Bush is renominated for president by the Republican Party.
1992, August 24:	Hurricane Andrew batters Florida and Louisiana.
1992, November 3:	Bush is defeated for reelection by Democratic nominee Bill Clinton.
1992, December 24:	Bush pardons six former government officials convicted or indicted for lying to Congress about arms for hostages deals with Iran during the Reagan administration.

Clinton

1946, August 19:	Bill Clinton is born in Hope, Arkansas.
1968-1970:	Clinton studies as a Rhodes scholar at Oxford University in England.
1975, October 11:	Clinton marries Hillary Diane Rodham in Fayetteville, Arkansas.
1978:	Clinton is elected governor of Arkansas.
1980:	Clinton is defeated for reelection.
1982-1992:	Clinton again serves as governor of Arkansas.
1992, July 15:	Clinton is nominated for president by the Democratic Party.
1992, November 3:	Clinton is elected president.
1993, January 20:	Clinton is inaugurated as president.

1993, February 5:	Clinton signs a family leave bill.
1993, February 26:	Terrorists bomb the World Trade Center in New York City.
1993, April 19:	Eighty cult members die in a fire at the Branch Davidian complex in Waco, Texas, following an assault by federal law enforcement officials.
1993, September 13:	The Palestine Liberation Organization (PLO) and Israel sign a peace pact at the White House.
1993, November 20:	Congress passes the North American Free Trade Agreement (NAFTA).
1994, May 6	Paula Jones files a lawsuit alleging that Clinton sexually harassed her while he was governor of Arkansas.
1994, August 5:	Kenneth Starr is appointed an independent prosecutor to investigate Clinton's role in an Arkansas real estate transaction called Whitewater.
1994, November 8:	Republicans win control of both houses of Congress for the first time in forty years.
1995, April 19:	Domestic terrorists bomb the Alfred P. Murrah Federal Building in Oklahoma City, killing 169 and injuring nearly 500.
1995, December 16:	Republicans in Congress shut down the federal government in a budget disagreement with Clinton.
1996, August 29:	Clinton is renominated for president by the Democratic Party.
1996, November 5:	Clinton is reelected president.
1997, January 20:	Clinton is inaugurated as president for a second term.
1998, August:	Clinton testifies before a grand jury about his relationship with former White House intern Monica Lewinsky.
1998, August 20:	U.S. warplanes attack suspected terrorist sites in Afghanistan and Sudan in retaliation for bombings at the U.S. embassies in Kenya and Tanzania.
1998, October 23:	The Wye River Accords are signed between Israel and the PLO.
1998, December 19:	The U.S. House of Representatives votes two articles of impeachment against President Clinton, for perjury and obstruction of justice, with regard to the Lewinsky investigation.
1999, January 7:	The impeachment trial begins in the Senate.
1999, February 12:	The Senate acquits Clinton on both counts; neither count receives a majority vote, much less the two-thirds required by the Constitution for removal.
1999, March 24-June 9:	NATO launches air strikes against Serbia to stop the killing of ethnic Albanians in the Kosovo province.
2000, April 22:	Five months after surviving an escape attempt from Cuba in which his mother drowned, six-year-old Elian Gonzalez is seized from his Miami relatives by federal agents and soon returned to his father in Cuba.
2000, July 1:	The Campaign Finance Disclosure Act is enacted.
2000, August 14:	Clinton addresses the Democratic National Convention in support of candidate Al Gore.

2000, September 20:	Independent counsel Robert Ray closes the six-year Whitewater investigation, clearing Clinton and his wife of criminal wrongdoing.
2000, October 10:	Trade relations with China are dramatically altered with the passage of the China-PNTR (Permanent Normal Trade Relations) Bill.
2000, November 7:	Hillary Clinton wins a U.S. Senate seat from New York.
2000, November 16:	Bill Clinton visits Vietnam, the first president to do so since 1969.
2001, January 5:	Clinton signs an executive order, called the "Roadless Initiative," that protects one-third of U.S. forest land from logging and road construction.
2001, January 19:	In his last act as president, Clinton pardons ninety people, including his former Whitewater business partner Susan McDougal and former housing secretary Henry Cisneros, who had resigned in 1996.

G. W. Bush

1946, July 6:	George Walker Bush is born in New Haven, Connecticut.
1964-1968:	Bush attends Yale University.
1968-1973:	Bush serves as an F-102 pilot in the Texas National Guard.
1973-1975:	Bush earns an MBA from Harvard.
1977, November 5:	Bush marries Laura Welch.
1978:	Bush runs for U.S. Congress but loses the race.
1994:	Bush is elected governor of Texas.
1998, November:	Bush wins a second term as Texas governor.
2000, November 7:	The presidential election between Bush and Vice President Al Gore is too close to call: Florida, with its twenty-five electoral votes, finds that it has a razor-thin difference of a few hundred votes between the candidates.
2000, November 9:	An election recount and subsequent legal problems begin.
2000, November 26:	Kathleen Harris, Florida's secretary of state, declares Bush the winner in the state by 537 votes.
2000, December 13:	Gore concedes the election to Bush.
2001, January 29:	The White House Office of Faith-Based and Community Initiatives is established, which, in part, removes requirements that religious organizations separate their charitable functions from their religious functions.
2001, January 20:	Bush is sworn in as the forty-third president of the United States.
2001, September 11:	Terrorists kill nearly three thousand people in attacks on the World Trade Center in New York City and the U.S. Pentagon in Washington, D.C.
2001, October 7:	In a televised address, Bush announces the commencement of Operation Enduring Freedom and the launch of air strikes against Afghanistan's Taliban regime, whom Bush accuses of harboring terrorists.
2001, October 26:	The Patriot Act is passed, revising the rules regarding information-gathering and criminal procedure with respect to cases of suspected terrorism.

2002, January 8:	The No Child Left Behind Act is passed in order to improve the quality of American schools.
2002, October 16:	Bush signs a joint resolution enacted by Congress authorizing the use of military force against Iraq.
2002, November 25:	The Homeland Security Act is passed, creating the Department of Homeland Security.
2002, November 27:	Bush announces that Henry Kissinger will head the independent council investigating the September 11 terrorist attacks.
2003, February 5:	Secretary of State Colin Powell appears before the United Nations Security Council to make a case for entering a war with Iraq.
2003, March 19:	Bush announces that early stages of U.S.-led attack on Iraq have begun.
2003, May 2:	Aboard the USS *Abraham Lincoln*, Bush announces that "major combat operations in Iraq have ended."
2003, September:	After asking Congress for an additional $87 billion for the Iraq War, Bush admits that no hard evidence ties Iraqi president Saddam Hussein to the September 11 attacks.
2003, November 5:	The Partial-Birth Abortion Ban Act is passed.
2003, December 8:	The Medicare Prescription Drug, Improvement, and Modernization Act is signed into law.
2004, January 22:	The Interior Department opens nearly nine million acres of wilderness on Alaska's North Slope to oil drilling.
2004, February:	After questions regarding the lack of weapons of mass destruction found in Iraq, Bush creates a bipartisan commission to investigate U.S. intelligence failures.
2004, May:	Photos depicting abuse by American military personnel of Iraqi prisoners at Abu Ghraib Prison creates a scandal for the Bush administration.
2004, June 28:	The United States hands over formal sovereignty of Iraq to an interim government.
2004, November 2:	Bush is reelected president.
2005, January 20:	Bush is inaugurated as president for a second term.
2005, January 30:	Iraqi elections are held.
2005, January-April	Bush tours the United States and lobbies for a reform of Social Security.
2005, August 28	Hurricane Katrina hits the Gulf Coast states, causing billions of dollars in damage and more than a thousand deaths.

Michael Witkoski; revised by Sarah M. Hilbert

Presidential Election Returns, 1789-2004

Year	Candidate (party)	Electoral Vote	Popular Vote
1789	**George Washington (Federalist)**	69	
	John Adams (Federalist)	34	
	Others	35	
	Not cast	8	
1792	**George Washington (Federalist)**	132	
	John Adams (Federalist)	77	
	George Clinton (Anti-Federalist)	50	
	Thomas Jefferson (Anti-Federalist)	4	
	Aaron Burr (Anti-Federalist)	1	
	Not cast	6	
1796	**John Adams (Federalist)**	71	
	Thomas Jefferson (Democratic Republican)	68	
	Thomas Pinckney (Federalist)	59	
	Aaron Burr (Democratic Republican)	30	
	Others	48	
1800	Aaron Burr (Democratic Republican)	73	
	Thomas Jefferson (Democratic Republican)	73	
	John Adams (Federalist)	65	
	Charles Pinckney (Federalist)	64	
	John Jay (Federalist)	1	
1804	**Thomas Jefferson (Democratic Republican)**	162	
	Charles Pinckney (Federalist)	14	
1808	**James Madison (Democratic Republican)**	122	
	Charles Pinckney (Federalist)	47	
	George Clinton (Democratic Republican)	6	
	Not cast	1	
1812	**James Madison (Democratic Republican)**	128	

Year	Candidate (party)	Electoral Vote	Popular Vote
	DeWitt Clinton (Federalist)	89	
	Not cast	1	
1816	**James Monroe (Democratic Republican)**	183	
	Rufus King (Federalist)	34	
	Not cast	4	
1820	**James Monroe (Democratic Republican)**	231	
	John Quincy Adams (Democratic Republican)	1	
	Not cast	3	
1824	Andrew Jackson (National Republican)	99	155,872
	John Quincy Adams (National Republican)	84	105,321
	William H. Crawford (National Republican)	41	44,282
	Henry Clay (National Republican)	37	46,587
1828	**Andrew Jackson (Democratic)**	178	647,231
	John Quincy Adams (National Republican)	83	509,097
1832	**Andrew Jackson (Democratic)**	219	687,502
	Henry Clay (National Republican)	49	530,189
	John Floyd (Independent)	11	
	William Wirt (Anti-Mason)	7	
	Not cast	2	
1836	**Martin Van Buren (Democratic)**	170	762,678
	William Henry Harrison (Whig)	73	548,007
	Hugh L. White (Whig)	26	
	Daniel Webster (Whig)	14	
	W. P. Mangum (Independent)	11	
1840	**William Henry Harrison (Whig)**	234	1,275,017
	Martin Van Buren (Democratic)	60	1,128,702
1844	**James K. Polk (Democratic)**	170	1,337,243
	Henry Clay (Whig)	105	1,299,068
1848	**Zachary Taylor (Whig)**	163	1,360,101
	Lewis Cass (Democratic)	127	1,220,544
	Martin Van Buren (Free-Soil)	—	291,501
1852	**Franklin Pierce (Democratic)**	254	1,601,474
	Winfield Scott (Whig)	42	1,386,578
1856	**James Buchanan (Democratic)**	174	1,927,995

Year	Candidate (party)	Electoral Vote	Popular Vote
	John C. Frémont (Republican)	114	1,391,555
	Millard Fillmore (Know-Nothing)	8	873,053
1860	**Abraham Lincoln (Republican)**	180	1,866,352
	John C. Breckinridge (Democratic)	72	845,763
	John Bell (Constitutional Union)	39	589,581
	Stephen A. Douglas (Democratic)	12	1,375,157
1864	**Abraham Lincoln (Republican)**	212	2,216,067
	George B. McClellan (Democratic)	21	1,808,725
1868	**Ulysses S. Grant (Republican)**	214	3,015,071
	Horatio Seymour (Democratic)	80	2,709,615
	Not counted	23	
1872	**Ulysses S. Grant (Republican)**	286	3,597,132
	Horace Greeley (Democratic, Liberal Republican)	*	2,834,125
	Thomas A. Hendricks (Democratic)	42	
	B. Gratz Brown (Democratic, Liberal Republican)	18	
	Charles J. Jenkins (Democratic)	2	
	David Davis (Democratic)	1	
	Not counted	17	
1876	**Rutherford B. Hayes (Republican)**	185	4,033,768
	Samuel J. Tilden (Democratic)	184	4,285,992
	Peter Cooper (Greenback)	—	81,737
1880	**James A. Garfield (Republican)**	214	4,449,053
	Winfield S. Hancock (Democratic)	155	4,442,035
	James B. Weaver (Greenback)	—	308,578
1884	**Grover Cleveland (Democratic)**	219	4,911,017
	James G. Blaine (Republican)	182	4,848,334
	Benjamin F. Butler (Greenback)	—	175,370
	John P. St. John (Prohibition)	—	150,369
1888	**Benjamin Harrison (Republican)**	233	5,440,216
	Grover Cleveland (Democratic)	168	5,538,233
	Clinton B. Fisk (Prohibition)	—	249,506
	Alson J. Streeter (Union Labor)	—	146,935
1892	**Grover Cleveland (Democratic)**	277	5,556,918
	Benjamin Harrison (Republican)	145	5,176,108

Year	Candidate (party)	Electoral Vote	Popular Vote
	James B. Weaver (Populist)	22	1,041,028
	John Bidwell (Prohibition)	—	264,133
1896	**William McKinley (Republican)**	271	7,035,638
	William Jennings Bryan (Democratic, Populist)	176	6,467,946
	John M. Palmer (National Democratic)	—	133,148
	Joshua Levering (Prohibition)	—	132,007
1900	**William McKinley (Republican)**	292	7,219,530
	William Jennings Bryan (Democratic, Populist)	155	
	Eugene V. Debs (Socialist)	—	94,768
1904	**Theodore Roosevelt (Republican)**	336	7,628,834
	Alton B. Parker (Democratic)	140	5,084,491
	Eugene V. Debs (Socialist)	—	402,400
1908	**William Howard Taft (Republican)**	321	7,679,006
	William Jennings Bryan (Democratic)	162	6,409,106
	Eugene V. Debs (Socialist)	—	402,820
1912	**Woodrow Wilson (Democratic)**	435	6,286,214
	Theodore Roosevelt (Progressive)	88	4,126,020
	William Howard Taft (Republican)	8	3,483,922
	Eugene V. Debs (Socialist)	—	897,011
1916	**Woodrow Wilson (Democratic)**	277	9,129,606
	Charles Evans Hughes (Republican)	254	8,538,221
	A. L. Benson (Socialist)	—	585,113
1920	**Warren G. Harding (Republican)**	404	16,152,200
	James M. Cox (Democratic)	127	9,147,353
	Eugene V. Debs (Socialist)	—	917,799
1924	**Calvin Coolidge (Republican)**	382	15,725,016
	John W. Davis (Democratic)	136	8,385,586
	Robert M. La Follette (Progressive, Socialist)	13	4,822,856
1928	**Herbert Hoover (Republican)**	444	21,392,190
	Alfred E. Smith (Democratic)	87	15,016,443
	Norman Thomas (Socialist)	—	267,420
1932	**Franklin D. Roosevelt (Democratic)**	472	22,821,857
	Herbert Hoover (Republican)	59	15,761,841
	Norman Thomas (Socialist)	—	884,781

Year	Candidate (party)	Electoral Vote	Popular Vote
1936	**Franklin D. Roosevelt (Democratic)**	523	27,751,597
	Alfred M. Landon (Republican)	8	16,679,583
	Norman Thomas (Socialist)	—	187,720
1940	**Franklin D. Roosevelt (Democratic)**	449	27,244,160
	Wendell L. Willkie (Republican)	82	22,305,198
	Norman Thomas (Socialist)	—	99,557
1944	**Franklin D. Roosevelt (Democratic)**	432	25,602,504
	Thomas E. Dewey (Republican)	99	22,006,285
	Norman Thomas (Socialist)	—	80,518
1948	**Harry S. Truman (Democratic)**	303	24,179,345
	Thomas E. Dewey (Republican)	189	21,991,291
	Strom Thurmond (States' Rights)	39	1,176,125
	Henry A. Wallace (Progressive)	—	1,157,326
	Norman Thomas (Socialist)	—	139,572
1952	**Dwight D. Eisenhower (Republican)**	442	33,936,24
	Adlai E. Stevenson (Democratic)	89	27,314,992
1956	**Dwight D. Eisenhower (Republican)**	457	35,590,472
	Adlai E. Stevenson (Democratic)	73	26,022,752
	Walter B. Jones (Democratic)	1	
1960	**John F. Kennedy (Democratic)**	303	34,226,731
	Richard M. Nixon (Republican)	219	34,108,157
	Harry F. Byrd (Democratic)	15	
1964	**Lyndon B. Johnson (Democratic)**	486	43,129,484
	Barry Goldwater (Republican)	52	27,178,188
1968	**Richard M. Nixon (Republican)**	301	31,785,480
	Hubert H. Humphrey (Democratic)	191	31,275,166
	George C. Wallace (American Independent)	46	9,906,473
1972	**Richard M. Nixon (Republican)**	520	47,169,911
	George McGovern (Democratic)	17	29,170,383
	John Hospers (Libertarian)	1	
	John G. Schmitz (American)	—	1,099,482
1976	**Jimmy Carter (Democratic)**	297	40,830,763
	Gerald R. Ford (Republican)	240	39,147,973
	Ronald Reagan (Republican)	1	

Year	Candidate (party)	Electoral Vote	Popular Vote
	Eugene McCarthy (Independent)	—	756,631
1980	**Ronald Reagan (Republican)**	489	43,899,248
	Jimmy Carter (Democratic)	49	36,481,435
	John Anderson (Independent)	—	5,719,437
1984	**Ronald Reagan (Republican)**	525	54,455,075
	Walter Mondale (Democratic)	13	37,577,185
1988	**George H. W. Bush (Republican)**	426	48,886,097
	Michael Dukakis (Democratic)	111	41,809,074
	Lloyd Bentsen (Democratic)	1	
1992	**Bill Clinton (Democratic)**	370	44,909,889
	George H. W. Bush (Republican)	168	39,104,545
	Ross Perot (Independent)	—	19,742,267
1996	**Bill Clinton (Democratic)**	379	47,402,357
	Bob Dole (Republican)	159	39,198,755
	Ross Perot (Independent)	—	8,085,402
2000	**George W. Bush (Republican)**	271	50,456,002
	Albert Gore, Jr. (Democratic)	266	50,999,897
	Ralph Nader (Green)	—	2,882,955
2004	**George W. Bush (Republican)**	286	62,040,610
	John F. Kerry (Democratic)	251	59,028,111

Vice Presidents

Administration	Vice President (term)	Political Party	Born-Died	State
Washington	John Adams (1789-1797)	Federalist	1735-1826	Massachusetts
J. Adams	Thomas Jefferson (1797-1801)	Democratic Republican	1743-1826	Virginia
Jefferson	Aaron Burr (1801-1805)	Democratic Republican	1756-1836	New York
	George Clinton (1805-1809)	Democratic Republican	1739-1812	New York
Madison	George Clinton (1809-1812)	Democratic Republican		
	Elbridge Gerry (1813-1814)	Democratic Republican	1744-1814	Massachusetts
Monroe	Daniel D. Tompkins (1817-1825)	Democratic Republican	1774-1825	New York
J. Q. Adams	John C. Calhoun (1825-1829)	National Republican	1782-1850	South Carolina
Jackson	John C. Calhoun (1829-1832)	Democratic		
	Martin Van Buren (1833-1837)	Democratic	1782-1862	New York
Van Buren	Richard M. Johnson (1837-1841)	Democratic	1780-1850	Kentucky
W. H. Harrison	John Tyler (1841)	Whig	1790-1862	Virginia
Tyler	none	—	—	—
Polk	George M. Dallas (1845-1849)	Democratic	1792-1864	Pennsylvania
Taylor	Millard Fillmore (1849-1850)	Whig	1800-1874	New York
Fillmore	none	—	—	—
Pierce	William R. D. King (1853)	Democratic	1786-1853	Alabama
Buchanan	John C. Breckinridge (1857-1861)	Democratic	1821-1875	Kentucky
Lincoln	Hannibal Hamlin (1861-1865)	Republican	1809-1891	Maine
	Andrew Johnson (1865)	Democratic	1808-1875	Tennessee
A. Johnson	none	—	—	—
Grant	Schuyler Colfax (1869-1873)	Republican	1823-1885	Indiana
	Henry Wilson (1873-1875)	Republican	1812-1875	Massachusetts
Hayes	William A. Wheeler (1877-1881)	Republican	1819-1887	New York
Garfield	Chester A. Arthur (1881)	Republican	1830-1886	New York

Administration	Vice President (term)	Political Party	Born-Died	State
Arthur	none	—	—	—
Cleveland	Thomas A. Hendricks (1885)	Democratic	1819-1885	Indiana
B. Harrison	Levi P. Morton (1889-1893)	Republican	1824-1920	New York
Cleveland	Adlai E. Stevenson (1893-1897)	Democratic	1835-1914	Illinois
McKinley	Garret A. Hobart (1897-1899)	Republican	1844-1899	New Jersey
	Theodore Roosevelt (1901)	Republican	1858-1919	New York
T. Roosevelt	Charles W. Fairbanks (1905-1909)	Republican	1852-1918	Indiana
Taft	James S. Sherman (1909-1912)	Republican	1855-1912	New York
Wilson	Thomas R. Marshall (1913-1921)	Democratic	1854-1925	Indiana
Harding	Calvin Coolidge (1921-1923)	Republican	1872-1933	Massachusetts
Coolidge	Charles G. Dawes (1925-1929)	Republican	1865-1951	Illinois
Hoover	Charles Curtis (1929-1933)	Republican	1860-1936	Kansas
F. D. Roosevelt	John Nance Garner (1933-1941)	Democratic	1868-1967	Texas
	Henry A. Wallace (1941-1945)	Democratic	1888-1965	Iowa
	Harry S. Truman (1945)	Democratic	1884-1972	Missouri
Truman	Alben W. Barkley (1949-1953)	Democratic	1877-1956	Kentucky
Eisenhower	Richard M. Nixon (1953-1961)	Republican	1913-1994	California
Kennedy	Lyndon B. Johnson (1961-1963)	Democratic	1908-1973	Texas
L. B. Johnson	Hubert H. Humphrey (1965-1969)	Democratic	1911-1978	Minnesota
Nixon	Spiro T. Agnew (1969-1973)	Republican	1918-1996	Maryland
	Gerald R. Ford (1973-1974)	Republican	1913-	Michigan
Ford	Nelson A. Rockefeller (1974-1977)	Republican	1908-1979	New York
Carter	Walter Mondale (1977-1981)	Democratic	1928-	Minnesota
Reagan	George Bush (1981-1989)	Republican	1924-	Texas
G. H. W. Bush	Dan Quayle (1989-1993)	Republican	1947-	Indiana
Clinton	Al Gore, Jr. (1993-2001)	Democratic	1948-	Tennessee
G. W. Bush	Dick Cheney (2001-)	Republican	1941-	Wyoming

Cabinet Members by Administration

Washington

Secretary of State
Thomas Jefferson (1789-1794)
Edmund Randolph (1794-1795)
Timothy Pickering (1795-1797)
Secretary of the Treasury
Alexander Hamilton (1789-1795)
Oliver Wolcott, Jr. (1795-1797)

Secretary of War
Henry Knox (1789-1795)
Timothy Pickering (1795)
James McHenry (1796-1797)
Attorney General
Edmund Randolph (1789-1794)
William Bradford (1794-1795)
Charles Lee (1795-1797)

J. Adams

Secretary of State
Timothy Pickering (1797-1800)
John Marshall (1800-1801)
Secretary of the Treasury
Oliver Wolcott, Jr. (1797-1801)
Samuel Dexter (1801)

Secretary of War
James McHenry (1797-1800)
Samuel Dexter (1800-1801)
Secretary of the Navy
Benjamin Stoddert (1798-1801)
Attorney General
Charles Lee (1797-1801)

Jefferson

Secretary of State
James Madison (1801-1809)
Secretary of the Treasury
Samuel Dexter (1801)
Albert Gallatin (1801-1809)
Secretary of War
Henry Dearborn (1801-1809)

Secretary of the Navy
Benjamin Stoddert (1801)
Robert Smith (1801-1809)
Attorney General
Levi Lincoln (1801-1805)
John Breckinridge (1805-1807)
Caesar Rodney (1807-1809)

Madison

Secretary of State
Robert Smith (1809-1811)
James Monroe (1811-1817)
Secretary of the Treasury
Albert Gallatin (1809-1814)
George Campbell (1814)
Alexander J. Dallas (1814-1816)
William H. Crawford (1816-1817)
Secretary of War
William Eustis (1809-1813)
John Armstrong (1813-1814)

James Monroe (1814-1815)
William H. Crawford (1815-1817)
Secretary of the Navy
Paul Hamilton (1809-1813)
William Jones (1813-1814)
Benjamin Crowninshield (1814-1817)
Attorney General
Caesar Rodney (1809-1811)
William Pinckney (1811-1814)
Richard Rush (1814-1817)

Monroe

Secretary of State
John Quincy Adams (1817-1825)
Secretary of the Treasury
William H. Crawford (1817-1825)
Secretary of War
George Graham (1817)
John C. Calhoun (1817-1825)

Secretary of the Navy
Benjamin Crowninshield (1817-1818)
Smith Thompson (1818-1823)
Samuel Southard (1823-1825)
Attorney General
Richard Rush (1817)
William Wirt (1817-1825)

J. Q. Adams

Secretary of State
Henry Clay (1825-1829)
Secretary of the Treasury
Richard Rush (1825-1829)

Secretary of War
James Barbour (1825-1828)
Peter B. Porter (1828-1829)
Secretary of the Navy
Samuel Southard (1825-1829)
Attorney General
William Wirt (1825-1829)

Jackson

Secretary of State
Martin Van Buren (1829-1831)
Edward Livingston (1831-1833)
Louis McLane (1833-1834)
John Forsyth (1834-1837)

Secretary of the Treasury
Samuel Ingham (1829-1831)
Louis McLane (1831-1833)
William John Duane (1833)
Roger B. Taney (1833-1834)
Levi Woodbury (1834-1837)

Secretary of War
John Henry Eaton (1829-1831)
Lewis Cass (1831-1837)
Benjamin Butler (1837)
Secretary of the Navy
John Branch (1829-1831)
Levi Woodbury (1831-1834)
Mahlon Dickerson (1834-1837)

Attorney General
John M. Berrien (1829-1831)
Roger B. Taney (1831-1833)
Benjamin Butler (1833-1837)
Postmaster General
William Barry (1829-1835)
Amos Kendall (1835-1837)

Van Buren

Secretary of State
John Forsyth (1837-1841)
Secretary of the Treasury
Levi Woodbury (1837-1841)
Secretary of War
Joel R. Poinsett (1837-1841)
Secretary of the Navy
Mahlon Dickerson (1837-1838)
James K. Paulding (1838-1841)

Attorney General
Benjamin Butler (1837-1838)
Felix Grundy (1838-1840)
Henry D. Gilpin (1840-1841)
Postmaster General
Amos Kendall (1837-1840)
John M. Niles (1840-1841)

W. H. Harrison

Secretary of State
Daniel Webster (1841)
Secretary of the Treasury
Thomas Ewing (1841)
Secretary of War
John Bell (1841)

Secretary of the Navy
George E. Badger (1841)
Attorney General
John J. Crittenden (1841)
Postmaster General
Francis Granger (1841)

Tyler

Secretary of State
Daniel Webster (1841-1843)
Hugh S. Legaré (1843)
Abel P. Upshur (1843-1844)
John C. Calhoun (1844-1845)
Secretary of the Treasury
Thomas Ewing (1841)
Walter Forward (1841-1843)
John C. Spencer (1843-1844)
George M. Bibb (1844-1845)

Secretary of War
John Bell (1841)
John C. Spencer (1841-1843)
James M. Porter (1843-1844)
William Wilkins (1844-1845)
Secretary of the Navy
George E. Badger (1841)
Abel P. Upshur (1841-1843)
David Henshaw (1843-1844)
Thomas Gilmer (1844)
John Y. Mason (1844-1845)

Attorney General
John J. Crittenden (1841)
Hugh S. Legaré (1841-1843)
John Nelson (1843-1845)

Postmaster General
Francis Granger (1841)
Charles A. Wickliffe (1841-1845)

Polk

Secretary of State
James Buchanan (1845-1849)
Secretary of the Treasury
Robert J. Walker (1845-1849)
Secretary of War
William L. Marcy (1845-1849)
Secretary of the Navy
George Bancroft (1845-1846)
John Y. Mason (1846-1849)

Attorney General
John Y. Mason (1845-1846)
Nathan Clifford (1846-1848)
Isaac Toucey (1848-1849)
Postmaster General
Cave Johnson (1845-1849)

Taylor

Secretary of State
John M. Clayton (1849-1850)
Secretary of the Treasury
William M. Meredith (1849-1850)
Secretary of War
George W. Crawford (1849-1850)
Secretary of the Navy
William B. Preston (1849-1850)

Attorney General
Reverdy Johnson (1849-1850)
Postmaster General
Jacob Collamer (1849-1850)
Secretary of the Interior
Thomas Ewing (1849-1850)

Fillmore

Secretary of State
Daniel Webster (1850-1852)
Edward Everett (1852-1853)
Secretary of the Treasury
Thomas Corwin (1850-1853)
Secretary of War
Charles M. Conrad (1850-1853)
Secretary of the Navy
William A. Graham (1850-1852)
John P. Kennedy (1852-1853)

Attorney General
John J. Crittenden (1850-1853)
Postmaster General
Nathan K. Hall (1850-1852)
Sam D. Hubbard (1852-1853)
Secretary of the Interior
Thomas McKennan (1850)
A. H. H. Stuart (1850-1853)

Pierce

Secretary of State
William L. Marcy (1853-1857)
Secretary of the Treasury
James Guthrie (1853-1857)
Secretary of War
Jefferson Davis (1853-1857)
Secretary of the Navy
James C. Dobbin (1853-1857)

Attorney General
Caleb Cushing (1853-1857)
Postmaster General
James Campbell (1853-1857)
Secretary of the Interior
Robert McClelland (1853-1857)

Buchanan

Secretary of State
Lewis Cass (1857-1860)
Jeremiah S. Black (1860-1861)
Secretary of the Treasury
Howell Cobb (1857-1860)
Philip F. Thomas (1860-1861)
John A. Dix (1861)
Secretary of War
John Floyd (1857-1861)
Joseph Holt (1861)

Secretary of the Navy
Isaac Toucey (1857-1861)
Attorney General
Jeremiah S. Black (1857-1860)
Edwin M. Stanton (1860-1861)
Postmaster General
Aaron V. Brown (1857-1859)
Joseph Holt (1859-1861)
Horatio King (1861)
Secretary of the Interior
Jacob Thompson (1857-1861)

Lincoln

Secretary of State
William H. Seward (1861-1865)
Secretary of the Treasury
Salmon P. Chase (1861-1864)
William P. Fessenden (1864-1865)
Hugh McCulloch (1865)
Secretary of War
Simon Cameron (1861-1862)
Edwin M. Stanton (1862-1865)
Secretary of the Navy
Gideon Welles (1861-1865)

Attorney General
Edward Bates (1861-1864)
James Speed (1864-1865)
Postmaster General
Horatio King (1861)
Montgomery Blair (1861-1864)
William Dennison (1864-1865)
Secretary of the Interior
Caleb Smith (1861-1863)
John P. Usher (1863-1865)

A. Johnson

Secretary of State
William H. Seward (1865-1869)
Secretary of the Treasury
Hugh McCulloch (1865-1869)
Secretary of War
Edwin M. Stanton (1865-1867)
Ulysses S. Grant (1867-1868)
John M. Schofield (1868-1869)
Secretary of the Navy
Gideon Welles (1865-1869)

Attorney General
James Speed (1865-1866)
Henry Stanbery (1866-1868)
William M. Evarts (1868-1869)
Postmaster General
William Dennison (1865-1866)
Alexander Randall (1866-1869)
Secretary of the Interior
John P. Usher (1865)
James Harlan (1865-1866)
O. H. Browning (1866-1869)

Grant

Secretary of State
Elihu B. Washburne (1869)
Hamilton Fish (1869-1877)
Secretary of the Treasury
George S. Boutwell (1869-1873)
William A. Richardson (1873-1874)
Benjamin H. Bristow (1874-1876)
Lot M. Morrill (1876-1877)
Secretary of War
John A. Rawlins (1869)
William Tecumseh Sherman (1869)
W. W. Belknap (1869-1876)
Alphonso Taft (1876)
James D. Cameron (1876-1877)
Secretary of the Navy
Adolph E. Borie (1869)
George M. Robeson (1869-1877)

Attorney General
Ebenezer R. Hoar (1869-1870)
Amos T. Akerman (1870-1871)
G. H. Williams (1871-1875)
Edwards Pierrepont (1875-1876)
Alphonso Taft (1876-1877)
Postmaster General
John A. J. Creswell (1869-1874)
James W. Marshall (1874)
Marshall Jewell (1874-1876)
James N. Tyner (1876-1877)
Secretary of the Interior
Jacob D. Cox (1869-1870)
Columbus Delano (1870-1875)
Zachariah Chandler (1875-1877)

Hayes

Secretary of State
William M. Evarts (1877-1881)
Secretary of the Treasury
John Sherman (1877-1881)
Secretary of War
George M. McCrary (1877-1879)
Alexander Ramsey (1879-1881)
Secretary of the Navy
Richard W. Thompson (1877-1881)

Nathan Goff, Jr. (1881)
Attorney General
Charles A. Devens (1877-1881)
Postmaster General
David M. Key (1877-1880)
Horace Maynard (1880-1881)
Secretary of the Interior
Carl Schurz (1877-1881)

Garfield

Secretary of State
James G. Blaine (1881)
Secretary of the Treasury
William Windom (1881)
Secretary of War
Robert Todd Lincoln (1881)
Secretary of the Navy
William Hunt (1881)

Attorney General
Wayne MacVeagh (1881)
Postmaster General
Thomas James (1881)
Secretary of the Interior
S. J. Kirkwood (1881)

Arthur

Secretary of State
Frederick T. Frelinghuysen (1881-1885)
Secretary of the Treasury
Charles J. Folger (1881-1884)
Walter Q. Gresham (1884)
Hugh McCulloch (1884-1885)
Secretary of War
Robert Todd Lincoln (1881-1885)
Secretary of the Navy
William E. Chandler (1881-1885)

Attorney General
Benjamin J. Brewster (1881-1885)
Postmaster General
Thomas James (1881)
Timothy O. Howe (1881-1883)
Walter Q. Gresham (1883-1884)
Frank Hatton (1884-1885)
Secretary of the Interior
Henry M. Teller (1881-1885)

Cleveland (1st Administration)

Secretary of State
Thomas F. Bayard (1885-1889)
Secretary of the Treasury
Daniel Manning (1885-1887)
Charles S. Fairchild (1887-1889)
Secretary of War
William C. Endicott (1885-1889)
Secretary of the Navy
William C. Whitney (1885-1889)

Attorney General
A. H. Garland (1885-1889)
Postmaster General
William F. Vilas (1885-1888)
Don M. Dickinson (1888-1889)
Secretary of the Interior
L. Q. R. Lamar (1885-1888)
William F. Vilas (1888-1889)
Secretary of Agriculture
Norman J. Colman (1889)

B. Harrison

Secretary of State
James G. Blaine (1889-1892)
John W. Foster (1892-1893)
Secretary of the Treasury
William Windom (1889-1891)
Charles Foster (1891-1893)
Secretary of War
Redfield Procter (1889-1891)
Stephen B. Elkins (1891-1893)

Secretary of the Navy
Benjamin F. Tracy (1889-1893)
Attorney General
W. H. H. Miller (1889-1893)
Postmaster General
John Wanamaker (1889-1893)
Secretary of the Interior
John W. Noble (1889-1893)
Secretary of Agriculture
Jeremiah M. Rusk (1889-1893)

Cleveland (2d Administration)

Secretary of State
Walter Q. Gresham (1893-1895)
Richard Olney (1895-1897)
Secretary of the Treasury
John G. Carlisle (1893-1897)
Secretary of War
Daniel S. Lamont (1893-1897)
Secretary of the Navy
Hilary A. Herbert (1893-1897)

Attorney General
Richard Olney (1893-1895)
Judson Harmon (1895-1897)
Postmaster General
Wilson S. Bissel (1893-1895)
William L. Wilson (1895-1897)
Secretary of the Interior
Hoke Smith (1893-1896)
David R. Francis (1896-1897)
Secretary of Agriculture
J. Sterling Morton (1893-1897)

McKinley

Secretary of State
John Sherman (1897-1898)
William R. Day (1898)
John Hay (1898-1901)
Secretary of the Treasury
Lyman J. Gage (1897-1901)
Secretary of War
Russell A. Alger (1897-1899)
Elihu Root (1899-1901)
Secretary of the Navy
John D. Long (1897-1901)

Attorney General
Joseph McKenna (1897-1898)
John W. Griggs (1898-1901)
Philander C. Knox (1901)
Postmaster General
Joseph Gary (1897-1898)
Charles E. Smith (1898-1901)
Secretary of the Interior
Cornelius N. Bliss (1897-1898)
E. A. Hitchcock (1898-1901)
Secretary of Agriculture
James Wilson (1897-1901)

T. Roosevelt

Secretary of State
John Hay (1901-1905)
Elihu Root (1905-1909)
Robert Bacon (1909)
Secretary of the Treasury
Lyman J. Gage (1901-1902)
Leslie M. Shaw (1902-1907)
George B. Cortelyou (1907-1909)
Secretary of War
Elihu Root (1901-1904)
William H. Taft (1904-1908)
Luke E. Wright (1908-1909)
Secretary of the Navy
John D. Long (1901-1902)
William H. Moody (1902-1904)
Paul Morton (1904-1905)
Charles J. Bonaparte (1905-1906)
Victor H. Metcalf (1906-1908)
T. H. Newberry (1908-1909)

Attorney General
Philander C. Knox (1901-1904)
William H. Moody (1904-1906)
Charles J. Bonaparte (1906-1909)
Postmaster General
Charles E. Smith (1901-1902)
Henry C. Payne (1902-1904)
Robert J. Wynne (1904-1905)
George B. Cortelyou (1905-1907)
George von L. Meyer (1907-1909)
Secretary of the Interior
E. A. Hitchcock (1901-1907)
James R. Garfield (1907-1909)
Secretary of Agriculture
James Wilson (1901-1909)
Secretary of Commerce and Labor
George B. Cortelyou (1903-1904)
Victor H. Metcalf (1904-1906)
Oscar S. Straus (1906-1909)

Taft

Secretary of State
Philander C. Knox (1909-1913)
Secretary of the Treasury
Franklin MacVeagh (1909-1913)
Secretary of War
Jacob M. Dickinson (1909-1911)
Henry L. Stimson (1911-1913)
Secretary of the Navy
George von L. Meyer (1909-1913)
Attorney General
George W. Wickersham (1909-1913)

Postmaster General
Frank H. Hitchcock (1909-1913)
Secretary of the Interior
Richard A. Ballinger (1909-1911)
Walter L. Fisher (1911-1913)
Secretary of Agriculture
James Wilson (1909-1913)
Secretary of Commerce and Labor
Charles Nagel (1909-1913)

Wilson

Secretary of State
William Jennings Bryan (1913-1915)
Robert Lansing (1915-1920)
Bainbridge Colby (1920-1921)

Secretary of the Treasury
William Gibbs McAdoo (1913-1918)
Carter Glass (1918-1920)
David F. Houston (1920-1921)

Secretary of War
Lindley M. Garrison (1913-1916)
Newton D. Baker (1916-1921)
Secretary of the Navy
Josephus Daniels (1913-1921)
Attorney General
James C. McReynolds (1913-1914)
Thomas W. Gregory (1914-1919)
A. Mitchell Palmer (1919-1921)
Postmaster General
Albert Burleson (1913-1921)

Secretary of the Interior
Franklin K. Lane (1913-1920)
John P. Payne (1920-1921)
Secretary of Agriculture
David F. Houston (1913-1920)
E. T. Meredith (1920-1921)
Secretary of Commerce
William C. Redfield (1913-1919)
J. W. Alexander (1919-1921)
Secretary of Labor
William B. Wilson (1913-1921)

Harding

Secretary of State
Charles Evans Hughes (1921-1923)
Secretary of the Treasury
Andrew W. Mellon (1921-1923)
Secretary of War
John W. Weeks (1921-1923)
Secretary of the Navy
Edwin Denby (1921-1923)
Attorney General
Harry M. Daugherty (1921-1923)
Postmaster General
Will H. Hays (1921-1922)

Hubert Work (1922-1923)
Harry S. New (1923)
Secretary of the Interior
Albert B. Fall (1921-1923)
Hubert Work (1923)
Secretary of Agriculture
Henry C. Wallace (1921-1923)
Secretary of Commerce
Herbert Hoover (1921-1923)
Secretary of Labor
James J. Davis (1921-1923)

Coolidge

Secretary of State
Charles Evans Hughes (1923-1925)
Frank B. Kellogg (1925-1929)
Secretary of the Treasury
Andrew Mellon (1923-1929)
Secretary of War
John W. Weeks (1923-1925)
Dwight F. Davis (1925-1929)
Secretary of the Navy
Edwin Denby (1923-1924)
Curtis D. Wilbur (1924-1929)
Attorney General
Harry Daugherty (1923-1924)
Harlan F. Stone (1924-1925)
John G. Sargent (1925-1929)

Postmaster General
Harry S. New (1923-1929)
Secretary of the Interior
Hubert Work (1923-1928)
Roy O. West (1928-1929)
Secretary of Agriculture
Henry C. Wallace (1923-1924)
Howard M. Gore (1924-1925)
William Jardine (1925-1929)
Secretary of Commerce
Herbert Hoover (1923-1928)
William F. Whiting (1928-1929)
Secretary of Labor
James J. Davis (1923-1929)

Hoover

Secretary of State
Henry L. Stimson (1929-1933)
Secretary of the Treasury
Andrew Mellon (1929-1932)
Ogden L. Mills (1932-1933)
Secretary of War
James W. Good (1929)
Patrick J. Hurley (1929-1933)
Secretary of the Navy
Charles Francis Adams (1929-1933)
Attorney General
William D. Mitchell (1929-1933)

Postmaster General
Walter Brown (1929-1933)
Secretary of the Interior
Ray Lyman Wilbur (1929-1933)
Secretary of Agriculture
Arthur M. Hyde (1929-1933)
Secretary of Commerce
Robert Lamont (1929-1932)
Roy D. Chapin (1932-1933)
Secretary of Labor
James J. Davis (1929-1930)
William N. Doak (1930-1933)

F. D. Roosevelt

Secretary of State
Cordell Hull (1933-1944)
E. R. Stettinius, Jr. (1944-1945)
Secretary of the Treasury
William H. Woodin (1933-1934)
Henry Morgenthau (1934-1945)
Secretary of War
George H. Dern (1933-1936)
Harry H. Woodring (1936-1940)
Henry L. Stimson (1940-1945)
Secretary of the Navy
Claude A. Swanson (1933-1940)
Charles Edison (1940)
Frank Knox (1940-1944)
James V. Forrestal (1944-1945)
Attorney General
H. S. Cummings (1933-1939)
Frank Murphy (1939-1940)

Robert Jackson (1940-1941)
Francis Biddle (1941-1945)
Postmaster General
James A. Farley (1933-1940)
Frank C. Walker (1940-1945)
Secretary of the Interior
Harold Ickes (1933-1945)
Secretary of Agriculture
Henry A. Wallace (1933-1940)
Claude R. Wickard (1940-1945)
Secretary of Commerce
Daniel C. Roper (1933-1939)
Harry L. Hopkins (1939-1940)
Jesse Jones (1940-1945)
Henry A. Wallace (1945)
Secretary of Labor
Frances Perkins (1933-1945)

Truman

Secretary of State
James F. Byrnes (1945-1947)
George C. Marshall (1947-1949)
Dean Acheson (1949-1953)

Secretary of the Treasury
Fred M. Vinson (1945-1946)
John W. Snyder (1946-1953)

Secretary of War
  Robert P. Patterson (1945-1947)
  Kenneth C. Royall (1947)
Secretary of the Navy
  James V. Forrestal (1945-1947)
Secretary of Defense
  James V. Forrestal (1947-1949)
  Louis Johnson (1949-1950)
  George C. Marshall (1950-1951)
  Robert A. Lovett (1951-1953)
Attorney General
  Tom C. Clark (1945-1949)
  J. Howard McGrath (1949-1952)
  James P. McGranery (1952-1953)

Postmaster General
  R. E. Hannegan (1945-1947)
  Jesse M. Donaldson (1947-1953)
Secretary of the Interior
  Harold Ickes (1945-1946)
  Julius A. Krug (1946-1949)
  Oscar L. Chapman (1949-1953)
Secretary of Agriculture
  C. P. Anderson (1945-1948)
  C. F. Brannan (1948-1953)
Secretary of Commerce
  W. A. Harriman (1945-1948)
  Charles Sawyer (1948-1953)
Secretary of Labor
  L. B. Schwellenbach (1945-1948)
  Maurice J. Tobin (1948-1953)

Eisenhower

Secretary of State
  John Foster Dulles (1953-1959)
  Christian A. Herter (1959-1961)
Secretary of the Treasury
  George Humphrey (1953-1957)
  Robert B. Anderson (1957-1961)
Secretary of Defense
  Charles E. Wilson (1953-1957)
  Neil H. McElroy (1957-1959)
  Thomas S. Gates (1959-1961)
Attorney General
  H. Brownell, Jr. (1953-1957)
  William P. Rogers (1957-1961)
Postmaster General
  A. E. Summerfield (1953-1961)

Secretary of the Interior
  Douglas McKay (1953-1956)
  Fred Seaton (1956-1961)
Secretary of Agriculture
  Ezra T. Benton (1953-1961)
Secretary of Commerce
  Sinclair Weeks (1953-1958)
  Lewis L. Strauss (1958-1961)
Secretary of Labor
  Martin Durkin (1953)
  James P. Mitchell (1953-1961)
Secretary of Health, Education, and Welfare
  Oveta Culp Hobby (1953-1955)
  Marion B. Folsom (1955-1958)
  Arthur S. Flemming (1958-1961)

Kennedy

Secretary of State
  Dean Rusk (1961-1963)
Secretary of the Treasury
  Douglas Dillon (1961-1963)
Secretary of Defense
  Robert McNamara (1961-1963)

Attorney General
  Robert F. Kennedy (1961-1963)
Postmaster General
  J. Edward Day (1961-1963)
  John A. Gronouski (1963)

Secretary of the Interior
Stewart L. Udall (1961-1963)
Secretary of Agriculture
Orville Freeman (1961-1963)
Secretary of Commerce
Luther Hodges (1961-1963)

Secretary of Labor
Arthur Goldberg (1961-1962)
W. Willard Wirtz (1962-1963)
Secretary of Health, Education, and Welfare
Abraham Ribicoff (1961-1962)
Anthony Celebrezze (1962-1963)

L. B. Johnson

Secretary of State
Dean Rusk (1963-1969)
Secretary of the Treasury
Douglas Dillon (1963-1965)
Henry H. Fowler (1965-1968)
Joseph W. Barr (1968-1969)
Secretary of Defense
Robert McNamara (1963-1968)
Clark Clifford (1968-1969)
Attorney General
Robert F. Kennedy (1963-1965)
N. de B. Katzenbach (1965-1967)
Ramsey Clark (1967-1969)
Postmaster General
John A. Gronouski (1963-1965)
Lawrence F. O'Brien (1965-1968)
W. Marvin Watson (1968-1969)
Secretary of the Interior
Stewart L. Udall (1963-1969)

Secretary of Agriculture
Orville Freeman (1963-1969)
Secretary of Commerce
Luther Hodges (1963-1965)
John T. Connor (1965-1967)
Alexander B. Trowbridge (1967-1968)
C. R. Smith (1968-1969)
Secretary of Labor
W. Willard Wirtz (1963-1969)
Secretary of Health, Education, and Welfare
Anthony Celebrezze (1963-1965)
John W. Gardner (1965-1968)
Wilbur J. Cohen (1968-1969)
Secretary of Housing and Urban Development
Robert C. Weaver (1966-1968)
Robert C. Wood (1968-1969)
Secretary of Transportation
Alan S. Boyd (1966-1969)

Nixon

Secretary of State
William P. Rogers (1969-1973)
Henry Kissinger (1973-1974)
Secretary of the Treasury
David M. Kennedy (1969-1970)
John Connally (1970-1972)
George Shultz (1972-1974)
William Simon (1974)
Secretary of Defense
Melvin Laird (1969-1973)
Elliot Richardson (1973)
James R. Schlesinger (1973-1974)

Attorney General
John Mitchell, Jr. (1969-1972)
Richard G. Kleindienst (1972-1973)
Elliot Richardson (1973)
William B. Saxbe (1974)
Postmaster General
Winton M. Blount (1969-1971)
Secretary of the Interior
Walter J. Hickel (1969-1971)
Rogers C. B. Morton (1971-1974)

Secretary of Agriculture
Clifford M. Hardin (1969-1971)
Earl L. Butz (1971-1974)
Secretary of Commerce
Maurice H. Stans (1969-1972)
Peter G. Peterson (1972)
Frederick B. Dent (1972-1974)
Secretary of Labor
George Shultz (1969-1970)
James D. Hodgson (1970-1973)
Peter J. Brennan (1973-1974)

Secretary of Health, Education, and Welfare
Robert Finch (1969-1970)
Elliot Richardson (1970-1973)
Caspar Weinberger (1973-1974)
Secretary of Housing and Urban Development
George W. Romney (1969-1973)
James T. Lynn (1973-1974)
Secretary of Transportation
John A. Volpe (1969-1973)
Claude S. Brinegar (1973-1974)

Ford

Secretary of State
Henry Kissinger (1974-1977)
Secretary of the Treasury
William Simon (1974-1977)
Secretary of Defense
James R. Schlesinger (1974-1975)
Donald H. Rumsfeld (1975-1977)
Attorney General
William B. Saxbe (1974-1975)
Edward H. Levi (1975-1977)
Secretary of the Interior
Rogers C. B. Morton (1974-1975)
Stanley K. Hathaway (1975)
Thomas D. Kleppe (1975-1977)
Secretary of Agriculture
Earl L. Butz (1974-1976)
John Knebel (1976-1977)

Secretary of Commerce
Frederick B. Dent (1974-1975)
Rogers C. B. Morton (1975)
Elliot Richardson (1975-1977)
Secretary of Labor
Peter J. Brennan (1974-1975)
John T. Dunlop (1975-1976)
W. J. Usery (1976-1977)
Secretary of Health, Education, and Welfare
Caspar Weinberger (1974-1975)
Forrest D. Mathews (1975-1977)
Secretary of Housing and Urban Development
James T. Lynn (1974-1975)
Carla A. Hills (1975-1977)
Secretary of Transportation
Claude S. Brinegar (1974-1975)
William T. Coleman (1975-1977)

Carter

Secretary of State
Cyrus Vance (1977-1980)
Edmund Muskie (1980-1981)
Secretary of the Treasury
W. Michael Blumenthal (1977-1979)
G. William Miller (1979-1981)

Secretary of Defense
Harold Brown (1977-1981)
Attorney General
Griffin Bell (1977-1979)
Benjamin R. Civiletti (1979-1981)
Secretary of the Interior
Cecil D. Andrus (1977-1981)

Secretary of Agriculture
Bob S. Bergland (1977-1981)
Secretary of Commerce
Juanita M. Kreps (1977-1979)
Philip M. Klutznick (1979-1981)
Secretary of Labor
F. Ray Marshall (1977-1981)
Secretary of Health and Human Services
Joseph A. Califano, Jr. (1977-1979)
Patricia Roberts Harris (1979-1981)

Secretary of Housing and Urban Development
Patricia Roberts Harris (1977-1979)
Moon Landrieu (1979-1981)
Secretary of Transportation
Brock Adams (1977-1979)
Neil E. Goldschmidt (1979-1981)
Secretary of Energy
James Schlesinger (1977-1979)
Charles W. Duncan, Jr. (1979-1981)
Secretary of Education
Shirley Hufstedler (1979-1981)

Reagan

Secretary of State
Alexander Haig (1981-1982)
George Shultz (1982-1989)
Secretary of the Treasury
Donald Regan (1981-1985)
James A. Baker III (1985-1988)
Nicholas Brady (1988-1989)
Secretary of Defense
Caspar Weinberger (1981-1987)
Frank C. Carlucci (1987-1989)
Attorney General
William French Smith (1981-1985)
Edwin Meese III (1985-1988)
Dick Thornburgh (1988-1989)
Secretary of the Interior
James Watt (1981-1983)
William P. Clark (1983-1985)
Donald P. Hodel (1985-1989)
Secretary of Agriculture
John R. Block (1981-1986)
Richard E. Lyng (1986-1989)
Secretary of Commerce
Malcolm Baldrige (1981-1987)
C. William Verity, Jr. (1987-1989)

Secretary of Labor
Raymond J. Donovan (1981-1985)
William E. Brock (1985-1987)
Ann Dore McLaughlin (1987-1989)
Secretary of Health and Human Services
Richard S. Schweiker (1981-1983)
Margaret Heckler (1983-1985)
Otis R. Bowen (1985-1989)
Secretary of Housing and Urban Development
Samuel Pierce (1981-1989)
Secretary of Transportation
Andrew L. Lewis, Jr. (1981-1983)
Elizabeth Dole (1983-1987)
James H. Burnley IV (1987-1989)
Secretary of Energy
James B. Edwards (1981-1983)
Donald P. Hodel (1983-1985)
John S. Herrington (1985-1989)
Secretary of Education
T. H. Bell (1981-1985)
William J. Bennett (1985-1988)
Lauro F. Cavazos (1988-1989)

G. H. W. Bush

Secretary of State
James A. Baker III (1989-1992)
Lawrence S. Eagleburger (1992-1993)
Secretary of the Treasury
Nicholas F. Brady (1989-1993)
Secretary of Defense
Richard Cheney (1989-1993)
Attorney General
Dick Thornburgh (1989-1992)
William P. Barr (1992-1993)
Secretary of the Interior
Manuel Lujan, Jr. (1989-1993)
Secretary of Agriculture
Clayton K. Yeutter (1989-1991)
Edward Matigan (1991-1993)
Secretary of Commerce
Robert A. Mosbacher (1989-1992)
Barbara H. Franklin (1992-1993)

Secretary of Labor
Elizabeth Dole (1989-1991)
Lynn Martin (1991-1993)
Secretary of Health and Human Services
Louis W. Sullivan (1989-1993)
Secretary of Housing and Urban Development
Jack Kemp (1989-1993)
Secretary of Transportation
Samuel K. Skinner (1989-1992)
Andrew Card (1992-1993)
Secretary of Energy
James D. Watkins (1989-1993)
Secretary of Education
Lauro F. Cavazos (1989-1991)
Lamar Alexander (1991-1993)
Secretary of Veterans Affairs
Edward J. Derwinski (1989-1993)

Clinton

Secretary of State
Warren Christopher (1993-1996)
Madeleine Albright (1996-2001)
Secretary of the Treasury
Lloyd Bentsen (1993-1995)
Robert E. Rubin (1995-1999)
Lawrence H. Summers (1999-2001)
Secretary of Defense
Les Aspin (1993-1994)
William J. Perry (1994-1997)
William Cohen (1997-2001)
Attorney General
Janet Reno (1993-2001)
Secretary of the Interior
Bruce Babbitt (1993-2001)
Secretary of Agriculture
Mike Espy (1993-1995)
Dan Glickman (1995-2001)
Secretary of Commerce
Ron Brown (1993-1996)
Mickey Kantor (1996-1997)
William Daley (1997-2000)

Norman Y. Mineta (2000-2001)
Secretary of Labor
Robert B. Reich (1993-1997)
Alexis Herman (1997-2001)
Secretary of Health and Human Services
Donna Shalala (1993-2001)
Secretary of Housing and Urban Development
Henry Cisneros (1993-1997)
Andrew Cuomo (1997-2001)
Secretary of Transportation
Federico Peña (1993-1997)
Rodney Slater (1997-2001)
Secretary of Energy
Hazel O'Leary (1993-1997)
Federico Peña (1997-1998)
Bill Richardson (1998-2001)
Secretary of Education
Richard E. Riley (1993-2001)
Secretary of Veterans Affairs
Jesse Brown (1993-1998)
Togo D. West, Jr. (1998-2000)
Hershel W. Gober (2000-2001)

G. W. Bush

Secretary of State
    Colin Powell (2001-2005)
    Condoleezza Rice (2005-   )
Secretary of the Treasury
    Paul H. O'Neill (2001-2003)
    John Snow (2003-   )
Secretary of Defense
    Donald Rumsfeld (2001-   )
Attorney General
    John Ashcroft (2001-2005)
    Alberto Gonzales (2005-   )
Secretary of the Interior
    Gale A. Norton (2001-   )
Secretary of Agriculture
    Ann M. Veneman (2001-2005)
    Mike Johanns (2005-   )
Secretary of Commerce
    Don Evans (2001-2005)
    Carlos Gutierrez (2005-   )
Secretary of Labor
    Elaine Chao (2001-   )

Secretary of Health and Human Services
    Tommy G. Thompson (2001-2005)
    Michael O. Leavitt (2005-   )
Secretary of Housing and Urban Development
    Mel Martinez (2001-2003)
    Alphonso Jackson (2004-   )
Secretary of Transportation
    Norman Y. Mineta (2001-   )
Secretary of Energy
    Spencer Abraham (2001-2005)
    Samuel Bodman (2005-   )
Secretary of Education
    Rod Paige (2001-2005)
    Margaret Spellings (2005-   )
Secretary of Veterans Affairs
    Anthony Principi (2001-2005)
    Jim Nicholson (2005-   )
Secretary of Homeland Security
    Tom Ridge (2003-2005)
    Michael Chertoff (2005-   )

Executive Departments and Offices

Departments

Department of Agriculture
1400 Independence Avenue SW
Washington, DC 20250
Web site: www.usda.gov
Established: May 15, 1862; administered by Commissioner of Agriculture until 1889

Supervises agricultural production; uses subsidies and development programs to help farmers financially; helps food producers sell their goods overseas; operates food assistance and nutrition programs; and uses inspection programs to ensure that food is safe to eat.

Department of Commerce
1401 Constitution Avenue NW
Washington, DC 20230
Web site: www.doc.gov
Established: March 4, 1913; Department of Commerce and Labor created February 14, 1903

Promotes international trade, economic growth, and technological advancement; maintains American competitiveness in international markets; and gathers statistics for business and government planners.

Department of Defense
Office of the Secretary, the Pentagon
Washington, DC 20301-1155
Web site: www.dod.gov
Established: July 26, 1947, as National Military Establishment; name changed to Department of Defense August 10, 1949

Oversees and directs all military-related endeavors of the Army, Navy, Marine Corps, and Air Force, as well as the Joint Chiefs of Staff and several specialized combat commands; and engages in nonmilitary operations, including flood control and management of oil reserves.

Department of Education
400 Maryland Avenue SW
Washington, DC 20202
Web site: www.ed.gov
Established: October 17, 1979

Administers more than 150 federal education programs, including student loans, migrant worker training, vocational education, and special programs for the handicapped.

Department of Energy
1000 Independence Avenue SW
Washington, DC 20585
Web site: www.energy.gov
Established: October 1, 1977

Oversees and directs the research and development of energy technology and conservation, the civilian and military use of nuclear energy, the regulation of energy production and use, and the pricing and allocation of oil.

Department of Health and Human Services
200 Independence Avenue SW
Washington, DC 20201
Web site: www.dhhs.gov
Established: April 11, 1953; replaced Federal Security Agency created in 1939

Administers Social Security; funds Medicare and Medicaid; offers social services for certain segments of the United States, including poor families, Native Americans, and the elderly; oversees institutes dealing with mental health and substance abuse; works to control preventable and infectious diseases; conducts research on diseases, aging, and other issues; monitors the safety of the food supply; and tests and approves all drugs.

Department of Homeland Security
Washington, DC 20528
Web site: www.dhs.gov
Established: January 24, 2003, through the combination of twenty-two separate agencies

Works to prevent and deter terrorist attacks; protects against and responds to threats and hazards to the United States; and monitors borders.

Department of Housing and Urban Development
451 7th Street, SW
Washington, DC 20410
Web site: www.hud.gov
Established: November 9, 1965; replaced Housing and Home Finance Agency created in 1947

Promotes community development; administers fair-housing laws; and provides affordable housing and rent subsidies.

Department of the Interior
1849 C Street NW
Washington, DC 20240
Web site: www.doi.gov
Established: March 3, 1849

Protects and manages such things as national parks, monuments, rivers, seashores, lakes, outdoor recreation areas, historic sites, and wildlife refuges; supervises economic development and environmental protection of public land; and helps Native Americans living on reservations.

Department of Justice
950 Pennsylvania Avenue NW
Washington, DC 20530
Web site: www.usdoj.gov

Established: June 22, 1870; Office of Attorney General created September 24, 1789

Supervises U.S. district attorneys and marshals and federal prisons and other penal institutions; advises the U.S. president on petitions for paroles and pardons; represents the U.S. government in legal matters; gives legal advice to the president and other members of the Cabinet; and administers immigration laws.

Department of Labor
200 Constitution Avenue NW
Washington, DC 20210
Web site: www.dol.gov
Established: March 4, 1913; Department of Commerce and Labor created February 14, 1903; Bureau of Labor created in 1884

Protects the rights and working conditions of workers; promotes good relations between labor and management; tracks national economic changes and trends via the Bureau of Labor Statistics.

Department of State
2201 C Street NW
Washington, DC 20520
Web site: www.state.gov
Established: September 15, 1789; Department of Foreign Affairs created in 1781

Advises the president on foreign policy issues; works to carry out the country's foreign policy; maintains relations with foreign countries; negotiates treaties and agreements with foreign nations; represents the United States in the United Nations and other major international organizations; supervises embassies, missions, and consulates overseas.

Department of Transportation
400 7th Street, SW
Washington, DC 20590
Web site: www.dot.gov
Established: October 15, 1966

The department's nine agencies determine the nation's transportation policy and oversee such things as highway planning, development, and construction; aviation; urban mass transit; railroads; and the safety of waterways, ports, highways, and oil and gas pipelines.

Department of the Treasury
1500 Pennsylvania Avenue NW
Washington, DC 20220
Web site: www.ustreas.gov
Established: September 2, 1789

Tracks the financial state of the government and the economy; regulates the interstate and foreign sale of alcohol and firearms; supervises the printing of stamps for the U.S. Postal Service; and operates the Customs Service, which regulates and taxes imports. The Internal Revenue Service, a branch of the Treasury, regulates tax laws and collects federal taxes.

Department of Veterans' Affairs
810 Vermont Avenue NW
Washington, DC 20420
Web site: www.va.gov
Established: March 15, 1989; replaced Veterans Administration created in 1930

Provides benefits and services to veterans and their dependents, including pensions, education, rehabilitation, home loan guarantees, burial, compensation payments, and a medical care program.

Offices

Council of Economic Advisers
Old Executive Office Building
Washington, DC 20502
Web site: www.whitehouse.gov/cea
Established: February 20, 1946

Gathers data on economic developments and trends in order to help the president devise an economic policy that promotes employment, production, and purchasing power.

Council on Environmental Quality
722 Jackson Place NW
Washington, DC 20503
Web site: www.whitehouse.gov/ceq
Established: 1969

Coordinates federal environmental efforts; collaborates with federal agencies in the development of environmental policies and initiatives; works with the U.S. president to formulate programs, strategies, laws, and regulations that help preserve the environment and natural resources.

Domestic Policy Council
The White House
1600 Pennsylvania Avenue NW
Washington, DC 20500

Web site: www.whitehouse.gov/dpc
Established: 1993

Coordinates the domestic policy-making process in the White House and provides advice to the U.S. president; and ensures that policy is consistently implemented throughout federal agencies.

National Economic Council
The White House
1600 Pennsylvania Avenue NW
Washington, DC 20500
Web site: www.whitehouse.gov/nec
Established: January 25, 1993

Advises the president on matters related to U.S. and global economic policy; ensures that policy decisions and programs are consistent with the president's economic goals; monitors implementation of the president's economic policy agenda.

National Security Council (NSC)
Eisenhower Executive Office Building
Washington, DC 20504
Web site: www.whitehouse.gov/nsc
Established: July 26, 1947

Advises and assists the president on matters of national security and foreign policies; coordinates these policies among government agencies.

Office of Administration
Eisenhower Executive Office Building
725 17th Street NW
Washington, DC 20503
Web site: www.whitehouse.gov/oa
Established: December 12, 1977

Provides administrative support to all units in the executive office of the president, including personnel, financial management, data processing, library services, records maintenance, and general office operations.

Office of Faith-Based and Community Initiatives
The White House
1600 Pennsylvania Avenue NW
Washington, DC 20500
Web site: www.whitehouse.gov/fbci
Established: January 29, 2001

Enables religious and community organizations to target various national socioeconomic problems using social service grants from the agency; identifies and eliminates federal barriers to the full participation of faith-based programs in the provision of social services; and engaging in public education and outreach activities.

Office of Management and Budget
Executive Office Building
725 17th Street NW
Washington, DC 20503
Web site: www.whitehouse.gov/omb
Established: July 1, 1939

Assists the president prepare the federal budget and ensures that the other executive agencies comply with its provisions.

Office of National AIDS Policy
The White House
1600 Pennsylvania Avenue NW
Washington, DC 20500
Web site: www.whitehouse.gov/onap/aids.html
Established: 1992

Coordinates the efforts to reduce the number of new HIV/AIDS infections in the United States; advises the assistant secretary for health and other officials on the implementation and development of HIV/AIDS policy and priorities; and implements HIV/AIDS outreach programs.

Office of National Drug Control Policy
Executive Office of the President
Washington, DC 20503
Web site: www.whitehousedrugpolicy.gov
Established: January 29, 1989

Sets policies, priorities, and objectives for the nation's drug control program; and seeks to reduce illegal drug use, manufacturing, and trafficking, as well impede the rate of drug-related crime and violence.

Office of Science and Technology Policy
Eisenhower Executive Office Building
725 17th Street NW
Washington, DC 20502
Web site: www.ostp.gov
Established: May 11, 1976

Advises the president on the effects of science and technology on domestic and international affairs; works to ensure that the United States remains a world leader in science and technology.

Office of the United States Trade Representative
600 17th Street NW
Washington, DC 20508
Web site: www.ustr.gov
Established: January 15, 1963

Develops and coordinates U.S. international trade, commodity, and direct investment policy; and directs negotiations with other countries on such matters.

President's Foreign Intelligence Advisory Board

Web site: www.whitehouse.gov/pfiab
Established: 1956 as President's Board of Consultants on Foreign Intelligence Activities; name changed to President's Foreign Intelligence Advisory Board under President John F. Kennedy

Advises the president concerning the quality and adequacy of intelligence collection and analysis, of counterintelligence, and of other intelligence activities.

USA Freedom Corps (President's Council on Service and Civic Participation)

1600 Pennsylvania Avenue NW
Washington, DC 20500
Web site: www.whitehouse.gov/infocus/freedomcorps
Web site: www.usafreedomcorps.gov
Established: January 29, 2003

Coordinates national volunteer efforts; assists Americans in finding volunteer opportunities by using the resources of the federal government with the nonprofit, business, educational, and faith-based sectors.

First Ladies

President	First Lady	Born-Died	Marriage Year	State
Washington	Martha Dandridge Custis	1731-1802	1759	Virginia
J. Adams	Abigail Smith	1744-1818	1764	Massachusetts
Jefferson	Martha Wayles Skelton*	1748-1782	1772	Virginia
Madison	Dorothy "Dolley" Payne Todd	1768-1849	1794	North Carolina
Monroe	Elizabeth Kortright	1768-1830	1786	New York
J. Q. Adams	Louisa Catherine Johnson	1775-1852	1797	Maryland
Jackson	Rachel Donelson Robards*	1767-1828	1791	Virginia
Van Buren	Hannah Hoes*	1783-1819	1807	New York
W. H. Harrison	Anna Symmes	1775-1864	1795	New Jersey
Tyler	Letitia Christian	1790-1842	1813	Virginia
	Julia Gardiner	1820-1889	1844	New York
Polk	Sarah Childress	1803-1891	1824	Tennessee
Taylor	Margaret Mackall Smith	1788-1852	1810	Maryland
Fillmore	Abigail Powers	1798-1853	1826	New York
Pierce	Jane Means Appleton	1806-1863	1834	New Hampshire
Buchanan	none (never married)	—	—	—
Lincoln	Mary Todd	1818-1882	1842	Kentucky
A. Johnson	Eliza McCardle	1810-1876	1827	Tennessee
Grant	Julia Dent	1826-1902	1848	Missouri
Hayes	Lucy Ware Webb	1831-1889	1852	Ohio
Garfield	Lucretia Rudolph	1832-1918	1858	Ohio
Arthur	Ellen Lewis Herndon*	1837-1880	1859	Virginia
Cleveland	Frances Folsom	1864-1947	1886	New York
B. Harrison	Caroline Lavinia Scott	1832-1892	1853	Ohio
McKinley	Ida Saxton	1847-1907	1871	Ohio
T. Roosevelt	Alice Hathaway Lee*	1861-1884	1880	Massachusetts
	Edith Kermit Carow	1861-1948	1886	Connecticut

* Died before her husband took office.

President	First Lady	Born-Died	Marriage Year	State
Taft	Helen Herron	1861-1943	1886	Ohio
Wilson	Ellen Louise Axson	1860-1914	1885	Georgia
	Edith Bolling Galt	1872-1961	1915	Virginia
Harding	Florence Kling DeWolfe	1860-1924	1891	Ohio
Coolidge	Grace Anna Goodhue	1879-1957	1905	Vermont
Hoover	Lou Henry	1874-1944	1899	Iowa
F. D. Roosevelt	[Anna] Eleanor Roosevelt	1884-1962	1905	New York
Truman	Bess Wallace	1885-1982	1919	Missouri
Eisenhower	Mamie Geneva Doud	1896-1979	1916	Iowa
Kennedy	Jacqueline Lee Bouvier	1929-1994	1953	New York
L. B. Johnson	Claudia "Lady Bird" Alta Taylor	1912-	1934	Texas
Nixon	Thelma Catherine "Pat" Ryan	1912-1993	1940	Nevada
Ford	Elizabeth "Betty" Bloomer Warren	1918-	1948	Illinois
Carter	Rosalynn Smith	1927-	1946	Georgia
Reagan	Anne Frances "Nancy" Robbins Davis	1921-	1952	New York
G. H. W. Bush	Barbara Pierce	1925-	1945	New York
Clinton	Hillary Rodham	1947-	1975	Illinois
G. W. Bush	Laura Welch	1946-	1977	Texas

Presidential Libraries

Abraham Lincoln Presidential Library and Museum

Opened in October, 2004, the Abraham Lincoln Presidential Library contains more than twelve million books, documents, and artifacts relating to Illinois state history and the Lincoln era. The museum opened in April, 2005, and features multimedia "journeys" for Lincoln's life and presidency. Young people are encouraged to explore the hands-on exhibit titled "Mrs. Lincoln's Attic," while the Gettysburg Address and other important documents are displayed in the Treasure Gallery.

CONTACT INFORMATION:
112 North Sixth Street
Springfield, IL 62701
Ph.: (217) 558-8844
Web site: www.alplm.org/home.html

Rutherford B. Hayes Presidential Center and Library

Opened in 1916 as the Rutherford B. Hayes Memorial Museum and Library, it was the first of its kind in the United States. It holds more than one million manuscripts and books and has exhibits of objects including weapons used by Hayes as a Union general during the Civil War. The 25-acre site includes the Hayes family home.

CONTACT INFORMATION:
1337 Hayes Avenue
Fremont, OH 43420
Ph.: (419) 332-2081
Web site: www.rbhayes.org

Calvin Coolidge Presidential Library and Museum

The Calvin Coolidge collection was established in 1920 when Coolidge himself gave documents and memorabilia to Forbes Library. In 1956, the library board of trustees voted to establish the permanent Calvin Coolidge Memorial Room as a separate entity within the library. The collection grew to hold Coolidge's personal library from the White House and exhibits and manuscripts, both written and pictorial, that cover his youth, political career, and postpresidential years as a Northampton resident.

CONTACT INFORMATION:
Forbes Library
20 West Street
Northampton, MA 01060
Ph.: (413) 587-1014
Web site: www.forbeslibrary.org/coolidge/
coolidge.shtml

The Herbert Hoover Presidential Library

Dedicated on August 10, 1962, this 178-acre site includes the library, Hoover's birthplace, a reconstruction of his father's blacksmith shop, the Quaker meeting house that Hoover attended as a child, a schoolhouse, and the gravesite of Hoover and his wife. In addition to the library collection itself, life-size figures and interactive displays present the story of Hoover's life.

CONTACT INFORMATION:
PO Box 488
West Branch, IA 52358
Ph.: (319) 643-5301
Web site: www.hoover.nara.gov

Franklin D. Roosevelt Library and Museum

Dedicated on June 20, 1941, the Franklin D. Roosevelt Library is the oldest of the presidential libraries. The library was the conception of President Roosevelt himself, who realized the importance of keeping intact historic collections of official presidential papers and documents. Roosevelt helped design the building and donated land at his family estate at Hyde Park for its location. The library contains Roosevelt's papers and those of his wife, Eleanor, as well as the papers of more than one hundred friends and associates. Exhibits re-create the White House during Roosevelt's tenure as president and present FDR's life story. The Eleanor Roosevelt Gallery, added to the original library building in 1972, commemorates the president's active wife and her own many accomplishments. The 290-acre Franklin D. Roosevelt National Historic Site also includes the family home and Roosevelt's gravesite.

CONTACT INFORMATION:
4079 Albany Post Road
Hyde Park, NY 12538
Ph.: (845) 486-7770 or 1-800-FDR-VISIT
Web site: www.fdrlibrary.marist.edu

The Harry S. Truman Library

Officially dedicated on July 6, 1957, the library holds Truman's presidential papers and other documents relating to his life and career. There are also collections of books, periodicals, and other printed materials, as well as displays and objects including automobiles and a re-creation of the Oval Office while Truman was president. The gravesites of Truman and his wife, Bess Wallace Truman, are in the library's courtyard. The Truman Library is unique in that for many years the former president used it as his working office, sitting behind his desk from the White House.

CONTACT INFORMATION:
US Highway 24 and Delaware
Independence, MO 64050
Ph.: (816) 833-1400
Web site: www.trumanlibrary.org

The Dwight D. Eisenhower Presidential Library and Museum

Dedicated on May 1, 1962, the Eisenhower Library is part of a site that includes the family home on its original site, a museum, visitors' center, and the Place of Meditation, which has the graves of Eisenhower, his wife, Mamie, and their first son. The library holds documents relating to Eisenhower's presidency and life, especially his long military career. It contains over eleven million pages of manuscripts and thousands of photographs, books, and recordings. In addition are abundant audiovisual materials, in large part because the Eisenhower presidency was the first to be extensively covered by television.

CONTACT INFORMATION:
200 Southeast Fourth Street
Abilene, KS 67410
Ph.: (785) 263-6700
Web site: www.eisenhower.archives.gov

The John Fitzgerald Kennedy Library and Museum

Designed by internationally acclaimed architect I. M. Pei and dedicated on October 20, 1979, the Kennedy Library was substantially expanded and reopened in 1993 to better present the life and accomplishments of President John F. Kennedy to a new generation of Americans. The library makes extensive use of visual and audio presentations, many of them featuring the image and voice of President Kennedy. Exhibits re-create important moments of Kennedy's life and presidency, including the famous televised debate with Richard Nixon during the 1960 election. The library holds massive collections of Kennedy's own papers and those of other major figures of the twentieth century, over forty-two million manuscript pages in all. There are almost 200,000 photographs, six million feet of film and videotape, and one thousand audiotapes. The library has also collected almost all the known existing manuscripts of Nobel Prize-winning author Ernest Hemingway, including his original drafts for the novels *A Farewell to Arms* (1929) and *For Whom the Bell Tolls* (1940). The Kennedy Library's site at Columbia Point overlooks Boston Harbor, and the library is unique in that it can be reached by boat.

CONTACT INFORMATION:
Columbia Point
Boston, MA 02125
Ph.: (617) 514-1600 or 1-866-JFK-1960
Web site: www.jfklibrary.org

The Lyndon Baines Johnson Library and Museum

Dedicated on May 22, 1971, the Lyndon Baines Johnson Library is on the grounds of the University of Texas at Austin, and the library is associated with the university's graduate school of public affairs. The library holds the official papers of Johnson throughout his career as U.S. congressman, senator, vice president, and president. There are some forty million pages of manuscript. In addition, the library contains papers of Johnson's friends and associates, including his presidential cabinet. The extensive audiovisual files include numerous hours of oral history interviews. The displays and exhibits include dramatic presentations of the aftermath of President John F. Kennedy's assassination in Dallas in 1963, the escalating war in Vietnam, and the politics of the 1960's. Because of its location and the wealth of its holdings, the Johnson Library is the most visited and used of all presidential libraries.

CONTACT INFORMATION:
2313 Red River Street
Austin, TX 78705
Ph.: (512) 721-0200
Web site: www.lbjlib.utexas.edu

The Richard Nixon Library and Birthplace

Dedicated on July 19, 1990, this library sits on a nine-acre site that includes part of a Cali-

fornia orange grove once worked by the president's parents and the small wooden farmhouse where Nixon was born. The library's manuscript holdings contain materials from Nixon's public service, as well as papers and materials from his associates. Exhibits trace Richard Nixon's political career, including his meetings with world leaders and such triumphs as the establishment of détente with the Soviet Union and his historic visit to the People's Republic of China. One section presents the Watergate affair that led to Nixon's resignation in the face of impeachment. Richard Nixon and his wife, Pat, are buried in a formal garden on the grounds.

CONTACT INFORMATION:
18001 Yorba Linda Boulevard
Yorba Linda, CA 92886
Ph.: (714) 993-5075
Web site: www.nixonfoundation.org

The Gerald R. Ford Library and Museum

Dedicated on September 18, 1981, the Gerald R. Ford Library is on the campus of Ford's alma mater, the University of Michigan at Ann Arbor. The bulk of the library's holdings focus on Ford's years as president, but they also contain records of his brief time as vice president and his service in the House of Representatives. In addition, the papers of Betty Ford and of various advisers and associates are included in the collection. A companion facility, the Gerald R. Ford Museum, i located in Grand Rapids, Michigan. Exhibits trace Ford's political career, including his position as the first vice president and president to serve without being elected to those positions. There is also an exhibit on the United States' Bicentennial, celebrated during Ford's presidency.

CONTACT INFORMATION:
Library
1000 Beal Avenue
Ann Arbor, MI 48109-2114
Ph.: (734) 205-0555

Museum
303 Pearl Street, NW
Grand Rapids, MI 49504
Ph.: (616) 254-0400
Web site: www.ford.utexas.edu

The Jimmy Carter Library and Museum
    Dedicated on October 1, 1986, the Jimmy Carter Library is located on thirty-five acres of natural landscape near downtown Atlanta and features a peaceful, contemplative air. Conceived as an educational resource for students of the American presidency, the library highlights the development of that office during the twentieth century through films and exhibits. The library's collection is based on materials from the Carter presidency and includes manuscripts and papers from the president's wife, Rosalynn, and their staffs. Documents and materials for the period are included; these holdings are being increased systematically.
CONTACT INFORMATION:
441 Freedom Parkway
Atlanta, GA 30307
Ph.: (404) 865-7100
Web site: carterlibrary.galileo.peachnet.edu

The Ronald Reagan Presidential Library
    Dedicated on November 4, 1991, the Reagan Presidential Library is set in a landscape of unspoiled beauty and is designed in traditional California style. The library has a complete collection of all official records from the Reagan White House, including the records of many of the cabinet officers during the Reagan administration. In addition are numerous personal documents of the president and Nancy Reagan. There are more than forty-seven million documents in all. Photographs, videotapes, films, and audiotapes are part of the collection. Displays and exhibits trace Reagan's life and career, emphasizing his achievements as president. A gallery displays some of the thousands of gifts that Reagan and his wife received from foreign governments.

CONTACT INFORMATION:
40 Presidential Drive
Simi Valley, CA 93065
Ph.: (805) 577-4000
Web site: www.reaganfoundation.org/museum

The George Bush Presidential Library and Museum
    Groundbreaking ceremonies for the George Bush Presidential Library were held on November 30, 1994. Situated on the grounds of Texas A&M University, the library contains more than thirty-eight million pages of personal papers and official documents from George H. W. Bush's vice presidency and presidency. There is also an extensive audiovisual and photographic collection, as well as more than sixty thousand historical objects, including gifts from foreign nations and American citizens. The library has a classroom, the first of its kind in the presidential libraries network.
CONTACT INFORMATION:
1000 George Bush Drive West
College Station, TX 77845
Ph.: (979) 691-4000
Web site: bushlibrary.tamu.edu

William J. Clinton Presidential Library and Museum
    The Clinton Library and Museum serves as an archival and research facility, with seventy-six million pages of paper documents, nearly two million photographs, and more than seventy-five thousand museum artifacts. Replicas of the Oval Office and the Cabinet Room are open to visitors, and exhibits highlight domestic and foreign policies of the Clinton administration as well as the Clintons' life in the White House.
CONTACT INFORMATION:
1200 President Clinton Avenue
Little Rock, AR 72201
Ph.: (501) 374-4242
Web site: www.clintonlibrary.gov

Michael Witkoski; revised by Sarah M. Hilbert

Museums, Historic Sites, and Web Sites

EDITOR'S NOTE: *Among the following are homes of presidents or presidential couples, before or after their years in office. Many of these places are mentioned in the text of* American Presidents, *and all are open to the public. The first four listings contain information on all or most of the presidents or First Ladies; the sites listed thereafter are president-specific and appear in alphabetical order by president's name. All Web sites were visited by editors of Salem Press in September, 2005.*

General Resources on Presidents and First Ladies

American President Web site:
www.americanpresident.org

The American Presidents Web site:
www.americanpresidents.org/places
(Includes links to presidential places for each president)

National Archives and Records Administration Presidential Libraries Web site: www.archives.gov/presidential-libraries

National First Ladies' Library
331 South Market Avenue
Canton, OH 44702
Ph.: (330) 452-0876
Web site: www.firstladies.org

Presidential Museums, Historic Sites, and Web Sites

JOHN ADAMS AND JOHN QUINCY ADAMS

Adams National Historical Park
135 Adams Street
Quincy, MA 02169
Ph.: (617) 770-1175 (visitor information)
Web site: www.nps.gov/adam
(Includes home of John and Abigail Adams)

Massachusetts Historical Society
1154 Boylston Street
Boston, MA 02215
Ph.: (617) 536-1608
Web site: www.masshist.org
(Contains the Adams Papers Collection)

JAMES BUCHANAN

James Buchanan Home
1120 Marietta Avenue
Lancaster, PA 17603
Ph.: (717) 392-8721
Web site: www.wheatland.org
(Wheatland, home of James Buchanan and
　Harriet Lane)

JIMMY CARTER

Jimmy Carter National Historic Site
CONTACT:
300 North Bond Street
Plains, GA 31780
Ph.: (229) 824-4104
Web site: www.nps.gov/jica
E-mail: JICA_Site_Supervisor@nps.gov

GROVER CLEVELAND

**Grover Cleveland Birthplace, National
　Park, and Museum**
207 Bloomfield Avenue
Caldwell, NJ 07006
Ph.: (973) 226-0001
Web site: www.westessexguide.com/gcb

WILLIAM JEFFERSON CLINTON

Clinton Birthplace Home
117 South Hervey
Hope, AR 71802
Ph.: (870) 777-4455
Web site: www.clintonbirthplace.org
E-mail: Clinton@arkansas.net

CALVIN COOLIDGE

**President Calvin Coolidge State Historic
　Site**
Plymouth Notch, VT
CONTACT:
P.O. Box 247
Plymouth, VT 05056
Ph.: (802) 672-3773
Web site: www.vmga.org/windsor/
　plymouthhd.html

DWIGHT D. EISENHOWER

Eisenhower National Historic Site
97 Taneytown Road
Gettysburg, PA 17325
Ph.: (717) 338-9114
Web site: www.nps.gov/eise
E-mail: eise_site_manager@nps.gov
(Home of Dwight and Mamie Eisenhower)

MILLARD FILLMORE

Millard Fillmore Museum
24 Shearer Avenue
East Aurora, NY 14052
Ph.: (716) 652-8875
(Home of Millard and Abigail Fillmore)

GERALD R. FORD

Gerald R. Ford Exhibit
Gerald R. Ford Conservation Center
1326 South 32d Street
Omaha, NE 68105
Web site: www.nebraskahistory.org/
　conserve/exhibit.htm

Gerald R. Ford Museum
303 Pearl Street NW
Grand Rapids, MI 49504
Ph.: (616) 254-0400
Web site: www.ford.utexas.edu
E-mail: ford.museum@nara.gov

JAMES A. GARFIELD

James A. Garfield National Historic Site
8095 Mentor Avenue
Mentor, OH 44060
Ph.: (440) 255-8722
Web site: www.nps.gov/jaga
(Lawnfield, home of James and Lucretia
    Garfield)

ULYSSES S. GRANT

U. S. Grant Home State Historic Site
500 Bouthillier Street
Galena, IL 61036
Ph.: (815) 777-0248; (815) 777-3310
Web site: www.granthome.com/
    grant_home.htm

Ulysses S. Grant National Historic Site
7400 Grant Road
St. Louis, MO 63123
Ph.: (314) 842-3298 (visitor information);
    (314) 842-1867 (headquarters/recorded
    message)
Web site: www.nps.gov/ulsg
E-mail: ULSG_Site_Manager@nps.gov
(White Haven, home of Ulysses and Julia
    Grant)

WARREN G. HARDING

The Harding Home
380 Mt. Vernon Avenue
Marion, OH 43302
Ph.: (740) 387-9630; (800) 600-6894
Web site: www.ohiohistory.org/textonly/
    places/harding
(Home of Warren and Florence Harding)

BENJAMIN HARRISON

The President Benjamin Harrison Home
1230 North Delaware Street
Indianapolis, IN 46202
Ph.: (317) 631-1888
Web site:
    www.presidentbenjaminharrison.org
E-mail: harrison@surf-ici.com
(Home of Benjamin and Caroline Harrison;
    includes research library)

WILLIAM HENRY HARRISON

Berkeley Plantation
12602 Harrison Landing Road
Charles City, VA 23030
Ph.: (804) 829-6018
Web site: www.jamesriverplantations.org/
    Berkeley.html
(Ancestral home and birthplace of William
    Henry Harrison)

Grouseland
3 West Scott Street
Vincennes, IN 47591
Ph.: (812) 882-2096
Web site: www.grouselandfoundation.org
Email: info@grouselandfoundation.org
(Home of William Henry and Anna
    Harrison)

RUTHERFORD B. HAYES

Rutherford B. Hayes Presidential Center
Spiegel Grove
Fremont, OH 43420
Ph.: (419) 998-7737
Web site: www.rbhayes.org
E-mail: admin@rbhayes.org
(Spiegel Grove, home of Rutherford and
    Lucy Hayes)

HERBERT HOOVER

Herbert Hoover National Historic Site
CONTACT:
110 Parkside Drive, Box 607
West Branch, IA 52358
Ph.: (319) 643-2541
Web site: www.nps.gov/heho
E-mail: HEHO_Interpretation@nps.gov
(Includes presidential library and museum)

ANDREW JACKSON

Andrew Jackson State Park
196 Andrew Jackson Park Road
Lancaster, SC 29720
Ph.: (803) 285-3344
Web site: www.discoversouthcarolina.com/
stateparks/parkdetail.asp?PID=1797
(Includes Waxhaws Museum)

The Hermitage
4580 Rachel's Lane
Hermitage, TN 37076
Ph.: (615) 889-2941
Web site: www.thehermitage.com
E-mail: info@thehermitage.com
(Home of Andrew and Rachel Jackson)

THOMAS JEFFERSON

Monticello
931 Thomas Jefferson Parkway
Charlottesville, VA 22902
Ph.: (804) 984-9822; (804) 984-9800 (recorded
message)
Web site: www.monticello.org
E-mail: publicaffairs@monticello.org
(Home of Thomas and Martha Jefferson)

ANDREW JOHNSON

Andrew Johnson National Historic Site
CONTACT:
P.O. Box 1088
Greeneville, TN 37744
Ph.: (423) 638-3551 (visitor information);
(423) 639-3711 (headquarters)
Web site: www.nps.gov/anjo
E-mail: ANJO_Superintendent@nps.gov
(Includes home of Andrew and Eliza
Johnson)

President Andrew Johnson Museum and Library
67 Gilland Street
Greeneville, TN
CONTACT:
P.O. Box 5026
Tusculum College
Greeneville, TN 37743
Ph.: (423) 636-7348; (800) 729-0256, ext. 348
Web site: ajmuseum.tusculum.edu

LYNDON B. JOHNSON

LBJ Museum at San Marcos
120 West Hopkins, Suite 200
San Marcos, TX 78666
Ph.: (512) 396-3247
Web site: www.lbjsanmarcos.org

Lyndon B. Johnson National Historical Park
P.O. Box 329
Johnson City, TX 78636
Ph.: (830) 868-7128, ext. 244
Web site: www.nps.gov/lyjo
E-mail: LYJO_Superintendent@nps.gov

Lyndon B. Johnson State Historical Park
P.O. Box 238
Stonewall, TX 78671
Ph.: (830) 644-2252; (800) 792-1112
Web site: www.tpwd.state.tx.us/spdest/
    findadest/parks/lyndon_b_johnson
(Includes bus tours of LBJ Ranch, home of
    Lyndon and Lady Bird Johnson)

JOHN F. KENNEDY

John F. Kennedy National Historic Site
83 Beals Street
Brookline, MA 02446
Ph.: (617) 566-7937
Web site: www.nps.gov/jofi
(Birthplace and boyhood home of John F.
    Kennedy)

ABRAHAM LINCOLN

Ford's Theatre National Historic Site
511 Tenth Street, NW
Washington, DC 20024
Ph.: (202) 426-6924
Web site: www.nps.gov/foth
E-mail: NACC_FOTH_Interpretation@nps
    .gov
(Includes museum)

Lincoln-Herndon Law Office
6th and Adams Streets
Springfield, IL 62701
Ph.: (217) 785-7960
Web site: www.state.il.us/hpa/hs/
    Herndon.htm
(Includes presidential library)

Lincoln Home National Historic Site
413 South Eighth Street
Springfield, IL 62701
Ph.: (217) 492-4241, ext. 221
Web site: www.nps.gov/liho
E-mail: lincolnhome@nps.gov

The Lincoln Museum
200 E. Berry Street
Fort Wayne, IN 46802
Ph.: (260) 455-3864
Web site: www.thelincolnmuseum.org
E-mail: TheLincolnMuseum@LNC.com

WILLIAM McKINLEY

McKinley Memorial Library and Museum
40 North Main Street
Niles, OH 44446
Ph.: (330) 652-1704
Web site: www.mckinley.lib.oh.us
E-mail: mckinley@mcklib.org
(Includes birthplace memorial)

Saxton-McKinley House
331 South Market Avenue
Canton, OH 44702
Ph.: (330) 452-0876
Web site: www.firstladies.org/
    SaxtonMcKinleyHouse.htm
(Ancestral home of Ida Saxton McKinley;
    home of William and Ida McKinley; site
    of National First Ladies Library)

JAMES MADISON

The James Madison Museum
129 Caroline Street
Orange, VA 22960
Ph.: (540) 672-1776
Web site: www.jamesmadisonmus.org
E-mail: info@jamesmadisonmus.org

Montpelier
11407 Constitution Highway
Montpelier Station, VA 22957
Ph.: (540) 672-2728
Web site: www.montpelier.org
(Home of James and Dolley Madison)

Todd House
Independence National Historical Park
    Visitor Center
3d and Chestnut Streets
Philadelphia, PA
Ph.: (215) 597-8974
Web site: www.nps.gov/inde/todd-
    house.html
(Home of Dolley Payne Todd before she
    married James Madison)

JAMES MONROE

Ash Lawn-Highland
1000 James Monroe Parkway
Charlottesville, VA 22902
Ph.: (434) 293-9539
Web site: www.ashlawnhighland.org
E-mail: info@ashlawnhighland.org
(Home of James and Elizabeth Monroe)

**James Monroe Museum and Memorial
    Library**
908 Charles Street
Fredericksburg, VA 22401
Ph.: (540) 654-1043
Web site: www.umw.edu/
    jamesmonroemuseum
(Home of James and Elizabeth Monroe)

RICHARD M. NIXON

Nixon Presidential Materials
Web site: nixon.archives.gov/index.php
(The official online resource for the
    historical materials created and received
    by the Nixon White House)

FRANKLIN PIERCE

The Pierce Manse
14 Penacook Street
Concord, NH
CONTACT:
P.O. Box 425
Concord, NH 03302
Ph.: (603) 224-5954; (603) 225-2068
Web site: www.newww.com/free/pierce/
    pierce.html
(Home of Franklin and Jane Pierce)

JAMES K. POLK

The James K. Polk Ancestral Home
301 West 7th Street
Columbia, TN 38402
Ph.: (931) 388-2354
Web site: www.jameskpolk.com/new
E-mail: jkpolk@usit.net

RONALD REAGAN

The Reagan Exhibit
Eureka College
300 E. College Avenue
Eureka, IL 61530
Ph.: (309) 467-3721; (888) 438-7352
Web site: www.eureka.edu/tour/
    panoramas/reagan.asp
E-mail: reagan.eureka.edu/Legacy/
    exhibit.html

FRANKLIN D. ROOSEVELT

Eleanor Roosevelt National Historic Site
4097 Albany Post Road
Hyde Park, NY 12538
Ph.: (845) 229-9115
Web site: www.nps.gov/elro
E-mail: ROVA_webmaster@nps.gov
(Val-Kill Cottage, home of Eleanor
    Roosevelt)

Home of Franklin D. Roosevelt National Historic Site
4097 Albany Post Road
Hyde Park, NY 12538
Ph.: (845) 229-9115
Web site: www.nps.gov/hofr
E-mail: ROVA_webmaster@nps.gov
(Springwood, family home of Franklin D. Roosevelt)

The Little White House State Historic Site
401 Little White House Road
Georgia Highway 85 Alt.
Warm Springs, GA 31830
Ph.: (706) 655-5870
Web site: www.fdr-littlewhitehouse.org
(Franklin Roosevelt's residence in Georgia)

Roosevelt Campobello International Park
New Brunswick, Canada
CONTACT:
Executive Secretary
P.O. Box 129
Lubec, ME 04652
Ph.: (506) 752-2922
Web site: www.fdr.net/englishii
E-mail: info@fdr.net
(Summer home of Franklin and Eleanor Roosevelt)

THEODORE ROOSEVELT

Sagamore Hill National Historic Site
20 Sagamore Hill Road
Oyster Bay, NY 11771
Ph.: (516) 922-4447; (516) 922-4788
Web site: www.nps.gov/sahi
E-mail: sahi_information@nps.gov
(Home of Theodore and Edith Roosevelt)

Theodore Roosevelt Birthplace National Historic Site
28 East 20th Street
New York, NY 10003
Ph.: (212) 260-1616
Web site: www.nps.gov/thrb
E-mail: MASI_Superintendent@nps.gov

Theodore Roosevelt Collection
Houghton Library
Harvard University
Cambridge, MA 02138
Ph.: (617) 384-7938
Web site: www.theodoreroosevelt.org/
    modern/harvardcol.htm
E-mail: wfdailey@fas.harvard.edu

WILLIAM HOWARD TAFT

William Howard Taft National Historic Site
2038 Auburn Avenue
Cincinnati, OH 45219
Ph.: (513) 684-3262
Web site: www.nps.gov/wiho
E-mail: WIHO_Superintendent@nps.gov

HARRY S. TRUMAN

Harry S. Truman National Historic Site
223 North Main Street
Independence, MO 64050
Ph.: (816) 254-2720; (816) 254-9929 (visitor information)
Web site: www.nps.gov/hstr
E-mail: HSTR_Superintendent@nps.gov
(Truman home and farm)

JOHN TYLER

Sherwood Forest Plantation
John Tyler Highway
Charles City, VA 23030
Ph.: (804) 282-1441
Web site: www.sherwoodforest.org
E-mail: KTyler@SherwoodForest.org
(Home of John and Julia Tyler)

MARTIN VAN BUREN

Martin Van Buren National Historic Site
1013 Old Post Road
Kinderhook, NY 12106
Ph.: (518) 758-9689
Web site: www.nps.gov/mava
E-mail: MAVA_info@nps.gov
(Lindenwald, estate of Martin Van Buren)

GEORGE WASHINGTON

Mount Vernon Estate and Gardens
Mount Vernon, VA
CONTACT:
P.O. Box 110
Mount Vernon, VA 22121
Ph.: (703) 780-2000
Web site: www.mountvernon.org
(Home of George and Martha Washington)

WOODROW WILSON

Woodrow Wilson Birthplace and Museum
18-24 North Coalter Street
Staunton, VA 24402
Ph.: (540) 885-0897
Web site: www.woodrowwilson.org
E-mail: woodrow@woodrowwilson.org

Woodrow Wilson House Museum
2340 S Street, NW
Washington, DC 20008
Ph.: (202) 387-4062
Web site: www.woodrowwilsonhouse.org
(Home of Woodrow and Edith Wilson)

Glossary

AAA: the Agricultural Adjustment Act. Passed in 1933 as part of Franklin D. Roosevelt's New Deal, it intended to reduce farm production in order to increase farm income. Declared unconstitutional by the Supreme Court in 1936.

Alien and Sedition Acts: laws passed by the Federalist Party in 1789 that authorized the president to deport "undesirable aliens" and imprison persons who criticized the government or its officials. Widely unpopular, as well as unconstitutional, the acts were among the reasons the Federalists lost the 1800 elections.

American Independent Party: third party established in 1964 by George Wallace, governor of Alabama, as a protest against Democratic and Republican policies, but which helped tilt the election in favor of Richard M. Nixon, the Republican candidate.

amnesty: the authority of the president to grant a pardon to members of a group who have violated federal law. *See also* **pardon.**

Australian ballot: a secret ballot which allows voters complete confidentiality. It did not come into general use in the United States until the 1880's.

balanced ticket: the nomination of presidential and vice presidential candidates who appeal to the widest spectrum of potential voters—for example, having one candidate from the East Coast and the other from the Midwest or West.

bandwagon: a political campaign that is perceived as a winner. Uncommitted or undecided delegates or voters are encouraged to "jump on the bandwagon" instead of backing a losing candidate.

Bay of Pigs: the term used to describe the abortive anti-Castro invasion of Cuba in 1961.

Bill of Rights: the first ten amendments to the Constitution which guarantee the rights of individuals and of the states.

bloody shirt: a campaign technique used by Republicans in the years following the Civil War to remind voters that many members of the Democratic Party had opposed the war.

boss: the leader of a political organization, sometimes called a "machine," that can deliver votes in a specific area.

Buck Stops Here, The: the sign which Harry S. Truman had on his desk in the Oval Office, indicating that ultimate responsibility rests with the president.

Bull Moose Party: the party which nominated Theodore Roosevelt for president in 1912. *See also* **Progressive Party.**

bully pulpit: a phrase made popular by Theodore Roosevelt for the use of the presidency to inspire or lead.

cabinet: the heads of the major departments of the executive branch, such as state, treasury, defense, and commerce. Their dual purposes are to administer their specific agencies and to advise the president. Cabinet members are appointed by the president with the advice and consent of the Senate but can be removed at any time by the president.

Camp David: a presidential retreat in the Maryland countryside. Named by Dwight D. Eisenhower after his grandson.

Camp David accords: the agreement signed by Israeli prime minister Menachem Begin and Egyptian president Anwar el-Sadat on September 17, 1978, as mediated by President Jimmy Carter. The accords, which began the peace process in the Middle East, were named after the presidential retreat where the negotiations took place.

campaign: the activities associated with seeking public office, starting from announcing one's candidacy, through the nomination, to canvassing for votes in the general election. It includes fund-raising and the preparation and placement of advertising.

Checkers speech: the nationally televised address delivered by Republican vice presidential candidate Richard M. Nixon on September 23, 1952, in which he defended accepting special and secret contributions. Nixon claimed that the funds were used purely for political purposes and that the only gift kept by the Nixon family was their cocker spaniel, Checkers.

chief executive: the term for the president's role in implementing the decisions of Congress in particular and the federal government in general.

Civil Rights Act of 1964: a far-ranging civil rights law proposed by President John F. Kennedy and enacted under his successor, Lyndon B. Johnson. It outlawed discrimination in voter registration, public accommodations such as hotels and restaurants, and employment. It also gave the federal government the authority to take action to ensure these provisions. The most powerful civil rights act since Reconstruction, it was enacted only after the longest debate in Senate history to date (eighty-three days).

Civil Rights Act of 1968: legislation that prohibited discrimination in housing.

Civil Rights movement: a broad term to cover the different campaigns by African Americans from the late 1940's onward to secure their rights as American citizens. Its legislative results included the Civil Rights Acts of 1964 and 1968.

civil service reform: the replacement of the spoils system of awarding public offices with employment of government workers on the basis of open, competitive examinations. The Civil Service Act of 1883 was the original legislation in this effort.

closed primary: a primary election restricted to registered voters of the specific party conducting the election.

coalition: the uniting of various political groups to achieve electoral victory. For example, a traditional Democratic coalition consists of African Americans, urban ethnic groups, and organized labor.

code words: seemingly innocent words or phrases that carry a meaning which a candidate wishes to communicate to certain voters but not openly express. "Law and order" and "states' rights" as synonyms for "anti-civil rights" are examples.

Cold War: a period of hostility, but not actual warfare, between communist nations and the United States and its allies from 1948 to 1989.

commander in chief: as designated by the Constitution, the president as the person in charge of the armed forces of the United States.

conscription and selective service acts: the laws by which the federal government drafts citizens into the armed forces. Conscription acts were enacted during the Civil War (1862) and World War I (1918). A peacetime draft was established in 1940 and again in 1948. The draft was ended during the Nixon administration, although mandatory registration was retained.

conservative: as used in American politics, the term for those who generally favor the status quo, or existing situation, and who wish to make few if any changes, and then make them as deliberately as possible. Generally, conservatives reject or limit the role for government in addressing most social ills but favor a strong "law and order" approach to crime and a reduction of taxes, especially on business and the wealthy.

Constitution: a written document that establishes the procedures by which the United

States is governed. The original Constitution was drafted in 1787 and ratified by 1788. It has been amended numerous times since.

Constitutional Union Party. *See* **Know-Nothing Party**

convention: a meeting of members (delegates) of a political party to nominate candidates and to write and adopt a party platform. Presidential candidates are nominated at the national political conventions, held once every four years.

"corrupt bargain": the charge made against John Quincy Adams and Henry Clay by supporters of Andrew Jackson after the presidential election of 1824. Although Jackson had received a plurality of the popular and electoral votes, no candidate received a majority. When the House of Representatives decided the election, Clay's supporters voted for Adams. Later, Adams appointed Clay as his secretary of state.

cross of gold: the dramatic phrase used by William Jennings Bryan at the 1896 Democratic Convention in support of using more available silver as the basis for U.S. currency.

Cuban Missile Crisis: the confrontation between the United States and the Soviet Union over the presence of Soviet missiles based in Cuba. The Soviets withdrew the missiles after President John F. Kennedy placed a naval embargo around Cuba.

dark horse: the descriptive name for a person who seems to have little chance of winning a nomination or an election.

Democratic Party: in modern American politics, one of the two major parties. The oldest continuous political party in the world, it was founded prior to 1800 by Thomas Jefferson as the Democratic Republican Party; the name was changed by the time of Andrew Jackson. In general, it supports the traditional freedoms guaranteed under the Constitution along with government action to improve economic and social conditions.

Dixiecrat Party: a group of southern Democrats angered by the civil rights platform of the 1948 Democratic Party who nominated Strom Thurmond of South Carolina for president. Officially known as the States' Rights Party.

draft: to nominate by popular acclaim, generally at a national political convention, a person who has not been an announced candidate for president.

electoral college: the body of persons selected from each state to cast that state's electoral votes for president and vice president. According to the Constitution, each state has the same number of electoral votes as it has senators and representatives in Congress. Another three electors are from the District of Columbia, for a total of 538. The electoral votes of a state go to the candidate who wins the popular vote of that state.

Emancipation Proclamation: a wartime measure issued by Abraham Lincoln that abolished slavery in all states "in rebellion against the United States." Slavery was officially ended in the United States with the ratification of the Thirteenth Amendment in 1865.

Era of Good Feelings: the name given to the second term of James Monroe, who was re-elected without opposition and with only one dissenting vote in the electoral college.

executive order: a directive from the president based on powers granted to the president by Congress.

executive privilege: the asserted right of the president, as chief executive, to withhold information from Congress. Invoked by Richard M. Nixon during the Watergate crisis and Bill Clinton during the Lewinsky investigation but strongly restricted by the Supreme Court.

Fair Deal: the name given by President Harry S. Truman in his 1949 state of the union address to his domestic policies. The name deliberately evoked Franklin D. Roosevelt's New Deal.

favorite son: a candidate for president whose support comes largely from his or her own state. Sometimes indicating a serious candidate, it is more often a way to control a bloc of votes for bargaining purposes.

Federalist Party: the political party that formed around Alexander Hamilton during the administration of George Washington. It favored a strong central government and protection of wealth and property rights. It faded after John Adams's defeat by Thomas Jefferson in 1800.

filibuster: the debating of a bill at great length in Congress (or other legislative body) in order to defeat it. It is generally used by opponents who lack the votes to defeat a bill outright. The most notable use of the filibuster is in the Senate, whose rules allow almost unlimited debate.

fireside chats: the informal radio addresses used by Franklin D. Roosevelt to discuss issues directly with the American public.

First Lady: the traditional popular title for the wife of the president.

Fourteen Points: conditions prepared by Woodrow Wilson for drawing up a peace treaty following World War I. They formed the basis for the League of Nations.

gerrymander: to redraw political boundary lines, such as those for congressional districts, to favor one party over another. Named after Elbridge Gerry, who was governor of Massachusetts in 1812 when such a district was established. An editorial cartoonist drew the district to resemble a salamander and renamed it a "gerrymander."

Gettysburg Address: Abraham Lincoln's brief but eloquent remarks at the dedication of the National Cemetery at the site of the Civil War battlefield at Gettysburg. In his address, Lincoln redefined the United States as a union of people, rather than independent states, and thus undercut the legal arguments for secession and extreme states' rights.

Good Neighbor Policy: the term used by Franklin D. Roosevelt to describe the relations between the United States and Latin America.

GOP: an abbreviation for Grand Old Party; a nickname for the Republican Party.

Great Depression: the severe breakdown in the economy which began with the collapse of the stock market in 1929 and resulted in high unemployment, bank failures, bankruptcies, and intense social unrest. The measures of Franklin D. Roosevelt's New Deal were designed to address these conditions.

Great Society: the term used by Lyndon B. Johnson to describe his ambitious social programs proposed during 1965 and 1966, including the War on Poverty.

"Happy Days Are Here Again": the song played at Franklin D. Roosevelt's nomination at the Democratic Convention of 1932. Since then, it has been the unofficial theme of the Democratic Party.

"Happy Warrior, the": the nickname given to Governor Alfred E. Smith of New York by Franklin D. Roosevelt in his speech nominating Smith for the presidency at the 1928 Democratic Convention.

hat in the ring: a term meaning that a political candidate has officially announced his or her intentions to run for office. It derives from early boxing and wrestling matches, where a person would throw his hat into the ring to indicate that he was ready to fight.

Hatch Act: a 1939 federal law that prohibited political parties from forcing federal employees to contribute money or involuntarily take an active role in campaigning.

He Kept Us Out of War: the slogan used by Democratic presidential candidate Woodrow Wilson in the 1916 campaign. World War I had begun in Europe in 1914, and Wilson had pursued a course of strict neutrality.

Hundred Days, the: the period following the inauguration of Franklin D. Roosevelt in 1933, during which much of the New Deal legislation was enacted. The term has since become a convenient measuring point for the progress of any new administration.

I Like Ike: the popular slogan to express support for Dwight D. (Ike) Eisenhower in the presidential elections of 1952 and 1956.

impeachment: a formal accusation of wrongdoing against a public official. The Constitution provides that the House of Representatives has the power to impeach a president for "high crimes and misdemeanors." If impeached, the president is tried by the Senate.

In Your Heart, You Know He's Right: the slogan used by supporters of conservative Republican nominee Barry Goldwater in 1964. Democrats and independents countered with the rejoinder "Yes—extreme right."

inauguration: the formal action that installs the president in office.

incumbent: a candidate in an election who holds the office being voted on.

Interstate Commerce Commission: the oldest independent regulatory agency of the federal government, established in 1887 to regulate trade within the United States, set minimum standards of service and safety, and ensure fair prices.

Jacksonian democracy: a political and social movement, reaching its peak with the presidency of Andrew Jackson, that expanded the role of the average citizen in government.

Jeffersonianism: a belief in a limited government that respects the rights of individuals and does the least possible to restrict their liberties.

Keep Cool with Coolidge: the Republican slogan during the 1924 presidential campaign, used to make a virtue of the candidate's taciturn style.

Kennedy-Nixon debates: the first televised presidential debates, held during the 1960 election. John F. Kennedy is widely credited with having won the debates, which helped propel him to a narrow victory over Richard M. Nixon in the November election.

Kitchen Cabinet: an informal group that provides the president with advice. The term was popularized during the presidency of Andrew Jackson.

Know-Nothing Party: an antiforeign, anti-Catholic party (also called the Constitutional Union Party or the American Party) formed during the 1850's. Its members, when asked about the organization, responded "I know nothing."

lame duck: a politician serving out a term who is not eligible for reelection. Traditionally, lame ducks are seen as handicapped by their status.

Lame Duck Amendment: the Twentieth Amendment to the Constitution, which changed the presidential inauguration date from March 4 to January 20 and set the beginning of congressional terms on January 3 instead of March 4.

law and order: during the 1960's and 1970's, a code word used by politicians to signal an antiliberal, anti-civil rights position.

League of Nations: an international assembly to regulate disputes between states and preserve peace. Proposed by Woodrow Wilson at the end of World War I, it proved ineffective, largely because of lack of U.S. support.

liberal: in American politics, the term used to describe those who favor a stronger role of government in addressing issues and solving problems facing the nation as a whole. Traditionally, liberals have been concerned with civil rights and individual liberties, are tolerant of the views of others, and support progressive movements.

Lincoln-Douglas debates: a series of public appearances by Democrat Stephen A. Douglas and Republican Abraham Lincoln during the 1858 Illinois senatorial campaign. These debates made Lincoln a force in national politics and helped him gain the Republican nomination for president in 1860.

line-item veto: the authority of the president to veto specific portions of an appropriation bill without having to reject the entire bill.

Ma, Ma, Where's My Pa?: the derogatory chant used by Republicans against Democratic nominee Grover Cleveland, who as a young man may have fathered a child out of wedlock. Upon Cleveland's election, the Democratic response was "Gone to the White House, Ha-Ha-Ha."

machine: the name given to a political organization on the state or local level that is well organized and efficient in providing votes and public support for its candidates. The term is generally associated with big cities, such as the Daley Machine in Chicago or Tammany Hall in New York.

March on Washington: the massive, peaceful demonstration of supporters of civil rights legislation who converged on the capital in August, 1963. It was at this event that Dr. Martin Luther King, Jr., gave his famous "I Have a Dream" speech.

Medicaid: a health insurance program established in 1960 to assist poor persons who need medical care.

Medicare: a health insurance measure enacted in 1965 to provide medical care to the elderly.

missile gap: an issued raised by Democratic nominee John F. Kennedy in the 1960 election about a supposed shortfall in U.S. military capability relative to the Soviet Union.

Monroe Doctrine: a statement of U.S. foreign policy by President James Monroe in 1823 which declared that the Western Hemisphere was no longer subject to colonization or control by European powers.

muckrakers: journalists and other writers who expose illegal, dangerous, or improper activities by large corporations, government bodies, or government officials. They were especially influential during the late nineteenth and early twentieth centuries.

mugwumps: persons who are formally associated with one political party but who support another party. The term was first used to describe Republicans who refused to support their party's presidential candidate James G. Blaine.

New Deal: the term given to the policies of Franklin D. Roosevelt in fighting the Great Depression, especially during his first two administrations.

New Federalism: a term used by Richard M. Nixon to describe his plan to move much of the responsibility and authority of the federal government to the state governments.

New Freedom: the term used by Woodrow Wilson in the election of 1912 and during his first term as president to describe greater activism by the federal government and more involvement in public policy by citizens.

New Frontier: the popular name for the policies of John F. Kennedy during his presidency. Following his assassination and the inauguration of Lyndon B. Johnson, the New Frontier was replaced by the Great Society.

"no third term": a popular tradition in American presidential politics, originating with George Washington, that no president should serve more than two terms. The tradition was broken by the unprecedented four terms of Democrat Franklin D. Roosevelt and restored in 1951 with the passage of the Twenty-second Amendment. Ironically, two presidents who probably could have overcome the tradition of "no third term" were Dwight D. Eisenhower and Ronald Reagan, both Republicans.

NRA: the National Recovery Act. Part of the New Deal of Franklin D. Roosevelt, it helped address the Great Depression but was declared unconstitutional by the Supreme Court in 1935.

nullification: the theory that a state can nullify, or declare void within its borders, an act of Congress or a decision of the Supreme Court. The doctrine is in clear violation of the Constitution.

open primary: a primary election open to all registered voters of whatever party. Also known as a cross-over primary. *See also* **closed primary.**

Oval Office: the personal office of the president, often used to represent the presidency. This is an example of the rhetorical devices of synecdoche (the part stands for the whole), in which the office of the president signifies the White House, and metonymy (an object stands for a larger concept), in which the White House signifies the presidency itself.

pardon: the authority of the president to grant release from punishment or legal consequences of a crime before or after conviction. A pardon may be individual, as when President Gerald R. Ford pardoned former president Richard M. Nixon for crimes that he may have committed while in office, or general, as the blanket pardon that President Jimmy Carter granted to Vietnam draft evaders. *See also* **amnesty.**

plank: a part of a platform that deals with a specific issue.

platform: the official statement of principles and goals by a political party, generally drafted and adopted by the party at its national convention.

"Plumed Knight, the": the nickname for Republican presidential candidate James G. Blaine.

pocket veto: an automatic veto that takes place if Congress adjourns after sending a bill to the president and the president refuses to sign it.

popular vote: as distinct from the electoral vote, the number of individual voters who cast their ballots for a particular presidential candidate. Because of the electoral college system, a president can be elected with a majority of the electoral vote without a majority of the popular vote. This is especially true during elections featuring a strong third party. Abraham Lincoln, Woodrow Wilson, Harry S. Truman, John F. Kennedy, Richard M. Nixon, and Bill Clinton all won the presidency in this fashion. Rutherford B. Hayes and Benjamin Harrison won a majority of the electoral vote and an absolute minority of the popular vote, and thus were elected president.

Populist Party: a party loosely organized in the agricultural South and West during the late 1800's seeking greater representation and better treatment for farmers. For all practical purposes, it merged with the Democratic Party in 1896 with the nomination of William Jennings Bryan, who championed many of its causes.

president-elect: the term for the candidate who has been selected by the electoral college to be the next president but who has not yet been inaugurated.

presidential succession: the order in which the office of president is filled in case of death or disability. According to the Presidential Succession Act of 1947, the vice president, Speaker of the House, president pro tempore of the Senate, and secretary of state are the first four in line of succession.

primary: a process which allows voters to select the delegates to a party's presidential nominating convention in a special state election. The delegates chosen in such primaries are generally pledged or committed to voting for their candidate.

Progressive Party: although used by several parties in U.S. political history, a term most often referring to the party organized in 1912 to support the presidential candidacy of Theodore Roosevelt, who had been denied renomination for president by the Republican Party. Because of its close association with Roosevelt, it was popularly known as the Bull Moose Party.

Prohibition: the national ban on the sale of alcoholic beverages, as instituted by the Eighteenth Amendment in 1918. The Twenty-first Amendment, adopted in 1933, repealed the Eighteenth Amendment and ended national Prohibition, but it left states and counties with the power to enact local prohibition statutes.

Radical Republicans: during the Civil War and its immediate aftermath, those Republicans who favored immediate emancipation of slaves, vigorous prosecution of the war, and harsh treatment of the defeated Southern states.

Reconstruction: the period following the Civil War in which the states of the former Confederacy were brought back into the Union.

Republican Party: one of the two major parties in modern U.S. politics. It was founded in the 1850's in opposition to slavery. Traditionally, it has opposed greater government intervention, especially in social welfare, health care, and education, and has favored the reduction of taxes, especially on big business and capital gains.

Rum, Romanism, and Rebellion: a description of the Democrats as the party identified with "Rum [alcohol], Romanism [Catholicism], and Rebellion [the Civil War]" by minister Samuel D. Burchard in a statement supporting Republican James G. Blaine for president in 1884. The offensive words helped defeat Blaine in the election.

runoff primary: a second primary election held if no candidate in the first primary receives a majority of votes cast. It was originally used in a number of Southern states during the period when there was no substantial Republican Party and nomination in the Democratic primary was tantamount to election.

segregation: the policy of keeping races separated in housing, education, and other facilities, either by law (de jure) or custom (de facto).

Share the Wealth: the slogan used by Senator Huey P. Long during the 1930's as he contemplated a campaign for the presidency.

smoke-filled room: the popular shorthand term to describe the private deals made by professional politicians to nominate candidates and pass legislation. The term was coined at the 1920 Republican Convention, where party leaders nominated Warren G. Harding as a compromise candidate for president.

Social Security: legislation passed in 1935, as a major part of Franklin D. Roosevelt's New Deal, to provide public assistance to the elderly and disabled. The program has since been expanded and is a cornerstone of the domestic policy of the United States.

Southern strategy: a term to describe the approach, used by Richard M. Nixon in 1968 and subsequent Republican presidential candidates, to court Southern voters by covert attacks on the pro-civil rights policies of the Democratic Party.

split-ticket voting: voting for candidates of two or more parties for different offices. *See also* **straight-ticket voting.**

spoils system: the practice of hiring public officials according to their political affiliation, based on the premise that "to the victors belong the spoils."

State of the Union address: an annual message to Congress, required by the Constitution, during which the president customarily presents a legislative program for the coming year.

states' rights: the doctrine that the powers of the individual states are equal or superior to those of the federal government. This concept was used extensively by Southerners prior to the Civil War to justify secession and after it to defend segregation.

States' Rights Party: the official name for the Dixiecrat Party.

straight-ticket voting: voting only for the candidates of a single party. *See also* **split-ticket voting.**

Tammany Hall: the popular name for the Democratic Party machine in New York City, especially during the nineteenth century. It was named after the building in which the organization members met.

Teapot Dome scandal: the 1929 bribery conviction of Albert B. Fall, secretary of the interior under Warren G. Harding, for taking money to grant valuable oil leases, including those at Teapot Dome in Wyoming. The case became a symbol of corruption in the Harding administration.

third party: in modern American politics, an influential political party other than the Democratic Party or Republican Party. Generally arising over a specific issue and often representing no more than a protest against existing conditions, third parties can sometimes influence the outcomes of presidential elections.

ticket: the name given to the candidates for a political party running in a single election. For example, the Democratic ticket consists of all Democratic nominees for offices from the presidency to local offices.

Tippecanoe and Tyler Too: the slogan used by Whigs during the presidential election of 1840 to express support for William Henry Harrison, victor of the Battle of Tippecanoe, and his vice presidential running mate, John Tyler.

Tonkin Gulf Resolution: a measure passed by Congress in 1964 giving President Lyndon B. Johnson the authority to respond to attacks on U.S. forces by North Vietnam.

United Nations: an international body, formed after World War II, to secure the peaceful resolution of international disputes and to develop global cooperation. It was the successor to the earlier League of Nations.

veto: the act of the president returning a bill to Congress so that it does not become law. Two-thirds of the members present and voting are required to overturn a presidential veto.

vice president: the constitutional officer who assumes the presidency upon the death or incapacity of the president and who presides over the Senate, although voting only to break a tie.

Voting Rights Act of 1965: legislation that expanded the right to vote, especially to African Americans, by prohibiting the use of literacy tests to discriminate against potential voters. The act also expanded federal supervision of restrictions on voting, especially in Southern states that had traditionally set barriers to participation by African Americans.

VP, the Veep: informal names for the vice president.

War on Poverty: the popular name given to efforts of Lyndon B. Johnson's Great Society programs to improve social conditions in the United States. Specifically, the Economic Opportunity Act of 1964 declared "war on poverty" by assisting poor communities in the undertaking of antipoverty programs involving job training, vocational education, and job development.

Warren Commission: the body authorized by the Senate on December 13, 1963, to investigate and report on the assassination of John F. Kennedy. Named for Chief Justice Earl Warren, who headed it, the commission consisted of members of the Senate and House of Representatives (including future president Gerald R. Ford), former Central Intelligence Agency head Allen Dulles, and John McCloy, the former high commissioner of Germany. On September 28, 1964, the commission issued a report finding that Lee Harvey Oswald acted alone in the assassination of President Kennedy.

Watergate: the popular term for the burglary of Democratic National Committee headquarters in 1972 and the following cover-up and obstruction of justice that were orchestrated by the Nixon White House.

Whig Party: a major party in the United States from about 1834 to 1854. It was established by opponents of Democratic president Andrew Jackson who opposed his strong presidency. After winning the presidency in 1840 and 1848, it faded after 1852, and many of its members joined the new Republican Party.

WPA: the Works Project (or Progress) Administration. This part of the New Deal was designed to stimulate the economy through employment in public projects ranging from highways to the arts.

Yellow Dog Democrat: the name given to a voter who is so loyal to the Democratic Party that he or she would "vote for a yellow dog if it ran on the Democratic ticket."

Michael Witkoski

Bibliography

General References

Bennett, Anthony J. *The American President's Cabinet: From Kennedy to Bush.* New York: St. Martin's Press, 1996.

Gilbert, Robert E. *The Mortal Presidency: Illness and Anguish in the White House.* 2d ed. New York: Fordham University Press, 1998.

Graff, Henry F., ed. *The Presidents: A Reference History.* 2d ed. New York: Charles Scribner's Sons, 1996.

Hyland, Pat. *Presidential Libraries and Museums: An Illustrated Guide.* Washington, D.C.: Congressional Quarterly, 1995.

Kane, Joseph N. *Facts About the Presidents: A Compilation of Biographical and Historical Information from George Washington to Bill Clinton.* 6th ed. New York: H. W. Wilson, 1993.

Michaels, Judith E. *The President's Call: Executive Leadership from FDR to George Bush.* Pittsburgh: University of Pittsburgh Press, 1997.

Neustadt, Richard E. *Presidential Power and the Modern Presidents: The Politics of Leadership from Roosevelt to Reagan.* 4th ed. New York: Free Press, 1990.

Simpson, Brooks D. *The Reconstruction Presidents.* Lawrence: University Press of Kansas, 1998.

The Presidency

Burton, David H. *The Learned Presidency: Theodore Roosevelt, William Howard Taft, Woodrow Wilson.* Rutherford, N.J.: Fairleigh Dickinson University Press, 1988.

Campbell, Colin. *The U.S. Presidency in Crisis: A Comparative Perspective.* New York: Oxford University Press, 1998.

Congressional Quarterly. *Powers of the Presidency.* 2d ed. Washington, D.C.: Author, 1997.

Cronin, Thomas E., and Michael A. Genovese. *The Paradoxes of the American Presidency.* New York: Oxford University Press, 1998.

Freidel, Frank B., and William Pencak. *The White House: The First Two Hundred Years.* Boston: Northeastern University Press, 1994.

Frendreis, John P., and Raymond Tatalovich. *The Modern Presidency and Economic Policy.* Itasca, Ill.: F. E. Peacock, 1994.

Hart, John. *The Presidential Branch: From Washington to Clinton.* 2d ed. Chatham, N.J.: Chatham House, 1995.

Hess, Stephen. *Presidents and the Presidency: Essays.* Washington, D.C.: Brookings Institution, 1996.

Kessler, Ronald. *Inside the White House: The Hidden Lives of Modern Presidents and the Secrets of the World's Most Powerful Institution.* New York: Pocket Books, 1995.

Kiewe, Amos, ed. *The Modern Presidency and Crisis Rhetoric.* Westport, Conn.: Praeger, 1994.

Levy, Leonard W., and Louis Fisher, eds. *Encyclopedia of the American Presidency.* New York: Simon & Schuster, 1994.

Lorant, Stefan. *The Glorious Burden: The American Presidency.* Lenox, Mass.: Author's Editions, 1976.

Martin, Fenton S., and Robert Goehlert. *How to Research the Presidency.* Washington, D.C.: Congressional Quarterly, 1996.

Nelson, Lyle Emerson. *American Presidents: Year by Year.* 3 vols. Armonk, N.Y.: M. E. Sharpe, 2004.

Nelson, Michael. *Guide to the Presidency.* 2d ed. Washington, D.C.: Congressional Quarterly, 1996.

_____. *The Presidency and the Political System.* 4th ed. Washington, D.C.: CQ Press, 1995.

Nichols, David K. *The Myth of the Modern Presidency.* University Park: Pennsylvania State University Press, 1994.

Ragsdale, Lyn. *Vital Statistics on the Presidency: Washington to Clinton.* Washington, D.C.: Congressional Quarterly, 1996.

Riccards, Michael P. *The Ferocious Engine of Democracy: A History of the American Presidency.* Lanham, Md.: Madison Books, 1994.

Romero, Francine Sanders. *Presidents from Theodore Roosevelt Through Coolidge, 1901-1929: Debating the Issues in Pro and Con Primary Documents.* Westport, Conn.: Greenwood Press, 2002.

Smith, Craig A., and Kathy B. Smith. *The White House Speaks: Presidential Leadership as Persuasion.* Westport, Conn.: Praeger, 1994.

Sturgis, Amy H., comp. *Presidents from Hayes Through McKinley, 1877-1901: Debating the Issues in Pro and Con Primary Documents.* Westport, Conn.: Greenwood Press, 2003.

Thomas, Norman C., Joseph A. Pitka, and Richard Watson. *The Politics of the Presidency.* 4th ed. Washington, D.C.: CQ Press, 1997.

Thompson, Kenneth W. *Twenty Years of Papers on the Presidency.* Lanham, Md.: University Press of America, 1995.

Tsongas, Paul E. *Journey of Purpose: Reflections on the Presidency, Multiculturalism, and Third Parties.* New Haven, Conn.: Yale University Press, 1996.

Whitney, David C., and Robin Vaughn Whitney. *American Presidents.* 9th ed. Pleasantville, N.Y.: Reader's Digest, 2001.

Zernicke, Paul H. *Pitching the Presidency: How Presidents Depict the Office.* Westport, Conn.: Praeger, 1994.

Presidential Campaigns and Elections

Boller, Paul F. *Presidential Campaigns.* Rev. ed. New York: Oxford University Press, 1996.

Chace, James. *1912: Wilson, Roosevelt, Taft and Debs—The Election That Changed the Country.* New York: Simon & Schuster, 2004.

Congressional Quarterly. *Presidential Elections, 1789-1996.* Washington, D.C.: Author, 1997.

_____. *Selecting the President: From 1789 to 1996.* Washington, D.C.: Author, 1997.

Davis, James W. *U.S. Presidential Primaries and the Caucus-Convention System: A Sourcebook.* Westport, Conn.: Greenwood Press, 1997.

Hacker, Kenneth L. *Candidate Images in Presidential Elections.* Westport, Conn.: Praeger, 1995.

Haskell, John. *Fundamentally Flawed: Understanding and Reforming Presidential Primaries.* Lanham, Md.: Rowman & Littlefield, 1996.

Havel, James T. *U.S. Presidential Candidates and the Elections: A Biographical and Historical Guide.* New York: Macmillan, 1996.

Jamieson, Kathleen H. *Packaging the Presidency: A History and Criticism of Presidential Campaign Advertising.* 3d ed. New York: Oxford University Press, 1996.

McGillivray, Alice V., and Richard M. Scammon. *America at the Polls: A Handbook of American Presidential Election Statistics.* Washington, D.C.: Congressional Quarterly, 1994.

Morello, John A. *Selling the President, 1920: Albert D. Lasker, Advertising, and the Election of Warren G. Harding.* Westport, Conn.: Praeger, 2001.

Morris, Richard S. *Behind the Oval Office: Winning the Presidency in the Nineties.* New York: Random House, 1997.

Morris, Roy. *Fraud of the Century: Rutherford B. Hayes, Samuel Tilden, and the Stolen Election of 1876.* New York: Simon & Schuster, 2003.

Palmer, Niall A. *The New Hampshire Primary and the American Electoral Process.* Westport, Conn.: Praeger, 1997.

Pika, Joseph A., and Richard A. Watson. *The Presidential Contest: With a Guide to the 1996 Presidential Race.* 5th ed. Washington, D.C.: CQ Press, 1995.

Polsby, Nelson W., and Aaron B. Wildavsky. *Presidential Elections: Strategies and Structures of American Politics.* 9th ed. Chatham, N.J.: Chatham House, 1996.

Schantz, Harvey L., ed. *American Presidential Elections: Process, Policy, and Political Change.* Albany: State University of New York Press, 1996.

Schlesinger, Arthur M., Fred L. Israel, and David J. Frent, eds. *Election of 1840 and the Harrison/Tyler Administrations.* Broomall, Pa.: Mason Crest, 2002.

Southwick, Leslie H. *Presidential Also-Rans and Running Mates, 1788 Through 1996.* 2d ed. Jefferson, N.C.: McFarland, 1998.

Tenpas, Kathryn D. *Presidents as Candidates: Inside the White House for the Presidential Campaign.* New York: Garland, 1997.

Troy, Gil. *See How They Ran: The Changing Role of the Presidential Candidate.* Rev. ed. Cambridge, Mass.: Harvard University Press, 1996.

Woodward, Bob. *The Choice: How Clinton Won.* New York: Simon & Schuster, 1997.

Wright, Russell O. *Presidential Elections in the United States: A Statistical History, 1860-1922.* Jefferson, N.C.: McFarland, 1995.

First Ladies and Presidential Families

Anthony, Carl Sferrazza. *Nellie Taft: The Unconventional First Lady of the Ragtime Era.* New York: HarperCollins, 2003.

Baker, Jean H. *Mary Todd Lincoln: A Biography.* New York: W. W. Norton, 1987.

Brady, Patricia. *Martha Washington: An American Life.* New York: Viking, 2005.

Brendon, Piers. *Ike, His Life and Times.* New York: Harper & Row, 1986.

Bush, Barbara. *Barbara Bush: A Memoir.* New York: Charles Scribner's Sons, 1994.

Caroli, Betty B. *The Roosevelt Women.* New York: Basic Books, 1998.

Carter, Rosalynn. *First Lady from Plains.* Boston: Houghton Mifflin, 1984.

Clinton, Hillary. *Living History.* New York: Simon and Schuster, 2003.

David, Lester. *Ike and Mamie: The Story of the General and His Lady.* New York: Putnam, 1981.

Edwards, Anne. *The Reagans: Portrait of a Marriage.* New York: St. Martin's Press, 2003.

Fields, Joseph E., ed. *Worthy Partner: The Papers of Martha Washington.* Westport, Conn.: Greenwood Press, 1994.

Geer, Emily A. *First Lady: The Life of Lucy Webb Hayes.* Kent, Ohio: Kent State University Press, 1984.

Gelles, Edith B. *First Thoughts: Life and Letters of Abigail Adams.* New York: Twayne, 1998.

Keller, Rosemary S. *Abigail Adams and the American Revolution: A Personal History.* New York: Arno Press, 1982.

Kerr, Joan P., ed. *A Bully Father: Theodore Roosevelt's Letters to His Children.* New York: Random House, 1995.

Kilian, Pamela. *Barbara Bush: A Biography.* New York: St. Martin's Press, 1992.

King, Norman. *The Woman in the White House: The Remarkable Story of Hillary Rodham Clinton.* New York: Carol, 1996.

Klein, Edward. *All Too Human: The Love Story of Jack and Jackie Kennedy.* New York: Pocket Books, 1996.

Levin, Phyllis L. *Abigail Adams: A Biography.* New York: St. Martin's Press, 1987.

Miller, Nathan. *The Roosevelt Chronicles.* Garden City, N.Y.: Doubleday, 1979.

Milton, Joyce. *The First Partner, Hillary Rodham Clinton: A Biography.* New York: William Morrow, 1999.

Monk, William E. *Theodore and Alice, a Love Story: The Life and Death of Alice Lee Roosevelt.* Interlaken, N.Y.: Empire State Books, 1994.

Morris, Sylvia J. *Edith Kermit Roosevelt: Portrait of a First Lady.* New York: Coward, McCann & Geoghegan, 1980.

Nagel, Paul C. *The Adams Women: Abigail and Louisa Adams, Their Sisters and Daughters.* New York: Oxford University Press, 1987.

Packard, Jarrold M. *The Lincolns in the White House: Four Years That Shattered a Family.* New York: St. Martin's Press, 2005.

Radcliffe, Donnie. *Hillary Rodham Clinton: A First Lady for Our Time.* New York: Warner Books, 1993.

Ross, Ishbel. *Grace Coolidge and Her Era: The Story of a President's Wife.* New York: Dodd, Mead, 1962. Reprint. Plymouth, Vt.: Calvin Coolidge Memorial Foundation, 1988.

Saunders, Frances W. *Ellen Axson Wilson: First Lady Between Two Worlds.* Chapel Hill: University of North Carolina Press, 1985.

Schreiner, Samuel A. *The Trials of Mrs. Lincoln: The Harrowing Never-Before-Told Story of Mary Todd Lincoln's Last and Finest Years.* New York: Donald I. Fine, 1987.

Shachtman, Tom. *Edith and Woodrow: A Presidential Romance.* New York: Putnam, 1981.

Tribble, Edwin, ed. *A President in Love: The Courtship Letters of Woodrow Wilson and Edith Bolling Galt.* Boston: Houghton Mifflin, 1981.

Truman, Margaret. *Bess W. Truman.* New York: Macmillan, 1986.

Van der Heuvel, Gerry. *Crown of Thorns and Glory: Mary Todd Lincoln and Varina Howell Davis, the Two First Ladies of the Civil War.* New York: E. P. Dutton, 1988.

Warner, Judith. *Hillary Clinton: The Inside Story.* New York: Signet, 1993.

Wead, Doug. *All the Presidents' Children: Triumph and Tragedy in the Lives of America's First Families.* New York: Atria Books, 2003.

_____. *The Raising of a President: The Mothers and Fathers of Our Nation's Leaders.* New York: Atria Books, 2005.

Withey, Lynne. *Dearest Friend: A Life of Abigail Adams.* New York: Free Press, 1981.

Young, Jeff C. *The Fathers of American Presidents: From Augustine Washington to William Blythe and Roger Clinton.* Jefferson, N.C.: McFarland, 1997.

Young, Nancy Beck. *Lou Henry Hoover: Activist First Lady.* Lawrence: University Press of Kansas, 2004.

Presidential Quotations

Boritt, G. S., ed. *Of the People, by the People, for the People and Other Quotations by Abraham Lincoln.* New York: Columbia University Press, 1996.

Brallier, Jess M. *Presidential Wit and Wisdom: Maxims, Mottoes, Sound Bites, Speeches, and Asides—Memorable Quotes from America's Presidents.* New York: Penguin, 1996.

Frost-Knappman, Elizabeth, ed. *The World Almanac of Presidential Quotations: Quotations from America's Presidents.* New York: Pharos Books, 1993.

Gallen, David, ed. *The Quotable Truman.* New York: Carroll & Graf, 1994.

Kaminski, John P., ed. *Citizen Jefferson: The Wit and Wisdom of an American Sage.* Madison, Wis.: Madison House, 1994.

Lott, Davis N. *The President Speaks: The Inaugural Addresses of the American Presidents from Washington to Clinton.* New York: Henry Holt, 1994.

The White House

Abbott, James A., and Elaine M. Rice. *Designing Camelot: The Kennedy White House Restoration.* New York: Van Nostrand Reinhold, 1998.

Caroli, Betty Boyd. *Inside the White House: America's Most Famous Home, the First Two Hundred Years.* Garden City, N.Y.: Doubleday, 1992.

Freidel, Frank B., and William Pencak, eds. *The White House: The First Two Hundred Years.* Boston: Northeastern University Press, 1994.

Seale, William. *The White House: The History of an American Idea.* Washington, D.C.: American Institute of Architects Press, 1992.

The Presidents:

GEORGE WASHINGTON

Brookhiser, Richard. *Founding Father: Rediscovering George Washington.* New York: Free Press, 1996.

Callahan, North. *Thanks, Mr. President: The Trail-Blazing Second Term of George Washington*. New York: Cornwall Books, 1991.

Clark, E. Harrison. *All Cloudless Glory: The Life of George Washington*. Washington, D.C.: Regnery, 1995.

Dalzell, Robert F. *George Washington's Mount Vernon: At Home in Revolutionary America*. New York: Oxford University Press, 1998.

Edgar, Gregory T. *Campaign of 1776: The Road to Trenton*. Bowie, Md.: Heritage Books, 1995.

Ellis, Joseph J. *His Excellency: George Washington*. New York: Alfred A. Knopf, 2004.

Hirschfeld, Fritz. *George Washington and Slavery: A Documentary Portrayal*. Columbia: University of Missouri Press, 1997.

Lewis, Thomas A. *For King and Country: The Maturing of George Washington, 1748-1760*. New York: HarperCollins, 1993.

Randall, Willard S. *George Washington: A Life*. New York: Henry Holt, 1997.

Smith, Richard N. *Patriarch: George Washington and the New American Nation*. Boston: Houghton Mifflin, 1993.

JOHN ADAMS

Adams, John. *John Adams: A Biography in His Own Words*. Edited by James B. Peabody. New York: Harper & Row, 1973.

Brown, Ralph. *The Presidency of John Adams*. Lawrence: University Press of Kansas, 1975.

East, Robert A. *John Adams*. Boston: Twayne, 1979.

Ellis, Joseph J. *Passionate Sage: The Character and Legacy of John Adams*. 1993. Rev. ed. New York: Norton, 2001.

Ferling, John E. *John Adams: A Bibliography*. Westport, Conn.: Greenwood Press, 1994.

_____. *John Adams: A Life*. Knoxville: University of Tennessee Press, 1992.

Grant, James. *John Adams: Party of One*. New York: Farrar, Straus and Giroux, 2005.

McCullough, David. *John Adams*. New York: Simon & Schuster, 2002.

Shepard, Jack. *The Adams Chronicles: Four Generations of Greatness*. Boston: Little, Brown, 1975.

Thompson, C. Bradley. *John Adams and the Spirit of Liberty*. Lawrence: University Press of Kansas, 1998.

THOMAS JEFFERSON

Adams, William H. *The Paris Years of Thomas Jefferson*. New Haven, Conn.: Yale University Press, 1997.

Ambrose, Stephen E. *Undaunted Courage: Meriwether Lewis, Thomas Jefferson, and the Opening of the American West*. New York: Simon & Schuster, 1996.

Bedini, Silvio A. *Thomas Jefferson: Statesman of Science*. New York: Macmillan, 1990.

Bernstein, R. B. *Thomas Jefferson*. New York: Oxford University Press, 2003.

Burstein, Andrew. *The Inner Jefferson: Portrait of a Grieving Optimist*. Charlottesville: University Press of Virginia, 1995.

Ellis, Joseph J. *American Sphinx: The Character of Thomas Jefferson*. New York: Alfred A. Knopf, 1997.

Gaustad, Edwin S. *Sworn on the Altar of God: A Religious Biography of Thomas Jefferson*. Grand Rapids, Mich.: Wm. B. Eerdmans, 1997.

Gordon-Reed, Annette. *Thomas Jefferson and Sally Hemings: An American Controversy*. 1996. Rev. ed. Charlottesville: University Press of Virginia, 2000.

Lautman, Robert C. *Thomas Jefferson's Monticello: A Photographic Portrait*. New York: Monacelli Press, 1997.

Lerner, Max. *Thomas Jefferson: America's Philosopher-King*. New Brunswick, N.J.: Transaction, 1996.

Mapp, Alf J. *Thomas Jefferson: Passionate Pilgrim*. Lanham, Md.: Madison Books, 1991.

Miller, Douglas T. *Thomas Jefferson and the Creation of America*. New York: Facts On File, 1997.

Randall, Willard S. *Thomas Jefferson: A Life*. New York: Henry Holt, 1993.

Risjord, Norman K. *Thomas Jefferson*. Madison, Wis.: Madison House, 1994.

Shackleford, George G. *Thomas Jefferson's Travels in Europe, 1784-1789*. Baltimore: The Johns Hopkins University Press, 1995.

Simon, James F. *What Kind of Nation: Thomas Jefferson, John Marshall, and the Epic Struggle to Create a United States*. New York: Simon & Schuster, 2002.

Stein, Susan. *The Worlds of Thomas Jefferson at Monticello*. New York: Harry N. Abrams, 1993.

JAMES MADISON

Banning, Lance. *The Sacred Fire of Liberty: James Madison and the Founding of the Federal Republic*. Ithaca, N.Y.: Cornell University Press, 1995.

Cerami, Charles. *Young Patriots: The Remarkable Story of Madison, Hamilton, and the Crisis That Built the Constitution*. Naperville, Ill.: Sourcebooks, 2005.

Goldwin, Robert A. *From Parchment to Power: How James Madison Used the Bill of Rights to Save the Constitution*. Washington, D.C.: AEI Press, 1997.

Ketcham, Ralph L. *James Madison: A Biography*. New York: Macmillan, 1971.

McCoy, Drew R. *The Last of the Fathers: James Madison and the Republican Legacy*. New York: Cambridge University Press, 1989.

Madison, James. *James Madison: A Biography in His Own Words*. Edited by Merrill D. Peterson. New York: Harper & Row, 1974.

Matthews, Richard K. *If Men Were Angels: James Madison and the Heartless Empire of Reason*. Lawrence: University Press of Kansas, 1995.

Miller, William L. *The Business of May Next: James Madison and the Founding*. Charlottesville: University Press of Virginia, 1992.

Moore, Virginia. *The Madisons: A Biography*. New York: McGraw-Hill, 1979.

Rakove, Jack N. *James Madison and the Creation of the American Republic*. 2d. ed. New York: Longman, 2002.

Rutland, Robert A., ed. *James Madison and the American Nation, 1751-1836: An Encyclopedia*. New York: Simon & Schuster, 1994.

_____. *James Madison: The Founding Father*. New York: Macmillan, 1987.

_____. *The Presidency of James Madison*. Lawrence: University Press of Kansas, 1990.

Wills, Gary. *James Madison*. Edited by Arthur M. Schlesinger. New York: Henry Holt, 2002.

JAMES MONROE

Ammon, Harry. *James Monroe: A Bibliography*. Westport, Conn.: Meckler, 1991.

_____. *James Monroe: The Quest for National Identity*. New York: McGraw-Hill, 1971.

Cunningham, Noble E. *The Presidency of James Monroe*. Lawrence: University Press of Kansas, 1996.

Monroe, James. *Political Writings of James Monroe*. Edited by James Lucier. Washington, D.C.: Regnery, 2001.

JOHN QUINCY ADAMS

Hargreaves, Mary W. M. *The Presidency of John Quincy Adams*. Lawrence: University Press of Kansas, 1985.

Hecht, Marie B. *John Quincy Adams: A Personal History of an Independent Man*. New York: Macmillan, 1972.

Lewis, James E. *John Quincy Adams: Policymaker for the Union*. Wilmington, Del.: SR Books, 2001.

Nagel, Paul C. *John Quincy Adams: A Public Life, a Private Life*. New York: Alfred A. Knopf, 1997.

Parsons, Lynn H. *John Quincy Adams*. Madison, Wis.: Madison House, 1998.

_____. *John Quincy Adams: A Bibliography*. Westport, Conn.: Greenwood Press, 1993.

Remini, Robert V. *John Quincy Adams*. New York: Times Books, 2002.

Richards, Leonard L. *The Life and Times of Congressman John Quincy Adams*. New York: Oxford University Press, 1986.

Shepherd, Jack. *Cannibals of the Heart: A Personal Biography of Louisa Catherine and John Quincy Adams*. New York: McGraw-Hill, 1980.

ANDREW JACKSON

Cole, Donald B. *The Presidency of Andrew Jackson*. Lawrence: University Press of Kansas, 1993.

Davis, Burke. *Old Hickory: A Life of Andrew Jackson*. New York: Dial Press, 1977.

Marszalek, John F. *The Petticoat Affair: Manners, Mutiny, and Sex in Andrew Jackson's White House*. New York: Free Press, 1997.

Remini, Robert V. *Andrew Jackson: A Bibliography*. Westport, Conn.: Meckler, 1991.

_____. *Andrew Jackson and His Indian Wars*. New York: Viking, 2001.

_____. *Andrew Jackson and the Course of American Democracy*. New York: Harper & Row, 1984.

_____. *The Jacksonian Era*. 2d ed. Wheeling, Ill.: Harlan Davidson, 1997.

_____. *The Life of Andrew Jackson*. New York: Harper & Row, 1988.

Sellers, Charles G., comp. *Andrew Jackson: A Profile*. New York: Hill & Wang, 1971.

Williams, Frank B. *Tennessee's Presidents*. Knoxville: University of Tennessee Press, 1981.

MARTIN VAN BUREN

Cole, Donald B. *Martin Van Buren and the American Political System*. Princeton, N.J.: Princeton University Press, 1984.

Moser, Harold D., and Carole B. Moser. *John Tyler: A Bibliography*. Westport, Conn.: Greenwood Press, 2001.

Mushkat, Jerome, and Joseph G. Rayback. *Martin Van Buren: Law, Politics, and the Shaping of Republican Ideology*. DeKalb: Northern Illinois University Press, 1997.

Niven, John. *Martin Van Buren: The Romantic Age of American Politics*. New York: Oxford University Press, 1983.

Silby, Joel H. *Martin Van Buren and the Emergence of American Popular Politics*. Lanham, Md.: Rowman & Littlefield, 2002.

Widmer, Edward L. *Martin Van Buren*. New York: Times Books, 2005.

Wilson, Major L. *The Presidency of Martin Van Buren*. Lawrence: University Press of Kansas, 1984.

WILLIAM HENRY HARRISON

Peterson, Norma L. *The Presidencies of William Henry Harrison and John Tyler*. Lawrence: University Press of Kansas, 1989.

Schlesinger, Arthur M., Fred L. Israel, and David J. Frent, eds. *Election of 1840 and the Harrison/Tyler Administrations*. Broomall, Pa.: Mason Crest, 2002.

Stevens, Kenneth R. *William Henry Harrison: A Bibliography*. Westport, Conn.: Greenwood Press, 1998.

JOHN TYLER

Chidsey, Donald B. *And Tyler Too*. Nashville: Thomas Nelson, 1978.

Merk, Frederick. *Fruits of Propaganda in the Tyler Administration*. Cambridge, Mass.: Harvard University Press, 1971.

Monroe, Dan. *Republican Vision of John Tyler*. College Station: Texas A&M University Press, 2003.

Morgan, Robert J. *A Whig Embattled: The Presidency Under John Tyler*. Lincoln: University of Nebraska, 1954. Reprint. Hamden, Conn.: Archon Books, 1974.

Peterson, Norma L. *The Presidencies of William Henry Harrison and John Tyler*. Lawrence: University Press of Kansas, 1989.

Walker, Jane C. *John Tyler: President of Many Firsts*. Blacksburg, Va.: McDonald & Woodward, 2001.

JAMES K. POLK

Bergeron, Paul H. *The Presidency of James K. Polk*. Lawrence: University Press of Kansas, 1987.

Dusinberre, William. *Slavemaster President: The Double Career of James Polk*. New York: Oxford University Press, 2003.

Haynes, Sam W. *James K. Polk and the Expansionist Impulse*. Edited by Oscar Handlin. 2d ed. New York: Longman, 2002.

Leonard, Thomas M. *James K. Polk: A Clear and Unquestionable Destiny*. Wilmington, Del.: SR Books, 2001.

Williams, Frank B. *Tennessee's Presidents*. Knoxville: University of Tennessee Press, 1981.

ZACHARY TAYLOR

Bauer, K. Jack. *Zachary Taylor: Soldier, Planter, Statesman of the Old Southwest*. Baton Rouge: Louisiana State University Press, 1985.

Holman, Hamilton. *The Three Kentucky Presidents: Lincoln, Taylor, Davis*. 2d ed. Lexington: University of Kentucky Press, 2003.

Roberts, Jeremy. *Zachary Taylor*. Minneapolis: Lerner, 2005.

Smith, Elbert B. *The Presidencies of Zachary Taylor and Millard Fillmore*. Lawrence: University Press of Kansas, 1988.

MILLARD FILLMORE

Crawford, John E. *Millard Fillmore: A Bibliography*. Westport, Conn.: Greenwood Press, 2002.

Dix, Dorothea L. *The Lady and the President: The Letters of Dorothea Dix and Millard Fillmore*. Edited by Charles M. Snyder. Lexington: University Press of Kentucky, 1975.

Grayson, Benson L. *The Unknown President: The Administration of President Millard Fillmore*. Washington, D.C.: University Press of America, 1981.

Rayback, Robert J. *Millard Fillmore: Biography of a President*. Buffalo, N.Y.: Buffalo Historical Society, 1959.

Scarry, Robert J. J. *Millard Fillmore*. Jefferson, N.C.: McFarland, 2001.

Smith, Elbert B. *The Presidencies of Zachary Taylor and Millard Fillmore*. Lawrence: University Press of Kansas, 1988.

FRANKLIN PIERCE

Bisson, Wilfred J., and Gerry Hayden. *Franklin Pierce: A Bibliography*. Westport, Conn.: Greenwood Press, 1993.

Gara, Larry. *The Presidency of Franklin Pierce*. Lawrence: University Press of Kansas, 1991.

Nichols, Roy F. *Franklin Pierce, Young Hickory of the Granite Hills*. Rev. ed. Philadelphia: University of Pennsylvania Press, 1964.

Welsbacher, Anne. *Franklin Pierce*. Minneapolis: ABDO, 2002.

JAMES BUCHANAN

Binder, Frederick M. *James Buchanan and the American Empire*. Cranbury, N.J.: Associated University Presses, 1994.

Birkner, Michael, ed. *James Buchanan and the Political Crisis of the 1850's*. Selinsgrove, Pa.: Susquehanna University Press, 1996.

Cahalan, Sally S. *James Buchanan and His Family at Wheatland*. Lancaster, Pa.: James Buchanan Foundation, 1988.

Smith, Elbert B. *The Presidency of James Buchanan*. Lawrence: University Press of Kansas, 1975.

ABRAHAM LINCOLN

Bak, Richard. *The Day Lincoln Was Shot: An Illustrated Chronicle*. Dallas: Taylor, 1998.

Burlingame, Michael. *The Inner World of Abraham Lincoln*. Urbana: University of Illinois Press, 1994.

Chadwick, Bruce. *The Two American Presidents: A Dual Biography of Abraham Lincoln and Jefferson Davis*. Secaucus, N.J.: Carol, 1999.

DiLorenzo, Thomas. *The Real Lincoln: A New Look at Abraham Lincoln, His Agenda, and an Unnecessary War*. Roseville, Calif.: Forum, 2002.

Donald, David H. *Lincoln*. New York: Simon & Schuster, 1995.

_____. *Lincoln at Home: Two Glimpses of Abraham Lincoln's Family Life*. New York: Simon & Schuster, 2000.

Einhorn, Lois J. *Abraham Lincoln, the Orator: Penetrating the Lincoln Legend.* Westport, Conn.: Greenwood Press, 1992.

Freedman, Russell. *Lincoln: A Photobiography.* New York: Clarion Books, 1987.

Garrison, Webb B. *The Lincoln No One Knows: The Mysterious Man Who Ran the Civil War.* Nashville, Tenn.: Rutledge Hill Press, 1993.

Good, Timothy S., ed. *We Saw Lincoln Shot: One Hundred Eyewitness Accounts.* Jackson: University Press of Mississippi, 1995.

Hamilton, Charles. *Lincoln in Photographs: An Album of Every Known Pose.* Dayton, Ohio: Morningside, 1985.

Hanchett, William. *Out of the Wilderness: The Life of Abraham Lincoln.* Urbana: University of Illinois Press, 1994.

Harrell, Carolyn L. *When the Bells Tolled for Lincoln: Southern Reaction to the Assassination.* Macon, Ga.: Mercer University Press, 1997.

Harris, William C. *With Charity for All: Lincoln and the Restoration of the Union.* Lexington: University Press of Kentucky, 1997.

Holzer, Harold, ed. *The Lincoln-Douglas Debates: The First Complete, Unexpurgated Text.* New York: HarperCollins, 1993.

Kunhardt, Philip B., Jr., Philip B. Kunhardt III, and Peter W. Kunhardt. *Lincoln: An Illustrated Biography.* New York: Alfred A. Knopf, 1992.

Matthews, Elizabeth W. *Lincoln as a Lawyer: An Annotated Bibliography.* Carbondale: Southern Illinois University Press, 1991.

Neely, Mark E. *The Abraham Lincoln Encyclopedia.* New York: McGraw-Hill, 1982.

————. *The Last Best Hope for Earth: Abraham Lincoln and the Promise of America.* Cambridge, Mass.: Harvard University Press, 1993.

————. *The Lincoln Family Album.* New York: Doubleday, 1990.

Oates, Stephen B. *Abraham Lincoln: The Man Behind the Myths.* New York: Harper & Row, 1984.

Paludan, Phillip S. *The Presidency of Abraham Lincoln.* Lawrence: University Press of Kansas, 1994.

Peterson, Merrill D. *Lincoln in American Memory.* New York: Oxford University Press, 1994.

Platt, Thomas B. *Abraham Lincoln: A Biography.* New York: Book-of-the-Month Club, 1986.

Rawley, James A. *Abraham Lincoln and a Nation Worth Fighting for.* Wheeling, Ill.: Harlan Davidson, 1996.

Reck, W. Emerson. *A. Lincoln: His Last Twenty-four Hours.* Jefferson City, N.C.: McFarland, 1987.

Simon, Paul. *Lincoln's Preparation for Greatness: The Illinois Legislative Years.* Urbana: University of Illinois Press, 1989.

White, Ronald C. *The Eloquent President: A Portrait of Lincoln Through His Words.* New York: Random House, 2005.

Williams, Frank J., William Pederson, and Vincent Marsala. *Abraham Lincoln: Sources and Style of Leadership.* Westport, Conn.: Greenwood Press, 1994.

Wills, Garry. *Lincoln at Gettysburg: The Words That Remade America.* New York: Simon & Schuster, 1992.

Wilson, Douglas L. *Lincoln Before Washington: New Perspectives on the Illinois Years.* Urbana: University of Illinois Press, 1997.

ANDREW JOHNSON

Benedict, Michael L. *The Impeachment Trial and Trial of Andrew Johnson.* New York: W. W. Norton, 1973.

Brabson, Fay W. *Andrew Johnson: A Life in Pursuit of the Right Course, 1808-1875.* Durham, N.C.: Seeman Printery, 1972.

Castel, Albert E. *The Presidency of Andrew Johnson.* Lawrence: Regents Press of Kansas, 1979.

Gerson, Noel B. *The Trial of Andrew Johnson.* Nashville: Thomas Nelson, 1977.

McCaslin, Richard B. *Andrew Johnson: A Bibliography.* Westport, Conn.: Greenwood Press, 1992.

Mantell, Martin E. *Johnson, Grant, and the Politics of Reconstruction*. New York: Columbia University Press, 1973.

Nash, Howard P. *Andrew Johnson: Congress and Reconstruction*. Rutherford, N.J.: Fairleigh Dickinson University Press, 1972.

Rehnquist, William H. *Grand Inquests: The Historic Impeachments of Justice Samuel Chase and President Andrew Johnson*. New York: William Morrow, 1992.

Schroeder-Lein, Glenna, and Richard Zuczek. *Andrew Johnson: A Biographical Companion*. Santa Barbara, Calif.: ABC-Clio, 2001.

Sefton, James E. *Andrew Johnson and the Uses of Constitutional Power*. Boston: Little, Brown, 1980.

Smith, Gene. *High Crimes and Misdemeanors: The Impeachment and Trial of Andrew Johnson*. New York: William Morrow, 1977.

Trefousse, Hans L. *Andrew Johnson: A Biography*. New York: Norton, 1989.

_____. *Impeachment of a President: Andrew Johnson, the Blacks, and Reconstruction*. Knoxville: University of Tennessee Press, 1975.

ULYSSES S. GRANT

Arnold, James R. *Grant Wins the War: Decision at Vicksburg*. New York: John Wiley & Sons, 1997.

Bunting, Josiah. *Ulysses S. Grant*. New York: Henry Holt, 2004.

Goldhurst, Richard. *Many Are the Hearts: The Agony and the Triumph of Ulysses S. Grant*. New York: Reader's Digest Press, 1975.

Grant, Julia Dent. *The Personal Memoirs of Julia Dent Grant*. New York: Putnam, 1975.

Grant, Ulysses S. *Memoirs and Selected Letters: Personal Memoirs of U. S. Grant, Selected Letters 1839-1865*. New York: Library of America, 1990.

Kaltman, Al. *Cigars, Whiskey, and Winning: Leadership Lessons from General Ulysses S. Grant*. Paramus, N.J.: Prentice Hall, 1998.

Korda, Michael. *Ulysses S. Grant: Unlikely Hero*. New York: Atlas Books/HarperCollins, 2004.

McFeely, William S. *Grant: A Biography*. New York: W. W. Norton, 1981.

Perret, Geoffrey. *Ulysses S. Grant: Soldier and President*. New York: Random House, 1997.

Scaturro, Frank J. *President Grant Reconsidered*. Lanham, Md.: University Press of America, 1998.

Simpson, Brooks D. *Let Us Have Peace: Ulysses S. Grant and the Politics of War and Reconstruction*. Chapel Hill: University of North Carolina Press, 1991.

Smith, Jean Edward. *Grant*. New York: Simon & Schuster, 2002.

RUTHERFORD B. HAYES

Barnard, Harry. *Rutherford B. Hayes and His America*. Indianapolis: Bobbs-Merrill, 1954.

Davison, Kenneth E. *The Presidency of Rutherford B. Hayes*. Westport, Conn.: Greenwood Press, 1972.

Hoogenboom, Ari A. *The Presidency of Rutherford B. Hayes*. Lawrence: University Press of Kansas, 1988.

_____. *Rutherford B. Hayes: Warrior and President*. Lawrence: University Press of Kansas, 1995.

Morris, Roy. *Fraud of the Century: Rutherford B. Hayes, Samuel Tilden, and the Stolen Election of 1876*. New York: Simon & Schuster, 2003.

Perry, James M. *Touched with Fire: Five Presidents and the Civil War Battles That Made Them*. New York: PublicAffairs, 2005.

Williams, T. Harry, ed. *Hayes: The Diary of a President, 1875-1881*. New York: David McKay, 1964.

JAMES A. GARFIELD

Ackerman, Kenneth D. *Dark Horse: The Surprise Election and Political Murder of President James A. Garfield*. New York: Carroll & Graf, 2003.

Bates, Richard O. *The Gentleman from Ohio: An Introduction to Garfield*. Durham, N.C.: Moore, 1973.

Booraem, Hendrik. *The Road to Respectability: James A. Garfield and His World, 1844-1852*.

Lewisburg, Pa.: Bucknell University Press, 1988.

Clark, James C. *The Murder of James A. Garfield: The President's Last Days and the Trial and Execution of His Assassin.* Jefferson, N.C.: McFarland, 1993.

Doenecke, Justus D. *The Presidencies of James A. Garfield and Chester A. Arthur.* Lawrence: Regents Press of Kansas, 1981.

Leech, Margaret, and Harry J. Brown. *The Garfield Orbit.* New York: Harper & Row, 1978.

Peskin, Allan. *Garfield: A Biography.* Kent, Ohio: Kent State University Press, 1978.

Rupp, Robert O. *James A. Garfield: A Bibliography.* Westport, Conn.: Greenwood Press, 1997.

Shaw, John, ed. *Crete and James: Personal Letters of Lucretia and James Garfield.* East Lansing: Michigan State University Press, 1994.

CHESTER A. ARTHUR

Doenecke, Justus D. *The Presidencies of James A. Garfield and Chester A. Arthur.* Lawrence: Regents Press of Kansas, 1981.

Karabel, Zachary. *Chester Alan Arthur.* New York: Times Books, 2004.

Reeves, Thomas C. *Gentleman Boss: The Life of Chester Alan Arthur.* New York: Alfred A. Knopf, 1975.

GROVER CLEVELAND

Brodsky, Alyn. *Grover Cleveland: A Study in Character.* New York: St. Martin's Press, 2000.

Graff, Henry F. *Grover Cleveland.* New York: Times Books, 2002.

Hollingsworth, J. Rogers. *The Whirligig of Politics: The Democracy of Cleveland and Bryan.* Chicago: University of Chicago Press, 1963.

Jeffers, H. Paul. *An Honest President: The Life and Presidencies of Grover Cleveland.* New York: W. Morrow, 2000.

Marszalek, John F. *Grover Cleveland: A Bibliography.* Westport, Conn.: Meckler, 1988.

Tugwell, Rexford G. *Grover Cleveland.* New York: Macmillan, 1968.

Vexler, Robert I., ed. *Grover Cleveland, 1837-1908: Chronology, Documents, Bibliographical Aids.* Dobbs Ferry, N.Y.: Oceana, 1968.

Welch, Richard E. *The Presidencies of Grover Cleveland.* Lawrence: University Press of Kansas, 1988.

BENJAMIN HARRISON

Calhoun, Charles W. *Benjamin Harrison.* New York: Times Books, 2005.

Socolofsky, Homer E., and Allan B. Spetter. *The Presidency of Benjamin Harrison.* Lawrence: University Press of Kansas, 1987.

WILLIAM MCKINLEY

Bristow, Joseph L. *Fraud and Politics at the Turn of the Century: McKinley and His Administration as Seen by His Principal Patronage Dispenser and Investigator.* New York: Exposition Press, 1952.

Damiani, Brian P. *Advocates of Empire: William McKinley, the Senate, and American Expansion, 1898-1899.* New York: Garland, 1987.

Gould, Lewis L. *The Presidency of William McKinley.* Lawrence: Regents Press of Kansas, 1980.

_____. *The Spanish-American War and President McKinley.* Lawrence: University Press of Kansas, 1982.

Gould, Lewis L., and Craig H. Roell. *William McKinley: A Bibliography.* Westport, Conn.: Meckler, 1988.

Johns, Wesley A., and Paul Avrich. *The Man Who Shot McKinley.* South Brunswick, N.J.: A. S. Barnes, 1970.

Leech, Margaret. *In the Days of McKinley.* New York: Harper, 1959. Reprint. Westport, Conn.: Greenwood Press, 1975.

McElroy, Richard L. *William McKinley and Our America: A Pictorial History.* Canton, Ohio: Stark County Historical Society, 1996.

Morgan, H. Wayne. *William McKinley and His America*. 1963. Rev. ed. Kent, Ohio: Kent State University Press, 2003.

Phillips, Kevin. *William McKinley*. New York: Henry Holt, 2003.

Rauchway, Eric. *Murdering McKinley: The Making of Theodore Roosevelt's America*. New York: Hill and Wang, 2003.

Spielman, William C. *William McKinley, Stalwart Republican: A Biographical Study*. New York: Exposition Press, 1954.

THEODORE ROOSEVELT

Berman, Jay S. *Police Administration and Progressive Reform: Theodore Roosevelt as Police Commissioner of New York*. New York: Greenwood Press, 1987.

Brands, H. W. *T.R.: The Last Romantic*. New York: Basic Books, 1997.

Burton, David H. *Theodore Roosevelt*. New York: Twayne, 1972.

Cadenhead, Ivie E. *Theodore Roosevelt: The Paradox of Progressivism*. Woodbury, N.Y.: Barron's, 1974.

Collin, Richard H. *Theodore Roosevelt's Caribbean: The Panama Canal, the Monroe Doctrine, and the Latin American Context*. Baton Rouge: Louisiana State University Press, 1990.

Cutright, Paul R. *Theodore Roosevelt: The Making of a Conservationist*. Urbana: University of Illinois Press, 1985.

Egloff, Franklin R. *Theodore Roosevelt, an American Portrait*. New York: Vantage Press, 1980.

Gardner, Joseph L. *Departing Glory: Theodore Roosevelt as Ex-President*. New York: Charles Scribner's Sons, 1973.

Gould, Lewis L. *The Presidency of Theodore Roosevelt*. Lawrence: University Press of Kansas, 1991.

Grant, George. *Carry a Big Stick: The Uncommon Heroism of Theodore Roosevelt*. Nashville, Tenn.: Cumberland House, 1996.

Harbaugh, William H. *Power and Responsibility: The Life and Times of Theodore Roosevelt*. Rev. ed. New York: Octagon Books, 1975.

Hart, Albert B., Herbert R. Ferleger, and John A. Gable, eds. *Theodore Roosevelt Encyclopedia*. 2d ed. Westport, Conn.: Meckler, 1989.

Jeffers, H. Paul. *Colonel Roosevelt: Theodore Roosevelt Goes to War, 1897-1898*. New York: John Wiley & Sons, 1996.

McCullough, David G. *Mornings on Horseback*. New York: Simon & Schuster, 1981.

Markham, Lois. *Theodore Roosevelt*. New York: Chelsea House, 1985.

Meltzer, Milton. *Theodore Roosevelt and His America*. New York: Franklin Watts, 1994.

Miller, Nathan. *Theodore Roosevelt*. New York: William Morrow, 1992.

Morris, Edmund. *The Rise of Theodore Roosevelt*. 1979. Reprint. New York: Modern Library, 2001.

Norton, Aloysius A. *Theodore Roosevelt*. Boston: Twayne, 1980.

Ornig, Joseph R. *My Last Chance to Be a Boy: Theodore Roosevelt's South American Expedition of 1913-1914*. Mechanicsburg, Pa.: Stackpole Books, 1994.

Rauchway, Eric. *Murdering McKinley: The Making of Theodore Roosevelt's America*. New York: Hill and Wang, 2003.

Renehan, Edward J., Jr. *The Lion's Pride: Theodore Roosevelt and His Family in Peace and War*. New York: Oxford University Press, 1998.

Roosevelt, Theodore. *The Adventures of Theodore Roosevelt*. Washington, D.C. : National Geographic Society, 2005.

_____. *The Letters of Theodore Roosevelt*. Edited by H. W. Brands. New York: Cooper Square Press, 2001.

_____. *Theodore Roosevelt: The Rough Riders and an Autobiography*. Edited by Louis Auchincloss. 1899, 1913. Reprint. New York: Library of America, 2004.

Samuels, Peggy. *Teddy Roosevelt at San Juan: The Making of a President*. College Station: Texas A&M University Press, 1997

Wilson, Robert L. *Theodore Roosevelt, Outdoorsman*. Agoura, Calif.: Trophy Room Books, 1994.

WILLIAM HOWARD TAFT

Anderson, Judith I. *William Howard Taft: An Intimate History*. New York: Norton, 1981.

Burton, David. *William Howard Taft: Confident Peacemaker*. New York: Fordham University Press, 2004.

_____. *William Howard Taft: In the Public Service*. Melbourne, Fla.: R. E. Krieger, 1986.

Coletta, Paolo E. *William Howard Taft: A Bibliography*. Westport, Conn.: Meckler, 1989.

Mason, Alpheus T. *William Howard Taft, Chief Justice*. New York: Simon & Schuster, 1965.

Minger, Ralph E. *William Howard Taft and United States Foreign Policy: The Apprenticeship Years, 1900-1908*. Urbana: University of Illinois Press, 1975.

Taft, William Howard. *The Collected Works of William Howard Taft*. Edited by David H. Burton. 5 vols. Athens: Ohio University Press, 2001-   .

WOODROW WILSON

Buckingham, Peter H. *Woodrow Wilson: A Bibliography of His Times and Presidency*. Wilmington, Del.: Scholarly Resources, 1990.

Clements, Kendrick A. *The Presidency of Woodrow Wilson*. Lawrence: University Press of Kansas, 1992.

_____. *Woodrow Wilson, World Statesman*. Boston: Twayne, 1987.

Cooper, John M. *The Warrior and the Priest: Woodrow Wilson and Theodore Roosevelt*. Cambridge, Mass.: The Belknap Press of Harvard University Press, 1983.

Dean, John W. *Warren G. Harding*. New York: Henry Holt, 2004.

Esposito, David M. *The Legacy of Woodrow Wilson: American War Aims in World War I*. Westport, Conn.: Greenwood Press, 1996.

Heater, Derek B. *National Self-Determination: Woodrow Wilson and His Legacy*. New York: St. Martin's Press, 1994.

Heckscher, August. *Woodrow Wilson*. New York: Charles Scribner's Sons, 1991.

Knock, Thomas J. *To End All Wars: Woodrow Wilson and the Quest for a New World Order*. New York: Oxford University Press, 1992.

Mulder, John M., Ernest M. White, and Ethel S. White. *Woodrow Wilson: A Bibliography*. Westport, Conn.: Greenwood Press, 1997.

Saunders, Robert M. *In Search of Woodrow Wilson: Beliefs and Behavior*. Westport, Conn.: Greenwood Press, 1998.

Stid, Daniel D. *The President as Statesman: Woodrow Wilson and the Constitution*. Lawrence: University Press of Kansas, 1998.

Thorsen, Niels. *The Political Thought of Woodrow Wilson, 1875-1910*. Princeton, N.J.: Princeton University Press, 1988.

Weinstein, Edwin A. *Woodrow Wilson: A Medical and Psychological Biography*. Princeton, N.J.: Princeton University Press, 1981.

WARREN G. HARDING

Anthony, Carl S. *Florence Harding: The First Lady, the Jazz Age, and the Death of America's Most Scandalous President*. New York: William Morrow, 1998.

Downes, Randolph C. *The Rise of Warren Gamaliel Harding, 1865-1920*. Columbus: Ohio State University Press, 1970.

Ferrell, Robert H. *The Strange Deaths of President Harding*. Columbia: University of Missouri Press, 1996.

Frederick, Richard G. *Warren G. Harding: A Bibliography*. Westport, Conn.: Greenwood Press, 1992.

Gilbert, Robert E. *The Tormented President: Calvin Coolidge, Death, and Clinical Depression*. Westport, Conn.: Praeger, 2003.

Mee, Charles L. *The Ohio Gang: The World of Warren G. Harding*. New York: M. Evans, 1981.

Morello, John A. *Selling the President, 1920: Albert D. Lasker, Advertising, and the Election of Warren G. Harding*. Westport, Conn.: Praeger, 2001.

Murray, Robert K. *The Harding Era: Warren G. Harding and His Administration.* Minneapolis: University of Minnesota Press, 1969.

Russell, Francis. *The Shadow of Blooming Grove: Warren G. Harding in His Times.* New York: McGraw-Hill, 1968.

Sinclair, Andrew. *The Available Man: The Life Behind the Masks of Warren Gamaliel Harding.* New York: Macmillan, 1965.

Trani, Eugene P., and David L. Wilson. *The Presidency of Warren G. Harding.* Lawrence: Regents Press of Kansas, 1977.

CALVIN COOLIDGE

Booraem, Hendrik. *The Provincial: Calvin Coolidge and His World, 1885-1895.* Lewisburg, Pa.: Bucknell University Press, 1994.

Ferrell, Robert H. *The Presidency of Calvin Coolidge.* Lawrence: University Press of Kansas, 1998.

Greene, J. R. *Calvin Coolidge's Plymouth, Vermont.* Dover, N.H.: Arcadia, 1997.

McCoy, Donald R. *Calvin Coolidge: The Quiet President.* Lawrence: University Press of Kansas, 1988.

Sobel, Robert. *Coolidge: An American Enigma.* Washington, D.C.: Regnery, 1998.

HERBERT HOOVER

Barber, William J. *From New Era to New Deal: Herbert Hoover, the Economists, and American Economic Policy, 1921-1933.* New York: Cambridge University Press, 1985.

Best, Gary D. *Herbert Hoover, the Postpresidential Years, 1933-1964.* Stanford, Calif.: Hoover Institution Press, 1983.

_____. *The Politics of American Individualism: Herbert Hoover in Transition, 1918-1921.* Westport, Conn.: Greenwood Press, 1975.

Burner, David. *Herbert Hoover: A Public Life.* New York: Alfred A. Knopf, 1979.

Burns, Richard D. *Herbert Hoover: A Bibliography of His Times and Presidency.* Wilmington, Del.: Scholarly Resources, 1991.

Eckley, Wilton. *Herbert Hoover.* Boston: Twayne, 1980.

Fausold, Martin L. *The Presidency of Herbert C. Hoover.* Lawrence: University Press of Kansas, 1985.

Hoff-Wilson, Joan. *Herbert Hoover, Forgotten Progressive.* Boston: Little, Brown, 1975.

Krog, Carl E., and William R. Tanner., eds. *Herbert Hoover and the Republican Era: A Reconsideration.* Lanham, Md.: University Press of America, 1984.

Liebovich, Louis. *Bylines in Despair: Herbert Hoover, the Great Depression, and the U.S. News Media.* Westport, Conn.: Praeger, 1994.

Nash, George H. *The Life of Herbert Hoover.* 3 vols. New York: W. W. Norton, 1983.

Nye, Frank T., Jr. *Doors of Opportunity: The Life and Legacy of Herbert Hoover.* West Branch, Iowa: Herbert Hoover Presidential Library Association, 1988.

Olson, James S. *Herbert Hoover and the Reconstruction Finance Corporation, 1931-1933.* Ames: Iowa State University Press, 1977.

Robinson, Edgar E. *Herbert Hoover, President of the United States.* Stanford, Calif.: Hoover Institution Press, 1975.

Rosen, Elliot A. *Hoover, Roosevelt, and the Brains Trust: From Depression to New Deal.* New York: Columbia University Press, 1977.

Smith, Richard N. *An Uncommon Man: The Triumph of Herbert Hoover.* New York: Simon & Schuster, 1984.

Sobel, Robert. *Herbert Hoover at the Onset of the Great Depression, 1929-1930.* Philadelphia: J. B. Lippincott, 1975.

Tracey, Kathleen. *Herbert Hoover, a Bibliography: His Writings and Addresses.* Stanford, Calif.: Hoover Institution Press, 1977.

Walch, Timothy, ed. *Uncommon Americans: The Lives and Legacies of Herbert and Lou Henry Hoover.* Westport, Conn.: Praeger, 2003.

Walch, Timothy, and Dwight M. Miller, eds. *Herbert Hoover and Franklin D. Roosevelt: A Documentary History.* Westport, Conn.: Greenwood Press, 1998.

FRANKLIN D. ROOSEVELT

Abbott, Philip. *The Exemplary Presidency: Franklin D. Roosevelt and the American Political Tradition*. Amherst: University of Massachusetts Press, 1990.

Alsop, Joseph. *FDR, 1882-1945: A Centenary Remembrance*. New York: Viking Press, 1982.

Buhite, Russell D., and David W. Levy, eds. *FDR's Fireside Chats*. Norman: University of Oklahoma Press, 1992.

Davis, Kenneth S. *FDR: The New York Years, 1928-1933*. New York: Random House, 1985.

_____. *FDR: The New Deal Years, 1933-1937: A History*. New York: Random House, 1986.

_____. *FDR: Into the Storm, 1937-1940: A History*. New York: Random House, 1993.

_____. *FDR: The War President, 1940-1943*. New York: Random House, 2000.

Ferrell, Robert H. *The Dying President: Franklin Delano Roosevelt, 1944-1945*. Columbia: University of Missouri Press, 1998.

Freidel, Frank B. *Franklin D. Roosevelt: A Rendezvous with Destiny*. Boston: Little, Brown, 1990.

Goldberg, Richard T. *The Making of Franklin D. Roosevelt: Triumph over Disability*. Cambridge, Mass.: Abt Books, 1981.

Goodwin, Doris Kearns. *No Ordinary Time: Franklin and Eleanor Roosevelt: The Home Front in World War II*. New York: Simon & Schuster, 1994.

Graham, Otis L., and Meghan Wander, eds. *Franklin D. Roosevelt, His Life and Times: An Encyclopedic View*. Boston: G. K. Hall, 1985.

Jenkins, Roy. *Franklin Delano Roosevelt*. New York: Henry Holt, 2003.

Langston, Thomas S. *Ideologues and Presidents: From the New Deal to the Reagan Revolution*. Baltimore: The Johns Hopkins University Press, 1992.

Leuchtenberg, William E. *The FDR Years: On Roosevelt and His Legacy*. New York: Columbia University Press, 1995.

Maney, Patrick J. *The Roosevelt Presence: A Biography of Franklin Delano Roosevelt*. New York: Twayne, 1992.

Miller, Nathan. *FDR: An Intimate History*. Garden City, N.Y.: Doubleday, 1983.

Morgan, Ted. *FDR: A Biography*. New York: Simon & Schuster, 1985.

Mortimer, Edward. *The World That FDR Built: Vision and Reality*. New York: Charles Scribner's Sons, 1989.

Rozell, Mark J., and William D. Peterson, eds. *FDR and the Modern Presidency: Leadership and Legacy*. Westport, Conn.: Praeger, 1997.

Ryan, Halford R. *Franklin D. Roosevelt's Rhetorical Presidency*. New York: Greenwood Press, 1988.

Thompson, Robert S. *A Time for War: Franklin Delano Roosevelt and the Path to Pearl Harbor*. New York: Prentice Hall, 1991.

Underhill, Robert. *FDR and Harry: Unparalleled Lives*. Westport, Conn.: Praeger, 1996.

Ward, Geoffrey C. *Before the Trumpet: Young Franklin Roosevelt, 1882-1905*. New York: Harper & Row, 1985.

_____, ed. *Closest Companion: The Unknown Story of the Intimate Friendship Between Franklin Roosevelt and Margaret Suckley*. Boston: Houghton Mifflin, 1995.

_____. *A First-Class Temperament: The Emergence of Franklin Roosevelt*. New York: Harper & Row, 1989.

HARRY S. TRUMAN

Burns, Richard D. *Harry S. Truman: A Bibliography of His Times and Presidency*. Wilmington, Del.: Scholarly Resources, 1984.

Donaldson, Gary. *Truman Defeats Dewey*. Lexington: University Press of Kentucky, 1998.

Donovan, Robert J. *Conflict and Crisis: The Presidency of Harry S. Truman*. Columbia: University of Missouri Press, 1996.

_____. *Tumultuous Years: The Presidency of Harry S. Truman, 1949-1953*. New York: W. W. Norton, 1982.

Ferrell, Robert H. *Choosing Truman: The Democratic Convention of 1944*. Columbia: University of Missouri Press, 1994.

_____. *Harry S. Truman: A Life*. Columbia: University of Missouri Press, 1994.

_____. *Harry S. Truman: His Life on the Family Farms*. Worland, Wyo.: High Plains, 1991.

_____. *Harry S. Truman and the Modern American Presidency*. Boston: Little, Brown, 1983.

_____. *Truman: A Centenary Remembrance*. New York: Viking Press, 1984.

_____, ed. *Harry S. Truman and the Bomb: A Documentary History*. Worland, Wyo.: High Plains, 1996.

_____, ed. *Off the Record: The Private Papers of Harry S. Truman*. Columbia: University of Missouri Press, 1997.

Gullan, Harold I. *The Upset That Wasn't: Harry S. Truman and the Crucial Election of 1948*. Chicago: Ivan R. Dee, 1998.

Hamby, Alonzo L. *Man of the People: A Life of Harry S. Truman*. New York: Oxford University Press, 1995.

Kirkendall, Richard S., ed. *The Harry S. Truman Encyclopedia*. Boston: G. K. Hall, 1989.

McCoy, Donald R. *The Presidency of Harry S. Truman*. Lawrence: University Press of Kansas, 1984.

McCullough, David G. *Truman*. New York: Simon & Schuster, 1992.

Maddox, Robert J. *From War to Cold War: The Education of Harry S. Truman*. Boulder, Colo.: Westview Press, 1988.

Merrill, Dennis, ed. *Documentary History of the Truman Presidency*. 23 vols. to date. Bethesda, Md.: University Publications of America, 1995-   .

Miller, Richard L. *Truman: The Rise to Power*. New York: McGraw-Hill, 1986.

Neal, Steve. *Harry and Ike: The Partnership That Remade the Postwar World*. New York: Scribner, 2001.

Pemberton, William E. *Harry S. Truman: Fair Dealer and Cold Warrior*. Boston: Twayne, 1989.

Poen, Monty M., ed. *Strictly Personal and Confidential: The Letters Harry Truman Never Mailed*. Boston: Little, Brown, 1982.

Sand, G. W. *Truman in Retirement: A Former President Views the Nation and the World*. South Bend, Ind.: Justice Books, 1993.

Stone, I. F. *The Truman Era, 1945-1952*. Boston: Little, Brown, 1988.

Thompson, Kenneth W., ed. *The Truman Presidency: Intimate Perspectives*. Lanham, Md.: University Press of America, 1984.

Truman, Harry S. *Talking with Harry: Candid Conversations with President Harry S. Truman*. Edited by Ralph E. Weber. Wilmington, Del.: SR Books, 2001.

Wainstock, Dennis. *The Decision to Drop the Atomic Bomb*. Westport, Conn.: Praeger, 1996.

Walker, J. Samuel. *Prompt and Utter Destruction: Truman and the Use of Atomic Bombs Against Japan*. Chapel Hill: University of North Carolina, 1997.

DWIGHT D. EISENHOWER

Ambrose, Stephen E. *Eisenhower*. 2 vols. New York: Simon & Schuster, 1983.

_____. *The Victors: Eisenhower and His Boys, the Men of World War II*. New York: Simon & Schuster, 1998.

Beschloss, Michael R., and Vincent Virga. *Eisenhower: A Centennial Life*. New York: HarperCollins, 1990.

Bowie, Robert R., and Richard H. Immerman. *Waging Peace: How Eisenhower Shaped an Enduring Cold War Strategy*. New York: Oxford University Press, 1998.

Boyle, Peter G. *Eisenhower*. New York: Pearson/Longman, 2005.

Burk, Robert F. *Dwight D. Eisenhower, Hero and Politician*. Boston: Twayne, 1986.

D'Este, Carlo. *Eisenhower: A Soldier's Life*. New York: Henry Holt, 2002.

Ewald, William B. *Eisenhower the President: Crucial Days, 1951-1960*. Englewood Cliffs, N.J.: Prentice Hall, 1983.

Ferrell, Robert H., ed. *The Eisenhower Diaries.* New York: W. W. Norton, 1981.

Hold, Daniel D., and James W. Leyerzapf, eds. *Eisenhower: The Prewar Diaries and Selected Papers, 1905-1941.* Baltimore: The Johns Hopkins University Press, 1998.

Kinnard, Douglas. *Ike, 1890-1990: A Pictorial History.* Washington, D.C.: Brassey's, 1990.

Lasby, Clarence G. *Eisenhower's Heart Attack: How Ike Beat Heart Disease and Held on to the Presidency.* Lawrence: University Press of Kansas, 1997.

Lee, R. Alton. *Dwight D. Eisenhower: A Bibliography of His Times and Presidency.* Wilmington, Del.: Scholarly Resources, 1991.

_____. *Dwight D. Eisenhower, Soldier and Statesman.* Chicago: Nelson Hall, 1981.

Mayer, Michael S., ed. *The Eisenhower Presidency and the 1950's.* Boston: Houghton Mifflin, 1998.

Neal, Steve. *Harry and Ike: The Partnership That Remade the Postwar World.* New York: Scribner, 2001.

Pach, Chester J., and Elmo Richardson. *The Presidency of Dwight D. Eisenhower.* Rev. ed. Lawrence: University Press of Kansas, 1991.

Pickett, William B. *Dwight D. Eisenhower and American Power.* Wheeling, Ill.: Harlan Davidson, 1995.

Warshaw, Shirley Anne. *Reexamining the Eisenhower Presidency.* Westport, Conn.: Greenwood Press, 1993.

Wicker, Tom. *Dwight D. Eisenhower.* New York: Henry Holt, 2002.

Wykes, Alan. *The Biography of General Dwight D. Eisenhower.* Greenwich, Conn.: Bison Books, 1982.

JOHN F. KENNEDY

Andersen, Christopher P. *Jack and Jackie: Portrait of an American Marriage.* New York: William Morrow, 1996.

Benson, Michael. *Who's Who in the JFK Assassination: An A-Z Encyclopedia.* Secaucus, N.J.: Carol, 1993.

Brogan, Hugh. *Kennedy.* New York: Longman, 1996.

Chomsky, Noam. *Rethinking Camelot: JFK, the Vietnam War, and U.S. Political Culture.* Boston: South End Press, 1993.

Claflin, Edward, ed. *JFK Wants to Know: Memos from the President's Office.* New York: William Morrow, 1991.

Damore, Leo. *The Cape Cod Years of John Fitzgerald Kennedy.* New York: Four Walls Eight Windows, 1993.

Duffy, James P. *The Assassination of John F. Kennedy: A Complete Book of Facts.* New York: Thunder's Mouth Press, 1992.

Giglio, James N. *John F. Kennedy: A Bibliography.* Westport, Conn.: Greenwood Press, 1995.

_____. *The Presidency of John F. Kennedy.* Lawrence: University Press of Kansas, 1991.

Goldman, Martin S. *John F. Kennedy, Portrait of a President.* New York: Facts On File, 1995.

Hamilton, Nigel. *JFK, Reckless Youth.* New York: Random House, 1992.

Hellmann, John. *The Kennedy Obsession: The American Myth of JFK.* New York: Columbia University Press, 1997.

Hersh, Seymour M. *The Dark Side of Camelot.* Boston: Little, Brown, 1997.

Mailer, Norman. *Oswald's Tale: An American Mystery.* New York: Random House, 1995.

Matthews, Christopher. *Kennedy and Nixon: The Rivalry That Shaped Postwar America.* New York: Simon & Schuster, 1996.

May, Ernest R., and Philip Zelikow, eds. *The Kennedy Tapes: Inside the White House During the Cuban Missile Crisis.* Cambridge, Mass.: The Belknap Press of Harvard University Press, 1997.

O'Brien, Michael. *John F. Kennedy: A Biography.* New York: St. Martin's Press, 2005.

Posner, Gerald L. *Case Closed: Lee Harvey Oswald and the Assassination of JFK.* New York: Random House, 1993.

Reeves, Richard. *President Kennedy: Profile of Power.* New York: Simon & Schuster, 1993.

Salinger, Pierre. *John F. Kennedy, Commander in Chief: A Profile in Leadership.* New York: Penguin, 1997.

Schwab, Orrin. *Defending the Free World: John F. Kennedy, Lyndon Johnson, and the Vietnam War, 1961-1965.* Westport, Conn.: Praeger, 1998.

Scott, William E. *November 22, 1963: A Reference Guide to the JFK Assassination.* Lanham, Md.: University Press of America, 1999.

Sorensen, Theodore C. *The Kennedy Legacy.* New York: Macmillan, 1993.

Strober, Gerald S., and Deborah H. Strober, eds. *Let Us Begin Anew: An Oral History of the Kennedy Presidency.* New York: HarperCollins, 1993.

Thompson, Robert S. *The Missiles of October: The Declassified Story of John F. Kennedy and the Cuban Missile Crisis.* New York: Simon & Schuster, 1992.

LYNDON B. JOHNSON

Andrew, John A. *Lyndon Johnson and the Great Society.* Chicago: Ivan R. Dee, 1998.

Bernstein, Irving. *Guns or Butter: The Presidency of Lyndon Johnson.* New York: Oxford University Press, 1996.

Bornet, Vaughn D. *The Presidency of Lyndon B. Johnson.* Lawrence: University Press of Kansas, 1983.

Califano, Joseph A. *The Triumph and Tragedy of Lyndon Johnson: The White House Years.* New York: Simon & Schuster, 1991.

Caro, Robert A. *The Years of Lyndon Johnson.* New York: Alfred A. Knopf, 1982.

Dallek, Robert. *Flawed Giant: Lyndon Johnson and His Times, 1961-1973.* New York: Oxford University Press, 1998.

_____. *Lone Star Rising: Lyndon Johnson and His Times, 1908-1960.* New York: Oxford University Press, 1991.

Divine, Robert A., ed. *The Johnson Years.* 2 vols. Lawrence: University Press of Kansas, 1987.

Henggeler, Paul R. *In His Steps: Lyndon Johnson and the Kennedy Mystique.* Chicago: Ivan R. Dee, 1991.

Hunt, Michael H., and Eric Foner. *Lyndon Johnson's War: America's Cold War Crusade in Vietnam, 1945-1968—A Critical Issue.* New York: Hill & Wang, 1996.

Kotz, Nick. *Judgment Days: Lyndon Baines Johnson, Martin Luther King, Jr., and the Laws That Changed America.* Boston: Houghton Mifflin, 2005.

Muslin, Hyman L. *Lyndon Johnson, the Tragic Self: A Psychohistorical Portrait.* New York: Insight Books, 1991.

Redford, Emmette S., and Richard T. McCulley. *White House Operations: The Johnson Presidency.* Austin: University of Texas Press, 1986.

Reedy, George E. *Lyndon B. Johnson: A Memoir.* New York: Andrews & McMeel, 1982.

Roell, Craig, comp. *Lyndon B. Johnson: A Bibliography.* 2 vols. Austin: University of Texas Press, 1984.

Rulon, Philip R. *The Compassionate Samaritan: The Life of Lyndon Baines Johnson.* Chicago: Nelson-Hall, 1981.

Schulman, Bruce J. *Lyndon B. Johnson and American Liberalism: A Brief Biography with Documents.* Boston: Bedford Books of St. Martin's Press, 1994.

VanDemark, Brian. *Into the Quagmire: Lyndon Johnson and the Escalation of the Vietnam War.* New York: Oxford University Press, 1991.

RICHARD M. NIXON

Aitken, Jonathan. *Nixon: A Life.* Washington, D.C.: Regnery, 1993.

Colodny, Len, and Robert Gettlin. *Silent Coup: The Removal of a President.* New York: St. Martin's Press, 1991.

Genovese, Michael A. *The Nixon Presidency: Power and Politics in Turbulent Times.* New York: Greenwood Press, 1990.

Goldman, Martin S. *Richard M. Nixon: A Complex Legacy.* New York: Facts On File, 1998.

Kimball, Jeffrey P. *Nixon's Vietnam War.* Lawrence: University Press of Kansas, 1998.

_____. *The Vietnam War Files: Uncovering the Secret History of Nixon-Era Strategy*. Lawrence: University Press of Kansas, 2004.

Kutler, Stanley I., ed. *Abuse of Power: The New Nixon Tapes*. New York: Free Press, 1997.

_____. *The Wars of Watergate: The Last Crisis of Richard Nixon*. New York: Alfred A. Knopf, 1990.

Matthews, Christopher. *Kennedy and Nixon: The Rivalry That Shaped Postwar America*. New York: Simon & Schuster, 1996.

Morris, Roger. *Richard Milhous Nixon: The Rise of an American Politician*. New York: Henry Holt, 1990.

Nadel, Laurie. *The Great Stream of History: A Biography of Richard M. Nixon*. New York: Atheneum, 1991.

Nixon, Richard M. *Beyond Peace*. New York: Random House, 1994.

_____. *In the Arena: A Memoir of Victory, Defeat, and Renewal*. New York: Simon & Schuster, 1990.

Parmet, Herbert S. *Richard Nixon and His America*. Boston: Little, Brown, 1990.

Reeves, Richard. *President Nixon: Alone in the White House*. New York: Simon & Schuster, 2001.

Shawcross, William. *Sideshow: Kissinger, Nixon, and the Destruction of Cambodia*. 1979. Rev. ed. New York: Cooper Square Press, 2002.

Strober, Gerald S., and Deborah H. Strober. *Nixon: An Oral History of His Presidency*. New York: HarperCollins, 1994.

Volkan, Vamik D., Norman Itzkowitz, and Andrew W. Dod. *Richard Nixon: A Psychobiography*. New York: Columbia University Press, 1997.

Wicker, Tom. *One of Us: Richard Nixon and the American Dream*. New York: Random House, 1991.

Wills, Garry. *Nixon Agonistes: The Crisis of the Self-Made Man*. 1970. Reprint. Boston: Houghton Mifflin, 2002.

GERALD R. FORD

Cannon, James M. *Time and Chance: Gerald Ford's Appointment with History*. New York: HarperCollins, 1994.

Casserly, John J. *The Ford White House: The Diary of a Speechwriter*. Boulder: Colorado Associated University Press, 1977.

Firestone, Bernard J., and Alexej Ugrinsky, eds. *Gerald R. Ford and the Politics of Post Watergate America*. Westport, Conn.: Greenwood Press, 1993.

Ford, Gerald R. *A Time to Heal: The Autobiography of Gerald R. Ford*. New York: Harper & Row, 1979.

Greene, John R. *Gerald R. Ford: A Bibliography*. Westport, Conn.: Greenwood Press, 1994.

_____. *The Limits of Power: The Nixon and Ford Administrations*. Bloomington: Indiana University Press, 1992.

_____. *The Presidency of Gerald R. Ford*. Lawrence: University Press of Kansas, 1995.

Hartmann, Robert T. *Palace Politics: An Inside Account of the Ford Years*. New York: McGraw-Hill, 1980.

Howell, David, Margaret Mary Howell, and Robert Kronman. *Gentlemanly Attitudes: Jerry Ford and the Campaign of '76*. Washington, D.C.: HKJV, 1980.

Mieczkowski, Yanek. *Gerald Ford and the Challenges of the 1970's*. Lexington: University Press of Kentucky, 2005.

Reeves, Richard. *A Ford, Not a Lincoln*. New York: Harcourt Brace Jovanovich, 1975.

Schoenebaum, Eleanora W. *The Nixon/Ford Years*. New York: Facts On File, 1979.

TerHorst, Jerald F. *Gerald Ford and the Future of the Presidency*. New York: Third Press, 1974.

Thompson, Kenneth W., ed. *The Ford Presidency: Twenty-two Intimate Perspectives of Gerald R. Ford*. Lanham, Md.: University Press of America, 1988.

JIMMY CARTER

Anderson, Patrick. *Electing Jimmy Carter: The Campaign of 1976*. Baton Rouge: Louisiana State University Press, 1994.

Ariall, Dan, and Cheryl Heckler-Feltz. *The Carpenter's Apprentice: The Spiritual Biography of Jimmy Carter*. Grand Rapids, Mich.: Zondervan, 1996.

Biven, W. Carl. *Jimmy Carter's Economy: Policy in an Age of Limits*. Chapel Hill: University of North Carolina Press, 2002.

Bourne, Peter G. *Jimmy Carter: A Comprehensive Biography from Plains to Post-Presidency*. New York: Charles Scribner's Sons, 1997.

Brinkley, Douglas. *The Unfinished Presidency: Jimmy Carter's Journey Beyond the White House*. New York: Viking, 1998.

Dumbrell, John. *The Carter Presidency: A Re-evaluation*. New York: St. Martin's Press, 1993.

Glad, Betty. *Jimmy Carter: In Search of the Great White House*. New York: W. W. Norton, 1980.

Hyatt, Richard. *The Carters of Plains*. Huntsville, Ala.: Strode, 1977.

Jordon, Hamilton. *Crisis: The Last Year of the Carter Presidency*. New York: Putnam, 1982.

Kaufman, Burton I. *The Presidency of James Earl Carter, Jr.* Lawrence: University Press of Kansas, 1993.

Kraus, Sidney, ed. *The Great Debates: Carter vs. Ford, 1976*. Bloomington: Indiana University Press, 1979.

Lasky, Victor. *Jimmy Carter, the Man and the Myth*. New York: R. Marek, 1979.

Mazlish, Bruce, and Edwin Diamond. *Jimmy Carter: A Character Portrait*. New York: Simon & Schuster, 1979.

Morris, Kenneth E. *Jimmy Carter: American Moralist*. Athens: University of Georgia Press, 1996.

Neyland, James. *The Carter Family Scrapbook: An Intimate Close-up of America's First Family*. New York: Grosset & Dunlap, 1977.

Richardson, Don, ed. *Conversations with Carter*. Boulder, Colo.: Lynne Rienner, 1998.

Slavicek, Louise Chipley. *Jimmy Carter*. New York: Chelsea House, 2003.

Stroud, Kandy. *How Jimmy Won: The Victory Campaign from Plains to the White House*. New York: William Morrow, 1977.

Thornton, Richard C. *The Carter Years: Toward a New Global Order*. New York: Paragon House, 1991.

Troester, Rod. *Jimmy Carter as Peacemaker: A Post-presidential Biography*. Westport, Conn.: Praeger, 1996.

Wooten, James T. *Dasher: The Roots and the Rising of Jimmy Carter*. New York: Summit Books, 1978.

RONALD REAGAN

Abrams, Herbert L. *"The President Has Been Shot": Confusion, Disability, and the Twenty-fifth Amendment in the Aftermath of the Attempted Assassination of Ronald Reagan*. New York: W. W. Norton, 1992.

Bosch, Adriana. *Reagan: An American Story*. New York: TV Books, 1998.

Cannon, Lou. *President Reagan: The Role of a Lifetime*. New York: Simon & Schuster, 1991.

Cardigan, J. H. *Ronald Reagan: A Remarkable Life*. Kansas City, Mo.: Andrews & McMeel, 1995.

Davis, Patti. *Angels Don't Die: My Father's Gift of Faith*. New York: HarperCollins, 1995.

D'Souza, Dinesh. *Ronald Reagan: How an Ordinary Man Became an Extraordinary Leader*. New York: Free Press, 1997.

Edel, Wilbur. *The Reagan Presidency: An Actor's Finest Performance*. New York: Hippocrene Books, 1992.

Hannaford, Peter, ed. *Recollections of Reagan: A Portrait of Ronald Reagan*. New York: William Morrow, 1997.

Kengor, Paul, and Peter Schweizer, eds. *The Reagan Presidency: Assessing the Man and His Legacy*. Lanham, Md.: Rowman & Littlefield, 2005.

Levy, Peter B. *Encyclopedia of the Reagan-Bush Years.* Westport, Conn.: Greenwood Press, 1996.

Mervin, David. *Ronald Reagan and the American Presidency.* New York: Longman, 1990.

Morris, Edmund. *Dutch: A Memoir of Ronald Reagan.* New York: Random House, 1998.

Noonan, Peggy. *When Character Was King: A Story of Ronald Reagan.* New York: Viking, 2001.

Pemberton, William E. *Exit with Honor: The Life and Presidency of Ronald Reagan.* Armonk, N.Y.: M. E. Sharpe, 1998.

Reagan, Ronald. *An American Life.* New York: Simon & Schuster, 1990.

———. *A Shining City: The Legacy of Ronald Reagan.* Edited by Erik D. Felen. New York: Simon & Schuster, 1998.

Strober, Deborah H., and Gerald S. Strober. *Reagan: The Man and His Presidency.* New York: W. W. Norton, 1992.

Walsh, Kenneth T. *Ronald Reagan.* New York: Park Lane Press, 1997.

GEORGE H. W. BUSH

Barilleaux, Ryan J., and Mark J. Rozell. *Power and Prudence: The Presidency of George H. W. Bush.* College Station: Texas A&M University Press, 2004.

Bose, Meena, and Rosana Perotti. *From Cold War to New World Order: The Foreign Policy of George H. W. Bush.* Westport, Conn.: Greenwood Press, 2002.

Duffy, Michael. *Marching in Place: The Status Quo Presidency of George Bush.* New York: Simon & Schuster, 1992.

Greene, John Robert. *The Presidency of George Bush.* Lawrence: University Press of Kansas, 2000.

Himelfarb, Richard, and Rosana Perotti, eds. *Principle Over Politics? The Domestic Policy of the George H. W. Bush Presidency.* Westport, Conn.: Praeger, 2004.

Hyams, Joe. *Flight of the Avenger: George Bush at War.* San Diego, Calif.: Harcourt Brace Jovanovich, 1991.

Levy, Peter B. *Encyclopedia of the Reagan-Bush Years.* Westport, Conn.: Greenwood Press, 1996.

Parmet, Herbert S. *George Bush: The Life of a Lone Star Yankee.* New York: Charles Scribner's Sons, 1997.

Rozell, Mark J. *The Press and the Bush Presidency.* Westport, Conn.: Praeger, 1996.

Smith, Jean E. *George Bush's War.* New York: Henry Holt, 1992.

Stinnett, Robert B. *George Bush: His World War II Years.* Missoula, Mont.: Pictorial Histories, 1991.

Tarpley, Webster G., and Anton Chaitkin. *George Bush: The Unauthorized Biography.* Washington, D.C.: Executive Intelligence Review, 1992.

Valdez, David. *George Herbert Walker Bush: A Photographic Profile.* College Station: Texas A&M University Press, 1997.

BILL CLINTON

Allen, Charles F., and Jonathan Portis. *The Comeback Kid: The Life and Career of Bill Clinton.* New York: Birch Lane Press, 1992.

Campbell, Colin, and Bert A. Rockman, eds. *The Clinton Presidency: First Appraisals.* Chatham, N.J.: Chatham House, 1996.

Carpozi, George. *Clinton Confidential: The Climb to Power, the Unauthorized Biography of Bill and Hillary Clinton.* Del Mar, Calif.: Emery Dalton Books, 1995.

Clinton, Bill. *My Life.* New York: Alfred A. Knopf, 2004.

Clinton, Roger. *Growing Up Clinton: The Lives, Times, and Tragedies of America's Presidential Family.* Arlington, Tex.: Summit, 1995.

Denton, Robert E., Jr., and Rachel L. Holloway, eds. *The Clinton Presidency: Images, Issues, and Communication Strategies.* Westport, Conn.: Praeger, 1996.

Drew, Elizabeth. *On the Edge: The Clinton Presidency*. New York: Simon & Schuster, 1994.

Dumas, Ernest, ed. *The Clintons of Arkansas: An Introduction by Those Who Know Them Best*. Fayetteville: University of Arkansas Press, 1993.

Eszterhas, Joe. *American Rhapsody*. New York: Alfred A. Knopf, 2000.

Gallen, David, and Philip Martin. *Bill Clinton as They Know Him: An Oral Biography*. New York: Gallen, 1994.

Hamilton, Nigel. *Bill Clinton: An American Journey: Great Expectations*. New York: Random House, 2003.

Harris, John F. *The Survivor: Bill Clinton in the White House*. New York: Random House, 2005. An excellent nonpartisan view of Clinton's presidency.

Hohenberg, John. *The Bill Clinton Story: Winning the Presidency*. Syracuse, N.Y.: Syracuse University Press, 1994.

Maraniss, David. *First in His Class: A Biography of Bill Clinton*. New York: Simon & Schuster, 1995.

Metz, Allan. *Bill Clinton's Pre-presidential Career: An Annotated Bibliography*. Westport, Conn.: Greenwood Press, 1994.

Morris, Dick. *Behind the Oval Office: Getting Reelected Against All Odds*. Los Angeles: Renaissance Books, 1999.

Morris, Roger. *Partner's in Power: The Clintons and Their America*. New York: Henry Holt, 1996.

Oakley, Meredith L. *On the Make: The Rise of Bill Clinton*. Washington, D.C.: Regnery, 1994.

Odom, Richmond. *Circle of Death: Clinton's Climb to the Presidency*. Lafayette, La.: Huntington House, 1995.

Renshon, Stanley A., ed. *The Clinton Presidency: Campaigning, Governing, and the Psychology of Leadership*. Boulder, Colo.: Westview Press, 1995.

Stephanopoulos, George. *All Too Human: A Political Education*. Boston: Little, Brown, 1999.

Stewart, James B. *Blood Sport: The President and His Adversaries*. New York: Simon & Schuster, 1996.

Tyrrell, R. Emmett. *Boy Clinton: The Political Biography*. Washington, D.C.: Regnery, 1996.

Walker, Martin. *The President We Deserve: Bill Clinton, His Rise, Fall, and Comebacks*. New York: Crown, 1996.

Woodward, Bob. *The Choice: How Clinton Won*. New York: Simon & Schuster, 1997.

GEORGE W. BUSH

Bruni, Frank. *Ambling into History*. New York: Perennial, 2003.

Bush, George W. *A Charge to Keep*. New York: Morrow, 1999.

Frum, David. *The Right Man*. New York: Random House, 2003.

Gaddis, John Lewis. *Surprise, Security, and the American Experience*. Cambridge, Mass.: Harvard University Press, 2004.

Ivins, Molly. *Bushwhacked*. New York: Random House, 2003.

Minutaglio, Bill. *First Son*. New York: Times Books, 1999.

Podhoretz, John. *Bush Country*. New York: St. Martin's Press, 2004.

Sammons, Bill. *At Any Cost*. Washington, D.C.: Regnery, 2001.

_____. *Misunderestimated*. New York: HarperCollins, 2004.

Schier, Steven E., ed. *High Risk and Big Ambition*. Pittsburgh: University of Pittsburgh Press, 2004.

Thomas, Evan. *Election 2004*. New York: Public Affairs, 2004.

Toobin, Jeffrey. *Too Close to Call*. New York: Random House, 2001.

Kevin J. Bochynski

American Presidents
Third Edition

Index

AAA. *See* Agricultural Adjustment Act

Abbas, Mahmoud, 836

ABMs. *See* Antiballistic missiles

Abolitionist movement; and Lincoln, 297; and Polk, 233; and Van Buren, 186

Abortion, 762

Abu Ghraib prison, 837

Acheson, Dean, 597, 671

ACLU. *See* American Civil Liberties Union

Acting president, 694

Adams, Abigail, 52, 60, 134

Adams, Charles Francis, 524

Adams, John, 24, 50-66; as J. Q. Adams's father, 134; appointment of judges, 76; as a diplomat, 135; and the election of 1796, 3; legacy of, 4; opinion of J. Q. Adams, 135; opinion of Madison, 113; as vice president, 34

Adams, John Quincy, 134-149; and the campaign of 1824, 130, 157; and the campaign of 1828, 157; and the election of 1824, 5, 215; and the Holy Alliance, 127; opinion of Jackson, 125; opinion of Monroe, 118, 132; opinion of Polk, 215; opinion of Van Buren, 186; as secretary of state, 120; and slavery, 124; and Van Buren, 183

Adams, Louisa, 136

Adams, Sherman, 610, 619, 641

Adamson Act, 479

Addison's disease, 640, 642

AFDC. *See* Aid to Families with Dependent Children

Affirmative action, 701

Afghanistan, 746, 770, 831

African Americans; and Coolidge, 515; and Hoover, 529; in the military, 601; rights of, 423; and the Seminoles, 189; in the South, 592; voting rights of, 364, 675

African National Congress, 789

Agnew, Spiro T., 694, 698, 727

Agricultural Adjustment Act, 547

Agricultural Marketing Act, 524

Agriculture, 511, 524, 547

Aguinaldo, Emilio, 418, 425

Aid to Families with Dependent Children, 703

Air Commerce Act of 1926, 510

Al-Qaeda, 831

Alabama claims, 338, 345

Alaska, 323

Albanians, 814

Albany Regency, 183

Aldrich, Nelson W., 458

Algeciras Conference, 450

Alger, Horatio, 9

Alger, Russell A., 413, 419

Alien and Sedition Acts, 4, 48, 60, 74

Allen, Henry J., 532

Allende, Salvador, 708

Alliance for Progress, 631

Alliance of 1778, 75

Allied Powers, World War I, 483

Allies, World War II, 565, 572

Allison, David, 154

Allison, William Boyd, 366

Amendments, 26. *See also individual amendments*

American Civil Liberties Union, 784

American Civil War. *See* Civil War

American Federation of Labor, 478

American Indians, 160; assimilation of, 83; and Cleveland, 393; in Florida, 125; and W. H. Harrison, 198; and Hayes, 368;

and Hoover, 528; Jackson's opinion of, 156; and Nixon, 702; policies under Jackson, 160, 162; removal of, 131, 145, 160, 162, 189; self-determination of, 702; treaties with, 131, 160, 162; and Western settlement, 36

American Revolution. *See* Revolutionary War

American System, 145, 163, 167, 216, 278

Americans with Disabilities Act, 787

Ames, Fisher, 33, 45, 59

Ames, Oakes, 348

Anderson, John, 759

Anderson, Robert, 273

Andropov, Yuri, 764, 782

Antiballistic missiles, 713, 764, 830

Antietam, Battle of, 298

Anti-Masons, 167, 247

Antitariffites, 167

Antiwar protests, 685, 714, 758, 800

Apartheid, 789

Appropriation, 122

Aquino, Corazon, 771

Arab countries, 711

Arafat, Yasir, 836

Argentia Conference, 565

Arkansas, 801

Armistice, 489

Arms control, 713, 764, 768-769

Arms reductions, 530

Armstrong, John, 100, 106, 108

Army, U.S., 59

Army Appropriations Act, 322

Aroostook River, 188

Arthur, Chester A., 375, 379-385; and the campaign of 1880, 374; as New York Customhouse collector, 368

Arthur, Ellen, 380

Article 231, 493

Articles of Confederation, 25, 71, 95

Arts patronage, 557

Ash, Roy, 697-698

Ash Commission, 705

Ashcroft, John, 828

Ashley, James, 324

Assassination; of Garfield, 377, 381; of Kennedy, 653, 657; of Lincoln, 311, 319; of McKinley, 426, 436

Assassination attempt; against Ford, 733; against Reagan, 759, 782

Aswan Dam, 629

Atlantic Charter, 565, 572

Atomic bomb, 570, 583-584, 598

Atomic energy, 621

Atomic Energy Commission, 620-621, 705

Attorney general, 29

Atwater, Lee, 783, 794, 823

Axis powers, World War II, 571

Ayatollah, the. *See* Khomeini, Ayatollah Ruhollah

B-1 bomber, 742, 764

Babcock, Orville E., 344, 351

Baker, Bobby, 671

Baker, Howard, 781

Baker, James A., III, 783-784, 794, 828

Baker, Newton D., 476

Balanced budget, 704, 762

Ballinger, Richard H., 459

Ball's Bluff, Battle of, 301

Baltic republics, 788

Baltimore, 108

Bancroft, George, 219, 222, 235, 312

Bank of the United States, 30, 35, 76, 101, 113, 122, 145, 165, 169, 207, 216; Jackson's veto of recharter bill, 166; Tyler's veto of recharter bill, 208

Bank War, 171, 181, 207

Banking crisis, 546

Banking reform, 477

Banknotes, 339

Bankruptcy, 194

Banks, 189. *See also* Bank of the United States; National banks; State banks

Barbary pirates, 41, 77, 112

Barbour, James, 141

Barkley, Alben W., 587

Barnburners, 253

Barnett, Ross, 652

Barron, James, 88

Barry, William Taylor, 159
Baseball, 824
Bates, Edward, 287
Batista, Fulgencio, 631
Battles. *See names of individual battles*
Bay of Pigs, 647
Begin, Menachem, 745
Beijing, 789
Beirut, 765, 767
Belknap, W. W., 351
Bell, John, 7, 285
Bennet, William S., 462
Benton, Thomas Hart, 155, 158, 172, 180, 185
Bentsen, Lloyd, 780
Bering Sea, 409
Berkeley (Virginia), 927
Berlin, 590, 632, 648-649, 769
Berlin Decree, 88
Berlin Wall, 649, 769, 788
Berrien, John M., 158
Biddle, Nicholas, 122, 166, 170-171
Big Stick Diplomacy, 444-445, 449
Big Three, 572
Bill of Rights, 27, 95
Bin Laden, Osama, 831
Birmingham, Ala., 652
Birney, James G., 220
Bishop, Maurice, 765
Black, Hugo L., 550
Black, Jeremiah S., 264, 273
Black Friday, 343
Black Hawk's War, 162, 238
Black suffrage, 319, 322
Black Tuesday, 525
Blaine, James G., 9, 352, 359, 374-375, 381-382, 385, 390, 408-409
Blair, Francis Preston, 164, 177-178
Blair, Montgomery, 287
Bland-Allison bill, 366
Bleeding Kansas, 258
Bliss, Cornelius N., 413
Blockade; of Berlin, 590; of Cuba, 649; by Great Britain, 87, 106
Bloody shirt, 345
Blount, William, 152-153

Blount, Willie, 155
Blum, John Morton, 429, 444
Bohlen, Charles, 622
Bolsheviks, 492
Bomb. *See* Atomic bomb; Hydrogen bomb; Nuclear weapons
Bombing; in Beirut, 767; of Cambodia, 708, 710; of Japan, 584; of Libya, 755, 770; of North Vietnam, 677; of Quemoy and Matsu, 627
Bonaparte, Napoleon. *See* Napoleon I
Bonds, 339, 398
Bonus riot, 533
Booth, John Wilkes, 311, 319
Borah, William E., 493
Borden, Robert L., 462
Border states, 289, 296
Bork, Robert, 762, 785
Bosnia, 811
Boulder Dam, 510
Bourbon Democrats, 383, 390, 398
Boutwell, George S., 342-343
Boxer Rebellion, 424, 521
Boycotts, 624
Braddock, Edward, 21
Bradley, Joseph P., 360
Brady, Nicholas, 784
Brady bill, 808
Branch, John, 158
Brandeis, Louis D., 476, 478
Breckinridge, John C., 7, 269, 271, 285, 318
Brennan, William, 793
Brewster, Benjamin J., 383
Brezhnev, Leonid, 746, 764, 782
Briand, Aristide, 516
Brinkmanship, 619, 625
Bristow, Benjamin H., 350, 352, 359
Britain. *See* Great Britain
British West Indies. *See* West Indies
Broken voyage concept, 87
Brooks, Preston, 258
Brown, Pat, 756
Brown, Walter, 523
Brown v. Board of Education of Topeka, Kansas, 623

Browne, William E., 272

Bruce, Louis R., 702

Bryan, William Jennings, 10, 400, 412, 473, 475, 477

Brzezinski, Zbigniew, 745, 748

Buchanan, James, 262-274; and the election of 1856, 6; legacy of, 341; and Mexico, 228; as secretary of state, 222

Buchanan, Patrick, 794, 826

Buchen, Philip, 724

Budget and Accounting Act, 500

Budget deficit. See Deficit; National debt

Budget Reform Act, 706

Buena Vista, Battle of, 240

Buffalo, N.Y., 389

Bulge, Battle of the, 574

Bull Moose Party. See Progressive Party

Bull Run, First Battle of, 293

Bull Run, Second Battle of, 298

Bureau of Indian Affairs, 528, 702

Burleson, Albert, 476

Burlington Treaty, 369

Burns, Arthur, 697-699

Burnside, Ambrose E., 302

Burr, Aaron, 33, 46, 63, 74, 81; conspiracy of, 90; duel with Alexander Hamilton, 80; and the election of 1800, 3, 65; and Jackson, 154; trial of, 91

Burt, Silas W., 368

Bush, Barbara, 778

Bush, George H. W., 760, 776-796, 805, 819; and the campaign of 1980, 759; and the campaign of 1992, 806; and Clinton, 805, 815; and the election of 1992, 16; legacy of, 16

Bush, George W., 795, 818-840; as Texas governor, 824

Bush, Jeb, 795

Bush, Laura, 821-822

Bush, Prescott, 777, 819

Bush Doctrine, 833

Businessman's Cabinet, 406

Butler, Anthony, 173

Butler, Benjamin F., 295, 324, 326, 341, 345, 348

Butterfield, Alexander, 717

Byrnes, James F., 580

Cabinet, 29, 165, 512, 706; of J. Adams, 56, 141; of Arthur, 381; of Buchanan, 264, 271, 273; of G. H. W. Bush, 784; of G. W. Bush, 828; of Cleveland, 393; of Coolidge, 509; of Eisenhower, 618; of Garfield, 375; of Grant, 342; of Harding, 499; of B. Harrison, 405; of Hayes, 362; of Hoover, 524; of Jackson, 158, 162, 165; of Jefferson, 75; of A. Johnson, 322, 324; of Kennedy, 643; of Lincoln, 286, 302; of McKinley, 413-414; of Madison, 97; of Monroe, 120; of Pierce, 255; of Reagan, 759; of Van Buren, 186; of Washington, 29; of Wilson, 475

Cabot, George, 80

Caddell, Patrick, 739

CAFTA. See Central American Free Trade Agreement

Calhoun, John C., 120, 137, 144, 146, 157, 162-164, 168, 192, 242, 248

Califano, Joseph, 741

California, 222, 227, 232, 241, 243, 249, 554, 756

Cambodia, 708-710; bombing of, 710

Camelot, 637, 653

Camp David accords, 745, 749

Campaigns, 5, 15, 202, 783;
   of 1796, 53;
   of 1800, 63, 74;
   of 1808, 456;
   of 1824, 130, 137, 157;
   of 1828, 147, 157;
   of 1832, 167;
   of 1836, 173, 185;
   of 1840, 194, 201;
   of 1844, 217, 220;
   of 1848, 240;
   of 1852, 249, 252;
   of 1856, 249, 263;
   of 1860, 271, 284, 317;
   of 1864, 7, 306, 309, 318;
   of 1868, 329, 337;

of 1872, 346;
of 1876, 352, 359;
of 1880, 353, 374;
of 1884, 385, 390;
of 1888, 395, 404;
of 1892, 397;
of 1896, 412;
of 1900, 424;
of 1912, 451, 464, 473;
of 1916, 479;
of 1920, 495, 498;
of 1924, 509;
of 1928, 517, 523;
of 1932, 533, 544;
of 1936, 557;
of 1940, 563;
of 1944, 574;
of 1948, 592, 595, 602;
of 1952, 604, 617;
of 1956, 641;
of 1960, 642, 663, 694;
of 1964, 653, 668;
of 1968, 684, 696;
of 1976, 723, 727, 731, 733, 739-740, 758, 780-781;
of 1980, 748, 759, 781;
of 1988, 783;
of 1992, 794, 805;
of 2000, 825
Canada; border with, 125, 137; and McKinley, 414; support for rebellion in, 187; and Taft, 462; and the War of 1812, 105
Canning, George, 88, 99, 127
Cannon, Joseph G., 438, 460
CAP. See Community Action Program
Capitol, 65, 116; burning of the, 108
Caroline affair, 188
Carranza, Venustiano, 481-482
Carter, Jimmy, 736-753; G. H. W. Bush's opinion of, 781; and the campaign of 1976, 733; and the campaign of 1980, 759; and the election of 1976, 15
Carter, Rosalynn, 738
Carter Doctrine, 746

Casey, William, 772
Cass, Lewis, 165, 240, 253, 264
Casserly, John J., 730
Castlereagh, Viscount, 105, 108
Castro, Fidel, 631, 647, 780
Catholicism, 640, 654
Caucuses. See Congressional party caucuses
CCC. See Civilian Conservation Corps
Ceausescu, Nicolae, 788
Censure; of Jackson, 171-172; of Joseph McCarthy, 662
Central America, 243
Central American Free Trade Agreement, 839
Central High School, 623
Central Intelligence Agency, 647, 708, 714, 780
Central Powers, 483
Chamberlain, Daniel, 363
Chamberlain, Neville, 562
Chandler, William E., 383
Chandler, Zach, 360, 363
Chase, Salmon P., 242, 287, 302, 306, 326, 333
Chase, Samuel, 81
Checkers speech, 15, 693
Cheney, Dick, 785, 825-826
Chernenko, Konstantin, 764, 782
Cherokees, 131, 160-161, 189
Chesapeake. See USS Chesapeake
Chiang Kai-shek, 516, 600, 627
Chief justice of the United States, 467
Chile, 708, 789
China, 209, 424; and G. H. W. Bush, 780, 789; conquest by Japan, 531; and Coolidge, 516; and Eisenhower, 627; and Hayes, 369; and the Korean War, 600; and McKinley, 423; and Nixon, 696-697, 708, 712; Nixon's visit to, 712; and T. Roosevelt, 445; and Taiwan, 627; treaties with, 369; and Truman, 597
Chinese immigration, 369
Chotiner, Murray, 692
Chou En-lai, 627
Churchill, Winston, 517, 565, 571, 626
CIA. See Central Intelligence Agency

CIO. *See* Congress of Industrial Organizations

Civil rights, 593, 601, 623, 676; and Carter, 737; and L. B. Johnson, 662; and Kennedy, 652; and Nixon, 701; and Truman, 594

Civil Rights Act of 1957, 641, 662

Civil Rights Act of 1964, 665

Civil Rights Act of 1968, 779

Civil Rights movement, 593, 624, 676, 679; and Kennedy, 646

Civil service reform, 340, 345, 347, 349, 367, 371, 384

Civil War, 7, 289, 310, 336, 357

Civilian Conservation Corps, 548

Clark, Champ, 462, 473

Clark, William, 79

Clay, Henry, 5-6, 102, 125, 137, 139, 141, 157, 166-167, 192, 207, 216, 218, 220, 242, 249, 278

Clayton Act, 478

Clayton-Bulwer Treaty, 243, 423

Clean Air Act, 787

Clemenceau, Georges, 491-492

Cleveland, Frances, 388

Cleveland, Grover, 386-401; and the campaign of 1888, 404; and the election of 1884, 9; as New York governor, 384; and Spain, 415

Clifford, Clark, 592, 594, 683

Clinton, Bill, 797-817, 824-825; as Arkansas governor, 802; and the campaign of 1992, 794; and the election of 1992, 16; impeachment of, 17, 719

Clinton, DeWitt, 105, 141, 183

Clinton, George, 34, 83, 96, 101

Clinton, Hillary Rodham, 799, 801, 804, 809, 815

Coal mines, 441

Cobb, Howell, 264, 266

Coelho, Tony, 785

Cohn, Roy, 622

Colby, William, 780

Cold War, 492, 585, 605-606, 625, 650, 696, 708, 745; cost of the, 629; end of the, 787

Colfax, Schuyler, 333, 340

Colombia, 445, 502; treaties with, 446

Colonialism, 128, 572

Colorado River, 510

Colson, Charles, 714

Columbia University, 616

Commander in chief, 291

Commercial treaties, 142

Committee for the Re-election of the President, 714, 716

Committee on Public Information, 488

Commonwealth of Independent States, 793

Communism, 515, 603; in Eastern Europe, 788; expansion of, 625, 677; in the United States, 602, 621, 692, 756

Communist Party; during World War II, 567

Community Action Program, 665

Compromise of 1850, 243, 249, 252, 316

Confederate army, 293

Confederate States of America, 285

Confederation, 25

Confiscation acts, 295-296

Congress; conflict with Jackson, 170; election of the president, 1; founding of, 27; and Lincoln, 292; power over territories, 124; role in internal improvements, 122

Congress of Industrial Organizations, 557

Congressional party caucuses, 5, 43, 130

Conkling, Roscoe, 359, 368, 374-375, 380-381

Connally, John, 698

Conner, Fox, 614

Connor, Bull, 652

Conscientious objectors; during World War I, 488

Conscription Act of 1863, 304

Conscription Act of 1917, 488

Conservation, 442, 459, 528, 548

Conservatism, 551, 760; dynamic, 618; and F. D. Roosevelt, 551

Conservatives, 185

Constitution, 272

Constitution of Kansas, 267-268

Constitution, U.S., 1, 25, 34, 95, 291, 841-854; amendments to the, 3, 26, 74, 300, 309, 319-320, 322, 467, 727; interpretation of the, 34; presidential succession in the, 207; ratification of the, 26

Constitutional Convention, 3, 29

Constitutional Union Party, 7, 285

Constitutions, 52

Containment, 587, 589, 596, 618, 677, 713

Continental Army, 24

Continental Congress, 23, 26, 51, 70, 95

Contraction of the currency, 339

Contras, 767, 771, 782, 790

Convention of 1818, 125

Conventions, 5, 281. *See also* Constitutional Convention; Convention of 1818; Democratic National Conventions; Hartford Convention; Philadelphia Convention

Coolidge, Calvin, 501, 506-518; legacy of, 11

Coolidge, Grace, 508

Copperheads. *See* Peace Democrats

Cornell, Alonzo B., 368

Corrupt bargain, 5, 139, 157, 215

Corruption, 271, 348, 350, 354, 504; in war production, 582

Cortelyou, George B., 414, 425

Cost-of-living adjustments, 703

Coughlin, Charles, 555

Council of Economic Advisors, 591, 704

Council on Environmental Quality, 705

Council on Executive Reorganization. *See* Ash Commission

Covode, John, 271

Cox, Archibald, 718

Cox, Jacob D., 334, 342, 345

Cox, James M., 495, 498, 543

Coxey, Jacob S., 399

Cramer, Charles F., 504

Crash of 1929. *See* Stock market crash of 1929

Crawford, William H., 120, 137, 141, 157

Credibility gap, 674

Crédit Mobilier scandal, 348

Credit system, 192

Creek War, 155

Creeks, 131, 155

Creel, George, 488

CREEP. *See* Committee for the Re-election of the President

Creeping socialism, 619

Creswell, John A. J., 342

Crime of '73, 366

Crittenden, John J., 249

Crittenden Resolution, 293

Cross of gold speech, 10

Crowninshield, Benjamin, 121

Cuba, 142, 338, 415; acquisition of, 253, 258, 271; and Cleveland, 399; and Eisenhower, 632; and Grant, 344; invasion of, 632, 647; and Kennedy, 647; and McKinley, 419, 423; revolution in, 631; and T. Roosevelt, 449; and Taft, 456

Cuban Missile Crisis, 649

Currency, 30, 174, 185, 190, 339, 343, 366, 477; contraction of the, 339; debasement of, 174; paper, 192

Currency Act of 1874, 335, 348

Curtis, Charles, 532

Cushing, Caleb, 255

Custis, Martha Dandridge, 22

Czechoslovakia, 562, 590

Czolgosz, Leon, 426

D day invasion, 574, 616

Dallas, Alexander J., 109

Dallas, George M., 219

Dana, Francis, 135

Daniels, Josephus, 476

Dark horse candidates, 6, 217, 253, 781

Daugherty, Harry M., 499, 504, 509

Davis, David, 360

Davis, James J., 509, 524

Davis, Jefferson, 239, 255, 309, 316, 319

Davis, John W., 510

Dawes, Charles G., 509, 512

Dawes Act of 1887, 393

Dawes Plan, 510, 516

Day, William R., 413

Dean, John W., III, 714, 716

Deane, Silas, 51

Dearborn, Henry, 75, 105

Death penalty, 824

Debs, Eugene V., 399, 473, 489, 501

Debt. *See* Deficit; National debt; State debts; War debt

Declaration of Independence, 51, 70, 72, 292

Defense industry, 570

Defense of the Constitutions of the United States of America, A (Adams, J.), 52

Defense spending, 597, 761

Deficit, 16, 559, 761-762, 773, 793

Deficit spending, 560-561, 704

De Klerk, F. W., 789

De Lafayette, Marquis, 22, 131

De Lesseps, Ferdinand. *See* Lesseps, Ferdinand de

Demilitarized Zone, 625

Democracy, 293

Democratic National Convention of 1844, 217

Democratic National Convention of 1964, 668

Democratic National Convention of 1968, 15, 685

Democratic Party, 4-5, 8; and Buchanan, 268; and Carter, 741; and the Civil War, 303; and Cleveland, 389; and Clinton, 804; factions in the, 252; founding of the, 146; and Jackson, 172; and A. Johnson, 317; and F. D. Roosevelt, 561; in the South, 594; split of the, 285; and Truman, 580; and Tyler, 207. *See also* Democratic Republican Party; National Republican Party

Democratic Republican Party, 3, 32, 44, 60, 95; factions in the, 129; and Jefferson, 90

Dependents' Pension Act, 397, 408

Depression, 398, 524. *See also* Great Depression

Depression of 1819, 122, 138

Depression of 1857, 265

Deregulation, 705, 782

De Santa Anna, Antonio López, 231, 240

Desegregation; of the armed forces, 601; of public schools, 623, 647, 701

Détente, 650, 654, 712, 768

Devens, Charles A., 362

Dewey, George, 418, 434

Dewey, Thomas E., 13-14, 574, 595

Díaz, Porfirio, 369, 480

Diem, Ngo Dinh. *See* Ngo Dinh Diem

Dienbienphu, 625-626

Dillon, Douglas, 645

Dingley tariff, 413

Dinwiddie, Robert, 21

Direct vote, 1

Dirksen, Everett, 665, 726

District of Columbia, 242-243, 296

Dix, John A., 255

Dixiecrat Party. *See* States' Rights Party

Dixon, Edgar, 620

Dodge Commission, 421, 424

Dole, Bob, 732, 783, 811

Dole, Elizabeth, 772, 784

Dollar Diplomacy, 463, 467

Dolliver, Jonathan P., 458

Domestic Council, 699

Dominican Republic, 447, 678. *See also* Santo Domingo

Domino theory, 626

Donelson, Andrew Jackson, 165

Donelson, John, 153

Doughboys, 488

Doughfaces, 6, 124

Douglas, Helen Gahagan, 692

Douglas, Stephen A., 6, 242, 249, 256, 267, 271, 284-285, 318

Douglas, William O., 726

Douglas-Lincoln Debates. *See* Lincoln-Douglas debates

Douglass, Frederick, 322, 334, 368

Draft, 488; and Clinton, 800, 806

Draft evaders, 733, 800, 806

Draft riots, 304

Dred Scott decision, 265, 296

Duane, William John, 170

Dukakis, Michael, 783-784

Dulles, Allen, 648

Dulles, John Foster, 618, 625
Dupuy de Lome, Enrique, 417
Duties, 382
Dynamic conservatism, 618

Eagleburger, Lawrence, 789
East Berlin, 632
East Florida, 86, 101, 103, 125
East Germany, 788
Eastern Europe, 586, 630, 788
Eaton, John Henry, 158, 162
Eaton, Peggy, 162
Eaton scandal, 162, 165
Eavesdropping, 707
Economic Opportunity Act, 666
Education, 675, 802, 824, 829
Egypt, 629, 681, 711, 745
Ehrlichman, John, 698-699, 714, 729
Einstein, Albert, 570
Eisenhower, Dwight D., 609-635; and the
    campaign of 1948, 595; and the campaign
    of 1952, 604; and the election of 1952, 14;
    and L. B. Johnson, 662; and Nixon, 692;
    in World War II, 574
Eisenhower, Mamie, 610, 614
Eisenhower Doctrine, 628, 631
El Salvador, 782, 790
Election laws, 364
Elections, 1-2, 6, 216;
    of 1796, 3, 46, 55;
    of 1800, 3, 65, 74;
    of 1804, 81;
    of 1808, 91, 96, 456;
    of 1812, 105;
    of 1816, 118;
    of 1824, 5, 139, 157, 215;
    of 1828, 5, 147, 158;
    of 1832, 167;
    of 1836, 174, 186;
    of 1840, 194;
    of 1844, 6, 210, 220;
    of 1848, 235, 241;
    of 1852, 6, 253;
    of 1856, 6, 263;
    of 1860, 7-8, 271, 285;
    of 1864, 309;
    of 1868, 8;
    of 1874, 350;
    of 1876, 8, 352, 359;
    of 1880, 9, 370, 375;
    of 1884, 9, 392;
    of 1888, 404;
    of 1892, 398, 409;
    of 1896, 10, 413;
    of 1904, 11, 441;
    of 1910, 461;
    of 1912, 11, 466, 474;
    of 1920, 498;
    of 1924, 510;
    of 1928, 523;
    of 1930, 532;
    of 1932, 12, 533;
    of 1936, 12;
    of 1938, 561;
    of 1940, 13, 564;
    of 1944, 13, 574;
    of 1948, 13;
    of 1950, 604;
    of 1952, 14, 605;
    of 1956, 625;
    of 1960, 14, 643, 695;
    of 1964, 15;
    of 1968, 685, 696;
    of 1972, 704;
    of 1976, 734, 741;
    of 1980, 759;
    of 1984, 768;
    of 1992, 16, 794, 807;
    of 1996, 811;
    of 2000, 827;
    of 2004, 837
Electoral college, 2-3, 29, 46, 55, 71, 216
Electors, 2-3
Electric power, 620
Elementary and Secondary Education Act,
    675
Ellsberg, Daniel, 714
Ellsworth, Oliver, 33
Emancipation Proclamation, 291, 294,
    297-298, 304

Embargo, 746
Embargo Act, 89, 98, 136
Emergency Relief Appropriation Act, 556
Emory, William H., 326
Employment Act of 1946, 591
Energy, atomic, 621
Energy, Department of, 742
Energy crisis, 742
England. *See* Great Britain
Enlightenment, 69
Environmental Protection Agency, 698, 705, 779
EPA. *See* Environmental Protection Agency
Equal Employment Opportunity Commission, 701
Equal Pay Act, 702
Equal Rights Amendment, 702
ERA. *See* Equal Rights Amendment
Era of Good Feelings, 119, 137, 183
Era of Sectionalism, 138
Erskine, David, 98-99
Ervin Committee, 717
Espionage Act of 1917, 488
Essex Junto, 80
Establishment, the, 679
Europe, 484, 516, 530; aid following World War II, 589
Eustis, William, 98
Ev and Jerry Show, 726
Evarts, William M., 326, 362, 382
Evil empire, 764
Excise taxes, 44
Executive departments and offices, 914-918
Executive Order 8802, 569
Executive power, 28
Executive privilege, 91
Exodusters, 364
Expansion. *See* Western expansion

Factions. *See* Parties
Fair Deal, 600-601
Fair Employment Practices Commission, 569
Fair Labor Standards Act, 560
Fairbanks, Charles W., 432
Fairfax, Thomas Lord, 20

Fairfield, John, 188
Fall, Albert B., 499, 504
Fallen Timbers, 38
Fallows, James, 750
Family and Medical Leave Act, 808
Family Assistance Program, 703
FAP. *See* Family Assistance Program
Farewell address, 174; of Jackson, 174; of Truman, 605; of Washington, 46-47, 50, 75
Farm relief, 511, 524, 547
Faubus, Orville, 623-624
FBI. *See* Federal Bureau of Investigation
FDR. *See* Roosevelt, Franklin D.
Federal Bureau of Investigation, 714
Federal Campaign Reform Act, 732
Federal deficit. *See* Deficit; National debt
Federal Emergency Relief Administration, 549
Federal Employment Stabilization Board, 528
Federal Farm Board, 524, 528
Federal Farm Loan Board, 479
Federal government; role of the, 30, 700
Federal Reserve Act, 478
Federal Reserve System, 477
Federal Trade Commission, 478, 513
Federalist, The, 95
Federalist Party, 3, 27, 32, 74; and J. Adams, 50; and the Louisiana Purchase, 80; and Washington, 44, 48; and the XYZ affair, 59
Federated American Engineering Societies, 522
Fenno, John, 33
FEPC. *See* Fair Employment Practices Commission
FERA. *See* Federal Emergency Relief Administration
Fessenden, William Pitt, 328
Fifty-four Forty or Fight, 224
Filibusters, 601, 646, 662, 665
Fillmore, Abigail, 246
Fillmore, Millard, 241, 245-251
Finch, Robert, 698

Fireside chats, 509, 546

First Bank of the United States. *See* Bank of the United States

First Battle of Bull Run. *See* Bull Run, First Battle of

First Continental Congress. *See* Continental Congress

First World War. *See* World War I

Fish, Hamilton, 344-345

Fisk, Jim, 343

Flood Control Act of 1928, 512

Florida, 45, 86, 101, 104, 125, 156

Flowers, Gennifer, 806

Floyd, John, 271

Folger, Charles J., 384, 389

Forbes, Charles, 504

Force Act, 206

Ford, Betty, 723

Ford, Gerald R., 699, 721-735; and the campaign of 1976, 759; and the campaign of 1980, 782; pardon of Nixon, 718, 728

Ford's Theatre, 929

Foreclosures, 550

Forest Service, 443

Formosa Resolution, 627

Forney, John W., 256

Forsyth, John, 187

Fort Duquesne, 21

Fort Sumter, 273, 288

Fortas, Abe, 685

Foster, Augustus J., 101, 105

Foster, Vince, 809

Founding Fathers, 1

Four Freedoms, 564

Fourteen Points, 489-490, 493, 565

Fourteenth Amendment, 320, 322, 594

France, 38; and J. Adams, 56, 62; Half-War with, 58; and Indochina, 625; and Jackson, 173; and Jefferson, 71, 78; and Madison, 100; seizure of American ships by, 40, 95, 100; trade with, 100; and Washington, 39

Franco, Francisco, 562

Franklin, Benjamin, 52, 71

Franks, Tommy, 832, 835

Fredericksburg, Battle of, 302

Free market economy, 760

Free-Soil Party, 241, 256

Freedmen's Bureau, 320

Freedom of Information Act, 719

Freeman, Orville, 645

Frelinghuysen, Frederick T., 382

Frémont, John C., 6, 295, 306, 309

French Revolution, 38, 54

Freneau, Philip, 33

Fries, John, 61

FTC. *See* Federal Trade Commission

Fugitive Slave Act, 295

Fulbright, J. William, 644

Gadsden, James A., 259

Gadsden Purchase, 260

Gag rule (slavery), 187, 233

Gage, Lyman J., 413

Gallatin, Albert, 75, 97, 100, 106

Garfield, James A., 373-378; and the election of 1876, 360; and the election of 1880, 9, 370; opinion of Grant, 333, 336

Garfield, Lucretia, 374

Garner, John Nance, 542, 544

Garrison, Lindley M., 476

Gary, Joseph, 413

Gas shortage, 750

Gazette of the United States, 33

Geary, John W., 258

General Electric, 756

Genet, Edmond, 39

Genet v. Sloop Betsy, 40

Geneva Disarmament Conference, 511, 530

Georgia, 131, 161, 343, 737

Germany, 485, 562; reunification of, 788; surrender of, 583

Gerry, Elbridge, 57, 62, 98, 105

Gettysburg Address, 300, 305

Ghent, Treaty of, 111, 136

Gingrich, Newt, 17, 785

Girondists, 39

Glasnost, 764

Glass, Carter, 477

Global warming, 830

Godoy, Manuel de, 45

Gold, 10, 340, 343, 366, 398

Gold standard, 351, 366, 398, 408, 704

Gold Standard Act of 1900, 414

Goldberg, Arthur, 645, 684

Goldwater, Barry, 15, 634, 653, 669

Gompers, Samuel, 478

Gonzales, Alberto, 838

Good, James W., 523

Good Neighbor Policy, 502, 515, 530

Gorbachev, Mikhail, 764, 768, 782, 787, 793

Gore, Al, Jr., 804, 807, 826

Gould, Jay, 343

Gramm-Rudman Balanced Budget Act, 762

Granger, Francis, 247

Grant, Julia, 334

Grant, Ulysses S., 332-355; and the campaign of 1868, 328; and the campaign of 1880, 374; and the Civil War, 304, 310; and the election of 1868, 8; and A. Johnson, 321; as secretary of war, 324-325; and slaves in the Civil War, 295

Great Britain; aid in World War II, 564; and American expansion, 36; blockade by, 87, 106; border dispute in Oregon, 223; and Cleveland, 399; and Coolidge, 517; 1812 war with, 105-106, 108, 110, 155, 199, 238; and Grant, 344; and Jefferson, 86; and McKinley, 414; and Madison, 98; and Monroe, 125; search for deserters by, 87; seizure of American ships by, 40, 62, 87, 95; support for the Confederacy, 338; trade with, 41-42, 98; treaties with, 42, 88, 111, 125, 226, 243, 423; and Van Buren, 187

Great Communicator, 755, 772

Great Depression, 12, 524, 526-527, 543, 545, 569

Great Emancipator, 299

Great Society, 15, 556, 655, 666, 674-675, 679, 686, 696

Great War. *See* World War I

Greece, 588

Greeley, Horace, 8, 297, 346

Green, Duff, 164

Greenback Party, 9

Greenbacks, 339, 343, 348, 366

Greenspan, Alan, 732

Greenville, Treaty of, 38

Gregory, Thomas W., 476

Grenada, invasion of, 765

Groton School, 540

Grouseland, 927

Guadalcanal, Battle of, 571

Guadalupe Hidalgo, Treaty of, 232

Guiteau, Charles Julius, 377, 381

Gulf War. *See* Persian Gulf War

Gunboat Diplomacy, 530

Guthrie, James, 255

Habeas corpus, 290, 303

Habeas Corpus Act, 303

Haig, Alexander, 729, 759

Haiti, 79, 86

Haldeman, H. R., 698, 714, 716

Half-Breeds, 359

Half-War with France, 58

Hall, Nathan K., 246

Halleck, Henry Wager, 301

Halloween Massacre, 780

Hamilton, Alexander, 29, 31-33, 95; as commander of the army, 59-60; conflict with J. Adams, 54, 59; conflict with Jefferson, 71; creation of the Bank of the United States, 35; defense of the electoral college, 2; duel with Aaron Burr, 80; and Great Britain, 42; view of the French Revolution, 39; and the Whiskey Rebellion, 45

Hamilton, Paul, 98, 106

Hamlin, Hannibal, 279, 285

Hammerschmidt, John, 801

Hampton, Wade, 363

Hancock, Winfield Scott, 9, 325, 375

Hanna, Mark, 10, 412-413, 436, 441

Hannegan, Robert, 582

Hard money, 174, 185, 340, 351, 366, 408

Harding, Florence, 499

Harding, Warren G., 497-505; and Coolidge, 507; and the election of 1920, 495; legacy of, 11; and Taft, 467

Harlan, John Marshall, 367

Harrison, Anna, 199

Harrison, Benjamin, 402-410; and the campaign of 1888, 396; and the election of 1888, 10

Harrison, Caroline, 404

Harrison, William Henry, 197-203; and the campaign of 1836, 174; and the campaign of 1840, 194; and the election of 1840, 5; as B. Harrison's grandfather, 402; and the Indian wars, 103; as Indiana Territory governor, 78; and Jackson, 178; and the War of 1812, 106

Hartford Convention, 110

Hartmann, Robert, 723, 728, 730

Harvard University, 540

Hawaii, 399, 409, 414, 419, 568

Hay, John, 377, 414, 421, 426

Hay-Herran Treaty, 446

Hay-Pauncefote Treaty, 423-424

Hayakawa, S. I., 745

Hayes, Lucy Ware Webb, 357, 358

Hayes, Rutherford B., 356-372; and the campaign of 1876, 352; and the election of 1876, 8; opinion of Garfield, 373; opinion of Grant, 333

Hazlett, Swede, 612-613, 616

Head Start, 673

Health, Education, and Welfare, Department of, 620

Health insurance, 675, 808

Hell's Canyon, 620

Hendricks, Thomas A., 392

Henry, Patrick, 48

Hepburn Railroad Act, 442

Hermitage, the, 154, 928

Herrera, José Joaquín, 228

HEW. See Health, Education, and Welfare, Department of

High crimes and misdemeanors, 328

Hill, Anita, 793

Hinckley, John, Jr., 759, 782

Hiroshima, 583-584

Hiss, Alger, 692

Historic sites, 925-932

Hitler, Adolf, 13, 561-562, 573, 583

Ho Chi Minh, 625

Hoar, Ebenezer R., 345

Hobart, Garret A., 415

Hodges, Luther, 645

Hofstadter, Richard, 429, 432-433, 438

HOLC. See Home Owner's Loan Corporation

Hollywood, 755

Holocaust, 573

Holt, Joseph, 273, 319

Holy Alliance, 127, 143

Home Owner's Loan Corporation, 550

Homestead Act of 1862, 305

Hoover, Herbert, 519-536; and the campaign of 1928, 517; and the campaign of 1932, 545; and the election of 1928, 12; and F. D. Roosevelt, 544; as secretary of commerce, 499, 509; and Wilson, 495

Hoover, Lou, 520

Hoover Dam, 528

Hoover Moratorium, 527, 530

Hoover Plan, 530

Hopkins, Harry, 549, 556

Hostage crisis, 747-749

Hostages, 748, 750, 771, 782

House, Edward M., 475

House Committee on Un-American Activities, 692

House of Burgesses, 22, 70

House of Representatives; and the election of 1824, 139, 157; role in treaty making, 43; Speaker of the, 459

Housing Act of 1949, 601

Housing and Urban Development, Department of, 675

Houston, David F., 476

Huerta, Victoriano, 481-482

Hughes, Charles Evans, 480, 499, 502, 509, 515

Hughes, Karen, 824

Hull, William, 105

Human rights, 747

Humphrey, George, 618

Humphrey, Hubert H., 15, 594, 641-642, 668, 671, 685, 696

Humphrey, William E., 513

Hundred Days, 12, 548, 556

Hungary, 630

Hunt, E. Howard, 716

Hunt, William, 377

Hunter, David, 295

Hurricane Katrina, 795, 839

Hussein, king of Jordan, 631

Hussein, Saddam, 16, 790, 792, 795, 833

Hyde, Arthur M., 523

Hydrogen bomb, 598

I Like Ike, 611

ICBMs. *See* Intercontinental ballistic missiles

ICC. *See* Interstate Commerce Commission

Ickes, Harold, 550

Ike. *See* Eisenhower, Dwight D.

Illinois, 277

Immigration; from China, 369

Impeachment, 82, 328, 813; of Samuel Chase, 82; of Clinton, 17, 719, 813; of William O. Douglas, 726; of A. Johnson, 324, 326; of Nixon, 718, 801; of John Pickering, 82; of Tyler, 209

Imperialism, 444

Importation; from Great Britain, 89

Impressment, 88

Improvements, internal, 140, 163, 164, 234, 258; role of Congress in, 122

Inaugural address; of J. Q. Adams, 139-140; of Buchanan, 265-266; of G. H. W. Bush, 787; of Grant, 337, 341; of Hayes, 362, 364; of Jefferson, 83; of Kennedy, 645; of Lincoln, 286-287, 291, 309; of Monroe, 119; of Polk, 220; of F. D. Roosevelt, 546; of Van Buren, 186; of Washington, 28

Inauguration; of Grant, 333; of W. H. Harrison, 202; of Jefferson, 74; of Lincoln, 285, 318; of Monroe, 116; of Taft, 457; of Van Buren, 180

India, 782

Indian affairs. *See* American Indians

Indian Defense Association, 529

Indian Self-Determination and Educational Assistance Act, 703

Indian wars, 37

Indiana, 78, 103

Indiana Territory, 198

Indochina, 599, 625-626. *See also* Vietnam

Industrialization, 119

INF Treaty. *See* Intermediate-Range Nuclear Forces Treaty

Inflation, 190, 339, 348, 681, 741

Ingham, Samuel, 158

Intercontinental ballistic missiles, 633, 713

Intermediate-Range Nuclear Forces Treaty, 769, 782

Internment of Japanese Americans, 570

Interstate Commerce Commission, 442, 460, 513

Iowa, 781

Iran, 747, 766, 770, 782; hostage negotiations with, 748, 750, 771

Iran-Contra affair, 771, 782

Iraq, 766, 770, 790, 833, 837

Iraq War, 835

Irish Mafia, 640

Islam, 831

Isolationism, 13, 444, 562, 582, 585

Israel, 629, 681, 711-712, 745, 766-767

Italy, 562; surrender of, 572

Jackson, Andrew, 150-179; and the campaign of 1824, 137; and the campaign of 1828, 146; and the election of 1824, 5, 139, 215; and the election of 1828, 5; and Lincoln, 278, 287; and Mexico, 227; and Monroe, 125; and Polk, 212, 216; and the Seminoles, 125; and Tyler, 205; and Van Buren, 183; at Van Buren's inauguration, 180; and the War of 1812, 109, 111

Jackson, Francis James, 99

Jackson, Rachel Donelson Robards, 152, 158

Jacksonians, 145-147

Jacksonville agreement, 514

Jacobins, 39

James, Thomas, 376
Japan, 597; conquest of China, 531; and
   T. Roosevelt, 445, 564, 567; surrender of,
   584; and Truman, 583
Japanese Americans, 570
Jardine, William, 509
Jaworski, Leon, 716
Jay, John, 29, 42, 95
Jay Treaty, 42, 44, 86
Jefferson, Martha, 68
Jefferson, Thomas, 35, 54, 56, 67-93, 95;
   conflict with Alexander Hamilton, 33;
   and the Democratic Republican Party, 4,
   33; and the election of 1796, 3, 46; and
   the election of 1800, 3, 63, 65; and Great
   Britain, 40; legacy of, 4; and Monroe, 117;
   opinion of J. Adams, 51, 53; opinion of
   J. Q. Adams, 141; opinion of Madison,
   94, 112; view of the French Revolution,
   39; and Washington, 34
Jeffords, James, 829
Jenkins, Walter, 670
Jesup, Philip, 189
Jim Crow laws, 596
Job Corps, 665, 673
Johnson, Andrew, 282, 315-331; and Hayes,
   357; legacy of, 341
Johnson, Eliza, 317
Johnson, James Weldon, 515
Johnson, Lady Bird, 659, 671
Johnson, Louis, 596
Johnson, Lyndon B., 644, 657-688; and the
   campaign of 1960, 642; and the Civil
   Rights movement, 624, 641; and the
   election of 1964, 15; and Kennedy's
   legacy, 655; opinion of Ford, 726; as vice
   president, 646
Johnson, Richard M., 185, 187
Joint Chiefs of Staff, 709
Joint Committee on Reconstruction, 320
Joint Committee on the Conduct of the
   War, 292, 301
Jones, Paula, 810; lawsuit, 810-812
Jones, William, 106
Jonkman, Bartel C., 725

Jordan, 712
Jordan, Hamilton, 737
Judicial review, 76
Judiciary Act of 1789, 29, 76
Judiciary Act of 1801, 76
Judiciary Act of 1802, 76, 91

Kansas, 256, 266; slavery in, 266
Kansas crisis, 257
Kansas-Nebraska Act, 256, 265, 283
Keating-Owen Act, 479
Kefauver, Estes, 641
Kellogg, Frank B., 509, 515
Kellogg-Briand Pact, 514, 516
Kelly Act of 1925, 510
Kemp, Jack, 784
Kendall, Amos, 165, 170
Kennedy, Anthony, 762
Kennedy, Edward, 748
Kennedy, Jacqueline Bouvier, 639, 640, 645
Kennedy, John F., 636-656; and the
   campaign of 1960, 633, 663, 694; and the
   election of 1960, 14
Kennedy, Joseph P., 637-638, 643
Kennedy, Robert, 640, 643, 663, 668,
   684-685, 696
Kennedy-Nixon Debates, 642, 695
Kentucky Resolutions, 71, 95
Kerner Commission, 680
Kerry, John, 837
Key, David M., 363
Keynes, John Maynard, 491, 559
Khomeini, Ayatollah Ruhollah, 747, 749
Khrushchev, Nikita, 629, 632, 649, 693
King, Martin Luther, Jr., 624, 652, 684
King, Rufus, 33, 113, 141
King, William R. D., 257, 263
Kirbo, Charles, 737
Kirkpatrick, Jeane, 772
Kissinger, Henry, 697-698, 706, 709, 732
Kitchen Cabinet, 165
KKK. *See* Ku Klux Klan
Klan, the. *See* Ku Klux Klan
Kleberg, Richard M., 658
Know-Nothing Party, 249

Knox, Frank, 563
Knox, Henry, 29, 33, 63
Konoye, Fumimaro, 567
Korean War, 598-599, 602, 607; end of the, 625
Kosovo, 814
Kosygin, Aleksey, 681
Ku Klux Klan, 344-345, 515, 555
Ku Klux Klan Act, 345
Kuomintang, 516
Kuwait, 770, 790
Kyoto Protocol, 830

Labor movement; and T. Roosevelt, 439
Lafayette. *See* De Lafayette, Marquis
Laffer, Arthur, 760
La Follette, Robert M., 464, 510, 554
Laird, Melvin, 698-699, 709
Lamont, Robert, 524
Lance, Bert, 742
Land Act of 1796, 45
Land speculation, 36, 122, 174
Landon, Alfred M., 558
Landrum-Griffin Act of 1959, 641
Lane, Franklin K., 476
Lane, Harriet, 264
Lansing, Robert, 476
Laos, 650, 709
Latin America, 125-126, 142, 382, 449, 502, 530, 631, 767
Laurier, Wilfrid, 462
Lawnfield, 927
Lawyers, 278
LBJ. *See* Johnson, Lyndon B.
LBJ Ranch, 929
League of Nations, 11, 493, 495, 502, 516
Lebanon, 631, 765-767
Leclerc, Charles, 78
Lecompte, Samuel, 257
Lecompton constitution, 267-268
Lee, Charles, 63
Lee, Henry, 44
Lee, Robert E., 298, 310
Legal Tender Act, 348
Lend-Lease Act, 564

Lenin, V. I., 492
Lenzer, Terry, 706
Lesseps, Ferdinand de, 369
Lewinsky, Monica, 812; investigation, 812
Lewis, John L., 570
Lewis, Meriwether, 79, 85
Lewis and Clark expedition, 79, 85-86
Liberal Republicans, 8, 346, 359
Liberalism, 784; and F. D. Roosevelt, 551
Liberty League, 552
Libraries, presidential, 815, 921-924
Libya, 836
Liddy, G. Gordon, 716
Lincoln, Abraham, 275-314, 715; and the election of 1860, 7; and A. Johnson, 318; legacy of, 8, 341
Lincoln, Levi, 75
Lincoln, Mary, 277
Lincoln, Robert Todd, 381
Lincoln-Douglas debates, 284
Literacy tests, 676
Lithuania, 788
Little Ben, 403
Little Rock, Ark., 623
Livingston, Robert, 79
Lloyd George, David, 491-492
Lodge, Henry Cabot, 434, 494
Lodge, Henry Cabot, Jr., 640, 642
Logan, George, 100
London Naval Treaty, 530
Long, Huey P., 555, 558
Long, John D., 413, 434
Louisiana, 45, 78, 80, 90, 349, 351, 363, 555; slavery in, 80
Louisiana Purchase, 78-80, 117
Loyalty oaths, 319
Luce, Clare Booth, 565
Lusitania, 485
Lynchings, 515, 529

McAdoo, William Gibbs, 476
MacArthur, Douglas, 533, 600, 614
McCain, John, 826
McCammant, Wallace, 512
McCarran Internal Security Act of 1950, 603

McCarran-Walter Immigration and
   Nationality Act, 603
McCarthy, Eugene, 684-685
McCarthy, Joseph, 603-604, 621, 623, 640,
   662
McCarthyism, 602, 623, 640, 692, 756
McClellan, George B., 7, 296, 298, 301, 309
McCord, James W., Jr., 716
McCormack, John W., 646
McCracken, Paul, 704
McCrary, George M., 362
McDougal, James and Susan, 809
McDowell, Irvin, 301
McFarlane, Robert, 771
McGovern, George, 704
McHenry, James, 56, 64
Machine politics, 341, 376, 581
McKenna, Joseph, 413
McKinley, Ida, 412
McKinley, William, 411-427; and Harrison,
   406; legacy of, 10; and T. Roosevelt, 434
McKinley tariff, 397-398, 408, 412
McLean, John, 141
McNamara, Robert, 645, 682
McNary-Haugen bills, 511
Macon, Nathaniel, 100
Macon's Bill No. 2, 100
McReynolds, James C., 476
MacVeagh, Wayne, 377
Madawaska River, 188
Maddox, Lester, 737
Madero, Francisco, 481
Madison, Dolley, 96, 108, 114
Madison, James, 94-115; conflict with
   Alexander Hamilton, 33; at the
   Constitutional Convention, 29; and
   William Marbury, 76; and Monroe, 117;
   opinion of the presidency, 28; opposition
   to congressional elections, 1; as secretary
   of state, 75; view of the French
   Revolution, 39; view on national debt, 31;
   and the Virginia and Kentucky
   Resolutions, 60; and the War of 1812, 4
Maine, 124, 417, 434; border with New
   Brunswick, 188

Manassas, First Battle of. See Bull Run, First
   Battle of
Manchuria. See China
Mandela, Nelson, 789
Manhattan Project, 571
Manifest destiny, 259-260
Mansfield, Mike, 646
Manufacturing, 130
Marbury, William, 76
Marbury v. Madison, 76
March on Washington, 652
Marcos, Ferdinand, 771
Marcy, William L., 255
Marshall, George C., 589, 614-615
Marshall, John, 57, 63, 65, 91
Marshall, Thomas R., 475
Marshall, Thurgood, 679, 793
Marshall Plan, 588, 590
Maryland, 242
Mason, Stevens Thomson, 43
Mass media, 508
Massachusetts, 507
Massive retaliation. See Brinkmanship
Mathews, George, 102-103
Matsu, 627
Matthews, J. B., 623
Matthews, Stanley, 360, 368
Maynard, Horace, 368
Mayo, Henry T., 482
Maysville Road, 122, 164, 216
Meat Inspection Act, 442
Medicaid, 675, 686
Medi-Cal, 758
Medicare, 675, 686
Meese, Edwin, III, 771
Mellon, Andrew, 509, 523
Mellon Plan, 509
Mencken, H. L., 429
Mendès-France, Pierre, 626
Mercer, Lucy, 542, 575
Meredith, James, 652
Mero District, 151
Merritt, Edwin A., 368
Merry, Anthony, 90
Mexican-American War. See Mexican War

Mexican Revolution, 480, 482

Mexican War, 6, 213, 229, 239; and Lincoln, 280-281

Mexico, 90, 227, 480; and Buchanan, 270; and Coolidge, 515; and Hayes, 369; and Jackson, 173, 227; and Polk, 223, 228; and Taft, 481; treaties with, 232, 270; and Van Buren, 187; and Wilson, 481

Middle East, 711, 745, 766

Milan Decree, 89

Military, 598; African Americans in the, 601

Military buildup, 598-599, 763

Military-industrial complex, 570

Militia, 44, 99; in Maine, 188; in Tennessee, 153; in Virginia, 21

Miller, Thomas, 504

Milošević, Slobodan, 814

Mineta, Norman Y., 828

Minh, Ho Chi. *See* Ho Chi Minh

Minimum wage, 560, 787

Mining, 514, 521

Minnesota, 554

Missile gap, 633, 642

Missiles. *See* Antiballistic missiles; Intercontinental ballistic missiles

Missionaries in Oregon, 223

Mississippi, 352

Mississippi Freedom Democratic Party, 669

Mississippi River, 45

Mississippi Valley; secession of the, 90

Missouri, 123, 581; slavery in, 124, 295

Missouri Compromise line, 234

Missouri Compromise of 1820, 124, 137, 233, 265, 283; repeal of the, 256

Mitchell, John, Jr., 714, 716

Mitchell, Billy, 510

Mitchell, William D., 524

Model Cities Program, 679

Mohammad Reza Shah Pahlavi, 747

Moley, Raymond, 545-546

Mondale, Walter, 743, 768

Money. *See* Currency; Hard money; Specie

Mongrel Tariff of 1883, 382

Monopolies, 478

Monroe, Elizabeth, 118

Monroe, James, 56, 116-133; conflict with Jackson, 157; and the election of 1816, 4, 113; negotiation of the Louisiana Purchase, 80; negotiation with Great Britain, 88; as secretary of state, 98

Monroe Doctrine, 127-128, 137, 226, 400, 447, 464, 530, 632

Monterrey, 240

Montgomery, Ala., 624

Monticello, 71, 92, 928

Montpelier, 929

Moore, John Bassett, 481

Moore, Sarah Jane, 733

Morality, 438, 762

Morgan, J. P., 440-441

Mormons, 270

Morrill Land Grant Act, 305

Morris, Robert, 33, 36

Morrow, Dwight, 509-510

Morton, Levi P., 407

Morton, Oliver P., 359, 362

Motley, John Lothrop, 344-345

Mount Vernon, 20, 22, 932

Moynihan, Daniel Patrick, 697-698

Mr. Madison's War, 112

Muckrakers, 438

Mugwumps, 391

Mundt-Nixon bill, 692

Murchison letter, 397

Murphy, Charles F., 541

Muscle Shoals, 510, 548

Museums, 925-932

Muskie, Edmund, 771

Mussolini, Benito, 562

My Life (Clinton), 815

NAACP. *See* National Association for the Advancement of Colored People

Nader, Ralph, 826

NAFTA. *See* North American Free Trade Agreement

Nagasaki, 584

Nagy, Imre, 630

Napoleon I, 78, 86, 88, 95, 99-100

Napoleonic Wars, 84

NASA. *See* National Aeronautics and Space Administration

Nasser, Gamel Abdel, 629, 711

Nathan, Richard, 698

National Aeronautics and Space Administration, 645

National Association for the Advancement of Colored People, 515, 529, 592

National Bank. *See* Bank of the United States

National Banking Act of 1863, 247

National banks, 339

National Building Survey Conference, 525

National Business Survey Conference, 525

National Credit Association, 527

National debt, 30-31, 569, 806; under Grant, 343; under Monroe, 121

National Defense and Education Act of 1958, 641

National Drought Committee, 526

National Endowment for the Arts, 675

National Endowment for the Humanities, 675

National First Ladies' Library, 925

National Gazette, 33

National Guard, 623; and G. W. Bush, 821

National Industrial Recovery Act, 550

National Labor Relations Act, 557

National Labor Relations Board, 551

National Recovery Administration, 550

National Republican Party, 137

National Security Act of 1947, 596

National Security Council, 694, 707, 771

National Security Council-68, 598

National Security Study Memoranda, 707

National Union Party, 321

National Youth Administration, 659, 666

Nationalism, 112

NATO. *See* North Atlantic Treaty Organization

Natural resources, 442

Navigation Acts of 1818 and 1820, 129

Navies, 530

Navy, U.S., 59; search by Royal Navy, 88

Nazi Party, 562, 565, 573

Nebraska, 256

NEP. *See* New Economic Policy

Neutrality, 39, 485

Neutrality Act, 562

New Brunswick, border with Maine, 188

New Deal, 12, 529, 535, 544, 548, 551, 580, 696; and L. B. Johnson, 659; and Truman, 581

New Deal, second, 556

New Echota, Treaty of, 189

New Economic Policy, 703

New England; secession of, 80, 111

New Federalism, 700

New Freedom, 11, 477

New Frontier, 637, 642, 645

New Hampshire, 781

New Jersey, 472

New Mexico, 232, 241, 243

New Nationalism, 461, 473, 479

New Orleans, 839

New Orleans, Battle of, 111-112, 155

New World Order, 777, 787

New York Customhouse, 368

New York State, 389, 435, 541, 544

Newell, Frederick, 443

Newlands Reclamation Act of 1902, 443

Newsreels, 509

Ngo Dinh Diem, 627, 651

Ngo Dinh Nhu, 651

Nhu, Ngo Dinh. *See* Ngo Dinh Nhu

Nicaragua, 767, 771, 790; and Coolidge, 515

Nicholls, Frances T., 363

Nicholson, A. O. P., 256

1950's, 611

1960's, 696

NIRA. *See* National Industrial Recovery Act

Nixon, Pat, 690-691

Nixon, Richard M., 613, 689-720; and G. H. W. Bush, 780; and the campaign of 1960, 642; and the election of 1960, 15; and the election of 1968, 15; and Ford, 727; and Kennedy, 640; pardon of, 722, 728; resignation of, 718, 721, 727

Nixon Doctrine, 709

Nixon, Dixon and Yates, 620

Nixon-Kennedy Debates. *See*
    Kennedy-Nixon Debates
No Child Left Behind Act, 829
Nobel Peace Prize, 450
Noblesse oblige, 430, 444, 539
Non-Importation Act, 89
Nonintercourse Act of 1809, 98, 100
Noriega, Manuel, 790
Normalcy, 11, 495, 498
Normandy, 574
Norris, George W., 459, 513, 515, 548
Norris-LaGuardia Act, 528
North, Oliver, 772, 782
North American Free Trade Agreement,
    794, 808
North American Land Company, 36
North Atlantic Treaty Organization, 597,
    616, 649, 764, 814
North Carolina, 27
North Korea, 598, 625
North Vietnam, 677; negotiations with, 711
Northwest Territory, 37, 198
Notes on the State of Virginia (Jefferson), 70
Novanglus essays, 51
NRA. *See* National Recovery Administration
NSC. *See* National Security Council
NSC-68. *See* National Security Council-68
Nuclear Nonproliferation Treaty, 684
Nuclear Regulatory Commission, 705
Nuclear Test Ban Treaty, 650
Nuclear treaties, 650, 684, 713, 769
Nuclear weapons, 597, 713; in Vietnam, 626
Nullification, 163-164, 167, 205, 216
NYA. *See* National Youth Administration

Oath of office. *See* Presidential oath
Obregón, Álvaro, 482
O'Brien, Lawrence, 640, 716
O'Connor, Sandra Day, 762, 772
O'Donnell, Kenneth, 640
OEO. *See* Office of Economic Opportunity
Office for Faith-Based and Community
    Initiatives, 829
Office of Economic Opportunity, 705
Office of Homeland Security, 831

Office of Management and Budget, 705
Office of Minority Business Enterprise, 701
Office of Price Administration, 691
Ohio, 38, 78, 357
Oil, 742, 790
Oil industry, 822
Old Guard Republicans, 554, 558
Old Hickory, 201
Old Republicans, 123
Old Rough and Ready, 240
Old Tippecanoe, 201
Olds, Robert, 515
Olney, Richard, 399
Olson, Floyd, 554
Open Door notes, 423
Operation Desert Storm, 792
Operation Mongoose, 649
Operation Overlord, 572, 616
Operation Torch, 571
Operation Vulture, 626
Oppenheimer, J. Robert, 621
Orders in Council, 89, 98-100, 104-105
Oregon Country, 125-126, 218; border
    dispute with Great Britain, 223
Oregon Trail, 224
Osceola, 189
Ostend Manifesto, 259, 263
Oswald, Lee Harvey, 653, 664
Otis, Harrison Gray, 60, 111
Otis, James, 51
Overton, John, 153

Packard, Stephen B., 363
PACs. *See* Political action committees
Pahlavi, Mohammad Reza Shah. *See*
    Mohammad Reza Shah Pahlavi.
Pakenham, Edward, 155
Palestine Liberation Organization, 766
Palestinians, 745, 766, 836
Panama, 446-447, 502, 744; invasion of, 790
Panama Canal, 369, 445, 448, 456, 515, 743
Panama Canal Act, 448
Panama congress, 143
Pan-American Congress, 409
Pan-American Union, 409

Panic of 1819, 121-122, 213
Panic of 1837, 181, 189, 192
Panic of 1873, 347, 366
Panic of 1893, 398
Panic of 1907, 463
Panic session, 170
Paper currency, 192
Pardons, 319; of Nixon, 718, 722, 728
Paredes, Mariano, 228
Paris, Treaty of, 51
Parker, Alton, 441
Parker, John J., 532
Parks, Rosa, 624
Parochial schools, 640-642, 647, 675
Parrott, William S., 228
Parties, 29, 32, 44, 71, 146, 183, 280; and
    J. Q. Adams, 139, 146; and Jackson, 184;
    and Monroe, 119; rise of, 5; and Van
    Buren, 146, 184
Partisan press, 33
Patents, 140
Patriot Act, 832
Patronage, 287, 322, 341, 349, 354, 377
Paul, Randolph, 573
Payne-Aldrich Tariff Act, 458
Peabody, Endicott, 540
Peace Corps, 655, 705
Peace Democrats, 303, 309
Peace movement; during the Civil War, 303
Peace of Paris. See Kellogg-Briand Pact
Pearl Harbor, 566, 568
Pendergast, Tom, 581
Pendleton, George H., 357
Pendleton Act, 384
Pennsylvania, 44, 265
Pensions, 393, 408
Pentagon, 830
Pentagon Papers, 714
Pentagonal strategy, 708
Peress, Irving, 622
Perestroika, 764
Perot, Ross, 16, 794, 806
Perry, Matthew C., 249
Perry, Oliver Hazard, 106
Pershing, John J., 482, 614

Persian Gulf, 766
Persian Gulf War, 16, 790-792
Petticoat politics, 164
Philadelphia Convention, 1, 26
Philadelphia Plan, 701
Philippines, 418, 421, 425, 455, 615, 771
Philippines Commission, 422, 455
Phillips, Howard, 706
Pickering, John, 81
Pickering, Timothy, 54, 56, 65, 80, 111
Pierce, Franklin, 252-261; and the election of
    1852, 6
Pierce, Jane, 254
Pike, Zebulon M., 86
Pinchot, Gifford, 443, 458
Pinckney, Charles Cotesworth, 56-57, 65, 80,
    91, 96
Pinckney, Thomas, 45-46, 55
Pinkney, William, 88, 100-101
Pinochet, Augusto, 789
Piracy, 41, 77, 112; slave trade as, 129
Platt, Thomas, 376, 406, 436
Platt Amendment, 423, 425, 456
Pledge of Allegiance, 784
PLO. See Palestine Liberation Organization
Plumbers' unit, 714
Plumed Knight, 409
Pocket veto, 308
Poinsett, Joel R., 186
Poland, 574, 630
Polio, 543
Political action committees, 719
Political parties. See Parties
Polk, James K., 212-236; and the election of
    1844, 6; and Jackson, 178; and Lincoln,
    281
Polk, Sarah Childress, 214
Pope, John, 298, 301, 325
Porter, John Addison, 414
Portsmouth Conference, 450
Postal service, 368
Postal system, 376
Potomac Company, 36
Potter investigation, 367
Powell, Colin, 828

Powell, Jody, 737
POWs. *See* Prisoners of war
Prayer in schools, 762
Preemption Act, 209
Presidency, 1-18, 382, 413-414, 438, 772;
    election to the, 2; establishment of the,
    27, 48; power of the, 27, 280-281, 287,
    290, 376, 443; rituals and the, 27
Presidential campaigns. *See* Campaigns
Presidential elections. *See* Elections
Presidential oath, 291
Presidential power. *See* Presidency, power
    of the
Presidential succession. *See* Succession
President's Emergency Committee for
    Employment, 526
President's Organization on Unemployment
    Relief, 527
Press; partisan politics and the, 33;
    relationship with the president, 414, 508,
    674
Press conferences, 509, 645
Primaries, 11
Princeton University, 471
Prisoners of war; in the Korean War, 625
Privateers, 40
Proclamation of Amnesty and
    Reconstruction, 307
Proctor, Redfield, 417
Profiles in Courage (Kennedy), 136, 640
Progressive Party, 11, 465, 473
Progressive Republican League, 464
Progressivism, 10, 439, 461, 479, 520, 522,
    535
Prohibition, 503, 524, 529
Prophet, The, 198
Protectionism, 513
Protective tariffs. *See* Tariffs
Protests. *See* Antiwar protests
PT 109, 638
Public debt. *See* National debt; State debts;
    War debt
Public works, 550, 620
Public Works Administration, 550, 660
Puerto Rico, 142, 424

Pullman Strike, 399
Pure Food and Drug Act, 442
PWA. *See* Public Works Administration

Qaddafi, Muammar al-, 770, 836
Quakers, 521, 691
Quay, Matthew, 404, 406
Quayle, Dan, 784-785
Quemoy, 627
Quids, 90
Quitman, John, 258

Race relations, 592, 662
Racism, 364, 569; and T. Roosevelt, 445
Radford, Arthur, 626
Radical Republicans, 306, 318, 337
Radio, 509
Radio Act of 1927, 510
Rafshoon, Gerald, 737
Railroad, 365, 399, 440
Railroad, transcontinental, 260, 305
Railroad strike of 1877, 365
Railway Labor Act, 510
Rambouillet Decree, 100
Randolph, A. Philip, 596
Randolph, Edmund, 29, 33, 43
Randolph, John, 82, 89, 97, 159
Randolph, Patsy Jefferson, 68
Rawlins, John A., 344
Rayburn, Sam, 646, 658, 660, 727
Reagan Revolution, 773, 785
Reagan, Nancy, 756-757
Reagan, Ronald, 754-775, 805, 823; and
    G. H. W. Bush, 782; as California
    governor, 756; and the campaign of 1976,
    733; and the campaign of 1980, 781;
    legacy of, 16, 776; and the Panama
    Canal, 744
Reaganomics, 761
Rebozo, Bebe, 716
Recession of 1990, 793
Reciprocity with Canada, 462
Reconstruction, 311, 319-320, 322, 337,
    341-342, 351, 363; and Lincoln, 307, 310
Reconstruction Acts, 322-323, 326

Reconstruction Finance Corporation, 527, 620

Red Army, 571-572

Red Scare, 489, 602, 621

Redfield, William C., 476

Reed, Thomas B., 406

Reeder, Andrew, 257

Regan, Donald, 759

Regulation, 704

Rehnquist, William, 762

Relief Act of 1821, 123

Relief programs, 549, 556

Reorganization, 705

Reparations; for Civil War claims, 338; for World War I, 493, 516, 530

Report on Manufactures, 30

Republican National Committee, 780

Republican Party, 6, 8, 249; and Arthur, 380; and Buchanan, 263; and the election of 1870, 345; founding of the, 256, 284; and Garfield, 374; and Hoover, 531; and A. Johnson, 318, 321; and Lincoln, 300, 308; and Reagan, 756; and T. Roosevelt, 436; in the South, 349, 351, 363; and Taft, 457; and Texas, 779

Research Committee on Social Trends, 524, 528

Resignation; of Spiro T. Agnew, 698, 727; of Nixon, 718, 722

Resumption Act, 366

Revolutionary War, 23, 54, 117, 134, 151, 292

Reykjavik summit, 769

Rhode Island, 27

Ribicoff, Abraham, 645

Rice, Condoleezza, 828, 838

Richards, Ann, 824

Richardson, Elliot, 718

Richmond, 307

Ridge, Tom, 831

Riots, 533; draft, 304; race, 321, 680

Rives, William C., 185-186, 192

Roberts, John, 839

Robertson, William H., 376

Rockefeller, Nelson, 653, 698, 731

Rodham, Hillary. *See* Clinton, Hillary Rodham

Rodino, Peter, 718

Rodney, Caesar, 98

Roe v. Wade, 762

Rogers Plan, 711

Romania, 788

Romney, George, 653

Roosevelt, Edith, 431

Roosevelt, Eleanor, 538, 540

Roosevelt, Franklin D., 537-578; and the campaign of 1932, 533; and the campaign of 1944, 580, 582; and Hoover, 534; and L. B. Johnson, 659; legacy of, 8, 12-13; and the Soviet Union, 585

Roosevelt, Theodore, 420, 428-453; and the campaign of 1900, 424; and the campaign of 1912, 464, 473; and the election of 1904, 11; and the election of 1912, 11; and the elections of 1910, 461; and B. Harrison, 405; opinion of Tyler, 204; as F. D. Roosevelt's cousin, 540; and Taft, 456-458, 464; and trusts, 462; and Wilson, 479

Roosevelt Corollary, 447

Root, Elihu, 413-414, 530

Rosenberg, Julius and Ethel, 621

Rough Riders, 435

Rove, Karl, 824

Ruckelshaus, William D., 718

Rule of 1756, 86

Rules Committee, 459

Rum, Romanism, and Rebellion, 392

Rumsfeld, Donald, 705

Runaway slaves, 242

Rush, Richard, 141, 145

Rusk, Dean, 644, 683

Russell, Richard, 661

Russia, 136; and Wilson, 492. *See also* Soviet Union

Russian Revolution, 486, 492

Rutherfurd, Lucy Mercer. *See* Mercer, Lucy

Sachs, Alexander, 570

Sackville-West, Lionel, 397

Sadat, Anwar el-, 712, 745
Sagamore Hill, 931
St. Clair, Arthur, 37, 77
St. John River, 188
St. Lawrence River, 528
Salary grab, 348
SALT. *See* Strategic Arms Limitation Talks
Samoan Islands, 409
San Juan Hill, 419
San Lorenzo, Treaty of, 45
Sanders, Carl, 737
Sandinistas, 767, 790
Sandino, Augusto, 515
Santo Domingo, 344-345. *See also* Dominican
    Republic
Saturday Night Massacre, 718
Saudi Arabia, 790
Savings and loan industry, 16, 787
Saxton McKinley House, 929
Scalia, Antonin, 762
Scandals, 503, 806, 809. *See also* Crédit
    Mobilier scandal; Eaton scandal;
    Iran-Contra affair; Jones, Paula, lawsuit;
    Lewinsky, Monica, investigation; Teapot
    Dome scandal; Watergate scandal;
    Whitewater investigation
Schine, G. David, 622-623
Schlesinger, James, 742
Schofield, John M., 328
Schurz, Carl, 362, 367
Schwarzkopf, Norman, 792
Scott, Thomas A., 360
Scott, Winfield, 6, 188-189, 230-232, 240, 249,
    301
Scowcroft, Brent, 771, 784, 789
Scranton, William, 711
Screen Actors Guild, 755
SDI. *See* Strategic Defense Initiative
Secession, 168, 272, 307, 320; of the
    Mississippi Valley, 90; of New England,
    80, 111; of the South, 7, 242, 248, 285, 318
Second Bank of the United States. *See* Bank
    of the United States
Second Battle of Bull Run. *See* Bull Run,
    Second Battle of

Second Continental Congress. *See*
    Continental Congress
Second Declaration of Independence, 194
Second Industrial Conference, 522
Second party system, 192, 196
Second World War. *See* World War II
Secretary of commerce, 522
Secretary of the treasury, 170
Securities, 30, 36
Sedgwick, Theodore, 33
Sedition Act of 1798, 60
Sedition Act of 1918, 488
Segregation, 14, 594, 601; in the armed
    forces, 596
Segregationists, 737
Seminoles, 125, 156, 162, 189, 238
Senate, 51, 63; confirmation of cabinet
    positions, 512; rejection of Charles B.
    Warren, 512; rejection of John Tower, 784;
    rejection of Robert Bork, 762; rejection of
    William Short, 97; role in foreign policy,
    77; vote on impeachment, 82
September 11, 2001, attacks, 819, 830, 832
Serbia, 814
Settlement. *See* Western settlement
Settlers, 224
Seven Days' Battles, 301
Seven Years' War, 21
Seventeenth Amendment, 467
Sevier, John, 153
Seward, William H., 7, 242, 247, 285, 287,
    302, 323, 329
Seymour, Horatio, 8, 304
Shafter, William R., 419
Shah of Iran, the. *See* Mohammad Reza
    Shah Pahlavi.
Shannon, Wilson, 257
Shays's Rebellion, 95
Shenandoah Valley, 20
Shepherd, Alexander H., 349
Sheppard-Towner Act, 501
Sheridan, Philip, 309, 324
Sherman, James S., 459
Sherman, John, 360, 362, 366-367, 374, 407,
    413

Sherman, William Tecumseh, 307, 309-310, 321

Sherman Antitrust Act, 407, 440, 455, 462, 478

Sherman Silver Purchase Act, 397-398, 407

Sherwood Forest (Virginia), 932

Short, William, 97

Shultz, George, 698-699

Shuttle diplomacy, 712

Sick, Gary, 748

Silver, 366, 398, 407

Silver Democrats, 400

Simon, William, 732

Sinclair, Upton, 554

Sirica, John J., 717

Sit-ins, 624

Six-Day War, 681

Six Nations, 37

Sixteenth Amendment, 467

Slave trade, 129

Slavery, 4-6, 233, 293; abolition of, 296; and Buchanan, 263; and expansion, 260; and Great Britain, 42; and A. Johnson, 316; in Kansas, 266; and Lincoln, 283; in Louisiana, 80; and Madison, 114; and the Mexican War, 240, 248; in Missouri, 124, 295; and Monroe, 124; and Pierce, 254; and Polk, 233; and Taylor, 243; and Van Buren, 186

Slidell, John, 228, 265

Smith, Alfred E., 12, 523, 543-544

Smith, Jesse M., 504

Smith, Robert, 75, 97

Smith, Samuel, 108

Smith, William French, 759

Smith, William Loughton, 33

Smoot-Hawley Tariff, 526

Social Security, 557, 620, 662, 703, 838

Social service system, 528

Socialism, 554

Solid South, 9, 383, 477

Somalia, 795

Sorensen, Theodore, 640, 645

Soulé, Pierre, 259

Souter, David, 793

South; and African Americans, 592; civil rights protests in the, 624; Democratic Party in the, 594; and protective tariffs, 163; Republican Party in the, 349, 351, 363; secession of the, 7, 242, 248, 285, 318; violence in the, 345; voting fraud in the, 349

South Africa, 789

South Carolina, 65, 167-168, 206, 273, 288, 363

South Korea, 598, 625

South Vietnam, 677

Southard, Samuel, 141

Southeast Asia Resolution. See Tonkin Gulf Resolution

Southeast Asia Treaty Organization, 627

Soviet Union, 515, 585, 764; and G. H. W. Bush, 787; and Carter, 745; coup in the, 793; and Eisenhower, 633; end of the, 793; and Germany, 563; as joint peacemaker with the United States, 711; and Kennedy, 649; and Nixon, 712; and the Persian Gulf War, 790; and Reagan, 763-764, 768; and F. D. Roosevelt, 567, 585; and Truman, 585; and World War II, 585

Space program, 645, 662

Spain, 562; and J. Adams, 61; and American expansion, 36; border with, 125, 137; and Cleveland, 415; end of New World empire, 142; and Grant, 344; and Jefferson, 86; and McKinley, 415; and Monroe, 125; treaties with, 45, 421

Spanish-American War, 414, 416, 418, 434

Speaker of the House of Representatives, 459

Special interests, 742

Specie, 190-191, 339, 343, 366

Specie circular, 174, 190

Speculation, land, 36, 122, 174

Speeches; of J. Adams, 57; of G. H. W. Bush, 784, 791; of G. W. Bush, 832, 835; of Clinton, 807, 810, 812; of Eisenhower, 621; of L. B. Johnson, 676, 683; of Kennedy, 648; of Nixon, 710, 718; of Reagan, 765, 769

Spiegel Grove, 927
Spoils system, 160, 367, 384
Spooner Amendment, 425
Springfield Junto, 280
Springwood, 931
SSI. *See* Supplementary Security Income
Stalin, Joseph, 571-572, 574
Stalingrad, Battle of, 571
Stalwarts, 359, 363, 368, 374, 381
Stamp Act, 51
Stanbery, Henry, 323, 326
Stanton, Edwin M., 273, 319, 322, 324-325
Star Route case, 368, 376, 383
Star Wars. *See* Strategic Defense Initiative
Starr, Kenneth, 17, 810, 812
Starr Report, The, 813
State banks, 191
State debts, 30, 32
State governments; role of, 700
State legislatures, 1
State of the Union address; of Cleveland, 396-397; of Jackson, 160; of Madison, 103, 107, 113
States' rights, 53, 60, 90, 121, 168
States' Rights Party, 14, 594
Stealth bomber, 764
Stevens, Ted, 622
Stevens, Thaddeus, 319, 323, 326
Stevenson, Adlai E., 14, 394, 604, 625, 641, 644, 692
Stewart, Alexander T., 342
Stiles, John R., 724
Stimson, Henry L., 509, 524, 563, 778
Stimson Doctrine, 531
Stock market crash of 1929, 524
Stoddert, Benjamin, 63
Stone, Harlan F., 513
Strategic Arms Limitation Talks, 713, 746
Strategic Defense Initiative, 764-765, 769
Strikes, 365, 399, 507, 554, 560
Stuart, Gilbert, 22
Stump speech, 321
Submarine warfare, 485
Submerged Lands Act, 619
Succession, 207, 855

Suez Canal, 629
Suffrage. *See* Black suffrage; Universal suffrage; Woman suffrage
Summit meetings, 768
Sumner, Charles, 258, 319, 323, 344-345
Superpowers, 708
Supplementary Security Income, 703
Supply-side economics, 760, 782
Supreme Court; appointments by Bush, 793; appointments by L. B. Johnson, 684; appointments by Reagan, 762; and civil rights legislation, 593, 601; and the Dred Scott decision, 265; establishment of the, 29; and the New Deal, 556; and F. D. Roosevelt, 559
Surplus, 394, 397
Surratt, Mary, 319
Swartwout, Samuel, 159
Symington, Stuart, 642

Taft, Helen, 456
Taft, Robert A., 14, 589, 617
Taft, William Howard, 454-468; and the campaign of 1912, 473; as chief justice, 513; and the election of 1912, 11; and the League of Nations, 495; and Mexico, 481; and T. Roosevelt, 451
Taft-Hartley Act, 640, 660
Taggart, Samuel, 100
Taiwan, 627, 708, 780
Taliban, 831
Talleyrand, 57, 62, 86
Tallmadge, James, Jr., 123
Tallmadge, Nathaniel P., 192
Tammany Hall, 390, 541
Taney, Roger, 165, 170-171, 303
Tariff commission, 513
Tariff of Abominations, 145, 206
Tariff reform, 266, 395, 398, 477
Tariffs, 30, 113, 130, 145, 163, 167, 206, 216, 234, 340, 394-395, 408, 413, 458, 513
Tax reform, 742, 761
Tax Reform Act of 1986, 761
Taxes, 16, 510; cutting of, 652, 664, 761, 829; elimination of, 76; under L. B. Johnson,

680; role of federal, 31; on the wealthy, 557; during World War II, 569

Taylor, Margaret, 238

Taylor, Zachary, 237-244; and the election of 1848, 6, 235, 281; and Fillmore, 247; and the Mexican War, 228, 230-231

Teapot Dome scandal, 504

Tecumseh, 198

Television, 14-15, 641, 645, 695

Television commercials, 696

Teller Amendment, 418, 423

Temperance, 346

Tennessee, 152, 213, 316

Tennessee River, 510, 528

Tennessee Valley Authority, 510, 548, 620

Tenure of Office Act, 322, 325-326, 342

TerHorst, Jerald F., 729

Territories, 124

Terrorism, 766-767, 770-771, 819, 831-832

Tet Offensive, 682-683

Texas, 657, 824; annexation of, 6, 178, 187, 210, 218, 222, 228; attempts to purchase, 173; claims in New Mexico, 242-243, 249; and the Republican Party, 779

Third parties, 6, 9

Third term, 13

Third World, 630, 708

Thirteenth Amendment, 300, 309, 319

Thomas, Clarence, 793

Thomas, Lorenzo, 326

Thompson, Jacob, 264, 272

Thompson, Richard W., 362

Thornberry, Homer, 685

Thousand points of light, 786

Thurman, Allen G., 357

Thurmond, Strom, 14, 594, 829

Tiananmen Square, 789

Tilden, Samuel J., 8, 350, 352, 359

Tippecanoe, 103, 198

"Tippecanoe and Tyler Too," 194, 202, 207

Todd, John Payne, 114

Tollgates, 121

Tompkins, Daniel D., 120

Tonkin Gulf Resolution, 667

Torrijos, Omar, 745

Tower, John, 771, 784

Tower Commission, 771

Townsend, Francis, 555

Townsend Plan, 555

TR. See Roosevelt, Theodore

Trade, 142; conflict with Great Britain over, 86; with France, 86, 100; with Great Britain, 41-42, 98; in the West Indies, 129, 142

Trail of Tears, 161, 189

Transcontinental railroad, 260, 305

Transcontinental Treaty of 1819, 126

Transportation, 119, 122

Treason, 91

Treasury, U.S., 29-30, 76, 108, 181, 191; independence of the, 193, 222, 234; secretary of the, 170

Treasury reserve, 398

Treaties, 43, 461; with American Indians, 131, 160, 162; with China, 369; with Colombia, 446; commercial, 142; with Great Britain, 42, 88, 111, 125, 226, 243, 423; with Mexico, 232, 270; nuclear, 650, 684, 713, 769; with Panama, 745; with Spain, 45, 421. See also individual treaties

Treatment, the, 661

Trilateral Commission, 739

Tripoli, 77

Tripp, Linda, 812

Trist, Nicholas, 232

Truman, Bess, 580

Truman, Harry S., 558, 579-608; and the campaign of 1944, 574; and the election of 1948, 13; legacy of, 13; opinion of Germany and the Soviet Union, 567

Truman Doctrine, 588-589

Trumbull, Lyman, 328

Trusts, 407, 439-440, 458, 462, 467

Tsongas, Paul, 806

Tsunami, 795, 815

Tucker, Karla Faye, 824

Turkey, 588

TVA. See Tennessee Valley Authority

Twelfth Amendment, 3, 74

Twenty-fifth Amendment, 727

Two China policy, 708, 780
Two-party system, 175
Tyler, John, 200, 204-211; annexation of Texas, 223; and the campaign of 1840, 194; and the election of 1844, 6
Tyler, Julia, 208
Tyler, Letitia, 206

U-2 incident, 633
UAC. *See* Urban Affairs Council
Underwood-Simmons Tariff Act, 477
Unemployment, 732
Union army, 293
Union Party, 558
Unions, 439, 557, 569, 641
United Mine Workers, 514
United Nations, 574, 780; founding of the, 583
United Nations Security Council, 790
United States Telegraph, 164
United States v. Nixon, 718
Universal suffrage, 337; and Lincoln, 278
University of Mississippi Law School, 652
Urban Affairs Council, 697
USS *Chesapeake*, 88
Utah, 243, 270

Vallandigham, Clement L., 304
Valley Forge, 25
Van Buren, Angelica Singleton, 182
Van Buren, Hannah, 182
Van Buren, Martin, 159, 180-196; and the American System, 163; and the campaign of 1828, 146, 157; and the campaign of 1836, 173; and the campaign of 1844, 217; and the Eaton scandal, 163; and the Free-Soil Party, 241; legacy of, 5; opinion of J. Q. Adams, 141; and political parties, 146; as secretary of state, 158
Vance, Cyrus, 745, 748
Vandenberg, Arthur, 532, 590
Vera Cruz, invasion of, 482
Versailles, Treaty of, 492-493, 495, 531
Veterans, 393, 397, 408; from the Civil War, 393; from World War I, 533

Veterans Bureau, 501, 504
Veto, 169, 280, 308, 382, 732
Vice presidency, 53, 507, 663, 693; election to the, 2
Viet Cong, 676, 682
Vietnam; and Eisenhower, 625; and L. B. Johnson, 667, 677; and Kennedy, 650-651, 654. *See also* Indochina
Vietnam War, 676, 678, 681, 685, 687, 709-710; and G. W. Bush, 821; and the campaign of 1968, 696; and Clinton, 800; end of the, 711; lack of declaration of, 678
Vietnamization, 709
Villa, Pancho, 481-482
Virginia, 61, 70, 94
Virginia dynasty, 67, 113, 117
Virginia House of Burgesses. *See* House of Burgesses
Virginia Plan, 95
Virginia Resolutions, 48, 95
Voice of America, 622
Voodoo economics, 782
Voorhis, Jerry, 692
Voting rights, 675
Voting Rights Act of 1965, 676

Wade, Benjamin F., 328
Wade-Davis bill, 308
Wade-Davis Manifesto, 308
Wagner, Robert, 515, 528, 557
Wagner Act, 557
Walker, Robert J., 266
Wallace, George, 652, 696
Wallace, Henry A., 14, 547, 574, 580, 582, 587, 589, 592
Wanamaker, John, 405
War Between the States. *See* Civil War
War debt; from the Revolutionary War, 30-31; from the War of 1812, 109; from World War I, 515, 531
War Democrats, 303
War Hawks, 98
War of 1812, 105-108, 110, 155, 199, 238
War of Independence. *See* Revolutionary War

War on Poverty, 655, 665, 679, 686
War powers, 290-291
War Powers Act, 515
Ward, Ferdinand, 353
Warm Springs (Georgia), 931
Warren, Charles B., 512
Warren, Earl, 623-624, 664, 685
Warren Commission, 653, 664, 726
Wars. *See* Civil War; Korean War; Mexican War; Persian Gulf War; Revolutionary War; Spanish-American War; Vietnam War; War of 1812; World War I; World War II
Washington, D.C., 65, 68, 106, 290; burning of, 108
Washington, George, 19-49; legacy of, 4; and political parties, 3; reinstatement as commander in chief, 59; retirement of, 50
Washington, Martha, 20
Washington Conference, 502
Washington Globe, 164
Washington Union, 255
Watergate scandal, 15, 700, 706, 713, 727, 780; legacy of, 718
Wayne, Anthony, 37, 197
Weapons of mass destruction, 834, 836
Web sites, 925-932
Webster, Daniel, 166, 174, 192, 242, 249
Webster-Ashburton Treaty, 189, 209
Weed, Thurlow, 247
Weinberger, Caspar, 759
Welfare reform, 703, 758
Welles, Gideon, 287
West Bank, 745, 766
West Berlin, 632, 649
West Florida, 86, 101
West Indies, 129, 142
West Point, 335, 613
Western expansion, 119, 221; and the Mexican War, 230
Western settlement, 36, 45
Westmoreland, William, 677, 683
Wheatland, 926
Wheeler, Burton K., 564
Wheeler, William A., 361

Wheeler-Rayburn Act, 557
Whigs, 5, 170, 173, 184-185, 192, 194, 201, 207-208, 240, 284; and Lincoln, 278, 280; and Tyler, 209
Whiskey Rebellion, 44
Whiskey Ring, 350
Whitaker, John, 699
White, Frank, 803
White, Hugh Lawson, 174
White Haven, 927
White House, 108, 116, 381, 414, 438; burning of the, 108; remodeling of the, 645
White House staff, 414; of Eisenhower, 619; of Kennedy, 645
White Leagues, 349
Whitewater investigation, 17, 809
Whitman, Walt, 306
Whitney, William C., 389, 393
Why England Slept (Kennedy), 637
Wickersham, George W., 462
Wilbur, Ray Lyman, 524
Wilkinson, James, 90, 106
Willey, Kathleen, 812
Willkie, Bruce, 703
Willkie, Wendell L., 13, 563
Wilmot, David, 233
Wilmot Proviso, 233, 248, 256
Wilson, Edith, 471, 472
Wilson, Ellen Axson, 471
Wilson, Henry, 347, 350
Wilson, Henry Lane, 481
Wilson, William B., 476
Wilson, Woodrow, 469-495; and the campaign of 1912, 465; legacy of, 11, 437; and T. Roosevelt, 439, 451, 541
Wilson Dam, 548
Wilson-Gorman bill, 398
Winder, William H., 107
Windom, William, 377, 408
Wirt, William, 108, 121, 141
Wisconsin, 554
Wise Men, 683
Wolcott, Oliver, Jr., 56
Woman suffrage, 473

Women's rights, 701
Wood, Leonard, 434
Woodbury, Levi, 165
Work, Hubert, 509
Work relief, 556
Works Progress Administration, 556, 660
World Court, 516, 530
World Trade Center, 830
World War I, 11, 451, 479, 483, 487, 502;
    and Hoover, 521
World War II, 13, 563-564, 571; and
    G. H. W. Bush, 778; and Eisenhower,
    615; home front during, 569; impact on
    the Soviet Union, 585; impact on the
    United States, 585; and Kennedy, 638;
    and Truman, 582
WPA. *See* Works Progress Administration
Wright, Jim, 785

Wright, Silas, 219
Writ of habeas corpus. *See* Habeas corpus
Wythe, George, 70

XYZ affair, 57

Yalta Conference, 574, 585, 622
Yarborough, Ralph, 779
Yates, Eugene, 620
Yazoo land companies, 36-37, 90
Yeltsin, Boris, 793
Yom Kippur War, 712
Young, Owen D., 530
Young Hickory, 212

Zapata, Emiliano, 481
Zimmerman, Alfred, 485
Zweicker, Ralph, 622